D1266893

ASTAIRE DANCING

ASTAIRE DANCING

THE MUSICAL FILMS

JOHN MUELLER

ALFRED A. KNOPF NEW YORK 1985

FOR JAM AND ESM,
AND FOR KARL, KAREN,
AND SUSAN

THIS IS A BORZOI BOOK
PUBLISHED BY
ALFRED A. KNOPF, INC.

 Published in the United States by Alfred A. Knopf, Inc., New York, and simultaneously in Canada by Random House of Canada Limited, Toronto. Distributed by Random House, Inc., New York.

Grateful acknowledgment is made to the following for permission to reprint previously published material:

Chappell Music Company. Excerpts from lyrics to "That's Entertainment" by Howard Dietz and Arthur Schwartz. Copyright © 1953 by Chappell & Co., Inc. Copyright Renewed. Excerpts from lyrics to "Stereophonic Sound" by Cole Porter. Copyright © 1955 and 1958 by Cole Porter. Copyright Renewed, assigned to Robert H. Montgomery, trustee of the Cole Porter Musical and Literary Property Trusts. Chappell & Co., Inc., owner of publication and allied rights. Excerpts from lyrics to "A Foggy Day" by George Gershwin and Ira Gershwin. Copyright © 1937 by Gershwin Publishing Corp. Copyright Renewed, assigned to Chappell & Co., Inc. Excerpts from lyrics to "Things Are Looking Up" by George Gershwin and Ira Gershwin. Copyright © 1937 by Gershwin Publishing Corp. Copyright Renewed, assigned to Chappell & Co., Inc. Rights for the United Kingdom administered by Chappell International Music Publishers International. International Copyright Secured. All Rights Reserved. Used by permission.

The Estate of Johnny Mercer. Excerpts from lyrics to "A Lot in Common With You" by Johnny Mercer and Harold Arlen. Used by permission.

Warner Bros. Music. Excerpts from lyrics to "Something's Gotta Give" by Johnny Mercer. Copyright © 1954 (Renewed) WB Music Corp. All Rights Reserved. Rights for the United Kingdom administered by TRO Essex Music Limited. All Rights Reserved. Used by permission.

The Welk Music Group. Excerpts from lyrics to "On the Beam" by Jerome Kern and Johnny Mercer. Copyright © 1942 T. B. Harms Company. Copyright Renewed (c/o The Welk Music Group, Santa Monica, California, 90401). International Copyright Secured. All Rights Reserved. Used by permission.

Library of Congress Cataloging-in-Publication Data
Mueller, John E.
Astaire dancing.
Includes index.
1. Dancing in moving-pictures, television, etc.—United States—Case studies. 2. Astaire, Fred.
3. Moving-pictures, Musical—United States—History and criticism. I. Title.
GV1779.M84 1985 791.43'09'09355 84-47874
ISBN 0-394-51654-0

Manufactured in the United States of America

FIRST EDITION

ACKNOWLEDGMENTS

This was a complicated book to put together, and I had a lot of help. My wife, Judy, read every syllable (a few of them twice), and made hundreds of apt and pithy recommendations for improvement. Then Eva Resnikova, at Knopf, made thousands more, an appallingly high percentage of which were inescapably on target. I am also especially grateful to Bob Gottlieb at Knopf for his encouragement and expert guidance, for his enthusiastic (one might go so far as to call it exuberant) engineering of the design, and for his many comments, few of them mildly expressed. Also at Knopf, Ellen McNeilly elegantly solved some of the most difficult technical problems, particularly with the frame enlargements; Iris Weinstein designed the approach and artfully juggled pictures, text, and footnotes to make things work out; Andy Hughes masterfully coordinated the production; and Terry Zaroff went far beyond the usual duties of a copy editor, helping enormously with infelicities of text and footnotery.

For agreeing to submit to interviews, I would like to thank Fred Astaire, Pandro Berman, Hermes Pan, Ed Sims, and Charles Walters, and for answering letters and telephone calls of inquiry, Robert Russell Bennett, Gerald Bordman, Cy Feuer, Hugh Fordin, John Green, Claire Luce, Eleanor Powell, Stanley Green, Hilda Schneider, Charles Schwartz, Anton Dolin, and Burton Lane.

From the start this book has benefited from the counsel and encouragement of Richard Gollin, Miles Kreuger, and Marcia Siegel. I also thank James Mark Purcell for expert information on film costs and earnings, Clifford McCarty for comments on music credits, John Cocchi for reviewing and improving the cast lists, Charles L. Turner for assistance at one point of difficulty, John Langeland and Harold Stanley for word-processing advice, Howard Levine for documentation on recordings of Bing Crosby, and Richard Niemi and Paul Hunter for helping to arrange my schedule at the University of Rochester.

Also contributing valuable comments, observations, assistance, and suggestions: Arlene Croce, Ron Haver, Rick Jewell, David and Darcy Paletz, Paul Becker, Caro Thompson, Kate Light, David Parker, Laura Shapiro, Marcia Butzel, Bill Rosar, William Riker, Elizabeth Hinkleman, Robert Cornfield, Iris M. Fanger, Elsie Mueller, Stephen Youngkin, Jane Goldberg, Karl Mueller, Michael Feinstein, Mary Corliss, Phyllis Baboolal, Leila Sussman, Michael Lasser, Ralph Locke, Karen Mueller, Beth Genné, Eric de Kuyper, Jessica Voeten, John Kuiper, Sidney Rosenzweig, Mary Ann de Vlieg, Dirk Lauwaert, Judy Allen, Lois Maki, Suzanne Shelton, Vernon Harbin, Jack Haley, Jr., Rick Altman, John Hanrahan, George Grella, Mary Ostrander, George Pratt, James Parish, Bob Lockyer, Carol Teten, Ernie Smith, Jim Cavanaugh, George Dorris, Deborah Jowitt, Reba Adler, Mike Kriegsman, Catherine Diringer, Claire Leonard, Martin Williams, Ernest Gilbert, Susan Mueller, Herbert Nusbaum, Michel Uytterhoeven, Frankie MacCormick, John and Claudia Morgan, Frosti McClurken-Croslin, Russell Roberts, Harriet Crawford of the Columbia Pictures Music Library, Mary Ellen Benenati of Chappell Music, and David Chierichetti and Sid James of RKO.

For the expert work on processing the frame enlargements I would like to thank Ben Emerson, and, for other assistance in this area, Jerry O'Neill, Raymond Gramiak, John Groves, Tom Thorpe, and Ted Stigler. For many of the stills I am grateful to Ron Haver and the Film Department of the Los Angeles County Museum of Art, John Kobal, and Carlos Clarens.

Two archivists have been particularly helpful and extraordinarily generous with their time and counsel: Ned Comstock of Special Collections at the University of Southern California, and John Hall of RKO. I would also like to thank the staffs of the library of the American Academy of Motion Picture Arts and Sciences, Eastman House/International Museum of Photography, Museum of Modern Art, Film Studies Center of the University of Rochester, Institute of the American Musical, UCLA Theatre Arts Library, American Film Institute–Hollywood, Rochester Public Libraries (Rundel and Arnett branch), Special Collections at Boston University, Songwriters Hall of Fame Archive, National Film Theatre (London), and the Dance, Theatre, Music, and Recorded Sound collections of the New York Public Library.

The typing was handled with notable elan and proficiency by Mary Heinmiller, with additional contributions by Janice Brown and Donna French.

The films discussed in this book were all originally intended to be shown in theatres to audiences of substantial sizes. I am particularly grateful to the receptive (but not uncritical) audiences at the University of Rochester, which helped recreate this condition and which caused me to better appreciate the pacing of many of the films. Audiences at the University of Iowa were similarly helpful in several cases. For his cheerful and enthusiastic assistance in arranging the Rochester film showings, I would like to thank George Morrison, and for other assistance on that project, Ted Stigler, Shelly Duran, Sylvia Moukous, Frank Scarcelli, and Dee Emler.

Contents

For ease of reference, in this book each film, musical number, and frame enlargement is numbered or lettered. For example 20 F 16 refers to frame 16 in musical number F ("Puttin' On the Ritz") in film 20 (Blue Skies). The film title and number appear at the top of each page.

ASTAIRE DANCING

Introduction

It is not uncommon for people who achieve great success in popular entertainment to try their hands, sometimes a bit self-consciously, at Real Art. Fred Astaire has never been tempted by such an undertaking. He is extremely wary of "inventing 'up' to the arty," as he puts it, and finds such efforts "really dangerous." For him, artistry is something that "just happens." It is the central contention of this book that Astaire "just happens" to have created a large body of works of the highest artistic value, that he is one of the greatest dancers and choreographers who ever lived, that he is one of the master artists of the century.

Assertions like these sometimes seem surprising to people whose primary interest is film or popular entertainment. To many people involved with dance, however, they are obvious and unexceptional. George Balanchine, perhaps the greatest of all ballet choreographers, said of Astaire: "He is terribly rare. He is like Bach, who in his time had a great concentration of ability, essence, knowledge, a spread of music. Astaire has that same concentration of genius; there is so much of the dance in him that it has been distilled." This opinion is echoed by such important modern-dance choreographers as Merce Cunningham and by some of the most prominent dancers of our time. Rudolf Nureyev calls Astaire the "greatest American dancer in American history" and praises the "inventiveness, vocabulary of steps, logic" in the choreography. Margot Fonteyn in a recent book on dance history repeatedly refers to Astaire as a "genius" and calls him "one of the greatest dancers of all time." Mikhail Baryshnikov agrees: "He's a genius . . . a classical dancer like I never saw in my life." And Jerome Robbins, prominent as a choreographer both in ballet and in musicals, relates: "When I was in the Soviet [Union] recently I was being interviewed by a newspaperman and he said, 'Which dancers influenced you the most?' And I said, 'Oh, well, Fred Astaire.' He looked very surprised and shocked and I said, 'What's the matter?' He said, 'Well, Mr. Balanchine just said the same thing.' "

Astaire's masterpieces are embedded in a medium whose unabashed mission is popular entertainment and financial gain, but that should not—as *New York Times* dance critic John Martin observed in 1941—"overshadow the fact that he is also an artist of high distinction." This book will assess and analyze the range and depth of Astaire's contribution as a major artist, but given his considerable discomfort on the issue, the label "art" will largely be avoided.

THE YEARS BEFORE HOLLYWOOD

The primary concerns of this book are the musical films that Astaire made in Hollywood. There are scores of masterful dance works in these films and each can be looked at in detail—indeed, because he worked primarily in film, Astaire is that great rarity, a master choreographer the vast majority of whose works have been precisely preserved. One reason the quality of the dances is so high from the beginning is that Astaire was no neophyte when he came to Hollywood: he was thirty-four years old and had been performing professionally on the stage for nearly three decades. Born in Omaha, Nebraska, in 1899, Astaire was the son of an immigrant Austrian brewery employee who was also a stage-struck amateur musician. Because Astaire's sister, Adele, showed such prodigious talent in dancing-school recitals, her mother took her to New York in 1904 for professional training. Her brother, younger by a year and a half, came along, and both were enrolled in Claude Alvienne's dancing school.

Within a year Alvienne had worked out a twelve-minute vaudeville act for the youngsters, and by 1905, when Fred was only six, they were performing it professionally in New Jersey. At one point in their routine, which also made use of a huge wedding cake wired with electric lights, Fred appeared in top hat, white tie, and something like knickers. He did a tap dance in toe shoes and played the piano; later in the zany number, after his sister had become a glass of champagne, he reappeared as a lobster. The debut was successful enough so their father could arrange an extensive vaudeville tour for the child act at $150 a week—this at a time when a skilled worker earned, on average, less than $2 a week. Other tours followed, after the act was trimmed a bit, in part on Fred's suggestions—at age seven, his first choreography.

In a few years the children had outgrown their material and could no longer get bookings. They stayed out of show business for two years, attending regular school sessions in New Jersey, but eventually they were enrolled in Ned Way-

Fred and Adele Astaire—in their first vaudeville act, around 1906 (above), and in "A Rainy Saturday" in 1911 (below)

burn's dancing school in New York for six months. For a fee of $1,000 Wayburn wrote a sketch for them called "A Rainy Saturday," which they played in small-time vaudeville theatres for about two years with marginal success.

Wayburn's script depicts a pair of children trapped inside by rain. After a great deal of banter, they conclude the dialogue portion by imitating their parents—Adele bawling Fred out for coming home late in a drunken condition, Fred striking a series of poses trying to get a word in edgewise which suggest that his talent for comic mime and mimicry was already considerable. Two song-and-dance numbers were incorporated into the sketch, one in the middle, one as a finale. In both cases Fred was called upon to do the singing, and in the finale Adele played the piano. Wayburn also made comic use of the fact that Adele was taller than her brother, and he cannily incorporated a few lines to be spoken offstage by Mrs. Astaire, representing the children's mother in the skit.

Under the guidance of another vaudeville dancer, Aurelio Coccia, whom Astaire considers the most influential man in his dancing career, the Astaires eventually cut the dialogue from their act, reconstructed the songs and dances, and added new ones (in two of which Fred played the piano). They soon had a "streamlined show stopper." By their last season in vaudeville, when Fred and Adele were still in their mid-teens, they had become featured performers earning $350 a week.

In 1917 the Astaires were given an opportunity to move from vaudeville to the musical stage, and they leaped at the chance. From then until 1932 they appeared in ten musical productions on Broadway. There were a few flops, but most were hugely successful, particularly two musical comedies with songs by George and Ira Gershwin (*Lady, Be Good!* in 1924 and *Funny Face* in 1927) and a revue with songs by Arthur Schwartz and Howard Dietz (*The Band Wagon* in 1931).

In the 1920s the Astaires toured with three of their Broadway shows to London, where their success was even greater than in New York. They regularly hobnobbed with royalty, and Adele, always the object of male admiration, soon met an appealing aristocrat, Charles Cavendish, the second son of the Duke of Devonshire. She agreed to drop out of show business and marry him after her next hit show. When this was achieved with *The Band Wagon,* she settled down in 1932 to married life in a twelfth-century two-hundred-room castle in Ireland, a wedding present from her father-in-law.

Since she was never adequately filmed, it is difficult to assess Adele Astaire's qualities as a performer, but it is even more difficult to find a witness who has anything negative to say about her. Bright-eyed, pixie-voiced, bubbling with humor, she personified the 1920s flapper, and captivated audiences and critics everywhere. Some of her photographs suggest that she could also be affectingly vulnerable. Offstage, she was equally charming. As P. G. Wodehouse and Guy Bolton recalled: "Adele had the faculty of making any party from two to fifty-two a success. Such words as enchanting, delicious, captivating did not seem like tired adjectives when applied to her. She could be impish, she could be wise, she could be tender, she could be honest and friendly—are we conveying the impression that we like Adele Astaire?"

Adele's brother was perfectly content to let her have the limelight. As she recalled, "He was always staying in the background himself, pushing me forward." Even in his autobiography, published decades later, Fred Astaire delights in recalling such critical appraisals as "The girl seems to have talent but the boy can do nothing." Photographs of the pair often show them in a characteristic pose: Adele looking directly at the camera, Fred gazing solicitously at Adele.[1]

But although Fred Astaire may have been self-effacing around his talented sister, his own gifts did not exactly go unnoticed. Reviewing one of the Astaires' few unsuccessful shows in 1930, Robert Benchley calmly observed in *The New Yorker,* "I don't think that I will plunge the nation into war by stating that Fred is the greatest tap-dancer in the world." Among those with limitless admiration for Astaire was Serge Diaghilev, the great Russian ballet impresario, who was particularly impressed by the dancer's charm and musicality.

As their stage careers progressed, Fred Astaire became more and more interested in and involved with the choreography for the routines: "All the numbers we used to do, they were all Fred's ideas," according to his sister. He also did some occasional choreography for other shows—in 1930, for example, he helped a young dancer from Texas, Ginger Rogers, with a musical number in *Girl Crazy,* the Gershwin show that first gained her notice. And, beginning with *Lady, Be Good!,* he started performing in solo numbers, mostly of his own devising.

Even in vaudeville, where successful routines once set were almost never varied, Astaire was, according to one fellow vaudevillian, "never satisfied," constantly practicing and struggling. Particularly influential on Astaire's outlook on

[1] The enormous affection these performing partners felt for each other is expressed eloquently, and with characteristic Astaire indirection, by Adele in a 1936 article in *Variety*: "You know those four little worry wrinkles that drop away from a dachshund's eyes and make it look so sad and so terribly appealing? Sometimes Fred's got that look to me. Maybe that's why I love dachshunds—they remind me of Fred. When I get back to Ireland I'm going to get eight of them. Big dachshunds that will have little dachshunds romping sadly around. I can look at them and see Fred."

Fred and Adele Astaire

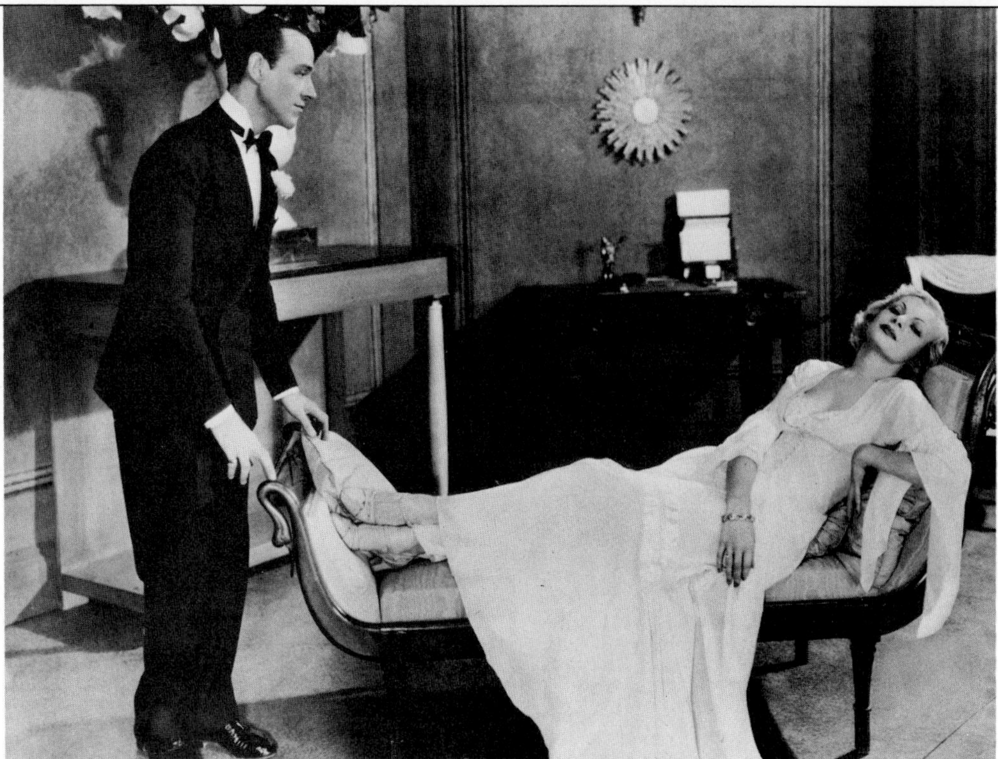

Astaire and Claire Luce in *Gay Divorce* (1932)

dance at this time were, besides Coccia, the great Danish ballerina Adeline Genée and three dancing teams: Vernon and Irene Castle, Eduardo and Elisa Cansino, and Bert Kalmar and Jessie Brown. Astaire was also impressed by a black tapper, John Bubbles, whose sense of invention never seemed to flag. And in the 1920s Astaire worked with ballet dancer Anton Dolin to "learn how to twiddle my feet like you."

Cast adrift by his sister's retirement, Astaire sought to reshape his career. He settled on the featured role in *Gay Divorce,* a "musical play" by Dwight Taylor with songs by Cole Porter. The show was a critical failure when it opened in New York in November 1932, but it held the boards for most of a year on the strength of the performances, some judicious price cutting, and the popularity of its hit song, "Night and Day." *Gay Divorce* was important not only because it proved Astaire could flourish without his sister, but because it helped to establish the pattern of most of his film musicals: it was a light, perky, unsentimental comedy, largely uncluttered by subplot, built around a love story for Astaire and his partner that was airy and amusing, but essentially serious—particularly when the pair danced together.

Astaire's partner in this musical was the lithe and voluptuous Claire Luce. When the Astaires were still teen-agers, they had sometimes played opposite each other romantically, but after 1923, "when we became well known as real brother and sister," they avoided such stories, and while their duets were affectionate and playful, at no time, obviously, could these dances do much to explore romance or sensuality. Now that the restriction was lifted, Astaire apparently approached his task with some uncertainty. Luce recalls that she had to encourage him to take hold of her: "Come on, Fred, I'm not your sister, you know." But he soon got the hang of it, and fashioned to the show's hit song his first great romantic duet. However, he never saw himself as a true romantic lead and had an antipathy to "mushy" dialogue scenes and to such clichés as passionate kisses: "Saying 'I love you' was the job of our dance routines," he explains.

In 1931 Astaire met and soon fell in love with his own patrician: the beautiful young Phyllis Livingston Potter, who came from one of Boston's most aristocratic families and who had never seen him on the stage. He launched a determined pursuit, and they were married in July 1933.[2] They had two children: Fred, Jr., born in 1936, and Ava, born in 1942.

THE HOLLYWOOD MUSICALS

In 1933, Astaire's agent, Leland Hayward, worked out a Hollywood deal at RKO: Astaire would do a film there at $1,500

[2] The daughter of Dr. Howard Baker of Boston, she had married Eliphalet Nott Potter, Jr., in 1927. Divorced in 1932 in Reno, they carried on a custody fight over their child, Eliphalet Nott ("Pete") Potter III, that was not resolved until a few hours before Phyllis' marriage to Astaire.

a week, and if the studio liked the results, it would put him in two more at a higher salary. And so in July 1933, shortly after *Gay Divorce* closed on Broadway and two days after his marriage, Astaire flew to California with his new wife to try out the film business.

Astaire's screen potential was a matter of some debate in Hollywood. Some, like David O. Selznick, the producer who signed him at RKO, saw strong possibilities: "I am tremendously enthused about the suggestion . . . of using Fred Astaire. If he photographs . . . he may prove to be a really sensational bet . . . Astaire is one of the greatest artists of the day: a magnificent performer, a man conceded to be perhaps, next to Leslie Howard, the most charming in the American theater, and unquestionably the outstanding young leader of American musical comedy." Another RKO producer, Merian Cooper, had seen *The Band Wagon* and recalls that he found Astaire "a helluva dancer, there wasn't anybody in his class." After Astaire's screen test, however, there was less confidence. Selznick retreated a bit: "I am a little uncertain about the man, but I feel, in spite of his enormous ears and bad chin line, that his charm is so tremendous that it comes through even on this wretched test." On the other hand, MGM associate producer Johnny Considine asserted, "You can get dancers like this for 75 dollars a week."[3]

Astaire had to prove himself. Certainly his great success in the theatre was no guarantee: many Broadway musical stars had come to Hollywood in the late 1920s and early 1930s and most had failed, buried in flimsy vehicles quickly turned out by tasteless hacks.

1933–1939: THE ROGERS YEARS

Astaire's debut in films was not entirely auspicious. Before beginning at RKO, he worked a few days at MGM, where he had a dancing bit in *Dancing Lady,* a melodramatic backstager fashioned in conscious imitation of the year's big hit, *42nd Street.* Though his appearance was incidental, Astaire shows an arresting screen presence when he goes into his brief, truncated dance with the film's star, Joan Crawford.

Then, over at the financially shaky RKO, he was fifth-billed in an exuberant, fluttery musical with a score by Vincent Youmans: *Flying Down to Rio.* In this Astaire mostly repeated the juvenile characterization he had developed on Broadway with his sister. By RKO's standards, *Flying Down to Rio* was a massive hit: of the roughly two hundred films the studio had produced since its creation in 1929, only three (*Rio Rita, Little Women,* and *King Kong*) had been more profitable. And it was obvious that Astaire's performance was a major factor in that success. The clearest trumpeting of his potential and the reasons for it came in the review in *Variety:* "The main point of *Flying Down to Rio* is the screen promise of Fred Astaire. . . . He's assuredly a bet after this one, for he's distinctly likeable on the screen, the mike is kind to his voice and as a dancer he remains in a class by himself. The latter observation will be no news to the profession, which has long admitted that Astaire starts dancing where the others stop hoofing." Even as the film opened, Radio City Music Hall's newspaper ads gave him top billing alongside the film's putative star, Dolores Del Rio.[4]

The message was clear: the thin, balding, self-conscious, ingratiating, romantically unimpressive tap dancer from New York was a moneymaker. Samuel Goldwyn petitioned to borrow RKO's new hot property, but RKO refused. Exercising its option, it arranged to feature him in two vehicles of his own. Along for the ride was Ginger Rogers, now a con-

Astaire with his wife, Phyllis, in 1933

[3] There is a legend that an Astaire screen test inspired the evaluation "Can't act. Can't sing. Balding. Can dance a little." This seems to be just one of those Hollywood "stories," however. RKO producer Pandro Berman says he never heard it in the early 1930s and that it emerged only years later.

[4] Studio executive Benjamin Kahane noted Astaire's appeal in an internal memo and calmly took credit for it: "Fred Astaire steals picture and think properly handled we have created another new and fresh screen personality."

tract player at RKO, who had been set opposite Astaire in *Flying Down to Rio* more as a comedy foil than anything else. They went together well, everyone seemed to agree.

Before either of his first two films had been released, Astaire traveled to London, where, on November 2, 1933, he opened in a slightly revised version of *Gay Divorce* to great popular—and, in this case, critical—acclaim. Adele was in the audience: "I'd never seen him from out front before. It was also the frst time I realized that Fred had sex appeal. Fred. Wherever did he get it?" London reviewer James Agate had a similar reaction. The "secret" of Astaire, he suggested, was sex—sex "bejewelled and be-glamoured and be-pixied."

Personnel changes at RKO placed the twenty-nine-year-old Pandro S. Berman as overseer of Astaire's career at the studio and producer of his films there. When *Flying Down to Rio* had firmly established Astaire's potential, Berman went shopping for properties for Astaire and for Astaire-Rogers. He went to London to see *Gay Divorce* (the only time he saw Astaire onstage), liked it, and bought it. On the way, he saw Jerome Kern's *Roberta* in New York and bought that for the pair (and for the singer Irene Dunne) as well.

Since *Roberta* continued to run on Broadway, *Gay Divorce* (retitled *The Gay Divorcee*) was chosen as the first of the major Astaire-Rogers pictures, with filming to begin in mid-1934 after Astaire had concluded his London stage engagement. In London, however, Astaire became understandably alarmed at the prospect of finding himself alloyed into another "team." He wrote a series of letters to his agent that seem quite amazing in retrospect:

> What's all this talk about me being teamed with Ginger Rogers? I will *not* have it Leland—I did not go into pictures to be *teamed* with her or anyone else, and if that is the program in mind for me I will not stand for it. I don't mind making another picture with her but as for this *team* idea it's *out!* I've just managed to live down one partnership and I don't want to be bothered with any more. I'd rather not make any more pictures for Radio if I have to be teamed up with one of those movie "queens." . . . This is no flash of temperament on my part Leland and does not call for one of your famous bawling out letters—please understand that. I'm just against the idea—that's all and feel that if I'm ever to get anywhere on the screen it will be as *one* not as two.

Pandro Berman's response to Astaire's agent was calm and assured: Astaire was not yet ready to be a star in his own right, he telegraphed, and needed to be bolstered with good support; "Ginger Rogers seems to go rather well with him and there is no need assume we will be making permanent team of this pair except if we can all clean up lot of money by keeping them together would be foolish not to." As it happened, they all did "clean up lot of money."

Astaire had other offers, a British film and another Dietz-and-Schwartz revue in New York. Since the money in such ventures could rival or surpass what he was getting in Hollywood, at times he doubted the wisdom of going to the coast: "I'm a bit sour on pictures at the moment—having read several movie magazines that call me a *rival* to *Hal LeRoy!!!* Boy—if they're going to start putting me in that class I think I'll stay on the stage where *mere billing and advertisement cannot* make stars. Unless I can do something outstandingly important I don't think I want to be bothered with movies."

But in general it seems Astaire was keen on pursuing a Hollywood career. In his autobiography he recalls that he found working for the camera much more interesting than working in the theatre, and before the London opening of *Gay Divorce* he told a reporter: "Your work on the screen never varies from performance to performance. You give your best performance all the time. . . . I'm a pretty severe critic of my own work, and there's no fun for me in not being at my best. The beauty of a film, too, is that it is working while you are resting. I think that's a marvellous idea!"

The Gay Divorcee scored even better at the box office than *Flying Down to Rio.* As film historian Richard Jewell observes, its importance to RKO "cannot be overemphasized." The studio desperately needed class and prestige as well as a box-office triumph. The Astaire-Rogers team was an almost overnight success, and exhibitors would seek to book all of RKO's pictures just to be assured of the Astaire-Rogers films.

Roberta followed in short order, out-grossing *The Gay Divorcee* and firmly establishing Astaire and Rogers as the king and queen of the RKO lot (see Table 1). Moreover, in this film they reached their full development as a team—the breathless high spirits, the emotional richness, the bubbling sense of comedy, the romantic compatibility are all there in full measure. In *Flying Down to Rio* they had been coparticipants; in *The Gay Divorcee* they were partners; in *Roberta* they became coconspirators.

The conspiracy deepened as they did six more films in the 1930s to make them one of the legendary partnerships in the history of dance. Rogers was outstanding among Astaire's film partners not because she was superior to the others as a dancer but because, as a skilled, intuitive actress, she was cagey enough to realize that acting did not stop when dancing began. She seemed uniquely to understand the dramatic import of the dance, and, without resorting to style-shattering emoting, she cunningly contributed her share to the choreographic impact of their numbers together. The point of many of these was joy; indeed, the reason so many women have fantasized about dancing with Fred Astaire is that Ginger Rogers conveyed the impression that dancing with

The Astaire-Rogers partnership at a peak: "Cheek to Cheek" in *Top Hat* (1935)

him is the most thrilling experience imaginable.[5] The plots in these films tend to work and rework successful formulas, but they contain a bit more variety than they are often given credit for. Two plot devices supposedly typical of the series—mistaken identity and having Astaire fall in love with Rogers at first sight—occur in only two or three of the nine films. And the leads, contrary to the usual assumption, are about as likely to portray working people as they are independently wealthy ones. Another common observation about these Astaire films, as well as later ones, is that they are "escapist," because they have little to say about specific contemporary political and economic ephemera, such as the Great Depression. But much the same charge could be leveled against the plays of Shakespeare and the operas of Mozart. Astaire's films are about love, and many of the dances deal profoundly with this distinctly nonephemeral subject.

For their films Astaire created a rich series of romantic and playful duets as well as an array of dazzling and imaginative solos for himself. Although the plot lines sometimes lurch improbably, Astaire was concerned from the beginning with making sure his numbers were motivated in the script. Playing off against the feisty yet arrestingly vulnerable Rogers, he gradually built out from the likable, happy-go-lucky, asexual juvenile he had played in his very earliest films. His screen persona developed more depth, sexual definition and security, and, eventually, maturity. Astaire and Rogers were not particularly close off-screen, but, countering occasional rumors to the contrary, both firmly and repeatedly insist their working relationship was cordial and cooperative: "We *never* fought."

Astaire's consummate musicality, together with the opportunity of working on such a classy, highly profitable project, made his films attractive to many of the top popular-song composers of the day, and Berman cannily used these inducements to obtain their services. As Irving Berlin told George Gershwin in 1936, "There is no setup in Hollywood that can compare with doing an Astaire picture." The result is a series of films whose musical values often match their choreographic splendor. The films are also notable for their often stunning Art Deco decor.

Under such conditions, Astaire was in a very good bargaining position, both creatively and financially. Berman says he instructed the directors of the films to give Astaire complete freedom on the dances and as much rehearsal time as he wanted, and had little difficulty convincing the studio powers to accept Astaire's requests for higher fees. Astaire's salary escalated dramatically. The $10,000 he received for *Flying Down to Rio* was doubled for each of his next two films, doubled again for the next one, *Top Hat,* and then doubled yet again for each of the next two, *Follow the Fleet*

[5] One of life's little handicaps for Astaire has always been this fantasy—as explicitly materialized in a late Astaire nonmusical, *The Pleasure of His Company.* At parties he would be plagued by women who wanted to dance with him and partly in consequence, he came to loathe both social dancing and parties. Gene Kelly apparently suffers from the same problem: "The girls always think we're going to throw them over a table or toss them up in the air. Their muscles tense up right away. So Fred and I go and sit in a corner and pretend we're talking business."

and *Swing Time*. Beginning with *Top Hat,* he also received a percentage of the gross. RKO's investment was sound: of the hundreds of motion pictures it produced between 1929 and 1936, the six Astaire-Rogers films in that period were among the nine most profitable. In both 1935 and 1936, two of their films ranked among the top ten money earners, an achievement unsurpassed and only very rarely equaled in the history of Hollywood (see Table 2). At the time Astaire was also doing a great deal of recording and radio work.[6]

In April 1936, shortly after *Follow the Fleet* was released, Astaire negotiated a five-film contract with the studio. In it he sought to establish a profile independent of Rogers, who had been featured in three profitable films on her own since *The Gay Divorcee* while he was busy working out the choreography for their joint films. Accordingly, this contract had a "Ginger Rogers" clause stipulating that she could appear in no more than three of the five films unless Astaire agreed otherwise.

The first two films under this contract, *Swing Time* and *Shall We Dance,* both with Rogers, showed a distinct—though far from catastrophic—falling-off in revenue, and Astaire and Rogers agreed to work separately for a year. The gross revenue of Astaire's Ginger-less effort during this period, the unjustly neglected *A Damsel in Distress,* was only two-thirds that of *Shall We Dance,* and it was the first Astaire film to lose money overall. Sobered, Astaire agreed to have Rogers in the two remaining films under his contract, *Carefree* and *The Story of Vernon and Irene Castle.* In different ways the films tried imaginatively to depart from the team's well-worn formulas, and both earned respectable grosses—about as much as *The Gay Divorcee.* But since they cost so much to produce (chiefly because of the stars' steadily escalating salaries—Astaire's was now well over $100,000), both films lost money (see Table 1).

Rogers was growing discontented. In 1938, when *The Story of Vernon and Irene Castle* was in production, she told reporter Ed Sullivan: "I don't want to make a musical for the next year. Don't get me wrong—I'm not ungrateful for what musicals have accomplished for me. However, for the last four years I've been doing the same thing with minor variations, in musicals. Drawing myself up haughtily and saying 'No, but definitely no,' or slapping Fred in the face to register pique, or skulking through scenes with (a) a tear-stained face, or (b) a sour puss." She soon set out on a series of films without Astaire at RKO. Most of these were highly successful, and one of them, *Kitty Foyle* of 1941, earned her the Academy Award for best actress. She became the studio's hottest property and one of the eight or ten highest-paid salary earners in the country.

Meanwhile, Astaire was asking $150,000 per film at RKO. The studio, suggesting that this figure made profiting impossible, refused to pay more than $75,000. On that unglamorous note Astaire left to seek better fees elsewhere, and his partnership with Rogers, which seemed to have run its course anyway, was dissolved—at least temporarily.

1940–1946: TRANSITION AND EXPERIMENT

The next years were nomadic ones for Astaire. He wandered from studio to studio, appeared with a variety of partners, and prospered. Between 1940 and 1946 he made three films at MGM (where he got his $150,000), and six others—two at Columbia, three at Paramount, and one back at RKO—where his salary usually was $100,000 plus a share of the profits.[7]

For the most part missing in these nine films is convincing romance—a major departure from the Rogers years. In *Broadway Melody of 1940,* his first film away from RKO, Astaire found himself opposite a tap dynamo, Eleanor Powell, to whom he found it difficult to relate romantically; although the two have several duets, they scarcely touch each other. In *Second Chorus* he spent almost all his time badgering Burgess Meredith and almost none of it romancing the beautiful Paulette Goddard. Astaire also seems to have had some difficulty warming to Rita Hayworth in *You'll Never Get Rich* and, to a lesser extent, in *You Were Never Lovelier*—perhaps he found her stupendous beauty a bit off-putting. In two films with Bing Crosby, *Holiday Inn* and *Blue Skies,* Astaire played a supporting role, chasing the woman but losing her to Crosby, and real romance with Lucille Bremer only occasionally burdens *Ziegfeld Follies* and *Yolanda and the Thief.* Affecting romance returns in full measure only in *The Sky's the Limit,* in which Astaire is cast

[6] In 1935 Adele Astaire, toying with the idea of making a comeback, had a friend approach RKO about the possibility. The studio had no interest at the time, since it was riding the crest of the Astaire-Rogers success. When she visited Hollywood that year there were rumors she and her brother would do a film version of *Lady, Be Good!* In 1936 she wrote: "If people would only realize when they ask me why I don't do a picture with him—they ask me that all the time, and were quite keen on it while I was in Hollywood—if they'd only realize that he's gone 'way ahead of me. Why, I couldn't begin to keep up with him. I couldn't even reach the steps he throws away." In 1937, however, she was enticed into working on a film in Britain with Jack Buchanan and Maurice Chevalier. She dropped out after two days of filming; as she recalled later, "I thought, 'Oh boy, if my brother Fred sees this—I'm gone!' "

[7] As Purcell has pointed out in analyzing the rankings in Table 2, Astaire's post-Rogers hit films were greatly benefited by top box-office costars: Bing Crosby in *Holiday Inn* and *Blue Skies,* Judy Garland in *Easter Parade.* Despite their rather low rankings, however, *You'll Never Get Rich, You Were Never Lovelier,* and *The Sky's the Limit* were good moneymakers: they were modestly budgeted and came out during a time when the size of the audience for movies had greatly expanded.

opposite Joan Leslie, the actress in these years who most recalls Rogers in her combination of feistiness and vulnerability. (If he sometimes did not find his female costar very electrifying, Astaire still had many effective sparring matches with the men who played his rivals or tormentors in these films: Crosby, Meredith, Robert Benchley, Adolph Menjou.)

The dances, however, retain their usual high quality. His tap duets with Powell may be emotionally unevocative, but they are brilliant nonetheless, as are several of the duets—particularly the playful ones—with Goddard, Leslie, Bremer, Hayworth, and *Holiday Inn*'s Virginia Dale. In his solos Astaire often seems to be seeking to expand the tap vocabulary, in part by capitalizing on its capacity for sheer noisemaking, an effect made most of in his firecracker solo in *Holiday Inn*. This quality is also used for emotional purpose to express giddy joy in *You'll Never Get Rich,* rage and frustration in *The Sky's the Limit,* and an arresting sense of audience confrontation in *Blue Skies*. In addition, Astaire explored drunkenness in three dances, two of them (in *Holiday Inn* and *The Sky's the Limit*) with remarkable depth.

Musically, Astaire continued to attract the best: Porter, Berlin, Kern, Harold Arlen, Harry Warren (the chief omissions in Astaire's career were Richard Rodgers and, among lyricists, Lorenz Hart). The average quality probably wasn't quite so high as it had been in the 1930s films, but these later films are musical treasures nonetheless. New to the Astaire films was the brilliant lyricist Johnny Mercer, whose efforts grace three of the films and help make one of them, *The Sky's the Limit,* truly remarkable. Major musical contributions in these films also come from several on-screen bands whose sounds Astaire often found choreographically invigorating: the crisp assertiveness of Artie Shaw, the cheery boogie of Freddie Slack, the bright jazziness of Chico Hamilton, the perky Latinisms of Xavier Cugat, the supportive sparkle of Bob Crosby.

All the films in this group are comedies; but whereas the first few mostly seek to emulate the zany insouciance of the Rogers films, toward the end other approaches were tried. *The Sky's the Limit* is an affecting dark comedy about the impact of World War II on life and love. *Ziegfeld Follies* presents a sumptuous (though sometimes overcalculated) opulence, and most of the numbers have an arrestingly hard edge; Astaire also seems to have found its precedent-shattering revue form liberating and turned out a duet with Bremer that deals with a kind of extravagant, highly charged lovemaking he had never explored so richly before. *Yolanda* attempts to achieve vaporous fantasy, while in the two Crosby films Astaire is content to be a romantic also-ran, interestingly pathetic in the otherwise mostly tedious *Blue Skies*.

By 1946 Astaire had decided to retire from motion pictures. He was influenced in this by his mother, who reasoned that he had been working long enough, toiling over forty years since he had started in show business at the age of five—the equivalent of a lifetime of labor, as she figured it. His films in the thirties had created a boom in the dancing-school business, and, at the urging of his wife and in response to hundreds of thousands of letters, he planned to try to cash in on this bonanza by establishing his own chain of dancing schools—an investment that may have seemed more secure than his future in the movies as an aging dancer.[8] He had no desire to experience a long, pathetic period of decline. As he told *Time* magazine at the time, "There comes a day when people begin to say, 'Why doesn't that old duffer retire?' I want to get out while they're still saying that Astaire is a hell of a dancer."

Accordingly, he posed for a series of photographs during the filming of "Puttin' On the Ritz," his brilliant solo in *Blue Skies,* and in late 1945 *Life* magazine published a set of these under the title "Astaire's Last Dance." The magazine announced that his "decision to retire stems not from his joints —which are as resilient as ever—but from an apprehension that his inventiveness is running dry."[9]

Like most of Astaire's apprehensions, this one was considerably exaggerated, as his next films were to demonstrate. But the "retirement" gave him time to reflect, and to realize that he was not yet ready to abandon show business.

1948–1957: THE LAST MUSICALS

The dancing-school venture was to prove successful, but only after considerable difficulty and trauma. The first school opened in New York on March 7, 1947; in October Astaire had an opportunity to return to the movies, and he jumped at it. Gene Kelly, who was scheduled to appear opposite Judy Garland in *Easter Parade* at MGM, broke his

[8] In 1936 an appreciative editorial in a dance publication observed, "The infectious and well-nigh miraculous perfection of Astaire has set burning in millions of people a desire to dance. We can't count the dollars of profit that Astaire has steered toward the dance field, but we know they've been coming." In 1934 a manufacturer of metal taps for dancing shoes reported a 280-percent increase in business; in 1935 the rise was 400 percent.

[9] According to one report, Astaire exited dramatically. When filming was completed, "he carefully removed his toupee. He stared at it for a moment, like Hamlet contemplating Yorick's skull. Then, in full view of the entire cast and crew, he slammed the hair piece to the floor and jumped on it with undisguised venom. 'Never, never, never,' he shouted, 'never will I have to wear this blasted rug again.' " Stephen Harvey suggests the reason for Astaire's retirement may also have been that "his style no longer matched the contemporary mood" as he saw "Gene Kelly now gaining the admiration that had greeted him ten years earlier." This conjecture may be partly valid, though it should be noted that Kelly had only begun to establish his own style and approach at that time.

ankle and was unable to work. At his suggestion, producer Arthur Freed approached Astaire about taking over.

Of the ten Astaire films released between 1948 and 1957, seven were made at MGM, and six of these were produced by Freed. In general, the conditions were congenial and the salary ($150,000 per film) was generous. Freed was the dominant figure in Hollywood musicals during that era, producing dozens of them, with an excellent record of financial success and a deserved reputation for quality (see Table 3). His films tend to be slick, colorful, well paced, tasteful, literate (or at any rate coherent), and energetic.

Astaire certainly helped contribute both to the earnings and to the reputation of the Freed musicals. *Easter Parade,* with the affectingly vulnerable Garland, was a major hit, and Freed, who had planned an Astaire-Garland pairing as early as 1943, sought several times to team the couple again in another film. (His efforts failed, because of Garland's mental and physical instability.)

Garland was replaced in Astaire's next film, *The Barkleys of Broadway,* by Ginger Rogers, whose career had slumped somewhat since the early 1940s. The pairing still had plenty of electricity, but it was not tried again. Most of Astaire's other partners in these later musicals were ballet-trained: Vera-Ellen in *Three Little Words* and *The Belle of New York,* Cyd Charisse in *The Band Wagon* and *Silk Stockings,* Leslie Caron in *Daddy Long Legs,* and, to a more limited extent, Audrey Hepburn in *Funny Face.* For variety there was Jane Powell, a singer-actress who could move quite well, in *Royal Wedding,* and Betty Hutton, an irrepressible comedienne, in *Let's Dance.* Astaire occasionally had difficulty using his partners' various talents to advantage, but for the most part he did quite well; in *The Belle of New York* he seems to have relished the opportunity to choreograph for a dancer who could keep up with him comfortably.

Somewhat more problematic was the issue of Astaire's age. In his late forties and early fifties when these films were made, he would hardly be convincing as the young, carefree romantic he had portrayed in the 1930s. It would have been possible to cast him in a nonromantic role, of course, but no one seemed quite ready for that. One approach, used in several films, was to ignore the problem and hope no one would notice, or at least mind. Another was to supply him with a partner of his own generation—a solution that worked well in *The Barkleys of Broadway,* the one time it was tried. Finally, several films took the age disparity and used it as a central plot device—variations on the *Pygmalion* theme in *Easter Parade, Daddy Long Legs,* and *Funny Face,* generational conflict in *The Band Wagon.*

Although this group of films contains a number of masterful dances, their average quality is not quite so high as before. Two films, *Three Little Words* and *Funny Face,* are, overall, remarkably undistinguished choreographically by the standards Astaire had set himself earlier, however appealing they may be in other ways. In some of the films Astaire seems to have put himself more under the guidance of other choreographers than usual, and that sometimes shows. And occasionally in romantic duets his partner seems to have proved intractable—as in *The Barkleys of Broadway, Let's Dance,* and *Daddy Long Legs.* But if the average is lower, the peaks are still there: playful duets, sometimes of the screwball variety, in *Easter Parade, The Barkleys of Broadway, Let's Dance, Royal Wedding, The Band Wagon, Silk Stockings,* and especially *The Belle of New York;* solos in *The Barkleys of Broadway, Royal Wedding,* and *The Belle of New York,* and a brilliant solo fragment in *Three Little Words.* In many of these dances Astaire developed his talents for mime and mimicry to new heights.

Musically, there is a considerable falling-off in these films. As it happened, Astaire's career in musicals coincided with a golden age for the American popular song, which was coming to an end by the 1950s. Two of Astaire's films from this period, *The Barkleys of Broadway* and *Let's Dance,* have original scores of unprecedented banality. Others are better, but it is undoubtedly a sign of the times that four of the films —*Easter Parade, Three Little Words, The Band Wagon,* and *Funny Face*—rely mostly on songs resuscitated from the 1920s and 1930s. Moreover, many of the songs are slowed and weighted down with lugubrious symphonic orchestrations and arrangements, one of the more unfortunate trademarks of the MGM musical.

This period was marked by a great personal tragedy for Astaire—the agonized death of his beloved wife from cancer in 1954 at the age of forty-six (see also p. 368).

THE YEARS AFTER THE HOLLYWOOD MUSICALS

By the mid-1950s the era of the classic Hollywood musical as Astaire had experienced it—indeed, defined it—was coming to an end. Revenues were declining, costs were rising, the studio system was falling apart, competition with television was growing, popular music was moving into the age of rock and roll. (There are satiric swipes at some of these developments in Astaire's last film of the period, *Silk Stockings.*) Astaire and other proponents of the classic Hollywood musical, such as Freed and Kelly, were out of business as Hollywood created fewer and fewer musical films, typically ex-

On a television special with Barrie Chase in 1958

travagant transmutations of Broadway musicals, perfunctory song-and-story vehicles for Elvis Presley, or well-scrubbed beach-and-bunny capers aimed at the adolescent crowd.

Undaunted, Astaire moved into other fields. He was highly successful in television, where he appeared on numerous shows as host and/or performer, and where he produced four carefully crafted, multiple-award-winning musical specials between 1958 and 1968. His partner in the specials was Barrie Chase, a limber young dancer who had had bit dancing parts in two of his films in the 1950s.

In 1968 Astaire appeared in one more musical film, as the gnarled, dotty title character in *Finian's Rainbow,* an enchanting stage musical systematically destroyed on the screen by its inexperienced and overcalculating director, Francis Ford Coppola. After that Astaire helped to host *That's Entertainment,* two compilation films by MGM to salute its by then vanished golden age of musicals.

Meanwhile, Astaire explored other fields as well. Shattering Hollywood tradition, he wrote his autobiography himself (in longhand). And he tried his hand at straight acting roles, with considerable success. In films he played a misanthropic scientist in *On the Beach* (1959), a debonair playboy in *The Pleasure of His Company* (1961), a diplomat in *The Notorious Landlady* (1962), a British secret agent in *The Midas Run* (1969), con men in *The Towering Inferno* (1975) and *The Amazing Dobermans* (1976), a country doctor in *The Purple Taxi* (1977), a conscience-stricken murderer in *Ghost Story* (1982). On television over the years he has played a number of characters, usually suave ones, in dramatic specials and series.

As he entered his eighties, Astaire, a lifelong horse-racing enthusiast, romanced and then—in 1980—married Robyn Smith, a successful jockey in her mid-thirties who had never seen any of his films.

As others honored and feted him for his achievements at glamorous occasions, in New York, Los Angeles, and Washington, D.C., Astaire continued to maintain that his dancing past interested him very little. When an interviewer asked him for his proudest achievement, he replied: "A four wood I hit on the 13th hole at Bel Air Country Club in June of 1945. It landed right on the green and rolled into the cup for a hole in one." But looking over his old film clips at a gala in his honor in 1981, he did go so far as to observe with pleasure, and with some apparent surprise, "I didn't realize I did all that stuff . . . but I'm glad to say I liked what I saw."

THE AUTHORSHIP OF THE CHOREOGRAPHY

The creation of most of Astaire's dances in films involved a degree of collaboration, and someone else is usually listed as "dance director" or "choreographer" in the film's credits. However, the guiding creative hand and the final authority in the Astaire numbers—especially in the solos and duets—was Astaire himself. In an interview in 1973, he put it this way: "You know, I was creative to a large degree. I don't say I created everything I ever did, because I always like the help of anybody who had any ideas—*grab* them, you know—but a good deal of the stuff that I did was my own creation." And there was also Astaire's style, integral to the choreography: "Nobody could ever teach me what to do about that."

Most important among those who aided Astaire and contributed ideas to his dances was Hermes Pan, a choreographer and idea man Astaire met early in his film career. Pan, who worked on seventeen of Astaire's thirty-one musical films (including all of the Rogers pictures) and on three of his four television specials, is sometimes seen to be a mysterious behind-the-scenes figure who actually created the Astaire phenomenon.[10] A curious reporter from the magazine *American Dancer* set out in 1936 to test the validity of this rumor and concluded: "Fred Astaire creates his own numbers to a great extent. . . . [But] no dancer, no matter how great he is, or how clever, can correct himself. He must have someone to assist and criticize him if he is to grow and be successful, and this is what Hermes Pan does for Fred Astaire."

In part, this need for an in-house critic is dictated by the film medium itself. In the theatre one can test a routine on the audience and change it before the next performance, but there is no such luxury in films. By the time an audience sees a number, it is usually too late to make changes other than cutting it completely.

Other descriptions and interviews attest to Astaire's dominance in the creative process. But the best evidence comes from the films themselves. Although Astaire was teamed with a considerable number of dance directors and assistants during his long career, the choreography generally retains the same remarkably high quality and apt artistic sensibility no matter who his collaborator is. One can also look at the dances that some of his choreographic collaborators created on their own. Though skillful, they frequently fall back on

[10] Pan came by his improbable name naturally: an American of Greek descent, he shortened his original surname, Panagiotopulos.

Hermes Pan in action in 1936

the kind of tap or show-biz clichés that Astaire consistently avoided, and they often have a naïve relationship to the music, something never found in Astaire's dances. Perhaps the purest test is the dances in *The Sky's the Limit,* a film for which Astaire had no choreographic collaborator or assistant: each is as masterfully crafted as any Astaire ever danced.

Astaire's dance directors or assistants usually worked with him in the duets and solos and sometimes contributed ideas subject to his approval. They would also be responsible for remembering the choreography (since filming might happen weeks, or even months, after the dance was created), arranging the chorus dances, and choreographing any dances in which Astaire did not appear.[11] Sometimes others would contribute to the numbers—ideas, concepts, steps. According to Astaire, George Gershwin liked to come to rehearsals when they worked together on Broadway and would "often jump up from the piano and demonstrate an idea for a step, or an extra twist to something I was already experimenting with" —and several of these ideas were used. Astaire also notes that the finish to a dance number in one of his films was developed from an idea contributed by an MGM prop man. Then, too, Astaire's partners often made suggestions: "Barrie would contribute," says Astaire, "and so would Ginger, after we got going; she'd say, 'How about this,' and I'd say, 'Fine, we'll use it.' "[12]

ASTAIRE'S WORKING METHODS

A perfectionist, Astaire spent weeks creating the choreography for his films, most of it before actual filming began. In a secluded rehearsal space provided by the studio he would work with his partners and his choreographic collaborators and assistants to music provided by a rehearsal pianist—Hal Borne in the 1930s, Tommy Chambers, Walter Ruick, and others later on.

The process of creation was long and agonizing.[13] As Astaire recalls:

> You go to a rehearsal hall months ahead. . . . When you come in you don't know *any*thing of what you're going to do. . . . For maybe a couple of days we wouldn't get anywhere—just stand in front of a mirror and fool around. . . . Then suddenly I'd get an idea, or one of them would get an idea. . . . So then we'd get started. . . . There was no telling when you might finish. You might get practically the whole idea of the routine done that day, but then you'd work on it, edit it, scramble it, and so forth. It might take sometimes as long as two, three weeks to get something to go.

Though Astaire spent enormous amounts of time in the rehearsal studio, his work before the cameras—when costs to the studio were highest—was remarkably efficient. Table 4 gives the log for the production of perhaps his most famous dance, the solo in *Royal Wedding* in which he dances on the walls, ceiling, and floor of a hotel room. Astaire had been planning such a dance for years and had worked out the choreography during ten weeks of preproduction rehearsals. When it came time to shoot the number, Astaire spent thirteen more days rehearsing it, in August and early September, during which time he made some silent photo tests and re-

Ginger Rogers with dance director Robert Alton on the set of *The Barkleys of Broadway* (1949)

[11] This division of labor is not unusual in dance history. At the Paris Opéra in the nineteenth century, for instance, choreographers took charge of the chorus and the general structure of the ballet, but soloists usually fashioned their own material. Indeed, since choreography is fashioned directly on human beings, collaboration in one form or another is very often involved, as in the case of the great British ballet choreographer Frederick Ashton, who often likes to have his dancers improvise while he selects and edits their ideas.

[12] Mark Sandrich, who directed five of the Astaire-Rogers musicals, once remarked: "You would be surprised how much [Rogers] adds to the numbers. Fred arranges them, and then when they get to rehearsing, Ginger puts in her own suggestions. And they're sensible ones. Fred discusses every one with her at length, and a good many of them are used." As Rogers laconically puts it, "We all pitched in."

[13] Another function of those long rehearsal sessions was to get Astaire back into dancing shape. Beyond a bit of golf, he never did much exercising between pictures.

corded the singing and music for the complete number.[14] Then, fully prepared, he was able to accomplish the filming of this exceptionally complicated number in less than a day and a half: he started on the morning of September 7, and well before lunch on September 8 he was posing on the set for still photographs, usually the last operation in a musical number.

In working out the choreography, Astaire would establish how the music for the number would be paced and arranged, and would determine the essentials about how it should be shot. He was very often involved in other aspects of the film as well—in script conferences, auditions, and discussions over the selection of key production personnel.[15] In 1936, Ginger Rogers gave a spirited account of what it was like to work with Astaire:

> How do you think those Astaire routines were accomplished? With mirrors? . . . Well, I thought I knew what concentrated work was before I met Fred, but he's the limit. Never satisfied until every detail is right, and he will not compromise. No sir! What's more, if he thinks of something better after you've finished a routine, you do it over. . . . He may get a hunch in the middle of the night. And he doesn't confine his mental gymnastics to dancing. Sometimes he'll think of a new line of dialogue or a new angle for the story. Ask the boys around the studio. They never know what time of night he'll call up and start ranting enthusiastically about a fresh idea. . . . No loafing on the job of an Astaire picture, and no cutting corners.

As this suggests, Astaire would worry a lot—before, during, and after production. The loose, carefree character he played in so many films was anything but autobiographical.[16] "I have a horror of not delivering," he observes; he found it difficult to see himself in the rushes, and preferred movies to the stage because he did not have to go to his own opening nights. Despite his extraordinary success, he says, "I always need a lot of convincing about the acceptance of my work"—a statement that many who worked with Astaire would consider an understatement of monumental proportions. As the director Vincente Minnelli recalls:

> He lacks confidence to the most enormous degree of all the people in the world. He will not even go to see his rushes. He'll stay out in the alley and pace up and down and worry and collar you when you come out and say "How was so and so?" . . . It would be much simpler if he would go and look at them himself, you know. But he always thinks he is no good.

Or lyricist-scriptwriter Alan Jay Lerner:

> I remember when I was doing a film with Fred Astaire, it was nothing for him to work three or four days on two bars of music. One evening in the dark grey hours of dusk, I was walking across the deserted MGM lot when a small, weary figure with a towel around his neck suddenly appeared out of the giant cube sound stages. It was Fred. He came over to me, threw a heavy arm around my shoulder and said: "Oh Alan, why doesn't someone tell me I cannot dance?" The tormented illogic of his question made any answer insipid, and all I could do was walk with him in silence.

Reflecting on Astaire's temperament, director Charles Walters has suggested that Astaire's "problem" is that he doesn't really enjoy performing, that he's "not a ham," and might well have been happier as a dance director.

Astaire warns against the notion that he is "too lightfooted and lightheaded to know what it's all about." In contrast, "I am really bad-tempered, impatient, hard to please, critical." Sometimes his temper is directed at others—particularly at critics, a pet peeve. After some snide notices in *Time* in the 1950s, he let himself go in public, telling a reporter the reviews were "stupid, small-minded, incomprehensive and block-headed." Astaire's attitude toward criticism is described by his sister: "He can't believe [his work is] any good. So when people tell him they like it, he thinks they're being nice. Trying to let him down easy. Yet one little criticism, and he gets mad. He blows up, but quickly it's over. Then afterwards he says, 'Yes, you were right. It stinks.' "

As this suggests, the anger and creative anguish are mostly directed at himself. Trudy Wellman, a secretary who worked on *Top Hat,* recalls the shooting of Astaire's solo in the title number: "He gets very annoyed with himself, just with himself. . . . He would take that cane and he would break it across his knee, just like that, and, of course, we were all shocked because we knew we only had 13 canes. . . . It was a good thing we had that 13th cane because that was the take we printed." And once, after some sixty years of almost unrelieved success on stage, film, and television, Astaire observed, "I've never yet got anything 100% right. Still," he said, brightening a bit, "it's never as bad as I think it is."

---

[14] Prerecording of the sound tracks was standard procedure in virtually all of Astaire's numbers. Thus, during filming Astaire would mouth his own words and perform to the playback. For clarity, taps and other sounds would be dubbed in later. Unlike most Hollywood performers, Astaire dubbed his own taps, while his dance assistant usually dubbed those of his partner. Astaire recalls, "I used to do it because I—I don't know, I wanted to kill myself, I guess, or something; but God, it's an awful job." During the 1930s there were a few numbers in which the singing and dancing sounds were recorded by microphones on the set, and a few others in which Astaire performed to live piano whose sound was later replaced (postrecorded) by that of an orchestra.

[15] Astaire also concerned himself with how the film was promoted, marketed, and even projected: in the mid-1930s he got Radio City Music Hall to cease a practice in which portions of dances from a film were projected over the film's opening titles.

[16] As one interviewer observed, "Astaire has found out that he is most convincing as a successful breezy character, while less popular as a struggling person. He is a little bewildered about this, since he has struggled a great deal in his life and wonders why people don't believe that he too knows how to worry."

Astaire's self-doubt, insecurity, and shyness, and his hypercritical ability to see in his works imperfections that are invisible to anyone else, could make him difficult, even exasperating, to work with. Nevertheless, the rehearsal atmosphere was often leavened with humor and practical joking; as Hermes Pan recalls, "We worked hard, but we had a lot of laughs, too."[17] Moreover, co-workers fully appreciated that Astaire's efforts were directed toward improving the product, not simply exalting his own ego. Joan Fontaine, one of Astaire's partners, has acidly observed that Astaire was just about the only leading man in Hollywood whose "first concern was the film, not himself." Reflecting on a lifetime of experience on stage and screen in 1975, director Rouben Mamoulian observed: "Of all the actors and actresses I've ever worked with, the hardest worker is Fred Astaire. He behaved like he was a young man whose whole destiny depended on being successful in his first film. He rehearses between takes, after takes—there's no limit to his professionalism."

The appreciation for Astaire's professionalism by his more ordinary co-workers is touchingly suggested by an incident in 1944. Principal filming for *Ziegfeld Follies,* fraught with delays and difficulties, was completed only a few days before Astaire was scheduled to leave on a USO tour. At the end he was working with a temperature of 102, a reaction to the vaccination shots he had been given for his overseas trip. Such dedication inspired someone in the cast to circulate a petition in tribute:

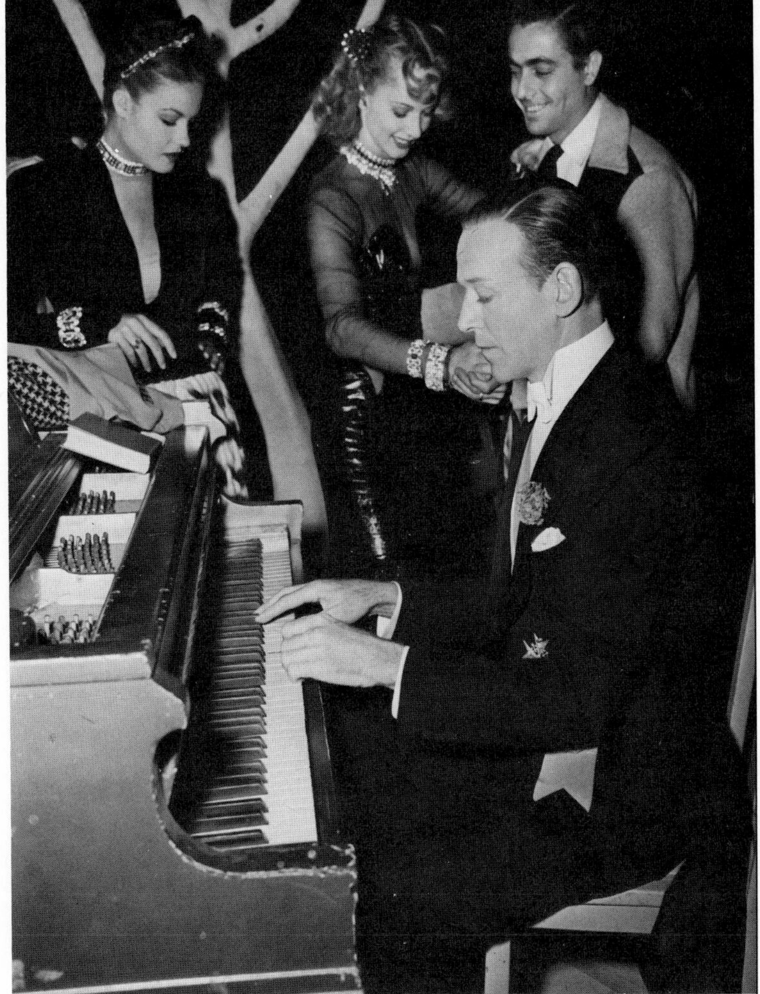

On the *Ziegfeld Follies* set in 1944

Los Angeles, California
August 31st, 1944.

TO WHOM IT MAY CONCERN:

We, the undersigned, devote this space to the expression of our gratitude to those who made it possible for us to be associated for a while with FRED ASTAIRE, a man endowed with qualities so innumerable that all the superlatives we could find would still fail to adequately describe his genuine greatness.

Never have we seen a man, whose name has been star-caliber for so long and whose talent is outstanding, give out with as much hard work for the many months of most difficult and tiresome routines, and yet maintain through it all such a fine spirit of tolerance, consideration and cooperation with respect to every one around him. —It was a pleasure and a great privilege at all times to serve such a man.

The indomitable spirit shown by Mr. Astaire while working under high tension shall remain an inspiration to every one of us, even long after the picture has been forgotten.

All of us who worked on the picture

cc to:
Mr. Eddie Mannix
Mr. Louis B. Mayer
Mr. Arthur Freed
Mrs. Fred Astaire
Mr. Nicholas Schenck

[17] Much of this off-screen humor was broad and rough, a release, perhaps, from the kind of understated wit that was an Astaire specialty on the screen. On one occasion in the 1930s Astaire asked Pan if he wanted a drink of water; when Pan said yes, Astaire threw water all over him, and this developed into a running gag still being played in the 1950s. Rehearsing with Rita Hayworth, Astaire once took hold of her after having dipped his hands and arms in a bucket of ice; "keeping the laughs going . . . was part of the day's work," he relates.

ASTAIRE'S CHOREOGRAPHY: STYLE AND CONSTRAINTS

As his working procedures suggest, Astaire's dances were crafted with meticulous care. Yet despite all the thought and planning that went into them, they emerge on the screen with an engaging freshness and spontaneity; they never look overrehearsed. Ironically, Astaire argues, the extensive rehearsals allow for the spontaneity: "I think it's probably the secret of the success of the numbers that you know it so well you never have to think about what the next step is. . . . It looks like it just happens. . . . It only comes from rehearsing. It just becomes part of you."

Nor are the dances overchoreographed. Indeed, an economy of construction is one of their most striking qualities. No number is a grab bag of effects; rather, each seeks to explore a limited number of choreographic ideas, each has its own distinctive movement vocabulary—two or three central ideas that are carefully presented and developed as the dance proceeds. As Astaire observed in a 1937 interview: "Working out the steps is a very complicated process—something like writing music. You have to think of some step that flows into the next one, and the whole dance must have an integrated pattern. If the dance is right, there shouldn't be a single superfluous movement. It should build to a climax and stop!" When he was asked whether he had ever made the statement "Get it as perfect as you can—and then cut two minutes," he replied, "That's a good phrase. If I said it, I'm delighted."

Although the dances are economical, they are in no sense simple. Beneath the uncluttered texture lurks an amazing and endlessly revisitable world of nuance and subtle complexity. In preparing a ballet tribute to Astaire in 1983, Jerome Robbins, together with two New York City Ballet dancers, spent twelve hours analyzing one Astaire dance—and still felt they had not grasped all the detail. "Astaire's dancing looks so simple, so disarming, so easy," observed Robbins, "yet the understructure, the way [he] sets the steps on, over or against the music, is so surprising and inventive." Ginger Rogers thoroughly agrees:

> Just try and keep up with those feet of his sometime! Try and look graceful while thinking where your right hand should be, and how your head should be held, and which foot you end the next eight bars on, and whether you're near enough to the steps to leap up six of them backward without looking. Not to mention those Astaire rhythms. Did you ever count the different tempos he can think up in three minutes?

The dances are also stylistically eclectic. What Astaire calls his "outlaw style" is an odd and singularly unpredictable blend of tap (making use, however, of the entire body) and ballroom with elements from other dance forms worked in. But he denies being a specialist in any form and says he resents any rules and restrictions that would follow from adherence to a specific approach. What holds everything together is Astaire's distinctive sensibility: the casual sophistication, the airy wit, the transparent rhythmic intricacy, the

Hermes Pan working with Ginger Rogers in 1936

apparent ease of execution, the consummate musicality. These qualities are apparently inbred in this most natural of dancers who, dapper and lithe (5 feet 9 or 10, 135 to 140 pounds), had few problems to overcome as a dancer. One was an inability to be clumsy, a defect unlikely to inspire much sympathy from others; when awkwardness was called for, he often resorted to extreme, and ultimately unconvincing, measures, such as walking on the outsides of his feet (see 7 B 2). He frequently tried to disguise his other problem, his disproportionately large hands (suggested in 16 F 2), by curling his middle two fingers (see, for example, p. 54).

As Robbins suggests, Astaire's dances are particularly notable for their inventiveness. The constant quest for originality, for doing something new and fresh in each dance, was almost an obsession. Not only did he assiduously avoid clichés—which made him virtually unique in Hollywood—but he was highly wary of creating his own clichés and would often run his previous films to refresh his memory about what he had done before.[18] Astaire's sensitivity on the issue was amusingly displayed when he appeared as the sole

[18] In his stage career, however, Astaire would sometimes carry over an idea from one dance to the next—particularly the "oompah trot" or "runaround," which became something of a trademark for his sister and himself. He brought several choreographic ideas from his stage days to his films—including, in 9 D, the runaround.

guest on the Dick Cavett television show in 1971. Two solos, filmed fifteen years apart, were shown. As it happened, each used the same bit of business—a cane or a closed umbrella was sailed through the air to land perfectly in a waiting receptacle (see 16 E 14 and 29 G 4). Astaire was a bit flustered and almost apologetic to discover that he had repeated this three-second stunt.

The result of Astaire's inventiveness is a series of dances similar in choreographic sensibility and yet amazingly dissimilar in means. The few ideas that are repeated in Astaire's dances are mostly incidental steps, particularly transitional ones. Even the most important among these, the Astaire double helix—a witty do-si-do-like maneuver in which Astaire and his partner make spinning spirals around each other until they wind up in each other's arms (a splendid example is illustrated in 7 B 14–19)—which appears in perhaps one-third of Astaire's duets, was varied in a surprising number of imaginative ways over the course of his film career.

Interestingly, the same basic idea sometimes reappears in different guises in several dances in the same film—a sort of choreographic leitmotif varied and developed as the film progresses, as if Astaire were seeking to explore all its possibilities in the manner of an étude. Thus all the dances in *Roberta* make prominent use of steps with crossed legs, all the duets in *Top Hat* use sequential imitation, most of the dances in *Shall We Dance* contrast ballet and popular dance styles, and the dances in *The Belle of New York* frequently apply the ballet pose known as *attitude*, with the bent leg raised in back.

The variety in Astaire's dances is particularly remarkable because he was working within considerable constraints, some of them self-imposed. One constraint was choreographic: whole areas of dance movement were little explored. Ideas from ballet, modern dance, Latin dance, acrobatics, and Broadway jazz dance are used sparingly; he almost never uses falls (he didn't even go down on his knees until his twelfth film), and even the use of lifts is limited. Moreover, the vast majority of his dances are solos and duets; there are just a few trios, and only very occasionally does he incorporate a chorus meaningfully into his choreography.

Another constraint on the dances follows from the limited range of emotions they explore. Astaire's films are light romantic comedies, and the plots are similar in essential strategy. The vast majority follow the ABC pattern. A: attraction, when boy and girl meet; B: breakup (over mistaken identity, disagreements, or whatever); C: conciliation, when they resolve their differences.[19] Astaire's dances are at the service of the plot and tone of the film, and accordingly most of the duets deal with romance. There is considerable emotional range in the various pleasures and pains of love, of course, but it scarcely encompasses all human passions. To expand the possibilities, Astaire and his partner could have stepped out of character in some of their duets—since many take place onstage in the films, this would have been easy. But Astaire did not explore this approach very often. Only one of his duets in the 1930s, for example, is performed out of character—he and Rogers play a pair of doom-eager socialites in an onstage number in *Follow the Fleet* (6 J)—and even there romance remains an essential element.

While the duets mostly reflect the romantic theme of the film, so, often, do the solos, showing the dancer happily, or not so happily, in love. At other times the solos are fairly objective display pieces in which Astaire usually remains more or less in character.

A third constraint on Astaire's dances derives from the music. With very few exceptions, they use arrangements of popular songs of the Tin Pan Alley type—songs remarkable for their spareness of form and emotion. As Charles Hamm observes in his excellent study of the popular song in America, the restrictions seem as tight as those embraced by haiku poets: an optional verse followed by a chorus that tends to be made up of four eight-measure strains which are most commonly arranged in AABA or ABAC patterns. The songs exhibit "little tonal contrast or variety" and are limited in subject matter almost exclusively to romantic love. Astaire may have found the popular song's efficiency of form and style in keeping with his economical approach to choreography.[20] But unlike contemporary ballet choreographers, whose choice of music often ranges from Bach to Webern and from rag to rock, Astaire remained contentedly constrained in his musical options.[21]

A fourth constraint was financial. Astaire has always acknowledged his interest in making money (he never needed adversity to summon his muse) and fully accepted the necessity of pleasing a wide audience in order to be successful in the business: "If you don't make a buck you're just out of luck because that means you haven't got it." At the same time, he

[19] Because of their brevity and of the time given over to musical numbers (see Table 7), Astaire's musical films rarely are able to develop much in the way of a separate subplot, and are more like short stories than like plays or novels—or even like stage musicals. Richard Rodgers is said to have argued that a musical plot that takes more than two or three minutes to tell is too complicated for Broadway; for films of the Astaire era, *one* minute might be a more realistic limit.

[20] The high value songwriters of the era put on economy is ebulliently expressed by lyricist Irving Caesar: "I'll tell you the best popular song ever written. . . . The most perfect popular song: (singing) 'I wonder who's kissing her now.' That's the *entire* story right there—you don't have to know another word. . . . A real top popular song in my opinion must have the title, and the great melody under it, embody the entire song so that after you've sung the first line . . . your own imagination creates the rest."

[21] Moreover, virtually all of Astaire's dances are in double meter; in his entire film career he only did one fully-realized waltz (11 L).

was wary of playing down to the audience: "if you do that they're not going to like it." Of course he was also interested in satisfying himself, and, indeed, if all he really wanted was to please the audience, he hardly needed to work so hard.

Finally, the film medium itself created restraints. One reason Astaire rarely used dancing choruses was that he felt they did not go over well on the screen; similarly, he almost always stayed close to his partner in duets, because the camera cannot deal well with wide spaces, and perhaps part of the double-helix maneuver's appeal for him was that it doesn't take up much space. Of course the medium also furnished certain opportunities, which will be discussed later.

ASTAIRE'S CHOREOGRAPHY: SOURCES OF THE MOVEMENT VOCABULARY

As noted, Astaire's dances are crafted with extreme care and remarkable economy. Each tends to be built around two or three central ideas which are then carefully manipulated and developed in the course of the number.[22] The inspiration for a dance's distinctive movement vocabulary could come from a variety of sources.

STEPS

Many of the ideas are purely choreographic—that is, Astaire would stumble on an interesting step in rehearsal and would then develop it, exploring its various possibilities. For example, the "I'll Be Hard to Handle" duet in *Roberta* (4 D) frequently has the partners playfully swinging one leg across the other, and this simple idea is developed and elaborated in several ways in the course of the dance.

THE MUSIC

An essential source of inspiration for Astaire was the music: "I find that I have to have music that will give my idea some inspiration before I start working out the actual steps. If the music is bad, I am completely stumped. I can't do anything."[23]

While the relation of Astaire's dances to the music is always intimate and affectionate, it is never slavish. One of the particular glories of his choreography—his eye-music, to use Stravinsky's term—is the way he plays with the music, going against it at times, altering and shading the tempo within a single phrase, stopping for a while and then spurting ahead to catch up. A nice example occurs in the "Cheek to Cheek" duet in *Top Hat.* At one point the orchestra plays a musical phrase exactly the same way twice. The first time the choreography matches it directly, nuance for nuance; the second time the choreography goes against it, a sensuous legato dance phrase arching over the music's bouncy rhythms. Yet in both cases the choreography fits the music with taste, precision, and apparent inevitability (5 E 13–16).

Astaire has a remarkable facility for deriving inspiration from the melodic line or from the accompaniment—sequentially or simultaneously—when it suits him. The "Night and Day" duet in *The Gay Divorcee* (3 E), for example, has a yearning, insistent melody placed over an agitated counter-rhythm. The choreography moves intricately back and forth from one musical line to the other in the course of the dance.

Specific musical characteristics of a song would often suggest choreographic ideas to Astaire. For example, part of the melody for "Something's Gotta Give" in *Daddy Long Legs* (28 H) derives its appeal from a temporary feeling of hesitation—holding back slightly and then falling forward into a satisfying resolution. Astaire picks up this idea of holding back and then pushing ahead and builds it into the choreography. In several dances in the early 1940s, he made witty use of a characteristic of many contemporary big-band arrangements: endings that occur suddenly, without buildup, fanfare, or ornament.

Astaire is also very aware of the drama suggested by the popular-song form. Most of the songs in his films are of the AABA form—that is, made up of one central melodic idea repeated three times, with the third statement separated from the second by a strain (called the "release") of contrasting musical material. The dramatic high point in such songs tends to be at the beginning of the final statement of the A strain, its reappearance having been artfully delayed by the release strain. Astaire often makes specific choreographic use of this formal characteristic: it is at this point, for example, that he first firmly clasps his partner close to him in each of two seductive duets, "Change Partners" in *Carefree* (10 E 13) and "They Can't Take That Away from Me" in *The Barkleys of Broadway* (22 I 21).

While Astaire was inspired by the music, the inspiration went the other way, too, for if Astaire is a dancer's dancer, he is also a musician's musician. Alec Wilder, in his extensive

[22] In effect, he seems to subscribe to George Balanchine's observation: "Gestures . . . have certain family relations. As groups they impose their own laws. The more conscious an artist is, the more he comes to understand these laws, and to respond to them."

[23] However, this does not mean he needed to have the finished score before he could begin choreographing. Often he would begin working to music composed by himself or by his rehearsal pianist. When the score subsequently arrived, steps and music would be adapted and arranged to fit each other.

study, *American Popular Song*, observes: "Every song written for Fred Astaire seems to bear his mark. Every writer, in my opinion, was vitalized by Astaire and wrote in a manner they had never quite written in before: he brought out in them something a little better than their best—a little more subtlety, flair, sophistication, wit, and style, qualities he himself possesses in generous measure." (For some results, see Table 5.) Composers generally agree: Burton Lane considers Astaire "the world's greatest musical performer." As Irving Berlin appreciatively wrote, "He knew the value of a song and his heart was in it before his feet took over."

Berlin went on to stress that his admiration was not only for Astaire's dancing but also for his singing—for the musicianship with which Astaire handled the music, and the integrity with which he handled the lyric. In fact, Berlin says that he would rather have Fred Astaire sing his songs than anyone.[24] Jerome Kern, always a severe critic of the way his songs were sung, also preferred Astaire to all others. Oscar Levant concludes: "Fred Astaire is the best singer of songs the movie world has ever known. His phrasing has individual sophistication that is utterly charming. Presumably the runner-up would be Bing Crosby, a wonderful fellow, but he doesn't have the unstressed elegance of Astaire." However Crosby might view that assessment, his own thoughtful tribute to Astaire is of interest: "He has a remarkable ear for intonation, a great sense of rhythm and what is most important, he has great style—style in my way of thinking is a matter of delivery, phrasing, pace, emphasis, and most of all presence."[25] Jazz critic Whitney Balliett has written of Astaire: "He makes every song fresh and full-faced, as if each were important news."

A song writer of some distinction himself, Astaire often influenced the composition of a song.[26] And, like other Hollywood choreographers, he usually determined how the music would be shaped and arranged when he created the choreography. This would include not only the overall form of the dance (an AABA song might be arranged AABABA, for example) but also the development of the accompaniment line—particularly since he danced to the accompaniment as well as to the melody. As part of this, of course, he would also often determine the song's tempo—whether it was to be bright or somber, staid or lilting.

Irving Berlin auditioning an *Easter Parade* song for Judy Garland, MGM studio head L. B. Mayer, and producer Arthur Freed, 1948

Because of Astaire's musical sensitivity and integrity, these musical decisions could be made without complaint from the composers: as Jerome Kern said, "Astaire *can't* do anything bad." In fact, as the composers probably were well aware, Astaire sometimes improved their work. John Wilson quotes Irving Berlin: " 'You give Astaire a song, and you could forget about it. He knew the song. . . . He didn't change anything. And if he did change anything'—Mr. Berlin's sly chuckle rattled over the telephone line—'he made it better.' " As Wilder puts it, Astaire "made listeners think lots of songs were better than they really were. . . . He could make 'Trees' sound good."

One final musical area should be mentioned: orchestration. Some of Astaire's dances clearly influenced, or were influenced by, the orchestration. A delightful instance is the "Oops" duet in *The Belle of New York* (26 G), where some of the humor derives from an ingenious synchrony of choreography and orchestration. Nonetheless, if there is one musical area in which the Astaire films at times show weakness, it is here. In some films Astaire was brilliantly served by his orchestrators (Robert Russell Bennett in *Swing Time* and *A Damsel in Distress*, for example), but in others (*Top Hat* and some of the MGM musicals of the 1940s and 1950s) there is occasionally a sappiness and a lush, overblown sentimental-

[24] On the life-long friendship that evolved between Astaire and Berlin, see p. 78.

[25] One important composer who was less impressed by Astaire's voice, apparently, was George Gershwin. Astaire says he does not like his own singing voice.

[26] Astaire calls songwriting a "serious hobby of mine" and considered giving up performing to devote himself to composing. He has published quite a few songs, one of which, "I'm Building Up to an Awful Let-down," with an agile lyric by Johnny Mercer, reached hit status in 1936, to the composer's infinite delight. Though uncredited, Astaire furnished music used in two of his film dances, 20 O and 24 B (see also 18 O). As he has demonstrated in several numbers, Astaire is also an accomplished pianist and drummer.

ity in the orchestration that contrasts markedly with Astaire's understated, uncluttered, transparent style.

THE LYRIC

The words of the song also contribute to the dance's movement vocabulary. Much of the "Oops" dance, not too surprisingly, is a filigree of intricately timed mishaps. Astaire's solo "I Won't Dance" in *Roberta* is designed, in part, to show that his legs are not entirely under his conscious control, a condition suggested by the lyric (4 F). And in that film's "I'll Be Hard to Handle" duet, Ginger Rogers graphically demonstrates to Astaire the validity of the song's title (4 D). Sometimes the lyric specifically describes the dance's movement quality or even its basic step: "The Continental," "The Yam," "The Shorty George," "The Sluefoot." And, of course, the lyric in quite a few songs determines the general look of the dance, if not the exact steps: "Puttin' On the Ritz," "Let's Face the Music and Dance," "I Can't Be Bothered Now," "A Couple of Swells," "Oh, Them Dudes," "The Ritz Roll and Rock." In some cases the lyric has suggested the dance's structure, if not its movement vocabulary. In *The Sky's the Limit,* Astaire partly structured his powerful solo "One for My Baby" to follow the narrative suggested by Johnny Mercer's evocative lyric (17 F).

In a sense, the seriousness with which Astaire treated the lyric is actually confirmed in numbers where he abandons the lyric because the words do not suit the emotional situation. The lyric is not sung as part of the "Smoke Gets in Your Eyes" duet in *Roberta* because the dance is about loving dependency and the lyric is about shattered romance (4 H). And there is no singing in the "Dancing in the Dark" number in *The Band Wagon* (27 E), probably because the dance is about a slowly awakening love whereas the lyric suggests a more fully developed romance.

THE GIMMICK

Many of Astaire's dances, including many of the best remembered, are built around a gimmick, sometimes relating to dialogue or the plot. According to the scripts of *Royal Wedding* and *The Belle of New York,* love makes one feel one can dance on the ceiling or walk on air, and dances in these films ingeniously make those conceits literal (25 H, 26 D). In *Carefree,* Astaire dances and plays golf simultaneously (10 A) to show Rogers he can do two things at the same time (she is unimpressed). The lyric also may inspire (or reinforce) a gimmick developed in a dance: firecrackers in *Holiday Inn* (15 M), flying shoes in *The Barkleys of Broadway* (22 G), a dance on sand in *The Belle of New York* (26 K).

But many of Astaire's gimmick dances were fashioned quite independently of the films' scripts and the precise musical contexts. In fact, some of them were thought up years before the films were even made—and then often at four in the morning, says Astaire, the time when he gets some of his best ideas. Astaire simply filed the ideas, waiting for a suitable time to use them. Thus the ceiling dance, though it related to a line in the script, was an idea he had been carrying around for some time; so was the golf dance. A few had autobiographical inspirations. An abortive dance aboard a rocking ship in *Royal Wedding* (25 C) derived from an actual incident that had happened to Astaire and his sister in 1923, and a comedy duet with Judy Garland in *Easter Parade* (21 E) in which her dress begins to shed feathers is doubtless a reference to a similar and oft-recalled event that occurred in connection with the filming of the "Cheek to Cheek" duet in *Top Hat* thirteen years earlier.

Whatever their inspiration, most of Astaire's gimmick dances involved setting up obstacles that he seems to take a Buster Keaton–like pleasure in overcoming. Some of the obstacles were physical; if he could dance while playing golf, he could also dance on roller skates (8 H) or while drumming (9 J) or while conducting an orchestra (13 K). Some obstacles involved film effects such as slow motion (10 B, 21 J) or process photography (7 F, 20 F, 22 G, 26 D).

Astaire's success in overcoming these obstacles was not uniform. Sometimes the choreography suffered when Astaire concentrated on the effect. Of the two gimmick dances in *Royal Wedding,* the ceiling dance is the more spectacular, but it tends to wear somewhat on re-viewing because the choreography must be reined in to allow for smooth transitions as Astaire's floor rotates under him. The other dance, in which he partners a clothes tree (25 B), seems actually to expand his choreographic opportunities, and the resulting number seems infinitely re-viewable.[27]

ASTAIRE'S PARTNERS

"He made them all look good," it is often said. This assertion may be a bit exaggerated, since a few of Astaire's partners,

[27] Astaire animates the inanimate in several other dances: a cane in *Blue Skies* (20 F), a cape in *Funny Face* (29 G), a chair in *Silk Stockings* (30 D). Astaire's rule about not repeating himself applied to his gimmicks more than anything else. However, he did repeat one gimmick (though always in different ways): the notion of having portions of the floor move as he danced. The earliest use of this idea occurs in the fun-house trio in *A Damsel in Distress,* which takes place in part on a revolving turntable (9 D). The idea is elaborated in the "This Heart of Mine" production number in *Ziegfeld Follies* (18 G) and reappears briefly in a number in *The Barkleys of Broadway* (22 K).

however appealing they might be as actresses, seemed to present insurmountable obstacles as dancers, even to Astaire. Chief among these are the essentially untrained Joan Fontaine, the inadequately trained Audrey Hepburn, and the apparently ill-trained Leslie Caron, each of whom appeared in only one Astaire picture. And then there is Astaire's embarrassed but mercifully brief confrontation with ballet contortionist Harriet Hoctor in a dance in *Shall We Dance* (8 J). But in general the proposition is apt. Astaire's choreography and dancing are suited to his partners' abilities: to emphasize strengths and avoid weaknesses (a tactic applied in Astaire's choreography for himself, too, of course). And so, conversely, the partners' abilities can be considered an important source of the dances' movement vocabulary.

Thus Astaire's dances with Rogers make frequent use of her glamorously pliant back; their duets intricately explore the ballroom and tap vocabulary she was comfortable with. Dances with the ballet-trained Cyd Charisse and Vera-Ellen, by contrast, tend to be more space-devouring and full-out, with elaborate, if precise, arm movements and with leg extensions never found in the Rogers dances. Similarly, Astaire's duets with tap virtuoso Eleanor Powell make obvious use of her talents, and Astaire was clearly intrigued by Rita Hayworth's Spanish-dancing background—their duets often rely on sunny, sultry Latinisms.

Astaire's self-limiting approach is usually credited to his modesty and generosity. Without denying these qualities, it should be observed that what Astaire was doing in these duets was also plain good showmanship. A duet can only be as effective as its weaker half, and efforts to build up one partner at the expense of the other are likely to backfire. This is particularly the case for Astaire, because he liked to have the performers dance side by side much of the time, a configuration that gives maximum exposure to both dancers. And, of course, Astaire had plenty of opportunity to show his stuff in his solos elsewhere in the films.

The congenial duets were achieved at no small effort by Astaire. As Hermes Pan once observed, "Except for the times Fred worked with real professional dancers like Cyd Charisse, it was a twenty-five year war." The extent of Astaire's gift to his partners can be gauged by looking at what happens when these dancers are delivered into the hands of other choreographers. Thus Eleanor Powell delivers a clumsy pseudo-ballet number in *Broadway Melody of 1940* (12 G), and Rita Hayworth flounces around vacantly in *You Were Never Lovelier* (16 D), while Vera-Ellen and Charisse have some leggy solos that range from the banal to the merely serviceable (23 G, 26 I, 30 F).

THE PLOT: ASTAIRE AND THE INTEGRATED MUSICAL

The particular glory of the American musical, whether of the Broadway or the Hollywood variety, has been the songs and dances, not the plots. Nonetheless, musical numbers are often judged by how well they service the plot, and a considerable literature has emerged on the issue of the ideally integrated musical—one in which song, dance, and story are artfully blended.

It is often held that the earliest integrated dance number—a dance that advances the plot—is either George Balanchine's "Slaughter on Tenth Avenue" in *On Your Toes* of 1936 or Agnes de Mille's dream ballet "Laurey Makes Up Her Mind" in *Oklahoma!* of 1943. But before Balanchine and de Mille had done any work on Broadway, Fred Astaire was choreographing dances that were profoundly integrated into the plot—or, to put it another way, he was crafting dramatically eventful dances whose movement vocabulary was carefully related to, and developed from, the plot situation.

That Astaire was fully conscious of the issue is clear. During his last year on Broadway he told a reporter, "If I may say it, the success of the majority of my dances has been due in great measure to the fact that I have introduced my numbers not only at the psychological moment but in a manner that would logically blend with the ideas of the play." Later, in Hollywood, he observed, "To catch the public, dances must have a personality and a pattern. The times my dances have clicked are the times they had a reason, when they told a part of the story, and when they belonged in the plot." And in a 1937 interview: "It is extremely important for a dance cue to flow naturally in and out of the story. . . . Each dance ought to spring somehow out of a character or situation."

An early example is the romantic duet "Night and Day," which Astaire choreographed on Broadway and which was reproduced on film in *The Gay Divorcee* in 1934 (3 E). The dance is one of seduction. At the beginning the woman is irritated by Astaire's attentions, and she tries several times to get away from him during the course of the dance; at one point, in fact, she shoves him away and sends him staggering across the floor. But each time he encircles her, blocking her exit, enveloping her determinedly in an ardent dance of desire. Her defenses weaken until finally she is attracted, mesmerized, and won. There is no conceivable way the dance could be removed from the musical without leaving a noticeable gap in the plot, and it may well be the first dance number, either on Broadway or in Hollywood, to tell a plot-advancing story in its choreography.

Astaire made many dances that advance the plot this way

With Ginger Rogers in "Night and Day" in *The Gay Divorcee* (1934)

With Rogers in *Flying Down to Rio* (1933)

With Rogers in "The Continental" in *The Gay Divorcee*

With Lucille Bremer in *Yolanda and the Thief* (1945)

With Rita Hayworth in *You Were Never Lovelier* (1942)

With Cyd Charisse in *Silk Stockings* (1957)

—most typically duets, like "Night and Day," in which the relationship between the dancers becomes importantly altered during the course of the dance. Examples are "Isn't This a Lovely Day" in *Top Hat* (5 C), "Pick Yourself Up" in *Swing Time* (7 B), "Oops" in *The Belle of New York* (26 G), "Dancing in the Dark" in *The Band Wagon* (27 E), and "All of You" in *Silk Stockings* (30 D). In *Carefree,* produced five years before *Oklahoma!,* he even choreographed a dream dance that advanced the plot: Ginger Rogers falls asleep and comes to realize that she is in love with her psychiatrist, not her fiancé (10 B).

In addition to dances that directly advance the plot, Astaire created many that express character or elaborate and give depth to the emotional situation—dances that are intricately derived from the plot situation and expand upon it. Thus, although the script hints several times at the emotional attraction between the Astaire and Rogers characters in *Roberta,* it is only in their dance duet, "I'll Be Hard to Handle," that we really see the depth of this attachment and the delight each takes in the other's presence (4 D). Similarly, despair over a shattered romance is expressed in a dance in *Swing Time,* the mutual dependency of two married people deeply in love in a dance in *The Story of Vernon and Irene Castle* (a duet in *The Barkleys of Broadway* suggests the sexual elements of this dependency), the giddy joy of discovering love is requited in a solo in *You'll Never Get Rich,* and the anguish of being torn from the woman he loves by the duties of war in a solo in *The Sky's the Limit.* This also holds for many dances that take place onstage in the films; very often, even in these dances that seem simple insets, bearing only passing relation to the plot, one can see the attraction between the characters the dancers portray. When they leave the stage at the end of the number, one gets the distinct feeling, not so much that the dance has ended but, rather, that this is all the dancers are willing to show in public (for example, in 4 G, 7 D, 22 D).

The close relation so many of Astaire's dances bear to plot and character has led some dance critics, such as Arlene Croce and Anna Kisselgoff, to suggest that it is better to think of the Astaire musicals as dance films with plots rather than as story films with dances. This distinction is useful, and is surely far closer to the truth than the assertions of students of the Hollywood musical who suggest that Astaire's dances—particularly those in his films of the thirties—were not integrated, that they were "merely adornments," or "like cherries in a cherry cake: self-contained, very little affected by their environment, easily removable." Or of those who argue that the rise of the "fully integrated musical"—a "unity of expression" where "a story is told *through* songs and dance, not despite them"—had to wait until the 1940s and the emergence in Hollywood of Arthur Freed and Gene Kelly.[28]

Astaire's dances are fashioned with a sense of context that is often remarkably profound. But to experience this profundity one must carefully explore the dances' rich and subtle choreographic language.

ASTAIRE'S USE OF THE CAMERA

When he arrived in Hollywood, Astaire was quick to see the alternatives in filmmaking: "Either the camera will dance," he once observed, "or I will." It is very clear which he chose. However, the camera is no mere passive observer in Astaire's filmed dances; it, too, is choreographed.

Working by trial and error and largely without precedents, Astaire created a method for the filming of dance that was to dominate Hollywood for a generation; as Gene Kelly has observed, "The history of dance on film begins with Astaire." According to Astaire, his approach was forged in considerable part by indirection, not by self-conscious crusading: as directors discussed their ideas with him, he would assert his point of view mostly by vetoing approaches or results he didn't like. However, Hermes Pan and Ginger Rogers recall that Astaire was intensely concerned about the filming of his dances from the beginning.

While Astaire's approach was fundamentally cautious and conservative, he was also open to new ideas and to the development of old ones: once he had gained control over the filming of his numbers in the 1930s, and once he had firmly established his basic aesthetic for filmed dance, he began to open out, to expand, to make wider use of the medium—but always with an eye toward putting the medium at the service of the dance.

EDITING

Astaire made the camera an involved but unobtrusive spectator at his dances, comfortably distant enough to show the dancers fully from head to toe. The revolution he produced in Hollywood lay not so much in discovering the (rather obvious) full-figure shot as in successfully insisting that this camera perspective be almost the *only* acceptable one for the entire dance.

[28] This is not the view, incidentally, of Kelly's principal collaborator, Stanley Donen: "This may seem a funny thing to say, but in my opinion, [our movies] were really a direct continuation from the Astaire-Rogers musicals."

He determined not only how the camera would be positioned, but also how the dance sequences would be cut, editing them to preserve the integrity of the dance and effectively preventing the intrusion of cluttering and disorienting inserts in the dance sequences. As he observed in a 1937 interview: "In the old days they used to cut up all the dances on the screen. In the middle of a sequence, they would show you a close-up of the actor's face, or of his feet, insert trick angles taken from the floor, the ceiling, through lattice work or a maze of fancy shadows. The result was the dance had no continuity. The audience was far more conscious of the camera than of the dance."

A myth flourishes that most of Astaire's numbers are entirely unedited, presented in a single shot. Actually, almost all have at least one cut in them. He did experiment with the idea of unedited dances in his early years in Hollywood, and most of his few single-shot dances date from this period.[29] Some of the confusion may arise from the fact that many of his dances in the thirties were *filmed* in a single take and then edited later. That is, sometimes three cameras would record the entire dance from three slightly different perspectives, and then the results would be edited. But even this approach was largely abandoned by the end of the 1930s, by which time, according to Hermes Pan, they knew how the dance would look and could choose the correct angle before shooting. As Astaire notes, the one-take dances were "a terrifying, tiresome thing to do. . . . You could have done it much easier by cutting, . . . using the medium. The numbers I like the best that we did are those that were not stuck on just one thing."

While nearly all of Astaire's dances do contain at least one cut, the cutting is invariably done with enormous care and finesse. The vast majority of the cuts are modest shifts of perspective in order to follow the dancers as they travel, or to show them, or the choreography, to better advantage. Rarely does the size of the dancer relative to the camera frame change much. The cuts generally occur at times when the choreography is in transition or during a dance pattern that repeats, not when a special choreographic point is being made. They are never predictable, nor are they very noticeable (which is probably one reason why the single-shot notion persists).[30] But the cutting, of course, did allow the dance to be done in sections when that seemed advantageous.

Several aspects of Astaire's approach to film editing are of particular interest.

Director Mark Sandrich with Rogers and Astaire on the set of *Top Hat* (1935)

First, while few of Astaire's dances are presented in a single shot in the finished film, the number of shots used is almost always small. Typically a three-minute dance will be shown in two or three shots; few, even the most elaborate, use more than seven. This is a very different technique from the one prevailing when he first came to Hollywood. In *Flying Down to Rio* there is a ninety-second duet in the "Carioca" production number that is presented in twelve shots by director Thornton Freeland (see Table 6), and the same number of shots is used by director Mark Sandrich for the romantic duet "Night and Day" in Astaire's following feature, *The Gay Divorcee*. Then Astaire took over. The romantic duet in his next film, *Roberta*, is captured in two shots, and things stayed that way for twenty-five years.

Second, Astaire quickly got rid of cluttered camera perspectives. Three of the shots in the "Carioca" duet (4, 7, and 13 in the table) are framed in the foreground by posed observers, and Sandrich shot part of the "Night and Day" duet through Venetian blinds and another part from under a table (see 3 E 9, 11). Such distracting effects were never to be seen again in Astaire's dances.

Third, Astaire insisted the dance be allowed to finish fully on camera, rather than having the camera cut away from the dancers just as they conclude. This maddening finish occurs only once in an Astaire dance, in the early "Carioca" duet (shot 15 in the table). Thereafter, the camera always stayed on the dancers at the end of the dance, allowing both the audience and the performers to savor the moment of completion.

Fourth, Astaire brought the reaction shot under control.

[29] These are 3 C, 4 D, the duet in 5 F, 6 J, 7 D, 9 J, 10 B, and 13 C. There are also a few short dance episodes captured in a single shot: some of the exhibition dances in *The Story of Vernon and Irene Castle* and Astaire's solo within a production number in *Blue Skies* (20 O), for example.

[30] As Astaire notes, " 'Top Hat'—you think that was all one take? It *looks* like one take, because we were very careful to see that it did." Occasionally Astaire would cut between takes from the same angle, leaving a scarcely noticeable glitsch in the action at the cut; samples can be found in several solos, among them 13 K, 14 F, and 25 H.

At auditions for *Flying Down to Rio* in 1933—dance director Dave Gould, Astaire, director Thornton Freeland, associate producer Lou Brock, and RKO associate producer Lee Marcus

When a dance is performed for an on-screen audience, directors often feel they have to insert shots of the audience into the dance, apparently in the belief that people watching the film are incapable of remembering what the setting for the dance is, or need guidance about how to react to the dance. The ninety-second "Carioca" duet of 1933 is punctured by two such reaction shots (6 and 11 in the table). Astaire continued to allow the reaction shot as a device when there seemed a good plot reason for one; for example, a reaction shot of Ginger Rogers is inserted in an Astaire solo in *The Story of Vernon and Irene Castle* to make it clear that he is showing off for her benefit (11 B 10). But the device is used sparingly—less than one number in ten includes a reaction shot—and it is characteristically applied with great care, and usually only near the beginning of the number.[31]

Fifth, after his first films Astaire avoided what might be called the re-establishing shot. Many directors, in an apparent effort to vary the texture, like to cut back from time to time during a dance to a long-shot perspective. This is distracting and can undercut the force of the dance as the dancers are suddenly reduced in size relative to the frame. Such re-establishing shots appear throughout the "Carioca" duet (shots 4, 7, and 13 in the table) and, to a lesser extent, in the "Night and Day" duet a year later. Another example occurs as late as 1935 in the "Cheek to Cheek" duet in *Top Hat*. (In this case the cut back to a wider perspective is particularly damaging: occurring just as the dancers are exploding into a leap, it serves to vitiate the impact of the movement; see 5 E 17.) Such editing was almost never to appear again in Astaire's filmed dances.

Sixth, Astaire quickly triumphed over that most mindless of editing effects, the inserted close-up shot of the dancer's flickering feet. Such inserts appear in his two earliest film solos (2 E 9 and 3 B 2) and then never again for twenty-five years. "In every kind of dancing, even tap," he observed in 1937, "the movement of the upper part of the body is as important as that of the legs."[32]

Seventh, although Astaire banned inserted foot shots, he gradually came to accept the judicious use of medium shots showing only the upper body. In the early *Flying Down to Rio* and *The Gay Divorcee*, there are dances in which an upper-body medium shot is inserted (as in shot 9 in the

[31] For an apparent parody of the reaction-shot device, see 26 G 21. A reaction shot that seems to have been used to cover a dancing error or a mismatch of shots occurs in a duet in *Follow the Fleet* (6 D 10), and in a number in *Easter Parade*, a reaction shot is used to cover a change from slow motion to regular-speed photography in the dance (21 J 7). Other jarring reaction shots occur in 16 I 1 and 28 A.

[32] By the time of *Top Hat* in 1935, Astaire was making a joke about close-ups of the feet (see p. 87).

Director William Seiter with Rita Hayworth and Astaire on the set of *You Were Never Lovelier* (1942)

table). At first Astaire seems to have decided these were disruptive, and (with one minor exception: 6 H 12) no upper-body shots occur in any of the dances in his next six films. But whereas inserted shots of the feet distract from the dance and underline meaningless virtuosity, there is, at least in principle, a choreographic point to including upper-body shots, since these can sometimes help to emphasize the emotion of the dance—for example, the teasing sexiness that is so much a part of the "Continental" duet in *The Gay Divorcee* (3 F 12).

A major drawback to including upper-body shots in the dance is that an inserted shot involves two disruptions: a cut to the closer shot and then a cut back to the full-figure shot. By the time he came to film the romantic duet "Change Partners" in *Carefree,* Astaire had come up with an ingenious compromise which he found congenial. The upper-body shot was cut in at the point where it was dramatically appropriate. But then, instead of cutting back to the full-figure perspective, the camera *tracked* back to that position (10 E 13–14). Thus not only was the closer shot cut in with only a single disruption, but the shift at the cut allowed the combining of different takes and furnished another way to break down the dance into photographically viable segments. This procedure was used quite often in Astaire's next twenty films, particularly for duets.

SPACE

Any choreographer working with the camera must deal with the space defined by the camera's peculiar point of view: a narrow triangle with its acute angle at the lens. Choreographing for the camera is something like choreographing for a one-eyed spectator who is wearing blinders, and the most interesting dimension tends to be to and from the camera rather than from side to side, as it is onstage.

Astaire rarely seemed interested in experimenting with this spatial phenomenon in his Hollywood films; instead he nullified it. As the dancers move, the camera usually moves with them, keeping them fairly tight in the frame. If they move away from the camera, the camera closes in on them; if they move toward the camera, it backs up—something that is easier to discuss than to carry out. One is made aware that the dancers are traveling by reference to the floor or to the background, rather than by their progress through the camera's frame.

Keeping the camera tightly on a soloist requires no choreographic adjustment; keeping it tightly on both members of a duet (or on all three dancers in Astaire's rare trios) puts a distinct constraint on the choreography in that the dancers must stay close together (for a rare exception, see 8 G 6–7). Since the subject of most of Astaire's duets is romance in one way or another, this was not terribly difficult, but it re-

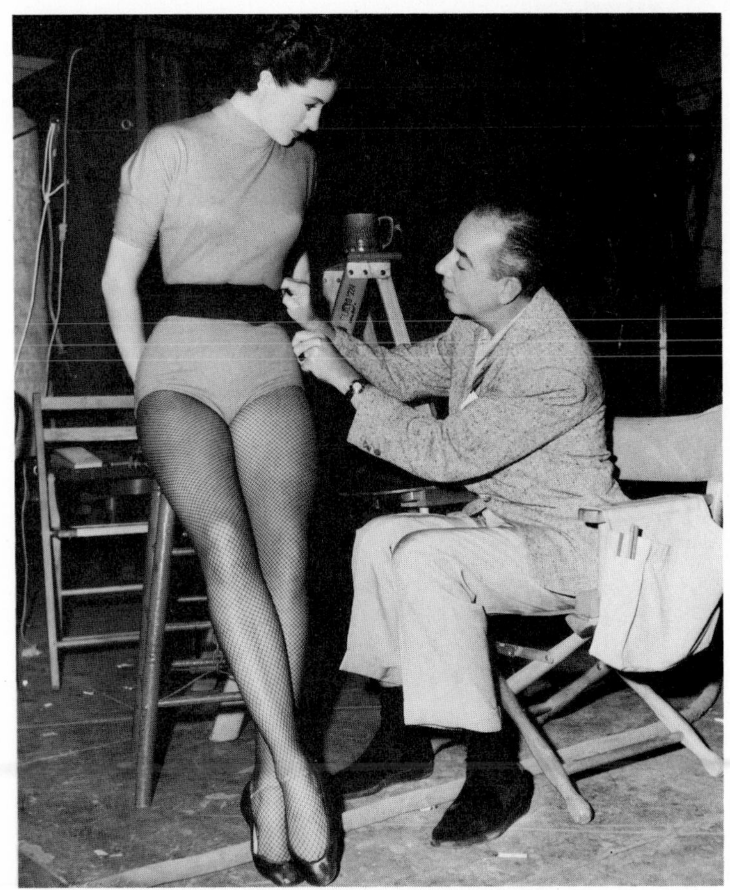

Director Vincente Minnelli with Cyd Charisse on the set of *The Band Wagon* (1953)

mained a definite choreographic restriction.[33] It is also notable that the performers in Astaire's duets frequently dance side by side, a configuration that comfortably fills the camera frame but is comparatively unusual in stage dancing.

Given the imaginativeness of Astaire's choreography, it is a bit strange that he didn't make more use of the dimension to and from the camera. Here and there one finds brief experiments. In the "Cheek to Cheek" duet in *Top Hat,* the dancers move dramatically to and from the camera in one passage (5 E 23), but this doesn't seem to have worked out very well, and the experiment was not repeated.

Nor did Astaire have much interest in using the camera's space to define entrances and exits. For entrances one might fix the camera and then have the dancer move into its range. This seems never to have been done. And there are about two dozen Astaire numbers that end with the disappearance of the dancer or dancers behind some visible obstacle—typically the wing of a stage or a doorway. Never do they disappear simply by maneuvering off-camera.[34]

Astaire's approach here seems to have owed more to aesthetic choice than to lack of imagination. His guiding principle was to let the dance speak for itself and to keep the camera work observant but unobtrusive. Furthermore, his films always involved real people in real situations (or in real fantasies), and he did not wish to distract from this by having the camera call attention to itself. He had little interest in being obviously cinematic.

Interestingly, in Astaire's television specials, created between 1958 and 1968, the use of the space defined by the camera is often much different than in his film work. There is far more movement to and from the camera, much more depth in the positioning of the dancers, and many entrances and exits by the dancers to and from the fixed camera's space. This may have been due in part to the relative immobility of television cameras of the era. Or it may have meant Astaire was gradually getting used to using the camera's depth; his films of the 1950s do show more sensitivity to this element.[35]

But the difference in approach may also derive from the format of these television variety shows, which differed in important respects from Astaire's Hollywood films. On television, Astaire acknowledged that the camera existed—he looked at it, talked to it. The dances were linked to no plot and to no real characters; above all, they were frankly being performed *for* the television camera and audience, with the camera an accepted fact of format, obtrusive by definition. By contrast, following accepted Hollywood convention, Astaire seems almost never to have looked directly into the camera during his entire motion-picture career (a rare exception is documented in 24 D 3).

Another difference between Astaire's film and television work is in his use of dissolves, which never occur in his films except to indicate a major change of locale or a passage of time. In general, dissolves are much more common on television. For dance, this is not a particularly good idea, since dissolves inevitably blur the picture temporarily. Yielding to television practices, however, Astaire did occasionally use dissolves in his television specials, though he used them far less frequently than is usually the case for dance in this medium.

SPECIAL EFFECTS

If Astaire was conservative about editing and about camera manipulations, he was equally cautious about special effects. He came to Hollywood at a time when Busby Berkeley was putting the camera through gyrations, and in his first couple of films Astaire appeared in production numbers in which all sorts of special effects were used—including process photography, a kind of double-exposure technique that allowed chorus girls to seem to dance on the wings of flying airplanes. Nevertheless, he remained unimpressed for a long time. All the dance routines he created for his films until 1936 were shaped so they could have been performed on the stage of a theatre. On the other hand, if "special effect" is defined to be something possible on film but impossible in the theatre, then even in those early years there was one "special effect" Astaire was extremely interested in exploring: perfection in every performance. He came to demand large numbers of takes and retakes until the dance was recorded exactly the way he wanted it.

It was not until his seventh film, *Swing Time,* that he tried out process photography: in the "Bojangles" solo he danced with, and against, shadows of himself (7 F). Such effects were used from time to time in later Astaire films: in *Blue Skies* he danced with a chorus of nine Astaires (20 F), in *The Barkleys of Broadway* he did combat with a herd of dancing shoes

[33] The wide screen used in a few of Astaire's films in the 1950s allowed more leeway on this—if one wasn't concerned about how it would look on television (see especially 28 H and 30 C). Of the wide-screen processes, Astaire apparently preferred the widest, CinemaScope. Gene Kelly, on the other hand, found it "an abomination."

[34] This discussion of the way Astaire used the space defined by the camera applies particularly to his standard solos and duets. It does not relate as directly to the extended fantasy-dream ballets that are found in some of his films of the 1940s and 1950s. These were largely directed by others (most effectively by Vincente Minnelli) and sometimes used different standards and approaches, though always with a sensitivity for the dance element that Astaire would approve.

[35] Astaire says he found no important difference in working for television, except that three separated cameras were used at one time rather than one, as in films.

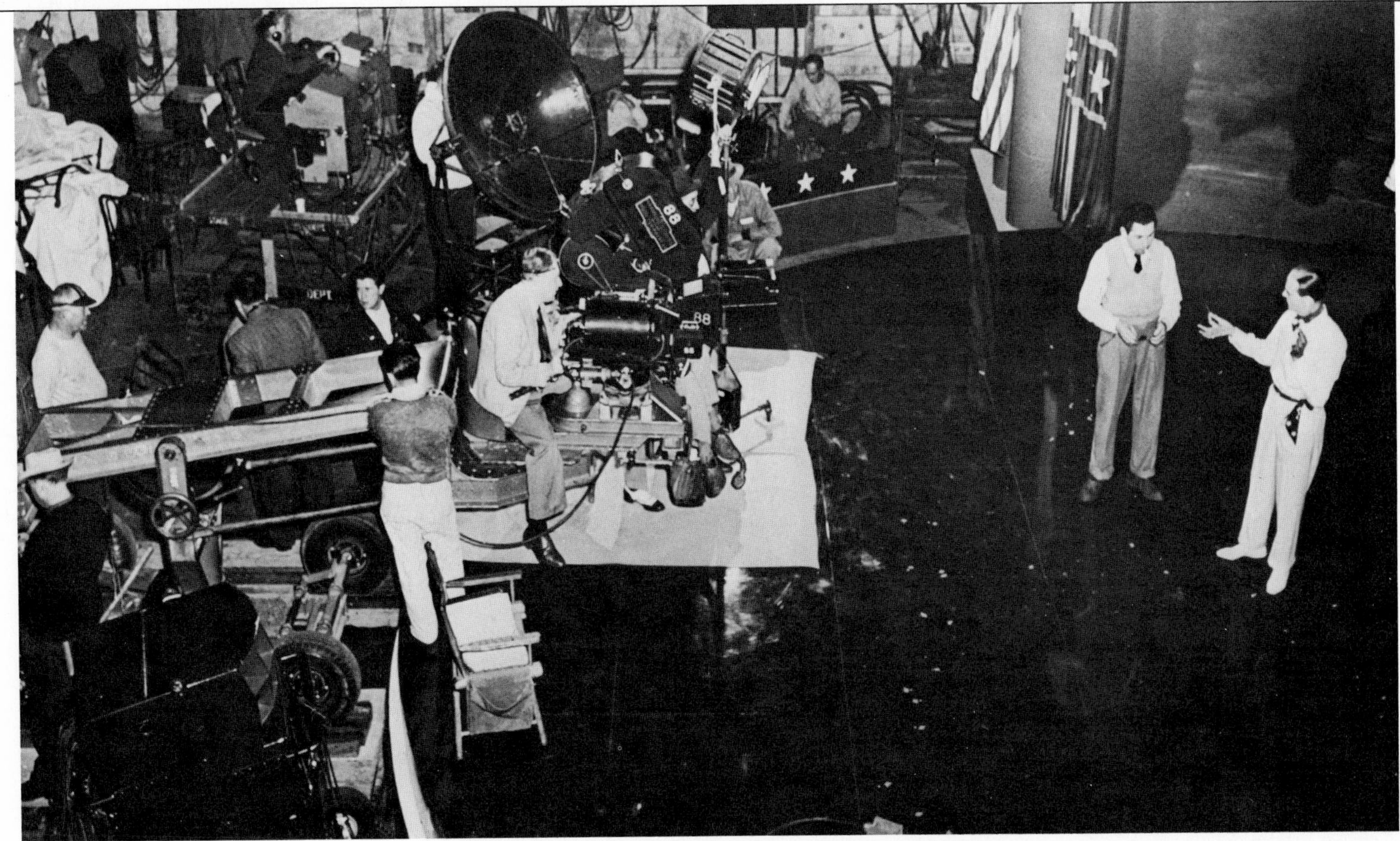

Working on the firecracker number in *Holiday Inn* (1942)

(22 G), in *The Belle of New York* he danced on air (26 D), and in several films there are brief segments in which dancing is superimposed over other scenes.

Swing Time also brought a more important development for Astaire: the opening out of space. In the "Never Gonna Dance" duet, he and Rogers traveled for the first time from one stage area to another within a single dance (7 G), something that would have been difficult (though not impossible) to do on stage. Thereafter he was on the loose, cavorting around a ship's boiler room, through a fun house, down a country glade, and all over a country club in his next three films. In later films he was to dance through Grand Central Station, lurch drunkenly from barroom to barroom, frolic down the street alongside a trolley, glide across fields, caper through a succession of empty movie sets, and wander through several fantasy-dream ballets.

The *Swing Time* experience is characteristic of Astaire. The opening out of space was a "special effect" which really expanded his choreographic opportunities and it is one he was to use quite often. Process photography was a gimmick, a trick of limited value, and he used it only occasionally.

Astaire employed other special photographic effects in other dances. He tried slow motion in *Carefree* and once again in *Easter Parade* (10 B, 21 J). Neither instance is terribly successful, probably because both tended to cut Astaire off from the music—his inspirational and rhythmic anchor.[36] And while he never got around to dancing with a mouse, he applied animation (sparingly) occasionally—for added explosion effects in his firecracker solo in *Holiday Inn* (15 M) and to simulate a star in a duet in *Daddy Long Legs* (28 E).

Many of the most memorable effects in Astaire's numbers are essentially dance or movement effects, but ones that would be possible only on film, the golfing effects in a solo in *Carefree,* for example (10 A). The use of multiple takes and the filming of the numbers in segments made such feats feasible in motion pictures. Even the most famous special effect of all—the *Royal Wedding* solo in which he dances up the wall and across the ceiling—is, to a considerable degree, a *dance* effect (25 H). To be sure, the number is only possible because the room and the camera could be fixed inside a rolling drum, but the number works so well because Astaire

[36] By contrast, he gets a slow-motion effect in part of the "Puttin' On the Ritz" solo in *Blue Skies* by *dancing* in slow motion—and by making his cane appear to be doing so as well (20 F 9–10). The effect is stunning and brilliantly musical.

The March Milastaire number in *You'll Never Get Rich* (1941)

"We Saw the Sea" in *Follow the Fleet* (1936)

"Shootin' the Works for Uncle Sam" in *You'll Never Get Rich*

"Who Wants to Kiss the Bridegroom?" in *The Belle of New York* (1952)

is able to dance seamlessly through the transitions as his floor rotates under him. The illusion is chiefly made by the man, not the machine.

Just as Astaire's choreography characteristically explores and develops a limited number of movement ideas in each dance, usually only one special-effect idea is applied at a time, and it is explored and developed with great care and theatrical cunning as the number progresses. Thus Astaire's confrontation with disembodied dancing shoes in a number in *The Barkleys of Broadway* gradually builds from idle fancy to a maniacal threat (22 G).

Astaire does not use internal cutting to simplify an effect or a stunt: lengthy shots remain the rule. The toss of the cane into the umbrella stand in one solo (16 E 14) is seen in a single shot, though it would be far easier to devote one shot to the toss and another to a close-up of the landing.

An effect that became integral—rather than incidental—to his dance approach derived from the technique of prerecording the music for the numbers. On the stage, song-and-dance numbers tend to be just that—the performer sings, then dances. The reason for the ordering, of course, is that the dancing usually leaves the performer too winded to sing with full control. With the songs prerecorded, there is no reason to maintain this convention. One can sing after dancing as well as before it, or one can do both at the same time. Nonetheless, Astaire largely stayed with the conventional pattern throughout the 1930s. Perhaps he was comfortable with it and saw no need to alter his habits; or perhaps he felt that a return to singing late in the number would seem contrived and unnatural to the audience. But the most likely reason is that he simply liked the idea of letting dance have the climactic moments of the number.

Whatever the reason, it was not until 1942, in *Holiday Inn,* that the routine was thoroughly altered: in the "You're Easy to Dance With" duet, he sings and dances all the way through the number (15 C), an idea that probably came from the lyric, which certainly suggests simultaneous singing and dancing. In later films there are numbers in which Astaire returns to singing during, or at the end of, the dance, but such numbers are still very much in the minority.[37] Actually, the biggest change was not in having the singing encroach on the dancing, but the reverse: using the potential of prerecording, he came to make more of a dance out of the movement that occurs during the singing of the song. In a sense, then, his dances got longer. In the 1930s, though movement during the singing was always eminently watchable, there was often not much of it, especially in duets. In the early 1940s this changed. One of the first examples is the "A Lot in Common with You" duet in *The Sky's the Limit,* where much of the movement under the song is quite vigorous, wittily underlining the lyric and establishing movement themes to be developed in the dance proper (17 C).

APOCALYPSE THEN

During the era in which the Hollywood musical attained its greatest popularity—from the early 1930s to the late 1950s—Astaire's approach to the filming of dance generally prevailed, as can be seen in the films of Gene Kelly, Ray Bolger, and others. The camera was not always so circumspect as in Astaire's films, but the idea that dance should be allowed to speak for itself was generally accepted.[38]

As an influence on the making of dance films, Astaire's greatest legacy may have been in public television. Sporadically in the 1950s and 1960s, and then with considerable momentum in the mid-1970s, public television set about trying to use the medium to display some of the riches of dance; for the most part, it approached dance with a sensibility that Fred Astaire would surely approve.

In Hollywood, on the other hand, Astaire's approach was soon abandoned. No longer did directors *let* dance happen; instead they sought to *make* it happen. Dance was not trusted to be effective on its own. Astaire himself took part in one of the films that marked the apocalypse—his last Hollywood musical, *Finian's Rainbow,* in 1968. As directed and edited by Francis Ford Coppola (who was born four years after *Top Hat*), the dances are presented with the same impatient insensitivity as in Thornton Freeland's *Flying Down to Rio* of thirty-five years earlier: each is a desperate phantasmagoria of arty angles, disorienting and purposefully unmatched cuts, and abrupt and uninformative close-ups.[39] Dance is photographed and edited as if it were a car chase in a Roger Corman epic.

It was the new (old) Coppola approach, not Astaire's, that came to dominate Hollywood films. In Herbert Ross' *The Turning Point* (1977), for example, Leslie Browne's big solo,

[37] The return to singing at the end of the dance is much more common in Gene Kelly's numbers.

[38] Charles Walters, a director of several musicals (including three featuring Astaire), observes that by the time he came to Hollywood, in the 1940s, the notion that dance should be allowed to flow, to proceed without undue disruption, was the accepted norm.

[39] Actually, a more precise precedent for *Finian's Rainbow* might be a chorus section of the "Continental" production number in *The Gay Divorcee* (3 F 21) in which director Sandrich subjects the dance to a rapid series of cuts, frantically trying to enliven the proceedings. This kind of editing—it might be called the Odessa Steps syndrome—seems largely to have vanished in Hollywood as a method for portraying dance until it was revived in the 1960s.

which is allowed to run all of eighty seconds, is presented in sixteen shots as a series of fancily photographed dance scraps embroidered around close-ups of other actors reacting melodramatically in the wings. In Hollywood, choreography and dancing became "cinematized," reduced to a series of fragmentary gestural effects frenetically photographed. In Fred Astaire's terms, they ceased to exist.

ASTAIRE'S CONTRIBUTION

Over the course of his long film career, Fred Astaire appeared in 212 musical numbers, of which 133 contain fully developed dance routines. At least seventy-five of these dance numbers seem to me to be at or near the masterpiece level, and there is a great deal of highly impressive choreography and dancing among the less masterful dances as well. There are some clinkers, but these are remarkably few in number, and most were largely or entirely choreographed by others. In quantity, and especially in quality, Astaire's contribution is unrivaled in films and, indeed, has few parallels in the history of dance.

Astaire made an impact in other ways, too. He helped enormously to define and develop a film genre; he brought out the best in many composers and lyricists; he influenced a generation of filmmakers and choreographers; and his example inspired quite a few people to take up dance as avocation or profession. Of course, he also activated the fancies and fantasies of millions in his audiences over the years, and he will continue to do so as long as films are shown.

But his most important contribution is in the films and dances themselves, not in their impact on other creators or in the momentary diversion they often supplied. What follows is an attempt to describe, analyze, and evaluate Astaire's contribution. The detailed consideration of his thirty-one musical films provides a frame for the chief purpose of this book: a kind of textual analysis in context of this amazing array of fine dances.

It should not be assumed that the patterns and themes developed in these analyses were explicit in Astaire's mind when he fashioned his dances. Indeed, a highly intuitive creator, he vigorously denies formulating any explicit plans or patterns or schemes when choreographing: "I don't think about what I do; I can't explain how I do it." But whatever the process of creation, Astaire's dances show a clear aesthetic sensibility and sense of craft that can be at least partly explicated and assessed. And perhaps these discussions will help to furnish a broadened and richer appreciation of—to borrow a phrase from lyricist Yip Harburg—this elegant legacy.

1.

Dancing Lady

1933

Fred Astaire was originally contracted to begin his career in Hollywood on August 1, 1933, at RKO, where he was assigned a role in *Flying Down to Rio.* At the time, however, MGM had under production a Clark Gable–Joan Crawford opus, *Dancing Lady,* and wanted him to do a bit of dancing in it. Astaire agreed to fly to California with his new wife in mid-July—at MGM's expense—to undertake the assignment.

Dancing Lady is unusual in Astaire's career, not merely for the brevity and essential irrelevance of his appearance in it, but because the film's whole tone and shape are substantially different from the kind of musical film he was to develop at RKO in the 1930s. He came to specialize in light, casual comedies in which musical numbers are used to give depth and visceral seriousness to a central romance; *Dancing Lady,* by contrast, is a serious romantic melodrama on which comedy and musical numbers are casually grafted.

Astaire found the experience of working on the film beneficial. It gave him an opportunity to learn about how movies were made without bearing any important responsibility for the outcome, and it served to introduce him to the film audience in a classy manner: in a high-budget picture (twice that of *Flying Down to Rio*), one established star, Clark Gable, calls him by his real name and asks him to dance with another one, Joan Crawford. The film's very considerable box-office success also pleased him, of course.

Astaire's contribution to the film consisted of a brief rehearsal routine and a certain amount of cheery, eye-catching singing and dancing as part of an onstage production number. In both cases he partnered Crawford. Neither appearance does much to establish Astaire's choreographic profile, except in one respect: the artful way in which he adapts his style to accommodate Crawford's particular strengths and limitations as a dancer. Already in this first, fleeting effort in films, Astaire was seeking, with consummate showmanship, to make his partner look good.

He managed to make an impression. Several audience members at the previews mentioned they liked the dancer who partnered Crawford, and he was favorably noticed in the reviews. Astaire's reaction: "I was pleased with lots of things but kept thinking of what I would like to try if I ever got in a position to make my own decisions."

THE SCRIPT AND THE PRODUCTION

Dancing Lady was created as a vehicle for Joan Crawford. Her previous two films had failed, and to recover she needed a success. At Crawford's urging, MGM studio head L. B. Mayer took a personal interest in the film and assigned his son-in-law, David O. Selznick, to produce it. Selznick was not very interested in musicals but he understood Crawford's situation and soon arrayed around her the necessary support —including Clark Gable, reluctantly cast opposite her. Also on hand was Merrill Pye, whose sleek, uncluttered Moderne decor is one of the film's most striking features.

Earlier in 1933, Warner Bros. had brought out the Busby Berkeley backstage hit *42nd Street,* and *Dancing Lady* was one of the imitations turned out in Hollywood during the next year. The setting is Broadway, and a central character is the no-nonsense, high-strung, hard-boiled stage director Gable, who is trying to put on a show, in the face of considerable adversity. Crawford is the chorus girl who takes over the "top spot" and helps materially (we are to believe) to put the show over in the end. Like *42nd Street, Dancing Lady* is fairly realistic in its depiction of what goes on backstage: the uncertainties, the tension, the sweat and grime, the compromises with backers, the attractions of the chorus girl as object of lust and willing plaything.

The film is reasonably successful at blending in a second plot, the dawning romance between Crawford and Gable, complicated by the panting pursuit of Crawford by a millionaire dandy, played by Franchot Tone.[1] For the most part, the Crawford-Gable romance is implied rather than developed, and its progress is charted in a series of clinches in which the two stars find themselves almost, but not quite, kissing—an elaborate audience tease resolved only at the final fade-out.

The script with two separate, if linked, story lines was not to become typical of Astaire. Thereafter his films were

[1] The on-screen triangle partly reflected offscreen realities. Crawford and Gable reportedly had been lovers earlier and would be so again later. At the time of filming, Crawford had become romantically involved with Tone, and in 1935 they were married; their stormy alliance lasted four years.

usually love stories undiverted by major subplot, and although most of his films had a show-business background, he never did another true backstager until *The Band Wagon* twenty years later. Nor was Astaire in a hurry to emulate the elaborate trick-photography effects used in *Dancing Lady*'s production numbers.

THE MUSIC

Under contract at MGM were Richard Rodgers and Lorenz Hart. Selznick planned to ask them to do the score for the film, but a trial song they came up with, "That's the Rhythm of the Day," proved to be a bit of a dud. Although Selznick used the song in the film (in a number that did not include Astaire), he looked elsewhere for the rest of the score, finally settling on the young Burton Lane, who turned in several useful songs including "Everything I Have Is Yours," his first film song and his first hit. The title song was contributed by the team of Jimmy McHugh and Dorothy Fields, and another was written by Nacio Herb Brown and Arthur Freed. Such a grab bag of composers and lyricists was not to be typical of Astaire's films.

Astaire was later to work productively with Lane, Fields, and Freed, but, regrettably, this is the closest he ever came to working with Rodgers and Hart.[2]

THE CHOREOGRAPHY

Directing the dances were Sammy Lee (who had worked with Astaire before, on the Broadway show *Lady, Be Good!*) and Eddie Prinz. In the big numbers the choreographers were obviously trying to emulate the extravaganzas of Busby Berkeley but had little of Berkeley's sense of design and logic. According to Astaire, the dances "required a lot of rehearsing and I mostly did as I was told."

[2] The second closest was Astaire's 1961 nonmusical *The Pleasure of His Company*, in which he sings "Lover," the Rodgers-and-Hart classic written in 1932.

With Joan Crawford—in "Heigh-Ho, the Gang's All Here" (left) and in "Let's Go Bavarian" (right)

THE NUMBERS

A
HOLD YOUR MAN
(2′ 11″)

At a seedy burlesque house, Crawford and her fellow chorines display their wares to an audience that includes a slumming socialite, Tone, who is immediately attracted to Crawford (A 1, 2). His response registers as a puzzling but intriguing blend, at once boyish grin and lascivious leer.

B
CRAWFORD'S AUDITION
(46″)

When the dancers are arrested for indecent exposure, Tone pays Crawford's fine and then makes a play for her, but she proves unwilling. Flushed with ambition, she rushes uptown the next day to try to audition for a new show that Gable is casting—a job he finds difficult, what with "all the real talent gone to Hollywood," as the Hollywood scriptwriters have him gratuitously comment.

Crawford has no success at getting a tryout until Tone uses his influence with the show's producer. Her audition (performed to "Alabama Swing" by James P. Johnson) for the reluctant Gable (B 1, 2) is good enough to land her a job in the chorus. (Fluttering around backstage are the century's rudest mechanicals, the Three Stooges, here associated with their vaudevillian straight man and originator, Ted Healy.) As a dancer, Crawford specialized in an assertive, labored, lumbering tap—more or less of the Ruby Keeler school—blended with kicking Charleston figures. The effect is heavy—she tends to look down and give in to her weight—a style, in other words, just the opposite of Astaire's.

C
EVERYTHING I HAVE IS YOURS
(1′ 52″)

The film's hit song is sung by Art Jarrett at a posh party where Tone continues his pursuit of Crawford (C 1). The Lane-Adamson song had been discovered by one of the film's writers when he heard the composer play it at a party. Originally the script called for Crawford to sing the song, but she didn't have the range for it. So it was given to Jarrett, with Crawford contributing a couple of scat phrases so that studio publicity could say she "sang" the song in the film.

D
DANCING LADY
(1′ 56″)

Eventually the persistent Tone goes so far as to ask Crawford to marry him; she agrees to do so if the show fails. Meanwhile, Gable has decided to change the show to make it as modern as "riveting machines," and for that he needs it to be led by "a girl who has to beat time to the city's rhythm, a girl who's crazed to dance." Chorus dancer Crawford has the quality he needs and, to her infinite delight, he elevates her to the "top spot." After promising to work very hard, she is next seen rehearsing a bouncy routine supported by male chorus as Gable looks on with something other than utter objectivity (D 1).

E
HEIGH-HO, THE GANG'S ALL HERE
(REHEARSAL) (33″)

Next it is time to rehearse the "gang number." To partner Crawford, Gable calls for Fred Astaire, who comes on camera and is introduced to Crawford (E 1, 2). Although this sequence launched Astaire's film career, he was appalled when he saw it on the screen: "Gosh, I look like a knife!" Their routine is cut short when she

A1 A2 B1 B2 C1 D1 E1 E2 E3 E4 F1 F2

crumples in agony with a leg cramp, but what is shown gives evidence of Astaire's ability to fashion dance for the talent at hand. It makes use of the hard-driving, floor-slamming steps Crawford seemed to specialize in, but it delivers them with an arresting lightness of the upper body and sometimes uses the downward plunge to generate a contrasting airy jump on the rebound (E 3, 4).[3]

F

HEIGH-HO, THE GANG'S ALL HERE / LET'S GO BAVARIAN

(5′42″)

Astaire vanishes from the film when Crawford collapses, and doesn't reappear until it is nearly over. Meanwhile, there is quite a bit of plot to play out.

Gable solicitously massages Crawford's leg back into working order (F 1). When she tries to use it again, she falters; he grabs her as she starts to fall and for a moment there they almost kiss (F 2). Then the show is canceled, because Tone, in order to get Crawford to marry him according to their agreement, has secretly withdrawn his financial backing. Gable almost kisses Crawford again when she tells him how sorry she is (F 3). Eventually Gable decides to finance the show himself. Crawford rejoins the cast after she finds out about Tone's underhanded intervention, and she and Gable have another face-off (F 4).

The big night arrives, and the show opens with an elaborate production number—a Broadway-inspired routine embellished by a few self-conscious Busby Berkeleyisms. There is glitter and glitz but little point or coherent imagery. However, Fred Astaire does finally get to perform, and he really lights up the proceedings when he is allowed to go into action.

The number opens in a glamorous penthouse where the chorus is singing a bouncy Lane-Adamson song. The group is seen first from out front, where the theatre audience sits, and then, once only, from the rafters, where Berkeley's camera was often perched (F 5). Eventually the chorus clears out of the way to make room for Crawford and Astaire, who stroll jauntily on from upstage. As they strut forward they play a sweet joke: they need to maneuver through a space too narrow to accommodate their side-by-side stroll; without interrupting their momentum, they manage the obstacle by facing each other for an instant and sidling through (F 6–7).

Unruffled, they arrive downstage and, ambling brightly to the melody's rhythm, spiritedly sing the song (F 8). The brief dance duet that ensues—the finished version of the routine they were rehearsing earlier—begins with a camera gaffe that Astaire never allowed to happen again: he and Crawford separate so far they almost leave the camera frame (F 9).

As the rehearsal routine had suggested, the duet is choreographed with Crawford's talents in mind, though the puffy, enveloping gown she wears makes it difficult to see what she is doing. Most of the choreography involves heavy stomping lightened by an upward-craning carriage of the head and upper body (F 10, 12), alternating

[3] The filming of this sequence was problematic. It required Astaire and Gable to be in the same shot, but Gable was ill when it came time to do the shot, and Astaire was soon to leave to begin work at RKO on August 1. Gable was well enough to come to the set for two hours on July 30 to do the shot (E 1) where he introduces Astaire and Crawford. He is also shown sitting in the foreground during the brief dance (E 3, 4), though a double may have been used for this shot. Crawford claims she was dancing with a broken ankle in the film.

F 3 F 4 F 5 F 6
F 7 F 8 F 9 F 10
F 11 F 12 F 13 F 14

with some bounding, spinning jumps (F11). This fast and jazzy routine has a witty, sophisticated sense of rhythm. It ends oddly and interestingly: while pivoting on one foot, the dancers repeatedly stomp the floor heavily with the other, seemingly causing the music to slow down (F12). When they stop their stomping, the music is "freed" and instantly resumes its normal, cheery tempo.

Then the dancers catch up with the music and spin over to a circular carpet, which proceeds to fly off with them, leaving the rest of the merrymakers behind, waving unconcernedly (F13).

Crawford and Astaire teeter around the edge of their flying carpet for a while but soon regain their composure and dance a bit on their airborne floor. Once, in fact, they do one of Astaire's favorite steps—a spiraling, double-turning transition maneuver, the Astaire double helix, which he was to use frequently (and variously) in later film duets (F14).

In due course the carpet sets them down among a crew of beer-drinking revelers in Bavaria, a locale apparently chosen because Astaire had done a successful German number, "I Love Louisa," onstage in *The Band Wagon* two years earlier.[4] All sing and clink goblets. Astaire and Crawford quickly catch the spirit and, emerging in appropriate Bavarian attire (F15), get to sing and romp a bit before the number comes to an abrupt end: four pretty girls blowing beer foam at the camera. Astaire is seen no more in the film.[5]

G

THAT'S THE RHYTHM OF THE DAY

(5′42″)

The show ends with the kind of "modern" number Gable had demanded earlier in the film. A stately minuet is rudely interrupted by Nelson Eddy, who urges the dancers to catch the "rhythm of the day" and sings an upbeat Rodgers-and-Hart song in which "electric" is ingeniously rhymed with "correct trick" (G1).[6]

Unfortunately, the staging does not exhibit comparable ingenuity. The minueters are led through a barrier at mid-stage and emerge on the other side in modern garb (G2). After they have romped around agitatedly for a while, the day's celebrated rhythm abruptly gives way to a (presumably anachronistic) Tchaikovskiesque waltz, which accompanies the churnings of a glittering carousel (G3) and a "mirror of Venus" (G4). To end it all, Crawford rides into view on a carousel horse wearing a spangled, $5,000 gown (G5).

Following the rules of the genre, the show is a big success. In the congratulatory aftermath, Gable is a bit dazed and finds himself yearning for Crawford (G6). He is accordingly cheered when she casts Tone off and joins Gable for their inevitable, if long-delayed, kiss (G7).

[4] However, the "Let's Go Bavarian" song was not created with Astaire in mind: it had been written by Lane and Adamson before they came to Hollywood.

[5] Production notes suggest the Bavarian number was intended to be quite a bit longer, involving a chorus dance, two Astaire-and-Crawford "specialty dances," and a waltz danced by Winnie Lightner and Ted Healy (who were to arrive in a carriage drawn by oxen). The number was to conclude with Astaire and Crawford doing Astaire's "oompah trot" runaround to music provided by an on-camera German band.

[6] This was Eddy's second film in Hollywood and this brief assignment his only appearance in it. When MGM re-released the film in 1936 on a double bill, he and Astaire were given equal billing with Crawford and Gable in the advertising.

F15 G1 G2 G3
G4 G5 G6 G7

2.

Flying Down to Rio

1933

Far from the least of the achievements of *Flying Down to Rio* was its considerable financial success, which helped to pull RKO out of receivership and away from bankruptcy. One major reason for the film's success, it quickly became apparent, was the arresting performance of the fifth-billed Fred Astaire. His appeal as a screen performer converted any doubters while, according to his own testimony, it pleasantly surprised Astaire himself. *Flying Down to Rio,* then, was an important, even crucial, event in Astaire's career. Had the film failed, or had he not stood out in it, his detractors might well have had their first impressions reinforced and he might have been dropped, particularly since musicals were risky, expensive investments.[1]

Astaire's role in the film reflects the Broadway persona he had developed in his shows with his sister, Adele: the talented nice-guy juvenile who has no girl to romance. He was to try out romance in his next film (with spectacular success), but the juvenile aspect of the characterization, with its clear box-office appeal and its equally clear typecasting restrictions, was to linger with him for years, until he got partway out from under it in *Carefree* (1938), then shed it entirely in *The Sky's the Limit* (1943).

Although Astaire's abilities as a dancer helped him attract notice in *Flying Down to Rio,* his dancing opportunities in the film are actually rather slim: he has one brief virtuosic solo and a couple of slight duets, all mercilessly cut up by director Thornton Freeland. But enough was there to entrance audiences and to make them want more. They were soon to get much more, and much better.

ASTAIRE AND ROGERS

Playing opposite Astaire was Ginger Rogers, a young contract player at RKO who had previously appeared in nineteen features and four shorts, only two of which (*42nd Street* and *Gold Diggers of 1933*) were musicals. A show dancer, singer, and comedienne whom Astaire had known briefly on Broadway, Rogers was assigned the role almost by default, replacing Dorothy Jordan, who dropped out of the film in order to marry its executive producer.

Of particular appeal were Astaire and Rogers' dance duets embedded in a lengthy production number, "The Carioca." The number created such a dance craze that Astaire and Rogers were quickly billed by studio publicists as "The King and Queen of 'The Carioca.'"

As Arlene Croce observes, *Flying Down to Rio* is an Astaire-Rogers movie "only in the sense that the two of them are in it." In particular, although the two characters hang around with each other quite a bit in the film, there is no suggestion of romance between them: Rogers might as well be Astaire's sister. Nonetheless, the film did help to establish some of the characteristics of subsequent films—the tone of airy, essentially inconsequential comedy, for example, and the use of elaborate, eye-arresting Art Deco sets.

THE MUSIC

In one area *Flying Down to Rio* is an important forerunner of films to come: it is blessed with a superb score, something that was to become a happy commonplace in Astaire's films of the thirties. The four varied Vincent Youmans songs are models of grace and imagination. Unfortunately, this was the last musical score Youmans was to complete: plagued by tuberculosis and alcoholism, he thereafter worked only intermittently. But he set a high standard for composers like Cole Porter, Jerome Kern, Irving Berlin, and George Gershwin to maintain. *Flying Down to Rio* is the only Astaire film with lyrics by the brilliant Gus Kahn, working here in tandem with Edward Eliscu. Kahn's lyrics are especially notable for their wit and intricate internal rhyme.

THE SCRIPT

It should also perhaps be noted that the film has a plot. It involves a love triangle in which sexy blond Gene Raymond chases sexy dark Dolores Del Rio all the way down to Rio de Janeiro, only to find she is already engaged to his best friend,

[1] On these developments in Astaire's career, see pp. 7–8.

With Dolores Del Rio

the long-suffering, doe-eyed Brazilian tenor Raul Roulien, who turns noble at the end and surrenders his fiancée. All three are billed ahead of Rogers and Astaire in the titles.

Roulien, a Spanish-language film player who largely vanished from Hollywood after this picture, brings a certain touching believability to his role, but Raymond and Del Rio, who didn't, are pure plastic. Their love affair is carried out with the self-obsessed posturings of Hollywood sex symbols or operatic prima donnas, and their desperate efforts at repartee continually founder in a sea of directorial incomprehension and heavy-handedness.

When this plot line doesn't get in the way, however, the film has many things to recommend it besides the sprightly score and the cheerful flutterings of Astaire and Rogers. For example, there is the sassy impertinence of much of the dialogue, which slipped by in those days when Hollywood's censorship board had not yet been forced to take itself too seriously.[2] And there is the film's unabashed, exuberantly absurd celebration of modern technology, culminating in a musical number that takes place on the wings of flying airplanes: "Too big for the earth," the film's blurb trumpeted, "so they staged it in the air!"

THE CHOREOGRAPHY

Dave Gould, the film's dance director, seems to have been chiefly responsible for engineering the two big production numbers. Gould was not much of a dancer himself and was mainly interested, like Busby Berkeley, in massed effects and eye-catching camera work.

Assisting Gould was Hermes Pan, a young dancer and choreographer who was to become very important to Astaire. They met on the set when Astaire was working on a solo and was stumped at one spot. Pan came up with an idea that pleased Astaire, and the incident led to a long friendship and a highly productive partnership.

Another important member of the Astaire team was also enlisted on the *Rio* set—Hal Borne, a pianist with extensive classical training who was doing "sideline." He is seen playing the piano (D 2), but, a newcomer to Hollywood, he had not yet obtained the requisite union status to be recorded. Astaire heard him play (even if the movie audience didn't) and liked what he heard: "I think we got a piano." Borne was to work as Astaire's rehearsal pianist and to contribute to the musical arrangements of his numbers throughout the 1930s.

[2] For a discussion of the changes in censorship policies that were to occur in 1934, see p. 55.

"Flying Down to Rio"

With Ginger Rogers in "The Carioca"

THE NUMBERS

A
MUSIC MAKES ME
(1′44″)

The film is notable for its brash and remarkably unfettered sexual references. Its tone is set in the first scene, when the Miami hotel manager (the priggish Franklin Pangborn), with his assistant in tow (the perennial Eric Blore, who seems to be wearing less hair than in later films), inspects the hotel personnel and disapprovingly observes that one of the maids has worn the backs of her heels down, "getting familiar" with the guests. He warns the hotel band and its sassy singer (Ginger Rogers) against such activity.

The band leader (Gene Raymond) and his agile sidekick and accordionist (Fred Astaire) arrive just in time to launch the band into a number.[3] It is sung from the bandstand by Rogers, who, dressed more revealingly than in any later film, discloses here, as William Park has perceptively and approvingly observed, "one of the greatest figures of all time" (A 1). The wonderful song has a lively, wraparound melody and tricky rhythmic shifts. Rogers sings it with sly insinuation, making it quite clear she understands, and revels in, the provocative sexual import of its sparkling lyric.

B
ORCHIDS IN THE MOONLIGHT
(1′23″)

On a dare, a visiting Brazilian, Dolores Del Rio, bats her eyelashes at handsome Raymond, and he soon trots over to her table. This prompts one of her American companions (Mary Kornman) to emit the film's most famous crack—"What have these South Americans got below the equator that we haven't?"—a line that bothered the censors even in those freer days (B 1).[4]

The Raymond–Del Rio flirtation leads to the band's being fired, but they soon pick up an engagement in Rio de Janeiro, which happens to be Del Rio's home town. Raymond employs a ruse so he can fly Del Rio to Brazil in his own small plane. After landing for repairs on a moonlit beach in Haiti, he composes a tune for the occasion and plays it on a piano he keeps in the plane, while Del Rio responds by breathing heavily. In a scene notable for its vague pacing and strained effort at light romance, the couple kiss (B 2) and quarrel.

C
THE CARIOCA
(11′38″)

In Rio, Raymond tells his friend Raul Roulien about the moonlit episode with Del Rio, unaware that Roulien is engaged to Del Rio (C 1).

That evening the band members troop over to the Carioca Casino to scout the local opposition band. The Brazilian group proves to be very good indeed, and soon the place is jumping—everybody is out on the floor dancing as the band spins out chorus after chorus of an infectious fast tango, "The Carioca." Astaire becomes intrigued and, scarcely looking at Rogers, says, "I'd like to try this just once—come on" (C 2); he

[3] Astaire had developed a proficiency on the accordion for "Sweet Music," a number that he performed with his sister Adele in *The Band Wagon* on Broadway in 1931. The number, complete with Astaire's accordion playing, was recorded at the time.

[4] The line, according to a sternly disapproving *Vanity Fair* review, was "lifted bodily from a current dirty joke."

A1 B1 B2 C1
C2 C3 C4 C5
C6 C7 C8 C9

drags her out onto the dance floor, a rather historic moment.

Unfortunately, neither of the brief, camera-cluttered routines they do as part of the "Carioca" number is very impressive. As Astaire later put it, "I thought Ginger and I looked all right together but I was under the impression that we weren't doing anything particularly outstanding." Still, everything is relative—the "Carioca" dance duets are probably better than any ever before seen in Hollywood and, for that matter, better than most seen later outside of Astaire's own films.

The gimmick here is to dance with foreheads pressed together, an inspiration of Hermes Pan's. Astaire's eclectic dance style is evident in the very first phrase of the first duet, which deftly blends tap and ballroom figures. It includes a brief tap warm-up (C3), a demonstration of the Carioca pose without the use of the hands (C4), a quick lift (C5), a coordinated spin, and a development of the Carioca idea as the dancers whirl around, keeping their heads touching (C6).

The music repeats, and the choreography mostly repeats as well—something that was certainly not characteristic of Astaire's later dances. The rest of the dance involves some close-partnered Carioca-ing (C7) leading to a series of fast ballroom spins around the floor (C9), some rhythmically complex tap phrases in which the dancers trade off complementary barrages (C10), and a bit more Carioca-ing with some shoulder-shrugging shimmying mixed in (C11, 12).[5] Often Astaire embellishes the dance by fluttering his hands (as in C4, 10, 11). Meanwhile, the dance is systematically dismembered by director Freeland's inserted reaction shots (C8, 13).

Next Astaire and Rogers comically bump heads as they try to resume the Carioca configuration (C14), then stagger around dazed for a moment (C15, 16). We never learn how it all turns out, because Freeland chooses to cut to the audience just as the dance is about to end (C17), something that was never again to happen in an Astaire dance.[6]

[5] The patterns in which the dancers spell each other and seem to chase the music with little bursts of activity are later developed with great wit and imagination in the bandstand duet in *Top Hat* (5 C).

[6] For an extended discussion of the pre–Astaire-era camera work in this dance, see pp. 27–29.

As Astaire and Rogers retire from the floor, the area is filled by a surge of dancers while a pair of female singers, perched on a nearby balcony, divide the song between them. The choreography consists of various scraps, some involving pressing the heads together, but without much in the way of logic or development, since no sequence is ever built into an extended phrase. Instead, the dancers merely spin out a step variant and repeat it a few times; once the point is made, the camera cuts or dissolves to another pattern. Thus the only tangible impression given is one of churning activity (C18).

Then the arrangement turns hot. A black woman (Etta Moten) appears and repeats the song insinuatingly (C19), while the stage is filled with black couples doing their upbeat, and more explicitly sexual, version of the dance. At one point, the camera holds steady long enough to show a lead couple rendering a few appealing scampers and skitters (C20).

After Astaire and Rogers have returned to do nineteen seconds of hot Carioca-ing on top of a set of clustered, revolving pianos (C21), the blacks reappear, undulating sexily while the camera cuts rapidly from one activity to another. At the

C10 C11 C12 C13
C14 C15 C16 C17
C18 C19 C20 C21

end, the whites join them and pose prettily on revolving turntables as the blacks frolic, separate but equal, in the foreground (C 22). There is little in the way of a real choreographed ending; the camera simply fades out with the music.

As a musical number, "The Carioca" is something of a shambles, though the non-Astaire portions are probably more imaginative than comparable material in its two direct imitations, "The Continental" in *The Gay Divorcee* (3 F) and "The Piccolino" in *Top Hat* (5 F).

Astaire and Rogers dance for barely two minutes of its length, yet that is enough to suggest their screen appeal. Astaire's skill as a dancer is fully evident, as is his infectious exuberance as a performer. And Rogers joins in, not simply a convenient foil but playful and eager, a real co-participant. She clearly understands what he is doing and has the instinctive intelligence and ability to contribute to the effect.

D
ORCHIDS IN THE MOONLIGHT
(REPRISE) (7′42″)

The next few scenes give Astaire quite a bit of comedy business, which he handles appealingly, if a bit self-consciously. Encountering Del Rio at a local pastry shop, he tries to warn her away from masher Raymond but is thrown out by the management. When he runs into her again at the Aviator's Club that evening, he fears another altercation and hides from her. Meanwhile, the club's band strikes up the tune Raymond had composed on the beach in Haiti, and crowds of dancers tango sultrily (D1, 2). Del Rio's escort, Roulien, croons the song to her, embellished by swirling photographic effects that take place behind them (D3).[7] She finds the song even more seductive now that the lilting tune has been suitably fleshed out with a sumptuous Kahn-Eliscu lyric—and agrees to marry Roulien at once. But Raymond shows up, and the triangle is exposed (D4). To escape the awkward situation, Del Rio snaps up the uncomfortable Astaire and tangos away with him (D5).

E
MUSIC MAKES ME
(DANCE) (1′25″)

The next day Astaire is seen trying to rehearse a motley collection of chorus girls—including a provocative quartet known as the "Yes Girls" (E1)—for a show that will open a new hotel owned by Del Rio's father. Raymond subversively conducts his band nearby in a bouncy rendition of "Music Makes Me," which utterly distracts Astaire from his directorial duties. The music makes him perform a brief virtuosic tap number. It's another teaser, and a dazzling one.

The basic idea of the dance is to suggest that the music has taken possession of Astaire's body—his feet in particular—and is forcing him to execute the blistering routine contrary to his conscious will. The notion is introduced as, chewing on a wad of gum, he crouches to instruct his pupils and finds one foot uncontrollably tapping to the band's music (E2). He succumbs, rising to issue a brief tap flurry, but then tries to return to the instruction.

The music is too much for him, however—he is impelled into an extended tap routine, in which he conveys his predicament in various ways. For example, his feet corkscrew around each other as if uncoordinated (E3), and one leg draws away from his body as if to go off on its own (E4). Astaire's legs keep seeming to trip him up, and he staggers across the floor, dancing all the while, his thrashing arms contributing

[7] This sequence was variously color-tinted in the original prints, an effect that *Variety* termed "an intrusion."

C22 D1 D2 D3
D4 D5 E1 E2
E3 E4 E5 E6

greatly to the effect (E3, 6, 10).[8] One particular step is repeated several times: Astaire forces his feet close together, as if trying to bring them under some control, but they demonstrate that they can rap out a blistering pattern even in that tight position (E5, 8, 9).

The ending is wonderfully amusing. As the music comes to a snappy finish, Astaire, relieved at last of his stimulus, hits one quick barrage on the last note (E11) and then, without pause, simply resumes his role as instructor, as if it were of no note that he had just whipped off fifty-two seconds of brilliant tap dancing (E12).

Despite the dance's brevity, director Freeland has no qualms about dismembering it. Inserted is an unnecessary reaction shot of two approaching policemen (E7) and a close-up of Astaire's flickering feet (E9); and two shots are taken from the side (a pointless jolt of angle), where the perspective is cluttered by the foreground clustering of chorus members (E6, 8). All these directorial conceits were soon to be eliminated or brought under tight control by Astaire.

[8] For later dances that further develop some of these ideas, see 4 F and 22 G.

F

FLYING DOWN TO RIO

(4′29″)

The plot has developed a wrinkle: local political connivance has kept Del Rio's father from getting an entertainment permit for the opening of his hotel. Without entertainment, the hotel will flop, we are assured, and an evil business syndicate, made up of three shadowy Greeks, will triumph. Quick as a flash, Raymond dreams up a plan: with the aid of the Aviator's Club (and the RKO special effects department) they will supply a number outside municipal control, a number staged on airplanes.

Astaire sings the song from the ground—his only singing assignment in the film—with jauntiness and contagious enthusiasm (F1). He then signals to the air corps, and all heads crane skyward to gaze at the improbable spectacle of dozens of scantily clad, windblown chorus girls lashed to the wings of airplanes and gesticulating semaphorically in time to the music (F2–4). (At one point these bizarre antics are embellished with a bit of terror: a trapeze performer loses her grip and falls—to be caught by the wing-riding crew of an airplane below.) As in the other chorus routines in the film, there is no logic or development to the images presented, nor is there a distinctive choreographed ending. The camera simply jumps from one idea to another by means of a cut, a dissolve, or a wipe until the music runs out. Although the number is sometimes seen to reflect (and to imitate) the approach of Busby Berkeley, Berkeley's careful interlinking of cumulative images is nowhere in evidence.

The show is a success, the hotel is saved, and the Greeks are dispatched. Still to be resolved is the romantic triangle, a task handled with bright wit.

While flying one of the planes in the musical number, Roulien becomes resigned to the fact that Del Rio loves Raymond. He lands and, still wearing his parachute, hustles her off to board a passenger plane flying up from Rio on which he knows Raymond has booked passage. Shortly after takeoff, Roulien, with a great show of nobility, presents Del Rio and Raymond to the plane's pilot to be married (F5). He then abruptly jumps out of the plane, cheerfully parachuting back down to Rio.

At the fade-out, Astaire and Rogers are shown tipsily gazing skyward at the scene—musing, perhaps, about their next picture (F6).

E7 E8 E9 E10

E11 E12 F1 F2

F3 F4 F5 F6

3.

The Gay Divorcee

1934

After the success of *Flying Down to Rio,* and the apparent success within it of the Fred Astaire–Ginger Rogers team, RKO quickly moved to capitalize on the new combination. Their first vehicle was a screen version of *Gay Divorce,* a musical play by Dwight Taylor with music and lyrics by Cole Porter, which had done well on Broadway and in London with Astaire and Claire Luce in the lead roles.[1] Astaire and Rogers had had secondary roles in *Flying Down to Rio;* in *The Gay Divorcee* they would essentially be on their own, carrying the romantic interest in the film and a large share of the comedy as well. In charge of the film (and, ultimately, of Astaire's whole career at RKO in the 1930s) was producer Pandro Berman, then twenty-nine years old, and he selected as director Mark Sandrich, aged thirty-three, who was to serve in a similar capacity in most of the other Astaire-Rogers pictures at RKO.

The resulting film was a great success at the box office. It initiated the Astaire-Rogers phenomenon of the 1930s and established most of the elements that were to make up the aesthetic of those films: vaguely plausible plots blending light, rather frivolous comedy with significant love stories for Astaire and Rogers that avoided gush and sentimentality; the imaginative, fanciful, gleaming Art Deco decor; the superb Tin Pan Alley–derived songs; and the masterful dancing and choreography.

When *Flying Down to Rio* came out, Astaire says, "I was amazed that the reaction could be so good because I knew I hadn't yet scratched the surface with any real dancing on the screen." Now that he was given his opportunity to show what he could do, he rose to the occasion by putting on some of his finest dance numbers, including a duet, "Night and Day," that is among the greatest dance works ever created—by Astaire or anyone else.

[1] Luce had some film experience—she had had a prominent role in John Ford's *Up the River* in 1930 with Spencer Tracy—and in late 1933 RKO gave some thought to using her in the film. The enormous success of the Astaire-Rogers pairing in *Flying Down to Rio,* however, ended all consideration of that idea.

THE SCRIPT

In *The Gay Divorcee* Astaire plays a young and successful professional dancer who happens to run into Ginger Rogers at a British customs station. He manages at once both to irritate her and to fall hopelessly in love with her. One reason she is unwilling to give in to Astaire's ardent, puppylike advances is that she is undergoing a difficult and unpleasant transition: unhappily married, she is in the process of obtaining an English divorce by arranging to spend the night with a professional co-respondent at a seaside resort.

By luck, Astaire runs into her there, and though she tries to flee, he is able to break her resistance down in the course of a song and dance. But she is only momentarily dazzled: through a conversational quirk, she becomes convinced he is the professional co-respondent, and she is horrified to be attracted to a man in such low calling. She regains her previous haughtiness and marches out, giving the thunderstruck Astaire her room number and telling him to be there at midnight.

The mistaken identity is milked for all it's worth, but things are soon clarified and all ends happily as evidence is found of her husband's infidelity (or bigamy) which will allow her conveniently to divorce *him* and to marry Astaire.

Fluttering around Astaire and Rogers are four comedy characters (or caricatures): Alice Brady as Rogers' scatterbrained aunt, Astaire's sidekick Edward Everett Horton as an amusingly incompetent lawyer, Erik Rhodes as the self-important professional co-respondent, and Eric Blore as a solicitous, busybody waiter at the seaside hotel.[2]

Certain elements of the plot in *The Gay Divorcee* are sometimes held to be typical of all the Astaire-Rogers films

[2] Blore and Rhodes had played the same roles in the stage version. RKO originally tried to get Helen Broderick (who was later to perform memorably as Rogers' older friend in *Top Hat* and *Swing Time*) to take on the role Brady plays, but Broderick was unavailable at the time.

This page and opposite: Two moments in "The Continental"

The end of "Night and Day"—with Claire Luce in the stage play (above) and Ginger Rogers in the film (below)

—his instantly falling in love with her, for example, or the gimmick about mistaken identity. But these elements are only occasionally found again in their other films (and then mainly in *Top Hat,* which is to a degree a remake of *The Gay Divorcee*). More typical are the general characteristics of the characters they play. The character Astaire plays is brash, likable, and assured, with a Keaton-like resourcefulness (for example, he uses the "Road Closed" sign he happens to carry around in his car to gull Rogers into a conversation). As an actor he seems a bit ill-at-ease, but this often has a certain charm about it. Rogers exudes a slightly acid haughtiness tempered with an almost palpable vulnerability—a characteristic she was greatly to develop and refine in later films.

CHANGES FROM THE STAGE SHOW

A few aspects of the film's plot differ significantly from the stage play. One of these is the addition of a boy-meets-girl scene, which in the play had occurred before the action begins.[3] This initial-encounter scene was to be included in the vast majority of later Astaire films (including most of the ones he did with Rogers), probably because of its dramatic and comic possibilities. For example, in *The Gay Divorcee* Astaire cheerfully manages to annoy Rogers on their first meeting by tearing her dress.[4]

Another interesting difference is the Astaire character's occupation. In the play he was a writer, but Hollywood apparently did not trust its audience to have sufficient imagination to accept the idea that a writer could dance as well as Astaire does, so the film character is a professional dancer. This is typical of the industry's odd penchant for "realism" while working in a medium with unbounded opportunities for fantasy.[5]

[3] In the play, as in the film, it was love at first sight for the character Astaire plays. His first words to her are reported in the play to have been "I'm sorry to intrude, but I love you."

[4] In the stage version the two people had immediately taken to each other, but she had run off because of her embarrassment over her upcoming divorce, intending to call him when she was finally free. Thus in the play Astaire had only to overcome a pathetic, self-deprecating attitude on her part; in the film he has also to contend with her general annoyance with him, and the possibilities for witty contest between them are accordingly extended.

[5] The title was changed from that of the stage play, apparently because it was felt that, while one can imagine a divorcée who is happy, it is improper to suggest that a divorce itself could be happy—as one might characterize a widow as "merry" but not the process of becoming a widow. According to accepted lore and to Pandro Berman, the title change was required by Hollywood's censorship office; however, the request is not recorded on any of that office's letters in the RKO files, and, in fact, the production code certificate posted at the start of the film gives *The Gay Divorce* as the title. Actually, the title RKO finally chose doesn't make too much sense, because Rogers doesn't become a divorcée until after the film is over. There was so much discomfort with the title that at one point a reward of $50 was offered to the employee who could come up with a better one, but apparently no one collected.

THE FILM AND THE CENSORS

The Gay Divorcee was filmed at an extremely awkward time for Hollywood. Under considerable pressure from religious groups, led by the Legion of Decency of the Catholic Church, Hollywood's self-censorship organization, the Hays Office, announced on June 22, 1934, that henceforth it would get tough with suggestive movies, enforcing its directives by levying fines of $25,000 for violations of the Production Code.

With the film about to go into production, the censors recommended that, since a degree of suggestiveness was at the very heart of the plot and humor in the script, RKO give careful consideration to "the suitability of picturizing" the story at a time when so much criticism was being leveled at the industry. Too much money had been put into the film by then, however, and the censors, who were inclined to be understanding about such matters, let the script go through with assurances from the studio that the sexual suggestiveness would be delicately handled.

Accordingly, the final film is something of a hybrid: in conception it contains much of the jaunty naughtiness often found in pre-1934 musicals (including *Flying Down to Rio*), but in execution much of the naughtiness has been excised. Thus the garment Rogers wears, which in the film is called a "negligee," looks more like a decorative suit of armor, and the dress-tearing incident is carried out with such decorum that it's difficult to see that any damage has been done. Throughout, suggestive lines from the play are toned down. In the film, when Rogers tells Astaire to come to her room, the line is "I'll be waiting for you in my room. Two-sixteen. At midnight." In the play the line closes the first act: she hands him her room key and says "Here. Come to my room at ten o'clock. And bring your pajamas."

THE CAMERA

The Gay Divorcee marks Astaire's emergence as a self-conscious filmer of dances. Disappointed at the way previous directors had handled his dances, he was able to assert himself in this film, and he began to develop the aesthetic that dominated his future films and became the prevailing attitude toward the filming of dance in Hollywood for a generation. However, Astaire had yet to establish full control; a couple of his numbers in this film—most regrettably, "Night and Day"—are marred by the kind of cluttered camera perspectives he later successfully banished from his motion pictures.

Betty Grable and Edward Everett Horton

THE MUSIC

Of the thirteen Cole Porter songs used in the New York and London productions of the stage show, only the big hit "Night and Day" was thought good enough to be carried over to the film. Berman says he asked Porter to write more songs for the film, but since Porter was not interested, other composers were called in. Two new songs by Con Conrad and Herb Magidson were added: "The Continental," which won an Oscar for the best song in 1934 (the first year that category was included in the Academy Awards), and the unpretentious "A Needle in a Haystack," which deserved to. Two additional tunes, determinedly bouncy, were composed for the film by Harry Revel and Mack Gordon.

THE CHOREOGRAPHY

Although little of the music was carried over from the stage version, Astaire incorporated into the film many of the choreographic ideas that had worked so well on the stage, refashioning them for new contexts and new music. Also working on the choreography were Astaire's colleagues from *Flying Down to Rio*: dance director Dave Gould turned out another pseudo–Busby Berkeley number, while Hermes Pan worked as his—and, more importantly, Astaire's—assistant.

THE NUMBERS

A
DON'T LET IT BOTHER YOU
(1'40")

The film opens with a scene that seems to have no real function except to introduce Fred Astaire in his new persona as star. It takes place in a Paris nightclub, where a chorus of leggy showgirls is singing (with intermittent French accents) a rather shallow Revel-Gordon song and performing a precision (well, synchronized) finger-doll dance (A 1). The dance was choreographed by Frank Warde, characterized in RKO publicity materials as a "big time vaudeville artist." Then the camera pans to show the finger-doll efforts of Horton and Astaire, who are applying, one presumes, their own choreography (A 2). Judging from this brief exhibition, one would predict a greater future in dance for Astaire than for Warde. The chorus's dance is just so much finger-wiggling, while Astaire's routine has rhythmic articulation, wit, and musicality. But what is truly impressive and telling is the obvious thought and care Astaire has given to this tiny bit of throwaway business.

Amusingly, Astaire's dance takes place up and down a little staircase formed by the base of the table lamp. As it happens, most of the dances in *The Gay Divorcee*—and also in his next film, *Roberta*—have at least some sequences on stairs. A warm-up, perhaps.

B
DON'T LET IT BOTHER YOU
(REPRISE) (1' 20")

When Astaire and Horton are unable to pay their bill because they have forgotten their wallets, Astaire, annoyed and embarrassed, is forced to do a short dance to prove he is the famous dancer Guy Holden, in order to establish credit with the proprietor of the nightclub. The solo itself is just a scrap, but it establishes the Astaire presence and serves as a teaser for the dancing yet to come. It begins with a trumpet fanfare from the orchestra that startles the dancer.[6] Although he is further irritated by being publicly frightened, Astaire settles down and, hands in pockets, begins a minimal tap shuffle. The music soon impels him into action, however, and the solo widens out with tap spins and sprawling arms (B 1). When the music pauses, Astaire reverts to a jogging figure and builds from that to a vigorous cadenza (B 2). The dance ends with some space-devouring spins and (when Horton discovers his "missing" wallet in his jacket pocket) a disgusted collapse to the floor.

The dance is dismembered by intermixed shots of Horton and of the proprietor—shots that are, however, relevant to the plot. The dance also includes two kinds of shots that were to be all but banished from future Astaire dances: shots in which the dancing is partly obscured by foreground obstacles—in this case by the head of an audience member (B 1)—and inserted close-ups of dancing feet (B 2).[7]

[6] The fanfare idea appears to have been something of an inside joke. See p. 70n.

C
A NEEDLE IN A HAYSTACK
(3' 34")

Preparing to clear customs upon arriving in England, Rogers gets her dress caught in a steamer trunk. Astaire, answering her calls for help (C 1), clumsily tears the dress, immediately falls in love with her, and pleads with her to phone him at his apartment.

He hangs around his London room hoping she will call or send a note, but he finally gives up and resolves to go out and scour the streets of the city searching for her, even if that's like looking for a needle in a haystack. First, however, he sings and dances about it.[8]

In this, his first full-blown solo in a film, Astaire was determined to show what he had to offer. The solo, as might be expected, is virtuosic —but the brilliance is controlled, understated, leavened with wit, and serves to emphasize a point in the plot. Among other things, the number clearly and firmly establishes—declares —Astaire's choreographic credo: the economy of structure, the originality, the jokes that seem to

[7] The inserted close-up of Astaire's feet in his solo in his previous film, *Flying Down to Rio* (2 E 9), had at least some small justification, since it showed a motif used throughout the dance; for the close-up here there is no such excuse. Throughout Astaire's career the shot occurs only once more: in the lamentable *Finian's Rainbow* thirty-five years later (31 L 4).

[8] This number replaces Porter's "After You, Who?," a rather despairing song sung by Astaire early in the play as he recalls their moments together. A bit later, when he tries to cheer himself up by anticipating how he will strut his stuff at the seaside hotel, he does an upbeat solo to the same music. It was because he liked this song that Astaire decided to do the stage show, according to Porter.

A 1 · A 2 · B 1 · B 2 · C 1 · C 2 · C 3 · C 4

emerge naturally and almost incidentally out of the choreographic texture, the careful attention to music, lyric, and situation. The number is also the first in which his camera aesthetic emerges: in the dance portion he is always shown full-figure, and although the dance involves vaulting over furniture and throwing props around, it is recorded in a small number of shots—in this case, one.

The song, by Conrad and Magidson, was probably the first film song written specifically for Astaire. It is suitably lilting and classy, with a lyric that perfectly suits the situation. Though the songwriters provided a fine wistful verse for the song, it is not used in the film: instead Astaire sings the chorus twice (in his later films he almost never sang a song completely through more than once unless there was a change in the lyric). The first time he is sitting on a couch, fairly seething with determination to find Rogers (C 2). The second time he begins to get dressed to go out on his search, deftly backhanding his robe to his valet (C 3), then searching through a selection of neckties, picking one, and putting it on; in the process, the words "beat of your feet" cause him absently to deliver a brisk little tap barrage, which startles the otherwise unflappable valet.[9]

Astaire wanders over to the hearth as he finishes singing. The dance, we are to believe, is begun incidentally and by forces beyond his control. As he sinks into thought—reflecting, no doubt, on the difficult quest before him—he is amused to find that his right foot (indeed, his whole right leg) has begun to dance (C 4). Gradually the rest of his body joins in, propelling him at one point into a goofy little waddle (C 5) and then finally into movements that are so broad they cannot be contained on the hearth and carry him into the center of the room. The music for this part of the number is a breezy jazz-band arrangement with a witty, soaring clarinet obbligato.

When the orchestra returns to the top of the song, Astaire accordingly returns to the top of the dance—but this time with the suggestion that he is doing it consciously (C 6; compare C 4).

Much of the humor in the dance emerges from Astaire's unruffled alternations between brilliant virtuosity and controlled serenity. For example, his air of genial calm (C 6) is abruptly abandoned for a rhythmically complex cadenza of tap spins and hops (C 7); then, just as suddenly, he sinks back into a nonchalant attitude as if nothing had happened.

Next he abruptly bolts across the room (C 8) and inserts himself into the jacket his valet patiently holds for him; so attired, he unexpectedly vaults over the couch (C 9)—arriving on the other side in a state of unperturbed calm. Finally, he whips off a series of three cabrioles—angled jumps during which the legs thrash in the air (C 10)—as well as a vigorous tap barrage (C 11), and then jumps onto a chair, where, subsiding again into complete composure, he catches the hat and umbrella tossed to him by the valet (C 12) and then calmly strolls out the door as the music ends (C 13).[10]

The handling of the three cabrioles is unusual. Ordinarily, Astaire's choreography is remarkably unpredictable, and he rarely repeats a major effect without varying it in some interesting, usually witty, way. But in this case the cabrioles lay directly on the music, and the first two could be used to "predict" the third.[11]

D
LET'S K-NOCK K-NEEZ
(4′ 33″)

Not too surprisingly, Astaire eventually does run into Rogers on the street and, after a car chase, he immediately, if offhandedly, proposes marriage. She remains irritated, though she is also evidently attracted (D 1). Again she runs out on him.

In the company of her aunt, Rogers visits Horton at his law office, and he eagerly promises to

[9] Astaire had done a getting-dressed-and-going-out number in the 1931 stage revue *The Band Wagon* to "New Sun in the Sky." The idea came to him while he was dressing one morning, an activity to which he brings the same meticulous, if agonized, perfectionism as to his dancing: often, it has been reported, "he will tie and untie a dozen of his 150-odd cravats before settling on one for the day."

[10] The cabrioles appear to have been anticipated by an earlier leap (C 8) that can be seen (in retrospect) as a kind of aborted or half-formed cabriole—as if Astaire had started a cabriole, but decided in mid-leap against doing such a showy step at that point because he was not yet completely dressed.

[11] The cabrioles were a carryover from one of Astaire's solos (probably "After You, Who?") in the stage show, and they had been new for him there. The anonymous drama reviewer for the London *Morning Post* noted that Astaire "uses quite a number of ballet steps—cabrioles and brisés and so on—in a way that has never been attempted before." On Astaire's ballet training at the time, see p. 6.

C5 C6 C7 C8

C9 C10 C11 C12

work his "brain to the bone" for her (D2). To facilitate her divorce under British law, he arranges for her to spend an innocent (but legally provocative) night with a professional co-respondent at a seaside resort. Meanwhile, Astaire decides to try to forget the elusive Rogers. Unaware that she is Horton's client, he agrees to tag along with his bumbling friend on the divorce mission to the resort.

At the resort Horton is casually accosted by the seventeen-year-old Betty Grable (already a veteran of ten motion pictures). Supported by a chorus of beach bunnies and their beaux, they are soon romping desperately about to a Revel-Gordon ditty whose melody seems to derive some of its inspiration (though not enough) from Porter's "I've Got You on My Mind" in *Gay Divorce*. The censors, ever on the alert for suggestiveness, at first found the song's title unacceptable.

This number threatens to add new depth to the word "trivial." It requires the performers repeatedly to bash their knees together (D3) and then limp off in agony. The dance is largely innocent of transitions: when the performers finish spreading one repetitive idea over a four- or eight-measure musical phrase, the camera simply cuts to someone doing something else. The best moment is at the end, when Astaire enters in the background, quietly watching (D4). Standing still, he commands more attention than all the frantic performers in the foreground.[12]

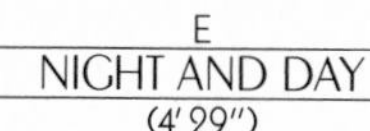

E

NIGHT AND DAY

(4′29″)

Later, when Astaire happens to glance down from a balcony at the hotel, he is surprised and delighted to discover Rogers among a crowd of diners. She sees him at the same time and flees, but he catches up with her in one of those empty, secluded dancing areas that were to populate Astaire's films in such convenient profusion. She wants nothing more than to get away—her previous experiences with him have mostly been irritating to her. Furthermore, she is intensely embarrassed to be recognized by anyone at the place where she will be undergoing the humiliating experience with the professional co-respondent.

In the course of a brief conversation Astaire learns, to his great joy, that she had called him at his London apartment (after he had left for the seaside), thereby suggesting that her previous hostility toward him should not be taken entirely at face value. As she turns to leave, he entraps her with a song and then seduces her with a dance. She is distant and cool at the beginning, but by the end she is dazzled and won.[13]

The number, originally choreographed for the stage show, uses at least three devices to chart the emotional transformation.

The first might be called architectural. At the beginning of the dance, Rogers tries repeatedly to flee, and her routes of escape are clearly shown, but Astaire always blocks her path. Toward the end of the dance she does manage to free herself, but, realizing now that she doesn't really want to get away, she moves to an upstage corner where there is no exit and, self-entrapped, quietly waits for him to collect her.[14]

The second makes use of an odd shuffling or supplicating "mating" dance phrase. Astaire does it three times in the number, and each time Rogers' response is different: first she shrugs it off; later she echoes the step but then abruptly turns on her heel and strides away; and finally she responds willingly and in kind, telling him in dance terms that she has been won.

The third was probably largely contributed by Rogers. In the early part of the dance, she often moves stiffly and standoffishly, or as if entrapped. Gradually, however, her focus turns inward and she begins to dance as if for herself alone. When Astaire sweeps her into his arms, she is jolted out of her reverie, but she is still unwilling to give in completely to him. Soon, however, she willingly flows into his arms.

In addition to its intricate love story, the dance

[12] According to Croce, the routine was choreographed by Hermes Pan. He was to do better work later on.

[13] Although the issue of seduction seems quite clear in this duet, it appears that the first person to comment on it in print was Arlene Croce, in a 1965 article. However self-evident the issue may seem, the reviews of the film seem never to mention it, even indirectly, nor does it appear to be noted in the pre-1965 literature on Astaire or on the musical.

[14] This stylized dramatic progression is similar to the famous adagio in the second act of *Swan Lake* as it is often staged. The swan queen, timorously responding to the prince's ardent advances, suddenly tries to flee and darts away toward the wings; but the prince intercepts her and blocks her path. Later she again starts to run for the wings. This time, however, he does not run after her. She stops and of her own accord returns to him, placing herself in his arms.

C13 D1 D2 D3

D4 E1 E2 E3

is notable for its highly imaginative use of the music, reflecting in its patterns not only the soaring line of the melody but also, very often, the sensuous rhythms of the accompaniment and of a bubbling violin countermelody. Also interesting is the way the choreography deals with the dramatic shifts between loud and soft in the musical arrangement.

Cole Porter wrote "Night and Day" specifically with Astaire's voice in mind. In some respects it is difficult to sing. It covers an octave and a half, with many important parts (including the final notes) occurring at extremes.[15] It also includes quite a bit of tricky chromaticism, as well as two jumps of an octave and one of a seventh at dramatic points. At first Astaire doubted he could sing it, but when the producer of the stage show suggested that it therefore be dropped, Porter stood firm. The resulting success of the song in the show proved to be a special gift to Astaire, for the song was an instrument by which he grew as a performer.

The lyric suits the situation well. Astaire sings of the hours he has spent thinking of her, the many repeated notes suggesting the agonized monotony of waiting in his "lonely room."[16] However yearning the lyric, the song is taken at a bright clip so that it picks up a lightly swinging lilt, a quality that influences the choreography.

As Astaire ardently sings, the dancers' movement introduces the central dramatic theme of the number: Rogers' desire to leave and Astaire's determination that she stay. At first she seems willing to stick around for a while as he begins to pour out his heart to her in song. She looks at him with a mixture of bewilderment and faint pleasure—but also embarrassment, and much of the time she looks somewhat sadly away from him (E1). Midway through the song, she gets up and starts to leave. He pursues her, arresting her progress, and as he finishes the song he blocks her exit entirely.[17]

While the orchestra plays the verse, she tries to get past him to exit to the right, but he runs ahead of her to block her again (E2). She tries the left exit and then the right one once more, with the same result. As she turns and strides determinedly toward the left exit again, he chases after her and rather roughly grabs her by the wrist (E3)—the first time he has touched her.

Startled, she looks back at him; as the orchestra begins the music of the chorus, he does his little supplicating dance for her, a hopeful expression on his face (E4). It doesn't work, though: when he releases her hand, she starts out again for the exit. He springs after her and, with a catlike pounce, grabs her wrist (E5) and pulls her firmly into his arms. They glide across the floor in an odd partnering pose—eyeball-to-eyeball rather than cheek-to-cheek (E6).

Some beautiful, musically complex partnering follows—he spins her out of his arms and then back in. When she spins away from him, Rogers has some difficulty maintaining the desired flowing effect (E7)—a problem she was to overcome in later films.

Now Astaire winds Rogers into his arms and holds her close, imprisoning her in her own right arm (E8). As her focus begins to turn inward, he watches her intently, fluttering his free hand—almost as if he were trying to mesmerize her. At one point they echo the bubbling lilt in the music with a hopping pattern.

Exactly what happens in the next phrase of the dance will never be known, because Sandrich shows most of it filtered through a set of Venetian blinds (E9).[18] When we return to the dance, however, something remarkable is going on. Rogers, under the ever-watchful eye of Astaire, has sunk further into her sensuous reverie as she gives herself over to the impulses of the music (E10). This seems to continue as the camera glimpses the dancers from under a table (E11)—another inane directorial inspiration. This was the last time such a shot was to be seen in an Astaire dance. But even apart from these episodes, the number is filmed in a "prehistoric"

[15] Charles Schwartz argues that the repeated notes in mid-range "made things as easy as possible for Astaire." However, a song is made easy not by having *most* of the notes within a comfortable range, but by having them *all* that way.

[16] However evocative Porter's lyric may be in general, there is one very clumsy phrase: "Under the hide of me" (contrived to rhyme with "inside of me"). Porter was reportedly blocked on the lyric until he attended a luncheon at the home of Mr. and Mrs. Vincent Astor during a rainstorm and heard Mrs. Astor complain about a broken eave: "That drip, drip, drip, is driving me mad." Instantly Porter jumped up and said, "I think that will work." Porter claimed that the music "was inspired by a Mohammedan call to worship that he had heard in Morocco," though at other times he gave out more mundane stories about its origins.

[17] For a parody of this maneuvering, see the movement under the singing of the song in "My One and Only Highland Fling" in *The Barkleys of Broadway* (22E).

[18] The phrase includes an early instance of the Astaire double helix (see p. 19).

E4 E5 E6 E7
E8 E9 E10 E11

manner: Sandrich takes eight shots to present the dance proper (from E 4 on). By contrast, the romantic duet in Astaire's next film (4 G) is rendered in two shots.

At this point the dancing and the music build to a climax with some simultaneous, but separate, turns for the dancers. As the music returns to the beginning of the song, it suddenly decreases in volume, and Rogers abruptly snaps out of her reverie, startled to find herself confronting the yearning Astaire again (E 12). This is the first time she has really looked at him, at least since she entered her self-absorbed reverie. He quickly moves to take her in his arms, and the next portions of the dance are partnered. But Rogers is still unyielding: she dances warily, sometimes with her left arm dangling at her side (E 13), or as if forcing him to maintain a distance (E 14).

Beginning here, the musical arrangement incorporates a bouncy little violin melody that runs counter to the main theme. This countermelody is often reflected in the choreography for the next sections of the dance.

Although Rogers remains aloof, Astaire decides to try again with his little supplicating step (E 15; compare E 4). This time she responds with a related step of her own as he watches (E 16). But any hopes he might have are dashed as she suddenly turns away and begins once more to walk out determinedly on him (E 17). Again he chases her, grabbing her arm as before and pulling her back sharply into the dance (E 18). His persistence will soon be rewarded.

Rogers' change of heart occurs at what might seem to be the most frustrating point in the dance for Astaire. She shoves him away by pushing the heel of her hand against his chin (E 19). This sends him staggering across the floor (E 20) in perhaps the most extraordinary single moment in this astonishing dance. The movements—Rogers' action and Astaire's reaction—are highly stylized; that is, Rogers does not put her weight behind her gesture, and therefore Astaire's extravagant sprawl across the floor is not realistically justified. The actions, therefore, never cease to be dance movements, and there is no choreographic jolt when Astaire recovers from his stagger and returns smoothly to the bouncy rhythm of the music.

But now Rogers has changed. Rather than taking advantage of her clear opportunity for escape, she runs upstage, where there is no exit, and, watching Astaire over one shoulder, she waits quietly for him to come and get her (E 21). After looking quickly around to see where she has gone, he does exactly that, purposefully leading her back to the main dancing area. They flow across the floor with the dance's only lift (E 22), and at one point Astaire spins himself around, daringly wrapping himself in her arm (E 23).[19]

Now comes the big test. For the third time Astaire tenders his little dance of supplication (E 24; compare E 15, 4). This time she answers willingly and in kind (E 25). Then, as if to symbolize their new relationship, Astaire for the first time in the dance turns his back on her, confident at last that she won't try to run away (E 26).

The rest of the duet is a dance of celebration and consummation. When they turn to face each other, the music builds dramatically and she melts into his arms; for the first time they dance close, cheek to cheek, her arm encircling his upper back and neck (E 27; compare E 6, 13, 14).

[19] This maneuver seems to be developed from a step, the "Wind Up," devised by Vernon and Irene Castle (see II I 7–9). Astaire uses versions of it in several dances: it reappears more pointedly in the "Cheek to Cheek" duet in *Top Hat* (5E 19) and, in quite a different way, in 14G 15 and 18G 4. It is parodied in 15G 11 and in 21E 4.

E12 E13 E14 E15
E16 E17 E18 E19
E20 E21 E22 E23

The dance ends with some voluptuous partnered maneuverings around the area and with some brisk spins by Rogers in Astaire's arms. For a moment they pause and he presses her closely into his body (E 28); then he deposits her softly on a bench as the music subsides (E 29; compare p. 54). He backs away, brushes off his hands—in satisfaction, one presumes, with a job well done (E 30)—and calmly offers a cigarette to his dazzled partner (E 31).[20]

In later films there were to be other duets—playful as well as romantic—in which seduction was an issue. But none surpasses "Night and Day" in sheer choreographic richness and in the lavish invention of partnering patterns. Amazingly, this highly original, extravagantly inventive, richly textured dance was the first romantic duet Astaire ever choreographed. In *Gay Divorce,* his first show without his sister, Adele, Astaire played opposite the lovely Claire Luce. As he recalled, "Claire was a beautiful dancer and it was her style that suggested to me the whole pattern of the 'Night and Day' dance. This was something entirely different from anything Adele and I had done together. That was what I wanted, an entirely new dancing approach."

Equally amazing is Rogers' contribution to the success of the dance. She understands what is going on and seems to realize instinctively how to put it across (although she sometimes seems a bit confused about how to react during Astaire's singing). She was to improve and gain more confidence as a dancer, but even in this early test she shows herself to be well up to the dramatic demands of the dance. If Astaire had never choreographed like this before, Rogers had never been asked to dance like this before. In fact, Astaire's initial reluctance to play opposite her in *The Gay Divorcee* was due not only to his understandable, if somewhat obsessive, unwillingness to become half of another "team" but also to his concern that Rogers was incapable of taking over a dance that had been built on a very different kind of dancer.[21] "Ginger was a Charleston dancer when I first met her," Astaire once remarked, "and she hadn't had any real experience [with] dances . . . like 'Night and Day.' " His conclusion is a masterpiece of understatement: "By the time we got Ginger into this thing she just sold it beautifully."

If an "integrated" dance number is one that advances the plot, then "Night and Day" may be the first truly integrated dance number in the history of both the American musical theatre and the Hollywood musical (see also pp. 23 and 26). At the same time, there is a strong contrast in tone between the rich seriousness of the dance number and the studied frivolity of the story in which it is embedded—a contrast that was to become typical of the films Astaire and Rogers made together.

F
THE CONTINENTAL
(16′ 17″)

Frivolity dutifully returns. After their duet, Astaire accidentally pronounces the password phrase by which Rogers is supposed to recognize the professional co-respondent in her divorce case (F 1). Hurt and outraged, she turns haughty, tells him to be at her room at midnight, and

[20] This business is neatly parodied in the aftermath of the romantic "Smoke Gets In Your Eyes" duet in *Roberta* (see p. 74).

[21] Once the film was arranged with Rogers as his partner, Astaire made the suggestion to RKO—astonishing in retrospect—that "Night and Day" be dropped, on the grounds that the song had become overfamiliar. On Astaire and the "team" issue, see p. 8.

E 24 E 25 E 26 E 27
E 28 E 29 E 30 E 31
F 1 F 2 F 3 F 4

stalks away. Astaire is dumbfounded by her abrupt emotional shift (F2) but does show up, somewhat uncertainly, at the appointed hour. The confusion over Astaire's identity allows for some amusing dialogue, but fairly soon, to Rogers' great relief, they discover their mistake.

Now the real co-respondent shows up: Erik Rhodes as a foppish Italian tenor who is given to telephoning his wife to keep her apprised of his activities (F3).[22] Rhodes finds Astaire an unwelcome interloper but is eventually mollified and settles down to a game of solitaire. Then Astaire and Rogers wander out onto the balcony and soon get involved in a gargantuan production number—one of the longest numbers in the history of the Hollywood musical.[23] It has little to do with the plot but a lot to do with the business of musicals in the early 1930s, in its attempt to combine the formulas of the Busby Berkeley extravaganzas with the dance-craze appeal of the Astaire-Rogers combination in *Flying Down to Rio*'s "Carioca" number.[24]

Rogers begins the number by brightly singing the song to Astaire (F4). It is a long one, consisting of two different AABA sections plus an insistent vamping phrase that links them. The lyric is filled with coy suggestiveness: "Beautiful music, dangerous rhythm . . . something daring . . . it does what you want it to do . . . two bodies swaying . . . you kiss while you're dancing . . . rhythm that you can't control."

The first duet (1′ 51″). After some evasive tactics to distract Rhodes, Astaire and Rogers enter the dance floor, where festivities are in progress, and dance to the second of the two AABA portions of the song (played twice through for the duet).

According to RKO publicity materials, "The Continental" ("the smartest dance yet created") is a "combination of smooth gliding rhythms and hot breaks." The duet combines this idea of contrasts with a play on the teasing suggestiveness of the lyric. In the first phrases of their dance, Astaire and Rogers contrast some delicate footwork and gliding patterns (F5) with some hot tap steps (F6). Then they develop the duet's diagonal arm signature (F5) into the suggestion of a nuzzle as they hover near each other, their hands fluttering, their faces close but not touching (F7).[25]

During the transitional vamp between the two renderings of the melody, there is an ingenious and playful manipulation of a partnered hopping step (F8). In this Rogers demonstrates, as she had in the Carioca, the infectious joy and pleasure—ecstasy, even—that she suggests she feels in dancing with Astaire, a quality that was to be a major contribution to the success of their playful duets in later films.

As the melody returns, so does the contrast of cool composure with "hot breaks." Here the

[22] On the Rhodes character, see also p. 81n. For the London version of *Gay Divorce*, Porter wrote an amusing song for Rhodes to sing to his distant spouse: "Tonight I'm forced to compromise / A radiant blond with ravishing eyes, / But don't worry, Maria, I love only you."

[23] It should not be assumed that tolerance for long numbers was any greater in 1934 than it is now. Many people attending the previews complained about the length of "The Continental," but apparently to no avail. (Actually, the time span of the number does include some two and a half minutes of nonmusical plot business.)

[24] In ads for *The Gay Divorcee* Astaire and Rogers were billed as "the King and Queen of the Carioca," and extensive efforts were made by RKO to get dancing teachers and ballrooms interested in the picture and in its new "dance sensation." Demonstrations were arranged, instruction kits were mailed out, and theatre parties were organized.

[25] Some photographs from a dance in *Gay Divorce* show Astaire and Claire Luce in this pose. So apparently it is another choreographic idea brought over from the stage musical.

F5 F6 F7 F8 F9 F10 F11 F12 F13 F14 F15 F16

coolness is shown in some Continental hand kissing, carried out with exaggerated decorum (F 9). (This is about as close as Astaire ever got to kissing while dancing.) Alternating with it are some jazzy Americanisms (F 10).

Next comes a beautiful sequence in which the dancers seem to hold back against the flow of the music and then happily give in to its compelling insistence with more partnered hopping, their arms linked in a basket-weave pattern (F 11).

The ending of the duet, to a musical coda fashioned from the cycling vamp melody, is built entirely around the fluttering, teasing, diagonal arm motif introduced earlier. It is even shown once in a medium shot (F 12), a camera perspective that, though it heightens the teasing sexiness of the dance here, was virtually banished from Astaire's dances for his next six films (for a discussion, see pp. 28–29). As the fluttering continues, Rogers' beautifully pliant back is displayed to advantage (F 13). Finally Astaire ends the tease: he reaches out for Rogers abruptly and snaps her into his arms (F 14–16), where, quite obviously, she belongs.

Thus, though the duet is playful and exhibitionistic, it is, as the ending makes clear, erotic and deeply serious at the core.

The chorus dance. Astaire and Rogers are startled out of the private world they have created for themselves on the public dance floor by the applause of the audience and by the invasion of scores of chorus dancers who cascade down the steps and onto the floor. Now Rhodes appears on the balcony and enthusiastically croons the song (F 17).

The various routines delivered by the chorus do not support the putative choreographic point of the dance—the "smooth gliding rhythms" combined with "hot breaks." However, there is quite a bit of decorative drill work (F 18) and, at several points, exhibitions of kissing while dancing, which, far from suggesting anything remotely erotic, serves to demonstrate how absurdly awkward that idea can be (F 19).[26] Most of the camera work involves abrupt cuts or dissolves from one dance idea to the next, which, as Croce notes, "hardly compare with the unfolding logic—or the surrealistic illogic—of Busby Berkeley's numbers."

Next comes the "jazz" section. Songstress Lillian Miles appears and, in a sassy upbeat, sings new material telling how the Continental is sweeping all nations. Although waiter Eric Blore contributes a nifty dance bit (F 20), the section mostly shows the chorus, in new costumes, energetically thrashing about. In parts, Sandrich and Gould use extremely rapid cutting and tilted cameras, apparently in a desperate effort to breathe some life into the choreography (F 21).

The final duet (1′42″). According to rehearsal pianist Hal Borne, it was Astaire's idea to do the dance "in many languages," and, for a finale, Rogers and Astaire return to salute the Continent again. They do a tango up a staircase, a czardas at the top, and a broad Viennese waltz back down again. It all concludes with some American tap stuff (F 22) and an exuberant dash up the stairs and out the revolving doors.

[26] Hermes Pan, who says he "worked out the steps" in this number, remembers it as "blood, sweat, and tears." They worked twelve hours a day on it "and no overtime."

G

TABLE DANCE—THE CONTINENTAL

(REPRISE) (1′25″)

The next morning, problems are neatly and amusingly resolved. When Horton arranges for Rogers' husband to discover her with Rhodes, the husband refuses to accept the charade as grounds for divorce. But all is saved when waiter Blore recognizes the husband as a man who has frequented a hotel with another woman (G 1).

With her husband's infidelity established, Rogers will have no trouble divorcing him, and to celebrate she and Astaire do a gleeful waltz parody around her hotel room, the steps of which carry them absurdly over the furniture and out the door (G 2).[27] This tricky dance, set on the music with a naive directness uncharacteristic of Astaire, was created for the stage show and was based on an idea of the show's dance director, Carl Randall. Astaire says it was "a spectacular thing on the hazardous side" that usually generated "unlimited encores." When the dancers occasionally fell in performance, they would "just get up and do it over properly" and then "the audience would give twice as much applause." Claire Luce's recollections are not so mellow, however. She damaged her hip during a London performance and, though in pain, finished the dance; the resulting aggravated injury led to the end of her career as a dancer.

[27] An unusual aspect of this dance is the way the dancers exit off-camera at one point and then reappear dancing into the next shot, thereby avoiding the necessity of matching shots. It is a form of labor-saving never found again in Astaire's solos and duets.

F17 F18 F19 F20

F21 F22 G1 G2

4.

Roberta

1935

In addition to its sumptuous Jerome Kern score and its superb dances, *Roberta* is especially significant as the film in which Fred Astaire and Ginger Rogers became fully established as a team. The pairing had been introduced in *Flying Down to Rio* and was greatly enriched in *The Gay Divorcee,* but only in *Roberta* do the two performers seem comfortable and confident enough fully to achieve the spirited gaiety, the irrepressible charm, and the emotional depth that became the trademarks of their collaboration. It is in *Roberta* that Astaire and Rogers transcend partnership and become co-conspirators.

The central romantic story in the film is carried by others —the somber Irene Dunne and the lumbering Randolph Scott—and the function of Astaire and Rogers is to supply comedic embroidery. They are cast as childhood sweethearts who meet again in Paris and rekindle old compatibilities. So while there is a love story for them to play out, there is no major drama to it—no chase, no seduction, no plot complications. Yet their three duets explore romance with more variety and depth than any other Astaire film except *Swing Time:* the dances show love in play, love in erotic dependency, love in ecstatic afterglow. The film also includes one of Astaire's finest and most virtuosic tap solos, "I Won't Dance."

All the dances are characterized by their extensive use of crossover steps, as if Astaire were seeking to explore the various nuances of this maneuver. The dances are also remarkable for their freshness and buoyant spontaneity—qualities that, though often achieved in Astaire's other dances, were never realized more compellingly or with such gratifying consistency as in *Roberta.*

THE SCRIPT

The last of Astaire's films to be substantially taken from a Broadway musical until *Silk Stockings* in 1957, *Roberta* is based on the Jerome Kern–Otto Harbach stage success of 1933–34. Harbach's script was derived in turn from Alice Duer Miller's popular novel of 1933 *Gowns by Roberta,* and it followed the novel's basic plot fairly closely, though a bit of sprightly humor (utterly lacking in the novel) was added and a college band was incorporated into the proceedings to enlarge the musical possibilities. The critics found the stage show dreary—John Mason Brown pronounced it "as eventful as a ride on the shuttle"—but it survived and enjoyed gradually increasing business as its memorable score (particularly the song "Smoke Gets In Your Eyes") gained wide popularity.

At least four writers worked on the *Roberta* screenplay—among them Allan Scott, who was to be an important contributor to the next five Astaire-Rogers films. In general, the Hollywood writers brightened the stage book considerably and improved its pacing while excising its more risqué jokes. At the same time, they managed to retain the show's basic plot devices and much of its wonderful score.

The central joke in *Roberta* involves the juxtaposition of oafish masculinity with delicate femininity. When his elderly aunt dies, a rather dense and prudish but handsome American football player inherits her Parisian fashion salon. In trying to run the shop, he throws over his obnoxious American girlfriend and falls in love with his aunt's assistant, who, as it happens, is an émigrée Russian princess.

Producer Pandro Berman bought the film rights to *Roberta* in part as a vehicle for Irene Dunne, a singing star who could be at once regal and approachable on the screen. She was given the role of the princess in the film and received billing ahead of Astaire and Rogers. As the oafish halfback, whose signature exclamation is "Gee, that's swell!," the studio cast Randolph Scott, an athletic cowboy type and a nonsinger.

The Astaire-Rogers pairing in the film was developed by manipulating roles in the stage play. Astaire's role was created by combining two characters from the show: its comedy lead—a jokey bandleader (played by Bob Hope in his first important theatrical assignment)—and, to a lesser extent, a hoofing band manager (played by George Murphy).[1] Rogers took the role of a flamboyant nightclub singer, created in the

[1] Hope approached Berman about doing the film, but the producer had already destined the role for Astaire. Although pleased with the film, Berman later termed his failure to bring Hope to RKO one "of those mistakes you make." Astaire had seen the show, with Hope in the cast, before making the film.

With Irene Dunne

show by the vivacious, Polish-born Lyda Roberti, the "original blonde bombshell," as Hope calls her. There had been no romantic attraction between these characters in the stage play—Roberti had designs on the football player, in fact—but this was easily fixed.

Unlike *The Gay Divorcee,* the film of *Roberta* contained none of the performers from the stage version—though Rogers takes great pleasure in importing Roberti's accent.[2] Also left behind were two highly praised aspects of the stage production: the sleek dress designs of Kiviette, and José Limon's choreography for the fashion show.

THE MUSIC

Of the eight central songs in Kern's stage score, four are given full treatment in the film: the bouncy "Let's Begin," the sassy "I'll Be Hard to Handle," and two misty ballads, "Smoke Gets In Your Eyes" and "Yesterdays." In addition, Kern came up with a new song for the film, "Lovely to Look At," which quickly became a big hit. Finally, the perky "I Won't Dance," written by Kern for a show that had flopped in London in 1934, was purchased at Astaire's suggestion and incorporated into the film; it went on to become a hit after the film was released. There's not a weak song in the bunch, and together they constitute one of the finest scores in all of Astaire's films.

With the filming of *Roberta,* Kern left New York for good, to work for the rest of his life almost entirely in Hollywood, where he found the weather, pace, and financial arrangements very much to his liking. At RKO he met Dorothy Fields, who wrote the lyric for "Lovely to Look At" and revised the lyrics for some of the other songs. She and Kern became close friends and later collaborated on other film scores, including, most notably, *Swing Time.*

THE FILMING OF THE DANCES

Working with William Seiter, *Roberta*'s accommodating director, Astaire firmly established his point of view about using the camera in his dances. None of the four major dance episodes has any obstructing or cutaway shots, and all are recorded in a minimal number of shots—between one and three.[3]

THE FATE OF THE FILM

Roberta has suffered an undeserved obscurity. In 1945 MGM bought the film and pulled it out of circulation, with a view toward doing a remake. This finally came about in 1952 with *Lovely to Look At,* in which the Astaire role was divided between Red Skelton and Gower Champion, and the Rogers role between Ann Miller and Marge Champion. Only in the 1970s was *Roberta*—now prefaced by the MGM lion logo—made available once again.

THE CHOREOGRAPHY

Aiding Astaire on choreography was Hermes Pan, who here received his first screen credit—as "assistant dance director." *Roberta* is unique among Astaire's thirties films in that he receives explicit choreographic credit: "Dances arranged by . . ."

[2] Nevertheless, many in the *Roberta* stage cast eventually migrated to Hollywood: not only Hope and Murphy, but also Roberti, leading man Ray Middleton, middle-aged bon vivant Sidney Greenstreet, and bit player Fred MacMurray.

[3] Seiter, a congenial and pleasant fellow who had directed three earlier Rogers films at RKO, was assigned to the film by his friend Berman because Mark Sandrich (who had directed *The Gay Divorcee*) was busy preparing *Top Hat.* Seiter directed Astaire again in *You Were Never Lovelier* in 1942, and Rogers again in *In Person* in 1935.

With Ginger Rogers in "Smoke Gets In Your Eyes"

With Rogers in "I Won't Dance"—the pianist is Hal Borne

THE NUMBERS

A
ORGAN NUMBER (INDIANA)
(1′26″)

As the film opens, Astaire's band, the Wabash Indianians, lands in France to fulfill an engagement. First off the ship is the hatless Hal Borne, who plays the band's pianist. In the real world he was Astaire's rehearsal pianist and co-arranger (A 1).

The owner of the cafe that has engaged the band meets them. Outraged when his expectation of finding a group of feathered Indians is frustrated, he informs them that the deal is off. He remains unmoved even when Scott (apparently the band's manager) forces him to listen to a screwball audition: wearing gloves that look like organ keys, the musicians cluster together and hum through an Indiana hymn as Astaire genially pretends to be playing their hands as a keyboard (A 2) (a vaudevillian gag brought over from the stage play, where the idea had been suggested by Bob Hope).

B
LET'S BEGIN
(2′22″)

Scott remarks that he has an elderly aunt who runs a chic Parisian fashion salon under the name Roberta. The cheerful if destitute musicians go there to solicit help, and Scott is warmly greeted by his aunt (B 1). Later he meets a haughty customer, Ginger Rogers, and learns she is an influential cafe singer. He persuades her to listen to the band, which is waiting outside.

For its second impromptu audition of the film, the band, led by Astaire, launches into a rendition of one of Kern's rare genuinely rollicking—swinging, even—tunes. The song is given an appropriately bouncy treatment. Astaire, aided by three other band members, spiritedly sings the chorus once through (B 2) and then is joined by the trick-voiced and bewigged comedian Candy Candido—Astaire's startled reaction as Candido joins him is one of the number's special delights (B 3). In a wispy falsetto occasionally alternating with a basso profundo, Candido parries Astaire in another rendering of the song.

The number concludes with a zany little dance routine for Astaire, Candido, and Gene Sheldon. Regarding the other two as intruders, Astaire challenges them to keep up with him and leads them into various pratfalls. At the end he pilots them in some high-kicking prances (B 4) that prove to be too much for them; as they topple to the ground, Astaire recognizes Rogers on the balcony as his hometown flame, and the number is cut short when he dashes off after her.

C
RUSSIAN SONG
(1′25″)

Astaire and Rogers meet in the presence of Scott and his aunt. For professional purposes, Rogers is pretending to be a countess and has affected a suitably indescribable accent, her imitation of Lyda Roberti. Astaire is amused and plays along (C 1). In private, she promises to try to get his band a job.

Meanwhile, it is time for the aunt's nap. Accompanied by the guitar playing of the doorman (an émigré Russian prince), Dunne, her assistant in the salon, serenades her with a lullaby apparently written by Kern (C 2).

A 1 A 2 B 1 B 2
B 3 B 4 C 1 C 2
D 1 D 2 D 3 D 4

D

I'LL BE HARD TO HANDLE

(5′ 39″)

At the Cafe Russe, Rogers is rehearsing with Astaire and his band to warm them up for their audition with the proprietor. In her song—delivered in full accent—she cheerily warns (or brags) about her ferocious temper as Astaire watches admiringly (D1).[4]

After her song she joins him, and as the band goes over the number once more in the background, they reminisce about their youthful romance back in Indiana. Astaire idly punctuates their banter with some casual tap salvos (D2). When he kids her about a beauty contest she once won (he claims to have fixed it himself), she rushes at him in mock fury; he playfully blocks her blows—and the dance is on (D3).

[4] The song's lyric has been substantially altered from the stage version, where the singer rails against the idea of marrying, preferring instead a life of freedom, or, in one version, the life of "a tart." The clever "shellfish"/"selfish" rhyme was written for the film version by Dorothy Fields. A film clip of Roberti's stage performance of the song (in Miles Kreuger's Institute of the American Musical) suggests Rogers is imitating some of Roberti's mannerisms as well as her accent.

The spirit of play dominates the dance, which is especially notable, even by Astaire's standards, for its remarkable spontaneity. As Croce observes, it's "three minutes of what looks like sheerest improvisation." Part of the illusion is created by having the sound recorded live on the set (the usual practice was to dub in the taps later). Though this causes some of the tap sounds to be a bit muffled, it also allows Rogers' little squeals of breathless delight as Astaire swirls her around the dance floor to emerge with exceptional naturalness.[5]

"I'll Be Hard to Handle" is the first in a series of playful duets, matchless in their sheer joyousness, that are the greatest single achievement in the Astaire-Rogers series. It is also the first of Astaire's duets to be shown in one shot. The duet makes extensive use of steps in which one leg is crossed over the other. Small and simple at the beginning, these are soon elaborated, as one leg sweeps out and across the other with momentum enough to propel the dancers around the floor.

[5] For *Roberta,* Astaire had a circular floor of hard maple constructed to replace the red (which photographs gray) linoleum often used in his previous films (see p. 64). The idea was to get the dances to record more clearly.

The dance is in three parts: an opening frolic, a tap dialogue that takes the form of an argument suggested by the song's lyric, and a final jubilant foray around the floor.

The first portion opens with a series of eight-measure phrases, each of which ends with an unaccompanied tap fusillade. The crossover step is introduced in the context of a casual promenade that opens the dance (D4). Then Astaire snaps Rogers up and swirls her across the floor in a phrase that features some exquisite tempo modulations and, at the end, dissolves wryly back into the crossover step (D5, 6). A crossover step also appears in the dodging pattern they do next, face to face (D7). As the music slows suddenly, the dancers mock its broad pace by partnering grandly, repeating their crossover step. Then, when the music returns to tempo, they revert to casualness, and the crossover idea becomes more playful and definite, the crossed leg thrust out a bit, and eventually used to locomote a tour of the floor (D8). The step becomes most flamboyant at this point, when it is developed as the impetus for a traveling, hopping pattern (D9) and then in a thrusting, staggering version as the dancers cling (D10). This leads to

D5 D6 D7 D8

D9 D10 D11 D12

D13 D14 D15 D16

another tap break, a sudden pause (D11), a quick turn, and an amused lapse into a jaunty tap stroll (D12).

Interrupted in this happy perambulation by a bugle call, the couple snap to a salute and respond with a brief tap flurry.[6] The music now ceases to be audible, but its remembered dimensions provide the pacing for the second portion of the dance, an ingenious tap dialogue. As Astaire and Rogers trade two- and four-measure phrases back and forth, a mock drama is played out. Having somehow managed to offend her, he becomes more and more obsequious (D13), but she only gets furiouser and furiouser (D14)—very hard to handle. Finally, she slaps him, then makes it worse by stamping on his foot, causing him to hobble around extravagantly as she gloats in triumph and satisfaction (D15). This argument, up to the slap, takes thirty-two measures, paralleling the first four strains of the (unheard) song, and was obviously rehearsed to the music.

Further mayhem is prevented by another bugle call, to which Rogers responds by saluting (D16). The band strikes up again, and instantly the dancers begin their final frolic (D17), which includes a quick reprise of their crossover hops (D18; compare D9) and of their staggering partnered step (D19; compare D10). The duet concludes with a swirl across the floor in which Rogers ecstatically gives herself over to Astaire's lead, and a happy, exhausted collapse into two chairs (D20).

They have been so wrapped up in their play that they are startled when their audience of waiters and cleaning women applaud. The performers respond by taking a bow with mock formality.

E

YESTERDAYS

(2′21″)

After some struggle, Rogers is able to persuade the cafe owner to hire Astaire's band.[7]

Meanwhile, at the fashion salon, Scott's aunt prepares to take another nap. She requests a song from Dunne, who serenades her with one of Kern's most haunting ballads, the nostalgic "Yesterdays," sung to guitar accompaniment (E1).[8] The lights fade and the watchers silently leave the room as the aunt falls asleep. Suddenly she slumps lifelessly (E2); then, as the orchestra repeats the song in the background, a newspaper headline announcing her death is shown, followed a bit later by a shot of Dunne sadly alone in the room (E3). This situation, difficult to

[6] The bugle-call routine is something of an inside joke that seems to have derived from a rehearsal gag. When Astaire would arrive at the rehearsal stage and close the door behind him, Hal Borne would punch out the first two measures of the bugle call "Assembly" on the piano, and Astaire would respond "by tapping out the last two bars with his feet. Then they knew it was Fred arriving." The device is used as a running gag in *Follow the Fleet* and turns up in several dances: 3 B, 6 E, 9 J, and, most elaborately, an army-camp solo, 14 F.

[7] As the cafe owner comes in, Rogers regains her accent and urges the band to "geeve it to heem and make it sveet and chot," a sly reference to the stage version's Lyda Roberti, who first gained success on Broadway in 1931 with a Harold Arlen song, "Sweet and Hot."

[8] On stage the song was sung in reminiscence by the aunt herself, played by the sixty-eight-year-old Fay Templeton, who came out of retirement for this, her last role, after sixty years in the theatre. Kern's melody, reflecting Templeton's limitations, has a range of only a tenth—unless one chooses, as Dunne does here on her second rendering, to take an optional high note at the end. Harbach's lyric has a passage of flowery ineptitude in which the word "forsooth" appears. At RKO's urging he rewrote this passage but retained the rhyme of "sequestered days" with "yesterdays," a linkage that is not only clumsy, but inappropriate, since the singer is fondly recalling her free and *un*sequestered youth.

D17 D18 D19 D20
E1 E2 E3 F1
F2 F3 F4 F5

bring off successfully in musical comedy, is handled here with impressive taste.

F
I WON'T DANCE
(5′ 33″)

Scott inherits the dress shop, but eventually he and Dunne agree to run it together. When Scott finds one of their dresses to be too revealingly vulgar, he orders it discarded from the collection. As an opportune plot-thickener, Scott's obnoxious girlfriend from the United States shows up and, egged on by Astaire, decides to buy the dress Scott hates. Dunne protests, but not too much.[9]

The big night of the band's opening at the Cafe Russe arrives. Scott is there with his girlfriend, but they soon get into an argument over her dress, and she walks out on him (F1) and is never seen again. As Scott sourly decides to drink his sorrows away, the camera cuts to the bandstand, where Fred Astaire is about to do a terrific number.

[9] Played by the orchestra in the background under these scenes are two ballads from the stage show, "The Touch of Your Hand" and "You're Devastating."

First Astaire bats out a hot piano arrangement of the song—playing what he had called "feelthy piano" earlier in the film (F2). (The arrangement is actually for two pianos: the other half is being played by the unseen Hal Borne.) When it is finished, Astaire springs up from the piano bench and shoots the audience a winning aw-shucks smile (F3). Then Rogers comes sashaying in and, in song, requests that he dance with her. This is impossible, he sings back: she is so lovely that once she is in his arms his heart won't let his feet operate properly.[10] She takes the compliment with good humor but reminds him of how charming he is when he does the Continental. At this point a trumpet plays a phrase from that number in *The Gay Divorcee,* and the performers hit one of the diagonal arm poses that figured in this duet (F4; compare 3 F5)—the only instance of an explicit choreographic reference in one Astaire film to another. (For an inexplicit, and perhaps unconscious, reference, see 15 A6, 9.)

[10] The lyric, with such wonderful inspirations as the rhyme of "asbestos" with "heaven rest us," was totally rewritten for the film by Dorothy Fields. It would make somewhat more sense if it were titled "I *Can't* Dance." Perhaps the producers didn't want to tamper with the title that had previously been established by lyricist Oscar Hammerstein. In the earlier version it was sung by a woman who refuses to dance because she fears giving in to dangerous romantic longings.

As he concludes the song, she continues to implore. Two of the decorative Cossacks in the restaurant now come to her aid, hauling Astaire bodily to the dance floor (F5) and setting him down firmly. (Actually they don't have it quite right—the idea of the song is not that he won't dance, but that he won't dance with *her.*) As the orchestra starts up again, Astaire spins off some casual tapping, embellishing it with a few loud barrages that send the Cossacks running for cover. Freed of his captors, Astaire ingratiatingly scuffles around the dance floor, greeting the audience (F6) and at one point working a handshake slap with one of the patrons into the percussion (F7).

The tap solo that ensues is a virtuosic, crazy-legged affair—it is as if Astaire were setting out graphically to develop the song's suggestion that he has no conscious control over his feet. There is a lot of limb slinging, and, between furious tap flutters, he is constantly finding one leg wrapping itself around the other. Often he

F6 F7 F8 F9
F10 F11 F12 F13
F14 F15 G1 G2

goes so far that his legs become entwined, as if he were trying to stand on the same spot with both feet.[11]

A frenetic cross-legged tap passage across the floor, punctuated by a pulled-in pose on tiptoe (F8), sets the dance in motion. The leg-wrapping idea begins with three sets of slow hopping spins on one foot (F9), the last of which triggers a quick, bounding cluster of tap-hops. The music soon slows, and the leg crossing and slinging are elaborated in various ways, the most spectacular occurring when one leg is flung in a wide arc around the other (F10), corkscrewing the body (F11) and leading to some brilliant leg-over-leg sprawls (F12). The dance's ending is fast and furious—a set of rapid, spinning taps with windmilling arms (F13), culminating in another pulled-in, cross-legged pose (F14) and an exuberant lunge toward the audience (F15).[12]

[11] These ideas are somewhat similar ones Astaire used in a brief solo in *Flying Down to Rio* (2 E).

[12] A reporter at the rehearsals dutifully recorded the names Astaire applied to some of the steps in this solo as he created them: the "chicken stew," the "taffy twirl," and, in honor of a recurrent small visitor, the "spider twist."

G
SMOKE GETS IN YOUR EYES
(5'40")

Now Dunne enters the Cafe Russe and is treated with royal respect. At a private table, accompanied by a band of roving balalaika strummers, she sings the show's hit tune for the rapt diners (G1).

The lyric derives from an old Russian proverb conveniently invented by Harbach: "When your heart's on fire, smoke gets in your eyes," a rather overly vivid way of saying that love is blind. In the midst of her serenade the drunken Scott staggers over and accuses her of being vindictive in selling the ugly dress to his (former) girlfriend (G2); they argue, he walks out, and Dunne returns to the table tearfully to reprise the last lines of the song, which have suddenly taken on a degree of personal meaning for her: "yet today my love has flown away. . . ."[13]

[13] The lyric for this famous song is remarkably inept. Despite the ingenious story it tells, its logic is muddled; also, stresses in the words often fail to match those in the melody, and there are unnecessary filler words, redundancies, and absurdly highflown language ("chaffed" rhymes with "laughed").

H
LOVELY TO LOOK AT/ SMOKE GETS IN YOUR EYES
(13'5")

During the huffy disagreement between Scott and Dunne that ensues, Astaire has, by default, taken over the management of the fashion salon, a job he finds a bit beyond his talents. In a deft comedy scene, he makes executive decisions about fabrics by improvising efficient, if capricious, aesthetic criteria: "Use whatever we've got most of." Rogers, meanwhile, hangs around making appropriately acidic comments (H1).

The scriptwriters generate a pretext for Dunne to visit the salon, and Astaire and Rogers are soon able to convince her to help them with the big forthcoming fashion show, which, they decide excitedly, will be set to music.

The fashion show is a long, multifaceted musical sequence with bits of plot embedded in it, rather along the lines of "The Continental" in *The Gay Divorcee*. It opens with a group of sportily attired models. Astaire frolics among them, delivering a jaunty sales pitch to the tune of "Don't Ask Me Not to Sing," which was taken from the stage show, where it formed the basis of

H1 H2 H3 H4 H5 H6 H7 H8 H9 H10 H11 H12

a comedy number (H2). Things get more serious as the new hit tune Kern wrote for the film, "Lovely to Look At," is played as a series of cocktail dresses are paraded. Then Dunne emerges to sing the song (H3). The melody, played ten times in all, is used as the background for the rest of the fashion show, which now focuses on formal gowns—one of them modeled by a blond, twenty-four-year-old Lucille Ball (H4).[14]

The last of the gowns, a comparatively simple number cut low in back, is modeled by Ginger Rogers. She joins Astaire at the bandstand, and together they sing one last chorus of the Kern classic. As they do so, Rogers takes Astaire's arm and gazes fondly at him; the contentment and the warm mutual dependency of their relationship becomes palpable (H5).

As the lovers stroll to the dance floor, the music blends effortlessly into a reprise of "Smoke Gets In Your Eyes."[15] The romantic duet that ensues is ostensibly performed for the audience at the fashion show. Throughout, however, the dancers' focus remains on each other, and it is clear that the essential audience for the duet numbers only two.

A gently throbbing accompaniment in the musical arrangement provides a beguiling, pulsating lilt to Kern's lush melody, which creates the illusion that the song is being taken at quite a clip. In fact it is being rendered at a substantially slower pace than Dunne's sung version earlier in the film.[16]

The dancers are attracted as much by the accompaniment as by the soaring melody, as the pensive, loving stroll (H6) merges into a sumptuous, varied, continually unfolding love dance. Gradually, they let go of each other's hands and separate in a figure that makes use of crossed arms as well as the film's choreographic signature, crossed legs (H7). After some soft turns, they complete the first phrases by floating across the floor in one flowing, gently rocking pattern, face to face, dancing closely together but not touching (H8).

As the music begins to repeat the main theme, the dancers resume their side-by-side stroll, this time in a slightly jaunty mood (H9). The next phrases form an extended, seamless transition to full partnering. Astaire takes Rogers by one hand as they sink briefly into a cross-legged pose (H10). Later he partners her tenderly at the waist, or with hands overhead (H11). Through all of this, the easy, rocking pulsations continue. Then Astaire dramatically swoops around Rogers (H12), closes in on her, and presses her tightly to him (H13).

This leads to some rapid partnered turns across the floor, during which Rogers leans back voluptuously in Astaire's arms—the first full exploitation in their dances of her remarkably limber back (H14). These romantic spins then ex-

[14] According to legend, someone once observed to Kern that, at only sixteen measures, the song was rather short. "That's all I had to say," Kern is alleged to have responded. The lyric Fields wrote for what Berman called this "curiously uneven melody" so pleased the producer that he put it in the film without checking with Kern. Happily for everyone (especially Fields), Kern loved it.

[15] The transition is breathtakingly simple. Astaire sings the last line of "Lovely to Look At" but omits the final word ("tonight"); the orchestra plays out the melody, the last note of which, without pause or separation, becomes the first note of "Smoke Gets In Your Eyes."

[16] As Astaire recalls: "It's a very good song to dance to and I always loved that dance. Very slow we did it, very slow. Ginger said to me during rehearsals, 'Awfully slow, isn't it?' and I said, 'Yes, that's the way I think it should be,' and she said, 'Okay.' " Wilder suggests there are elements in the song's construction that "keep the melody from flowing"; the arrangement here seems to have solved that problem.

H13 H14 H15 H16 H17 H18 H19 H20 H21 H22 I1 I2

plode with the music into a series of traveling leaps (H 15), sweeps (H 16), and pivots (H 17; compare H 7)—a sequence that is brilliant, almost becoming too grandiose. (In these, and in a few other spots—particularly in some of the unpartnered turns—Rogers appears to have been pushed a bit beyond her capabilities at the time, though she was developing rapidly.) As the dancers spin their way upstage and the music reaches a dramatic climax, Rogers plunges into another deep, supported backbend (H 18). The music subsides and, without pause, Astaire tenderly raises her. They walk forward softly in the dance's most memorable image: nestled together, he gently presses her head to his shoulder (H 19, 20).

The music suddenly shifts again, becoming light and bouncy,[17] and the dancers noodle around somewhat unimaginatively, finally spinning an elaborate double-helix pattern around each other (H 21). They emerge from this face to face, clasp hands, and pause, gazing at each other as the camera cuts to another angle—the only cut in the dance.

The music turns mellow again, and the dance ends with a beautiful gliding sweep up the stairs, a pause at the top as the dancers sink back to catch the music's soft pulsations, some gentle turns, and a final return to the loving, arm-in-arm stroll, which carries them offstage (H 22).

[17] In these remarkable shifts Astaire found that the music could support many more moods than the torchy sorrow of the lyric. Kern was ambivalent about his melody, having written it originally as a bright instrumental for a tap routine; the idea of making it into a ballad was apparently Harbach's.

I
I WON'T DANCE
(REPRISE) (50")

In a backstage anteroom, Rogers flops into an easy chair, exhilarated and exhausted. She and Astaire now play out a brief scene that is an audacious parody of one they had in *The Gay Divorcee,* after the seductive "Night and Day" duet. Although the "Smoke Gets In Your Eyes" duet has been in no sense seductive, Rogers prefers to pretend she has been won over. As Astaire stands around looking uncertain, she mischievously remarks, "My oh my, that was lovely. I guess I'll have to give in to you" (I 1). At his evident confusion, she obligingly clarifies: "I thought you were about to want to marry me." "Well, I was." "Well, I accept." "Well, thanks very much." "Well, you're welcome, my fine feathered friend." They shake hands to seal the bargain (I 2). Clearly the scriptwriters realized that any serious dialogue would sound foolish and redundant after the rich and evocative dance, and they wisely came up with this zany exercise in indirection.

Very soon the pair will dance again, but first the Dunne-Scott romance has to be tied up. This is achieved in less than five minutes. After various forgivenesses are exchanged, confusions cleared up, and expressions of affection delivered, he says, "Gee, that's swell," picks her up, and kisses her (I 3).

Now the camera can cut back to Astaire and Rogers, who have returned to the stage to deliver an ecstatic encore to finish the film. *Roberta* may be filled with superb dancing, but nothing in it surpasses this exultant postlude. Performed in the same space as the "Smoke Gets In Your Eyes" duet, the dance also follows the same architectural outline and can be taken as a giddy parody: it begins at the top of the stairs, progresses around the floor, and ends with a return up the stairs into a loving embrace. But where the earlier duet showed love in contemplative, gliding mutual dependence, this one shows it in euphoric, scampering celebration. And, like all the dances in *Roberta,* this final routine makes prominent use of a crossover step, here a lagging-leg tap figure that is first seen right after the dancers enter (I 4).

The grand joke in the dance is the way it shifts between two speeds: fast and faster. The dancers explode onto the stage, bound confidently down the stairs, deliver the crossover step again, and alternate gleeful prances around each other with sudden scoots into an even faster speed. Astaire now bolts upstage and waits, clapping in rhythm as Rogers frolics by herself and then skitters after him (I 5). Together they promenade, holding each other at the waist—the only partnered dance figure in the number (I 6). There are some brisk, rhythmically unpredictable dodging forays near the camera (I 7), and then a bubbling scramble upstage. In a final progression forward, the lagging crossover step is blended with other buoyant tap steps (I 8; compare I 4) in a dizzying sequence of explosive speed shifts. Then there is a goofy zigzag frolic back to the stairs, and the dance, and the film, end as the celebrants scamper up the steps to embrace jubilantly at the top (I 9, 10).

I 3 I 4 I 5 I 6
I 7 I 8 I 9 I 10

"Smoke Gets In Your Eyes"

5.

Top Hat

1935

It is the comparative absence of unevenness in *Top Hat* that makes it, all things considered, the most successful of the Fred Astaire–Ginger Rogers films. The dances and decor in *Swing Time* may be a bit finer, the script and direction in *The Gay Divorcee* or *Carefree* a bit more crisply paced, the music in *Swing Time* or *Roberta* a bit more striking, the ancillary comedy capers in *Shall We Dance* a bit more endearing, the acting in *Swing Time* or *Carefree* a bit richer; but *Top Hat* comes out very high in all these categories and adds up to surpassingly satisfying entertainment, and a top moneymaker, the Astaire-Rogers film with the best box office both when it was released and today.[1]

THE SCRIPT

The principal scriptwriter for *Top Hat* was Dwight Taylor. He had written the Broadway play on which *The Gay Divorcee* was based and, as Arlene Croce observes, "There's a lot of *The Gay Divorcee* in *Top Hat,* enough to qualify it as a remake." Once again the footloose Astaire meets and instantly falls in love with Rogers, pursues her, wins her over in a dance, suddenly loses her when she mistakes him for someone else, gets her back when the confusion is eventually cleared up, and happily dances off with her at the end. The leads are surrounded by many of the same comedy actors playing similar roles in the two films: Erik Rhodes as a dandified Italian, Eric Blore as a meddling English servant, and Edward Everett Horton as Astaire's bumbling sidekick. Only Helen Broderick, as Rogers' acerbic confidante, is new—and, actually, only in the flesh: RKO had tried to cast her in *The Gay Divorcee,* in the part Alice Brady plays, but Broderick was unavailable at the time.

There is one important structural change from the earlier film: the addition of a second plot-advancing dance duet. In both films Astaire wins Rogers over with a dance—a romantic duet ("Night and Day," 3 E) in *The Gay Divorcee,* a playful one ("Isn't This a Lovely Day") in *Top Hat.* But in *Top Hat,* after the couple break up, he almost wins her back again with a second duet ("Cheek to Cheek").

The mistaken-identity mechanism in *Top Hat* is more contrived and drawn out, but also dramatically more interesting, than in *The Gay Divorcee.* In the earlier film Rogers turned haughty and walked out on Astaire because she felt he had a low-caste occupation, that of a professional co-respondent. In *Top Hat* she does so because she thinks he's the husband of her best friend. This confusion is maintained at great length through airy artifice—we are asked to believe Astaire has met, become enamored of, chased, sung to, danced with, won the love of, and proposed marriage to Rogers without once ever telling her either his first or his last name. But her dilemma—falling in love with a man who turns out to be (she supposes) a philanderer—has considerable dramatic potential. In early versions of the script this dilemma was explored with some depth; in the film, however, it has been reduced considerably, though it still informs the essential mood of the beautiful "Cheek to Cheek" duet.

Top Hat was the first screenplay written specifically for Astaire, and documents suggest that his initial reaction to it was considerable dismay: its similarity to the earlier film disturbed him, and he was upset that he was again cast in the role of a juvenile—and, as he saw it, a rather unpleasant one. His concerns were assuaged by the time the film was completed; indeed, his role in this film is one of the most appealing in his career. But his final escape from typecasting as a juvenile would take several more years to accomplish.[2]

[1] In 1953 RKO issued a cut version of *Top Hat.* To reduce the film to seventy-eight minutes, utter mayhem was committed: portions of *all* the substantial musical numbers were removed. Even the memorable sand dance was lopped from "No Strings." Prints of this version still exist and are shown. *Caveat emptor.*

[2] In a handwritten letter to producer Pandro Berman in the spring of 1935, Astaire expressed his concerns about the script as it was evolving:

> In the first place—as this book is supposed to have been written *for me* with the intention of giving me a chance to do the things that are most suited to me—I cannot see that my part embodies any of the necessary elements except to *dance-dance-dance.*
>
> I am cast as a *straight juvenile* & rather a cocky and arrogant one at that—a sort of objectionable young man without charm or sympathy or humor.
>
> I cannot see that there is any real story or plot to this script.
>
> It is a series of events patterned *too closely after Gay Divorce,* without the originality & suspense of that play.
>
> I have practically no comedy of any consequence except in the scene in the cab.
>
> I am forever pawing the girl or she is rushing into my arms. . . .
>
> After I go to the Lido—I dissolve into practically *nothing*—it seems saying or doing nothing at all interesting or humorous. The lead into "Cheek to Cheek" is hopeless as at present designed. It would be impossible to get a sincere note into that number out of the situation which precedes it. The fact that Rogers *slaps* me in the *face* in two different episodes is certainly wrong. . . .

In Venice—Rogers learns of Astaire's identity

TAP DANCE AS MOTIF

In most of his films Astaire plays a professional dancer who happens to spend a great deal of time dancing in unlikely places—boiler rooms, guardhouses, business offices, toy shops, city streets. *Top Hat,* however, is the Astaire film that best capitalizes on, and thoroughly delights in, the essential absurdity of this activity. In the film Astaire tells Rogers he suffers from an "affliction": "Every once in a while I suddenly find myself dancing." This urge becomes a motif in the film, as Astaire's dancing feet, usually irritating somebody or other, send the plot skittering along.

THE MUSIC AND THE ASTAIRE-BERLIN FRIENDSHIP

Irving Berlin's songs for *Top Hat* are impressive both for their lyrics and their music, though the full effect is marred occasionally by lapses in the orchestration. The score was a spectacular success. All five songs became hits in 1935, a fact Berlin was frequently to recall with justified pride.[3] Astaire remembers that the success of the film score helped to revive Berlin's self-confidence, which had been lagging at the time. Berlin had already composed music for a few films, but had never really settled in Hollywood, finding the work there neither satisfying nor lucrative. Wooed by several studios, he was eventually offered both fees and a percentage of the profits, and evidently found this sufficiently interesting. Beginning with *Top Hat,* he was to spend a great deal of time working on the West Coast.

Astaire had danced to Berlin tunes on the stage as early as 1915 and had often visited Berlin's New York music-publishing firm, but the pair did not meet until the 1930s, when they were working on *Top Hat.* A lifelong relationship of friendship and mutual admiration ensued: Berlin even calls Astaire his "closest and best friend." Berlin was to contribute to more Astaire films (six) than any other composer, and found Astaire particularly satisfying to work for: "He's a real inspiration for a writer. I'd never have written *Top Hat* without him. He makes you feel secure."

THE CHOREOGRAPHY

Dance director and Astaire's choreographic collaborator for the film was Hermes Pan.

[3] In the broadcast of "Your Hit Parade" on September 28, 1935, all five songs were among the top fifteen. On the October 5 broadcast, "Cheek to Cheek," "Top Hat," and "Isn't This a Lovely Day" were ranked first, second, and fourth, respectively. (See also Table 5.)

THE NUMBERS

A
OPENING SEQUENCE
(21″)

After the RKO logo is shown, Astaire, seen from the waist down, frolics onto a shiny stage floor, backed by a male chorus sporting canes. As he hits a pose, his name appears. Rogers follows in like manner (A 1), and together they swirl toward the camera as the picture dissolves to show a top hat, which is kept under the rest of the titles (A 2).[4] This opening is so bright and splendid, it seems odd that other Astaire films didn't incorporate dance into title material. But the only other one that did was the Astaire-Rogers reunion film, *The Barkleys of Broadway.*

B
NO STRINGS (I'M FANCY FREE)
(3′53″ and 1′24″)

The first scene takes place in a stuffy London club, where Astaire disturbs the somnolent members by accidentally rustling his newspaper (B 1). Then Horton, an unlikely show-business impresario, comes to pick him up, and as they depart, Astaire shatters the club's atmosphere of studied indolence by vengefully blasting out a raucous tap barrage.

This neatly introduces the film's tap-dance motif, which is given its most glorious development in the next scene. Horton, in his hotel suite, suggests to Astaire that he ought to consider getting married, but Astaire finds his present state preferable and sings confidently of his stringless connections and his tieless affections, conditions that are soon to change (B 2). The song springs naturally and without cue from the dialogue, and Astaire sings it through twice for Horton.[5] During the last phrase, he bolts into a ballet jump, complete with beats of the legs, and this sends him into a brief solo dance that builds in intensity (and noisiness) as it progresses from limber tap shuffles in place to traveling patterns to rapid-fire heel jabs (B 3) to an exuberant circumnavigation of the room during which he hammers the decor with his hands. As he returns to the center of the room to deliver his most floor-punishing steps so far, the camera cranes downward to the room below, where Rogers, roused from sleep, registers annoyance (B 4). As usual, irritation becomes Ginger.

There follows a sequence of phone calls among Rogers, the hotel management, and Horton during which Astaire playfully builds Horton's actions into his frolic—startling him with a behind-the-back tap burst (B 5) and ostentatiously escorting him to the telephone (B 6). Horton leaves to investigate the complaint, while Astaire continues to slam around the room.

He accidentally topples a small statue from its pedestal but catches it in mid-air and has begun to incorporate it into his dance when Rogers,

[4] The titles in *The Band Wagon* (1953) make sardonic reference to this top hat (see 27 A 1). When Irving Berlin's name appears on the screen, the background music provides a signature and welcomes him to Hollywood by rendering a portion of "Alexander's Ragtime Band." A similar device was used to welcome George Gershwin to RKO in *Shall We Dance.*

[5] There are some delightful images in Berlin's lyric—as when Astaire proclaims himself to be free "as an unwritten melody." Berlin wrote a fine introductory verse for the song, but it is not sung in the film. Singing a song twice without a change in lyric was extremely unusual for Astaire; to add a little variety, during the repetition he mixes drinks for Horton and himself.

A 1, A 2, B 1, B 2, B 3, B 4, B 5, B 6, B 7, B 8, B 9, B 10

fleeing the falling plaster in her room, abruptly breaks in on him (B7). He is amazed, delighted, and instantly attracted. They engage in chipper repartee, and it is clear from Rogers' face as she turns away from him to leave that she has not found the encounter entirely unpleasant (B8). Astaire explains (and once demonstrates) his helpless affliction, which causes him to dance at odd moments (B9), but Rogers appears unimpressed and, smiling to herself, she returns to her room (B10).

As Horton returns, Astaire spreads on the floor sand from a convenient (and freshly cleaned) cuspidor. He carefully pats the sand smooth and then lulls Rogers to sleep with a gently loping sand dance—an image at once tender and erotic (B11). The palliative is thoroughly effective, coaxing not only Rogers off to sleep, but also Horton and, finally, Astaire himself (B12, 13).

This beautiful scene is one of the most memorable in Astaire's career. But the structure of the number—a substantial dance routine interrupted by a fairly extensive dialogue sequence—is unique in Astaire's films, and in no way altered his belief that the choreography should do the really important communicating.[6]

[6] The number was the idea of scriptwriter Taylor and is found in his earliest writings for the film. Buster Keaton, in a 1936 sound short called *Grand Slam Opera,* does a wonderful working-class parody of the number. His galumphing tap dance over the furniture (and mantel) in his seedy rooming-house apartment wakes the woman in the room below; when she protests, he lulls her to sleep by doing a sand dance using material from a nearby fire bucket (after first removing a chewed cigar). At the end he sinks sleepily into his broken-down bed and pulls the covers over himself.

C
ISN'T THIS A LOVELY DAY (TO BE CAUGHT IN THE RAIN)?
(4′ 13″)

Astaire launches his pursuit of Rogers the next day. He sends her a roomful of flowers and surreptitiously takes the place of a hansom-cab driver in order to accompany her to the park, where she is to go horseback riding. It is the irrepressible tapping of his feet in the driver's seat above her that signals to Rogers who the driver really is (C1).[7]

A thunderstorm breaks out while Rogers is riding in the park and she takes shelter in a covered bandstand. After Astaire follows her in, they engage in a scientifically fanciful discussion about the causes and characteristics of your average rainstorm, and he is soon inspired to sing her a relevant song in which he explains that the rain's pitter-patter really doesn't matter as long as he can be with her.[8] He sings most of the song to her back, but the camera has a good view of her lively and varied expressions as she listens attentively. It is clear that her initial feelings of annoyance and uncertainty about being trapped by her pursuer have faded by the time he completes the song (C2).

[7] Because the play on the word "damn" in this scene ("Who was the horse's dam?" "It didn't give a dam.") was found objectionable by Hollywood's censorship office, the film was shot so that Rogers blots out the "dam" of the response by slamming the trap door of the cab—an improvement over the original. The office also warned that the flower salesman's "Her niceties are very nice" in an earlier scene must be read without suggestiveness, a warning apparently ignored by RKO. Reviewing the film in England, Graham Greene found the film "quite earnestly bawdy" and was delightedly amused that British censors hadn't had the wit to notice.

[8] Originally this number was supposed to occur at a zoo, but Berlin came up with this song, and so, as he put it, "they made it rain in order to put the song in."

Woven into the wonderful dance that follows is a witty game of flirtation. He plays the role of the pursuer and she the pursued, but it is Rogers who controls the game. Astaire has made his feelings for her plain, and the audience knows from her expressions during his singing (as well as those earlier in the film) that she reciprocates them. All that remains is for her to communicate this to Astaire—which she does in the dance, but all in good time. So, even though Astaire does win Rogers over in the course of the number, it is not really a dance of seduction, since she is not acting with misgivings or against her better judgment.

Two choreographic devices are used to trace the progress of the dance game. One of these is the idea of sequential imitation—one dancer does a step and the other responds in kind. This idea is used throughout, but it becomes subtly transformed during the course of the dance. At the beginning the imitations are done in mock spite; in the middle they are done as a kind of gift from one dancer to the other; and at the end they are done in a spirit of cooperation. Thus a single choreographic idea is developed to suggest an emotional progression. The other device involves touching. Often during the first two minutes of this two-and-a-half-minute dance the performers seem to be about to touch, but then hesitate and pull back. Although Astaire would clearly like to have his arms around Rogers from the beginning, he doesn't touch her until she has played out her part and invites him into her

B11 B12 B13 C1
C2 C3 C4 C5

arms. This structure is similar to the classic minuet, which is also a ritual of flirtation involving a game of touching.

To begin the dance, Astaire strolls to the middle of the bandstand floor and whistles part of the tune. When his back is turned, Rogers joins him in the stroll, mocking his casual whistling and manly stride (C3). (The sense of equality expressed in these maneuverings is supported by the clothes they wear, by the way each throws the other later, and by the congenial handshake at the end.) Astaire is surprised at her behavior —and delighted (C4). The imitation notion is introduced as a challenge: he raps out a snappy little tap step; then, behind his back, Rogers briskly answers in kind (C5) and, a bit later, embellishes the comment with another subversive fusillade.

Leaving the issue of competition aside for a while, they dance forward liltingly, side by side; they are in unison but remain on opposite sides of the space (C6). Then they turn to face each other—and almost fall into each other's arms. But they stop before touching, and several seconds are given over to a game in which they somewhat awkwardly grope toward each other, think better of it, pull back, try a brief tap phrase in unison, stop to face each other again, fold their arms in, reach out, pull back (C7).

Meanwhile, the music has speeded up, and they break through their indecision by postponing the issue of touching. As they catch the pulse of the music, they swing into a hopping step in which they travel face to face, their arms flowing left and right in mirrored unison (C8). The phrase carries them around the space, breaking down the implied barrier between them. Some witty frolicking follows, including a scamper up and down the step at the front of the bandstand. The sequence alternates sly hesitations with brilliant bursts of activity and includes a crisp pirouette that seems to come out of nowhere (C9).

The imitation theme now returns: Rogers does a sequence of tap spins (C10) and Astaire responds by doing his version of the same steps (C11). But now things are importantly changed. The imitations that opened the dance were performed challengingly and mockingly, Rogers doing hers behind Astaire's back. In this reprise, the steps are done *for* the other dancer: as one does the step, the other stands back and admires.

But they still haven't touched. As they face off once again, a crack of thunder jars them. Now the music builds expectantly back toward the main melody and, still facing, the dancers visualize its implications by darting back and forth with a series of dragging steps (C12). There is a turning leap and a tap barrage in unison; then, as the main melody finally emerges full force, Rogers opens her left arm decisively and invites Astaire in (C13). Wasting no time, he explodes into her arms and they spin joyously around the stage (C14).

They separate again for a brief sequence of unison stops and starts, exuberantly chasing the music and each other around the space. Then they embrace again and, in a final reference to the imitation theme, this time cooperative, he throws her (C15) and she throws him (C16). When their momentum propels them off the bandstand, they are suddenly reminded that it is raining—something they had come to forget in the course of the dance game (C17). They fold themselves back under the cover of the bandstand, and, at the fade-out, shake hands (C18).[9]

D
TOP HAT, WHITE TIE AND TAILS
(4′ 24″)

At her hotel, Rogers gleefully catalogues her activities for Erik Rhodes, a pompous dandy of an Italian dress-designer for whom she works as a model (D1): "I've seen him, I've talked to him, I've danced with him!" Rhodes is unimpressed.[10]

Because Rogers has never troubled to ask Astaire his name, she now, through a series of mixups, confuses him with Horton, who is the husband of her best friend, Helen Broderick.[11] She slaps the astonished Astaire (D2) and then

[9] In *Broadway Melody of 1938* Eleanor Powell and George Murphy do a sort of parody of this number. They too dance on a covered bandstand to escape from a rainstorm. At the end, however, they leave the shelter to frolic in the puddles, the last of which is so deep they almost drown.

[10] The Rhodes character is, of course, closely modeled on the one he played in *The Gay Divorcee,* and for a while both films were banned in Italy because the character was deemed offensive. Hollywood's censorship office warned RKO "to avoid any idea of his being 'pansy' in character." Another passage in this scene also caused concern: after Rhodes reads a telegram to Rogers in garbled manner, she observes, "Sounds like Gertrude Stein." When the film came out, the RKO legal office was apoplectic—the use of Stein's name had not been cleared with her, and, since the reference in the film might be considered derogatory, there was the danger of a costly lawsuit.

[11] The mixup is accomplished in part through some business involving a briefcase, an idea lifted from a Hungarian play that is sometimes credited as the basis for the *Top Hat* plot. According to Croce, this is the only idea from the play that survives in the film.

C6 C7 C8 C9

C10 C11 C12 C13

goes with Rhodes to Venice to tell Broderick about the events. Meanwhile, Horton, sensing scandal, assigns his "invaluable manservant," Eric Blore, to shadow Rogers (D3). Astaire finds out about Rogers' flight and, as he is about to go onstage, demands that Horton charter a plane so they can carry the pursuit to Venice. (Earlier Horton had told Astaire they would fly to Venice for the weekend, so this bit of business is either confused or redundant.)

Although the routine Astaire now performs is not linked in any important way to the plot, it is the number around which the film was built. Its origins are in the stage version of *Funny Face* (1927), in which Astaire had performed a solo backed by a top-hatted male chorus. He elaborated the idea in *Smiles* (1930): the chorus men (as well as harmonicist Larry Adler) became targets in a shooting gallery, while Astaire used his cane as a mock gun and used tap effects to suggest rifle and machine-gun bursts. The number, "Say, Young Man of Manhattan," was a great success in an otherwise unsuccessful show. When Astaire suggested doing a version of it in a film, Irving Berlin brought "Top Hat, White Tie and Tails" out of his trunk. This song in turn suggested the film's title.

The song has become a signature piece for Astaire, and the number is one of his most famous routines. It makes extensive use of one of Astaire's most remarkable qualities as a dancer: his ability to alter the tempo within a single dance phrase. In this case he often explores the extremes, by suddenly bursting into explosive motion from a pose of utter quiet, or abruptly shifting from wild activity to repose.

An interesting aspect of the number is its vaguely unpleasant air: the eerie street scene and the shooting gallery episode, however amusingly performed, carry ominous overtones. The slamming intensity of tap dancing can sometimes seem furious and threatening—a quality Astaire was to explore more fully in the 1940s (see especially 17 F and 20 F).

As the number begins, the chorus is strutting and lunging about before a beautiful backdrop that economically suggests a Paris street scene. As the men make way, Astaire enters and strides confidently to the front of the stage. He pauses and watches with interest as they form ranks behind him—thus making it clear from the beginning that they are an important part of his act.

He now begins to sing appealingly, using a telegram from the previous scene as a prop—it's an invitation, he says, to attend a formal affair.[12] As he croons, he literally underlines in mime the lyric about putting on top hats, straightening up white ties, and brushing off tails. Behind him the men of the chorus lean at a rakish angle, making an arresting composite picture (D4). Astaire steps out (appropriately enough) as he renders the snappy release strain: "I'm stepping out, my dear, to breathe an atmosphere that simply reeks with class," a phrase that crackles with apt insolence, high spirits, and vivid yet economical imagery. The music for this strain is the song's highlight—it is rhythmically off-balance, and resolved, with great wit, only at the end (here, on the word "class").[13] As he sings this portion of the song, Astaire trades tap barrages with the chorus as added comment (so sequential imitation is used a bit in this number, too).

The dance begins with some jaunty pacing from side to side. Although Astaire and the chorus men behind him do exactly the same step, Astaire clearly stands out because of the inflections he puts into the simple walk—hesitations, subtle articulations of the hands, arms, and shoulders, tiltings of the head (D5). As the men pause, Astaire lashes out with a swirling tap phrase and then waits expectantly as they respond in pale, if raucous, imitation (D6). The chorus then exits to the back and sides of the stage in an imaginative sequence of overlapping, direction-shifting hitch steps and walks.

All alone with Berlin's agile music, Astaire bolts through a blistering solo in which taps with the cane embellish the clattering of his nimble feet—his first use of a cane in a dance in films (D7).[14] Best of all are the whimsical and utterly unpredictable pauses he structures into the solo. In one of these he seems to be waiting for the audience to catch up, or wryly saying, "How'd you like *that,* folks?" In another he seems to be contemplating the next step, as if to suggest that this intricate dance is being improvised (D8).

The solo widens out in space. Astaire's journey apparently takes him to a strange and threat-

[12] In the original script the "Top Hat" number was placed later, in Venice. It was to be a big production number triggered by an invitation to Astaire to attend a party, in which case he would have had a real invitation to work with.

[13] On the relationship between this song and Berlin's earlier "Puttin' On the Ritz," see p. 267n.

[14] On the high mortality rate for these canes during shooting, see p. 16.

C14 C15 C16 C17

C18 D1 D2 D3

ening neighborhood. The stage darkens, and he variously mimes open friendliness (D9), wariness, surprise (D10), edgy readiness (D11), and jaunty confidence, snapping from one attitude to the next with amazing precision. Astaire writes that he could not "routine" this section; instead he ad-libbed the dance here to get the spontaneous effect he wanted.

Threat becomes manifest as the chorus reappears at the stage horizon and looms in the distance. Astaire methodically dispatches them all, using his cane as a weapon and his taps as the blast. He finds a considerable number of ways to fire—from the front, from behind his neck, during turns, from over his shoulder (D12), and as if manning a submachine gun. At one point he mocks the whole exercise by using his arm as a rifle and a tap of the cane as the blast, and then, at the end, resorts to bow and arrow to take care of the most difficult target (D13). One last triumphant tap barrage, a quick ingratiating lunge at the audience, and it is over.

E
CHEEK TO CHEEK
(4′59″)

The rest of the film takes place at what is supposed to be the Lido in Venice, though it is rendered with spectacular, audacious unreality: a massive, glowingly white set in which shimmering curlicue Art Deco islands, linked by arched footbridges, are set among winding canals. (Croce suggests that the extreme fancifulness of the decor may have been prompted, in part, by a desire to distract the audience from the real Venice, which was at that time in Fascist hands.)

The plot, equally fanciful, continues to milk the mistaken-identity theme. Rogers informs the acerbic Helen Broderick of the carryings-on of the man Rogers presumes to be Broderick's husband; meanwhile, the eavesdropping Blore, aided by a pair of water wings, swims by unobserved (E1). To Rogers' amazement, Broderick, a pillar of common sense around whom the other characters flutter, greets the news with calm amusement.

With Broderick's approval, Rogers concocts a plan apparently designed to frighten Astaire into marital responsibility: she goes to his room, plants a kiss on him (E2), and invents a tale about an affair they had the year before in Paris. The ruse has no impact: though he is bewildered, Astaire simply goes along with the gag and ends up frightening Rogers (E3). This pointless episode is allowed to drag on for nearly four minutes.

It turns out that Broderick is something of a matchmaker and has decided Rogers and Astaire would make an ideal couple. Accordingly, she arranges for them to meet at a dinner—only to discover that they already know each other (E4). To Rogers' intense discomfort and confusion, Broderick mischievously urges her to dance with Astaire, and "don't give me another thought."

Astaire sings Berlin's now classic song[15] to Rogers as they dance together on the crowded floor, gently illustrating the lyric when he sings "cheek to cheek" and "I want my arm about you" (E5). The Astaire-Rogers dances are so memorable that they can make one forget how much of the magic emerges during the singing of the songs. Rogers looks warm, attracted, pleased, receptive, and a little sad, while Astaire is ardent and charming, his face reflecting his vocal efforts as he seeks to do justice to the song with its considerable range.[16]

When Astaire comes to the end of the song, he and Rogers drift across a bridge to a deserted ballroom area that happens to be nearby. They are dancing cheek to cheek as they do so, but soon they break apart and do not cling so closely again until the end of the number.

As in "Isn't This a Lovely Day," the dancers' roles here are those of pursuer and pursued, though the emotional situation is quite different. In this duet they are no longer flirting—they are in love. But Rogers feels guilty and deceived and is trying to avoid Astaire's advances, seeking to fall out of love with him. Consequently, Astaire's objective in this number is to get her to forget her misgivings (which he doesn't understand) and to get her to yield to him.

The seduction is seen, in part, in the ardor and the forcefulness of the partnering—Astaire's

[15] The song is an exceptionally long one—seventy-two measures. It follows the standard form AABA except that the B (or release) strain is unusually elaborate, consisting of two ideas—a rather bouncy passage (which is played twice) and a more grandiose passage that neatly melts back to the main melody. The lyric is as memorable as the melody; for example, in the reference to cares that vanish "like a gambler's lucky streak." Jay asserts that the melody is "based on" Chopin's popular A-flat major polonaise (no. 6), which, like "Cheek to Cheek," uses a prominent, twice-declared descending major second ("Heaven") in the opening portion of its main theme.

[16] Berlin is highly appreciative of how Astaire sang the song: "The melody line keeps going up and up, he *crept* up there. It didn't make a damned bit of difference. He made it."

D4 D5 D6 D7

D8 D9 D10 D11

attention is fully on Rogers, and he is constantly pulling her into the dance, surrounding her, encasing her in his arms, and, more startlingly, wrapping himself in her arms. The progression of the seduction is traced through a repeated choreographic nuance, the supported backbend. Several times Rogers falls backward in Astaire's arms, and each time the backbend gets deeper, longer, more luxurious, more sensuous, the last one suggesting utter surrender (E7, 12, 15, 16, 25).

In addition, there are two brief passages that apply the idea of sequential imitation that was so central to the bandstand number. For this duet, however, the idea is romanticized, and seems a serious, abstracted gloss on the earlier dance. They begin with this idea—first in long shot, then closer up—as they spin and lean, dodging back and forth past each other (E6). Then they move back into each other's arms in the standard ballroom position, and there are the first quick suggestions of the supported backbend, the idea being established twice in passing in the context of the ballroom dance (E7).

At the end of this phrase Astaire explores some of the dramatic potential of the ballroom position. If the dancers' outstretched hands (man's left and woman's right) become separated, and the man pulls his hand back, the woman, to close the position, must pull herself in toward his body (E8). The sly eroticism implicit in this ploy, touched upon here briefly, is more fully developed in later duets, such as 10 E12–13, 15 I9, 18 G5, 21 B3.

Next, side by side and with hands touching, they dance a loping, liltingly percussive phrase that plays with, and sometimes against, the music (E9). Then Astaire sends Rogers into a spin, collects her upstage, and deftly maneuvers her into a musically satisfying linked-arm stroll forward (E10). This idea is developed and made even more eloquent as he spins her away again, encircles her while she turns (E11), takes her in his arms, and then coaxes her into another backbend; this time there is a slight but voluptuous hesitation as she pulls out of it (E12).

As the music becomes bouncier, the dancers, side by side, render a light tap phrase that reflects the music fairly directly (E13). Next the music repeats exactly, but the choreography changes completely. The dancers flow across the floor in the standard ballroom position (E14), but

D12 D13 E1 E2 E3 E4 E5 E6 E7 E8 E9 E10 E11 E12 E13 E14

then, going against the music, Rogers suddenly falls into another, deeper backbend, one foot coming slightly off the floor, and for the first time there is a short pause at the deepest part (E 15). When this is repeated, the next backbend is even deeper and more surrendering (E 16).

An explosive, more grandiose passage of the music brings out a series of bold leaps and turns (E 17).[17] Gradually the music quiets down to form a transition back to the main melody.

The next section, with its tentative, pre-climactic quality, contains some of Astaire's most exquisite partnering. Rogers remains a bit distant, almost in a dreamlike state. They separate briefly, she looking away from him (E 18), and he grasps her outstretched hand and spins toward her, wrapping himself in her arm (E 19) (in contrast to the bandstand number, where he had entered her arms only after she explicitly invited him).[18] After a passage in which the idea of sequential imitation is reprised and elaborated (E 20; compare E 6), they emerge separated by a small space (E 21). Astaire quietly moves forward, clasps Rogers' waist from behind, and gently but forcefully pulls her backward into the next section of the dance—a gesture at once simple and ardent, tender and firm (E 22).

The music now reaches its climax, rendered by full—overfull—orchestra. The choreography tries to keep up, the dancers extravagantly tracing a path to and from the camera (E 23), then spinning out three broad and theatrical ballroom lifts (E 24). The dance phrase ends abruptly with a pause in the music as Rogers falls backward into the last of the supported backbends—this one completely surrendering (E 25).

The ending of the dance is as exquisite as any that Astaire (or anyone else) ever arranged. As the dancers hold their pose, the music quietly resumes and finishes out its last measures. The dancers, lost in their private world, ignore it for a moment, then are slowly pulled back into the dance by its insistent murmuring. Locked in each other's arms, they drift—cheek to cheek

[17] On the distracting camera work in the first part of this phrase, see p. 28.

[18] This striking maneuver is used, in different ways, in other Astaire duets (3 E 23, 14 G 15, and 18 G 4) and is parodied in 15 G 11 and 21 E 4. It seems to have been developed from the Wind Up, a step invented by Vernon Castle (see 11 I 7–9).

E 15 E 16 E 17 E 18 E 19 E 20 E 21 E 22 E 23 E 24 E 25 E 26 E 27 E 28 F 1 F 2

for the first time since the dance began—back upstage toward a low wall (E 26). There are a couple of light turns, and they come to rest next to the wall, while music and dance evaporate. As the dancers sink into repose, Astaire's right leg softly crosses over his left to finish out the musical phrase (E 27). Rogers is dazzled (E 28), and Astaire, the seduction complete, gazes at her with affection and gratification, slowly twiddling his thumbs.

The filming of this ravishing duet was attended by a much-recorded incident. The dress Rogers wears was covered with feathers that shed—like a chicken attacked by a coyote, says Astaire—when put into motion. After many delays (and a certain amount of frustrated anger from Astaire), the feathers were sufficiently sewn down to permit filming, though a few scattered feathers can be glimpsed against the black portion of the floor in some of the shots in the finished film. Astaire jokingly called Rogers "Feathers" for years after, and later parodied the event in a duet with Judy Garland in *Easter Parade* (21 E).[19]

F
THE PICCOLINO
(6′ 16″)

At the end of the "Cheek to Cheek" duet, Rogers realizes the full depth of her plight: she is hopelessly in love with a man who, she believes, is a deceiver, a rake, and the husband of her best friend. To vent her frustration she blurts out, "How could I have fallen in love with anyone as low as you!" and slaps Astaire again (F 1).

The film never takes her dilemma very seriously, though director Mark Sandrich does permit one beautiful close-up in which her expression clearly registers her despair (F 2).[20] In that mood she decides to resolve her problems through a desperate and wildly improbable stratagem: she marries the foolish Rhodes.

Astaire now discovers the truth about the confusion of identity and resolves to break up Rogers' marriage before it is consummated. (In the process he spouts such deadly lines as "All is fair in love and war, and this is revolution!") Neatly reflecting the "No Strings" scene, Astaire interrupts Rhodes and Rogers in their bridal suite by tap dancing in the room above them (F 3, 4). Sternly proclaiming his family motto, "For thee woman thee kees, for thee man thee sword," Rhodes angrily goes off to "keel heem."[21] With Rhodes out of the way, Astaire sneaks into Rogers' room and persuades her to go off with him on a gondola ride, during which he explains everything to her.

When Rhodes, Horton, and Broderick take off in a motorboat in pursuit of Astaire and Rogers, Blore, for reasons known only to the scriptwriters, removes the fuel so that they drift helplessly out to sea. Astaire and Rogers, meanwhile, are free to celebrate their confusion-delayed reconciliation by participating in "The Piccolino," a big production number that takes place all over the extravagant set. The number is built along the lines of "The Continental" and "The Carioca" in earlier Astaire-Rogers films, but, unlike its predecessors, "The Piccolino" never became a national craze.

It begins with a brief gondola parade, after which a dancing chorus enters and proceeds to clunk through some stagy ballroom poses and rippling-pattern routines. Rogers then gives a lively rendition of Berlin's amusing song about a Latin from Brooklyn who wrote a catchy melody while gazing at the stars (F 5). As the song is repeated by an off-camera chorus, the dance ensemble romps through some more patterned effects, using long sashes as props (F 6). This is mostly photographed from above in the Busby Berkeley manner, but without Berkeley's ability to supply an image-linking logic: when one idea is finished, the camera simply dissolves to the next.

Finally, the camera cuts back to Astaire and Rogers, who finish off the number with a brilliant two-minute dance shown all in one take. Two aspects of Astaire's choreographic approach are particularly evident in this duet: his ability to choreograph both to the melody and to the accompaniment, and his interest in exploring all the possibilities of a dance step—varying it, bending it, turning it inside out.

[19] Among the onlookers was Astaire's wife, who was amused by the dress (and who had trouble pronouncing *r*'s): "She looks like a wooster," she giggled to David Niven. Because the duet has some tap portions, Astaire and Pan were later required to create a tap track to be mixed into the sound. For Rogers' edification, they created a joke track in which were blended a woman's melodramatic sighs and, for the backbends, cracking sounds.

[20] The original script was different in this respect. Later, when Astaire is about to take her off so they can clear up their misunderstandings, Rogers was given an introspective song-soliloquy, "Get Thee Behind Me, Satan." To speed the plot, this sequence was dropped.

[21] In the original script this motto was "For the man the sword, for the woman the whip!" The censorship office would have none of that. Also lost was Rhodes' observation "It's a family tradition—my father killed a man before I was born."

F 3 F 4 F 5 F 6

F 7 F 8 F 9 F 10

Irving Berlin's song is one of his favorites among his own creations: "I love it, the way you love a child that you've had trouble with. I worked harder on 'Piccolino' than I did on the whole [*Top Hat*] score." The song combines a witty lyric set to a tune that contrasts with a bubbling, churning Latinesque undercurrent, or vamp, in the accompaniment. The choreography for the chorus relates almost exclusively to the melodic line (when it relates to the music at all), while Astaire, in his choreography for the duet, is at least as fascinated by the bubbling counter-rhythm of the accompaniment.

As Astaire and Rogers bound from their table, down the steps, and across the floor, the buoyant choreography suitably reflects the vamp rhythms in the music: the dancers seem to be in the air most of the time, as if skimming the floor (F 7). Then the melody enters, and they stop their rhythmic progression to deliver the Piccolino step clearly and concisely: the feet jut out to the side of the body (F 8).

The camera work here seems a happy in-joke. Astaire particularly disliked inserted close-ups in a dance sequence. There are no inserts of any kind in the "Piccolino" duet, but it *begins* with a close-up of the tapping feet of two as yet unidentified people who, as the camera pulls back, are revealed to be Fred Astaire and Ginger Rogers. (Thereafter, the camera judiciously shows the dancers full figure.) The camera movement seems a wry play on a tired Hollywood cliché, using the close-up in a way that aids, rather than hampers, the dance's continuity.[22]

[22] The joke was to be revived in the Astaire-Rogers reunion-film of 1949, *The Barkleys of Broadway* (22 A 1-2).

The music repeats, and the choreography remains basically the same: hopping, buoyant steps for the vamp, a straight rendering of the Piccolino step (with some traveling added) when the melody returns. The next phrases neatly shift between the melody and the accompaniment. Included is a final instance of sequential imitation—the dancers joyfully chase past each other in a revolving partnered figure (F 9).

As the main melody re-enters, the dancers return to the Piccolino step—expanding it somewhat and adding turns (F 10)—and this is followed by a complex amalgam of variations on the Piccolino step and on the bubbling patterns, including a game of stopping and starting, and some frisky back-kicks (F 11).

The main melody returns again, sappily rendered by the violins, but the dancers ignore it to stay with the bubbling pattern; Rogers seems to be lightly mocking the smarminess of the orchestration in the overly cute way she carries her upper body (F 12). With a final return to the vamp melody, the dancers take up the Piccolino step, which is extravagantly embellished with leaping turns and developed to allow them to travel sideways back to the table (F 13), where they sink happily into chairs and raise their glasses in a toast (F 14).

G
THE PICCOLINO
(REPRISE) (TAG) (33″)

It takes a bare three minutes to untangle the plot. There is a final confrontation in the bridal suite during which it is revealed that Rogers and Rhodes had never been legally married, since the ceremony had been performed by Blore, disguised as a clergyman (G 1).[23]

The film concludes with a chipper duet fragment showing Astaire and Rogers dressed to go out on the town. Euphorically they parade across the Venetian set (G 2), reprise the Piccolino step (G 3; compare F 8), kick up their heels (G 4; compare F 11), and swirl into the distance.

A NUMBER PARTIALLY CUT FROM THE FILM

H
THE PICCOLINO
(REPRISE) (TAG)

At the time of previews in July 1935, according to production records, a number of cuts were made in the film to improve its pacing and "to eliminate a feeling of any excess of dancing." One option contemplated was to cut the Astaire-Rogers duet out of the "Piccolino" number and to use it as the tag. However, "under pressure from the publicity department," this idea was dropped. Instead the tag duet was retained, but it was cut to include only its last half-minute. As originally shot, this number was probably two or three times longer and involved a dance that traveled across the set, up and over two staircase bridges, and then away. The extant portion of the dance finds the couple as they begin to descend from the second bridge (G 2).

[23] On some prints there remains a scene near the end showing Blore being arrested for impersonating a gondolier and for insulting police officers (who he mistakenly thinks do not understand English).

F 11 F 12 F 13 F 14

G 1 G 2 G 3 G 4

6.

Follow the Fleet

1936

Soon after its release, *Follow the Fleet* became the second most financially successful film in the Fred Astaire–Ginger Rogers series. This was largely due, however, to the momentum it derived from coming immediately after *Top Hat*. Bogged down by a sour, labored plot, this lengthy film contains little of its predecessor's bounce and sparkle and, accordingly, has retained little of its initial popularity.

It does, however, emulate *Top Hat* in two important respects: its Irving Berlin songs are at least as fine, and its dances are at least as splendid. But never in Astaire's career have so many fine musical numbers been so ill-served by the surrounding material.[1]

THE SCRIPT

Someone at RKO apparently decided it would be amusing to cast the aristocratic Astaire as an ordinary sailor—a way, perhaps, of varying the formula of the Astaire-Rogers films, in which everyone seemed to spend so much time enjoying effortless success and wallowing in casual luxury. And so in *Follow the Fleet* Astaire tries to disguise himself: he swaggers and chews gum. No one is taken in.

The basic plot was very loosely derived from *Shore Leave,* a 1922 Broadway play that had served in 1927 as the basis for the Vincent Youmans musical *Hit the Deck*. These successful shows had both been previously made into films, in 1925 and 1930 respectively. Their plots centered on a woman who falls in love with a sailor on a one-day leave. To please him, she salvages an old ship she has inherited, but he is too proud to accept the offering and runs away to sea. Eventually, however, he is happily ensnared.

In many ways *Follow the Fleet* is shaped like *Roberta*. Although they are given top billing, Astaire and Rogers do not take the central romantic roles. The pursued sailor is played by Randolph Scott, and the pursuing woman would have been played by his *Roberta* partner, Irene Dunne, had she been available. After a talent search conducted by director Mark Sandrich, the role was given to a twenty-one-year-old newcomer, songstress Harriet Hilliard, the recent bride of bandleader Ozzie Nelson.[2]

The film's greatest single failing is its inability to infuse the Scott-Hilliard romance with any appeal. There was a certain charm in Scott's good-natured and amusingly inept efforts at repartee and gallantry as the oafish football player in *Roberta*. His oafish sailor in *Follow the Fleet* is pure, unleavened lout, and his interest in Hilliard is merely a passing fancy: when she gets "serious," he hotfoots it out of her life. But at least he is honest with Hilliard—he flees when she hints at marriage and does not lie about his motives. So her inability to get the message and her desperate efforts to win him over with home-cooked dinners and salvaged ships are grim and pathetic. Except for the reconciliation at the end, the unequal dueling between the smug, arrogant Scott and the clinging, ineffectual Hilliard is believable enough; the problem is that it's singularly unpleasant to watch.

By contrast, the dueling between Astaire and Rogers is, as usual, both equal and appealing. Especially when it centers on one of their musical numbers, their warm, mutually dependent love-making, cloaked in banter and clowning, is chiefly what makes the film memorable. But even here sourness sometimes triumphs: there are extended sequences, for example, in which the pair play spiteful, ill-humored, and absurdly improbable pranks on each other.

As in *Roberta,* Astaire and Rogers are cast as former sweethearts who meet again and quickly rekindle old longings. They are also called upon to deliver almost all of the film's humor. Lucille Ball saunters through to deliver a couple of wisecracks with impeccable timing, and there is a mischievous monkey who gets a few laughs; but there are no

[1] In 1953 RKO released a cut version of the film, prints of which are still shown. Two song solos, "Get Thee Behind Me, Satan" and "But Where Are You?" were deleted, as was, most catastrophically, the Astaire-Rogers rehearsal scene that includes "I'm Putting All My Eggs in One Basket."

[2] *Follow the Fleet* was to be Hilliard's only major film, though she later achieved considerable fame on "Ozzie and Harriet," the popular radio and television series in which she costarred with her husband and sons. According to her husband, Ginger Rogers was particularly helpful on the set to the young Hollywood neophyte.

other comedy characters, or even comedy walk-ons, in the film—a mistake RKO never made again in the Astaire-Rogers series.[3]

THE MUSIC

The film's score is masterful. Berlin was riding high after the stupendous success of *Top Hat,* and, always invigorated by having Astaire to write for, he turned out a collection of songs for *Follow the Fleet* that are engaging and unusually innovative—while still scoring well on the hit parade (see Table 5).

"Get Thee Behind Me, Satan" is an understated and affecting mood piece; "Let Yourself Go" explores exhilarating shifts of key; and several songs have lyrics that contain clever and intricate rhyme schemes worthy of Lorenz Hart. The film's big, broad ballad, "Let's Face the Music and Dance," is dark and passionate, while the perky "I'm Putting All My Eggs in One Basket" may well be the most endearing song Berlin ever wrote (well, except maybe for "Mandy").

As in *Top Hat,* Berlin received, at best, workmanlike support from music director Max Steiner and his stable of arrangers and orchestrators. The music for the Astaire numbers is served up competently, if not very imaginatively, while the two songs sung by Hilliard are set with a cloying insensitivity that saps their vitality—which is particularly unfortunate because, as a singer, Hilliard needed all the help she could get.

THE CHOREOGRAPHY

Hermes Pan was again Astaire's choreographic assistant. As in *Roberta,* Pan had no separate chorus dances to create, but the film does contain Rogers' only tap solo in the Astaire series; Pan choreographed this and served her well.

[3] Ball's potential was evident to at least one member of the preview audience: "You might give the tall gum chewing blonde more parts and see if she can't make the grade—a good gamble." Ball had been under contract at RKO when she appeared in *Roberta* (see 4 114), and her tiny role in *Follow the Fleet* was her biggest to date. Lela Rogers, Ginger's mother, served as her drama coach. Twenty years later Ball purchased the entire studio to produce television programs.

With Ginger Rogers in "Let's Face the Music and Dance"

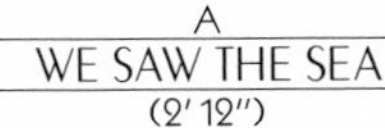

THE NUMBERS

A
WE SAW THE SEA
(2′ 12″)

The film opens on board a ship with Astaire leading his navy band in a bright rendition of this jaunty gloss on a sea ditty (A1). The navy gets some mild ribbing: the sailors declare they joined to see the world but instead merely saw the sea, and there is a lame reference to an admiral who has never been to sea. Satire of the navy had been handled better and far more provocatively by Gilbert and Sullivan fifty-eight years earlier, but, then, RKO had the support of the navy in making *Follow the Fleet.* (The film's technical adviser on things naval was Commander Harvey S. Haislip, who apparently has a bit part toward the end of the film as the stern executive officer who refuses Astaire's request for liberty.) On the other hand, Berlin's rhyming of "Black Sea" with "taxi" would have elicited gleeful approval even from W. S. Gilbert.

The number includes a brief routine in which Astaire is tossed around by the sailors. Astaire generally shied away from such dangerous, unfamiliar antics; indeed, this is the only example of this kind of manipulation in his film career.

B
LET YOURSELF GO
(SONG) (1′49″)

On shore in San Francisco, the sailors make a beeline for a dime-a-dance ballroom. Scott runs into the bespectacled Hilliard at the ticket booth and is singularly unimpressed. The feeling is not mutual, however, and Hilliard ponders her unattractiveness to men when she pays a backstage visit to her sister, played by Rogers. (To heighten the contrast between the two women, Hilliard's hair, normally blond, was darkened for the film.) Rogers advises her to act dumb if she wants to get a man, and calls in a showgirl, the skeptical Lucille Ball, who agrees to try to renovate Hilliard (B1).

Meanwhile, Rogers heads out to the ballroom's tiny stage, where, sometimes accompanied by a singing trio that includes the blond Betty Grable, she spiritedly sings a brilliant Berlin song (B2). Urgency is lent to the invitation in the lyric by two upward key shifts: first on the change from verse to chorus and then, most exhilaratingly, on a final repeat of the main strain.

C
GET THEE BEHIND ME, SATAN
(1′ 38″)

It turns out that the Astaire and Rogers characters had once had an act devoted to "High-Class Patter and Genteel Dancing." Astaire went to sea when Rogers refused to marry him, and he has been trying to look her up on his visit. Startled and pleased to discover her performing in the ballroom, he greets her by piping out a bit of a bugle call behind her back, to which she responds with a programmed, if involuntary, tap barrage—a running gag in the film that apparently derives from an Astaire rehearsal joke (see p. 70n). Their reconciliation scene is jocular but affectionate (C1).

Meanwhile, the newly glamorized Hilliard has entered the ballroom, and Scott is instantly attracted. He moves in on her, and she soon agrees to go off with him to "talk" (C2). As she waits for him to retrieve his hat from the checkroom, Hilliard muses in song on the danger and excitement of her temptation (C3). Her song was originally intended to be sung by Ginger Rogers in *Top Hat.* Resuscitated here, it manages to suit the plot fairly well—one of the few musical numbers in the film to do so. The song ruminates moodily in a minor key and is arresting, even haunting, but its impact is undercut by the distracting accompaniment of sweetly swarming violins.[4]

D
LET YOURSELF GO
(DANCE) (2′47″)

On the ballroom floor, Astaire and Rogers find themselves in the middle of a dance contest. The wonderfully amusing dance they do as part of the competition is wildly eccentric, featuring fluttering jumps in place and other steps involving leg wiggles, whose inherent absurdity is embellished by the floppy bell-bottoms they both wear.

They move onto the crowded floor with a funky sidling step which they then develop into

[4] When the film was released in Britain, the censors, according to reviewer Graham Greene, "supplied the best joke of the week by carefully preserving the devil from disrespect": they decided "Satan" was a naughty word and covered it with a "sharp, metallic click" each time it appeared on the sound track. This number and Hilliard's other solo, "But Where Are You?," are often cut when the film is shown on television.

A1 B1 B2 C1

C2 C3 D1 D2

a mock-serious limp-armed promenade as they circle the floor to join the contest (D1). Their chief competition, it so happens, specializes in slouchy waddles (D4). When the orchestra plays the anticipatory music from the song's verse, Astaire and Rogers respond to the challenge of their competition with various back-kicking jumps and jerky, doll-like spins, and even throw in a nonchalant lift for good measure (D2, 3). After each display they pause confidently and size up the others—Astaire chomping on his chewing gum all the while.[5]

They are a bit amazed at the tenacity (or the impudence) of the competition, but they soon have the floor to themselves, and as the orchestra strikes up the music of the song's chorus, they launch into an extended frolic. It begins with some brilliant galloping kicks in place (D5), punctuated by an amusing sudden pause in mid-romp (D6).

Sequences alternating frisky jumps with earthy heel-grinding come next (D7), followed by a partnered caper around the floor. Then more scampering and leg wiggling, often with windmilling arms (more by Astaire than by Rogers), leads to a series of hopping turns with one leg extended in the air (D8).

Emerging from these turns, they at first find themselves staggering around each other (D9). But while they gradually bring the staggering under control, the film cuts to a shot of Astaire's sailor buddies cheering wildly (D10). (This disfiguring insertion of a reaction shot in a dance in full flower was, of course, extremely unusual in Astaire's work; see p. 28.) After that momentum-arresting incident in this most exultantly on-rushing of dances the performers wrap things up with repeats of some of their opening steps, and with a brilliant, circling, partnered tap cadenza (D11). There is a final lunge, and, as Astaire resumes his nonchalant gum-chewing, a salute of triumph (D12, 13). They win.

E
I'D RATHER LEAD A BAND
(5′28″)

At Hilliard's apartment, she and Scott kiss and discuss nautical matters. She shows him a model of a ship she has inherited, which she hopes to have salvaged and then sail around the world with her "husband at the helm." That's the kind of talk that frightens the husky Scott (E1), and he makes a hasty exit. Meanwhile, Astaire has purposely gotten Rogers fired at the dance hall, intending to get her a better job with a big agent the next day. But his plan goes awry, to Rogers' intense disgust, when the fleet receives sudden orders to set sail.

Some English dignitaries visit Astaire's ship, and for their edification he performs a solo number backed by a male chorus. The number is unusually episodic for Astaire. It is in four unrelated parts: he sings about how he enjoys conducting, then blisters through a tap solo that has nothing to do with conducting, then conducts a mock military drill with the chorus, then blasts out a concluding solo as the chorus disbands.

The number does have a central theme, however, one that is musical in inspiration: in various ways it investigates the effect on the dance of major shifts in tempo. It is characteristic of Astaire's dances that the choreography plays witty games with the music—running ahead, falling behind, catching up, imitating directly, forging an independent path. But although there

[5] The competitors were recruited by Hermes Pan from Los Angeles dance halls. The couples were filmed separately and the footage was inserted into the Astaire-Rogers dance, a procedure that is slightly disorienting since the competitors are never shown in the same shot. The final contestants were an eighteen-year-old ex-dishwasher and a twenty-year-old unemployed stenographer.

D3 D4 D5 D6
D7 D8 D9 D10
D11 D12 D13 E1

are a few other Astaire dances in which the music enters the game by changing tempo once or twice (usually speeding up in bouncy numbers or slowing headily in romantic ones), it is in "I'd Rather Lead a Band" that these speed shifts are most fully explored. The tempo of the music goes from fast to slow to fast to nothing to slow to very fast.

To open the number, Astaire engagingly sings the song to his audience while turning from time to time to lead the band during brief breaks in the vocal (E 2). Not surprisingly, he throws his whole body into the task of conducting. (There is an incident in Astaire's rendering of the lyric that is endearing. The word "baton" is set in the music with the accent on the first syllable, as in high-style British, rather than on the second, as in sailor American. Taking his cue from this, Astaire gives the word a British-style pronunciation by swallowing the final "n". Then, to make everything work out properly, he swallows the final consonant in the word's intended rhyme, "sat on." RKO could try to make the man over as an ordinary gob, they could put him in a sailor suit and give him lots of gum to chew, but some things are simply not suppressible.)

Upon finishing the song, Astaire cheerily abandons the band area (and his baton). He was to make a dance out of conducting in a film four years later (13 K), but here he devotes himself to dancing for its own sake, launching into a bristling, space-jabbing tap dance that carries him around a large open space on the ship's deck (E 3). For quite a while everything is brisk and bubbling, but then he suddenly goes against the music by propelling himself into a slow, cool spin (E4). He reverts to rapid tapping again but then hits another lethargic spin, and this time the music begins to slow down with him. Following the fleet Astaire, it continues to slow as he adopts a loping tap figure (perhaps in a sense, he really is conducting). Next, Astaire contrasts a furious, slamming, foot-slapping tap-scribble over the languid accompaniment (E 5).

Suddenly the music shifts to a fast tempo again and the chorus marches on crisply as Astaire does a beautiful skittering tap frolic to its regular beat. When the men have halted in formation behind Astaire, the music stops and he puts them through a drill, simulating barked commands with his taps (E 6). This episode, performed in silence, was highly unusual for Astaire. During his career he created two other numbers that included unaccompanied tap segments, but in those (4 D and 12 H) the episodes were brief and cadenzalike and continued the implied momentum of the music. In this case the number's momentum is intentionally stopped. Though the episode is amusing, it has a dampening effect on the number's cumulative impact.

In response to one of Astaire's more complex tap commands, the men rap out a unison tap routine that turns them around and ends in a lunge. It takes a few more orders to get them straightened up again—for a while they list to port or to starboard (E 7). Astaire performs an arrogant mock inspection of the troops (E 8) and is suitably rewarded with a kick in the pants (E 9) —an episode that does not fit very well with the drill routine that frames it and slows the number down further.

Finally, Astaire resumes the drill and sets the chorus to marching in place. He does a sparkling contrapuntal solo to this accompaniment in which his taps seem to occur only during the silences between the beats marked by the chorus. When he hits a pose on one leg, the chorus is suddenly sent into double-time marching in place, and Astaire's tap obbligato speeds up correspondingly, with various sprawling and fluttering figures (E 10).

E2 E3 E4 E5
E6 E7 E8 E9
E10 E11 E12 E13

After Astaire and the chorus trade tap barrages, the music starts up again, and he is propelled into another skittering, scooting routine as the chorus maneuvers in a snappy double-time march behind him. One of the number's best moments comes next, but it is obscured by the unfortunate decision to film it in long shot. As the chorus continues its quick-stepping, which eventually carries it out of sight, Astaire's complementary solo brilliantly alternates between the bright, regular rhythm of the chorus and a set of decorative, crisp poses inspired by the music (E 11). It's one of the most impressive demonstrations of Astaire's astonishing ability to shift abruptly between frenetic activity and expectant calm.

In the poses of this section, his arms frame his head in various ways, anticipating the solo's final pose, which he hits after a quick set of tap spins that propel him toward the camera (E 12). It's a rather limp ending, but there is a nice touch at the fade-out: as his shipboard audience applauds, Astaire snaps to attention, bows, salutes, and remembers to gesture to the band he has supposedly been leading, calling for it to share in the applause (E 13).

F
LET YOURSELF GO
(SOLO DANCE) (1′ 9″)

Although it was through no fault of his own that Astaire was unable to fulfill his promise to get Rogers a better job, she is duly furious and unforgiving for his help in getting her fired from her previous job. In this state of mind, she has finally managed to obtain an audition with the big agent and has hopes of providing herself with a good job on her own.

At the agent's office, Rogers percolates nicely through a tap routine and the agent is suitably impressed. Her dance is neatly crafted; the phrases are stitched together with wit and care, and are sometimes imaginatively set at knowing variance with the musical phrases that accompany them—a big improvement over some of Pan's earlier independent choreography. It is also inventive: there is a pleasant bowing figure, an impertinent tap turn (F 1), and a repeated, Spanish-style traveling step with hands perched provocatively on hips (F 2).

The performance is sweet and winning, though Rogers seems a little cautious, as if afraid of slipping. Her shoulders tend to be tensed (as in F 1), an effect exaggerated by the fuzzy vest she wears. (Later in the film, Astaire parodies this characteristic of her dancing.) There is a beautiful step toward the end of the solo—a foot-dragging sweep with the arms circling overhead—which unfortunately fails to register, either because Rogers doesn't dance it full out or because Pan didn't allow enough time in the music for it to be completely articulated (F 3; for an instance of the same basic idea fully projected, see 8 G 16 and p. 117).

G
BUT WHERE ARE YOU?
(2′ 35″)

Astaire has returned to San Francisco and happens to be in the agent's outer office but does not know that the auditioner inside is Rogers. Learning that the auditioner is doing well and has yet to sing for the agent, Astaire seeks to sabotage her efforts (to save the job for Rogers) by dumping bicarbonate of soda in her drinking water. Rogers loses the job when she hiccups her way through the song (G 1). (Burping would have been more realistic, but that activity was banned by Hollywood's censorship office at the time.)

Hilliard, hopelessly in love with Scott after their one encounter, has, with him in mind, begun the costly process of salvaging the ship she inherited. He knows nothing of this and has done little to encourage her affections—he has, in fact, been busily chasing after a rich woman they both know (convincingly played by the acerbic Astrid Allwyn).

Hilliard and Scott meet again at a party, but he soon deserts her for more appealing prey. Hilliard has been hired to entertain the guests, and her song turns out to have personal relevance as she tearfully sings, "Have you forgotten the night that we met?" (G 2). The song has an attractive, unpretentious, almost country-folksy melody, but a lyric with a sentiment and a rhyme scheme that are too pat ("The sky is blue, but where are you?"). A lyric soprano like Irene Dunne might have been able to minimize the song's calculated naïveté. Hilliard, her wispy pop voice surrounded by overbearing violins, only emphasizes it.

H
I'M PUTTING ALL MY EGGS IN ONE BASKET
(6′ 51″)

Rogers is soon avenged for the bicarbonate caper when she contrives to have Astaire pick a fight with a man who happens to be a navy officer in

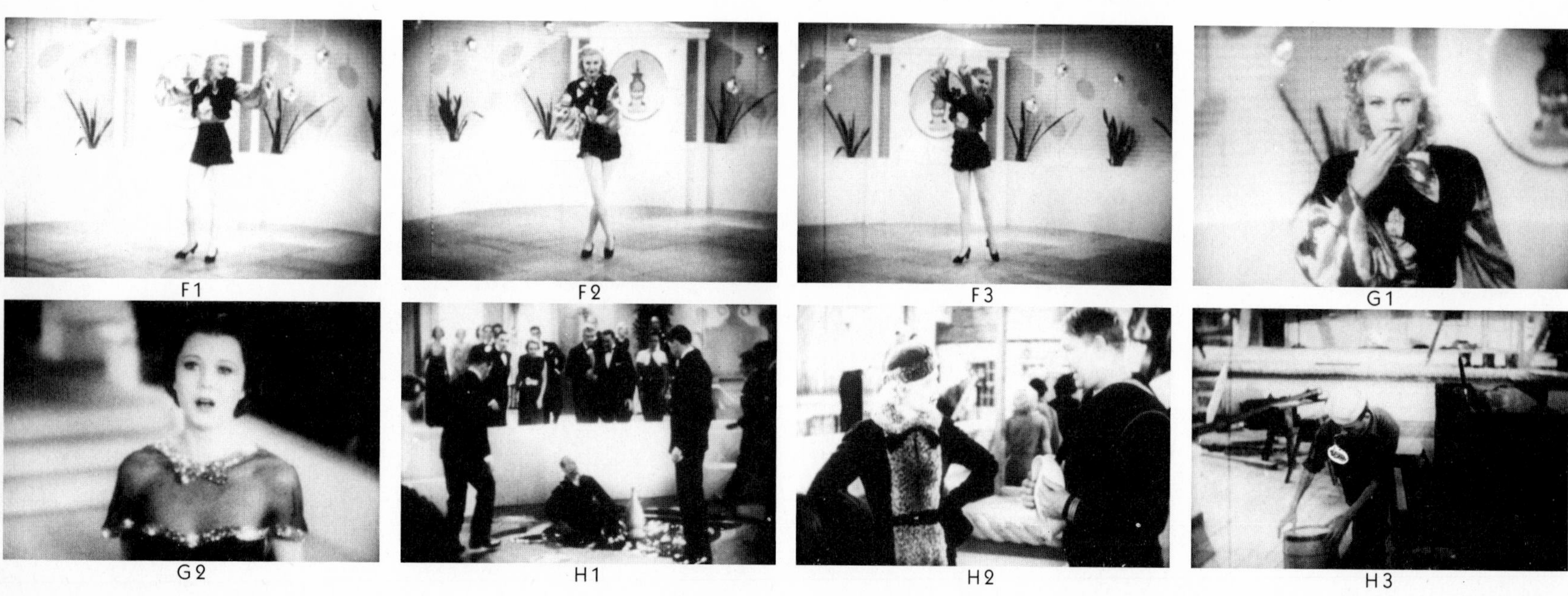
F1 F2 F3 G1
G2 H1 H2 H3

civilian clothes. Astaire loses ingloriously (H 1).

Finally reconciled, Astaire and Rogers now try to help pay for Hilliard's ship salvage: they will stage, and star in, a big benefit show on board the ship. Helping are Astaire's navy band and the showgirls from the ballroom where Rogers was previously employed.

A scene showing a rehearsal for this show is by far the film's finest sequence. As it begins, the sailors and the showgirls gather. One of the sailors makes an admiring remark to Lucille Ball and she crisply administers a deft putdown: "Tell me, little boy, did you get a whistle or a baseball bat with that suit?" (H 2).[6]

Astaire checks over the battered rehearsal piano; he tunes one of its strings and plays a few chords. Then, after rotating the small upended keg he is using as a stool (H 3), he sits down and, cigarette dangling in classic don't-shoot-the-piano-player fashion, ripples through a bouncy rendition of Irving Berlin's happiest tune (H 4). As usual, Astaire's animated piano playing is a visual, as well as an aural, treat.

He now joins Rogers and they decide to run through a number for the show, although, as she observes pointedly, they haven't yet "been through the dance completely." The rehearsal begins as they sing to each other—Astaire the verse and one chorus, Rogers a second chorus. Although this is supposed to be a number planned for the stage, it is clear from the affection with which they render the song that they take personally and very seriously its pledge of eternal fidelity, however jocularly the sentiment is phrased in the lyric. Particularly charming is the way each seems a little embarrassed—and very pleased, of course—by the other's declaration (H 5, 6).

This sequence is one of the most warmly affecting moments in Astaire's film career. Contributing in no small measure to its appeal is Berlin's disarming song. The melody has a brightly skipping—almost yodeling—quality. (Astaire points up the music's witty gyrations on its first occurrence, under the words "one basket," by angling a finger up and then down along with the music. He also traces the song's musical flights with his facial expression.) The felicitous lyric bubbles with sunny tenderness and witty internal rhyme. A splendid example of Berlin's word play (blended with some delightful modulations of key) can be found in a portion of the chorus that Rogers sings: "I've tried to love more than one / Finding it just can't be done / Honey, there's one I lie to / When I try to / Be true / To / Two."

As Astaire pulls Rogers onto the floor, the music speeds up, a change that brings out an innate goofiness in the melody, with its humorous jumps in pitch. This proves to be ideal accompaniment for the screwball dance that follows.

It begins with a loose-armed shuffle, a signature step that immediately sets the tone of the dance (H 7)—in Astaire's aesthetic, to ignore the arms and upper body, as here, is inherent and inescapable parody. The central kinetic joke involves choreographed disharmony: Rogers gets stuck on a step and repeats it endlessly while Astaire goes on and then has to break off in order to get her back in the groove (or out of her rut).[7] Especially amusing are the intricacy with which the "mistakes" are choreographed and the mischievous, childlike glee Rogers projects as she becomes so infatuated with one step that she forgets to go on to the next.[8]

The first step she falls in love with adds a little kick to the basic loose-armed shuffle, and the second involves a kick and an outward flick of the arms (H 8). Astaire is able to get her back in synchronization each time, and next they settle into another variation on the loose-armed shuffle—a jogging step with the shoulders held high (H 9). Astaire may here be poking fun at Rogers' tendency as a dancer to tense her shoulders; if so, she hugely enjoys the joke: she scrunches her shoulders almost to ear level, while he seems incapable of doing anything that untoward.

But even this orderliness proves temporary. Rogers soon becomes mesmerized with this step, and then twice collides with Astaire when he goes on to the next, sending him staggering across the floor. On the third try he avoids the collision by pulling out of the way at the last instant, and Rogers, having missed the connection, is sent sprawling instead—a maneuver she handles magnificently (H 10).

[6] In the final script, this scene is represented merely by a "scratch outline" pending completion of the dance number. Almost all the dialogue (including Ball's rejoinder) was created on the set.

[7] Pan has referred to the idea as "an old burlesque gag." Astaire tried it once again, though differently developed, in portions of a duet with Vera-Ellen sixteen years later (26 G). Perhaps the most extensive use of the idea is in the "mistake waltz" section of Jerome Robbins' 1957 ballet *The Concert*.

[8] Rogers' substantial talents in this area were to be more fully exploited in comedy episodes in *Carefree*, two years later.

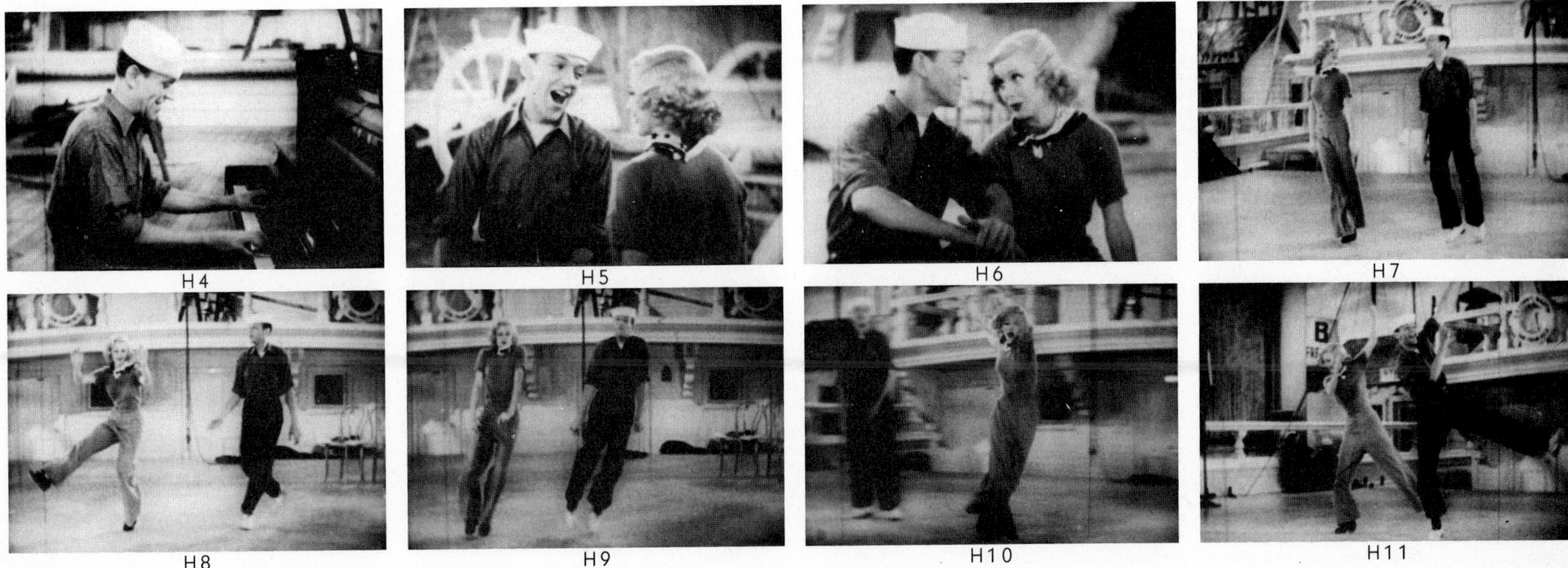

H4 H5 H6 H7

H8 H9 H10 H11

She recovers and joins him in a step involving wide arm swings (H 11). However, she soon gets caught up in this, too; in disgust, Astaire quits dancing and tries to suppress her movements physically, though in the process he gets slugged a couple of times by her swinging arms. As part of this routine, Astaire cranks one of Rogers' arms, seemingly causing the other to move—a gimmick familiar from children's games and the routines of tired comedians (H 12).[9]

Soon, however, the nonsense returns to a more inspired level. Going back to square one, Astaire finally gets Rogers settled again into the loose-armed shuffle step that had begun the dance—although Rogers now adds slightly raised shoulders (H 13; compare H 7). Grinning impishly, she gets locked into this step as well, and now Astaire gives up entirely. He walks over to a nearby chair, picks up a newspaper, and begins to read as Rogers continues her self-enchanted perambulations (H 14).

Suddenly the band switches to a waltz. Since a partnerless waltz is virtually a contradiction in terms, Astaire has no choice but to fling his newspaper aside and join her (H 15). No sooner have they started to mock the snooty airs of the waltz than the music turns jazzy; after a moment of puzzlement (H 16), they follow suit. Then, after another unexpected change in the music, they resume their broad waltz. For an instant they partner grandly and float apart holding hands (H 17). However, as Astaire pulls Rogers back in toward himself, the music abruptly returns to a pop mode. Accordingly, Astaire starts doing another dance and misses the partnering connection that had been dictated by the (now suddenly irrelevant) waltz. Rogers topples into a stupendous fall—twisting, full out, pell mell, terminal—one of her most glorious moments (H 18, 19).

With Rogers out of the way snarling on the floor, Astaire performs a hilarious set of screwball variations on the loose-armed shuffle—something well beyond Rogers' capabilities (H 20–22). She gets up, however, to join him for the finale—or, rather, finales. The music has a series of false endings, with which the dancers, with increasing desperation, try to get coordinated (H 23).

[9] For this sequence the camera cuts to a medium (or three-quarter) shot, the only one Astaire allowed in his dances in the six films he made between *The Gay Divorcee* (1934) and *Carefree* (1938).

I

TYPEWRITER BIT

(19″)

Astaire is next seen back at his ship, typing out the script for the show. He makes a funny rhythm routine out of his mundane task (I 1).

J

LET'S FACE THE MUSIC AND DANCE

(7′56″)

Such incidental felicities help make up for such things as the next scene's contrived comedy: Astaire rehearses a love scene for the show with Scott's rich lady friend and arranges things so that Scott overhears and thinks it's for real (J 1). Scott breaks off with the woman, and even Astaire's later confession that the scene was all a ruse has no impact. Now Scott learns that Hilliard has salvaged her ship for him. He is impressed and, we are to believe, immediately falls in love with her.

After some complications that require Astaire to jump ship, he and Rogers go on stage to perform in a production that is part of the benefit for the ship's salvage. This is the only duet in their RKO films in which Astaire and Rogers perform completely out of character, and it gives

H12 H13 H14 H15 H16 H17 H18 H19 H20 H21 H22 H23

them the opportunity to impersonate characters who could not be developed within the framework of the light comedy plots of their films. Here they play a couple of Monte Carlo socialites in a context that is supremely glamorous and almost absurdly serious.

In a brief prologue, Astaire is seen to lose his last money at the gaming table. He greets the loss with good humor (J 2) but suddenly finds himself shunned by polite society (J 3). Then the scene changes and he is shown wandering aimlessly on an airy, elegant terrace overlooking the ocean, where he is snubbed by the others in a beautifully staged sequence that is somewhere between dance and pantomime. Of particular interest is the yearning, imploring demeanor Astaire adopts as he is rejected by each set of passers-by (J 4). This sagging, limp-kneed pose will reappear in various contexts and guises throughout the rest of the number.[10]

In despair, he takes a pistol from his pocket and points it to his head, but then is distracted when he sees Rogers in the distance, about to leap to *her* death from the terrace rail (J 5); he rushes toward her and pulls her back. She is hostile and sullen when he ironically shows her his pistol and, smiling, indicates that he, too, had been planning suicide (J 6). Though she grabs for the weapon, he throws it away. Then he calmly shows her his empty wallet—and throws that away as well.

Although both characters are potential suicides, their personalities are shown in this episode to be quite distinct.[11] Rogers fairly radiates mystery and gloom, while Astaire approaches life—and death—with considerable openness and casualness: his initial response to his gambling loss is to shrug it off with a smile, and when he finds himself rejected by everyone, his calm reaction is to shrug life off with comparable equanimity. His discovery, then, of a fellow suicide (who happens to be a beautiful woman into the bargain) has the perverse effect of buoying his spirits: Rogers adds enough interest to his life to make ending it no longer so attractive. For the time being, at least, he has an interest in keeping both of them alive.

And so he sings to her about that. As she broods sadly, he implores her to face the music —to confront reality—and to dance while there is still music and moonlight and romance in the world, and before they're asked to pay the bill (J 7). Berlin's ballad is majestic and somber—the kind of throaty, melancholy melody the cello seems to have been invented to play (the orchestrators took the hint)—and Astaire sings it with appropriate ardor and insistence.[12]

Then he gradually draws the reluctant Rogers into dancing. He'd done that before in films and

[10] The limp-kneed yearning is again used by Astaire in his romantic duet in his next film, *Swing Time* (7 G) and the idea is startlingly parodied in a number in *Shall We Dance* (8 G 5, 6).

[11] The final script calls for Rogers to show Astaire a letter from which we are to deduce that "her sweetheart has evidently left her." Without this business in the filmed number, she is more mysterious, and the two characters are better differentiated.

[12] It seems likely that the whole number was developed from the mood suggested by the lyric (which itself seems to owe something to "Dancing in the Dark," a 1931 song with a lyric by Howard Dietz). However, while Berlin's song was probably written with Astaire in mind, the scriptwriters originally planned to have it sung by the Hilliard character when it was thought that her role would be taken by Irene Dunne. Since the song was too rich for Hilliard's voice, it was freed up. Somewhere along the line it was proposed that Tony Martin (who is one of the sailors, fourth from the left in D 10) sing it, but to Martin's disappointment, that plan came to nothing.

I1 J1 J2 J3
J4 J5 J6 J7
J8 J9 J10 J11

he would again; but here the dance is between strangers, not lovers, and the goal is emotional catharsis, not sexual—dance as therapy, not as lovemaking. Accordingly, there is little warmth and no fondness in it. The tone is exhibitionistic, not intimate: there is no cheek-to-cheek embracing, there are no ecstatic lifts. Most of the time Rogers seems to be in her own world, looking either away from Astaire or through him, and there is narcissism in her demeanor. Her arms are most often held tentatively in front of her, as if she were groping through a fog or trying lethargically to ward off intruders into her private despair. Her gown, with its impractical weighted sleeves and hem, is sleek but steely, almost a kind of armor. Though Astaire is attentive and commanding, he is also often essentially decorative as he flutters around his distant, aloof partner.[13]

The duet runs two minutes and fifty seconds and is shown in one continuous shot. It is in two parts. The first contains abrupt stops and hesitations, and lingering poses, as Astaire pulls Rogers around the floor and surrounds her with the dance, trying to impel her into continuous motion. Her dress becomes an important aspect of the choreography as it swirls around her during the hesitations.[14] The second part of the dance is constructed in one long, sweeping kinetic line, as if the dancers, having overcome initial reticence, now seek to achieve release through a cascade of movement.

At the beginning Astaire confronts Rogers and begins to sway from side to side, his arms held up and in front of him. She responds by tentatively imitating his swaying body (J 8). When he darts around her and tries again, she yields further to the body movement and brings her arms into play as well—thus establishing the groping arm position, one of the dance's central motifs (J 9).

With her arms still in that position, she allows herself to be swept across the stage by Astaire (J 10). He takes her by one hand as she draws away (J 11) and then spins her back in toward him (J 12) until they settle into a pose in which he holds her hands in his (J 13).[15] During much of this Astaire adopts the buckled-knee stance that is associated with his character and with the mood of the dance.

The hand holding that is established in this pose becomes the chief mode of partnered contact for the dancers. Astaire pulls Rogers around the stage (J 14), at times snapping her in toward himself and piloting her in a series of exotic promenades in which she has one knee raised (J 15). In the next phrases, set to the music of the release strain (the section with a lyric that begins, "Soon, we'll be without the moon"), they waft around the stage in figures that develop the sagging, bent-knee pose of Astaire and the groping arms of Rogers (J 16).

[13] Oddly, some of the posed publicity stills from this number show the pair grinning incongruously.

[14] Pan recalls that the swirling dress was a fortunate "accident"; it was not originally planned for in the choreography.

[15] As Rogers spins across in front of Astaire in this maneuver, her weighted sleeves pick up quite a bit of momentum. On the first take of this dance, Astaire forgot to get out of the way and was hit on the jaw and eye by a flying sleeve. "I kept on dancing," he recalls, "although somewhat maimed." At the end Astaire was asked about the take: "I replied that I didn't remember anything about the take—that I had been knocked groggy in the first round." To compensate, they did some twenty more takes that day. The rushes the next morning showed the first take to be perfect, and so that is the one preserved on the finished film. Rogers' haymaker is administered in J 12.

J12 J13 J14 J15
J16 J17 J18 J19
J20 J21 J22 J23

As the main melody returns, there is a beautiful transition to full partnering: Astaire spins around Rogers while she slowly turns (J 17); then he grasps her by the hand (J 18) and pulls her into his arms. They move slowly and tentatively in this position, then speed up, and are soon swirling across the floor (J 19).

They emerge from this holding hands at arm's length again (J 20), and the next section alternates such expressive stillnesses with spurts of movement. They dart past each other, wait, do a strange little hop in place (J 21), spin until they are facing each other, stop, swirl around the floor for a moment, and then stop, once more holding hands at arm's length (J 22). After a few more tentative dashes, spins, and hops, they face each other as the orchestra concludes its first rendering of the song (J 23).

It now returns to the beginning of the melody, playing it opulently, and the dancers, finding it irresistible, fall into each other's arms for their final, cascading dance to the finish. Among the ideas developed in this half of the dance are a rapid partnering figure embellished with a momentum-spurring back kick (J 24); a development of the groping-arm motif in which Rogers, while flowing across the floor in Astaire's arms, holds her arms in that position and turns (J 25); some partnering built on a low, twisting jump; a figure involving pistonlike arm pumping that seems somewhat less dramatic than the lush music it is set to (J 26); and some side-to-side arm swaying similar to that done earlier in the dance, but now delivered without tentativeness (J 27; compare J 9, 16).

The dance's conclusion is suitably exotic and entirely astonishing. As Rogers repeats her signature arm-groping motif, Astaire dances a rushing pattern around her, including a couple of quick jumps with leg beats (J 28). He then dashes past her, takes her hand (J 29), and pulls her spinning toward him. Suddenly, side by side, they each sink to one knee and pause (J 30)—the first time their momentum has been interrupted in the second half of the dance (since J 23). They take several steps backward, pause again (J 31), and then stride toward the wings. At the last moment they rear backward and turn their faces to the audience, each raising one leg (J 32). From that daring and extraordinary pose they lunge into the wings as the curtain rapidly closes.

K

WE SAW THE SEA

(TAG) (23")

Somewhere backstage during this duet, Hilliard and Scott have become reconciled and engaged. Mercifully, the film shows only a brief scene filled with mechanical smiles and obligatory kisses (K 1). There is a brisk cut to Astaire and Rogers, who also become engaged—in characteristic fashion. He tells her that he refuses to team up with her in show business (after serving his time in the brig for having jumped ship) unless she asks him to marry her. Rogers: "Well, will you?" (K 2). Astaire: "You'll have to ask Father." There is, as usual, no concluding kiss for Astaire and Rogers. In this film, however, they seem to have developed their nonkissing into a conscious audience tease. In two earlier scenes Astaire starts to kiss Rogers but is dissuaded—once by her refusal and once by a passing policeman. The tease would continue in *Swing Time.*

Follow the Fleet ends with a brief reprise of its only nautical song (K 3).

J24 J25 J26 J27

J28 J29 J30 J31

J32 K1 K2 K3

7.

Swing Time

1936

Although *Swing Time* suffers from a rambling, lurching, ill-balanced script, this defect is mitigated by the film's positive qualities: the affecting acting by the leads, the rich and memorable musical score, the splendid Art Deco sets, and, especially, the brilliance of the choreography and the dancing. When looked at as a "dance film," *Swing Time* is, as Arlene Croce suggests, the greatest of the Astaire-Rogers films.

The film is graced by four dance numbers: a spiky, inventive Astaire solo, and three duets that are among Astaire's most profound achievements. These duets explore different phases of the love relationship—exuberant courtship, ecstatic celebration, and painful separation—and are linked choreographically: a signature step introduced in the first duet reappears in the other two, transformed to suit the differing emotional situations.

THE MUSIC

The score, by Jerome Kern and Dorothy Fields, includes two songs that have become standards: "The Way You Look Tonight" and "A Fine Romance." Also notable is the high quality and the distinct individuality of the music that *didn't* become standard: the vigorous "Bojangles of Harlem," the haunting "Never Gonna Dance," and an instrumental, "Waltz in Swing Time," which is the finest piece of pure dance music ever written for Astaire. Greatly adding to the success of the score are the superb arrangements and orchestrations of Robert Russell Bennett (whom Kern had brought from Broadway to Hollywood in 1935), music director Nathaniel Shilkret, and, in some measure, Hal Borne, Astaire's rehearsal pianist.

There was something of a clash between Kern and Astaire over the music for the film. Astaire wanted at least two of the numbers to be thoroughly contemporary—to "swing." Kern, a generation older, respected the request but felt he simply couldn't write that kind of music. The gap was largely bridged by Bennett, who fashioned Kern's music to suit Astaire's sensibilities. Still, the film's title (chosen after *I Won't Dance, Never Gonna Dance, Pick Yourself Up,* and fifteen other possibilities had been rejected) is something of a misnomer, which bothered some critics at the time.[1]

THE SCRIPT

As in several other Astaire films, the songs for *Swing Time* were basically written independently, and then great efforts were made to work them into the script. By and large this was successful: except for the "Bojangles" solo, the numbers are all duly motivated by the plot.

Initially written by Howard Lindsay and then completely revised by Allan Scott, the script was still unfinished when filming began; the finale of the film, an effort to resolve all problems in a cascade of contagious laughter, was suggested in the script but assembled only at the last moment. The story is riddled with inconsistencies, implausibilities, contrivances, omissions, and irrationalities. While remembering the dances in *Swing Time* with great fondness, Astaire has dismissed much of the script as "stupid." Indeed, the quality of the script so alarmed dance editor Paul R. Milton that he declared in his magazine, "Two more pictures like *Swing Time* and Astaire will be washed up, through." He urged dancing teachers to write Astaire "to help him save himself while there is still time."

The plot pattern in most of Astaire's films is ABC: Attraction, Breakup, and Conciliation. *Swing Time* takes this formula and runs rampant with it. There are three breakups and three conciliations (two small and one large) in this roller coaster of a romance—the plot could be rendered ABCBCBC or perhaps AbcbcBC. The devices for generating tension tend to spring from the characters' inability to engage in rational conversation—instead Rogers pouts, storms out of the room, or petulantly agrees to marry someone else.

Many of these problems can be glossed over by the hardy

[1] In *The New York Times,* Frank S. Nugent blamed the "disappointment" of the film "primarily on the music." Kern, he said, "has shadow boxed with swing" and the songs mostly "are merely adequate, or worse. Neither good Kern nor good swing." In a 1936 letter, George Gershwin was somewhat patronizing about the music: "Although I don't think Kern has written any outstanding song hits, I think he did a very credible job with the music and some of it is really quite delightful. Of course, he never was really ideal for Astaire and I take that into consideration."

With Ginger Rogers in "Waltz in Swing Time"

stratagem of not thinking too hard about the plot. Two defects in the film are more difficult to ignore, however. One of these is an element of ill-humor in the script—particularly the drawn-out practical jokes and Astaire's continual confrontation with the unrelievedly unpleasant bandleader (Georges Metaxa). The second is George Stevens' occasionally leaden direction.

THE ACTING

Yet, taken as a whole, *Swing Time* is richly affecting. There seems a special glow to the Astaire-Rogers relationship: more than in any other of their films, we care about them, worry about their inevitable troubles, and rejoice in the sweetness of their equally inevitable reconciliations. In *Swing Time* the Astaire-Rogers partnership truly becomes, in Dorothy Fields' felicitous construction, "The la belle, la perfectly swell, romance."

Many musicals (and nonmusicals) suffer from what might be called second-act lag: they start out well enough, but the plot becomes strained about three-quarters of the way through, and they are saved, if at all, only by a smash finale. *Swing Time* has the opposite problem—it seems to take forever to get going, but once it finds its stride, it carries through to the end at a chipper clip. The film achieves this, and triumphs over the inadequacies of script and direction, not only through its high choreographic and musical values—more than any other Astaire film, this one chiefly moves during the numbers—but also through the quality of the acting. With each film of their partnership Rogers became more self-confident and Astaire less self-conscious. There are scenes in *Swing Time* that still betray awkwardness—an embarrassed kissing episode and the scene surrounding Astaire's "The Way You Look Tonight" serenade. But these are more than compensated for by three scenes that are among the most affecting in Astaire's film career: the charmed gaiety of "Pick Yourself Up," the touching hesitancies of "A Fine Romance," and especially the somber anguish of "Never Gonna Dance."

With Rogers in "Pick Yourself Up"

The leads are backed by a fine supporting cast. Although Helen Broderick is given a few lines that even she is incapable of making funny (something one would have thought impossible after her triumph in *Top Hat*), she sails through her part as Rogers' acerbic older friend. Eric Blore's role adds a nicely hostile edge to his usual pose of harried obsequiousness. New to the Astaire-Rogers coterie was the well-established Broadway comedian Victor Moore, who plays a crony of Astaire's. Moore finds an interesting, if limited, depth in the role—he is at once dependent and cagily resourceful.

GINGER ROGERS

Whether *Swing Time* is the greatest Astaire film or the greatest Astaire-Rogers film may be a matter of debate. Less debatable is the superior quality of Ginger Rogers' performance in it—her finest in the series. As a dancer she had grown enormously during the four years of their partnership, developing fluidity, confidence, and rich choreographic insight. Moreover, her acting is richly textured and engagingly convincing, and she is especially able in this film to leaven the defensive haughtiness of her character with a touching vulnerability. Many scenes—particularly the one in which she walks out on Astaire for the third time—show a remarkable triumph of actress over script material. Rogers gives much of the credit to director Stevens: "He gave us a certain quality, I think, that made [*Swing Time*] stand out above the others."[2]

ASTAIRE'S PHOTOGRAPHY

The film contains two landmarks in Astaire's development as a filmer of dances. "Never Gonna Dance" was the first dance he choreographed that would not be just about equally effective (though not *impossible*) in the theatre, a dance that travels from one stage area to another. And in "Bojangles of Harlem," where he appears to be dancing with shadows of himself, Astaire made his first use of trick photography.

THE CHOREOGRAPHY

Assisting Astaire was his usual RKO sidekick, Hermes Pan.

[2] At the time Rogers was reportedly having an affair with Stevens, something that may have favorably affected her (or his) performance.

"Bojangles of Harlem"

THE NUMBERS

A
IT'S NOT IN THE CARDS
(9″)

Originally the film began with a substantial on-stage musical number including Victor Moore doing some card tricks and ending with a brief dance for Astaire backed by a male chorus. According to Pan, it was generally agreed the number was not very good. Since it was unnecessary to the story and since the film was too long anyway, all the number was cut except a scrap from the end (A 1).[3]

The omission created a severe imbalance, for the film goes for a very long time before there is a musical number—twenty-five minutes before anyone sings, twenty-eight minutes before anyone dances.

[3] The excised number is described more fully below. There was not time enough to cut the number from the print sent to Radio City Music Hall for the scheduled pre-Labor Day premiere, so the number was seen there and is mentioned in three New York reviews. The music for the song is played at the beginning of the film and then as background under the first scenes. It is bright and catchy, its ending phrases slightly reminiscent of Irving Berlin's "I'm Putting All My Eggs in One Basket."

B
PICK YOURSELF UP
(SONG 1′ 52″, DANCE 2′ 1″)

In the excessively long opening scenes, Astaire misses his wedding to Betty Furness when his fellow dancers steal his pants. He then hops a freight train to New York, penniless but still in his fancy wedding duds (now including the pants), to seek his fortune as a way of proving his essential worthiness to his prospective father-in-law (B 1). Freight hopping is, of course, an image especially associated with the Depression, and having the formally attired Astaire ride the rails is sly satire of the image. It's about as close as any of the Astaire-Rogers films ever got to acknowledging that the Depression existed.

In New York, with Victor Moore tagging along, Astaire runs into Ginger Rogers on the street and has an altercation with her over a 25-cent piece. It turns out she is an instructor at the Gordon Dancing Academy, and he chases her there in order to return some money he has accidentally purloined.

Astaire playfully wangles a dancing lesson from her under the solicitous eye of Mr. Gordon himself (Eric Blore). Following the formula of *The Gay Divorcee* and *Top Hat,* her initial encounter with him has been annoying to her, and here he proceeds to increase her irritation by pretending to be inept as she grudgingly tries to teach him a few steps. She explains he must learn to walk before he can hope to dance, and together they pace the floor a few times. On one of these progressions, Astaire unconvincingly feigns awkwardness by walking on the sides of his feet (B 2).

She then tries to teach him a dance step that will prove to be very important in the film—a partnered turning, hopping step, three hops on one foot and then three on the other (B 3). When he keeps collapsing, she says in disgust, "I can't teach you anything." From the floor Astaire pleads, in song, for more lessons, and she sings back, "Pick yourself up, dust yourself off, and start all over again" (B 4). He takes advice and they try the step once more, but this time his studied collapse topples both of them.

Now thoroughly disgusted, Rogers concludes he is a hopeless case and advises him to save his money. This last remark outrages proprietor Blore, who fires Rogers on the spot. But Astaire

A1 B1 B2 B3 B4 B5 B6 B7 B8 B9 B10 B11

argues that, in fact, Rogers is a truly great teacher, and he does a snappy little tap barrage to show how much he has learned already. He then confidently sweeps the astonished Rogers into a sparkling dance.

"Pick Yourself Up" is one of the very greatest of Astaire's playful duets: boundlessly joyous, endlessly re-seeable. It is notable, among other things for its humorous contrasts of the self-consciously elegant with the unabashedly raucous. The dance also constitutes Ginger Rogers' most glorious two minutes and a superb example of how much she contributed to their duets—not so much steps as flavor and point. At first she is stiff and bewildered as she tries to comprehend the miracle that has transformed Astaire from klutz to whirlwind. Gradually her tentativeness gives way to surprised delight, her stiffness to fluidity, until, by the end, she is gleefully playing with the choreography and even mocking her own joy.

Kern's tune (which sounds better without Fields' somewhat determinedly unsophisticated lyric) is a bouncy polka that is taken substantially faster for the dancing than for the singing.

After his tap barrage, Astaire invites Blore to sit down and watch, and then with Rogers launches into the dance, which begins, appropriately enough, with the little partnered hops she had been teaching him earlier (B5; compare B3). This is soon developed, becoming looser and more jaunty (B6), and the rhythm is toyed with, changing from a three-step to a two-step pattern. Rogers is clearly amazed and delighted.

The dancers open out into a pose in which Astaire adopts a casual, shrugging, look-ma-no-hands demeanor (B7) while Rogers, following along, glances down in astonishment at his suddenly educated feet (B8). Inserted here are a couple of reaction shots of the incredulous Blore (B9), after which the dance is recorded in a single shot.

A cascade of tap scamperings around the floor shows Rogers ever looser and more spirited as she frolics with Astaire, who once again gives his wry shrug (B10). A neat joke about contrasts follows when a marked, swaying partnered figure (B11) changes abruptly into a casual linked-arm stroll (B12). This idea is varied with tap barrages that include some impertinent little kicks (B13). Next comes a splendid Astaire double-helix maneuver: the dancers make separate and independent circles, emerging smoothly into a partnered pose (B14–19).

Now the music slows, and the orchestration becomes mockingly delicate as the melody is given to violins and xylophone; the dancers, turning, slow with it and join in its mockery by becoming preciously light and airy—Rogers is particularly wonderful here (B20, 21). Then the orchestra shifts abruptly from this ethereal tinkling to earthy brassiness, and the dancers follow along with some heavy, down-driving slams (B22) and other kinetic exclamations.

Next is a loose side-by-side progression forward in which Rogers gleefully matches Astaire step for step (B23). Then the dancers make a joyous partnered survey of the terrain. Rogers lies back confidently and delightedly in Astaire's arms, her left arm placed daintily on his shoulder with exaggerated delicacy (B24) or allowed to waft airily (B25). When they arrive upstage, the orchestra pauses and the dancers cheerily trot forward side by side in a tap cadenza (B26). At the front they deliver an endearingly goofy, and totally unexpected, little jump (B27); as they land, Astaire again shrugs nonchalantly (B28). The jump sets the orchestra to playing again.

The arena is no longer large enough to contain the dancers' exuberance. They swing each

B12 B13 B14 B15

B16 B17 B18 B19

B20 B21 B22 B23

other back and forth over the railing that frames the space (B 29). Then they travel rapidly across the floor and hurdle the opposite railing (B 30), moderating their speed so they slow to a calm stroll just as they are disappearing through the doorway (B 31).

At the end Blore, blissfully oblivious of the utter plausibility of the transformation that has taken place before his eyes, hops over the railing in pursuit of the dancers (B 32) and exclaims delightedly (and accurately), "Sheer heaven!" He immediately rehires Rogers and sets about arranging an audition for the two as nightclub performers. Meanwhile Moore, who had previously caused Rogers' friend Broderick to lose her job as receptionist at the dancing academy, tries to mend the damage by swirling her about the floor in a brief parody of the Astaire-Rogers duet (B 33; compare B 24), concluding with an (ill-advised) effort at fence hopping (B 34).

C
THE WAY YOU LOOK TONIGHT
(1′56″)

To get appropriate clothes for the audition Blore has arranged, Astaire tries to apply his gambling skills: he plays strip piquet with a well-dressed drunk who is the correct size. But luck is against Astaire, and he loses his pants for the second time in the film. Rogers discovers him thus and is appalled to discover he is a "common gambler" (C 1).

Within a week Astaire has gambled himself into a bankroll and has rescheduled the audition. Rogers is still piqued, however. With the connivance of Broderick, Astaire enters Rogers' apartment and, while she is washing her hair in another room, serenades her with "The Way You Look Tonight." Understandably bewitched, she is drawn toward Astaire and the piano, forgetting that her hair is covered with shampoo (C 2). By the end of the song she is moved enough to forgive Astaire for his transgressions.

The song's lyric is a heartfelt declaration of love. Since the Astaire-Rogers romance has not yet progressed that far, the song is delivered as a randomly selected ballad Astaire happens to have on the tip of his larynx at the moment. It is staged as a light joke—while Astaire rhapsodizes about "the way you look tonight," Rogers is supposed to be in a contrasting state of disarray. However, as scriptwriter Lindsay recalls, "The producers lacked the courage to do this. . . . She entered with her hair covered with white foam, but so beautifully sculptured that it looked like a white wig."

There is no dance with the song, but later the music is reprised with great poignancy as part of the "Never Gonna Dance" number.

D
WALTZ IN SWING TIME
(2′43″)

Astaire and Rogers appear at the Silver Sandal nightclub for their audition but are frustrated when bandleader Georges Metaxa, who is in love with Rogers, petulantly refuses to play for them.[4] So they go to another nightclub, where Astaire wins the contract for Metaxa's entire band in a wager. (Rogers' distaste for gambling seems to emerge only when convenient for the scriptwriters.) Metaxa also works at the second nightclub and still refuses to play, and cannot be required to since it is after hours. But the re-

[4] Metaxa was a Romanian tenor here making his second screen appearance. The character he plays—ill-tempered, vindictive, pompous, arrogant—is an unnecessarily unpleasant feature of the script, though it is possible a better actor could have brought more depth to the role. It is characteristic of Astaire's films—at least until *Carefree* in 1938—that his rival was either laughable or contemptible.

B24 B25 B26 B27
B28 B29 B30 B31
B32 B33 B34 C1

sourceful Astaire tricks him into publicly pumping his baton, and the music begins.

Astaire and Rogers now plunge into their second magnificent duet of the film. The man for whom they are supposedly auditioning is in another part of town, at the *first* nightclub. However, since their sparkling dance is so obviously a rapturous celebration of love, to treat it merely as an audition would be to trivialize its significance.[5]

This dance—probably the couple's most virtuosic duet—is notable for its speed and for the sheer number of its steps: it has an almost baroque intricacy. At no time, however, do the lacing and interlacing get so involved that the dance becomes cluttered; it always retains great clarity.

The music is largely the composition of Robert Russell Bennett.[6] Astaire wanted a waltz that would really move—a waltz that would "swing." Bennett came up with a fast waltz—a waltz "in one"—that contains some syncopated sections in which a phrase in double meter is laid over the triple meter of the waltz. The piece is unified by a recurring fanfarelike melody played by trumpets. The remarkable composition is brisk and unsentimental, yet intimate and personal. Scored for pit band at Astaire's suggestion, the music combines the lilt of a waltz with the bright, eager, no-nonsense rush of a swing band composition.

The dance is presented all in one shot and is in three sections. The first is almost entirely partnered; even when the dancers lose contact momentarily, they are drawn back together again almost magnetically. It opens with brisk spins for Rogers under Astaire's arm (D1) alternating with fast, flowing partnered waltzing, including sequences in which Astaire partners Rogers from behind (D2). As the syncopated waltz begins, the dancers spin out some steps in which one leg is kicked (D3, 4; compare 4 D9).

There is a brief cadenza for the dancers, and the second section of the dance is introduced by a sequence that includes a most unusual step: a back kick that travels upstage (D5) and then downstage (D6).[7] This section of the dance is soloistic: the dancers mostly paralleling each other, touching only incidentally. But neither ever drifts into a separate world—they always seem to belong together even if they rarely come into explicit contact. As the music repeats the fanfare melody from the opening, the dancers alternate a skating idea (D7) with some brilliant hopping spins; this is probably the most difficult sequence Rogers ever had to perform, and she handles it splendidly. When the music subsides to a soft melody derived from part of "Never Gonna Dance," the dancers perform a fast, scribbling counterpoint over it. Quick flitting steps (D8) alternate with dragging hesitations (D9). There is also a brief use of a diagonal arm idea (D10) and an odd little scuffling heel-down tap step (D11).

The transition from the second (soloistic) section of the dance to the third, which is partnered, is probably the most beautiful Astaire ever choreographed (which makes it monumental indeed). Set to the fanfare melody, it takes a full eight measures. Rogers angles her body slightly backward, forming a voluptuous hurdle

[5] As Croce puts it, quite sensibly, "They can't wait another second and neither can we."

[6] According to Bennett, Kern supplied him with some basic themes and then told him to "put them together in any way that would satisfy Astaire." In 1981 Bennett simply stated that his contribution to the film included the "composing" of the "Waltz in Swing Time." Hal Borne insists there is also some of his material in the composition.

[7] This scooting back-kick idea was a favorite of Astaire's. He was to use it again in 12 A4, 19 F13, and repeatedly in 18 M.

C2 · D1 · D2 · D3 · D4 · D5 · D6 · D7 · D8 · D9 · D10 · D11

over which Astaire vaults (D12); he then turns and falls into her arms (D13). They separate, and the vault and embrace are repeated. Although this move is performed, like everything else in the dance, at great speed, Astaire still has time to hesitate and to make the action of taking her in his arms a clear and deliberate act of tenderness. Once again they separate, and once again he hurdles over her (D14). There is a slight pause (D15), and then, as the next passage of music begins, they plunge into each other's arms (D16) and stay there for the rest of the dance.

As they sweep into their final dance embrace, the orchestra announces a new melody, the only one in the composition that is a true, straightforward waltz. The step Astaire and Rogers perform as this broad and ingratiating melody enters (D16, 17) is the same partnered hopping step with which they had begun their earlier duet (B5, 6)—the step Rogers tried to teach Astaire in their aborted (but ultimately hugely successful) dancing lesson (B3). Embedded here at the climax of the "Waltz in Swing Time," the step becomes a nostalgic celebration of their first meeting. It will reappear in their final duet in the film (G17), where it is given new meaning. The dancers explode across the floor with their theme step, and for a moment the fast waltzing gets broader and even more celebratory.

Then they settle down, ecstatic, transported, their faces raised (D18). There is no more dazzle, no more intricacy or flash, as they circle the floor several times in an almost hypnotic tapping pattern, until they vanish from view behind a screen (D19).

E
A FINE ROMANCE
(2′28″)

In the next scene, Astaire and Rogers are shown beaming giddily at each other (E1). Together with Broderick and Moore, they have a date to drive to the snowy countryside in an open car.

In *Swing Time* Astaire and Rogers effectively communicate only in dance. He has fallen in love and can't bring himself to tell her about his fiancée back home, so he adopts a defensive aloofness that understandably puzzles her (E2). In the country she complains by singing a chorus of "A Fine Romance," with its amusingly bitter lyric.

Astaire had earlier told Moore to keep him from being alone with Rogers, and when Astaire, responding to Rogers' sarcastic invitation, finally works up the courage to kiss her, Moore obligingly breaks up their clinch with a well-aimed snowball. Now Astaire resolves to throw all caution to the wind, but Moore—without cause, point, or motivation—has in the meantime told Rogers about Astaire's engagement. She sours—and it is Astaire's turn to sing a chorus of the satiric "A Fine Romance."

Despite the contrivance of the script in this scene, it is one of the most charming in the Astaire-Rogers series. Rogers is particularly convincing, by turns puzzled, cautiously flirtatious, frustrated, petulant, and deeply hurt.

F
BOJANGLES OF HARLEM
(7′51″)

Astaire and Rogers are now employed at the newly refurbished Silver Sandal. Backstage, Broderick argues to Rogers that Astaire must love her, since he has decided not to return to his fiancée. On Broderick's dare, Rogers, all fluttery and nervous, goes to Astaire and gives him a kiss, which is accomplished out of sight behind a door. Then Stevens' camera lingers on the pair for a full thirteen seconds as they giggle and smirk self-consciously (F1).

Elated at Rogers' change of heart, Astaire goes onstage to perform "Bojangles of Harlem." The title refers to the nickname of the great black tap dancer Bill Robinson. It was the only time Astaire appeared in blackface, and the number makes some people uncomfortable today. Offense, of course, was not intended, and the number could even be seen as a homage to Robinson. Actually, however, Astaire was not particularly impressed by Robinson as a dancer, and tended to regard him as a one-trick artist who mainly tapped up and down stairs. Robinson's dances were very foot-oriented, with a basically immobile carriage of the upper body. Astaire, by contrast, was always interested in making use of the expressive possibilities of the entire body. This does not mean Astaire was unappreciative of the artistry of black dancers. He had boundless admiration for another black hoofer, John W. Bubbles, considering him a truly great performer, particularly for his spontaneity and his dazzling inventiveness.[8] In style Astaire is far closer to Bubbles than to Robinson. But the song

[8] See also pp. 6, 159n. As was true of most Hollywood films of the period, there are scarcely any blacks in Astaire's films. Astaire did make recordings with blacks during the 1940s and 1950s and prominently featured black bands on his television specials in 1958, 1959, and 1960.

D12 D13 D14 D15

D16 D17 D18 D19

was about Robinson, who was easily the best known black tapper in the world, having appeared in several popular Shirley Temple movies by the mid-1930s.

Someone—probably Dorothy Fields—prepared a phantasmagoric scenario for this number. Entitled "Hot Fields," it was designed as a parody of "Green Pastures" and involved thirty-three scenes including heaven, hell, Harlem, and an Emperor Jones jungle. Through this the Bojangles character journeyed, mostly by climbing up, or falling down, flights of stairs. Almost none of this scenario found its way into the film. Instead Astaire contented himself with a dance vaguely in "Negro dialect," as he had previously done "Chinese" and "German" dances on the stage and in *Dancing Lady* (1F)—and with the same benign unconcern about being offensive. The "Bojangles" solo is jaunty, cocky, rhythmically complex (even by Astaire's standards), and, in the slang of the time, "hot." In addition, the number makes use of some loose-pelvised hip thrusts. If there is a black reference, it is not Robinson but, rather, the *Porgy and Bess* character Sportin' Life, a role Bubbles had created on the stage the year before. The flashy sport jacket and bowler Astaire wears certainly suggest that character more than Robinson, who was usually dressed with conservative elegance. Otherwise, it is pure Astaire.

Interestingly, Astaire's makeup is not a true blackface. Normal stage makeup on whites is designed principally to highlight the eyes and the mouth by darkening them. Blackface does this in reverse: all areas *except* the mouth and eyes are darkened. Blackface is caricature mostly because of the large whitened area around the mouth, which creates the effect of exaggeratedly large lips. In Astaire's makeup only the lips themselves are whitened.

The music for the "Bojangles of Harlem" number is an amalgam. Astaire wanted a tune with bounce and syncopation, and Kern's instincts tended toward operettalike ballads.[9] Kern supplied a long, loping melody with some contrasting rhythmic sections. Much of the bounce in the number comes from Bennett's arrangement, which underscores the melody with jazz-oriented countermelodies. In addition, most of Astaire's solo portions in the number are set to a brilliant, cyclic vamping idea that modulates chromatically. This was apparently the contribution of Hal Borne and was worked out in rehearsals with Astaire. Borne plays it on the soundtrack on a piano doctored to sound almost like a harpsichord—a bright, brittle quality that suits the number beautifully.[10]

Having done numbers with an all-male chorus in his previous two pictures, Astaire now reverted to the more usual Hollywood accompaniment of an all-female chorus. This number, which takes place onstage at the nightclub, is opened by twenty-four women—twelve dressed in white, twelve in black, all in sepia makeup. They sing the verse of the song while performing some hip-swaying patterns (F2). The choreography by Hermes Pan is snappy and impudent, though somewhat repetitive.

Panels open to reveal gigantic shoe soles featuring lips and a derby hat to suggest a caricature of a black face (F3). As the women sing the chorus, they sidle over to the feet, pull them apart to reveal two huge legs at whose crotch sits Astaire, and then haul away the legs.

After that somewhat grim episode, Astaire frolics forward while the chorus concludes the song (F4).[11] His scampering, quick-footed dance instantly establishes the cocky, hyper-energized character he is portraying. Somewhat crouched over (quite the opposite of the almost regal Robinson), Astaire delivers a series of bright, skittery shuffle steps with flailing arms, giving the impression of hovering a few inches above the floor while tapping out his rhythm.

[9] Astaire's initial frustration is recalled by Dorothy Fields: "Fred took me aside, 'My God, can we ever get a tune that I can *dance* to? *Syncopated?*' And the two of us sat with Jerry, and Fred hoofed all over the room and gave him ideas . . . and finally Jerry came up with a very good tune, 'Bojangles of Harlem.' "

[10] According to Bordman, this section of the score appears in Kern's manuscript marked "Jig Piano Dance," and was not published with the song. Kern, getting wind of Borne's intervention, became furious, warning "that Borne was not to compose any music for the film and demanding RKO not pay him for any composition." But Borne says he "got paid a whole lot of money" for his contribution. Production records include a note indicating Astaire requested that Borne be given some credit in the titles, such as "additional musical arrangements by," but that never materialized.

[11] The shoe and amputation sequence was in the otherwise largely unused "Hot Fields" scenario. The song's lyric, which, fortunately, is mostly incomprehensible on the soundtrack, observes that the whole town is at Bojangles' heels, leaving flats, missing meals, and running "like rats going astray." Presumably because of this mayhem, it concludes by urging Bojangles to "throw those long legs away." However, when the chorus sings these last words, the legs have already been removed. The lyric is delivered with regrettable clarity on Astaire's 1936 recording of the song.

E1 E2 F1 F2

F3 F4 F5 F6

After reaching the front (there are a couple of especially nice moments when he pretends to be startled by the taps of the chorus behind him), Astaire performs to Borne's piano/harpsichord vamp melody a solo consisting of a darting sequence of quick tap shuffles, the rhythm embellished with occasional clacks generated by clappers affixed to the palms of his gloves. Toward the end of the solo he adopts an ingratiating, Al Jolson–like pose (F5) and then scampers away, only to return to deliver a series of tap turns and to hit the Jolson pose again as a finish.

Now Astaire confidently embarks upon the task of partnering all twenty-four women in the chorus simultaneously to a slowed-down rendering of the Kern melody by a jazz band. The choreography—clear, uncluttered, and highly imaginative—is built mostly on the hip-thrusting idea from the opening dance of the chorus, embellished now with a loose-ankled sidling step. The chorus forms itself into trios, one of which Astaire accompanies. As the women reform into lines, Astaire passes in front of them four times, picking up six dancers with each pass (F6), until he is partnering the whole group. At the end the formation splinters, and the women swirl into the wings, never to be seen again. Astaire's opening solo and his dance with the chorus are captured in a single take by Stevens' active boom camera.

Continuing his loose, hovering shuffle steps upstage, Astaire finds himself accompanied now by three gigantic male shadows (F7). This portion of the number involved optical printing, by which his solo and the dance of the three shadows were filmed separately and then combined on the same composite negative.[12] The basic idea of the shadow dance originated with Hermes Pan, who recalls that one day in the rehearsal studio there happened to be three different sources of light on him, which gave him three separate shadows as he moved. Intrigued by the effect, he showed it to Astaire: "I just pointed. I didn't have to say anything." The idea then evolved to the approach used in the film.

Astaire continues his loose-armed, scampering tap steps, now also incorporating some swaying hip thrusts to music built from Borne's piano vamp (F8). Throughout, the shadows stay in perfect synchronization—an effect that tends to distract from the dance since the viewer is likely to be set wondering whether the shadows are real, looking for instances of faulty coordination.[13] In due course, however, the problem is resolved—Astaire suddenly stops and the shadows continue (F9). Then there is something of a race. Astaire catches up with the shadows' routine and is soon outstripping them, until they become exhausted and, shrugging in defeat, stagger off.

To a brassy, slowed-down rendition of the Kern melody, Astaire has a final, triumphal solo, a tap extravaganza in which all the extremities take part—feet tap floor, hand clappers tap each other, hand clappers tap feet (F10). Then, easing into a casual swagger, Astaire ambles off stage, waving limply—a somewhat weak ending (F11).

G
NEVER GONNA DANCE
(5′54″)

As he takes his bow for the solo, Astaire is startled to see his fiancée in the audience. As she makes her way backstage to see him, some gangsters force Astaire to gamble, using a fixed deck to win back the contract for Metaxa's band. At this point Rogers comes upon the scene. She discovers that Astaire has broken a promise not to gamble, and then Astaire embarrassedly introduces her to his fiancée. Doubly hurt, Rogers walks out and promptly informs Metaxa that she will marry him.

From this clumsy and improbable episode, made convincing largely by Rogers' sensitive performance, the film moves to a scene that is one of the most moving in Astaire's film career. The somber Astaire encounters Rogers and the gloating Metaxa on the deserted floor of the nightclub (G1). When he asks to speak with Rogers, the wary Metaxa, on her urging, leaves his bride-to-be alone with Astaire, telling her that he will wait for her in the car. His exit path is important since it defines the architecture of

[12] Writing in a professional magazine in 1936, Vernon Walker, chief of camera effects at RKO, says the shadow dance was filmed first—Astaire "danced before a blank white screen, on which a Sun Arc projected a clear shadow." This shadow image was then apparently tripled optically. "Next, he did his foreground dancing under ordinary lighting, but before a blank screen." Finally, the shadow shot and the foreground shot "were combined by means of multiple optical printing." Synchronizing the dancing "was made easier by projecting the shadow-film onto a screen Astaire could watch while he did the foreground dancing." The two-minute trick solo is presented in five shots in the film and, according to studio records, was shot in three days, one of which ran to midnight.

[13] In "Puttin' On the Ritz" in *Blue Skies* (20 F), Astaire dances with a chorus made up of mirror images of himself, but in that dance he purposely breaks the illusion of synchrony early on.

F7 F8 F9 F10
F11 G1 G2 G3

the number that follows: he climbs one of the two staircases that lead to the upper landing (G 2) and leaves through the doorway at the top. Although she is delayed several times by Astaire, Rogers will, in the course of the dance, follow this same path, and when she flees through the doorway at the end of the number it is to join Metaxa, abandoning the forlorn Astaire.

The dialogue for Astaire and Rogers after Metaxa has left is thoughtfully written and beautifully acted. They are two people who have little more to say to each other but who cannot bear to part. The words are sparse and tentative, the logic elusive and essentially irrelevant.[14] Rogers quietly tells Astaire of her impending marriage to Metaxa, and there are various halting and self-conscious apologies from both sides. Astaire sadly bids her good-bye and wishes her "good luck . . . and all that." As she is about to leave, she looks at him directly and asks, "Does she dance very beautifully?" "Who?" Astaire responds. "The girl you're in love with." "Yes, very." "The girl you're engaged to, the girl you're going to marry." "Oh, I don't know. I've danced with you. I'm never going to dance again" (G 3).

Rogers turns and slowly starts to mount the stairs. But she stops to listen when Astaire begins to sing "Never Gonna Dance" to her (G 4, 5). The lyric for the song is filled with flighty, peculiar references: a "discreet" wolf who has taken everything from Astaire except his dancing feet, Groucho and Harpo Marx, radio amateur shows, clothes that dine where "they please." Some parts of the lyric don't even fit properly with the music. In its way it is as odd and illogical as the dialogue that precedes it, and in context it has a strange, affecting appropriateness. Kern's haunting music for the song is extremely unusual in form and in effect. It is a kind of rondo, ABACA, with the strident B and C sections contrasting sharply with the gently rocking rhythms of the main strain. The most memorable phrases come at the end of each of the A strains (not the beginning) and musically are almost a poignant afterthought as the singer sadly intones the title as part of four identical descending musical phrases: "Never gonna dance. Never gonna dance. Only gonna love. Never gonna dance."

Astaire's expression as he finishes is full of pain and yearning (G 5). Rogers quietly descends the stairs to be with him one last time, and a dance emerges—a dance about a shattered love affair, and about not dancing. Some of the music and choreography of their earlier relationship is reprised as Astaire seeks desperately to rekindle their romance by nostalgic association. But each attempt fails; the momentum of the dance repeatedly falters, and Astaire sinks deeper into despair.

When he had alienated Rogers earlier, Astaire had been able to win her back by singing "The Way You Look Tonight." A reprise of that music forms the score for the first part of the dance.[15]

As Rogers descends the staircase, Astaire takes her hand with great deliberateness and tenderness (G 6) and together they silently walk side-by-side around the floor, without looking at each other (G 7), an episode that, as Croce suggests, in part reflects the earlier dancing lesson (B 2). There are occasional pauses—silent, yet full of emotion (G 8)—and, rounding a corner, the stroll becomes briefly more decorative and vaguely dancelike (G 9), but it then returns to a pensive walk. Even when Astaire tries to partner Rogers (G 10), nothing catches; the familiar magic of their relationship is gone, and they go back to their gloomy stroll. A bit later she pauses, and, in a desperate move, he tries to wrap himself around her (G 11), but that, too, leads to nothing. Finally, as the melody subsides, the dancers ease to a stop near each other, but not touching (G 12). Then Rogers quietly abandons the slumped Astaire and begins to walk away purposefully, toward the staircase that leads to the waiting Metaxa (G 13).

To some transitional music Astaire runs after her, grabbing her wrist from behind and spinning her around to face him (compare 3 E 18 and 26 E 6). She is startled by this and perhaps a little frightened; Astaire's pose as she looks at him suggests both pain and desire (G 14). Now, without touching her, he tries to entice her into a dance as the orchestra boldly blares out a portion of "Never Gonna Dance." Facing him, she follows his gestures and begins to move (G 15). This leads to a fast, almost raucous section that blends stylized sweeps across the floor (G 16) with hurtling jumps.

Now Astaire makes his move: as the music

[14] In the various scripts for *Swing Time*, the dialogue for this scene got briefer—and better—with each revision.

[15] The music leads naturally from "Never Gonna Dance" to "The Way You Look Tonight" without transition. As Stanley Solomon has observed, the songs relate not only in the music, but also in the lyric: the word "never" is important in both songs—in the repeated title phrase of one and in the beautiful phrase "never, never change" in the other.

G 4 G 5 G 6 G 7

G 8 G 9 G 10 G 11

shifts to reprise the broad waltz from the "Waltz in Swing Time," Astaire flows into Rogers' arms and waltzes her around the floor with a partnered hopping step (G17) that is a direct reprise of the choreography to that music (D16, 17), itself a reprise of a step from their first duet at the dancing academy (B3, 5, 6). But even this explicit reminiscence doesn't work: this time the step leads nowhere, and the dance again disintegrates. The dancers separate and Rogers spins her way up one of the curved staircases, following Metaxa's path; Astaire ascends the other staircase and intercepts her on the upper landing (G18).

The furious dance on the landing is set to a frantic, compelling arrangement of the main strain of "Never Gonna Dance." Astaire repeatedly spins Rogers around the floor, sometimes traveling with her (G19), at other times propelling her on her own, like a top (G20). At the end he grabs her abruptly and holds her close one last time (G21). But she pulls away and dashes out the doorway (G22) as he sags, desolate and lost (G23; compare G13).

The entire dance through the flight up the stairs (G7–18) was accomplished in one continuous take. After the camera follows the dancers up the stairs with a dramatic crane shot, there is a cut to the dance on the landing, which was filmed separately. This dance on the landing was shot forty-seven times during a ten-hour shooting day, and Rogers' feet were bleeding before it was over.

H
THE WAY YOU LOOK TONIGHT / A FINE ROMANCE
(REPRISE) (57")

After "Never Gonna Dance," there are nine minutes remaining in the film, of which half are given over to laughing. In a scene that moves expertly from the somber mood of the dance duet to frivolous comedy, Astaire discovers his fiancée wants to marry someone else (H1). Complications are resolved, or at least submerged, in an all-laughing finale during which Astaire and Moore delay Metaxa's wedding by stealing *his* pants, framing the film in a sort of cheerful symmetry.

As Rogers joins in the laughing (H2), the previously venomous bandleader Metaxa unaccountably develops a sense of humor and is

G12 G13 G14 G15
G16 G17 G18 G19
G20 G21 G22 G23
H1 H2 H3 H4

transformed into a nice guy. He begins a song reprise that leads to the film's wonderful finale: Astaire and Rogers, overlooking a snowy Central Park, singing the film's two big hits, "The Way You Look Tonight" and "A Fine Romance," in counterpoint (H 3). At the end, as the sun breaks through the clouds, they fall into the closest they had come to a meaningful on-screen kiss in the series of films thus far (H 4).

A NUMBER CUT FROM THE FILM

I
IT'S NOT IN THE CARDS

At the beginning of the film a vaudeville routine was to be performed on stage by Victor Moore and Astaire, accompanied by six male assistants. In song, Moore asks repeatedly, "Do you want to see me do some card tricks?" Astaire responds negatively, but Moore does several anyway and fails miserably. Astaire sings, "You see it's not in the cards for you, Mister." Moore then explains how important card tricks are to him—as important as Mickey Mouse to Walt Disney, as important as fodder to a cow—to the accompaniment of harassing interjections by Astaire and the chorus (I 1). Moore resigns himself to failure and leaves the stage, and Astaire and the chorus do a brief spirited dance. In its finished form, the film begins during the final dance (A 1), as Moore reaches the wings. RKO music materials suggest the number was some four or five minutes long.

I1

The Silver Sandal set

8.

Shall We Dance

1937

Once the Fred Astaire–Ginger Rogers musicals, with their heavy emphasis on dance, had become an established success at RKO, an idea that seemed full of potential was to give one of the films a ballet setting. Although studio records suggest Astaire was not very enthusiastic about the idea, its attractiveness soared in 1936 when *On Your Toes* became a hit on Broadway. With music by Richard Rodgers and lyrics by Lorenz Hart, the show concerned an American hoofer who gets mixed up with a touring Russian ballet company. Highlights were its two satirical ballets (one of them the famous "Slaughter on Tenth Avenue") created by the great Russian émigré choreographer George Balanchine. Ironically, Rodgers and Hart had originally conceived their show as a film for Astaire. They tried to interest him in it in 1934, but Astaire was still insecure about his future in Hollywood, and, according to Rodgers, was "afraid his public wouldn't accept him in a role that would not allow him to wear his trademark attire of top hat, white tie and tails." The title song of the show contains one of Hart's tributes to Astaire: "The dancing crowds look up to some rare male—like that Astaire male."

Shall We Dance is an effort to exploit this successful formula.[1] Producer Pandro Berman even tried to secure the services of Balanchine for the film—a venture that would have brought about the most significant choreographic collaboration in the history of dance. Unfortunately, Balanchine, a great admirer of Astaire and Rogers, had recently become ballet master for the Metropolitan Opera and was committed for the period of filming.

Berman was more successful in his other effort to enrich the Astaire-Rogers formula with fresh New York talent: George and Ira Gershwin were enticed to the Coast to provide the film's score. As it happens, the attractive Gershwin score—songs and background music, brightly set by music director Nathaniel Shilkret and orchestrator Robert Russell Bennett—is one of the film's few outstanding features. The script's quest to find comedy in the contrast of the ballet and popular-dance worlds is halfhearted and inept, and the plot is built on a preposterous series of twists that become increasingly desperate as the film wears on. Most important, Rogers and Astaire, who had triumphed over inferior script material before, here seem to find themselves trapped in it. Their usual spontaneity is severely dampened, and the love story is less convincing than in any of their other films.

Perhaps in consequence of all this, the dance numbers fall significantly below standard, except for the "They All Laughed" duet, where the familiar glow is momentarily recaptured—and then thrown away. Most of the dances, appropriately enough, try to contrast ballet and popular dance, but none explores the differences with much wit or depth; for the most part ballet is shrugged off as pretentious and emptily decorative. Finally, and most egregiously, the film replaces the usual sumptuous Astaire-Rogers romantic duet with a grotesque episode in which Astaire finds himself partnering ballet contortionist Harriet Hoctor as part of a rambling production number.

THE GERSHWINS, ART, AND THE TRIP WEST

With economic decline on Depression-enervated Broadway and financial boom in Depression-stimulated Hollywood, the Gershwins started letting it be known that a Hollywood deal would be of interest to them. As early as October 1935, RKO received a report that they were "anxious to do an Astaire picture." Several studios expressed interest, but Ber-

[1] The source of the film's inspiration is suggested by some of the titles seriously considered for it. One of these was *On Your Ballet* which, one staff member observed sagely, is close to the original, but not actually a steal. Other titles tried to mimic the original's trisyllabic rhythms: *Watch Your Step, Stepping Stones, Stepping High* (which Astaire strongly vetoed), *Round the Town,* and *Stepping Toes,* a grotesque compromise that actually was the film's working title for a while. The final, rather blandly grand, title has this same rhythm and emerged in contest with *Dance with Me* and *Let's Dance.* Somewhere along the line *Twinkle, Twinkle* was also considered, but not, apparently, for long.

With Ginger Rogers in "Let's Call the Whole Thing Off"

man pursued the songwriters with the most ardor. At one point in the negotiations, Berman sent the Gershwins a night letter in which he sought both to close the deal and to reduce tensions with canny humor. It's a masterpiece of its kind:

> DEAR GENTS VERY MUCH SURPRISED TO HEAR FROM ARTHUR LYONS YOU HAVE DESCENDED TO COMMERCIAL MINDEDNESS, THOUGHT EVERYTHING BETWEEN US WAS IN A HIGHER REALM STOP NOT BEING A BUSINESS MAN MYSELF AND HAVING HEARD FROM THE TRADE YOU ARE ARTISTS WAS SURE WE HAD NOTHING MORE TO TALK ABOUT ESPECIALLY IN VIEW YOUR PROTESTATION OF WILLINGNESS TO SACRIFICE ALL FOR GOOD OLD RKO A SPIRIT WHICH I HAVE ADMIRED SINCE DEWITT CLINTON DAYS AND ONE WHICH LED ME BELIEVE WE HAD MADE A DEAL STOP SERIOUSLY I THINK YOU ARE LETTING A FEW THOUSAND DOLLARS KEEP YOU FROM HAVING LOT OF FUN AND WHEN YOU FIGURE THE GOVERNMENT GETS EIGHTY PERCENT OF IT DO YOU THINK ITS NICE TO MAKE ME SUFFER THIS WAY STOP PLEASE ADVISE LYONS CLOSE DEAL ACCORDING MY TERMS AND ALL WILL BE FORGIVEN BEST REGARDS

By June 1936, Berman had worked out a deal: $55,000 for one picture with an option for a second at $70,000. These fees were substantially lower than those received by Irving Berlin and Jerome Kern for earlier Astaire films, yet Berman had to struggle with studio executives to get the Gershwin fee as high as he did. The concern in Hollywood was that George Gershwin, who had had a series of flops on Broadway since 1931, could no longer write hits; moreover, with his *Porgy and Bess* opera of 1935 and with his extensive concertizing, he seemed to have gone irretrievably highbrow.

In an effort to reassure his potential employers, Gershwin wired his agent to tell them "RUMORS ABOUT HIGHBROW MUSIC RIDICULOUS STOP AM OUT TO WRITE HITS." He made good his threat: the three film scores he wrote before his sudden death in 1937 (*Shall We Dance, A Damsel in Distress,* and *The Goldwyn Follies*) contain several important hits. In general, these film songs are notable for their clear, tuneful directness and seem designed to communicate effortlessly with the audience. Nonetheless, the fears of the Hollywood brass were not entirely fanciful. The written responses of the audience at the *Shall We Dance* preview suggest some mystification about the music. Eight people commented on the music, only two favorably; the others complained that the music was "mediocre," "not up to usual standard," or had "no 'tone' or apparent 'melody.' " And while hits did emerge from the film, *Shall We Dance* was not nearly as successful in this respect as any of the four previous Astaire-Rogers films (see Table 5).[2]

THE SCRIPT AND THE PRODUCTION

When the Gershwins arrived in Hollywood, they discovered that the screenplay for which they were to supply songs existed only as a general idea. Accordingly, they spun out a collection of songs suitable for any occasion—several witty love songs and, with Astaire in mind, a snappy rhythm number. Although in his concert music George Gershwin had been particularly occupied with blending popular musical styles with classical forms, he apparently found the basic idea of the film—the contrast of jazz and ballet—uninspiring: none of the songs reflects this notion.

The scriptwriters, including that Astaire-Rogers perennial Allan Scott, then set about trying to shape a story around the songs. Mostly they failed. The musical numbers are almost all clumsily embedded in the script, and the finale is the only dance number that does much to develop the central love story.

Astaire is cast as a world-famous ballet dancer who is interested in tap dancing, Rogers as a world-famous tap dancer who is uninterested in anything Astaire does. As the film

[2] In a note to the producer, Lela Rogers, Ginger's mother, complained that the problem lay with the orchestrations, which she found "too intricate."

opens, Astaire has fallen in love with Rogers merely from seeing her picture—a script device that elevates to absurdity the love-at-first-glance formula of two previous Astaire-Rogers films. (The event was all but terminal: except for *The Belle of New York,* Astaire never again appeared in a musical in which the story has him falling in love with his partner at first sight.)

Astaire pursues Rogers with his usual charming ardor and wins her over, not in a dance number, but in a beautifully staged sequence in which they walk their dogs on board an ocean liner. Their budding romance is shattered twice when Rogers, aswirl in various plot contrivances, angrily stalks out on Astaire. Of course, she never allows him to explain, but the film does contain one original idea: the lovers' inevitable conciliation happens in the context of a musical number.

There is a certain amount of glib comedy associated with this rocky romance. Astaire gets to put on a broad Russian accent, and there are some fairly deft *double-entendre* cracks ("Now that you're married, ma'am, I can go to bed with a clear conscience." "So can I."). But Rogers seems less able to leaven her usual flighty haughtiness with convincing vulnerability, and the romance seems capricious and stilted. And, of course, it does not help matters that the film contains not a single fully realized love dance. For the rest, the film relies on the endearingly addled humor of the blundering Edward Everett Horton and the priggish Eric Blore, who are given considerable opportunity to display their comedy wares.

Overall, there is a certain decadence to the film: familiar formulas are overworked until they become cheerless and pat. This is typified by the sets—the airily opulent designs that enlivened earlier films in the series here become oppressively, enervatingly extravagant. Box-office returns showed a considerable dropoff from the previous Astaire-Rogers films: *Shall We Dance* was, in fact, the least profitable to date. It was clearly time to seek new formulas.

THE CHOREOGRAPHY

Assisting Astaire was Hermes Pan, and on hand to contribute to the ballet material was Harry Losee. Losee, who was flown out from New York, seems, oddly enough, to have had virtually no background in ballet. He had done some show dancing and had worked in modern dance with Ruth St. Denis and Ted Shawn. After *Shall We Dance,* he accepted a contract at Twentieth Century–Fox, where he worked on two Sonja Henie ice-skating musicals.

With Rogers in "They All Laughed"

Astaire with George and Ira Gershwin

With Harriet Hoctor in "Shall We Dance"

Hoctor and corps de ballet in "Shall We Dance"

THE NUMBERS

A
REHEARSAL FRAGMENTS

In the opening scene, a poster picture of Astaire is shown (A 1, 2).[3] Though his pose is meant to suggest ballet, it verges on caricature. In place of the sleek, softly rounded classical line, the pose is aridly decorative—corkscrewed almost to contortion, and topped by angular arms and fingers.

Next, the audience is invited to accept a wildly improbable bit of casting: the bumbling, eternally flustered Edward Everett Horton as the snobbish impresario of a Russian ballet (that is, a Ballet Russe–type) company. He has come to a palatial Paris ballet studio where his company is taking class to some sparkling piano music provided by Shilkret and Gershwin (A 3). Horton's casting does, however, make it easier to accept Astaire in his role as the ballet company's leading (and apparently only) male dancer. An American who performs under an assumed Russian name, Astaire has been subversively studying tap dancing on the side. He has ideas about combining "the technique of ballet with the warmth and passion of this other mood." To demonstrate his thesis to the horrified Horton, Astaire does two fluttering balletlike leaps—the first performed with rounded arms, the second with straight arms and followed by a tap barrage (A 4, 5). How the taps add "warmth and passion" to the leap is not immediately apparent.

B
RHUMBA SEQUENCE
(27")

Besides discovering tap dancing, Astaire has managed to fall in love with a popular singer and dancer played by Ginger Rogers. Though he has never actually met her, he has a flip-picture book showing her dancing. On this evidence ("that's grace, that's rhythm") he bases his plan to dance with her someday and then, of course, to marry her.[4]

The flip pictures dissolve to a stage on which Rogers is dancing a rhumba with a tall, dark partner before an ugly Art Deco set. This brief sequence, choreographed by Hermes Pan, is designed to show off Rogers, and, at the beginning especially, her self-effacing partner is scarcely visible while she glides about, undulating her hips in front of him (B 1). The fragment ends with a beautiful lift sequence: he carries her through a series of direction-shifting partnered hops; then he spins, swirling her around him as he does so.

C
BEGINNER'S LUCK
(59")

Rogers' partner makes a pass at her backstage, and she angrily shoves him into the stage set's pool and storms back to her apartment. She is discussing her frustrations with her manager, Jerome Cowan, when Astaire turns up. At the

[3] Under the opening titles there is a wry welcome to the Gershwins from RKO: as the songwriters' names are flashed on the screen, a fragment from *Rhapsody in Blue* is played. Irving Berlin was similarly saluted in his first RKO film, *Top Hat*.

[4] The Gershwins suggested an opening scene in which Astaire would discover Rogers' picture on a Parisian kiosk. Exultantly dancing down the street, he proclaims in song, "Hi-ho! Hi-ho! At last it seems I've found her." The number was never shot, however, because it would have cost too much to construct the set. The song "Hi-Ho!" was not published until 1967.

A 1 · A 2 · A 3 · A 4 · A 5 · B 1 · C 1 · C 2 · C 3 · C 4 · D 1 · D 2

doorway he overhears her express disgust with simpering admirers, whereupon he enters the room and storms about, adopting a demeanor of grand arrogance laced with a heavy pseudo-Russian accent that seems to owe a great deal to the fractured Italianisms of Eric Rhodes in *Top Hat* and *The Gay Divorcee* (C1). After Astaire has made his bounding exit (C2), he overhears that Rogers plans to take the next day's ship to New York. He arranges to travel on the same ship.

Back at his studio, he feels called upon to do a bit of tap rehearsing to Gershwin's "Beginner's Luck," but is frustrated when his record gets stuck and then winds down (C3, 4).

D

SLAP THAT BASS

(4′42″)

On board ship, Astaire makes for the boiler room—spacious, shiny, immaculately white, and preposterously unreal—where the black engine crew is holding a convenient jam session. One of their number, Dudley Dickerson, sings the verse of the upbeat Gershwin song (D1), and Astaire, catching the rhythm, sings the chorus (D2) and propels himself into a vigorous tap solo. Some nineteen minutes into the film, this is its first substantial musical number.

Unfortunately, the number scarcely justifies the wait. The song is too calculatedly bouncy and has inspired a dance that is too calculatedly playful, filled with choreographic noodling and inconsequential gimmickry. Here and there a few fragmentary ideas emerge—some nice rhythmic inflections near the beginning (D3) and some flowery "balletic" arm positions which Astaire hits and then pointedly abandons (D4). There is also some amusing heels-only tapping with the toes pointed skyward (D5). But these ideas are neither developed nor collected, and soon they are jettisoned as Astaire vaults up to a catwalk that winds along the wall.

At this point the solo becomes episodic and gimmick-laden. Astaire, in front of various chugging machines, performs tap passages relating to their beat or supplies silly visual imitations of their workings (D7).[5] At one point he hits, and then shrugs off, a vaguely balletic pose—an idea that, again, is incidental (D6). The number ends with a set of blistering spins down the catwalk (D8), a last twirling tap flurry, and a lunge into an applause-seeking pose (D9).

E

WALKING THE DOG

(2′38″, 1′41″)

Out of snobbishness, Horton disapproves of Astaire's attraction to the popular performer and has set himself the task of keeping them apart. But Astaire, by swaying from side to side, is able to convince Horton that the ship is rocking, and, fearing he is becoming seasick, Horton abandons his charge, leaving Astaire free to pursue Rogers.[6]

The pursuit is accomplished during two arresting sequences set to some wonderfully jaunty background music composed for the occasion by Gershwin. Published as "Promenade" in 1960, the music is beautifully set for a small orchestra,

[5] According to Pan, this idea arose when he and Astaire were walking past a studio cement mixer. "Fred began to dance against the rhythm and just about worked out the routine on the spot." It was then written into the script.

[6] In the film *Anything Goes*, released the year before *Shall We Dance*, Bing Crosby and Ida Lupino use the same device on Arthur Treacher, a fact that, rather amazingly, had no intimidating effect here.

D3 D4 D5 D6 D7 D8 D9 E1 E2 E3 F1 G1

the sound clean and transparent. It has been suggested that this was the composer's wry comment on the overblown orchestrations so common in Hollywood. Unfortunately, as the history of the Hollywood musical was to show, the jibe had no impact.

The sequences are pantomimic but have the impact of a carefully constructed dance number. Discovering Rogers walking her little dog, Astaire rents a large one and joins her in the stroll (E1). Irritated, she resists his playful advances. A bit later, Astaire calmly shows up walking a bevy of dogs, an act that appeals to Rogers' sense of humor (E2). In the next shot they are shown walking briskly, arm in arm, with only Rogers' little dog in attendance (E3).

F
BEGINNER'S LUCK
(1′ 10″)

When the couple pause at the ship's rail, Astaire tells Rogers of his love for her by singing the verse and a single chorus of another undistinguished Gershwin song (F1). Thus far, the chief musical interest has been in the background score. But soon the audience is to be bombarded with three blockbuster songs in a row.

G
THEY ALL LAUGHED
(4′ 24″)

There are a number of plot complications to be served up before the first of these songs is performed, however. Through a series of misunderstandings, people have come to believe that Astaire and Rogers are already married and, in fact, going to have a baby. Horton, ordered by Astaire to explain things to Rogers, deliberately alienates her, and she, in a characteristic huff, flees the ship in a mail plane with plans to drop out of show business and marry a Park Avenue socialite. In New York Rogers reassures her prissy, chinless fiancé about the marriage rumors, while the manager of her hotel—played by Eric Blore, who gets to do an amazing amount of his patented mugging in the film—fusses and sputters in confusion over whether the Astaire-Rogers marriage is myth or reality (G1).

As Rogers' manager, Cowan has an interest in breaking up her plans to leave show business for marriage. He contrives to get her to perform with Astaire at a rooftop nightclub, apparently hoping that Astaire will win her over (and away from her fiancé) during the course of a playful duet. It's as if Cowan had seen a couple of earlier Astaire-Rogers films, and "They All Laughed" does follow the general pattern of some illustrious predecessors: Rogers, standoffish at the beginning, soon warms to Astaire's challenge and charm, and thoroughly enjoys being with him by the end. Amazingly, however, the duet causes no perceptible alteration in the film's romantic development. Afterward Astaire continues to yearn for Rogers and she continues calmly to plan her wedding to her unlikely fiancé. Still, since the duet is by far the film's finest dance number, any criticism would be a form of churlish ingratitude.

It is unfortunate that the scriptwriters were unable better to integrate this superb song into the story. Its lyric, which does not reveal its true subject—love—until halfway into the chorus, is witty and brightly crafted. As used here, however, it is thrown away rather than used as choreographic motivation. Ira Gershwin says the lyric's origin was in the 1920s ad copy "They all laughed when I sat down to play the piano."

As the floor show begins, Rogers is invited to sing with the band. She does so with sweet liveliness while her fiancé beams witlessly from the audience (G2, 3). She is startled, however, when the bandleader, on Cowan's instructions, an-

G2 G3 G4 G5
G6 G7 G8 G9
G10 G11 G12 G13

nounces that Astaire will join her in a dance number.

On cue, Astaire bounds to the stage area and makes a grand show of fluttering extravagantly around her to some dramatic music that Gershwin called "Balloon Ballet" (G 4, 5). Astaire seems to be parodying not only the supposed pretentiousness of ballet but also, rather startlingly, those moments of sagging, bent-kneed yearning found in the intensely serious romantic duets in his previous two films (compare G5 to 6 J 4, 11, 13, 16, 20, 27, and 7 G 13, 14, 23). Much of the humor here derives from the choreography's extreme musical literalness—one dramatic gesture for each note in the music. Rogers, appalled and intensely embarrassed by the improbable human whirlwind wafting around her, pulls in on herself as if trying to become as small as possible.

In due course Astaire returns to earth and, taking Rogers lightly by the hand, bows to her with mock gallantry. Soon he flutters away across the floor so that the camera, in following him, loses her from the frame entirely—an event almost unique in Astaire's numbers (G 6). As he holds a portentous pose, the camera abruptly and amusingly pans to Rogers—one of the very few times in any of Astaire's dances that the camera deliberately calls attention to itself.

By now Rogers has regained some of her composure, and she raps out a perky tap routine in impudent contrast to Astaire's grand posturings. It carries her toward him (G 7) and ends as she pertly snaps her fingers. He responds by loping around her grandly, with exaggerated delicacy (G 8). Then he explodes into a raucous tap barrage (G 9) and comes to rest beside her. It's the first time he's displayed in public the results of his private study of her kind of dancing, and she's wary but impressed.

As the orchestra swings into a lively rendering of the song, the dancers lapse into some cool tap, side by side in place. The opening portions of this dance show the Astaire-Rogers partnership at one of its dizzying peaks: not much happens, and everything happens. The tone of this portion of the dance, set to opulent jazz clarinet, is quiet and unaffectedly conversational, yet it bubbles with intricate surprises. Many of these are rhythmic—sly tempo modulations and body inflections. Others come from the subtle game the two performers are playing with each other—the sidelong glances, the challenges they wordlessly extend and parry. At one point, for example, Astaire emphasizes a tap point with a drooping extended hand, a gesture that Rogers imitates—or mocks—a second later (G 10, 11).

This side-by-side tapping gradually becomes friskier, developing finally into a funny little backward lurch (G 12) that propels the dancers into a bouncy circumnavigation of the floor (G 13). The lurch capitalizes on a witty facet of the music—the breathless pickup notes that lead to the release strain (the first three notes under the words "They laughed at *me* wanting you"). These notes propel the song along without the pause that might seem logical at that point, and the choreographic joke is to suggest the notes catch the dancers unprepared as well.

Then there are some buoyant spins, another amusingly awkward lurch (G 14), and, as the clarinet is heard again, a casual return to the sauntering side-by-side tap of the opening.

As the orchestra comes to the end of the chorus, the tapping becomes more vigorous, and the dancers send the musicians into a second chorus with a series of heavy, half-falling tap slams (G 15). Soon the dancers are facing each other for the first time in sequences that alternate tapping with broad skyward swoops of the arms (G 16).

Next comes a brilliant blending—or miscegenation—of ballet and tap: Rogers spins perkily under Astaire's upraised arms in a ballet finger turn as he taps out a lively rhythm with his feet (G 17). This idea is repeated for a remarkably long time by Astaire's usual standards—it takes them around the stage almost twice—but they finally explode out of it to deliver a set of syncopated tap slams as they retreat toward the band area.

Two convenient white pianos become props for the dance's exhilarating finale. First Astaire lifts Rogers up so she is sitting on one of them. Then he brings her down into his arms—the first time in the dance they've been so close—and they spin across the floor (G 18). He deposits her on a step, collects her (G 19), romps back across the floor with her, and thrusts her up onto the piano again. For a second it looks as if he's going to end the dance by hopping up onto the other piano (G 20), but instead he reverses direction and vaults up next to Rogers. At the fade-out they are seen to be grinning happily (G 21).

H
LET'S CALL THE WHOLE THING OFF
(4′ 24″)

Taking no notice of what has clearly been going on in this splendid dance number, the script

G14 G15 G16 G17
G18 G19 G20 G21

plods onward. Cowan, still scheming to break up Rogers' ensuing marriage, has the sleeping Astaire photographed while being watched over by a lifesize Rogers mannequin (H1). This photograph is used by the newspapers as evidence that Astaire and Rogers are married. Rogers' fiancé, while apparently believing her when she proclaims the photo a fake, nevertheless suggests they postpone the announcement of their engagement.

To escape reporters, Astaire and Rogers sneak away in disguise. They regroup in Central Park and rent roller skates (H2). Resting on a bench, they get into a convenient disagreement over the correct pronunciation of "either" and "neither" and soon are launched into a song that muses somewhat cutely about such differences. Rogers sings one chorus of the song, although the lyric, which suggests she couldn't bear to part from Astaire, hardly matches her presumed feelings at this point in the plot. So she sings in a jocular manner, apparently trying to suggest she is not serious about the words' import. Ira Gershwin may have been inspired by the uneasy mutual dependency of the Astaire-Rogers partnership when he devised the lyric—and perhaps even by their diction, because in real life Astaire does tend to say "eyether" and Rogers "eether."

This leads, of course, to a dance on roller skates. A noble and amusing experiment, it is crafted with affection and care, but the gimmick ultimately proves more restrictive than liberating. When the dance begins, they are trying their skates out as tap shoes while still sitting on the bench. Not only does this generate a pleasant crunchy sound, but they find that they can spin their wheels in the air to create a churning resonance—an interesting discovery that is not developed further (H3).[7] Soon they are gliding about, arm in arm (H4) or in ballroom partnering position (H5). They pause to clank out some straight tap steps with the skates but before long are sprawling backward off-balance—a comic effect neither has the requisite skating skills to bring off well (H6).

After a few more gliding circumnavigations of the floor (H7), including a beautiful swoop around the upstage edge (H8), the dancers skate toward the viewer (H9) and pause as the camera cuts to a more distant shot—the only cut in the dance, but rather clumsily obvious by Astaire's standards. The dance concludes with a lengthy chugging promenade (H10) and a climactic glide (in a pose that looks suspiciously like a ballet arabesque) that sends the dancers toppling into the grass (H11, 12).

I
THEY CAN'T TAKE THAT AWAY FROM ME
(2′12″)

In order finally to settle the rumors about her marriage to Astaire, Rogers proposes they actually get married and then get divorced—a scheme that, if nothing else, adds an important new entry to the annals of hare-brained plot devices. The wedding is perpetrated in New Jersey, and on the fog-shrouded ferryboat ride back to New York, Rogers finds herself depressed. When Astaire ardently sings of the way he'll always remember her, tears well in her eyes (I1).[8] The setting is not ideal for a romantic dance, but the emotional situation is. Unfortunately, the moment is passed over.

J
SHALL WE DANCE
(10′35″)

Back in New York, Rogers' resistance to Astaire has crumbled. But now that he is in the driver's seat, Astaire for some reason decides to play hard to get, a ploy that misfires when he is suddenly visited by an old flame and Rogers discovers them together (J1). In an instant Rogers packs, storms out of her hotel room, and begins divorce proceedings.

The scandal over the marriage causes the ballet company's opera-house engagement to be canceled. They find work at the roof garden, however, and Astaire decides to mount a show there combining ballet and jazz in which he will dance with images of Rogers since he can't dance with the real thing.

The resulting production number continues the film's uncomprehending efforts to blend dance forms. It opens with a chorus of female ballet dancers (some of whom seem to be pre-

[7] In general the skating sounds, dubbed after the film was shot, tend to be unnaturally precise and are mixed in too loudly on the sound track.

[8] George Gershwin was apparently unhappy with the handling of this song, a special favorite of his: "They literally throw one or two songs away without any kind of plug." However, the song does get about as much play as, for example, "The Way You Look Tonight," in *Swing Time*: the lengthy song is sung once through (including the verse) and then reprised as part of a dance number later in the film.

H1 H2 H3 H4
H5 H6 H7 H8

H9 H10 H11 H12
I1 J1 J2 J3
J4 J5 J6 J7
J8 J9 J10 J11
J12 J13 J14 J15
J16 J17 J18 J19

teen-agers) puttering around. A ballet soloist, Harriet Hoctor, wafts in from the wings and is soon rendering an elliptical backbend on pointe, a specialty trick she had perfected as a vaudeville and Ziegfeld Follies headliner (J 2).[9]

She is approached by Astaire, dressed in black trousers and a white blouse. His manner is affected and tentative (J 3). In due course he partners her in a ghastly duet that seems designed mostly to show off Hoctor's fluid torso. They lean and pull and flutter about vapidly, registering no emotion whatever, except perhaps, on Astaire's part, embarrassment (J 4, 5). The choreography, presumably arranged by Losee and set to a reprise of "They Can't Take That Away from Me," shows little musical sensitivity, ignoring the ingenious rhythmic nuances.[10]

The duet, in fact, concludes before the music does, and Astaire watches Hoctor slip from his grasp and vanish into the wings. Now the stage is invaded by a chorus of women, each wearing a Ginger mask, as Astaire registers what one might take to be puzzlement (J 6). At this point the real Ginger happens to come to the nightclub to deliver the divorce summons to Astaire. Intrigued and touched by Astaire's gesture, she watches for a while and then asks Cowan to take her backstage (J 7).

Meanwhile, onstage, Astaire is supposedly torn between Hoctor and one of the Ginger dancers. He eventually opts for the Ginger impersonator, and Hoctor, in response, proceeds to deliver two variations on her backbend routine: your back kicks to the head (J 8) and your rapid swirlings (J 9). After flopping decoratively to the floor, she flits offstage with her corps de ballet, never to be seen again.

Astaire, now in white tie and tails, strides on stage confidently, as if relieved of some terrible burden. Framed by the Ginger girls, he spiritedly sings the title song. Then he bounds gleefully through a half-minute solo dance in which bold, dramatic gestures (J 10, 11, 13) are alternated with scampering tap frolics (J 12). Some of the dramatic poses are reminiscent of the duet with Hoctor (for example J 3), but here the limp tentativeness is gone: the gestures are delivered with assertiveness, clarity, and sumptuous musicality. If it is the film's intention to demonstrate that show dancing is superior to (what it takes to be) ballet, the message is here for once delivered with pungent effectiveness. The solo concludes with some explosive leaps and spins and a final openly declarative pose (J 14).

Having changed backstage into a chorus dancer's sleek black gown, Rogers now blends in among her impersonators (J 15). When Astaire becomes aware of the ruse, he systematically scampers from one dancer to the next until he finds the genuine article (J 16). To a reprise of the title song, Rogers and Astaire dance a brief duet of celebration which seems especially designed to exploit Rogers' beautifully flexible back in telling contrast to the Hoctor distortions (J 17, 18). At the end they sweep jubilantly downstage and sing "who's got the last laugh now?" (J 19).

[9] The twenty-nine-year-old Hoctor had been doing her backbend routine onstage since 1923 and returned to Broadway after this scene was shot. Although it was rumored she might become Astaire's partner in his next film, her only other film appearance was in MGM's *The Great Ziegfeld* of 1936. Comparing the two films at the time, she sweetly told an interviewer, "Naturally I prefer *Shall We Dance*, because in *The Great Ziegfeld* I danced with two lions. It is more fun to dance with Fred Astaire." Regrettably, the lion dance was cut from the film.

[10] Twelve years later, in *The Barkleys of Broadway* (22 1), Astaire choreographed a duet to "They Can't Take That Away from Me" that brilliantly atones for his complicity in this musical travesty.

With Rogers and lookalikes in "Shall We Dance"

9.

A Damsel in Distress

1937

During the 1930s Fred Astaire was concerned that, having survived the breakup of his partnership with his sister, Adele, he was now becoming bound up in another team effort, this one with Ginger Rogers. For this reason, he insisted in his 1936 five-film contract with RKO that one or two of these films be without Rogers. *A Damsel in Distress* is the lone Ginger-less film of the five, and it was the first of the few films in Astaire's career to lose money. Its neglect is unfortunate, for it is one of the most unrelievedly delightful films Astaire ever made.

Under the nimble direction of George Stevens, the film laces the felicitous fancies of Astaire and the screwball antics of George Burns and Gracie Allen into a cheery script derived from an affectionately satiric novel by P. G. Wodehouse. Blended into this concoction are songs by George and Ira Gershwin which are probably the best ever written for an Astaire film—and, therefore, for any movie musical.

Choreographically the film is a study in obstacles—as if Astaire consciously set out to make things as difficult as possible for himself. Perhaps to avoid any unpleasant comparisons with Rogers, he allowed himself to be cast opposite Joan Fontaine, the weakest dancer (or most obvious nondancer) he ever worked with.[1] Furthermore, he chose to do his duet with her out of doors, on rough turf amid trees and fences. Then he cooked up two trios with a pair of comedians (Burns and Allen), at all times having to rein in the choreography to the level of the weaker of the two. (Burns describes himself as "sort of a right-legged dancer. I could tap with my right foot, but my left foot wanted me to get into some other business.") Finally, his big solo is almost ludicrously restricted—it is staged to take place on one spot on the floor and is filmed all in one shot. That the quality of the dances in this film is so high is a breathtaking triumph of self-willed artist over self-imposed constraint.

THE FILM AND GEORGE GERSHWIN

The idea of making a movie out of the Wodehouse novel was George Gershwin's. RKO producer Pandro Berman purchased the film rights to the novel at Gershwin's urgings and then used this as part of an inducement package to bring the Gershwin songwriting team to Hollywood.[2]

Wodehouse has suggested that Gershwin was attracted to the book simply because its hero is a successful American composer of popular songs named George. But the parallels are actually much deeper. As it happens, the novel's George was beset with the same unease as the real George: an artistic and financial success, he was unable to find the ideal woman. The fictional George has just had "a success of unusual dimensions. . . . Yet he felt no elation. . . . He was lonely. . . . The solution of the problem of life was to get hold of the right girl and have a home to go back to at night. . . . He seemed to be alone in the world which had paired itself off into a sort of seething welter of happy couples." Biographers of Gershwin repeatedly note that he experienced the same malaise and anxiety: "He complained to intimate friends . . . that his life 'was all mixed up,' and that, despite his material and artistic successes, he could not find a suitable mate."

In the novel the hero's problems are miraculously solved. He is in London overseeing the British version of his New York hit show *Follow the Girl.* As he rides through town in a cab, a woman in distress hops in with him, and he shelters her from her pursuer. Although she soon vanishes as quickly as she had appeared, he almost immediately recognizes her as the woman of his dreams: "He was in love. . . . A curious

[1] Fontaine, nineteen years old when the film was shot, was an RKO contract player who had done several minor pictures for the studio. Although an American, she seemed to have the right aristocratic air for the part and was inexpensive. Her career flourished later—she garnered an Oscar for best actress in 1941 for her performance in Alfred Hitchcock's *Suspicion*—but she once told Astaire that *A Damsel in Distress* set her career back four years. The studio thought of casting Ruby Keeler in this role, and also very seriously pursued the fine (nondancing) comedienne Carole Lombard. Neither deal worked out. There was also some consideration of the British musical star Jessie Matthews, but she was unavailable.

[2] For a discussion of the wooing of the Gershwins, see pp. 115–16. As Wodehouse put it, Gershwin "used his considerable influence to have [the novel] done on the screen." Interestingly, Wodehouse once characterized his way of writing novels as "a sort of musical comedy without music."

happiness pervaded his entire being. . . . The sun was shining. . . . It had come at last. The Real Thing." Everything confirms his conclusion: when she writes him a note, he is amazed: "What a girl! He had never in his life met a woman who could write a letter without a postscript, and this was but the smallest of her unusual gifts." In one happy moment, then, his basic psychological problem has been resolved, and all he has to do now is (1) find out who she is, (2) pursue her with charm and ardor, (3) overcome various obstacles of station, background, and mistaken identity, and (4) marry her and live happily ever after—all of which is accomplished within the next two hundred pages.

There is no evidence that Gershwin spent a great deal of time riding around London in a cab with the doors unlocked, nor can it be claimed the two Georges are similar in all respects (the Wodehouse George, for example, is modest and unassuming); but the personal appeal of the novel to the lonely and lovelorn Gershwin seems obvious. The parallels are actually quite coincidental. Although Wodehouse and Gershwin had met (Gershwin had been a rehearsal pianist on a 1917 show in New York to which Wodehouse had contributed some lyrics), the composer was still very much an unknown in 1919, when the novel was published. Later Wodehouse worked with the Gershwins, and he and Ira in particular became lifelong friends.

THE MUSIC

The incredibly high quality of the score for *A Damsel in Distress* may well have been inspired at least in part by George Gershwin's personal identification with the moods and motivations of the hero in the novel. The songs were completed by May 1937, when the script was still largely unrealized, and accordingly must have been written primarily with the novel and a 1928 play version in mind. Indeed, the words of the film's most famous and most atmospheric song really tell the story of the novel more than the film script: "A foggy day in London town, had me low and had me down—suddenly, I saw you there—and through foggy London town the sun was shining ev'rywhere."

The Gershwins wrote nine songs for the film and eight were used, six of them prominently. Almost all of these reflect the novel or various English themes or identifications. Two, "A Foggy Day" and "Nice Work If You Can Get It," have become standards, while two others, "Things Are Looking Up" and "I Can't Be Bothered Now," are at least equally attractive. In addition there are two wonderfully witty tunes that form the basis for novelty numbers: "Put Me to the Test" and "Stiff Upper Lip." And finally, since the film takes place mostly in an English castle, the songwriters produced a comic madrigal, "The Jolly Tar and the Milkmaid," which is, as Oscar Levant somewhat exaggeratedly observes, "so deceptively authentic that most of those who heard it accepted it as seventeenth-century English," as well as (again in Levant's words) "a big robust tune, 'Sing of Spring,' which has the circumstance if not the pomp of Elgar."

The madrigal singers were included in part because of George Gershwin's disappointment over the way the songs were handled in his previous film, *Shall We Dance.* In a letter to a friend he complained the film included no "other singers than Fred and Ginger and the amount of singing one can stand of these two is quite limited. In our next picture . . . we have protected ourselves in that we have a Madrigal group of singers and have written two English type ballads for background music so the audience will get a chance to hear some singing besides the crooning of the stars."

Contributing in a major way to the remarkable musical success of *A Damsel in Distress* were the people in charge of arranging and orchestrating: music director Victor Baravalle (who was brought in at Astaire's urging), and arranger Robert Russell Bennett, here continuing the splendid work he had done on *Swing Time* and *Shall We Dance.* Astaire's rehearsal pianist, Hal Borne, also probably made a significant contribution. Because of them, the musical tone of the film is bright and brittle; assertive, witty, and imaginative; deeply felt but never mawkish or sentimental—just the way Gershwin would have wanted it.

THE SCRIPT

George Gershwin never saw the film: he died suddenly from a brain tumor on July 11, 1937. The script was completed only on September 25 and the film was first shown two months later.[3]

Wodehouse happened to be working in Hollywood at the time, and RKO had the intelligent idea of asking him to contribute to the script. He spent several weeks during the summer working on it, a job he found "uncongenial" though still

[3] Given the international shock caused by Gershwin's untimely death, it is remarkable that the film did so poorly at the box office. Miles Kreuger, however, suggests such deaths had a deflating effect on attendance, casting an eerie pall over the film. The films of the Astaire-Rogers series had all gotten a prestigious sendoff by being premiered at the Radio City Music Hall. However, that theatre passed by *A Damsel in Distress* (which made Astaire furious), and this might also have affected sales.

rather enjoyable because he was working with Stevens, whom he considered the best director around. At the time, he thought the book was "going to make a good picture." Considerably later, however, he was to alter the opinion: "Friends have often commented on the dark circles beneath my eyes and my tendency to leap like a jumping bean at sudden noises, and I find those phenomena easy to explain. It is only fifty years or so since I was involved in the shooting of *A Damsel in Distress*."

There were a number of changes from the novel, of course. Characters and events were compressed or eliminated, and scenes and relationships were altered to allow for the addition of Burns and Allen, whose inspired nonsense is one of the film's great pleasures. (In an effort to seek new formulas, Burns and Allen were borrowed from Paramount essentially as the comedy replacements for the likes of Eric Blore, Edward Everett Horton, and Helen Broderick. The change was permanent: none of these actors appears in either of the remaining Astaire-Rogers films at RKO.) The central woman—the damsel in distress—was given a more active role than in the novel, where she has few lines until the end. Some of the complexities of the plot were simplified: the novel has an ingenious structure of mistaken identities and purloined letters. And the character of the popular American composer named George was changed to a popular American dancer named Jerry.

There were two changes of particular note. In the novel, the hero pursues the damsel throughout and she only gives in at the end. In the film, the plot is reshaped into the standard Attraction-Breakup-Conciliation mold: Astaire wins her midway, loses her through a bit of fraud perpetrated by his press agent and by a conspirator in her castle, and then gets her back when confusions are clarified.

A second change involves the love-at-first-meeting theme. Astaire, unlike his counterpart in the novel, apparently does *not* fall in love with the damsel when he first meets her; he visits her castle mostly out of curiosity, it seems, and he appears to fall in love with her only after he becomes convinced (mistakenly) that she is in love with him. The love-at-first-glance theme had been used repeatedly in the Astaire-Rogers films—reaching maximum development in the preceding *Shall We Dance*, where Astaire falls hopelessly in love with Rogers from seeing only her picture. Presumably to get away from the cliché, this element was changed in *A Damsel in Distress*. Indeed, although Astaire was to make twenty-two more musicals, in only one, *The Belle of New York*, does the love-at-first-sight idea clearly reappear. In any case, the decision was unfortunate for *A Damsel in Distress*, because the love-at-first-sight element forms the motivating drive for the novel. It may even be that its presence in the novel was what made the producers think the story would be an appropriate vehicle for Astaire in the first place.

Actually, the love story is in general of less significance in this film than in most Astaire films. This is probably because Fontaine couldn't dance, which meant the love story had to be told almost entirely in words and song, whereas it was in dance that Astaire was usually best able to explore the range and depth of the love relationship. (In this film, for example, she falls in love with him, not during a dance, but when she slaps him after he tries to kiss her—hardly the usual Astaire scenario.) This does not mean the love story fades entirely from view, however. Stevens is too able a director and Astaire and Fontaine are too capable as actors for that to occur, and the love scenes (albeit brief) do have great charm and appeal. Furthermore, the music, particularly "A Foggy Day," is too deeply felt to suggest that love plays no role. But for the most part *A Damsel in Distress* is not so much a formula love story with great music and dances, like Astaire's Rogers films, as a wonderfully zany, yet affecting and memorable, comedy frolic (with great music and dances) through which a pleasantly engaging love story is threaded.

In this respect the general tone of the film is set not so much by Astaire as by Gracie Allen, who, with her usual daffiness, keeps everybody off-balance, brightens all her scenes, raises logic to new heights of absurdity, and inspires two fine dances—neither of which has much of anything to do with the plot.[4]

THE CHOREOGRAPHY

Hermes Pan was the dance director for the film, working with Astaire on the choreography. For the years 1935–37 there was an Academy Award for dance direction, and Pan received the 1937 Oscar in this category for the fun-house ("Stiff Upper Lip") number.[5]

[4] Allen's appeal has been thoughtfully characterized by Burns: "Contrary to opinion, Gracie is not a comedienne. She is an extremely good straight dramatic actress. It is the situations that are funny. The character she plays has what we call 'illogical logic'. She is completely earnest about what she is doing and saying, and I think it is the fact that she is so kind to the rest of the world for its lack of understanding of what is perfectly clear to her that makes people love her. She is right and everybody else is wrong, but she doesn't blame them—she just gently tries to explain to them, patiently, and puts up with everybody."

[5] He had received Academy Award nominations for the "Top Hat" and "Piccolino" numbers in *Top Hat* in 1935, and for the "Bojangles" number in *Swing Time* in 1936.

With Joan Fontaine

With Gracie Allen and George Burns in the fun-house number, "Stiff Upper Lip"

THE NUMBERS

A
I CAN'T BE BOTHERED NOW
(1′ 15″)

The film opens with a scene that sets up the scheming that gives the plot its momentum as well as its abrupt comedy shifts: the servants in Fontaine's castle have entered a betting pool on whom she will marry. Through fraud, the pompous butler (Reginald Gardiner) has drawn the name of the favorite, Fontaine's addled cousin, whom her domineering aunt is strenuously forcing on her. The page, meanwhile, has contrived to be assigned "Mr. X"—anybody *except* those named in the lottery. He knows Fontaine had fallen in love with an American the year before and expects him to win (A 1).

When Fontaine goes to London to meet her American, the butler follows in an attempt to prevent the meeting, and the page follows in an attempt to prevent the prevention. Pursued by the butler through the streets of foggy London, Fontaine jumps into a cab in which Astaire, a famous show dancer, happens to be riding. (The background music when Astaire is first seen riding through London is "A Foggy Day" rendered as a fugue—clearly this is to be no ordinary movie musically.) Astaire, amused, protects this damsel in distress from her pursuer (A 2).

After an altercation with the butler and with a London bobby, during which Fontaine escapes, Astaire himself flees. He soon comes across a Cockney street dancer who is doing an imitation of him (A 3).[6] When the crowd sees Astaire, they urge him to perform for them. He obliges, and his short number serves the function of delaying the pursuit by the butler and the bobby, who are stuck in the crowd, while Astaire maneuvers himself out onto the street. In the last instant of the dance, he hops aboard a moving bus to make his escape.

It is possible that Astaire at some point in his career performed a solo with more dazzle, wit, and contagious exuberance than this miniature, but if so he never filmed it. The number is performed in one exhilarating sweep. Astaire begins to sing breezily. (The song's lyric uses the word "shan't," an unlikely usage for an American—a wry commentary on the Wodehouse novel, perhaps, where the American hero is similarly inclined to utter improbable Britishisms.) Soon the compelling music takes over his body and he does a scrabbling little tap dance from side to side while illustrating some of the words: his furled umbrella is pointed skyward for "up among the stars," his left hand flutters outward for "throwing off the bars" (A 4). As song blends into dance, he is found cavorting amiably in a spread-legged tap figure (A 5), to which is soon added some sharp back kicks, which send his umbrella swinging in wide arcs (A 6). Next he adds the umbrella to the tap rhythm, shunting it from hand to hand in counterpoint to the rapping of his feet. Finally, he uses the umbrella to vault around the street (A 7), the last vault catapulting him onto the safety of a passing bus, from which he cheerfully waves as he vanishes from sight (A 8).

B
THE JOLLY TAR AND THE MILKMAID
(1′ 50″)

Meanwhile, back at the castle, everyone assumes Astaire is the American whom Fontaine loves, and her aunt orders her confined to the premises, although Fontaine's preoccupied father is sympathetic. The page forges a love letter to Astaire in Fontaine's hand, urging him to come to the castle and rescue her.

Reading the letter in the presence of his publicity team (George Burns and Gracie Allen), Astaire is amazed to discover Fontaine loves him after such a brief encounter and resolves to go to the castle to help her (B 1). This will also get him out of London, where Burns' overzealous publicity campaign has created the erroneous impression that Astaire is a great ladies' man—so much so that he is always being plagued by swarms of eager females.

Arriving at the castle on visitors' day, Astaire is barred from entering by the butler, who recognizes him from the London encounter. As Gracie Allen joins the castle tour and distracts the butler (by driving him to distraction), Astaire blends in with a group of madrigal singers and gains entry to the castle even under the inquisitive eye of Fontaine's aunt. As they sing the

[6] The dancer is Joe Niemeyer, a tap and eccentric dancer who had met Astaire in vaudeville in 1919. Their friendship was renewed when Niemeyer was hired, by sheer coincidence, for this bit role as Astaire's imitator. The role was to become a permanent one: Astaire invited Niemeyer, who was his size and a flexible dancer as well, to be his stand-in, a job Niemeyer enthusiastically carried out for twenty years. Niemeyer's other on-screen appearance in an Astaire film was in *The Belle of New York* (see 26 A).

A1 A2 A3 A4
A5 A6 A7 A8

Gershwins' mock madrigal, he heartily joins in (B 2).

The lyric tells of a milkmaid who turns down a sailor's advances because she is already the mother of three; the sailor then opines that a match would probably be unsuitable anyway, because he now recalls that he is already the husband of three. But the logic is difficult to follow in the choral arrangement, and most of the humor in the number comes from the gusto with which Astaire chimes in—harmonizing lustily, cheerfully taking the solo part to sing "I happen to be the mother of three," inserting a snappy tap-and-hip-bump phrase at one point, and, after starting to dash off at the end, returning hastily for the song's unexpected coda.[7]

C
PUT ME TO THE TEST
(2′58″)

With the aid of the page, Astaire gains an audience with Fontaine. The ensuing dialogue is artfully and amusingly arranged so that when she talks of the American she loves, Astaire assumes she is referring to him. To avoid her approaching aunt, Astaire flees to a balcony where the page provides a means of escape. Fontaine, assuming he has jumped, is mightily impressed.

Later, ensconced in a nearby cottage, Astaire is visited by Fontaine's father. Before the father enters, Astaire, thinking he comes with threats, jumps onto a table and takes down a sword with which to defend himself. The nimble little dance he makes out of this maneuver is one of the film's many delights. Meanwhile, the father, thinking Astaire is the American Fontaine loves, gives the union his blessing and assures him of her love. Astaire bounds into a jaunty dance after the father leaves, and Burns and Allen join in.

The dance has very little to do with the plot, but a great deal to do with Gracie Allen, and, like her, it has its own careful logic—at once compelling and absurd. For no reason, the three dancers happen to be armed with whisk brooms, which become an important prop in the dance, finding a multitude of likely and unlikely functions.[8] Gracie, who always seems to be in her own slightly askew world, soon finds herself out of synchronization with Astaire and Burns, who become piqued. This leads to a dance made up of a cascade of subtle kicks to the seat of the pants, in which, finally, three suits of armor participate. The dance combines the screwball charm of Burns and Allen with the meticulous symphonic craftsmanship of Astaire. Like Burns and Allen's art, it is filled with surprising, logically gnarled one-liners; like Astaire's art, the one-liners are savored, varied, developed, and connected into a broader coherent structure. The wonderful comic dance that emerges is filled with both incident and consequence.

It begins with Astaire rhythmically chanting a line from the script, "I've just begun to live," and leading Burns and Allen in a cocky stroll (C 1). The dancers interrupt their stroll for a quick tap barrage, and this serves as a fanfare to set the orchestra into action.[9] As it does so, the dancers, supremely satisfied with what they have accomplished, lapse back into their stroll.

The first part of the dance makes inventive use of the whisk brooms, structuring the sounds of various brushings of knee, elbow, and backside into the music's rhythms. At one point Astaire and Burns gallantly pause to brush off Allen (C 2); at another, the dancers whip off an incongruous bit of Irish or highland flinging[10] to

[7] The song was published in 1937, but was not recorded until 1976.

[8] The whisk-broom idea, notes Astaire, was brought in by George Burns. Burns has given two slightly different accounts of the origins of this dance in autobiographical books published twenty-five years apart. Anxious to please Astaire and to get the part in the film ("I wasn't going to lose a chance to work with Fred Astaire. Look what it did for Ginger Rogers"), Burns remembered a show-stopping act in vaudeville called Evans and Evans, a "two-dance" in which each used a whisk broom. One Evans had died (or retired) by 1937, but Burns located the other, brought him to Hollywood, and paid him for the rights to the routine and for instruction in how to do it. Burns, Allen, and Evans then auditioned the dance for Astaire, who loved it. Burns was pleased to have "located a dance Fred hadn't seen (some trick to begin with)" and to be in the position of teaching Astaire a dance: "and I can tell you something, he picked it up real fast; that boy's a pretty good dancer."

[9] Ira Gershwin wrote a lyric for this sprightly and engaging tune, but it is not used in the film. Inspired by the Wodehouse novel, the lyric is a pledge by a twentieth-century cavalier to do all sorts of daring deeds for his lady fair: climb the highest mountain, swim Radio City fountain, jump off the Eiffel (a trifle), ride a derby winner. The lyric, revised somewhat and with new music by Jerome Kern, was used in *Cover Girl* (1944). Regrettably, the Gershwin song has never been published or recorded.

[10] Allen, notes Burns, was a "great Irish dancer," a fact that may have inspired this passage. On the Burns and Allen radio show of July 26, 1937 (on which Hermes Pan was a guest), Allen was asked about the film and about how she rated as a dancer. "I'd say I'm between the world's best dancer, and the world's worst cluck." "Is that so?" "Yeah—I have to dance between Fred Astaire and George." As a running gag on the next three shows, she insisted on being called "Ginger."

B 1 B 2 C 1 C 2
C 3 C 4 C 5 C 6

an appropriate instrumental sequence (C3). At the end of the first chorus there is a deft whisk-broom-and-knee cadenza.

This sets off the second chorus, and, with great aplomb, the dancers flip their brooms into the air, catch them, and return to their self-satisfied stroll. Things (i.e., Gracie Allen) soon go awry, however. She falls out of step, causing Astaire and Burns to bump into her (C4). Annoyed, the men desert her and begin to stroll off fraternally, arm in arm (C5), but she is not so easily disposed of, and when they separate in order to perform a brisk pirouette, she coolly re-inserts herself between them (C6). There is a brief mimed argument over her impertinence, but the men apparently forgive her, and the trio regains its former composure, finding yet another use for the whisk brooms: as beards (C7).

Midway into the third chorus, the music abruptly launches into a tune called "Organ Grinder's Swing." Flustered only momentarily, the dancers soon work out the problem: Astaire becomes the organ grinder, Burns becomes the collector of tips, and Allen becomes (or continues to be) the dancing monkey (C8).

When they cheerfully return to their dance, however, Allen has once again fallen out of step —she thrusts back when the men thrust forward, and vice versa. With some effort and no little annoyance, the men eventually straighten her out, threatening dire consequences with their whisk brooms for future transgressions. Then, mollified, they brush her off again, and Astaire, presumably to hammer the message home, swats her once lightly over the head with his broom.

Allen is further punished as the trio ambles forward: Astaire neatly places a back kick to her rear (C9), and Burns adds one of his own for good measure. But she deftly wreaks vengeance by swinging from their arms and kneeing both their backsides simultaneously (C10), and then, with a satisfied smirk, strolls away (C11).

The dancers scoot around the floor defensively protecting their rear ends (C12). However, just when they have calmed down a bit, they are surprised by three suits of armor that assume life long enough to place kicks in appropriate spots (C13).[11] The dancers quickly retaliate: after deceitfully earning the armor suits' good will by giving them a brief dusting with their brooms, they lash out at them with a sharp back kick (C14). Alas, this is not a very good idea, the dancers realize, staggering away in pain and chagrin (C15).

Their final step is a version of an exit step (the "break a leg") often used by Bill Robinson. It is, accordingly, something of an inside joke: the step is quoted, but the queasy-leg aspect is given motivation, since that leg has just been injured in the kick. The camera work on this exit is unique in Astaire's films: the dancers essentially disappear by progressing off camera rather than behind some obvious cover, like a doorway or a stage wing—though there is a post at the extreme right of the frame that keeps the exit from being purely camera-related.

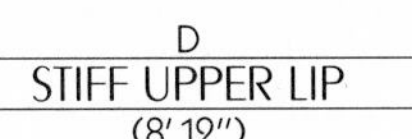

D
STIFF UPPER LIP
(8′12″)

At Fontaine's father's suggestion, Astaire arranges to run into her at a local fair. In a gondola going through the tunnel of love, she is cordial enough, but when he tries to kiss her she slaps him.

In the next gondola (D1) are Gracie Allen and Ray Noble (playing Fontaine's dim-witted cousin). They, too, are having a confusing conversation, though of course neither is aware of it: "I say, do you live here?" he asks, attracted. "No," she replies matter-of-factly, "where I live we sit in chairs." Throughout the rest of the film, Noble proves to be the perfect foil for Allen, accepting her logic with wide-eyed awe and following it blandly wherever it leads.[12]

With Astaire bewildered and soured by the slap, and Burns not having much fun at the fair, either, Allen feels called upon to cheer them up by singing an upbeat song urging them to maintain a stiff upper lip and expressing other appropriate British clichés—a stylistic tribute by Ira Gershwin to his old friend Wodehouse.[13]

As she concludes the song they are amused to discover that they are standing on one of two

[11] In reviewing the script before shooting, Hollywood's censorship office sternly warned: "There must be nothing vulgar in this business of the armor 'kicking Allen and Burns in the fanny.' "

[12] Noble, a musician who had attended Cambridge, came to the United States in 1934 and spent most of his career doing radio—leading bands and developing his comedy role as a dim-witted Englishman on the "Burns and Allen Show" in the late 1930s and on the "Edgar Bergen and Charlie McCarthy Show" in the 1940s and 1950s.

[13] The lyricist later happened to look up "stiff upper lip" and discovered, to his surprise, that the origins of the phrase are American, not British, a finding which is clearly preposterous, however true.

C7 C8 C9 C10

C11 C12 C13 C14

portions of the floor that are gently shuttling back and forth in opposite directions in precise time to the music. The first part of the dance takes place on these pulsating floorboards and is its highlight. When both feet are on the same board, the dancer's legs shuttle comically back and forth underneath a stationary torso; when each foot is on a different board, the legs shuttle in opposite directions (D2). They also briefly explore what the gimmick does to the ordinary activity of walking and, best of all, they twice hop back onto terra firma, lagging one foot on a floorboard, where it pulsates merrily (D3).

Things get more flamboyant (but somewhat less interestingly witty) when the dancers promenade happily on a pair of treadmills, which, among other things, allow them to do some traveling tap steps that stay in place (D4). Next they hop onto a large revolving turntable. Burns runs off, and Astaire and Allen linger to do an imitation of clockwork German dolls as the music is brightly scored to sound like a calliope. Then they launch into an old Astaire trademark: the "runaround" or "oompah trot," a comical repeated stiff-armed, shoulder-to-shoulder run that had been invented by choreographer Edward Royce for Fred and Adele Astaire to close a number in a 1921 show. The music in this section was given to the arrangers by Astaire, who noted that he had used it several times in the past and identified it as an old German folk song his father used to sing to him. The rotating turntable amplifies the delightful absurdity of the step, and the camera observes it first from outside (D5) and then from a position on the turntable itself, with the world swirling behind the dancers (D6). Astaire is spun off, a chorus of dancers comes on, and Gracie doggedly continues trotting.[14]

The rest of the number is rambling and diffuse. The chorus frolics inconsequentially for a while, and some drunks come on to be tumbled by the treadmills or mesmerized by a large churning barrel. Eventually Astaire and Burns pounce on Allen to bring her out of her hypnotic trot, and pull her into a room where they try various distorting mirrors for size (D7). The dance ends as the three suddenly find themselves sliding down a chute toward the camera (D8).[15]

[14] For another Astaire number that uses turntables and moving floor strips, in this case for extravagantly romantic purposes, see "This Heart of Mine" in *Ziegfeld Follies* (18 G).

[15] Hermes Pan came up with the idea of a dance in a fun house after visiting the Ocean Park amusement area one evening with some friends. The script was then modified to accommodate this.

E
THINGS ARE LOOKING UP
(3′46″)

Conveniently, Fontaine has fallen in love with Astaire, a condition that comes upon her "in a flash," as she twice puts it, shortly after she administers the slap in the tunnel of love. After telling her father of her abrupt change of heart, she goes to Astaire's cottage to explain things to him and to clarify the complex issues of mistaken identity.

Still smarting from the previous day's humiliation, Astaire is wary, then confused. Fontaine bolts from his cottage in irritation at his slowness of mind, but finally the truth dawns on him, and, elated, he chases after her (E1), takes her hand, asks her to confirm the miracle, and then enthusiastically serenades her with one of the Gershwins' most beautiful, yet underappreciated, ballads.[16]

C15 D1 D2 D3
D4 D5 D6 D7
D8 E1 E2 E3

Both the singing and the dance that follows take place in the context of a loving stroll through the woods back to her castle. It is the first (of few) dance numbers in Astaire's career to be filmed out of doors, and one of the first (of many) to travel from one locale to another.

The task here was to create a romantic number in which Fontaine's inadequacies as a dancer would be disguised.[17] One attempted solution was sometimes to allow the camera's view to be partially obstructed by trees, a device that adds atmosphere but doesn't really hide anything, and ends up calling attention to itself. The main method was choreographic: Fontaine is given simple steps she can do fairly well—walk, pause, bend, trot, pose, sit—while Astaire literally dances circles around her. For the most part this works well (she looks best when she is haughtily stalking, as in E1), but unfortunately Astaire and Pan pushed their luck by having her do a couple of leaps, which she executes with more galumph than flow, undercutting the desired mood and evoking groans from audiences, including, apparently, the first: Fontaine relates that at the gala premiere the woman sitting behind her loudly exclaimed during this dance, "Isn't she AWFUL!" Except for that, however, the number is quite alluring. Like the music, it is free and easy, unpretentious, and lilting—qualities that elude Astaire in his other out-of-doors duet, in *Funny Face* (29 H).

The dance grows naturally out of the stroll: Astaire and Fontaine slide smoothly around each other as they glide through a pair of turnstiles (E2), and then make a cheerful and loving game out of maneuvering around a tree (E3). Next comes one of Fontaine's leaps (E4)—especially unfortunate because it is performed in direct imitation of a leap by Astaire. Then they are off again, trotting gingerly down the path.

The next sequence is an ingenious, and generally successful, effort at obscuring Fontaine's weaknesses. As Astaire leads her off the path and up a trail, the camera is placed so that he partly obstructs its view of her—an extremely rare configuration in an Astaire duet (E5). Next he launches himself away from her and the camera follows him, leaving her completely (another virtually unique event). He darts back toward the path, hurdles a fence as she strolls back into the picture (E6), and tenderly takes her in his arms and turns her (E7).

Soon he seats her on a bench, dances a couple of turns around her, leaps about, and then partners her in the other of her awkward leaps (E8). Carried by her momentum, she hops away from him across a stream on some stepping stones, and the number ends in genial dialogue (Fontaine's strong suit) as she cordially invites him to the castle ball that evening (E9). In a significant departure from Astaire's usual practice, the camera cuts from one side of the performers to the other during this dance. Whereas most of the number is shot from the right side of the path (E1–6, 8), some shots at the end show the dance

[16] As with "A Foggy Day," the lyric is more appropriate to the novel than to the film: the singer recalls his "long ages" of "dull despair" and his "depression." While Astaire may have been depressed since the previous day's slap, it would be extravagant to call that period an "age." The first lines of the verse seem a nice touch—a reference, perhaps, to Astaire's charming propensity to burst into song whenever love hits him: "If I should suddenly start to sing/Or stand on my head—or anything/Don't think that I've lost my senses."

[17] Fontaine had had ballet lessons as a child, and for the film she studied tap with Ruby Keeler's brother—a procedure she found odd since she never had to do a single tap step in the film. However, it is clear that none of these lessons really taught her how to move, for she is tight, awkward, and self-conscious. Moreover, as Pan recalls, she was "terrified."

E4 E5 E6 E7

E8 E9 F1 G1

G2 G3 H1 I1

from the left side (E7, for example), a disorienting effect that probably could have been avoided. Astaire almost never did this again.

F

SING OF SPRING

(54″)

At the ball, the madrigal singers are back in force, lustily bawling away (F1).

G

A FOGGY DAY

(2′50″)

The butler, learning of Fontaine's love for Astaire and of her father's approval, has extorted the "Mr. X" ticket from the page. Accordingly, the enterprising page (somewhat overbearingly acted) now seeks to break up the romance and is initially successful—he shows Fontaine a newspaper publicity item (planted by Burns) in which she is listed as number 28 among Astaire's English conquests. Outraged and hurt, she sours on Astaire.

Meanwhile, unaware of her second change of heart in as many days, Astaire is again on his way down the path that leads to her castle, this time to attend the ball. As he strolls, he sings another beautiful Gershwin ballad (almost as fine as "Things Are Looking Up"), in which he reminisces fondly about that day in London when he met her, an event that changed his life from fog to sun. As if to jog his memory, the scene swirls in fog (G1).

For Astaire, the simplest walk is a dance, and the shifts of momentum, the slight hesitations, the quiet gestures combine with Stevens' evocative photography to make this stroll down a foggy country lane one of the most visually arresting dance moments in his career (G3).

It is serious as well—the only such moment in the entire film—and in its quiet way it calls to mind those deeply serious numbers in the Astaire-Rogers films. For inserted in the number are shots of Fontaine watching as he approaches the castle, her face filled with sympathetic sadness as she contemplates the calamitous news he must soon learn (G2).

H

NICE WORK IF YOU CAN GET IT

(SONG) (2′23″)

Well, perhaps things will still turn out happily. First, however, Astaire must find a way to get into the castle, for he has again been barred. Entry is facilitated by the butler, who, to Astaire's amazement, is now on his side. Once again Astaire is smuggled in as part of a singing group, this time performing a song that was to become one of the Gershwins' greatest hits.[18] The first chorus is sung in a beguilingly unglamorous manner by a sour-faced female trio in Andrews Sisters–style close harmony. Astaire amiably blends in, both musically and facially (H1).

[18] The idea for the lyric was inspired by an English cartoon in which two charwomen are discussing someone who "'as become an 'ore" and one of them remarks, "'at's nice work if you can get it."

I

AH! CHE A VOI PERDONI IDDIO

(2′6″)

When Astaire runs into Fontaine, she tells him off, to his intense bewilderment. Meanwhile, Gracie Allen and Ray Noble, with the friendly aid of George Burns, have become engaged.

As it happens, the butler is a compulsive opera singer. When the orchestra launches into a tune from von Flotow's opera *Martha,* he dashes outside and extravagantly sings (or, rather, mimes while opera tenor Mario Berini sings) the aria (I1). This daft bit of business (entirely appropriate in a Gracie Allen movie) derives from Reginald Gardiner's work on the stage, where he had achieved fame (and the notice of Hollywood) for his imitations of such unlikely items as a bell buoy with a toothache, ugly wallpaper, an effeminate French railway train, a chair in a sickroom, a lighthouse beacon, and the three Rhythm Boys.

J

NICE WORK IF YOU CAN GET IT

(DANCE) (3′38″)

Urged on by Fontaine's father, Astaire forces his way into her sitting room and, in a spirited comedy scene, demands to know what is going on (J1). She finally tells him about the newspaper report; he assures her it's a mistake; all is forgiven. By talking to her alone in her sitting room, he has, in the view of her aunt, compromised Fontaine, and to avoid any scandal, the

J1 J2 J3 J4 J5 J6 J7 J8

aunt condones the marriage.[19] However, when she comes to the door to tell the couple this, they panic, and Fontaine urges Astaire to escape by leaping once again from the balcony. His earlier escape had been accomplished with the page's surreptitious help, but this one, after considerable hesitation, is done solo, Tarzan-style (J2).

As Allen, after a few exquisite verbal transmogrifications, goes off to marry Burns instead of Noble (J3), Astaire re-enters the castle (through the door) and, before claiming Fontaine as his well-earned prize, feels called upon to blast his way through an exuberant solo. It was more typical of Astaire to end his films with a brief celebratory duet, not a long celebratory solo, but there were obvious extenuating circumstances in this case.

Astaire urges the castle ball's band into action and then scampers over to the drum set. There, like a child with a splendid new toy, he happily slams and bangs to see just how much punishment it can take. As noted, the solo is a *tour de force:* it is filmed in one continuous shot and takes place on one small spot on the floor. The camera perspective changes only slightly during the dance—retreating as Astaire frolics toward it and then closing in as he goes back to his drums. This was accomplished not by moving the camera but by using an early version of the zoom lens.

Astaire may have been partly prepared for the conditions of this solo by his radio work, particularly a weekly variety series built around him that ran thirty-nine weeks in the 1936–37 season in which his tap dances were confined to a four-foot-square mat.[20] The drum solo is an aural phantasmagoria, as he merrily raps away at snares and tomtoms and cow bells and cymbals and bass drums, adding to these noises the sounds of his tapping feet. (A minor problem is that the orchestra is mixed in so softly that it is often difficult to hear it over the drum.) But of course the dance is a visual treat as well. One of its best movements, for example, comes near the beginning, when he seems to let the sound of a cow bell ripple through his body (J4). In fact, most of the humor in the dance is visual, deriving particularly from the constant impossibility of predicting which item will next be hammered by which part of Astaire's anatomy. As he raps out a tattoo with drumsticks on one side, for example, he may suddenly lash out at a drum on the other side with his foot (J5).

The first part of the dance is largely exploratory—checking the equipment over with sticks (J4) and feet (J5)—and concluding with the first of several cocky promenades (J6). As the orchestra enters with the main melody, Astaire vents quite a bit of energy on one lone side drum. Not only does he rap it frequently with the drumsticks, but he keeps kicking it—pointedly (J7), incidentally, or in concert with another target in a jumping split kick that is a signature step of the dance (J8). Next a pair of pedal cymbals get the treatment (J9).

Grinning, Astaire jauntily parades around his space again, this time rapping out a rhythm on a new item, his shoes, thus proving one doesn't need a drum to be a drummer (J10). After an episode set to incidental bugle calls and brief orchestral phrases, he does another quick split kick (like J8) and then again gleefully frolics forward (J11).

Finally, he retreats to the drum set for his wrap-up—an unaccompanied cadenza. It begins almost entirely with noises made by drumsticks, but soon his feet are brought into play. Most spectacular is a complicated step that includes an angled jump in which his heels slam in quick succession against a side drum (J12). The solo concludes with a barrage of split kicks, a vigorous review of the noise-making arsenal, and a jump forward that ends as he slams down the pedal cymbals (J13).

Casually tossing his drumsticks over his shoulder, he struts from the band area to collect his fiancée (J14). Then, as they are about to leave, Astaire notices that the butler and the page are bent over, trying to pick up the remains of the "Mr. X" ballot, which had been shredded earlier when it seemed Fontaine had thrown him over. Astaire pauses briefly to plant a pointed reprise of his solo's signature step on the inviting targets (J15) and then exits triumphantly with his smiling damsel (J16).

[19] This scene caused no end of concern to the censorship board. They bought it only after insisting several times that the sitting room not in any way suggest a bedroom, and that it be made clear that the door to the outside corridor is not locked.

[20] He found this work rather unrewarding (except financially), in part because it limited the dance steps he could do. For example, he notes that his usual style was to get "up in the air a lot." But "if you got off the floor there was just nothing, but nothing, coming over the air."

J9 J10 J11 J12
J13 J14 J15 J16

10.

CAREFREE

1938

By 1938 the Astaire-Rogers formula was losing some of its appeal. The previous entry in the series, *Shall We Dance,* was in part an arid reworking of past themes and had shown a distinct falling off at the box office. It was clearly time to try a new approach.

Innovation (though not revolution) was pursued in *Carefree.* Although the script is a romantic comedy, the chain of events in the boy-chases-girl structure is partly revised, and the tenor of the humor is uncharacteristically boisterous. The dances retain the usual Astaire sensibility, but they are unusual in that they employ lifts far more than in the past (and even, once, a kiss), and each dance experiments with, or further develops, new filming methods. One idea, it seems, was to try to reduce the weight of the musical numbers. Although the numbers are well provided for in the script and often relate interestingly to one another, they are few and tend to be short (see Table 7). As a result, *Carefree* doesn't really "feel" much like a musical—very strange for an Astaire film of the era.

Although these innovations were not all equally fruitful, in most respects the film is a considerable success. The script is generally funny and well knit, the music (by Irving Berlin) appealing and memorable, the direction (by Mark Sandrich) fluid and well paced. The dances, while not uniformly among Astaire's finest, are engaging and imaginative. Above all, in *Carefree* Astaire and Rogers have recovered beautifully from the awkwardness that burdened *Shall We Dance:* at the peak of their powers as a performing team, they play off each other in both comic and serious moments with the confidence and mutual dependence of seasoned troupers and affectionate friends. Despite these virtues, however, the film was the least financially successful in the Astaire-Rogers series and is shown only rarely. It deserves better treatment.

THE SCRIPT

The screenplay, fashioned by Astaire perennials Allan Scott and Ernest Pagano from a collection of materials, is probably the most lucid and coherent in the Astaire-Rogers series. There are no incidental set pieces, no awkward insertions or jolts, no unmotivated lurches in direction, no scenes devoid of matter or point. Moreover, the plot does not hinge on mistaken identities or on petulant quarrels that exist only because the quarrelers don't have the wit to talk things over. Of course, it does depend on truth serums, revelatory dreams, and the magic of hypnosis, but that's all pretty believable—smacks of science, even.

For the first time in his film career, Astaire is cast in a role that carries no residue of his Broadway juvenile character. It is also his first film role as something other than a musical performer: he plays a psychiatrist. However, the scriptwriters didn't have quite enough courage to trust this device fully, so they have Astaire musing early in the film that he once wanted to be a dancer, but "psychoanalysis showed me I was wrong." Nor did they fully trust the script's other major innovation: having Rogers fall in love with Astaire first. She does chase him during the first half of the film, in happy reversal of the usual pattern, but things are arranged in mid-film to allow Astaire to resume his accustomed role of pursuer.

Rogers plays a radio singer who can't bring herself to become engaged to her ardent beau, Ralph Bellamy. Bellamy asks his friend Astaire to psychoanalyze her, and soon she falls in love with her analyst. Astaire hypnotizes her out of that infatuation but then comes to realize he is in love with her. After many capers and escapades he is able to undo the hypnotic suggestion, and all ends happily. Left outclassed is Bellamy, the first of Astaire's romantic rivals who isn't either laughable or contemptible (though he *is* rather boorish and humorless).

Comedy support is lent by Luella Gear, playing Rogers' aunt, who deftly delivers a considerable number of *double-entendre* cracks, and by Jack Carson, who plays Astaire's hulkish assistant. But the chief high-jinks are reserved for Rogers, who gets to go berserk twice: smashing windows, insulting passers-by, shooting up a country club, and generally having a good time. Rogers' considerable penchant for comedic mischief had gone largely unexploited in her earlier films with Astaire. Here she is unleashed and seizes the opportunity with glee.

For a while Rogers refused to appear on the *Carefree* set. She had major disagreements with the studio over money and over the assignment of Sandrich as director—he had often adopted a patronizing attitude toward her, and she had been promised he would never direct another of her films. Eventually differences were resolved, which was certainly fortunate for RKO, because the actress was soon to become the studio's top box office draw.

THE FILMING OF THE DANCES

By 1938 Astaire had largely settled on his aesthetic for recording dance on film, but he always remained open to new ideas. Perhaps inspired by the film's spirit of innovation, each of the four dance episodes in *Carefree* explores a new approach to the filming of dance.

In the first, Astaire's golf solo, internal cutting is used for the first time, to facilitate "impossible" physical feats. At one point, for example, the camera cuts to show him poised before a row of five golf balls (A 13). In the shot, he hits each of them down the course with a perfect drive. This segment, of course, was filmed many times until Astaire got it exactly right, and then the perfect take was inserted into the dance. The second dance tries out slow motion, a special effect Astaire was to use only once more (in 21 J). The third dance, "The Yam," travels from one location to another. The traveling idea had been tentatively introduced in *Swing Time* two years earlier (7 G) and had been developed in *A Damsel in Distress* (9 D, 9 E). In "The Yam" it is considerably elaborated.

Finally, in the romantic duet "Change Partners," Astaire settled on a technique for blending medium shots (shots showing the upper half of the body) into his dances: at a point where it is dramatically informative, the camera cuts to the medium shot (see E 12, 13) and then gently *tracks* back to the full-figure perspective (E 14), an operation that creates only one disruption in the dance. Astaire obviously liked this approach and used it often in later films.[1]

THE CHOREOGRAPHY

Hermes Pan assisted Astaire with the choreography. His screen credit reads "Ensembles staged by"—rather odd, since the film uses no dancing ensembles, though "The Yam" does call for a bit of crowd control in a couple of places.

[1] On these developments, see pp. 26–31.

With Ginger Rogers in "Change Partners"

With Rogers in "I Used to Be Color Blind"

THE NUMBERS

A
GOLF SOLO
(2′ 39″)

The film opens with Bellamy, drunk because Rogers has again broken off their engagement, staggering into Astaire's office and asking him to see her. While Bellamy is being detoxified, Astaire idly plays a few ripples on a harmonica (A1). Although Astaire feels certain Rogers is merely "one of those dizzy, silly maladjusted females who can't make up her mind," he agrees to see her. But Rogers learns of his prejudice when she arrives for her examination and, amused and spiteful, disrupts his routine and then stalks out (A2). Puzzled by her behavior, he concludes she might be an interesting case after all.

Astaire and Rogers run into each other at a country-club golf tee, where he is practicing his game. Her mocking comments throw him off, and he badly misses a couple of strokes. She pointedly reminds him of his theory that mental adjustment requires the conscious and the unconscious to be in coordination, and suggests he is out of alignment (A3). Challenged, he seeks to prove otherwise by launching into a dance to demonstrate that he is fully capable of doing two things at the same time. The precise psychoanalytic import of the dance is not entirely clear, but it certainly gives overwhelming evidence about his coordination: no therapy required.

The solo is in several sections, linked by a scattered logic that makes it something of a choreographic association test. In the first part Astaire shows he can play his harmonica and dance simultaneously. The dance is performed to the melody of Berlin's "Since They Turned 'Loch Lomond' into Swing," a tune that is appropriate (indeed, obligatory) because the golf pro who has been working with Astaire is a Scot named MacPherson; besides, golf is a game of Scottish origin.[2] It opens with a rollicking and varied caper that blends into its tap ripples a sweetly swirling spin on one foot (A4), some comic staggering (A5), and a bit of amiable sauntering. Appropriate to its inspiration, much of the dance is carried out high on the balls of the feet in Scottish fashion. Then Astaire calmly goes to the opposite extreme by rapping out, in happy coordination with a harmonica trill, a set of puttering heels-only steps across the turf (A6).

Now it occurs to Astaire that a Scottish sword dance would be in order. No swords being handy, he side-stomps over (on tiptoe with bent knees while playing a bagpipelike dance on his harmonica—A7) to a table on which rest two golf clubs. Abandoning his harmonica, he ceremoniously crosses the clubs on the ground and then hops merrily over them (A8). Astaire shows about as much concern for authenticity in the sword dance as he does in his psychoanalytic theories: for example, his dance incorporates such imaginative innovations as the delicate leg-shake-while-fluttering-flaps-of-sweater step (A9).

But it follows that if golf clubs make great swords, they make even better golf clubs, and so Astaire kicks one of the clubs away, cantilevers the other into his hand by stepping on its head, and, thus equipped, goes into a routine in which he golfs and tap dances at the same time. Astaire, an avid amateur golfer, reports that this idea had come to him several years earlier, while

[2] This jumpy tune has apparently never been published. Parts of it seem to owe something to the folk song "She'll Be Comin' 'round the Mountain." For this solo Astaire performed to Hal Borne's piano, and the orchestral sound was dubbed in later.

A1  A2  A3  A4

A5  A6  A7  A8

A9  A10  A11  A12

he was "fooling around" at the Bel Air country club. He showed the idea to Sandrich, who then had it worked into the script. Rehearsals for the number took two weeks, and five men were employed to shag the hundreds of golf balls.

In this episode, dance is sometimes subordinated to gimmick (unlike most of the earlier portions of the number), but the gimmick is so appealingly absurd that it is easy to pass by such minor choreographic improprieties. MacPherson helpfully bounces four golf balls to Astaire, who places them on the ground and then, in an inserted shot (the first cut in the dance), swats them away seriatim as an incidental effect in a chipper and complex tap dance rapped out with feet and club (A 10). A gloating glance of triumph in Rogers' direction (A 11) is followed by another swat and a change of clubs. Armed now with a driver, Astaire approaches a neat row of five balls. This proves to be a tease, however, for instead of hitting them with his club, he kicks them away with five flicks of his foot (A 12).

But now he moves up to another row of five balls and, in a second inset shot, mightily drives them down the course with five consecutive strokes timed (it hardly needs to be said) precisely on the music (A 13). A little frolic of triumph follows, but when he looks over to Rogers for well-earned adulation, he finds, to his amusement, that she has vanished.

B

I USED TO BE COLOR BLIND

(3′45″)

Astaire joins the aloof Rogers on a bicycle ride (B 1). He tries to psychoanalyze her while in motion, but this rather unorthodox approach goes awry when he loses control of his bicycle and crashes. He again meets his discomfort with amusement—a trait she apparently finds admirable (B 2).

They have warmed considerably to each other by that evening, when they dance together at the country club (B 3).[3] Rogers, now willing to be Astaire's patient, agrees to eat gobs of "dream-inducing food" in order to give him some data to work with. Joined by Bellamy and Gear, they order all sorts of bizarre food, to the sputtering bewilderment of the waiter, in a joke that is a bit overextended (B 4).

The dinner has its desired effect: that night Rogers drifts off into an exotic dream in which she dances rapturously with her analyst. This duet is of particular interest because it may well be the first "dream ballet" in American musical comedy and, unlike its more famous counterpart in *Oklahoma!* (created five years later), it advances the plot: as a result of the dance, Rogers comes to realize she is in love with Astaire (see also pp. 23–26).

Beyond that, however, the number seems a good idea that didn't work out very well. Part of the problem comes from the lyric, which, in context, seems at best odd and at worst absurd. As Astaire and Rogers wander through their black-and-white wonderland (B 5), he ardently sings about how she has filled his life with color, and invites her to gaze at rainbows and skies of blue. The original plan had been to shoot the film in color, and Berlin wrote the song with that in mind. However, the poor box office generated by Astaire's last film, *A Damsel in Distress,* caused RKO to economize.

The principal problem, however, derives from

[3] The dance music in the background is Berlin's "The Night Is Filled with Music." This lush ballad, as its title perhaps suggests, was originally intended to accompany Rogers' upcoming dream dance. It is used again as background dance music in a later scene at the club, just before "The Yam."

A 13 B 1 B 2 B 3 B 4 B 5 B 6 B 7 B 8 B 9 B 10 B 11

the strained effort to be fanciful. The whole number is filmed with fuzzy frame edges, a picture-cramping effect that is distracting and becomes irritating as the number wears on. Moreover, the set, which makes Astaire and Rogers look like a pair of Lilliputians cavorting over a lily pond, is coy. And the music is arranged to give a vaporous quality (unseen choirs oohing and aahing in the distance, for example), which tends to undercut the song's considerable vitality.[4]

The major fantasy element is the use of slow motion for the dance. The method used to segue into this effect is masterful. After singing the song to Rogers, Astaire takes her in his arms for the dance. At first they swirl around at a normal ballroom pace, but then he speeds up the swirling intoxicatingly (B6), and at that point the film modulates to slow motion (that is, the camera speed increases), slowing the dancers down again, this time unnaturally. This is all done without the aid of a cut. In fact, the dance is filmed all in one take, which means enormous care had to be taken to fit the dance to the music. Unfortunately, while the beginning and end match the music well enough, slow motion inevitably cut the rest of the dance off from the accompaniment, and the steps become musically unmotivated—a curious event for this most musical of choreographers.

The dance itself is an assortment of dreamy waftings—swirls, leaps, and, above all, floating lifts. Apparently in an effort to give these maneuverings greater amplitude, Rogers is dressed in a loose, filmy gown and Astaire in floppy pants, but the effect is cluttering (and fluttering) more than anything else. (In general, Rogers' costumes in this film show little of the flair and imagination of her attire in her earlier films with Astaire.)

The dance ends with Astaire and Rogers in the first full-out, no-kidding kiss in their films together. According to Astaire, this was done in part to undercut rumors that his wife was insisting that his screen romances with Rogers be essentially kissless: their fans, provoked perhaps by the kissing teases in *Follow the Fleet* and *Swing Time,* were becoming restless. On the contrary, Astaire had avoided kisses because he disliked mushy love scenes, because the Hollywood kiss was such a cliché, and because love is so eloquently expressed in his dances that using something so obvious would be tantamount to admitting choreographic failure.

What is particularly interesting about this kiss, however, is the amazing way in which Astaire has taken on that most hoary of Hollywood clichés and revitalized it with fresh eroticism. It is intricately prepared for in the choreography. Astaire spins Rogers in a wide swirling lift around his body (B7). As he slows, she gradually regains her footing but continues to turn in his arms (B8). Then, at last, she falls out of the turn and glides over backward as he holds her. They are now in the classic Hollywood-kiss pose: she lies surrenderingly in his arms as he leans over her (B9). But, going against the cliché, Astaire moves no farther; instead it is *Rogers* who consummates the kiss (after all, it's her dream). In languorous slow motion, she reaches upward, wraps her arms around his neck, and then gradually pulls her body up until her face meets his (B10). Even after their lips meet, she continues to tighten the embrace (B11).

Since the kiss is part of the overall choreography, the camera remains distant, showing the dancers' entire bodies through its ring of haze. To see an Astaire-Rogers kiss in close-up, the fans would have to wait for the next film; to that degree, the tease continued.[5]

C
THE YAM
(5′39″)

Rogers awakens and realizes she is in love with Astaire. Later that day, in his office, he asks her to relate her dream. To maintain his interest without disclosing her newly discovered yearnings, she concocts a gloriously convoluted and fanciful tale. This excites his professional interest ("a perfect mass of the most horrible neuroses and inhibitions"), and, in order to learn more, he gives her an anesthetic that will release her inhibitions temporarily. As he hovers over her (C1), her first reaction to the treatment is to re-enact her dream by rising up and kissing him—a clue

[4] In the recording Astaire made of the song several months before the film went before the cameras, on the other hand, the song is given an appropriately lively reading.

[5] The kiss was filmed for an extra fifteen seconds to allow for a dissolve. As a joke, the unedited take was shown by Sandrich at regular speed (making it unquestionably the world's longest kiss) with Astaire's wife in attendance. According to Astaire, she was amused.

C1 C2 C3 C4

C5 C6 C7 C8

he shrugs off as he leaves the room to wait for the anesthetic to take full effect.

Meanwhile, Bellamy, unaware of Rogers' condition, comes in and hauls her away to her radio show, for which she is late. Emotionally unfettered by the drug, Rogers has a comic soliloquy in which she runs rampant, sowing disarray wherever she goes. A high point is reached when she acts out everybody's innermost desire by smashing a sheet of plate glass with a blunt object—a policeman's billy club (C 2). She is finally brought under control, but only after she has insulted her sponsor on the air (C 3), batted her eyes mischievously at various passers-by (C 4), and kicked a policeman in the seat of the pants.

At the country club that evening, Rogers is determined to dance in real life with her dream partner. She tries to maneuver Astaire out onto the dance floor, singing a number with the club's band as part of her effort.

Carefree is sometimes referred to as a screwball comedy, and it is perhaps fitting that it includes a musical number built on a screwball dance step. According to the lyric, every time a held note occurs in the music, the dancers are required to fling their hands limply out to the side, palms up, and then waddle forward while rapping out a pert tap phrase. Rogers cheerfully demonstrates the step as she sings, and then patiently teaches it to Astaire, after she has coerced him out onto the dance floor by threatening to do more violence if he refuses (C 5). He picks up the step very quickly.

The high-spirited dance that ensues never strays from its delightfully nutty premise: no matter how complicated or frolicsome the choreography becomes, the dancers always dutifully lapse into the Yam step whenever there is a held note in the music. At the same time, the Yam step itself is developed as the dance progresses: without losing its basic integrity (if that's the word), it reappears in various guises—a twist of the body is added, or a turn, or it is performed in partnered formation. Its essential forward waddle makes the Yam a traveling step, and this may have inspired the number's most notable characteristic: the way it carries the performers around the rooms and terraces of the country club.

The dance begins as a kind of étude on the Yam: After Rogers teaches Astaire the step (C 5), he joins her in developing the idea. The step is performed partnered, for example (C 7), or as part of a spiraling, shuffling turn (C 9). It is contrasted with other material, such as a beautiful lunging, hopping partnered turn (C 6) or a jaunty, backstepping tap scamper (C 8). Gradually, too, the duet expands to cover more of the dancing area. Finally, Astaire snaps Rogers into his arms for a quick spin, and then, as the camera cuts to a longer shot, they separate and urge others to join them on the dance floor, pausing in this task to deliver the Yam step when required by the music (C 10).

Pursued now by the Yamming crowd, Astaire and Rogers burst into another room, where, between Yams, he nimbly bounces her off a couple of overstuffed chairs (C 11). Then, after Yamming their way into another section of the room, each delivers a solo fragment while the other watches: Astaire does a tap frolic, Rogers an impudent strut (C 12). Eventually their momentum carries them out onto the terrace, where Rogers sings about her preference for the Yam over such dance steps as the Suzie Q or the Black Bottom (C 13).[6]

After more hopping, scampering, and strutting, they find that the Yam has carried them back into the main dining area. Here, in the dance's most memorable image, they circle the room in a series of swooping, traveling lifts created by Hermes Pan: Astaire props his leg on each table in turn and swings the gleeful Rogers over the hurdles he has formed (C 14). All ends as they Yam happily forward to the spot where the dance began (C 15). The lift sequence is shown all in one shot, but there is an unfortunate cut after the last lift, just before the dance's brief epilogue (that is, between C 14 and C 15); this cut, uncharacteristic of Astaire, dampens somewhat the momentum of the dance's finale.

D
CHANGE PARTNERS
(SONG) (1′ 29″)

After the Yam is over, Rogers, whose dream fantasies about Astaire have presumably been confirmed now that she has danced with him in the flesh, decides to bare all. She tells Bellamy she is

[6] A bowdlerized version of the Black Bottom is performed. In the step's most provocative form, one jabs one's thumb at the side of one's rear end, then brings the thumb to the mouth and hisses ("sizzles") to suggest the thumb has been heated by this posterior contact. Rogers merely slaps her rear with one hand and then claps her hands together.

C9 C10 C11 C12
C13 C14 C15 D1

in love, but before she can tell him it is Astaire she is in love with, Bellamy leaps to the conclusion that *he* is the object of her new affections and excitedly announces their engagement. Later, Astaire and Rogers dance together (as the club's band appropriately reprises "I Used to Be Color Blind"), and she explains the predicament to him. He is not amused (D 1).

The next scene is one of the finest in the entire Astaire-Rogers series. In Astaire's office, Rogers agrees to let him hypnotize her so that she will fall out of love with him and into love with Bellamy. The pair play the unlikely scene with rapt seriousness, and it becomes deeply affecting when, in the process of hypnotizing Rogers, Astaire comes to realize he is in love with her himself (D 2).

Puzzled, he goes to another room to sort out his feelings in a dialogue with his subconscious (D 3). When he returns, however, Rogers has wandered off in a daze. He follows her to the country club, where she tries to act out his hypnotic suggestion that "men like him should be shot down like dogs" (D 4). After a certain amount of mayhem, she snaps out of her homicidal mood but continues to believe she is in love with Bellamy.

The Rogers-Bellamy wedding is now set for the next day (things happen fast in *Carefree*). At their engagement party at the country club on the eve of the wedding, Astaire tries to have a word with Rogers. As Bellamy steers her protectively around the crowded dance floor, Astaire sings Berlin's throaty ballad "Won't you change partners and dance with me?" (D 5). She won't.[7]

E
CHANGE PARTNERS
(DANCE) (1′ 53″)

With Bellamy detained on the telephone by Carson, Astaire is able to corner Rogers in a deserted pavilion and he attempts to hypnotize her so that he can erase the suggestion he had previously put in her mind. Since he is far from his laboratory apparatus, Astaire uses dance to bring her under his control.

In the romantic duets in *The Gay Divorcee* (3 E), *Follow the Fleet* (6 J), and *Swing Time* (7 G), Astaire had sought to mesmerize the reluctant Rogers into a dance. The idea, which was introductory and largely incidental there, becomes central here. Wonderfully and absurdly comic in conception, the dance is performed with an intense seriousness that gives it a unique daring and disarming charm. And, while each of Astaire's earlier romantic duets with Rogers tended to have a portion that is a bit overblown, this one avoids that slightly marring defect entirely.

It can be considered a duet for Rogers' voluptuously fluid body and Astaire's exquisitely articulate hands. Rogers responds pliantly to Astaire's controlling vision throughout, and when he sees that he has attained total power over her, he gradually becomes more forward. At first he manipulates her from a distance and partners her loosely; at the end he locks her in his embrace and cradles her in a resplendent lift. It's a very strange dance, with an almost necrophilic quality in the way the sentient, desirous Astaire toys with the half-conscious, compliant Rogers.

First Astaire gestures commandingly toward Rogers and then, without touching her, pilots her in a broad circle around him (E 1, 2). As she moves, her arms drift upward until they float

[7] Berlin had written the song years earlier for possible use in a Ginger-less Astaire film.

D2 D3 D4 D5
E1 E2 E3 E4
E5 E6 E7 E8

limply, at the sides of her body, as if trying vaguely to ward off some undefined danger (E 3). (The arm position, interestingly enough, is a dreamlike softening of the Yam arms; compare C 5 or 9.) He causes her to stop abruptly, then draws her backward toward him and partners her lightly from behind (E 4).

The same basic idea is then repeated, but with a more intimate conclusion. Again Rogers is sent wafting around the floor, and again she is commanded to stop (E 5). Now Astaire moves in on her and softly but firmly forces her defensive arms down to hang out of the way at her sides. Then he passes one hand over her face (E 6), and, as if rendered insensible, Rogers topples over backward into Astaire's tender embrace, in a pose similar to the one that concluded their dream duet earlier in the film (E 7; see B 9).

Then, for the third time, he sends her drifting across the floor, stops her, and advances toward her. Without touching her, he moves his hands caressingly around her body (E 8). He causes her to raise her arms to shoulder height and then deftly and daringly insinuates himself upon her so that she has one arm around his shoulder (E 9).

The music shifts to a lively waltz tempo, propelling the dancers into surging triple-meter patterns around the floor. Included are some low lifts in which Rogers, propped on Astaire's hip, swings her legs through the air (E 10).[8]

As the waltz portion subsides and the main melody returns, the dancers separate again. Astaire then commandingly draws Rogers toward him (E 11) and she settles in his embrace (E 12)—an event important enough for a cut to a medium shot (the only cut in the dance) showing Astaire's expression of ardent desire (E 13). As they cling, Astaire draws his left arm away from Rogers so that, to close the ballroom pose, she must reach in toward him, a slyly erotic notion Astaire used in several duets.[9]

As the camera tracks away, the dancers drift softly across the floor, almost heedless of the music (E 14). Then, in this film full of lifts, comes the most amazing one of all. Rogers and Astaire separate briefly, holding hands at arm's length (E 15). From this position he suddenly snaps her spinning in toward him, gathers her in his arms (E 16), and, turning, carries her across the floor as she succumbs to the force of the movement (E 17).

Finally, he sets her back on her feet tenderly, and together they sink onto a bench at the side of the pavilion. As Astaire watches her solicitously, Rogers stares blankly out into space (E 18).

In the meantime, however, Astaire's grand scheme is collapsing. Bellamy finally sees through the telephone ruse and, after giving Carson a kick in the pants, dashes to the pavilion, where he is able to snap Rogers out of her spell before Astaire has had time to put her mind in proper order.

The film ends with sprightly humor, though not with the usual musical number. On Rogers' wedding day, Astaire sneaks into her room with the object of knocking her unconscious so as to get her quickly into a condition suitable for the removal of hypnotic suggestions (E 19). He hasn't the heart to deliver the essential punch, however. Bellamy inadvertently comes to his aid by delivering an accidental haymaker to Rogers while trying to protect her. The ensuing fade-out shows Astaire escorting a smiling, black-eyed Ginger to the altar (E 20).

[8] This cantilevered hip lift was substantially developed twenty years later in a duet in *Silk Stockings* (30 H).

[9] Briefly in "Cheek to Cheek" in *Top Hat* (5 E 8), more extensively in *Holiday Inn* (15 I 9), *Ziegfeld Follies* (18 G 5), and *Easter Parade* (21 B 3).

E 9 E 10 E 11 E 12
E 13 E 14 E 15 E 16
E 17 E 18 E 19 E 20

11.

The Story of Vernon and Irene Castle

1939

By the end of the 1930s, the Fred Astaire–Ginger Rogers partnership seemed to have run its course. The popularity of their films together had fallen off, and the performers were interested in pursuing independent careers.[1] *The Story of Vernon and Irene Castle* was their last collaboration at RKO, and it is the least typical of Astaire's musical films.

Based on a true-life story, it portrays a famous dance team of an earlier era. Astaire and Rogers find themselves in a film that is fundamentally serious and confining, and some of their characteristic high spirits are accordingly curtailed. However, there is a subdued, unaffected quality to the film that is often endearing, as is some of the humor, which is gentle, understated, and incidental. At its best, the film, amiably directed by H. C. Potter, is poignant, warm, and charming; at its worst, it is a bit stilted and bland. Astaire and Rogers concluded their legendary partnership on a gentle, reflective note, without fanfare—but with class.

Like the film, the choreography does not readily call to mind other Astaire efforts. All the dances are performed as exhibitions, and all are based on the steps and styles of another time. While the choreography faithfully reflects the Castles and their era, however, there is a slight air of didacticism—even of arrogance, perhaps—in the way Astaire quietly embellishes the routines of the Castles, doing much more with their basic material than they did. Particularly memorable is an affecting waltz duet near the end—the last fully developed dance the Castles do in the film, and the last in the Astaire-Rogers series at RKO.

THE SCRIPT

Vernon and Irene Castle, a struggling young dance team in musical revue and musical comedy, became an overnight sensation when they danced an exhibition at a Paris nightclub in April 1912. Their phenomenal success was due not only to their dancing ability but also to their appeal offstage; as Irene Castle once laconically put it, "We were young, clean, married, and well-mannered."

Over the next few years they toured widely, helped to develop a new craze for ballroom dancing, performed in a feature film about themselves, danced in Broadway shows, established several nightclubs and dancing schools in the United States, wrote a book about dancing, and regularly set fashions—the most revolutionary of which was Irene Castle's widely imitated 1914 hair bob. They set the tone for a generation, an attractive mixture, as Arlene Croce observes, "of common sense and frivolity, of youthful exuberance and refinement." In 1916, Vernon Castle, English by birth, joined the Royal Flying Corps and served his country with bravery and distinction in World War I. After surviving considerable danger in France, he was transferred to Texas to train pilots for the war. There he was killed in a freak flying accident on February 15, 1918, at the age of thirty.

The film relates this extraordinary tale of meteoric success and abrupt tragedy with grace and taste. Biography was a major trend in U.S. cinema at the time (*The Great Ziegfeld* won the Academy Award for 1936, *The Life of Emile Zola* for 1937), but, more than most Hollywood true-life movies, *The Story of Vernon and Irene Castle* gives evidence of dramatic restraint and reasonable accuracy.[2] Events are inevitably shuffled and telescoped, and a few are invented, but on the whole the story is told straight and with minimal melodrama. In the process virtually all the usual Astaire-Rogers formulas are calmly abandoned. As writer Cecelia Ager impishly observed at the time:

> In *The Castles* everyone knows who everybody else is. Everybody's identity is clearly defined and completely understood from beginning to end and nobody is mistaken for somebody else, not even on the telephone. . . . Miss Rogers does not get mad at Mr. Astaire ever [actually, not quite true]. She likes him from the first moment she sees him and never pretends that she doesn't and the only change in her feeling toward him is the progressive degree of her passion. . . . They're married right off, nobody has to wish to God they would. . . . The ending is, necessarily, unhappy. There are two actual and satisfactory kisses. And it would take Solomon to balance any more justly the footage assigned to Miss Rogers with that assigned to Mr. Astaire.

[1] On the splitting up of the partnership, see p. 10.

[2] The lengthy if accurate title was accepted only after many alternatives had been considered. The preferred title was *Castles in the Air,* but this could not be cleared: MGM, which owned the film rights to it, would not release it because they planned to use it.

RKO AND MRS. CASTLE

According to RKO records, Irene Castle—then married to (though estranged from) her third husband, a Chicago sportsman and coffee heir—was paid $20,000 in 1937 for the rights to her story. She worked closely with scriptwriter Oscar Hammerstein II, who soon came up with a treatment that she approved enthusiastically. Hammerstein shaped this material into a rough screenplay by the end of the year, and during 1938 the script was continually reworked by other scriptwriters. Mrs. Castle, signed on as "technical adviser," greeted many of these changes with alarm, and had even more suggestions to make—particularly about costumes and hair styles—as production began at the end of the year. Since her contract gave her approval rights on the costumes and committed RKO to follow any treatment she approved, she was in a fairly good bargaining position. She was temporarily diverted to campaign for an antivivisection measure on the California ballot in November 1938, but then returned to plague producers and director with complaints and demands, culminating in a seven-page list delivered in February 1939, when filming was well under way. Her various letters of complaint carried threats of legal action, but eventually a settlement was worked out in which she withdrew her objections and received an additional payment of $5,000.

The objections ranged from the petty to the significant. She protested against departures from the Hammerstein script: invented scenes and dialogue that she felt misrepresented reality, omissions made largely to contain the length of the film. But most of Mrs. Castle's complaints were about matters of costume and hair style and were aimed primarily at Ginger Rogers. Conflict between the two women was probably inevitable. Irene Castle was, of course, highly sensitive about how she would be portrayed in the film, and was particularly concerned that the famous fashions she created be accurately rendered: she was hoping that publicity from the film would aid her commercial interests in this area. (Her contract gave her the right to exploit fashions she designed for the film—a venture that, in turn, would be good publicity for the film.) Rogers, for her part, had her own image to protect and her status as one of Hollywood's most popular actresses; as *Time* observed, "Irene Castle had her thousands of admirers, Ginger Rogers has her millions."[3]

[3] Despite their fame in the prewar era, the Castles were not exactly household words twenty years later. As Astaire recalls, "When I was doing the picture, my wife . . . said 'Who are these people?' . . . She didn't know who they *were*. . . . I was amazed."

Irene Castle modeling a dress in 1934 (above), and Ginger Rogers' version of the same dress (below)

Understandably, Rogers refused to cut her hair, and so the famous Castle bob is never adequately shown in the film. Moreover, as the accustomed mistress of her own wardrobe, Rogers, working with costume designer Walter Plunkett, insisted on modifying many of the fashions to suit modern sensibilities. Shoulder pads were inserted, and various decorative details were altered—even the shape of Mrs. Castle's famous Dutch bonnet was changed. Irene Castle considered these changes dowdy, cluttering, and puffy—or, to use her word, "plunketty"—and protested assiduously and in detail. From the perspective of a few decades later, it does seem that she knew what she was talking about. Comparisons of photographs of her original costumes with those worn by Rogers in the film suggest that Rogers' improvements were mostly damaging: the dresses lost some of their sleek line and became cumbersome and billowy by comparison, qualities particularly unfortunate in a dancing costume. Mrs. Castle made many (though not all) of her objections in good time for correction, but these were often ignored or vetoed by the production staff, who were flustered by what was felt to be her constant nitpicking.[4]

Mrs. Castle's antipathy to Rogers, however, did not begin at the costume-design stage: it went back to her earliest communications with RKO on the film. After consulting with Astaire in early 1937, she wrote RKO, "Fred was most insistent that Ginger Rogers should not play the role opposite him—as am I." (If that is an accurate reflection of Astaire's thinking at the time, it may have reflected his desire to make some films independent of Rogers. The ensuing failure of his Ginger-less *A Damsel in Distress* altered his opinion on that matter.) Mrs. Castle says RKO promised her a nationwide search for the actress to play her part, but she suspected the studio intended from the start to give the role to Rogers. According to producer Pandro Berman, her suspicion was correct.

Whatever reservations she had about Rogers, she had none whatever about Astaire. In fact, his casting as Vernon Castle was a provision in one of her contracts with RKO. The Castles had seen Astaire and his sister onstage in 1916, and afterward sent word to the thrilled youngsters that they thought them "wonderful." Fred Astaire never met Vernon Castle, but he did work with Irene Castle in the early 1920s, helping her with the choreography for her stage comeback. He was so embarrassed to be teaching the great dancer that he refused payment for the work—though she did get him to accept a present.

Fred and Adele Astaire had seen the Castles perform many times on Broadway. They were, Astaire writes, "a tremendous influence on our careers, not that we copied them completely, but we did appropriate some of their ballroom steps and style for our vaudeville act."

Oddly, despite his adulation of Vernon Castle—or perhaps because of it—Astaire's portrayal is probably the least authentic aspect of the film. Except for a few moments in the opening scenes, Vernon Castle comes off as sober, stoical, and a bit dull and humorless. Irene Castle's descriptions of her husband, on the other hand, stress the attributes that are very different. In one early biography she is constantly referring to his childlike qualities and to his irrepressible zest for life: "He was always galloping around somewhere . . . with never a care in the world or a thought for the future."[5] Similar observations come from Helen Hayes, who had worked with Vernon Castle. When she was ten, Hayes had a hopeless crush on him: "Vernon was a delight. He knew how to enter a child's world and, better still, how to make a child feel grown-up."

To a degree, then, Vernon Castle in real life had some similarity to the semijuvenile characters Astaire had so successfully portrayed in some of his earlier films. If Mrs. Castle had paid more attention to this element of reverent inauthenticity in the script, and less to the irreverent inauthenticity of some of Ginger Rogers' gowns, *The Story of Vernon and Irene Castle* might have turned out to be a livelier film.

Actually, judging from descriptions and from *The Whirl of Life,* the delightful, vaguely autobiographical film the Castles made in 1914, Astaire may have been substantially miscast in this film. His chief physical resemblance to Vernon Castle is his receding hairline (and, of course, his dancing ability). Castle was tall (five feet, eleven inches), very long-legged, and thin—giving the impression, as Hayes affectionately recalls, of a "string bean." Although Astaire is only an inch and a half shorter, he is far differently proportioned and substantially more filled out—135 pounds, as opposed to Castle's skeletal 118.

Moreover, unlike Astaire, Vernon Castle moved with (though he did not dance with) a trace of effeminacy; Mrs.

[4] For example, director H. C. Potter says, "She wanted one sequence shot over again only because Ginger, who was supposed to have come back from riding, had no hat on, and Irene said, 'I wouldn't be caught dead riding without a hat.' And oh, the arguments and pleadings that went on about that." However, RKO documents suggest that Mrs. Castle had made the request about the riding hat well before the scene was shot and therefore felt betrayed when her advice was ignored.

[5] In the early Hammerstein treatment, Irene Castle, upon hearing of her husband's death, says, "He was like a little boy. . . ." Realizing there was little in the script to give credence to this characterization, later scriptwriters changed this to "He was just beginning to live. . . ." In her autobiography, published thirty years later, Mrs. Castle continues to remember him as "happy-go-lucky," but suggests she felt considerable dismay over his profligacy: they "argued over money with the regularity of clockwork." Their manager suggests both Castles were profligate.

With Rogers, auditioning to "Waiting for the Robert E. Lee"

Castle, in fact, suggests that her husband went so eagerly into combat in order to dispel the popular view that he was not "a man's man." The lanky, eccentrically proportioned Vernon Castle was basically funny-looking, and he brilliantly exploited this quality as a stage comedian. Although Astaire tries to duplicate some of this in a couple of onstage routines in the film, the essential comic freakiness of Vernon Castle's stage persona was beyond his capabilities—Ray Bolger would have been a better approximation.

DANCE AND SENSUALITY

The Castles' success was due in considerable measure to their careful desensualization of dance. They emerged at a time when a craze for dance was beginning to sweep the country, creating a backlash of opposition from those who found such public clutching to be scandalous. The Castles, however, made close social dancing widely acceptable by de-emphasizing the sexual element. Irene Castle approvingly quotes critic Gilbert Seldes: "It was certainly the least sensual dancing in the world; the whole appeal was visual." In their dance manual, the Castles argue that their dances "properly danced are *not* vulgar; on the contrary they embody grace and refinement." Furthermore, they assure their readers that dancing "preserves youth" and reduces the consumption of alcoholic beverages and the incidence of gambling. The message, in short, was that dancing, properly done, was just good clean fun, and Mrs. Castle stresses the "humor that permeated all our dancing, the great sense of bubbling joy we shared together when we danced."

This approach to dance, which is effectively communicated in the Castles' dance exhibitions in *The Whirl of Life*, must have been especially useful to Astaire in his theatre days, when his dancing partner was his sister. But once Astaire started dancing with nonrelatives—Claire Luce on Broadway, Ginger Rogers on film—he showed little reluctance about putting the sexual element back in, though he managed to retain "grace and refinement" as well as plenty of humor and "bubbling joy."

Since sex was an important element in virtually all the Astaire-Rogers duets, the dances in *The Story of Vernon and Irene Castle* go against their own natural (and successful) impulses. Nevertheless, they manage to capture much of the Castle style in their exhibition dances in the film, and then in the last one, the waltz duet, they let us in on the deep emotional interdependency that they feel underlay these dances.

THE MUSIC

The score for the film is a pleasure. That's not exactly unusual in an Astaire film, particularly one from the 1930s, but the means used to achieve it are unique in Astaire's career.

Rather than commissioning a new score, the producers decided to assemble a collection of songs from the Castles' era. Over forty old songs are used for the numbers and for background music. The songs have been chosen with loving care and are played straight rather than being unduly modernized—for example, there are no saxophones, and banjos are used instead of guitars. Chiefly responsible for this tasteful and appealing pastiche were music director Victor Baravalle and arranger-orchestrator Robert Russell Bennett. Although *The Castles* was generously budgeted, the use of old songs did have a certain financial advantage: the rights to the songs cost $19,000, less than one-third the price of commissioning a score from composers of the status of those who had worked on previous Astaire films.

One new song was written for the film: a ruminating love ballad, "Only When You're in My Arms," with music by Con Conrad (who had contributed two fine songs to *The Gay Divorcee*) and lyrics by Bert Kalmar and Herman Ruby.[6] Like the film, the song is subdued and tender, but it does contrast stylistically with the rest of the score. Among other things, the song is in AABA form, something quite rare in popular songs before the mid-1920s.

THE CHOREOGRAPHY

Assisting Astaire with the choreography for the film was his usual RKO sidekick Hermes Pan. Although Astaire knew most of the Castle steps and style from his stage years, Pan did some additional research, especially on the Latin-derived steps.

[6] Eleven years later, Astaire was to portray Kalmar in *Three Little Words*.

Irene Castle signing her contract—behind her are Pandro Berman, George Stevens (originally designated to direct the film), and RKO executive Ned E. Depinet

Mrs. Castle was there to advise and correct, but it is not clear whether she was much help. Never much of a teacher or choreographer, she remarks in her autobiography that she had forgotten many steps within four years of her husband's death, though when the film came out she did tell an interviewer, "I had frequently to show Fred exactly how some of our old Castle steps were done." Her many memos in the RKO archives are devoid of any comments about the dancing, except to complain once that Rogers was making no effort to simulate her "very famous" coquettishly raised shoulders, "which practically everyone in the United States remembers as the trade-mark of the Castle dancing." Astaire, she reported to RKO, tells her "he has tried in every way to teach Miss Rogers a few of the principal characteristics, but she has shown no disposition to dance in any way except straight Ginger Rogers style."

On hand was Mrs. Castle's print of *The Whirl of Life*, the film she had made with her husband in 1914. The film contains several illuminating dance sequences, and Mrs. Castle complained that the print became worn from "continuous running" at RKO (though studio personnel responded that the film was mostly run by her and was damaged when she showed it at a private party).

THE NUMBERS

A
THE YAMA YAMA MAN
(1′50″)

The film begins, appropriately enough, with the meeting of the Castles.[7] Astaire, a second-string comic in a New York show, is interested in the show's leading lady, but she stands him up and he finds himself dateless on the beach at New Rochelle on a Sunday afternoon.

He and Rogers dive into the water in separate efforts to rescue a small stray dog from drowning, and bump into each other while swimming (A 1, 2). (Irene Castle, a skilled swimmer, pointedly suggested to RKO that the "poorly executed dive by Miss Rogers" be cut from the film.) In real life, the Castles had simply been introduced by a mutual friend at a swimming party. By altering events slightly, the scriptwriters have not only expanded the opportunities for gentle comedy, but also are able to furnish a limited glimpse of Vernon Castle's great fondness for animals. When she learns Astaire is an actor, Rogers brings him home to dry off and cajoles him into watching her impression of a famous number by Ziegfeld headliner Bessie McCoy.

McCoy (who also lived in New Rochelle) became an overnight Broadway sensation in 1908 with her solo "The Yama Yama Man."[8] Bright-eyed, stage-struck Irene had become mesmerized by the solo and worked out her own version, which she performed at amateur theatricals. Rogers' imitation of the imitation begins as she sings the song in a breathily emphatic manner that unfortunately severely undercuts the melody's beguiling lilt (A 3). She then plunges into a dance involving a great deal of cheery, childlike galumphing, including repetitive high kicks and an endearingly effortful split, all carried out with a winning, eager-to-please air (A 4). She was coached in the solo by Daphne Pollard, and Mrs. Castle apparently made no objections to the choreography, though she did criticize Rogers' makeup, crisply pointing out that the black spots should have been placed on cheek and chin rather than on both cheeks.[9] An eyewitness description of the dance by the real McCoy suggests that Rogers' rendition is wildly off the mark (though, of course, it may be a fair approximation of Irene Castle's version). A 1908 newspaper review contained this account: "She swings on her heel and leaps away into a wild fantastic headlong dance—the dance of a crazy king's clown, half girl, half wild boy, heady with the wine of the Spring air at twilight. . . . Her face flickers with changing moods. . . . She circles madly . . . like an imprisoned moth."

Throughout, Rogers is watched over by her wary, protective servant, played by Walter Brennan (A 5). The original servant was black; by giving the part to a white, the scriptwriters apparently felt they would have more freedom to develop the character, to assert his presence in the story, and to expand the opportunities for

[7] An opening title says the year is 1911, whereas the Castles actually met in 1910; this change was apparently made to facilitate the film's later compression of events.

[8] This song, written for McCoy's show *The Three Twins,* had music by Karl Hoschna and a lyric by Otto Hauerback (later Harbach).

[9] An objection corroborated by photographs—although Irene Castle seems to have put the cheek spot on the opposite side from McCoy. Neither Castle nor McCoy wore gloves with such exaggeratedly long fingers as Rogers. The baggy costume is supposed to suggest Pierrot, not the Yama Yama Man, a figure from children's fiction of the era.

A1 A2 A3 A4
A5 B1 B2 B3
B4 B5 B6 B7

humor. Irene Castle told RKO the character was "too prominent" in the film.[10]

B
BY THE LIGHT OF THE SILVERY MOON
(1′ 32″)

Uncomfortable but gracious as a captive audience, Astaire apparently warms to Rogers and to her family, which is extremely supportive of her, as the evening wears on.[11] At midnight, she accompanies him to the train station, where a stocky young man (Sonny Lamont) has been urged by fellow revelers to perform a tap dance. Astaire watches for a while and then, to Rogers' delight, casually intrudes on Lamont's routine and effortlessly shows up the lumbering amateur.

Astaire's solo serves a dramatic function by giving Rogers evidence of his skills as a dancer and by suggesting he already cares enough about her to show off for her benefit. The dance is close to a traditional soft shoe, with an easy, unclouded, ingratiatingly direct relationship to the music, showing little of the rhythmic complexity characteristic of Astaire's style. In his dance, Astaire keeps alternating between light footwork —as if to say to Lamont, "This is what you think you look like"—and a coarse, galumphing heaviness, as if to say, "This is what you actually look like."

Seated on a bench, he calmly watches Lamont begin his routine to a 1909 Gus Edwards song. Astaire then interrupts by rapping out a more imaginative tap phrase while still seated, forcing Lamont into more desperate efforts to show his stuff (B1). Astaire eventually sneaks out on the floor behind him and impudently echoes his steps (B2). Before Lamont can think up a defense, Astaire circles him in a mocking frolic and then intimidates him off the floor by rapping out a heavy tap burst behind his back (B3).

Astaire now has the arena to himself. He flutters out a set of delicate toe-taps punctuated by a rough kick to a nearby freight wagon (B4, 5). To make the air of insult quite unmistakable, Astaire flicks Lamont's tie (B6) and then returns to sardonic hyperdelicacy by tip-tap-toeing across the floor and around a pole (B7). He shifts abruptly to a heavy, staggering step that propels him backward to where Lamont is standing, forcing the hapless tapper to move farther out of the way (B8).

To finish, Astaire crosses the floor once again for a sailing swing around the pole (B9) and then, after a reaction shot of Rogers urging him on (B10), romps up on the freight wagon, kicks its forward rail (B11), glides down its tail ramp (B12), and lightly frolics over to Rogers to resume his seat at her side (B13). She is understandably impressed.

C
THE HEN PECKS
(2′8″)

When the train arrives, Astaire, urged on by the conductor, shyly kisses the appreciative Rogers on the cheek (C1).

Thrilled by her first in-person brush with a real theatrical personality, she ventures to New York with some friends to see him in action (C2). She is appalled to discover that his role is that of

[10] In her autobiography she says the racial transformation was to avoid giving offense to Southern audiences—a charge producer Pandro Berman finds absurd, since blacks were frequently depicted in servant roles in other films of the time.

[11] Apparently to help develop a rags-to-riches formula, the film shows Irene Castle's family to be substantially less well off than it actually was. She complained in a memo to RKO that the furnishings in the Foote home were "much too shabby and in bad taste." The Footes owned a yacht, not simply the rowboat used in the beach scene.

B8 B9 B10 B11
B12 B13 C1 C2
C3 D1 D2 E1

a punishment-receiving comic stooge to Lew Fields (C3). Although the scenes showing Rogers' outrage are not historically accurate, the barbershop sketch is—except that one should imagine the stooge played by a lankier man with extraordinarily long legs. Fields, the father of lyricist Dorothy Fields, had performed this reportedly show-stopping routine with Vernon Castle on Broadway and was called upon to stage it for the film.

D
REHEARSAL SEQUENCE
(17")

Rogers confronts Astaire backstage and impetuously accuses him of wasting his dancing talent (D1). He is irritated at being badgered by this naïve amateur but can't resist another visit to New Rochelle. After a bit of shy, awkward banter, and through the complicity of Zowie, the little dog they had jointly rescued (the original was a sturdy English bulldog), they are soon happily riding around in a rented automobile. Judging from Irene Castle's autobiography, the extreme innocence of the courtship depicted in the film is considerably exaggerated.

They are eventually seen in her living room rehearsing a dance routine to "King Chanticleer," a 1910 tune by Nat D. Ayer (D2). He is beginning to pursue a dancing career and has begun to work her into the act. She is breathlessly willing and eager to learn.

E
ONLY WHEN YOU'RE IN MY ARMS
(1'4")

After a sequence in which her parents try to stay out of the way, expecting Astaire to pop the question (a coy sequence Mrs. Castle said she couldn't stand, unfortunately without result), Astaire sings to Rogers the film's lovely new ballad with its apt lyric: "I can see myself doing the things that I never could do, it's true, but only when you're in my arms" (E1). He then proposes marriage and, when Rogers eagerly accepts, gives her a real kiss in close-up for the first time in their films (E2).

F
WAITING FOR THE ROBERT E. LEE
(1'36")

Now married, and adequately rehearsed, Astaire and Rogers audition for Lew Fields.[12] The bouncy little duet they perform is set to a ragtime-era classic, written in 1911 by Lewis F. Muir, and largely derives from the cakewalk and polka. There are also somewhat mellowed and refined references to the Texas Tommy, a cheerfully boisterous social dance the Castles tried to reform out of fashion later in the decade. The dance is a neatly crafted display piece, shaped with a vaudevillian's sense of presentation as well as with an auditioner's desire to show off all the tricks.

Astaire and Rogers trot out onto the stage and establish the opening with a crisp stamp of the foot (F1). Then, facing each other, they do some skipping steps, to one side and then to the other, and a strutting, circling do-si-do (F2). These two ideas are then varied: the side skips travel more and are partnered (F3), and the circling is done in place.

A kick is added to the skipping, light-footed base, partnered front to front (F4) or back to

[12] According to Irene Castle, it was she alone who auditioned for Fields, eventually winning a small part in his current show. However, according to Helen Hayes (who was watching from the wings), after Irene had been in the show for a while, the Castles did a duet audition for Fields in a scene very much like the one in the film.

E2 F1 F2 F3
F4 F5 F6 F7
F8 F9 F10 F11

back (F5). This is the step that, according to the supposed originator of the Texas Tommy, Ethel Williams, was the basis of that dance: "a kick and a hop three times on each foot." Then a brisk Astaire double helix sends the dancers swirling around each other (F6) until they end up front to front again and render one of the most notorious Texas Tommy steps: Rogers is spun away from Astaire and then wound back into his arms like a yo-yo (F7, 8).

As the song's chorus is repeated, a cheerfully agitated figure for violins becomes prominent. At first, bolting around the floor, their hands clasped behind each other's necks (F9), the dancers ignore that line in the music. But then, still in that formation, they burst into a brilliant series of quick cross-steps, reflecting the agitation of the violins (F10)—an idea that is pure Astaire.

For a topper, Rogers flops over as Astaire catches her (F11), and then Astaire steps over her (F12)—a maneuver that clearly anticipates some of the flashy, slightly sadistic partnering of the Lindy or jitterbug. The finish involves some snappy toeing-in and heeling-out (F13) and a final vaudeville-style lunge in unabashed anticipation of riotous applause (F14).

G
CASTLE WALK REHEARSAL
(45″)

Fields is unimpressed and sees no future for an act in which a man dances with his wife (G1), but a couple of French producers sign Astaire to appear in a revue in Paris. In a confusion invented for the film, he and Rogers believe the Frenchmen want their dancing act and are not disabused until they reach Paris.

The French revue is delayed for weeks and the couple, attended by Brennan, live off advances in the meantime. With their last sou, Astaire buys Rogers a Dutch bonnet she had admired in a shopwindow (G2).[13] As they rehearse sadly in their hotel room, an agent, investigating the noise, breaks in, likes what she sees, and arranges an audition for them at the Cafe de Paris (G3). The step they have been doing, Astaire informs her, might well be called the Castle Walk.

H
THE DARKTOWN STRUTTERS' BALL
(27″)

Astaire and Rogers go to the Cafe de Paris the night before their audition is to take place, in order to get a free meal and to size the place up. Rogers is wearing a version of Irene Castle's original garb—her wedding dress and her new Dutch bonnet. From the bandstand, a singer renders a well-known American ragtime tune in French (H1)—a bit of an anachronism, since the song was written in 1917, by Shelton Brooks.

I
TOO MUCH MUSTARD
(1′36″)

Following the Castles' actual experience of 1912, a Russian nobleman in the audience, learning of their presence, requests that the young couple dance for him. Though unprepared, they do a dance built on the Castle Walk to music written in 1911 by Cecil Macklin.

[13] The headpiece is referred to as a "Dutch cap" in the film, a term that in England is slang for a contraceptive. This jaunty euphemism has never made it across the Atlantic, but Vernon Castle, English by birth, was doubtless well aware of it. It seems odd that RKO wasn't sensitive to this issue, certain to cause tittering when the film was shown in Britain. Irene Castle unfailingly refers to the headdress as a "Dutch bonnet" in her writings and in her memos to RKO, and "bonnet" is a more accurate description of the item. Mrs. Castle was actually given the fashion-setting bonnet by a friend, not by her husband.

F12 F13 F14 G1
G2 G3 H1 I1
I2 I3 I4 I5

Here the film telescopes some events. Actually, the Castles had already appeared in the French revue and had danced in it an acrobatic duet something like the "Waiting for the Robert E. Lee" number. It was this dance that they performed on their legendary big night. Their rejection of acrobatic dances, and their self-conscious quest for refinement and simplicity in dancing, came later. (The Castle Walk, in fact, was born months later, after they had returned to New York.) But even though the dance Astaire and Rogers perform may be slightly advanced historically, it does neatly put on display at this crucial evening the kind of dancing the Castles eventually made popular and were best known for.

Irene Castle says the Castle Walk evolved accidentally. Being rather tired from dancing one night, "more as rest than anything else, we fell into a reverse of the usual proceeding. In all dances the weight is thrown down on the foot. For a change we threw the weight up." In their manual on "modern dancing" the Castles explain that the dance begins with a walk (the one-step); then "raise yourself up slightly on your toes at each step, with the legs a little stiff, and breeze along happily and easily, and you know all there is to know about the Castle Walk. To turn a corner . . . keep walking . . . in the same direction leaning over slightly . . . a little like a bicycle rounding a corner. . . . It sounds silly and is silly. That is the secret of its popularity!" Interestingly, *The New York Times'* dance critic John Martin complained, in a thoughtful 1939 article on the film, that the Astaire-Rogers version of the dance was insufficiently silly.

After a spinning flourish, Astaire and Rogers begin with a jaunty, stiff-legged Castle Walk twice around the floor (I1). There are Castle-devised embellishments: little hitch steps and an impudent back kick that happens exactly on a musical cue and thus seems to owe little to Astaire's aesthetic (I2). The walk is developed into a set of shunting side-steps (the Castle glide) and then into a nested walk in which both dancers face the same direction—a variation that allows for an amusing kicking lift from behind (I3).[14]

[14] Neither the hitch step nor the back kick is mentioned in the Castles' dancing manual, but the Castles include both, as well as a less flamboyant version of the lift, in their demonstration of this dance in *The Whirl of Life.* (However, in that version the hitch step and the back kick are done one after the other, not separated by more walking as in the Astaire-Rogers version.)

After a brief return to the standard Castle Walk (and back kick), there is a brilliant variation derived from suggestions in the Castle manual: a twisting, quick-paced circling of the floor in which forward steps are interlaced with side steps (I4). Also, starting with this phrase, the choreography begins to lie less directly on the music. A beautiful Astaire double helix in which the dancers brightly spin in independent circles around each other (I5) leads to another kicking lift (as in I3) and then to what seems to be a mincing exaggeration of the Castle Walk: a twisting, high-stepping partnered prance around the floor (I6). Significantly, the dance again is laid literally on the music for this satiric phrase.

Then, taking Rogers by one hand, Astaire sends her swooping in a wide circle around him. As she sweeps around, he turns, wrapping her arm around his neck so that he is soon wound into her arms (I7–9). This is a variation on a maneuver the Castles called the Wind Up, a version of which is found in several other Astaire duets (3 E23, 5 E19, 14 G15, 18 G4; parodied in 15 G11 and 21 E4). Interestingly, it is Rogers' *left* arm that gets wrapped around Astaire's neck, which means, of course, that she gets wound into proper ballroom position. In the Castle version it

I6 I7 I8 I9

I10 I11 J1 J2

J3 J4 J5 J6

is the woman's *right* arm that is wound around, which means that, once wound, the woman has to reverse arms smoothly in order to resume the usual ballroom position.

Astaire and Rogers conclude their exhibition dance with a turning version of the Castle Walk (labeled, appropriately enough, the Spin), which sends them swirling (pivoting on the right foot, just as in the book) exultantly around the floor until they break out of the turns and bow to the Russian nobleman (I 10, 11).

J
MEDLEY MONTAGE
(6′45″)

In the movies, unlike life, success is generally found to be less interesting than struggle, and so the film devotes just a few minutes to showing the Castles at the peak of their influence and popularity.

As soon as Astaire and Rogers return to their table, they discover that everyone in the place seems to be out on the dance floor Castle Walking. This leads to a well-paced montage illustrating their sudden, glittering success.[15] Their triumph at the cafe sends them twirling around the United States, selling books and records, setting fashions, inaugurating nightclubs, and endorsing hats, shoes, beauty creams, and cigars. Blended into the montage are several brief dances.[16]

The first is a tango, performed in appropriate, yet oddly distracting costumes, that takes place at Sans Souci, a New York restaurant the Castles owned. The choreography may be a bit genteel as tangos are supposed to go, but it deals with the dance's sexuality in the stylized manner Astaire preferred. Rogers and Astaire enter, then separate and, hands clasped behind them (a formation the Castles called the Innovation), pulsate chest to chest to the music's rhythms (J 1). Gradually they are drawn into each other's arms by the rocking insistence of the music (J 2). At the end, Rogers is sent into a set of dreamy spins and then topples decoratively, but surrenderingly, into Astaire's embrace—a maneuver she handles splendidly (J 3).[17] Also notable is the way the choreography plays around with the throbbing tango rhythm: although the dancers are always loyal to it, they often deal with it quite freely. It's a very tricky dance.

At Castle House, the first of the academies where they taught dancing and gave fashionable teas, two dances are shown. The first is the fox trot, represented only by a fragment. The Castles popularized this ballroom dance and are

[15] The original plan was to show Astaire and Rogers accompanied by black musicians, to represent the orchestras of Jim Europe and others who often worked with the Castles. The idea was scrapped, however, when Hollywood's censorship office gratuitously pointed out to RKO that this would "give serious offense to audiences throughout the southern part of the United States . . . and your studio is likely to be deluged with protests." A similar admonition was wired from RKO's New York office: "Southerners are certain to dislike use colored orchestra Castles picture and since it cannot make any difference entertainment wise . . . strongly advise use of white men. No one remembers or cares which they used and we should not take chance with colored."

[16] The dance music in the montage includes "The Rose Room" (tango) by Art Hickman (1917), "The Syncopated Walk" (fox trot) by Irving Berlin (1914), the traditional "Little Brown Jug" (polka), and "Dengozo" (maxixe) by Ernesto Nazareth (1915). The Castles danced "The Syncopated Walk" on Broadway in a hit show built around them, *Watch Your Step*, in 1914–15. This important event in their careers is otherwise unsaluted in the film, to Mrs. Castle's regret.

[17] The sensuality in this fragment, however abstracted, does not seem to be authentic Castle. As Mrs. Castle recalls, "If Vernon had ever looked into my eyes with smoldering passion during the tango, we would have both burst out laughing."

J7 J8 J9 J10

J11 J12 J13 J14

J15 J16 J17 K1

sometimes credited with inventing it, though Irene Castle said in 1938, "It was [bandleader] Jim Europe who suggested the fox trot to us, and for all I know, he invented it." The second is the polka in which the characteristic skittering hops gradually become more theatrical (J 4).

Next the Rogers bob, noticeably longer than the Castle bob, is shown sweeping the country (J 5). At Mrs. Castle's insistence, a shot of a woman with her hair cut more authentically is incorporated into the montage (J 6).[18]

The last dance segment, and the longest, is the maxixe, preferably pronounced "mashish," say the Castles in their manual. It takes place at Castles by the Sea, a supper club on Long Island where they often performed. The basis of this dance, a very hot item in 1914, is a version of the two-step: the dancers step to one side while swaying in the opposite direction, giving the dance an undulating voluptuousness. At the inauthentically brisk tempo used in the film, the dance emerges as more cheery than voluptuous, however.[19]

[18] According to one of Mrs. Castle's stories, the bob was mothered by necessity. When she swirled while dancing, hairpins would fly off and hit customers. In another story, she says she did it because she was going to the hospital for an operation and didn't want nurses to fuss with her hair.

[19] *The New York Times'* dance critic John Martin asserted in 1939 that the dance tempos "are all too fast for historical accuracy. . . . The maxixe especially has lost its essential quality for this reason." Ballroom dance expert Ed Sims thoroughly agrees about the maxixe, but not about the other dances. Although the Castles stress the need for slow dance tempos in their manual, the exhibition dances in *The Whirl of Life,* including some maxixe fragments, are taken at quick tempos, even allowing for vagaries of camera and projection speeds.

The basic move-one-way, sway-the-other joke is introduced clearly at the outset, when a series of such steps carry Astaire and Rogers around the floor (J 7). Next, in imitation of a figure in the music, they do another maxixe step—a set of tiny, puttering steps, which contrasts with the earlier expansive swaying (J 8). This is repeated, and then the whole idea is broadened: the swaying two-step becomes bigger and a turn is added (J 9), while the puttering steps become more focused (J 10). Then the contrast is further sharpened—and sometimes altered so that it does not directly reflect the music. A lunging kick is added to the two-step figure (J 11), and the puttering figure is usually done in close partnering, sometimes accompanied by complex arm shifts (J 12). There is a quick lift (J 13) and a fleeting reprise of the Castle Walk (J 14), and all ends harmoniously with a skating version of the swaying step (J 15) and a theatrical pose (J 16).

The montage ends with a spectacular effect: to symbolize the Castles' 1914 whirlwind circumnavigation of the United States, during which they performed in thirty-two cities in twenty-eight days, Astaire and Rogers are seen dancing across a huge map while, in their wake, miniature dancing couples spring up, until the whole map swarms with dancing Americans (J 17). The sequence was filmed from a forty-foot tower in daylight at the RKO ranch.

K
HELLO! HELLO! WHO'S YOUR LADY FRIEND?
(1′ 35″)

Their success is clouded by the news that war has broken out. Settled now in a spacious Long Island home, Astaire harbors thoughts of joining the British military.

He is next seen performing at a benefit for the Royal Flying Corps. Backed by a chorus of cadets, he romps through a solo that is set in Vernon Castle's style—an amusing routine built on scooting, careening, and leg slinging. This kind of dancing is usually labeled "eccentric" and is associated with dancers like Ray Bolger; its most memorable development in film is by James Cagney in *Yankee Doodle Dandy* (1942).[20] The solo is Astaire's only film venture into this kind of dancing, and he is obviously not its exemplar: on him the style loses its disjointed quirkiness. Purposeful awkwardness and studied uncoordination were not really within his capabilities—he simply could not make movement look unnatural or truly eccentric. But if the solo lacks stylistic authenticity, it abounds in its own kind of charm.

First Astaire strides out onto the stage and spiritedly sings the verse of the song—a British music-hall favorite from 1913, with music by Harry Fragson and a lyric by Worton David and Bert Lee. As the onstage chorus takes up the song, he romps across the stage (K 1) and is joined by a soldier in drag (representing the lady friend in question). The pair engage in a mock flirtation involving dropped handkerchiefs and whispered nothings.

This soon devolves into a shoving match, which ends as (s)he delivers an unladylike kick to the seat of Astaire's pants (K 2) and then briskly

[20] The Cagney role was reportedly first offered to Astaire, who turned it down, thinking it not right for him.

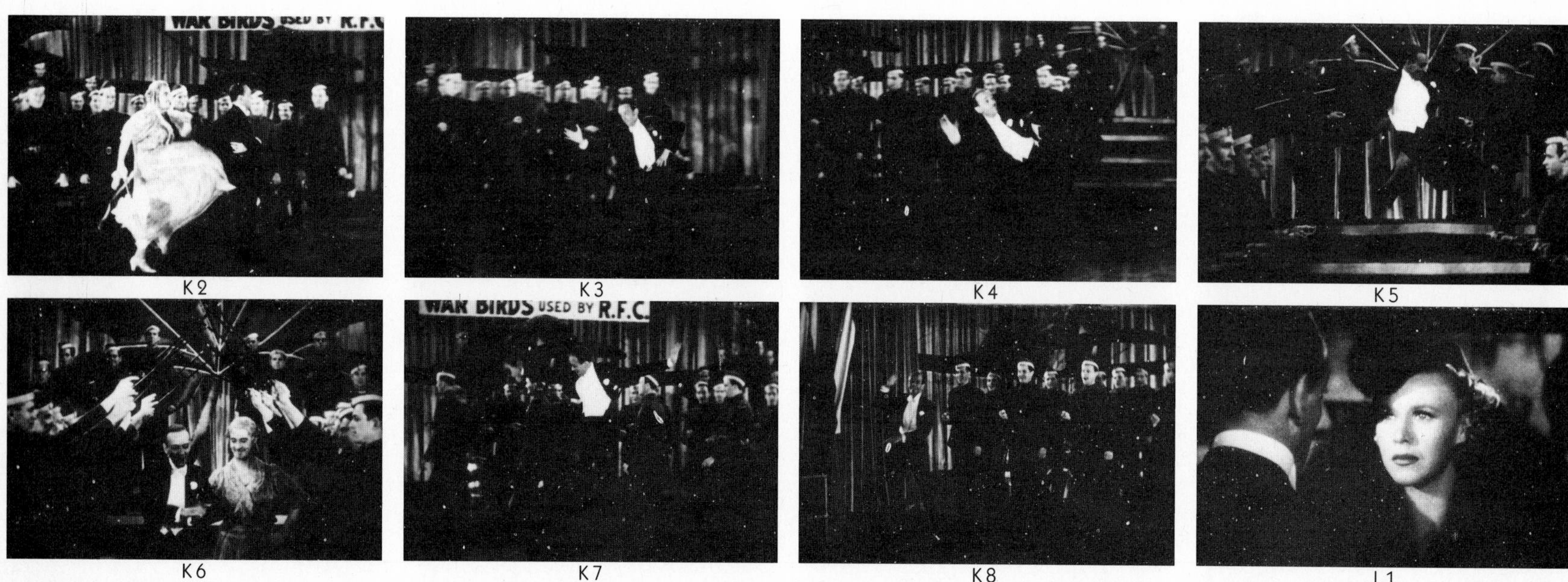

K 2 K 3 K 4 K 5

K 6 K 7 K 8 L 1

exits. Abandoned, Astaire launches into a cocky solo featuring swaggering, spread-legged slides across the floor (K 3), a scooting back-kick (K4), and soaring vaults (K 5). Presumably charmed by the exhibition, the lady friend rejoins Astaire for a congenial stroll through an arbor formed by the crossed swagger sticks of the chorus (K 6), then leaves again as Astaire finishes the number off with a leg-fluttering jump (K 7) and a cheery wave to the audience (K 8).

L
THE LAST WALTZ
(2′ 10″)

Moved by the sight of the young soldiers in the chorus, Astaire gives in to his conscience. He enlists in the Royal Flying Corps and then explains his decision to the worried Rogers (L 1).

Although the war benefit is a fiction created for the film, Astaire's depiction of Vernon Castle's deep concern about getting into the war is quite accurate. Castle was obsessed by the war and was often guilt-ridden over pursuing his lucrative stage and dancing career while his relatives and boyhood friends in England were in danger. And it is clear he felt keen social pressure, even across the Atlantic: "Sometimes, in the midst of a dance with Irene, with thousands of eyes following me . . . I'd be thinking not of being graceful as I could but of the reception I'd get from the home folks if I waited until the war was over to go back." Because his slight physical build made him an inappropriate ground soldier, he decided to go into flying and, to expedite things, took private flying lessons before enlisting.

Before going to France in 1916, he had leave in London, where his wife met him and they danced at a royal benefit. This reunion is moved in the film to the Cafe de Paris, and tension is added by having Astaire delayed because he volunteers to fly an additional mission in order to retake some photographs (Castle actually did fly such a photographic mission). Rogers is enormously relieved when he suddenly appears at the nightclub. He takes her in his arms and they begin to waltz (L 2).

This is the only genuine, fully developed waltz Astaire performed in his film career. By the time he reached Hollywood, the waltz seemed a dated and corny remnant of an earlier era, and, except here, he used the form only fragmentarily (3 F, 10 E, 18 G, 25 C) or for purposes of parody (3 G, 6 H). In this film, however, the waltz was appropriate, and Astaire tenders due homage.

The duet is considerably flawed. Set to three waltzes awkwardly spliced end to end, the choreography lurches from mood to mood and lacks much of the meticulous cumulativeness typical of Astaire's best dances. Moreover, Rogers' gown is defiantly undanceworthy: an overdecorated derivative of an evening dress Irene Castle had modeled in 1934. Rogers' version has sleeves with great hunks of dangling fur that slide around on her arms and swing uncontrollably as she moves, creating a ludicrous aftereffect (see p. 150).

For all that, however, this last dance of the Castles—and the last substantial duet for Astaire and Rogers in their legendary series of films at RKO—is deeply affecting. Far more than anything in the dialogue, it conveys the central message of the film, showing, with understatement and astonishing economy of means, two people who have been able to establish a richly loving and mutually dependent relationship even in the penetrating glare of the public spotlight.

The most moving aspect of the duet is the way the dancers gradually take mental leave of their nightclub audience to focus on each other. This idea is most fully developed in the last part of the dance, but it is set up at the very beginning: as the waltz opens, Astaire and Rogers hail friends at a ringside table (L 3); after that, their attention never returns to the onlookers.

The first section of the dance, set to the "Cecile Waltz" written in 1914 by Frank W. McGee, is gently exploratory—there are some soft, flowing turns around the floor and then solicitous, if distant, partnering as Astaire tenderly steers Rogers by touching her waist or fingertips (L 4).

The second section, set to Charles Ancliffe's "Nights of Gladness" from 1913, is bouncier—the waltz as polka. The dancers skip across the floor (L 5), or spin happily in each other's arms (L 6) as Rogers' gigantic fur sleeves flounce and slither absurdly.

The music then shifts to the "Missouri Waltz," arranged in 1914 by Frederick Knight Logan from music by John V. Eppel. To this the dancers perform a hesitation waltz, described by the Castles in their manual as requiring a six-count over two measures, pausing on the last two counts: "By counting 1, 2, 3, 4, 5, 6, and holding or hesitating the 5, 6, you can't very well go wrong." The hesitation notion is established simply enough: with Astaire partnering from behind, the dancers pace on the first four beats

L 2 L 3 L 4 L 5
L 6 L 7 L 8 L 9

and pause in place and rock lightly on the hesitations (L7)—an approach that has the effect of arresting the dancers' motion while continuing its implied momentum. This idea is then elaborated to incorporate a low floating lift on the hesitations (L8).

Now the dancers turn inward increasingly and abandon choreographic formula. Astaire holds Rogers from behind as they turn (L9); then, as she presses herself to his chest, he cradles her in a slowly swirling lift that rides over several measures of the music (L10). At this point the spotlight that had been following them drifts away and they are lit only by an isolating light above them. Then, as the overhead light goes out, there is a moment of darkness before the follow spot again picks them out. It's as if the people lighting the dance exhibition, noting how intensely personal the dance had become, were uncertain about invading the dancers' privacy.

Rogers regains her footing, makes one soft turn, and then returns to Astaire's arms. They rock gently in that position, and then all movement subsides—the ultimate hesitation—as they gaze at each other: secure, content, together, and alone in a crowded public arena (L11).

M
ONLY WHEN YOU'RE IN MY ARMS
(REPRISE) (39")

Early the next morning they are shown kissing again (M1). Next they learn that the United States has entered the war, and, in a quintessentially American interpretation of military history, Rogers jubilantly concludes, "That means the war is practically over!"

Telescoping events a bit, the film soon has Astaire transferred to Texas as a flight instructor, while Rogers does war-relief work and then begins a career in the movies. By telephone they excitedly plan a reunion in Texas—a fiction created by the scriptwriters, but one that neatly brings the elements of the story to a dramatic conclusion. Astaire arranges with the overbearing hotel manager to have a garden orchestra play a set of songs outside their window to remind Rogers of their life together. Then he returns to the airfield for a few hours. His fatal plane crash is shown with considerable accuracy: to avoid hitting another plane, he pulls his plane up; the engine stalls; and he crashes when he is unable to regain control.

Meanwhile, Rogers has arrived at the hotel. Brennan comes to her room and somberly tells her the tragic news (M2).

The film's ending was clearly a problem for director and writers. It was important to keep its inherent sentimentality within bounds and to handle the episode with taste and care. Therefore, in various script revisions, Brennan's speech and Rogers' tearful reminiscences to the garden orchestra's musical reprises were considerably tightened and shortened, to the point where preview audiences complained that Rogers seemed insufficiently emotional. Irene Castle agreed, pointing out to RKO: "Miss Rogers played the scene with more calm than anybody could, or would, who had suffered such a serious heartbreaking loss."[21] Responding to these complaints, Potter shot an additional segment showing Rogers crying and inserted it into the scene (M3).

The setting for the concluding dance fragment also underwent change. In Hammerstein's original treatment, the finale was almost phantasmagoric: there was to be an elaborate montage showing people dancing, dance teams, dance orchestras, and finally Astaire and Rogers as "themselves" doing fragments of their own dances, including the Continental. This was reduced simply to an intimate, ghostly duet, but all scripts called for Astaire's disembodied voice to say something to Rogers in invitation such as "I'll be with you always," "Face the music, darling. You've got to go on," "Chin up—chest out—and your best foot forward," or, simply, "Irene, dance with me."

In the film, the voice-from-the-grave idea is dropped. Instead, Rogers simply gazes tearfully out the window and, in double exposure, sees two dancing figures: Astaire in his military uniform and herself in her wedding dress and Dutch bonnet (M4). The dancers swirl away down a garden path to the melody of the film's love song and then vanish (M5, 6). This ending—simple, eloquent, and nostalgic—at once recalls the story of Vernon and Irene Castle and quietly marks the conclusion of an important phase in the careers of Ginger Rogers and Fred Astaire. From the war zone Vernon Castle once wrote to his wife, "We did have such wonderful times, didn't we, darling?"

[21] She helpfully added: "*Note:* The woman, who acted as Mrs. Castle's secretary and manager at the time Capt. Castle was killed, and gave her the shocking news, is here in L.A. and could be consulted by the director, as to what actually did happen. Very few imaginary emotions are as reliable and convincing as true ones from life."

L10 L11 M1 M2

M3 M4 M5 M6

Doing the maxixe with Rogers

12.

Broadway Melody of 1940

1940

Broadway Melody of 1940 is most notable for the terrific tap routines, for the absurdly overblown production numbers, for the sexlessness of the central love story, and for the insipidity of the character Fred Astaire plays. Its pleasures, in short, are real but limited.

In this, his first film after the series with Ginger Rogers at RKO, Astaire found himself at MGM embedded in a production that was determined to be lavish (though, to Astaire's disappointment, plans to do the film in Technicolor were scrapped, because it was feared that the ominous political conditions in Europe would reduce the film's market). The studio went out of its way to present him with a coherent script, a set of stylish songs by Cole Porter, a partner—Eleanor Powell—who was its hottest dancing property, and plenty of glittering stage sets. The result, as Astaire later recalled, was "a big Metro mess, but it was fun to do at the time."

Though Powell performed quite a bit of acrobatics and rather too much ballet in her film career, her specialty was tap. As a tap dancer (as, for that matter, in ballet and acrobatics) she was inclined to be of the pneumatic school, but in her tap duets with Astaire in this film her tendency toward flashy and predictable effects is brought firmly under control, and the results are wonderful. Astaire has a witty solo and does, in addition, some nice vaudeville-inspired dancing with another seasoned hoofer, George Murphy.[1] Yet despite the film's considerable dance appeal, there is a lack of variety overall, since the dance highlights all involve tap dancing and cluster in one expressive corner.

THE SCRIPT

Astaire and Murphy play a couple of struggling song-and-dance men in New York. Their act is seen by a big theatrical agent who picks out Astaire to be the dancing partner in his big new show opposite the big star, Powell. Through an accident of mistaken identity Murphy gets the job instead, but by the end this is straightened out and Astaire gets not only the part but, apparently, the girl as well.

This may not seem much of a plot, but it's Pulitzer Prize material compared with the film's direct antecedents at MGM, the *Broadway Melody*s of 1936 and 1938. Those films, both of which featured Powell, were mostly collections of vaudeville routines and production numbers scattered among a collection of subplots in search of a conclusion. The stories never made much sense, nor did anyone trouble to generate characters of depth or appeal.

Probably in deference to Astaire, the scriptwriters for *Broadway Melody of 1940* sought to put together a plot that had some coherence, or at least linearity. The story manages to stay focused on the Astaire-Powell-Murphy triangle, and each of the three is believably, if not very deeply, characterized. There is even a surprise plot twist or two. At the same time, the film does manage to incorporate a couple of off-the-wall episodes—a juggling exhibition and a screwball singing routine—that reflect some of the antics of the earlier *Broadway Melody*s.

Unlike the two earlier editions (but like the very first *Broadway Melody,* that of 1929) *Broadway Melody of 1940* is not a true backstage musical, a film where the struggle of putting on a show is a central theme. The locale is Broadway, and a show is put on during the course of the film, but its success is never in doubt and there are no squabbles with backers or haughty leading ladies. The only tensions (such as they are) concern the issue of who will be the leading man in Powell's show, not the fate of the show itself.

The script's least bearable aspect is the Astaire character. The nice guy of the 1930s films is here reduced to an utter sap as he moans ineffectually on the sidelines, lets people walk over him, and repeatedly engages in noble acts of self-sacrifice for Murphy until other people (Powell and, at the end, Murphy himself) manipulate events so that he finally gets his due. The doormat role in the movies of the time is more usually associated with George Murphy than with Astaire, but it is not worthy of either of them.

[1] Astaire agreed to do the picture only after MGM assured him he wouldn't hurt Murphy's position at the studio.

With George Murphy in "Please Don't Monkey with Broadway"

ASTAIRE AND POWELL

A major defect of the film is the near absence of romantic impetus. Whatever is going on between Astaire and Powell is left to the imagination more than revealed to the eye and ear of the beholder. According to the script, Astaire is in love with Powell from the start; she is pleased to learn of this, and in a deserted cafe they do a tap duet that they both thoroughly enjoy. Although they talk and dance together a great deal during the remainder of the film, their romance never seems more than perfunctory and mechanical. Astaire must not have been able to bring himself to feign genuine attraction, even in the dances, to the stiff and steely-grinned Powell, a problem he had with only a few partners in his career.[2] Accordingly, his duets with her, while clever and eventful, tend to be dispassionate displays of virtuosity, and the dancers rarely touch or even look at each other. It was decidedly not an artistic marriage made in heaven, and the pair never again appeared together in a motion picture.

THE MUSIC

Called upon to write his first Astaire score since *Gay Divorce* on Broadway in 1932, Cole Porter came up with a worthy collection of songs. The murmuring "I Concentrate on You" is the best-known new song, though it is unfortunately submerged in a fatuous production number. Better handled (and even better as songs) are the lilting "I've Got My Eyes on You" and the bouncy "Please Don't Monkey with Broadway." In addition, the film incorporates one of Porter's biggest hits, "Begin the Beguine," written in 1935. The snappy music for the "Jukebox Dance" was composed by Astaire's friend and sometime rehearsal pianist Walter Ruick, and the unappealing "All Ashore" was apparently written by Roger Edens.

THE CHOREOGRAPHY

Broadway Melody of 1940 was Astaire's first film away from Hermes Pan, who had collaborated on the choreography of his ten previous films. Furthermore, it was Astaire's first

[2] The closest analogy is with Ann Miller, another tap fireball, in *Easter Parade*. Astaire has two duets with her in which he is supposed to be viscerally attracted; both are singularly unconvincing in this respect (21 B, M).

(and only) film in which his female partner was accustomed to choreographing her own numbers. Astaire and Powell together created their duets in the film, although, as noted, those dances seem generally to be much closer in sensibility to Astaire than to Powell. At the start, the gap was considerable: "Fred dances on the off-beat, and mostly on the ball of the foot, while I am always on-beat, and get most of my taps from my heel," Powell wrote at the time. Then, too, Astaire, always very sensitive about his partners' height, may have found it disconcerting that Powell was almost as tall as he: Powell once wryly claimed she took a bath in Lux soap before meeting him, "hoping I'd shrink or something." All this, combined with Astaire's characteristic reserve, made their rehearsal sessions awkward, at least at the beginning—Powell recalls it took days before they got onto a first-name basis. Some of that discomfort seems to have infected their acting and dancing performances in the film, though they do look comfortable enough with each other in their final duets.

The chorus was marshaled by the film's dance director, MGM's Bobby Connolly, who had worked with Astaire on the New York and London stage versions of *Funny Face* in the late 1920s. Connolly's chief claim to fame was as the inventor of the Charleston-derived Varsity Drag for the 1927 Broadway musical, *Good News*. Another MGM choreographer, the uncredited Albertina Rasch, did the chorus work for "I Concentrate on You."

The arrangement of the numbers is a tease. A selling point of the film was the opportunity to see Powell and Astaire, two dancers who were independently famous, performing together for the first time, but that moment is put off until well into the second half of the film.

With Murphy

Rehearsing the jukebox dance with Eleanor Powell

THE NUMBERS

A
PLEASE DON'T MONKEY WITH BROADWAY
(3′ 18″)

In an amusing reversal from the usual pattern, the film *opens* with Astaire escorting a woman to the altar. It turns out that he is employed as a taxi dancer at the Dawnland Ballroom in New York, and part of his job is to pilot (or taxi) brides to the establishment's altar, where they then promptly get married (to someone else). Astaire's attitude toward his work is immediately apparent: he walks bored (A 1).

Hoping to be spotted by a Broadway agent, Astaire and his partner, Murphy, do a regular, unpaid specialty act at the ballroom. They romp through their routine and this turns out to be the lucky night—for one of them. An agent, the flappable Frank Morgan, happens to be in attendance and is impressed by Astaire's dancing. Murphy makes no effort to look inept, but the differences in ability are clear, and it is a bit unpleasant that the script emphasizes the obvious.

Recalling the number, Murphy is understandably proud: it's "a classic," he has written, "pure, solid vaudeville," so good "it could be televised today as an opening bit on any variety show." That's not a very exalted standard, but his enthusiasm is certainly justified.

The song has the requisite vaudevillian assurance and directness, and the number is carried out in an appropriate style: carefully structured hoke. Astaire and Murphy stride eagerly out onto the floor and cheerfully deliver the song, which is a plea to those seeking urban betterment to concentrate on Wall Street, Grant's Tomb, Sixth Avenue, City Hall, Brooklyn, and other insignificant parts of New York, but please, please (we beg on our knees), not to monkey with Broadway, an institution too fine for well-intentioned improvement. The performers barrel through two choruses of the song—the first sung in place, the second accompanied by strutting. To underline their final plea, they drop to their knees and lapse into broad harmony (A 2).

It is now time for the tap dance. The performers hop to it with unalloyed gusto and ingratiating charm. They begin with some oafish hot-footing and with a rapid shuffle step out to the sides. The differences between the two dancers are most obvious in these parallel passages. Astaire articulates the steps far more clearly and with far greater subtlety and dances with his whole body, while Murphy seems to be fully occupied simply trying to get all the steps in. The use of the head in the side-shuffle pattern (A 3) is a case in point. The choreography calls for each dancer to turn his head from side to side in coordination with his feet, but Astaire articulates this small movement so that it is a precisely timed gesture, whereas Murphy merely throws it in somewhere.

Next the dance expands in space, and the canes are brought into the act; the dancers even insert, during a traveling pattern, one of the backward-sliding back-kicks Astaire liked so much (A 4; compare 7 D 5–6, 18 M 5, 20, and 19 F 13).

Suddenly, high drama. Astaire slips and Murphy breaks his fall. Inconsistently with the personality he is given in the film plot, Astaire reacts to this friendly aid with singular bad humor by giving Murphy a kick in the seat of the pants (A 5). (According to Murphy, they first tried to do this with Astaire faking the kick, but it didn't work. Then Murphy suggested that Astaire do a real kick instead; "Fred instantly brightened. We did *eighteen* more takes!")

Tensions mount. While continuing to rap out a snappy pattern with their feet, the two men face off menacingly, cup their left hands at their hips, and thrust their canes into them, like swords into scabbards (A 6). Astaire pelts Murphy's face with his glove and shreds Murphy's proffered card. Insult having been heaped upon injury, the duel is on: back to back, they pace off as if planning to fight with firearms, then promptly turn and launch into a sword fight (with canes) instead. The incongruous tapping continues as they thrust and parry with Fairbanksian gusto—even managing to include some of those forays in which one duelist jumps while the other swats at his feet (A 7).

Justice soon triumphs. With one deft stroke, Murphy dispatches Astaire (A 8) and then fastidiously wipes the blood from his cane as his victim spins in agony.[3] Apparently it is bad

[3] The fatal jab comes at an appropriate spot in the music. Porter's song is of standard form, AABA, with each strain eight measures long. However, the B section really sounds as if it is going to be repeated (making the song AABBA), and the abrupt shift from B to A is unexpected and quite amusing (though some might see the sudden change of gears as a case of poor craftsmanship). The stab (A 8) comes exactly at this point of dislocation in the music.

A 1 A 2 A 3 A 4
A 5 A 6 A 7 A 8

stagecraft in ballroom tap duels, as in Shakespearean tragedy, to leave the stage littered with corpses, and so Murphy obligingly catches the toppling Astaire and drags him from the stage. As they leave, both executioner and executed tap out a vaudeville exit step and then tip their hats to the audience at the wings (A 9). A vintage close-order cross-over step is used to acknowledge the applause (A 10).

B
ALL ASHORE (I AM THE CAPTAIN)
(4′ 24″)

In trying to determine which name goes with which dancer (he refers to Astaire as "the one on the end"), Morgan mixes them up. Meanwhile, Astaire, unaware of Morgan's esteem, steals into a Broadway theatre and admiringly watches Powell perform.

Her number is introduced by a chorus of sailors, singing, leaning, and pulling ropes. Soon Powell enters by sliding down the mast (B 1). She sings and then launches into a tap routine that contains a few pleasantly surprising hesitations, an effect soon vulgarized into high kicks with delayed recoveries (B 2). Next, in between being slung around the stage by the crew (B 3), she manages to whip off a short rendition of her signature step—a multiple spin on one foot with the other rapping out an occasional tap pattern (B 4). She falls into a split and briefly becomes a rope on which the crew tugs energetically—a singularly unattractive image. A few more tosses and she joins the crew in an anxious salute to end the number.

C
BETWEEN YOU AND ME
(4′ 38″)

Back at his office, Morgan excitedly tells his partner and Powell about his great discovery (C 1).[4] Because of the name confusion, Morgan's partner offers Murphy the audition. Murphy happily agrees but tells Astaire he has turned down the offer. He knows full well that Astaire, the quintessential nice guy, will urge him to take it even though this may mean breaking up the act, and will also agree with puppylike eagerness to do the choreography—or "make up the steps," as Murphy puts it (C 2).

Murphy's audition is a full-blown and full-dress duet with Powell. He sings her a song and partners her in an energetic and fairly unimaginative ballroom exhibition duet. Starting with some odd and inconsequential tiptoeing steps, the dancers are soon wafting their way around the floor. Included are several lifts (sometimes a bit effortful), something Astaire shuns in his duets with Powell (C 3, 4).

The ending is given over to broad swirlings and partnered spin-outs, a nifty sequence involving a galloping tap pattern that scoots the width of the stage (C 5) and, underlined by obvious violin figures in the music, slides down ramps (C 6).

[4] When he is not sowing confusion in this film, Morgan participates in a running gag that concerns an expensive coat he bestows on his date of the evening and then tries, through various stratagems, to retrieve when he escorts her home. This was based on the real-life antics of a well-known Broadway (and later Hollywood) agent, Doc Shurr.

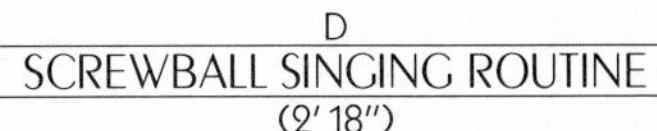

D
SCREWBALL SINGING ROUTINE
(2′ 18″)

Murphy's audition is enthusiastically received and he lands the job. Morgan, however, finally dopes out how identities were confused and informs Astaire, who self-effacingly urges secrecy. Fame and success quickly go to Murphy's head.

Meanwhile back at the rehearsals, Charlotte Arren, a comedienne not noted for her delicate effects, is auditioning as a singer. She warbles and screeches and crosses her eyes and exits on roller skates (D 1, 2).

E
I'VE GOT MY EYES ON YOU
(4′ 9″)

Murphy, hung over from a night on the town, is late for rehearsal. Astaire and Powell each try to cover for him, but with inconsistent stories. When Murphy arrives, he misreads Powell's gesture, makes advances, and gets told off by her.

On his way out of the theatre during a lunch break, Astaire comes across some memorabilia of his beloved: a small powder-puff ball (E 1) and a piece of sheet music with her picture on the cover (E 2). Unknown to him, Powell, who has deduced from a couple of his earlier slips of the tongue that he is in love with her, watches with amusement and increasing delight (E 3).

It's been over fifty minutes since Astaire last danced, but this solo certainly compensates for the wait. Warm and whimsical, it is a kind of courtship dance in absentia as Astaire frolics around the stage, showing off for Powell's pic-

A 9 · A 10 · B 1 · B 2

B 3 · B 4 · C 1 · C 2

ture or carrying it lovingly in his arms.[5] In fact the solo is the film's romantic high spot; as Stephen Harvey observes, "Astaire's most convincing display of affection toward his co-star takes place while she is discreetly off camera."

Accompanying himself at the piano, Astaire sings Porter's lovely and unpretentious song, which is particularly remarkable for its directness and its economy of construction—features not usually held to be Porter trademarks. Each of its four eight-measure strains is built out of the same basic material, but each has a separate shape and character, so that the song is a sort of theme with three developing variations. At the same time the strains are connected with logic and an easy flow, and each makes an essential contribution to the overarching line of the whole.

As he sings, Astaire pauses once to peek shyly at the cover of the sheet music (E4), then boldly closes the music entirely to sing the last strain directly to the picture. Aided by a jazz band on the soundtrack, Astaire plays the song through once more in a bouncy, faster arrangement, adding percussion from time to time by nimbly rapping the piano with one foot.

The dance begins as he snatches up the powder-puff ball and frolics around juggling with it—showing off for the picture. He tosses it around from behind his back and bounces it on his arm (E5). He pauses during a twisting turn and then, emboldened, pockets the ball and races back to the piano to take up the sheet music and swish around the floor with it in his arms, in wry semblance of a ballroom duet, including even an imaginary backbend (E6).

Propping the picture on a table, he engages it in an intricate mimed dialogue, a sequence that bubbles with impish wit. He asks her to dance for him but gives us to understand that she responds by suggesting he dance instead (E7). He cheerfully complies, hopping around in imitation of Powell's signature step, the tap spin (E8). He lets us know that she reacts angrily to this affront (E9) and, chastened, falls to one knee to plead for forgiveness (E10) and urge her to end this madness and to fly away with him. The music for this mime sequence is derived from the song's introductory verse, which is not sung in the film. A reaction shot of Powell is inserted here—the only one during the dance.

Powell apparently relents, and he gleefully scampers about with the picture, admiring it at arm's length (E11) or hugging it to his chest. His momentum takes him up a step onto a small garden set (E12). Most wonderful is the way Astaire pauses for the briefest instant as he finds himself on the garden set—he registers surprise at his new locale and assesses the new choreographic opportunities it presents. After hopping back and forth between floor and step, he embellishes this idea by springing on and off a bench three times. For the first and second of these jumps he prepares rather obviously, but the third is unpredictable—it happens when there seems to be neither space nor time enough to fit it in.

In the concluding portion of the dance, Astaire introduces and then develops a beautiful lagged leap in which one leg is thrown out while the torso and other leg seem to follow a bit later, as if in bemused afterthought. On the bench Astaire pauses and pointedly takes sight of his exit path in the distance (E13). Then he jumps down in the first of the lagged leaps (E14) and travels across the floor delivering variants of the step as he soars over each of three conveniently located easy chairs (E15). When he comes across another raised stage set, he blazes a brilliant path

[5] For another Astaire solo ostensibly motivated by his beloved's picture, see 25 H.

C3 C4 C5 C6

D1 D2 E1 E2

E3 E4 E5 E6

along its curb, frolicking on and off it (E16) and developing ideas from earlier.

Then comes one last spectacular trick: he takes the powder-puff ball from his pocket, flips it over his shoulder from behind his back, catches it on the sheet music, tosses it up onto a low overhang, and, as it plummets back to earth, effortlessly catches it in his hat, exactly on a musical cue (E17). Indeed, the flight of the powder puff has a musical logic of its own: as it rolls down the overhang, it encounters a lip at the edge and is bounced into the air at a point in the music that seems (in retrospect) to have dictated such behavior. The ball trick is not separated out in a single shot but is embedded in a lengthy shot that also includes the frolic on the curb (E16) preceding it and all the material following it.

The exit remains: a scooping variant on the lagged leap, which first takes him up onto a small stage set and then, as he cradles the sheet music, scoots him out a doorway (E18).

F
JUKEBOX DANCE (ITALIAN CAFE ROUTINE)
(2′33″)

At the conclusion of Astaire's solo, Powell comes out of hiding and applauds his efforts. He is flustered—and pleased—to discover she has been watching. She praises his skill and notes his patent superiority to Murphy as a dancer; still self-effacing, Astaire assures her of Murphy's enormous talent.

Powell maneuvers him into inviting her to lunch at a nearby cafe. Astaire is awkward in Powell's presence and gains a measure of self-confidence only when the conversation turns to dance. This idle chat leads, to no one's surprise, to the first of their duets. The dance and the music (a waiter obligingly puts a coin in the jukebox) evolve out of a basic tap rhythm that Powell demonstrates and Astaire echoes:

Both dance and music start simply: the dancers repeat the tap combination several times and travel forward with it over a pattern of rhythmically regular descending notes in the music (F1). Gradually both become more complex. The music adds countermelodies and counterrhythms, and the dancers carry their pattern to each side and once add an unexpected lurch (F2). Alternating hand claps and hops complicate the rhythm, while turns add to the visual pattern. Things soon become more playful, with episodes involving leg shaking (F3) and foot slapping (F4). This unison, parallel dancing furnishes an opportunity to compare the dancers and shows Astaire to have an edge on Powell as well as on Murphy (though to a lesser degree): he dances more fully with the whole body, and he articulates the steps more clearly and arrestingly (see F1, 3).

The time to touch—however gingerly—has arrived. It is signaled by the first clear break in unison dancing and, appropriately enough, it is Powell who issues the invitation (or challenge): she hits an abrupt tap slap, and Astaire quickly answers in kind. Together they glide somewhat tentatively around the floor, part briefly, and then, as the music speeds up, take hold of each other again and dance with far more confidence in a sequence that includes two beautiful patterns in which the dancers travel and turn simultaneously. In one, Powell hops backward while Astaire crosses his legs and swivels himself back and forth in her arms (F5). In the other, he holds a pose while she circles him in a rapid tap pattern, pivoting him as she does so—a reversal from the usual practice in ballet, where it is the man who promenades the woman (F6). As Astaire is turned, he embellishes the maneuver

E7 E8 E9 E10

E11 E12 E13 E14

E15 E16 E17 E18

by slapping the floor a couple of times with his free foot.[6]

The dancers bound out of the promenade into some fast parallel tapping where the differences in the use of the arms and upper body are again evident: Astaire is far more energized and articulate (F7). Next comes a witty use of Powell's flashy signature step, the multiple tap turn. Twice they whip out spins of this sort (F8), but instead of endlessly repeating the step to generate applause, they present it briskly—each turn is only doubled—and blend it into the fiery choreographic texture.

The finale includes slams forward, chases to the side, some blistering spins for Powell, and a repeat of the wonderful tap pivot/promenade (as in F6). At the end they spin out of the promenade and then deliver one emphatic tap blast as the music wraps itself up and vanishes (F9, 10). This kind of ending, which is also used to conclude the "Begin the Beguine" jazz-tap duet near the end of the film (12 H), was new for Astaire, whose previous dances tended to have more formal finales. The idea of having the dance suddenly evaporate—with logic but without anticipation or predictability—was probably inspired by some big-band arrangements of the time. It perfectly suited Astaire's sense of humor and artistic sensibility, and he was to use it again, and even more interestingly, in several later dances, all from the early 1940s (see 13 K, 14 F, 15 M, 17 C).

G
I CONCENTRATE ON YOU
(6′41″)

Astaire and Powell are so wrapped up in each other (we are to believe), they forget about the time and return to the rehearsal late. When Murphy sourly accuses Astaire of "chiseling" on him, Astaire, assertive for once, walks out (G1).

Next, Morgan bursts into the rehearsal, sputtering enthusiastically about his latest discovery: a unicyclist who rides "like the wind" and can stop "on a dime" at the lip of the stage. The stage area is hastily cleared, a drum is rolled, and his prodigy makes an uncertain entrance, wobbles across the stage, and topples gloriously into the orchestra pit (G2, 3).

Astaire's self-assertiveness is short-lived. On opening night he goes to wish Murphy good luck and finds him drunk and abusive. Then, while trying to strike Astaire, Murphy stumbles and knocks himself out. In an incredible act of self-abnegation, Astaire dons Murphy's costume and mask, successfully performs the opening number for him, and lets him have the credit.

The number, decked out in a harlequin motif, begins with a prologue containing some breathtakingly inept ballet dancing. Surrounded by a chorus, the tutued Powell putters vapidly in center stage while a long-suffering baritone (Douglas McPhail) croons the song in the background (G4).[7]

The masked Astaire materializes on a balcony. With what one might take to be understandable reluctance, he gradually makes his way down a staircase to Powell—sliding part of the way on

[6] This witty role-reversal idea is found in several duets of the great nineteenth-century Danish ballet choreographer, August Bournonville. Astaire uses a version of this promenade in several later duets: in *You Were Never Lovelier* (16 F10), *Yolanda and the Thief* (19 F14), *The Barkleys of Broadway* (22 I 19), and, fragmentarily, *Royal Wedding* (25 C5).

[7] Powell's principal dance training, surprisingly enough, was in ballet. She says she took only ten tap lessons (for $35) in her life. Porter's song strains somewhat for grand effect and tends to be self-consciously earnest. It also wallows in clichés ("your smile so sweet," "our arms intertwine"). And if Fortune, following the lyric, really went around saying things like "Nay, Nay!" she or he would have difficulty maintaining her or his credibility.

F1 F2 F3 F4
F5 F6 F7 F8
F9 F10 G1 G2

the banister (G5). Their duet consists mostly of coy poses, rendered tentatively and without conviction (G7, 8). The poses are mechanically embossed on the music, and often the dancers simply clunk from one to the next without meaningful transition—strongly suggesting that Astaire had little to do with the choreography. There are a few faster passages: a series of angled jumps with beats (cabrioles) that Astaire renders with requisite crispness (G6), and an appealing pattern that lopes, turns, and travels forward (G9). At the end the dancers clamber up the staircase, and Powell bends backward over the balustrade while Astaire hovers over her decoratively (G10).

This is one of the few Astaire dances in which he seems to have been unable to believe in what he was doing. His embarrassment is picked up with dry objectivity by the camera and transmitted to the audience.

H
BEGIN THE BEGUINE
(9′43″)

Urging Powell not to reveal what he has done, Astaire dashes back to Murphy's dressing room. Astaire helps the revived Murphy into his costume for the next number and tells him that it was he—Murphy—who had performed the Harlequin number (while unconscious). The next day Powell savagely disabuses the cocky Murphy of this notion. Then, when he shows up for the next performance drunk, Powell rushes to the Dawnland Ballroom, where Astaire has resumed his duties as bride escort (H1). Relieved to learn he is not an actual participant in the ceremony, Powell drags him back to the theatre to replace Murphy *again*. The message of the film seems to be that one absurdly self-abnegating turn deserves another: as it happens, the previously ill-tempered Murphy, having seen the error of his ways, has feigned drunkenness in order to give Astaire his big chance.

Meanwhile, onstage they are beginning the Beguine. According to Cole Porter, this famous song has mixed origins, employing elements of both rhumbalike dances he saw in a remote Paris nightclub as performed by natives of Martinique and music he heard on the island of Kalabahai in the East Indies. The song was introduced in 1935 in a rather unsuccessful Porter Broadway show, *Jubilee*, and was not a hit at the time. It became a real success only when it was recorded in 1938 by the jazz clarinetist Artie Shaw and his band in a bright and brilliant swing arrangement written by Jerry Gray.

It is perhaps understandable that a production number based on this song would be on the eclectic side. It is in three parts. The first is a tropical mix: the West Indies plus Polynesia. The second, a beautiful and intriguing duet for Astaire and Powell, begins in the tropics and then adds tap and Spanish dance elements. The third is pure American—a jazz-tap exhibition for the two stars set to a swing arrangement of the song featuring, as it happens, clarinet.

As the curtain rises, a soprano (H2) sultrily sings the song (or most of it[8]) and a female chorus wafts languorously across a mirrored stage with glass floor (the temperature had to be kept near freezing to prevent it from cracking under the lights). The dancers rely on an all-purpose step that they repeat agreeably, regardless of what may be happening in the music: a swinging kick alternating with a deep backbend (H3).

[8] One section of the song is not sung in the film (the second A section of the AABACC song). At 104 measures, "Begin the Beguine" is, according to Wilder, the longest popular song ever written, and it was apparently too long for the film's purposes here.

G3 G4 G5 G6
G7 G8 G9 G10
H1 H2 H3 H4

Throughout, they undulate their arms, in imitation, no doubt, of the swaying palms of the lyric (in the section of the song not sung in the film). These throbbing motions may suggest a Polynesian locale, but they are set to a Latin pulse.

Powell emerges from the background and does a brief, semaphoric solo in which incongruous high kicks (H4) are mixed with deep backbends (H5). As the chorus clears out, she is drawn to an image of a male dancer in the distance (H6).

The image proves to be only a reflection, and there is an arresting moment of dislocation as the man—Astaire—enters from behind her (H7). He approaches her, and an extraordinary duet ensues: there are no climaxes, and everything is controlled and even, dreamlike. The dancers continually circle each other, touching, competing, imitating, but they never really relate—as if each is unsure, in this extravagantly mirrored world, whether the other is real or illusion.

The opening portion of the duet is essentially an extended transition, during which the dancers repeatedly turn on their own axes while circling each other in a complex series of double-helix maneuvers (H8), setting up the circles-within-circles idea that will be used throughout the dance. Finally, they reach a brief moment of stasis, hand in hand (H9). As a portion of the melody enters, they move into a Spanish-style dance, front to front or side by side, featuring tight upper backs, hands clasped at the small of the back, and crisp heel-clicks (H10). And always the circling continues. Next there is a sequence of soft turns with the forearms held parallel to the floor in front and back, in the Spanish manner (H11).

After some more circlings the dancers pause briefly side by side and then flow gently back and forth, arms undulating in front of them, rather like the chorus earlier (H12). The music for the duet thus far has often toyed with elements of the Porter song; here it settles into a beguiling Latin vamp.

Then, as the orchestra finally announces the theme clearly, Astaire and Powell deliver a side-by-side tap episode that is cool and controlled yet filled with tantalizing pauses and eventful, if subtle, shifts, and embellished with some odd and imaginative arm movements (H13–15). (Powell is justifiably proud of the use of arms in this duet and recalls they worked for two weeks on this element alone.) The episode is in unison, except for one brief sequence in rapid imitation.

Finally, they join hands and pull close to each other for an instant—the duet's only suggestion of intimacy (H16). As the music builds, they respond by moving broadly across the floor, and Astaire swings Powell into the closest they come to a lift in any of their duets (H17). Things quickly settle down again, and soon there is a sequence in which the dancers dodge back and forth—at first separated (H18), then touching—all the while tapping out a brisk yet sensuous tap/Spanish rhythm.

The ending is stupendous. During the last sequence the orchestra hypnotically repeats seven times the music for the first part of the last line of the song, "When they begin . . . When they begin . . .," but the music never resolves. Instead, it breaks into a throbbing Spanish vamp melody, and the dancers separate for some Spanish-style floor jabbing with their hands on their hips (H19) and some quick partnered turns. Then, as the music continues its evocative churnings and gradually becomes louder, Astaire and Powell circle the floor face to face and render sequential tap spins—Powell turns, then Astaire re-

H5 H6 H7 H8

H9 H10 H11 H12

H13 H14 H15 H16

sponds—over and over again (H 20). Finally, they reach the exit and spin out of view (H 21).[9]

This three-minute duet is like nothing else Astaire ever did. Perhaps because it was part of a lengthy production number and was followed by a duet with plenty of sparkle and virtuosity, there was no need to bring the house down with spectacle or dazzle. Nor was there an emotional plot point to make. In addition, Astaire was here working with a dancer who was fully up to the technical demands of the dance—and, indeed, Powell looks splendid throughout. The result is an étudelike duet that is more abstract—more pure dance—than usual, and amazingly subtle and intricate.

Next the camera cuts to four bepompommed women who sing a jazzed-up version of part of the song in Andrews Sisters–style close harmony. Behind them is the dancing chorus, which forms itself into a long line and proceeds to bounce its way off camera. Reflected in a mirror at the back is a jazz orchestra (H 22).

As the singers sidle off, Astaire and Powell trot on, dressed in sporty white, and launch into a tap extravaganza that is the film's most famous sequence. The band plays an upbeat swing arrangement of the Porter song featuring a warm, vibrant clarinet.[10]

The playfully competitive duet is appealing for its contagious good spirits (Powell, for once, looks as if she's having a good time), its exhilarating speed, and its sheer virtuosity. At the same time, it remains essentially an exhibition dance: two experts enjoying a tap jam session, without really relating to each other except as congenial performers who happen to be sharing the stage.

The "Jukebox" and the "Spanish" numbers are essentially ballroom duets that make extensive use of tap. This final duet, however, eschews partnering entirely and relies on pure tap. Astaire and Powell here show how tap dance, usually considered to be a solo form, can be expanded without violating its essential premises. Of particular note is the ingenious use the duet makes of intricate and brilliantly paced shifts between unison and sequentially imitative movement—that is, between sololike material and duetlike material.

It all begins casually enough, with a jaunty stroll (H 23) that gradually becomes more theatrical, soon leading to a step that includes a couple of turning leg-swings (H 24). At the end of the strain the dancers abruptly come to a stop (H 25) and pause; then, as the orchestra begins the second strain, they scamper to catch up with it, and finally lapse again into the casual stroll.

So far everything has been in unison, but now there is a fleeting break: a tap step in lunge position starts in unison but then changes to a question-and-answer form (H 26). After some spins, Astaire leads, or entices, Powell across the floor in a tap combination that is the only thing like partnering in the duet (H 27). Face to face, they circle each other exuberantly and then, facing forward, deliver some exaggeratedly delicate tap

[9] Powell has discussed the rehearsal for this part of the dance (though she may be referring to a portion of their later duet—H 33): "We did that thing in the circle, counter rhythm. . . . Well, we had more fun working on it! . . . We had gone from eight right straight through to four, over and over. So the poor piano player, he was absolutely dying! . . . So we got a Big Ben alarm clock and we set it at one. And we promised no matter where we were, we would stop to allow this man to have time. We were crazy, he didn't have to be."

[10] Beyond this there is no plagiarism of the famous 1938 Artie Shaw recording, which takes the music about 40 percent slower than the film version and actually features the clarinet far less.

H17 H18 H19 H20

H21 H22 H23 H24

H25 H26 H27 H28

steps followed by a wonderful sequence of alternating tap ripples that travel to the side, giving the impression of a competitive chase (H 28). Back in unison, they frolic first away from the camera and then toward it, punctuating their return with a witty, musically inspired outward sweep of the arms (H 29).

During an extended sequence of leg swings that have the effect of pivoting the body around (H 30), the music fades away; next the dancers perform a tap cadenza that is the duet's most remarkable sequence. Following a set of turns that travel upstage, the dancers settle into a stationary tap vamp and then take turns embellishing it with little forward-traveling tap ripples (H 31): each dancer builds a snappy commentary on the tap foundation maintained by the other. Gradually the tap commentaries get closer and closer together, until they merge and the dancers are in unison again, emphasized by some brisk hand claps and floor slams that are perfectly together. Then they trip across the floor in a sequence of tiny traveling tap steps (H 32), settling finally into position side by side again. From there, still in unison, they rattle off a vigorous tap burst over and over again:

The brilliant finale begins as this tempo is picked up by the orchestra, and soon the dancers, continuing their basic tap rhythm, circle the floor and each other with a dazzling series of leaping turns (H 33).[11] Still spinning and tapping, they gradually maneuver until they are progressing toward the camera. After one last crisp turn (H 34) they slam soundly into a final pose as the music (and, therefore, the Beguine) ends; Powell's skirt, unaware the dance is over, swirls around in kinetic afterglow (H 35).

I

I'VE GOT MY EYES ON YOU

(REPRISE) (TAG) (59")

In the wings, Astaire and Powell learn of Murphy's self-sacrificing ruse (I 1). Exultantly, they drag him onstage for an encore to the film's most endearing song. The only defect of this joyous trio is its brevity. A deft combination of casual soft-shoe and virtuosic tap, it sparkles with humor and good spirits, and ends the film on a shimmering high.

While the orchestra plays the introduction, the dancers wait onstage for their cue and, in mime, Astaire invites the uncertain Murphy to join in (I 2). As the song is sung by a background chorus, the dance begins with a lilting soft-shoe combination that includes the obligatory brisk slaps to the thighs. After some close shots of each of the three beaming performers, the camera returns to a full-body shot for the rest of the dance, and the soft shoe continues with subtle hesitations and a corkscrew kick.

Soon the men come to a natural pause in the choreography, but Powell tries to show them up by rapping out a tap pattern with one foot while holding her arms in a coy, finger-to-chin "Who, me?" pose (I 3)—a signature pose of hers which Astaire had wryly quoted earlier in his solo (see E 8). The men feign irritation at her one-upwomanship: Murphy pulls her hand away from her chin, and Astaire tries to step on her tapping foot (I 4). When neither ploy works, they take her by the hands and turn her around. This launches her into another of her signature steps —a merry sequence of multiple spins (I 5; see also B 4) which Astaire also quoted earlier and which were incorporated into their first duet (E 8, F 8). As Powell gyrates, the men, amused, stand back and count her revolutions on their fingers. She emerges from the turns with apt timing to blend in with the men, effortlessly turning the dance back into a trio.

A crisp turn of one and a half revolutions has the result of pointing the dancers upstage. Undaunted, they casually stroll in that direction and shoot a backward glance at the audience, as if to assure viewers that the shift of direction was all part of the act (I 6). After a bit of tap scribbling over the music, there is a wonderful moment of rippling imitation: Astaire hits a tap burst or a tap turn to which Powell and Murphy reply in sequence and in kind.

For the finish, the trio progresses toward the camera with the leaping spin that had been used in "I Concentrate on You" (I 7; compare G 9), and with a series of turns with the Spanish arms from "Begin the Beguine" (I 8; compare H 11, 20, 21). This leads to the film's final image: all conflicts resolved, the dancers link arms and grin happily (I 9).

[11] The camera cuts to a more distant shot as they are about to begin their circular peregrinations (as in H 33), the only cut in the 2′45″ dance duet.

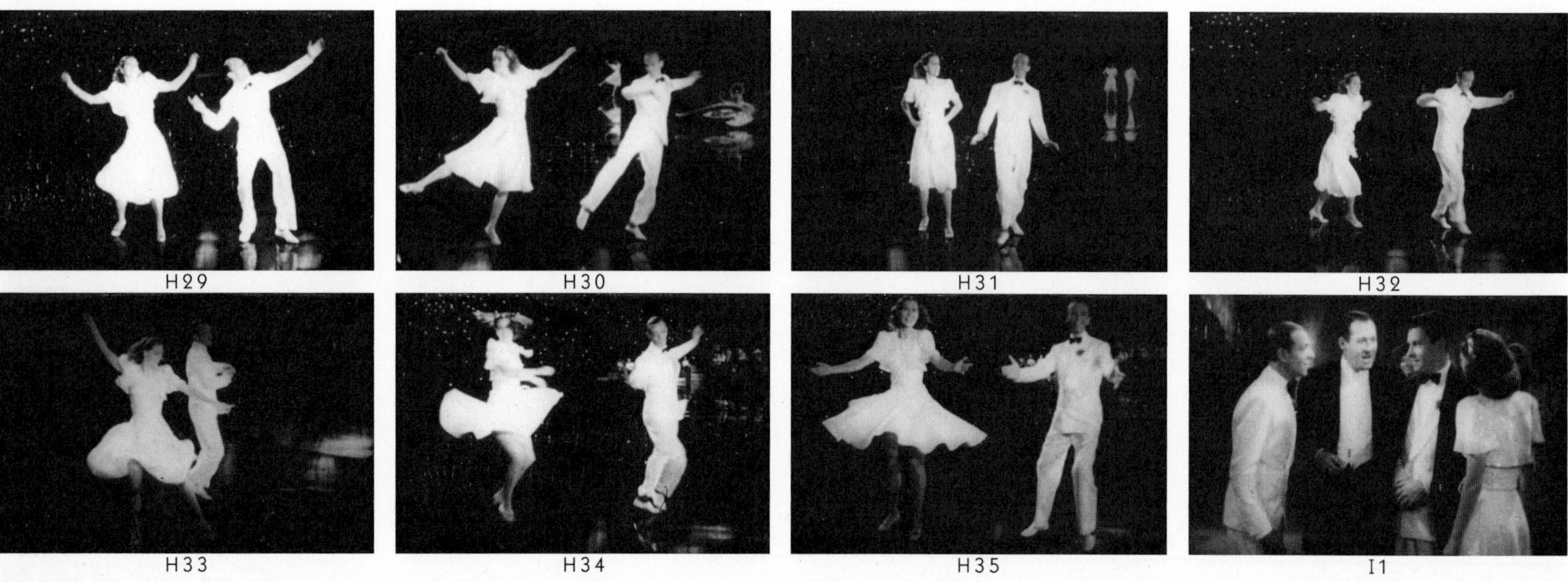

H29 H30 H31 H32

H33 H34 H35 I1

With Powell and Murphy in "I've Got My Eyes on You"

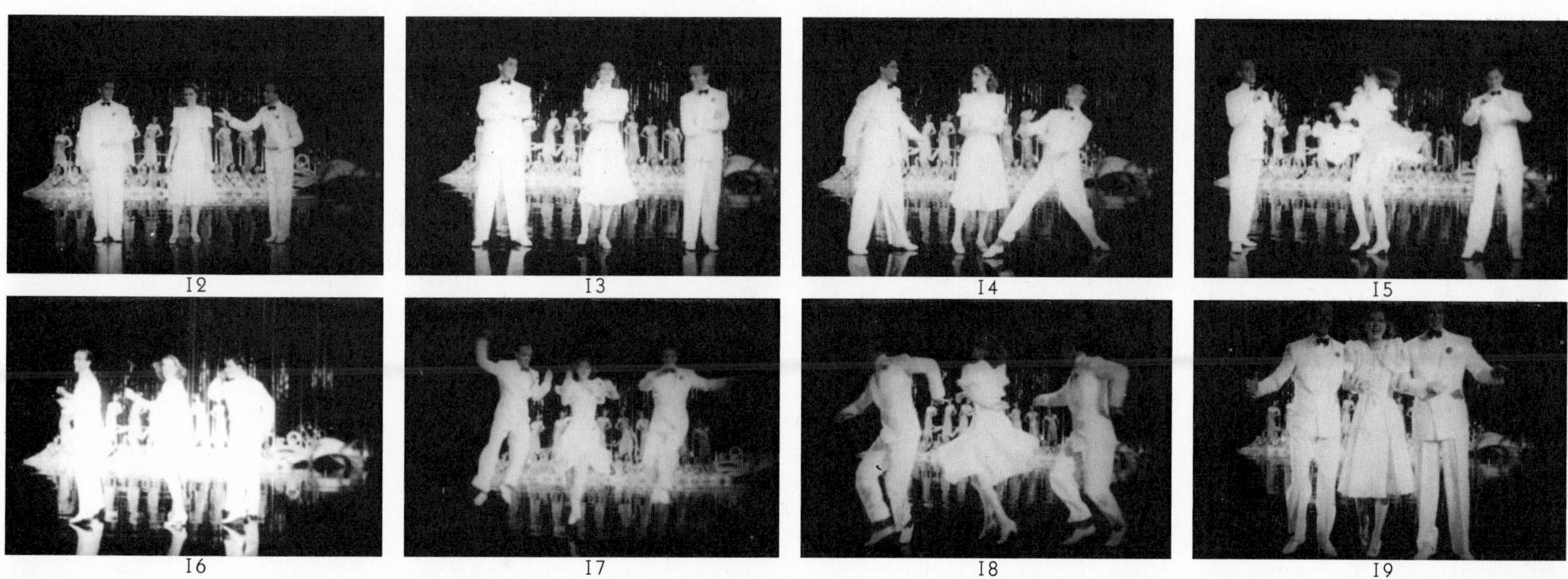

12 13 14 15

16 17 18 19

13.

Second Chorus

1941

In an interview conducted twenty-seven years after the event, Fred Astaire sourly described *Second Chorus* as "the worst film I ever made." The critical chorus has generally agreed and the film has collected several decades' worth of adjectives like "dismal" and "routine," and nouns like "failure" and "disaster." The condemnation seems excessive. Although the film is unlikely ever to be rediscovered as a forgotten masterpiece of the Hollywood cinema, it has its modest appeals.

Its cool reception stems partly from the fact that the film doesn't conform very well to the usual expectations of what a Fred Astaire film is supposed to be. It includes something of a romance between Astaire and the beautiful Paulette Goddard, but the love story is handled perfunctorily; it does not act as the motor of the plot or as its emotional center. Moreover, there is very little dancing—a playful duet for the couple early on, a solo for Astaire near the end, and a brief comedy dance in the middle.

The plot actually revolves around Astaire's acerbic competition with fellow trumpeter Burgess Meredith, an amusing combat that gives the film much of its bounce and drive. There are few dances, but there is quite a bit of good swing-era big-band music, much of it supplied by Artie Shaw and his band, then at the peak of fame. And the dances that did make it into the film, particularly the perky duet, are both ingenious and winning.[1] In short, while the film may not deserve adulation, it certainly merits attention and, at its occasional best, respect.[2]

THE SCRIPT AND THE PRODUCTION

The film's unusual shape derives from the way the script was assembled. Independently produced for Paramount release by Boris Morros, the film was apparently originally intended as a showcase for Artie Shaw, then one of the most famous men in the world, owing to a series of headline-grabbing events that had occurred to him over the course of the previous two years. In 1938 he had been catapulted to celebrity and wealth by his tremendously successful recording of Cole Porter's "Begin the Beguine." Then, early in 1939, he collapsed on the bandstand, and he spent weeks recovering from a rare illness that previously had almost always proved fatal. Back at work by the end of the year, he began to sour on the business aspects of the music world, and vanished—to Mexico, as it turned out—for weeks, walking away from a fortune. In 1940 he resurfaced in Hollywood, romanced various stars including Judy Garland, and then suddenly eloped with one of the era's great sex symbols, Lana Turner (the third of his eight wives). Next he made several recordings backed by studio musicians, of which one, "Frenesi," became a major hit. That summer he assembled a new band in Hollywood made up of select musicians from both coasts, added a string section, and featured trumpeter Billy Butterfield. It is this band—one of Shaw's finest—that appears in *Second Chorus.*

Astaire was attracted to the film, he says, by the opportunity to work with, and even to "dance-conduct," this "real swingin' outfit." The script was shaped to allow for Astaire's presence and talents, with much rewriting reportedly taking place after the production was already before the cameras (a phenomenon, however, that was hardly unique in Astaire's career).

The plot centers on the efforts of a pair of superannuated college dance-band trumpeters, Astaire and Meredith, to land jobs with Shaw's band. They spend most of their time trying to undercut each other but at the end work together to con a rich backer, played by the eternally befuddled Charles Butterworth, into supporting a public concert by Shaw. Their mutual friend Goddard watches all this with amusement, and Astaire, we are to believe, wins her heart when he ceases badgering Meredith and starts working in cooperation with him (albeit for a semifelonious end).

Artie Shaw, aged thirty at the time, plays himself in the film. He proves, not very surprisingly, to be a somewhat stiff actor, but the role has some modest depth to it—he is not simply a nice-guy idol, but a bit irritable and brusque, with

[1] Another extensive dance number was shot, but cut from the film. See 13 M.

[2] Astaire has referred to the film as "smaller-budget" and "a quicky," but everything is relative. It was undoubtedly less expensive than any of his four previous films, each of which cost more than $1 million to produce. But Astaire received $100,000 for *Second Chorus,* and if one assumes that at least that much was required to obtain the combined services of Goddard, Meredith, and Shaw, salaries for the stars alone pushed the film into higher budget categories: most of the films turned out at RKO in the 1940–41 season, for example, cost less than $200,000 to produce.

With Paulette Goddard

an autobiographically authentic desire to do concerts (as opposed to ballroom dates) and an antipathy toward freedom-restricting sponsorship by "crunchy-crinkle breakfast-food guys." The acting is largely left to Astaire and his two experienced and able associates: the craggy Meredith, better known for Serious roles on stage and screen, and the radiant and intelligent Goddard, fresh from an important role in *The Great Dictator,* a film created by her husband, Charles Chaplin.[3]

Among the other interesting characters associated with the film is the producer, Boris Morros. A Russian émigré, Morros was at the time beginning to work with Soviet agents; in 1947 he became an FBI counterspy. Morros' 1957 autobiography, which revealed his double life and was filmed in 1960 as *Man on a String,* scarcely mentions *Second Chorus.* His forgetfulness was continued by his heirs after his death in 1963, with the result that the film's copyright was apparently not renewed when due in 1969. Thus the film seems to have fallen into the public domain—the only Astaire film to do so.

[3] In 1944, two years after Goddard's divorce from Chaplin, she married Meredith, a union that lasted five years.

THE MUSIC

The film's music is something of a hodge-podge, but a pleasure nonetheless. Most of it is supplied by Shaw's band, and Shaw himself wrote a specialty piece, "Concerto for Clarinet," as well as the melody for the film's fine love song, "Love of My Life." Another song was written by Bernie Hanighen, a moderately successful pop composer of the time who never worked on another film. There is also a song by Hal Borne, Astaire's rehearsal pianist and musical associate from the 1930s. Supplying all the lyrics was the brilliant Johnny Mercer. This was Mercer's first (of five) Astaire films. He had, however, collaborated with Astaire before—it was he who wrote the lyric to Astaire's music for the 1936 hit song "I'm Building Up to an Awful Let-down."

THE CHOREOGRAPHY

Another old Astaire colleague working on the film was dance director Hermes Pan, who also puts in a fleeting appearance as a clarinetist in Astaire's college band.

With Goddard

THE NUMBERS

A
SUGAR
(1′ 1″)

After some title music supplied by the Shaw band, Astaire is seen leading his college band in a jazz standard by Maceo Pinkard (A1). Bobby Hackett was flown in from New York to dub Astaire's trumpet playing, while Meredith was dubbed by Shaw bandsman Billy Butterfield.

B
EVERYTHING'S JUMPING
(1′ 18″)

Goddard, who works for a collection agency, catches Astaire's eye from the audience, and when he eagerly trots over, she finagles him into accepting a summons for an overdue payment for some encyclopedias. Soon, however, he and Meredith get her fired and sign her as their band's manager. She handles that job with consummate skill, quickly arranging a series of appearances that include a Halloween dance at a country club (B1) and a college engagement. For the latter she uses all her charms to get the male selection committee to appreciate the superiority of Astaire's band to Artie Shaw's (B2). The object of her scorn is then shown playing a tune at a dance (B3).[4]

C
I AIN'T HEP TO THAT STEP BUT I'LL DIG IT
(3′ 38″)

Astaire and Meredith are still in college long after their natural term because they deliberately keep flunking courses, allowing them to hold their lucrative jobs with their band, named, appropriately enough, the Perennials. Astaire arrives at a rehearsal with the good news that he's flunked again, while Meredith has unaccountably passed. As Meredith rushes off, outraged, to see the dean, Astaire seems happy that a rival for Goddard's affections will no longer be with the band, and Goddard declares she smells "a mouse" (C1).

Picking up the rhythm of her retort, Astaire segues into Mercer's witty patter lyric about the embarrassing situation he's in. He ambles over to the band and, after conspiratorially trading jive lines with the musicians (C2), starts to develop the patter rhythm into a dance (C3). (Choreographer Hermes Pan is the musician at the left rear in C2 and the standing figure in C3.) Astaire's plan is to entice Goddard into a dance and distract her from her suspicions. Although she is fully aware of Astaire's ruse, Goddard cheerfully joins him in the game. This section is one of the most beguiling transitions from dialogue to musical number in Astaire's career.

He sings to Goddard Mercer's slang-parody lyric that muses about the kind of dance they should do: his hepness, Astaire explains, does not extend to such dances as the conga, mazurka, Charleston, or polka; but, if necessary, he is prepared to dig even these steps. Fortunately, no mazurkas are required, because Astaire quickly comes up with a new step—the Dig It (which publicists dutifully attempted to get the

[4] There is a topical joke in this sequence. At one point Goddard gets the band an especially genteel assignment by proclaiming its superiority to the "rowdy" Emil Coleman group. One observer of the big-band scene has characterized Coleman as "ultra-suave and urbane, a master at mesmerizing blue bloods who could be more impressed by the sight and name of a bandleader than by his music."

A1 B1 B2 B3 C1 C2 C3 C4 C5 C6 C7 C8

jitterbugging public to adopt when the film was released). The essential step seems inspired by a figure found often in Borne's jumpy melody (or vice versa) and involves snapping the feet together and then hopping in that hobbled position. During some bouncy transition music, Astaire demonstrates the step for Goddard's benefit (C 4) and then tries to cajole her into joining him. She makes a brief show of reluctance, then saunters out onto the floor, an event that Astaire celebrates by circling her while repeatedly hopping out his newly invented step (C 5).

The step, of course, has been devised with Goddard's limited dancing abilities in mind. It is artfully developed and embellished, but never so much that she has to strain to keep up: she looks comfortable and natural throughout. Moreover, Astaire always hovers around her, piloting—there is none of the side-by-side solo work often found in his duets with more able partners. Yet these restrictions don't seem to have limited the flow of Astaire's choreographic invention, for the dance is an utter delight. Shot all in one take—the last of Astaire's full-length duets to be so recorded—it was, according to Goddard, done "just once, one Saturday morning. . . . I'm glad it was all right, for I couldn't have done it again."

As the main melody enters, Astaire and Goddard amble forward and mark out the step a few times together. Once Goddard gets the hang of it, the step is elaborated, allowing them to shunt sideways (C 6). During the release section of the music (the B section of the AABA song), they swirl around each other (C 7) into some partnered figures concluding with a funny, musically derived staggering step that sends them careening toward the band (C 8). At the last second, however, Astaire brings the teetering under control, and the dancers resume Dig It–ing with two imaginative variations: extravagant (the side hop is embellished with a lift—C 9) and understated (the feet scarcely move but the hips jut to the side anyway in phantomlike response to the non-hop—C 10).

There are more versions of the step—partnered closely while traveling (C 11) and partnered distantly while stationary (C 12), for example. The return of the release strain leads to more partnered careening spun out of a beautiful scooting pattern around the floor (C 13, 14). After some dodging Dig It steps, the release is played a third time, and some jitterbugging (C 15) is developed into a step involving a fall to the side, an on-balance version of the staggering this portion of the music had inspired earlier (C 16; compare C 8, 14).

The ending is simple and thoroughly wonderful. Astaire and Goddard bounce around the floor with their tight-kneed hops, sometimes separately and sometimes partnered (C 17). Gradually they frolic toward the door, pause for an instant to wave to the boys in the band (C 18; compare C 15), and Dig It happily out of sight.

D
SWEET SUE
(2′2″)

In retaliation for his passing grade (which he received because Astaire submitted a plagiarized paper for him), Meredith has gotten Astaire fired. Then, suddenly, opportunity knocks for both men: because the band, under Goddard's management, has been taking so many engagements away from him, Shaw comes to the campus to hear what the upstart rival group sounds like. When he arrives, Astaire and Meredith try to show off for the big bandleader while playing a Victor Young standard (D 1). The music is imaginatively arranged for dueling trumpets, Hackett's singing, mellow tone (Astaire) contrasting with Butterfield's more assertive brassiness and swing (Meredith).

C9 C10 C11 C12 C13 C14 C15 C16 C17 C18 D1 E1

E

LOVE OF MY LIFE

(1′ 15″)

But Shaw turns out to have no interest in trumpet players and instead hires Goddard as his secretary-manager. Within two days she has worked her way into his confidence, and, at her urging, he agrees to let her combative college friends audition with the band. While waiting to join the band to play a number at a hotel ballroom for his audition, Astaire feels called upon to let Goddard know of his affection for her by ardently singing the film's fine love song (E1).

There has been little previous indication that romance was budding between them, but Goddard seems pleased. Shaw's melody has a rolling lilt, and Mercer's amusing and evocative lyric is singularly appropriate to the character who self-mockingly asks his love to join his hectic merry-go-round life—"to square my blunders and share my dreams."[5]

F

AUDITION SOLOS

(2′ 30″)

Mutual sabotage destroys both auditions. Astaire is ruined when he tries to play Johnny Green's "I'm Yours" with a set of wrong notes added to the music by Meredith (F1; the trumpeter on his left is Billy Butterfield). Then Meredith's rendition of Shaw's "Double Mellow" is cut short when Astaire pulls his chair off the bandstand from behind (F2).

G

RUSSIAN CAFE BIT

(2′ 35″)

Angrily expelled from her life by Goddard, the boys seek employment elsewhere. Meredith gets solo work at a racetrack, while Astaire is seen as an improbable member of a small band in a Russian nightclub, spiritedly bounding around in a mock-Moiseyev dance, sometimes with trumpet, to the traditional "The New Moon Is Shining" (G1–3). On seeing Goddard among the diners, he launches into a reprise of "Love of My Life" with a lyric in Russian gibberish (partly devised by producer Morros).

H

HOE DOWN THE BAYOU

(1′ 3″)

Next Goddard befriends a rich, timorous amateur mandolin player (Butterworth), and gets him to back a Shaw concert. Astaire and Meredith, thinking that Butterworth is "taking advantage" of Goddard, scare him off. But eventually they grasp the situation and, with some effort, square things with the gullible gentleman.

Seeking to benefit from their good deed (as Meredith philosophically puts it, "A little self-sacrifice goes a long way"), the boys contrive to have Butterworth force Shaw to include in his concert a "folk song" Astaire has written. Astaire plays the cheery Hanighen music, which he calls "Hoe Down the Bayou," on the piano for Butter-

[5] Other Mercer magic: "I hope in your horoscope there is room for a dope who adores you," which contains not only the "hope"/"scope"/"dope" rhyme, but also the rollicking resonance of the "in-your"/"horo"/"for a"/"adore"/"dores-you" match. Moreover, Mercer contributed an important element to the melody. According to Shaw, they had agreed to do a song called "Love of My Life" when Mercer added the pickup, "Would you like to be the," which gives the song much of its character and compelling flow. They finished the song in about a day but waited three weeks to show it to the studio executives. As the experienced Mercer explained to the bewildered bandleader, "If you bring a song right in, the movie people don't place any value on it."

F1 F2 G1 G2
G3 H1 I1 I2
J1 K1 K2 K3

worth (H 1), who is deliriously enthusiastic ("Solid North! Solid South! Solid, Jack!").

I
POOR MR. CHISHOLM
(1′ 9″)

Butterworth animatedly urges the song on Shaw (I 1), who finally agrees to let Astaire play it for him (I 2). The song turns out to come equipped with an agile Mercer lyric mocking Butterworth and his mandolin; Shaw, amused, agrees to use it.

J
CONCERTO FOR CLARINET
(3′ 22″)

Back at rehearsal, Shaw and band sail through a showy, episodic piece he wrote especially for the film (J 1). As Shaw says, "People make a big deal out of what was, in fact, written in a hurry. . . . I wrote out a framework. I didn't know what the hell I was going to play until we got to the studio. It worked alright. A lot of people copied it; some musicians even played it in schools. But I never intended it for posterity. . . . It filled a spot in the picture!"

K
POOR MR. CHISHOLM / HOE DOWN THE BAYOU
(2′ 11″)

Meanwhile, Butterworth has taken it into his head to play his mandolin at Shaw's concert. Meredith agrees to keep Butterworth out of the way if Astaire will get him a prominent trumpet assignment at the band concert. Though Astaire manages to do this (impressing Goddard in the process), Meredith and Butterworth have given each other champagne laced with a sleeping powder, and neither shows up.

At the big concert, Astaire finds himself conducting the band in the song he played for Shaw earlier.

The opportunity to build a dance number out of the task of conducting this fine band may have been what attracted Astaire to the film, but the idea itself is fundamentally flawed, as Astaire may have come to realize when he began working on the dance. A conductor's motions are necessarily synchronized with the music, whereas Astaire characteristically likes to depart from the music, to play intricate games with it, in his choreography—to tarry behind, to race ahead, to scribble over. The result is a bifurcated dance: in the first half Astaire works with the conducting idea, leading the orchestra beat for beat, and bleat for bleat; then, in the second half, he abandons that role and blasts out a virtuosic tap dance that rides imaginatively, but independently, over the music (which continues without benefit of conductor).

In the first half Astaire glides when the music is smooth (K 1), bolts explosively for sharp bursts (K 2), and links phrases with loose, lilting tap material (K 3). Then he becomes extremely literal, miming drum rolls with his hands and bass-drum beats with sharp kicks to the side (K 4). His musical independence is declared, appropriately enough, when he flips his baton in the air and catches it again (K 5). From that point on he is no longer the conductor but, rather, a performer adding his own line to the score.

At first most of this is loose and skittery—light spins and flitting, almost pussy-footing taps (K 6), all performed with sparkling rhythmic intricacy. Intensity mounts—interrupted by a humorous pause and snap of the fingers (K 7)—leading to a blistering sequence of tap turns and forceful floor slams (K 8, 9). After some traveling turns (K 10) he comes to a sudden halt, and his trumpet is tossed to him from outside camera range. He catches it effortlessly and

K4 K5 K6 K7
K8 K9 K10 K11
K12 K13 L1 L2

mimes the blowing of a wailing trumpet line while continuing his dance (K 11). For a finish there is a series of brilliant turns toward the camera, ending with a slam into place as dance and music wittily vanish together (K 12, 13). This kind of evaporative ending is often found in big-band arrangements; it suited Astaire's aesthetic beautifully and he used it in several other dances in films from the swing era (12 F, H, 14 F, 15 M, 17 C).

L
LOVE OF MY LIFE
(REPRISE) (11")

As Meredith and Butterworth doze the night away (L 1), Astaire and Goddard drive happily away from the concert. Astaire sings her a phrase of the film's love song, and they kiss twice to let us know the film did have something to do with romance after all (L 2).

A NUMBER CUT FROM THE FILM

M
ME AND THE GHOST UPSTAIRS

Shortly after she takes over as Astaire's band manager early in the film, Goddard lines up a Halloween date for the band at a country club (B 1). A scene showing the band's performance at this club was shot but cut from the film. Included in it was a comedy number that ran five and a half minutes, in which Astaire sang an amusing Hanighen-Mercer song while Hermes Pan, shrouded in a sheet, crept up behind him (M 1). There was some mimicking of Astaire by Pan, and then a raucous duet including various Lindy lifts and jitterbugging.

M 1

Goddard and Astaire with the Perennials—the clarinetist at the left is Hermes Pan

14.

You'll Never Get Rich

1941

Released two months before Pearl Harbor, and two years after war had begun in Europe, *You'll Never Get Rich* is a frothy, calculatedly superficial comedy about life in the army.

The United States was preparing for war, and the year before, Congress had passed, by one vote, the unpopular bill that set up conscription. Neither the draft nor the war apparently held any terrors for Columbia Pictures, however. Judging from *You'll Never Get Rich,* one of the first Hollywood films to have a World War II military setting, the draft was a convenient way to get out of amorous entanglements, and life in the army was, as Fred Astaire enthusiastically puts it in the film, "wonderful." As for the war, it simply didn't exist: it is never mentioned, as either present reality or future threat. Thus *You'll Never Get Rich* can be seen as a direct outgrowth of the kind of films Astaire made in the 1930s—the ones that never mentioned the Depression. The main difference is not in the setting but in the sets, with the fancifully luxurious decor of the RKO films replaced here by stern reality. The army camp in the film is a precise replica of a real one, except that the guardhouse was considerably enlarged to give Astaire room to perform his solos. Two years later Astaire was to make a pertinent film about the war, *The Sky's the Limit,* but *You'll Never Get Rich* is as cheerfully distanced from the grim side of contemporary reality as anything he had ever done.

And, seen in that light, the film is quite successful. Its convoluted, farcical plot percolates along at a happy pace, and it has a fine original score composed for it by Cole Porter—though the music is not always given its full due in the film. The choreographic highlights are a bright Astaire solo in the roomy guardhouse and a couple of duets: a Latinesque dance and a brilliant fragment that opens the film. Then there is the "Wedding Cake Walk," which has the distinction of being the most absurdly gaudy production number Astaire ever appeared in.

THE SCRIPT

The plot machinations are mostly impelled by the philanderings of Robert Benchley, one of the screen's great lechers. He wants to keep these activities secret from his wife in order to preserve his marriage—not because of sentiment or mellowed affection, but because all his property is in her name. Astaire, as the choreographer of a Broadway show Benchley is producing, becomes enmeshed in a scheme by which Benchley is trying to convince his wife (falsely) that he hasn't been panting after a chorus girl, played by the luminously beautiful Rita Hayworth. When Astaire is drafted, it seems a deliverance from these complex affairs, but the plot and Benchley follow him to the army camp, where some intricate business about a diamond bracelet continues and is elaborated. At the end, Benchley is still married and Astaire and Hayworth are planning their honeymoon.

Astaire carries quite a bit of the comedy himself in this film and does it well. Although there are comedy characters—Benchley in particular, and double-talk specialist Cliff Nazarro—the confusions and the layered misidentifications and misunderstandings mostly center on Astaire.

With all the complications of plot and circumstance, there seems little room in the film to develop the Astaire-Hayworth love story. It is handled rather perfunctorily in the script and is only tangential to the dance numbers. Astaire and Hayworth are mildly attracted to each other while working on their Broadway show at the beginning of the film, but they soon become alienated as the result of one of Benchley's schemes. Later, after being drafted, Astaire realizes that he is in love with her; but she remains aloof. Then they dance a romantic duet as part of a rehearsal for a camp show, and afterward she discovers "out of a clear sky" that she's in love with Astaire—a development that, oddly enough, has not been worked into the dance at all. After that they break up over a misunderstanding and eventually reconcile when the misunderstanding is cleared up. The romance develops mostly through a series of unmotivated dawning realizations, not through wooing and winning, or by thrusting and parrying. Rather mechanical, it shows little passion, pain, tenderness, or even warmth.

RITA HAYWORTH

This quality probably derives in part from the persona of Astaire's costar. Hayworth had been among those groomed

March Milastaire

for stardom by Columbia Pictures, led by the legendary vulgarian Harry Cohn. By 1941 she had appeared with increasing success in parts (mostly small) in thirty-three films and had caught the eye of the public. Columbia was now ready to build a film around her. The production was given a large budget (at least by Columbia standards), and Astaire and Porter were brought in to give it class. While the film was in production, *Life* put Hayworth on its cover and published a photograph showing her provocatively crouched in a negligee, which became one of the most reprinted and worshiped pinups of all time. Not to be outdone, *Time* put her on *its* cover and began its story with a set of grand proclamations: "It was news in Hollywood that a new star had been made. But it was news throughout the U.S. that the best tap dancer in the world, Fred Astaire, had a new dancing partner . . . and there could be no doubt that she was the best partner he ever had." Then *Life* completed the canonization by dubbing Hayworth the "Love Goddess."

Unfortunately, Hayworth seems to have believed some of this image making herself, and to have been hesitant to step down from the pedestal into the world of ordinary mortals. During the comedy sequences in the film she tends to adopt a pose of amused aloofness—like a queen (or a goddess)—rather than the haughtiness projected by Ginger Rogers. Aloofness is not very funny or touching; haughtiness is, in part because of the insecurity it tries to cloak. Throughout, Hayworth remains somewhat invulnerable and untouchable—qualities that seem to have kept Astaire from really warming to her. Hayworth's remarkable beauty, as well as her youth, may also have been off-putting to Astaire, who certainly never saw himself as the great Hollywood romancer and was generally more comfortable with women who projected a more earthy, accessible image. In an interview he once referred to Hayworth's "saintly quality." How do you make love to a saint?

For all that, Hayworth is a fine dancer. The daughter of Eduardo Cansino, a famous Spanish dancer Astaire had known well in vaudeville, she had danced professionally for years. Technically she seems able to handle anything Astaire cares to dish up, as demonstrated neatly in a short dance at the start of the film. She was also a quick study as a dancer: Astaire has said she learned steps faster than anyone he had ever known. But there is also an unbending aspect to her screen presence and to her dancing—a wariness, a distancing, even an iciness. In the words of the song Astaire sings to her in the film, she is "so near and yet so far."

A year later, Astaire made a second film with Hayworth, *You Were Never Lovelier,* in which he seems more comfortable with her. The two films, together with the intervening *Holiday Inn,* were to restore his security and (comparative) self-confidence after what he apparently viewed as his post-Rogers slump, *Broadway Melody of 1940* and, especially, *Second Chorus.*

The importance to Hayworth of the film and of her association with Astaire is suggested in an interview she gave almost thirty years later:

> I guess the only jewels in my life were the pictures I made with Fred Astaire. You know, in his book Fred said I was his best partner *[sic]*. I can tell you one thing—they're the only pictures of mine I can watch today, Fred and me dancing, without laughing hysterically. And *Cover Girl* too . . . I fought Cohn—and I won. I was trained to do this, honey. At 13, I was dancing. . . . How do you think I could keep up with *Fred Astaire* when I was 19 [actually 22]? I was *not* picked up at the corner drugstore like Lana. And OK so I happened to be pretty. . . . *Fred* asked for me. . . . Print *that. Fred Astaire.* Fred *knew* I was a dancer, he knew what all those dumb dumbs at Columbia didn't know.

THE MUSIC

None of the songs Cole Porter composed for the film became a hit, in part perhaps because ASCAP, of which Porter was a member, was involved in a dispute with the radio industry that lasted most of 1941, ending shortly before the film was released. The composers' organization was seeking higher fees for its songs, and radio refused to pay; consequently, all ASCAP songs were banned from the air, and the score did not get the pre-premiere exposure it would normally have received.

Also, though there are some splendid songs in the film, the best of them are somewhat submerged. A beautiful ballad, "Dream Dancing," is used only as background music; the witty "Boogie Barcarolle" is rendered as a brief instrumental; and the full effect of the superb "Since I Kissed My Baby Goodbye" is somewhat undercut by the style in which Astaire chooses to dance it. Porter reportedly regarded the songs as less than his best and at the same time was not pleased with the way they were used.

THE CHOREOGRAPHY

The dance director for the film was Robert Alton, a successful Broadway choreographer whose only previous film work had been on *Strike Me Pink* five years earlier. Later he joined MGM and worked on many films there until his death in 1957. Four of these were with Astaire, making Alton Astaire's most frequent collaborator after Hermes Pan.

Alton had much to do in *You'll Never Get Rich* since three of the numbers used a chorus—an unusually high number for an Astaire film. Alton's Broadway experience hadn't really prepared him for Columbia's dancers. "I insisted that they do tap and ballet dancing both, and do it well," he told one reporter, "and they came back with the claim that I was working them too hard. It seems that heretofore the average dancing girl in pictures merely had to walk through a routine, looking beautiful. She never really had to dance." The dancers threatened to strike unless their pay was raised from $55 a week to $66 a week with a $5.50 bonus for any day on which they had to do lifts. They won.

With Rita Hayworth in "The Wedding Cake Walk"

THE NUMBERS

A
REHEARSAL DUET
(32″)

At a Broadway theatre Astaire is rehearsing a chorus number.[1] He singles out Hayworth for correction and invites her to try the dance with him. She accepts, a little smugly, and then romps flawlessly through the routine, which is shot all in one take. The sequence introduces her not only as a glamour queen but also as a capable and confident dancer.

Set to twenty-four measures of some bright, jazzy piano music—"boogie" material from Porter's "Boogie Barcarolle"—the dance is built on a loose-legged shuffle step that sets up a basic rhythmic pattern (A1). Soon the choreography is playing games with this idea and with the music. The shuffle becomes wider and more rhythmically complex: it is developed into a percussive stamping pattern (A2), and then is alternated with a series of quick little jumps to the side (A3) which are not musically predictable. Abruptly the dancers abandon the shuffle pattern entirely to stroll jauntily for a while, grandly ignoring the implications of the rippling music (A4), only to catch up with it again to perform an intricate tap barrage with one leg hooked behind the other (A5). They spin briskly and finish with a pose that echoes the opening one (A6; compare A1). Even as he dances, Astaire keeps his eye on Hayworth, since the plot premise for the number is that he is checking on her dancing ability.

Such a parallel routine can be used to compare a great dancer with a good one. In this case the difference is seen particularly in the use of the arms. Hayworth holds hers out decoratively and somewhat stiffly or swings them gently with the flow of the dance. Astaire's arms are much more integrated into the dance pattern—looser, far more articulate. A wonderful nuance is the way he subtly flutters his left hand to embellish some of the shuffling sequences (as in A1), waves his hand to supply a mocking counterpoint in the stroll section (A4), and, to add brilliance to the final tap sequence, thrashes his left arm so fast it comes out as a blur in any single frame (A5).

[1] It is interesting that Astaire is specifically identified as a "choreographer" in the film, not a "dance director": the former term was not usual in Hollywood or Broadway at the time.

B
BOOGIE BARCAROLLE
(1′47″)

Now that he has convinced himself (and the movie audience) that Hayworth knows how to dance, Astaire immediately leads his dancers in a runthrough of a number they've been working on. As Porter's title suggests, the music for this number attempts to combine two disparate ideas: a soaring, balladlike melody is set over a jazzy (or boogie) rhythm. Astaire and Alton seek to express this musical concept by dividing the chorus into two sections: a balletic group and a jazz (or "modern," as it is called in the film) group. As the choreographer and rehearsal director in the film, Astaire moves from one group to the other, urging them on like a conductor.

The number works well musically and might be successful onstage. On film, however, it fails—perhaps reflecting Alton's inexperience at the time in the medium. When the camera focuses on one group, it loses the point of the contrast (as

A1 A2 A3 A4 A5 A6 B1 B2 B3 B4 B5 C1

in B1 and B3); when it tries to take in both groups, the picture is too cluttered for the contrast to be legible or interesting (B4). (The background of ladders and other backstage debris doesn't help, either.) The confusion is increased by the inclusion of a shot from the side—extremely unusual in an Astaire number—which would be disorienting under the best of circumstances but is especially harmful here because it obscures a maneuver in which the groups exchange stage positions (B2). The idea of contrasts is made really clear only at the end, when the camera pulls far back to take in the entire stage; but at that distance detail is lost and only grand effects register—rollicking jazz stuff in the middle, soaring ($5.50 per day) ballet lifts on the periphery (B5). In general, the choreography takes second place to the concept. The steps are repetitive and fairly simple: the ballet group is given to swooping arm gestures (B1 and on the right in B4), the jazz group to scampering, twisting tap steps (B3 and on the left in B4).[2]

[2] A more successful solution to the choreographic problem was found by George Balanchine for his satiric "Romeo and Juliet" ballet in *Goldwyn Follies* (1938).

C

DREAM DANCING

(1′16″)

Next, Benchley, the producer of Astaire's show, calls Hayworth to his office and gives her the diamond bracelet around which the plot will flutter (C1). But before he can tell her about a "little plan" he has in mind, his wife shows up. Hayworth intentionally leaves the engraved bracelet behind, obliging Benchley to explain to his skeptical wife that it is a present Astaire is planning to give to Hayworth. He arranges for the four of them to meet at a nightclub where his wife can witness the gift giving.

Astaire and Hayworth are seen gliding congenially over the nightclub's dance floor (C2). This is a dialogue sequence, not really a musical number, but the music the band plays for them as they dance and talk is "Dream Dancing," a wistful rhythm ballad written by Porter for the film. This is the song's only significant exposure in the film, though evidence in the film and cast documents suggests the film originally did include a performance of this song, sung from the bandstand by Gwen Kenyon (she is seen sitting in the background in C2).

D

SHOOTIN' THE WORKS FOR UNCLE SAM

(3′46″)

Under Benchley's watchful eye, Astaire dutifully presents the bracelet to Hayworth, but she is offended at being used and walks out. Later she gets even by making Astaire the butt of a practical joke: her boyfriend pretends to be her gun-toting avenging brother (D1).

Astaire is delighted when he is drafted, since this will take him far from Benchley's machinations (D2, 3). He is waiting at Grand Central Station for the train to the army camp when the women from his chorus descend on the place *en masse* (D4, 5) and, as a sendoff, back him up in a wonderfully improbable production number that suggests with nice irony that Astaire's two worlds in the picture—the Broadway musical stage and the army camp—are not all that different: both involve a lot of empty-headed close-order drill. Or, as Astaire puts it in the lyric, "I'm off, my queens, to learn some new routines."

Astaire joins in spiritedly—inspecting the troops, straightening the lines in the formation, and miming shooting when the word comes up in the lyric (D6). The dance consists mostly of a

C2 D1 D2 D3

D4 D5 D6 D7

D8 D9 D10 E1

parade around the terminal in which two opposing styles of locomotion are cleverly interwoven: an exaggerated military march (D 7) and a scampering jazz-tap figure (D 8). One strongly emphasizes the downbeat, the other emphasizes everything *but* the downbeat. The best jokes emerge at the places where jazz material reverts to march and kinetic flurry abruptly gives way to square order. The music is arranged to stress these abrupt shifts in the choreography.

In the last part of the number, Astaire and troops parade down a ramp to his train, still alternating march and anti-march (D 9). The music and his dancing continue as the scene dissolves to a drill at the army camp, where Astaire's inability to do a straightforward, uninflected march infuriates the drill sergeant (D 10).[3]

E

SINCE I KISSED MY BABY GOODBYE

(1′ 54″)

Astaire receives a letter from Hayworth returning the bracelet; this proves she is not a diamond digger and causes Astaire to think warmly of her.

Soon he is sentenced to two days in the guardhouse for various infractions. Fellow inmates include a black vocal quartet, the Four Tones (E 1), who happen to be singing a new Cole Porter tune, to which Astaire listens and then dances.[4] Except for a somewhat contrived effort in the lyric to evoke a down-home rural Southern atmosphere ("South-wind shakes the ole magnolia"), this ballad is a memorable one—dreamy, mournful, liltingly somber.

The forty-five-second solo fragment that Astaire performs to it is unusual for him in that it contrasts so strongly with the lyric. As the singers croon about the pain and depression that follow a terminated love affair, Astaire performs a noisy, crashing tap dance that takes him all over the guardhouse kicking the furniture.

If the viewer also ignores the lyric, the solo is quite impressive as Astaire rattles out a bright tap obbligato over the music and makes everything around him serve as a prop. He begins by pounding his chest while lying on his cot (E 2), then gives the wall a few sharp raps and rises to kick at his cot (E 3) and a post (E 4). The dance becomes increasingly boisterous as he travels across the floor and adds loud hand claps (E 5). It comes to an abrupt halt in mid-flight when the startled Astaire hears Hayworth's voice at the window (E 6).

F

MARCH MILASTAIRE (A-STAIRABLE RAG)

(2′ 25″)

She has unexpectedly come to the camp to visit her boyfriend, who is stationed there. For some reason Astaire tells her that he is not a prisoner but an officer in private's uniform inspecting the guardhouse. Amused, she invites him to visit her when in proper uniform (F 1). Upon release from the guardhouse Astaire does so, stealing an officer's uniform to try to impress her. The visit convinces him that he is in love with her, and she gives him some indication that she is not entirely repulsed by him.

Delirious with happiness, he returns to the guardhouse—this time for impersonating an officer—loudly declares, "I'm a man that's in love," and propels himself into another tap dance. Building on his earlier, truncated solo, he expresses his giddy delight and irrepressible joy by using his taps to make as much noise as possible, mostly by bolting into the air and then coming down as hard as he can with both feet slamming the floor.[5]

[3] The camp was modeled after Camp Haan, near Riverside, California, where director Stanley Lanfield and the scriptwriters spent five days absorbing atmosphere. Signed on as technical adviser was Captain Jack Voglin, a twelve-year veteran who had also worked in vaudeville and as a bit player in Hollywood. Voglin, a stickler for detail, allowed only two compromises: the enlarged guardhouse and the tailored private's uniform Astaire wears. His biggest problem was getting the extras to look like disciplined soldiers. His approach was to remind them that army pay is $21 per month while "you fellows check in at 9 and out at 6 and get $8 a day and a box lunch." He reports that the admonition worked miracles.

[4] As Stanley Green notes, "Only in the movies . . . could an army post in 1941 have a non-segregated guard house." (Of course, it's also true that only in the movies could one find a spontaneous song-and-dance number in Grand Central Station featuring dozens of leggy chorus girls.) Porter's lyric vaguely suggests Southern black dialect, and this may have inspired the use of the black singing group in the film.

[5] This idea need not necessarily express joy, of course. The "One for My Baby" solo in *The Sky's the Limit* (17 F) uses the same basic idea to express the opposite emotion.

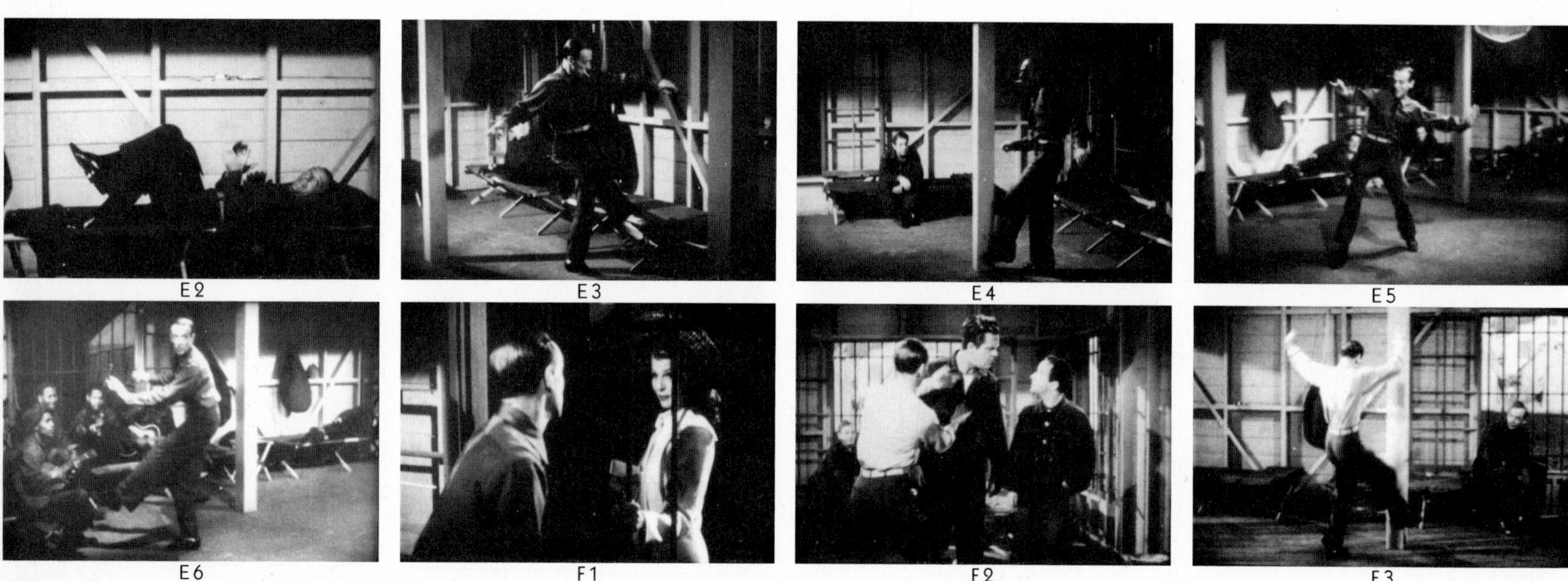

E 2 E 3 E 4 E 5

E 6 F 1 F 2 F 3

A second idea in the dance derives from the vigorous and supportive music, a version of "Bugle Call Rag." The music plays with the contrast that was also used in "Boogie Barcarolle" and in the marching section of "Shootin' the Works for Uncle Sam": the difference between square rhythms and ragged ones. In this case the music is composed so that pompous bugle calls are wittily alternated with music suggesting cool jauntiness. Astaire brings a similar contrast into the dance, though not always exactly where it happens in the music. Thus fierce floor-slams and stiff, militaristic poses are contrasted with light, gleeful tap-scampering (on bugle calls in other Astaire dances, see p. 70 n).

The dance is preceded by a neat link to the earlier solo: once again Astaire sets up tap rhythms by pounding on whatever is at hand, whether it's Big Boy Williams' chest (F 2) or the guardhouse post (F 3). To Astaire's delight, this sets the guardhouse drummer going and, with him, his jazz quintet (F 4). Pointing to the band with glee during the first bugle call (F 5), Astaire answers with a tap barrage ending in the first of the jumping slams to the floor (F 6), then eases into a cool tap shuffle. Next, the slamming idea is varied: during the second bugle call he stands on one leg and beats the floor sharply with the other (F 7; compare A 2 and E 5). As the music mellows, so does he, melting into a funny soft-armed limping shuffle forward (F 8).

Another two-legged slam, this time with the feet together, launches the clarinetist into a jazzy version of a bugle call. To this Astaire performs some slouchy, mincing slithers, including a pose (F 9) that closely resembles the Shorty George, a popular dance step around which he constructed an entire routine with Hayworth in their next film together (16 H). (At one point in this sequence it seems that the taps have been slightly misdubbed—very rare in Astaire's work.) Snapping into position, Astaire mocks the next bugle call with alternative left- and right-handed salutes, slapping himself on the thigh and forehead as he does so (F 10). This idea is then cleverly softened into a loose-legged side-to-side heels-down shuffle (F 11). As Astaire once again abruptly snaps into an exaggeratedly stiff pose (F 12), another bugle call is played, to which he dances a bent-over, loping figure. This leads to a maniacal flurry of stomps and slams, a progression across the floor in which one foot is repeatedly slammed against the floor (F 13) and a series of six crashing jumps (F 14, 15).

After the drummer is shown delivering a brief cadenza, the band (augmented now with other, off-screen instruments) resumes, and Astaire is launched into his brilliant, effusive finale. There is more one-legged floor slamming and a sequence of happy hand clapping (F 16). Then a new idea is introduced: a lag-legged figure (similar to a step in the earlier rehearsal duet—A 5) which is developed as a sequence of tap turns and as a series of twisting hops with flailing arms (F 17). The step is blended with some windmilling turns (F 18) out of which Astaire explodes with a final two-legged slam to the floor as music and dance evaporate together (F 19)—one of his witty, big-band-inspired wrap-up endings, the equivalent of a quick fade to black in the movies or a fast blackout in the theatre (the same approach is used in 12 F, 12 H, 13 K, 15 M, 17 C).

G
SO NEAR AND YET SO FAR
(4′ 1″)

Benchley now descends on the camp and proposes to put on a show there as part of an elaborate scheme to make time with his current chorus-girl prey (Osa Massen). Astaire agrees to work on the show because it will get him 1. out of the guardhouse for most of the day and 2. in a position to dance again with Hayworth.

The "So Near and Yet So Far" duet is presented as part of a dress rehearsal for this show. The situation is a perfect setup for an Astaire romantic duet. There's Rita, still aloof and cool, but ready to be warmed up. Cole Porter has supplied a serviceable song with a sensual rhumba flow, which suits her Spanish-dance background, and a remarkably appropriate lyric: the singer complains yearningly about how the object of his desire, while close physically, still retains an emotional distance.[6]

Strangely, the choreography does not make systematic use of the dramatic opportunity. There is a general progression in the dance from

[6] Otherwise, the lyric doesn't repay careful examination. That is, it would be unwise to linger too much over a couplet like this: "I just start getting you keen on clinches galore with me / When fate steps in and mops up the floor with me."

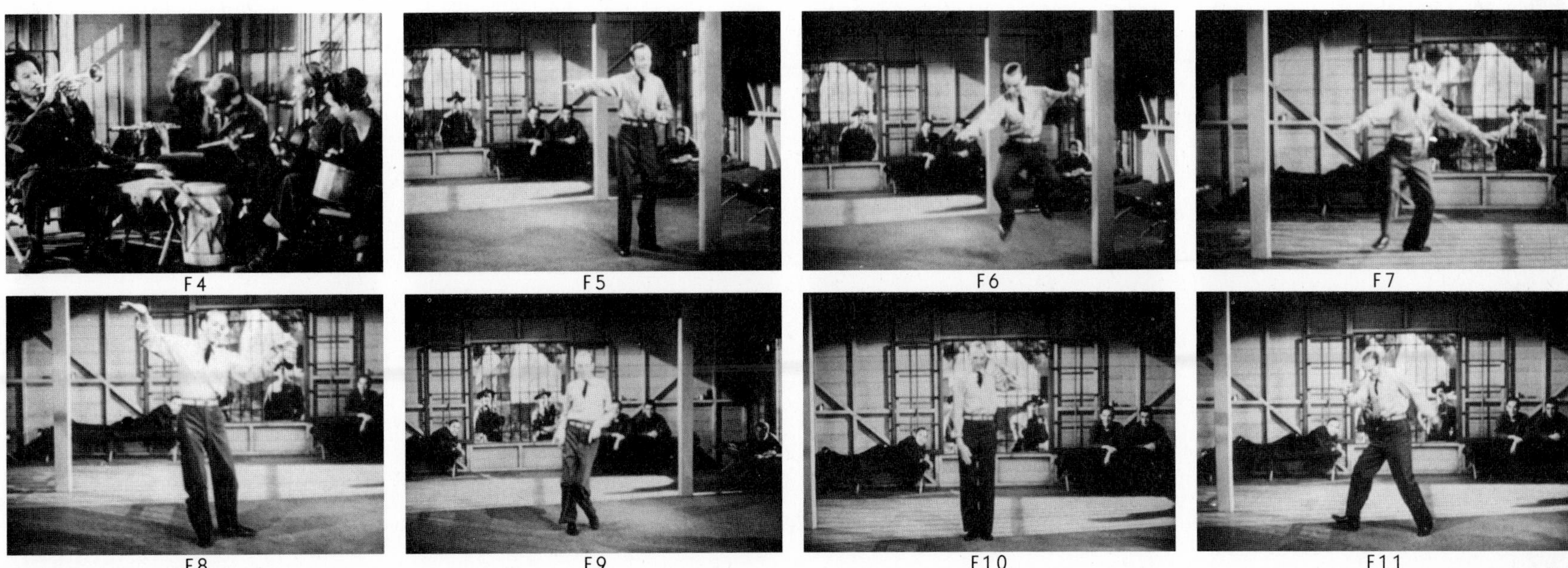

F4 F5 F6 F7

F8 F9 F10 F11

"far" to "near"—the partnering at the beginning is mostly distant, and at the end the dancers are snuggled closely together—but for the most part the duet is showy and impersonal, and the emotional aspects of the far-near progression are not developed with clarity. While Hayworth does inform her aunt a few minutes after the duet has ended that she has suddenly come to realize she is in love with Astaire, there is little in the duet to suggest that anything like that is happening to her.

Taken on its own terms, however, the "So Near and Yet So Far" duet is lovely, and Hayworth is appealing in it—especially her torso undulations, and the way her arms seem naturally to embellish the choreography. Besides the far-to-near progression, the duet is notable for its delicate and playful exploration of various Latin motifs and for its elaborate variations on the spiraling Astaire double-helix maneuver, two ideas blended throughout into the dance's frequent back-to-back circling patterns. Especially impressive are the transition from song to dance and the sensual ending with its soft turns and intricate arm work.

The near-and-far idea is introduced during the singing. The first time he sings "near," Astaire takes Hayworth's hand, and she gently but firmly pulls it away when he sings "far." The second time allows for some atmospheric close-ups of Hayworth as she leans toward Astaire on "near" (G1) and away, shielding her face with a glamorously raised shoulder, on "far" (G2). Her face suggests desirability without responsiveness, a quality that is, however, appropriate for the song. In sharp contrast to Ginger Rogers at such moments, she modulates her expression very little.

As Astaire approaches the end of the song, Hayworth stands just out of reach and undulates her hips enticingly (G3), then continues the motion while circumnavigating Astaire twice. The first time around he follows her with his eyes (G4) and completes the singing of the song. The second time, during some transition music, he turns, following her with his whole body (G5), until the couple end up in partnering position (G6) as the orchestra returns to the beginning of the song. This beautiful maneuver is a slow-motion version of the Astaire double helix, and having the woman manipulate *him* into the

F12 F13 F14 F15
F16 F17 F18 F19
G1 G2 G3 G4
G5 G6 G7 G8

dance is a witty reversal of the usual procedure in Astaire duets.

After some distant partnering and a few variations on rhumba-inspired undulations and glidings, the dancers play against the music's insistently churning rhythms by pausing in a series of positions suggestive of far (G7) and near (G8). There is a brief passage during which the dancers are close, but they quickly spin apart and are soon doing more rhumbalike movements in an arm's-length partnered position that puts them as far apart as possible while still touching (G9). Then there is a return to somewhat closer partnering (as in G6), embellished with light, dignified jumps. The next phrases are mostly a progressive elaboration of the double helix as the dancers repeatedly twist around each other back to back, sometimes in a stiff-backed manner that suggests flamenco (G10). Out of this maneuver there emerges a beautiful side-by-side partnered hopping pattern to some transitional music (G11).

The dancers punctuate the return to the beginning of the song by separating and snapping into declarative poses (G12). Then they sweep past each other twice in a livelier version of earlier back-to-back patterns (G13; compare G10). As the music suddenly becomes softer and more intimate, they cross the floor in a quiet and sensual pattern, lacing and unlacing their arms while continuing to turn (G14). Then Astaire suddenly spins and wraps himself in Hayworth's left arm (G15). He had used this idea in earlier dances, and would again in later ones, but only as part of a transition back to a partnered position (see pp. 158–59). Here it becomes an end in itself: the dancers pause in this pose and then, in that oddly stylized configuration, travel forward. Separating finally, they perform some brisk, vigorous jumps to the side—a Latinized version of a step in their earlier duet (G16; compare A3)—and then settle into a Spanish-style wrists-on-hips pose, which is developed into a series of increasingly rapid spins (G17). After an abrupt stop, they resume their exotic undulating.

Some churning steps in close partnering (G18) build to an explosive leap (G19) that ends in another held pose (G20). Slowly they draw together during some smooth back-to-back turns (G21). For their exquisite exit they return to the Latin undulations that reflect the music, repeating and

G9 G10 G11 G12
G13 G14 G15 G16
G17 G18 G19 G20
G21 G22 G23 H1

considerably extending the intricate interlaced-arm idea introduced earlier (in G14). At the very end, just as they are about to vanish into the wings, Hayworth leans back against Astaire's chest (G22, 23)—near at last.

H
THE WEDDING CAKE WALK
(5′5″)

Plot convolutions dominate the film's last half-hour. Hayworth has come to realize she is in love with Astaire (H1), but before she can tell him, he, alarmed that she might marry her boyfriend, goes AWOL to get a marriage license and the legendary diamond bracelet. Benchley arranges for Hayworth to discover Astaire and Massen in Astaire's apartment in town, hoping that Hayworth will think Astaire has been two-timing her, walk out on the show, and thus give Benchley's new favorite the role by default. This ruse fails to impress Hayworth until she discovers Massen's name on the bracelet (Benchley had it changed), and then she *does* walk out on the show (H2); whereupon Astaire, about to be hauled back to camp, vengefully telephones Benchley's wife and urges her to come to the show (H3). This she does, and discovers the affair, at which point Massen decides she had better leave (H4) and the show thus has no female lead. Now the disappointed soldiers petition Hayworth (who has become engaged to her boyfriend) until she reluctantly agrees to perform.

We are now fully ready for an elephantine production number that appears to be largely the work of Robert Alton. Performed as the grand finale of the army-camp stage show, it begins with Martha Tilton, supported by an eight-man drill team, brightly singing the song before the curtain (H5).[7] The curtains then part to reveal some clichéd chorus drill-work that builds (well, leads) to a mock wedding for Astaire and Hayworth (H6). The pair then lead the crew in some boogie routines, in the process jolting out some interesting rearward lurches (H7) as well as a couple of cakewalk struts (H8)—something one might have thought Alton would use more in the number. At the end Astaire and Hayworth repetitively jab a foot and arm outward alternately to each side (H9). When the camera pulls back we see that they are on top of a giant wedding cake in the shape of a tank (H10). Does this look like a country about to go to war? And win?

As the curtains close, Astaire rudely grabs the hostile Hayworth, kisses her (H11), and cheerfully proclaims from the top of the cake-tank that the onstage wedding was a real one since he had cleverly employed a genuine justice of the peace in the number (thus, one is forced to conclude, the number is one of those that advance the plot). When Astaire is again hauled off, Benchley steps forward and, with uncharacteristic nobility, clears up the confusion about the bracelet (H12). Hayworth believes him for the first time in the film and jubilantly rushes off to see her new husband in the spacious guardhouse (H13).

[7] Porter's song ends with the words "night and day" sung on three even, repeated notes, just as they are at the beginning and end of the famous song he had composed for Astaire nearly a decade earlier—a wry salute from composer to performer. To avoid potential legal problems, Porter secured permission for the quotation from RKO, which owned the film rights to the older song. The inside joke is somewhat obscured in the film: Tilton is being hauled offstage when she ends the song (H5), and the sound fades down a bit as she leaves. On Astaire's recording of the song, his delivery of the words makes the reference quite clear. In general, the song sounds better on that recording than in the film—it is rendered with more bounce and lightness.

H2 H3 H4 H5
H6 H7 H8 H9
H10 H11 H12 H13

With Hayworth in "Boogie Barcarolle"

15.

HOLIDAY INN

1942

Like its central performer, Bing Crosby, at his best, *Holiday Inn* has a relaxed, unsentimental charm. The film is tidily fashioned around a set of seasonally adjusted Irving Berlin songs celebrating the holidays of the year, and the colossal success of one of them, "White Christmas," has helped to make the film a December favorite and something of a classic.

Fred Astaire plays Crosby's partner, friend, sidekick, rival, and tormentor, and the two spend a lot of time questing for the same woman—Astaire by dancing, Crosby by singing. In the end singing wins, but the interest in this film lies in the competition, not the outcome. Between Crosby's warblings, Astaire performs several dance numbers: a playful duet that sparkles and shimmers, a gimmick solo that is ingenious but uneven, a smooth romantic duet that promises more than it delivers, a comedy trio that is agile and apt, a drunk dance that is both funny and profound, and a silly costume duet that is fairly catastrophic.

THE SCRIPT AND THE PRODUCTION

In the 1930s Irving Berlin had plans for a Broadway revue in which each number would deal with a different holiday. The revue never came about, but when he mentioned the idea in 1940 or 1941 to Mark Sandrich, then a producer-director at Paramount, Berlin received an enthusiastic response. Both agreed the idea was ideal as a film vehicle for Bing Crosby.

Since the revue form had been abandoned by Hollywood ten years earlier in favor of book musicals, a script was required. Elmer Rice and Claude Binyon fashioned a clever story in which all the action takes place on holidays, beginning on Christmas Eve in what is obviously meant to be 1940 and ending on New Year's Eve two years later; calendar inserts in the film are used to mark the progression of time. Crosby plays the proprietor of a country inn that is open only on holidays—this gives him "350 days a year to kick around in," the easy-going crooner observes. The plot revolves around his semifriendly competition with his former nightclub-act partner, a man who, unlike the Crosby character, is manic and hard-working. To play Crosby's rival, Sandrich signed Astaire, whom he had directed many times at RKO in the 1930s.

The Crosby-Astaire competition is focused on women. At the beginning, both are after the third member of their nightclub act, Virginia Dale. When Crosby decides to retire to the country, Dale at first chooses Astaire, but then she flutters off to marry a Texas millionaire. Next Astaire tries to move in on Crosby's newest flame, Marjorie Reynolds. Tricks are played, songs are sung, dances are danced, and soon Reynolds runs off to Hollywood with Astaire. At the end, however, she succumbs to Crosby again, and Astaire is given a reformed Dale as a consolation prize.

The film uses the talents of its two leading men to express the rivalry. In the opening number, an onstage routine, Crosby and Astaire explain how they plan to capture their quarry's heart with singing and dancing (respectively), and this song, with updated lyrics, is reprised at the end, to frame the story neatly. And, to a degree, each uses his talent to try to win the affections of Reynolds—Crosby croons agreeably into her ear except when Astaire is sweeping her around the dance floor. The disappointment is that this imaginative device isn't more fully exploited. It's used most effectively at the end of the film, when Crosby wins Reynolds back by joining her in the beautiful song that sets her dreaming nostalgically of the white Christmas when they first met. But almost all of Crosby's other songs are sung largely as display pieces. Even more unfortunate (and surprising) is that Astaire never gets to do a truly romantic dance with Reynolds. Their gliding caper to "Be Careful, It's My Heart" incorporates a bit of importuning seductiveness, but mostly it's a showpiece.

The film's weakest aspect is the Crosby character's diffidence in matters of love. When he and Reynolds become "sort of engaged," he manages to give her a hasty peck on the cheek. Then, to keep her away from Astaire, he plays a series of cruel tricks on her rather than simply pressing his obvious claim to her affections. Much of Crosby's characterization was undoubtedly shaped to accommodate his antipathy to playing mushy love scenes. Astaire shared this aversion, but was willing, especially when he had a compatible partner, to let affection show, particularly in the musical numbers, where he, not the director or writers, controlled the situation. By contrast, Crosby simply croons. It seems fitting that Crosby's most heralded achievement as an actor was in the role of a priest.

Bing Crosby in blackface for "Abraham"

The substantial salaries commanded by both Astaire and Crosby may have been the reason Sandrich cast two unknown (and therefore inexpensive) women opposite them. Reynolds and Dale are attractive and lively, but neither lights up the screen or ignites special chemistry as a dancing partner for Astaire. Reynolds, whose big chance this was, had previously appeared in small parts in dozens of motion pictures, most of them Westerns or horror movies. Although she had never before had a significant role in a musical, she was tested for *Holiday Inn* on the recommendation of dance director Danny Dare, who remembered her as a promising chorus dancer in a film he had worked on several years earlier. She went on to modest success in films and television. Dale, a member of a nightclub dance act, had appeared in several earlier film musicals; *Holiday Inn* proved to be her last.

THE MUSIC

Twelve of the fourteen songs used were freshly composed for the film. This was the "most new music ever presented in a single motion picture," publicists asserted at the time—a claim that may well be true. Unfortunately, with the important exception of "White Christmas," quality did not match quantity. The lyrics of most of the songs are especially disappointing—suggestive often of haste and overconfidence in their composition. A standout in this unimpressive crowd is the affectionate "You're Easy to Dance With."

Considerable musical brightening is provided by the background swing band led by Crosby's overshadowed brother, Bob. The group can't always keep Bing from lapsing into his all-too-characteristic musical lethargy, but it does make a significant contribution to all of Astaire's best musical moments.

THE SAGA OF "WHITE CHRISTMAS"

The staggering popularity of "White Christmas" is one of history's less obscure facts. The song appeared thirty-three times on the popular weekly radio and television program "Your Hit Parade," far more than any other. By the end of

With Marjorie Reynolds in "I Can't Tell a Lie"

With Virginia Dale in "You're Easy to Dance With"

1982, 143,310,326 records of the song had been sold in the United States and Canada alone, and it entered the *Guinness Book of World Records* as the greatest seller of any record. Bing Crosby's recording of the song (which he made in eighteen minutes) sold over twenty-five million copies alone.

Despite this record of success, the tune was something of a sleeper when it first appeared; in fact, there may have been some trouble getting the song into the film at all. According to one story, the religious Crosby was reluctant to sing such a secular song at first, feeling it would further commercialize the holiday. Actually, if Binyon's script had been followed, Crosby would never have sung "White Christmas" in the film at all. According to his scheme, the song is sung only once—by Reynolds in Hollywood at the end of the film; Crosby writes the evocative song to remind her of the white Christmases at his Connecticut inn, and, upon singing it, she is so moved that she abandons Hollywood and Astaire to return to Crosby (causing their agent to vow, "If I ever manage another team, it'll be Siamese twins!")

Even after the song was integrated into the film there seems to have been little expectation that it would become a major success. One of the film's arrangers, Walter Scharf, later recalled, "We thought 'Be Careful, It's My Heart' was going to be the big hit. . . . ['White Christmas'] seemed nice enough but no one thought it would be much else." Berlin says he expected no more than a modest success, and initial response to the film seemed to bear his expectation out. "Be Careful, It's My Heart" entered the "Your Hit Parade" listings as early as July 25, even before the film came out, and far overshadowed "White Christmas." While a few reviews singled out "White Christmas" for praise, most either casually enumerated it among the film's new tunes or failed to mention it entirely.

By the end of October, however, nearly three months after the film's release, "White Christmas" topped the "Your Hit Parade" chart, and it stayed in that position until well into the new year. What caused the change was not so much the approach of Christmas as the particular conditions of the time: 1942 was the first Christmas of the century during which the United States had a substantial number of troops involved in a foreign war, and the song perfectly expressed the yearning of these young men for home. Armed Forces Radio was flooded with requests for it. The song, written years earlier, took on, as Berlin once observed, "a meaning I never intended."[1] Crosby recalls, "I sang it many times in Europe in the field for the soldiers. They'd holler for it; they'd demand it and I'd sing it and they'd all cry. It was really sad."[2]

Although the song's connection with the war has now been largely forgotten, its association with Crosby helped him to become a special symbol of the Christmas season. In 1954 he made a hit film built around the song, and until his death in 1977 he appeared in yearly radio and television Christmas specials that were nostalgic, homey, and highly profitable, just like "White Christmas," the song he reportedly found too commercial in 1941.

THE CHOREOGRAPHY

On hand to help Astaire with the dances was Danny Dare, a Paramount regular who later, as Daniel Dare, became a producer on the lot. Dare is given credit in the titles for staging the dance ensembles, but since there are only some fragmentary chorus dances in this rather intimate film, he apparently had little to do in that capacity.

[1] Berlin wrote the song in the mid-1930s while he was in Hollywood working on an Astaire film at RKO; it was copyrighted as an unpublished song in 1940.
[2] This experience is re-created in two Crosby films: in a brief sequence in *Blue Skies* (see 20 P1) of 1946 and in the opening scene in *White Christmas* (1954).

THE NUMBERS

A
I'LL CAPTURE YOUR HEART
(3′ 16″)

Astaire and Crosby are members of a nightclub trio and each is in love with the third member, Virginia Dale, who, generous of affection, loves both of them back. Crosby wants to marry her and settle down on a farm, whereas Astaire wants to marry her and continue the act as a double. She prefers Astaire's bid but hasn't turned Crosby down yet.

In a plush Manhattan nightclub on Christmas Eve, the trio is shown performing an amusing routine that neatly plays on the Crosby/Astaire rivalry. Berlin has supplied a serviceable song in which Crosby brags about how he will capture her heart by singing, and Astaire responds with the confident claim that his dancing will do the trick. The song includes a suitable contrast for the characters: a mellow phrase for the singer and a snappy response for the dancer. This idea is intricately developed in the choreography, with the two performers seeking to one-up and undercut each other.

As the number opens, they eye each other warily while they wait for Dale on a street corner. Each is armed with a present—Crosby a box of candy, Astaire a bouquet of flowers (A 1). When Dale ambles into view, Crosby sings about his singing and Astaire sings about, and demonstrates, his dancing. When Astaire tries to extend his dance phrase to maneuver toward Dale, Crosby restrains him by the coattail. Next, without dropping a note or a step, they casually destroy each other's gifts: Crosby accidentally sits on Astaire's bouquet; Astaire purposely stomps on Crosby's candy box (A 2); Crosby plucks a surviving flower from the bouquet for his boutonniere and calmly pitches the rest away; Astaire retaliates by picking a piece of candy for himself and throwing the box away.

Things get really serious when Dale joins them. Crosby croons with a vengeance (A 3), and Astaire delivers a snappy tap phrase that concludes as he springs, with amazing quickness and agility, onto a nearby bench (A 4), where he raps out a little afterthought. Dale concludes from this that Crosby's failing is that he can't dance as well as sing, and that Astaire's problem is the same in reverse. Thereupon each contestant attempts a parody of the other. Astaire produces a rumbling croon adorned with a twittering whistle (A 5), and Crosby lumbers through a tap phrase that includes a labored jump onto the bench and ends with a wonderfully portentous port de bras (A 6). Dancers know that an eye-catching carriage of the upper body can distract attention from lower errors; Crosby's pose is either an astute parody or a desperate application of the homily.[3]

Faced with that evidence, Dale advises each to stick to his specialty, and in an aptly timed sequence she alternately sweeps around the stage with Astaire and harmonizes with Crosby. In the course of his dance Astaire tries to maneuver her toward the wings, but Crosby hauls the pair back to center stage (A 7). The competition is resolved in a draw: with convenient fickleness, Dale walks out on both of them. Undaunted, the two men briefly partner each other with mock daintiness (A 8), and amiably edge toward the wings. Crosby's arm motif is incorporated into the exit choreography, and he concludes the number with an impudent back kick that would

[3] Crosby's arm position bears a striking resemblance to a signature pose in Astaire's "Continental" number from *The Gay Divorcee* (see 3 F5, also 4 F4).

A 1 A 2 A 3 A 4
A 5 A 6 A 7 A 8
A 9 A 10 B 1 C 1

have been funnier if he had bothered to time it to the music (A 9, 10).[4]

B

LAZY

(1′ 23″)

Backstage, Dale finally tells Crosby she has decided to remain in show business with Astaire (B 1). Unperturbed, the singer retires to his newly purchased Connecticut farm. A montage sequence shows him struggling at hard labor (even on holidays) while in a voice-over he languorously croons a 1924 Berlin song with a distinctly contrasting message. The lyric of the old song shows a flair for witty rhyme ("wild wood"/"child would," "valise-ful"/"peaceful") which is quite absent in the songs composed for the film.

[4] In his autobiography Astaire says Crosby surprised him during rehearsals for this number: "Having heard that he didn't like to rehearse much, I was amazed when he showed up in practice clothes"—a somewhat ambiguous observation that might be taken to suggest Crosby worked hard on the number. It is said that Crosby had a wistful "ambition" to be a "tap dancer like Fred Astaire." The number provided Astaire with a snappy answer for the perennial question "Who's your favorite dancing partner?" "Bing Crosby," he could now reply. The pair were to dance together one more time, in a hokey routine in *Blue Skies* (20 H).

C

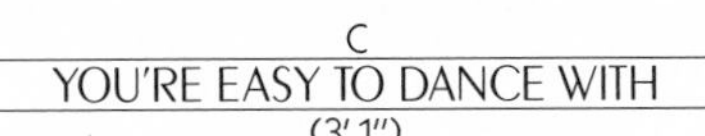

YOU'RE EASY TO DANCE WITH

(3′ 1″)

After a year of work (culminating in a rest stop at a sanitarium), Crosby decides to give up farming and to turn his spacious farmhouse into a country nightclub open only on holidays; the rest of the time he will spend in purposeless idleness. Crosby visits Astaire in New York on Christmas Eve, exactly a year after his "retirement" began, to tell him about the scheme. Staying on to catch Astaire's nightclub act, Crosby is seated at a table with an ambitious aspiring performer played by Marjorie Reynolds (C 1). They watch as Astaire and Dale percolate agreeably through the film's finest duet.

Dale does not look particularly easy to dance with: she does not move much like a skilled dancer, nor is she costumed with flair. But precisely because of that, this affectionate, understated duet is one of the finest examples of Astaire's ability to convey the illusion that any woman he dances with is a paragon of grace.

The number has an unusual form, probably inspired by the lyric. Instead of first singing and then dancing in his usual manner, Astaire chooses to do both simultaneously. There is a great deal of fully developed dance movement while Astaire (aided sometimes by a background chorus) sings the song through, and then, for the first time in his film career, he continues to sing portions of the song throughout the rest of the number. Moreover, to an unusual degree this number is about dancing together: almost everything is partnered, and there is very little of the independent, simultaneous solo work found in almost all of Astaire's other duets.

Berlin's attractive song is somewhat similar in construction, though far superior in effect, to "I'll Capture Your Heart": in the main strain (the A sections of the AABA song) a bouncy melody gives way to a contrasting, crooning declaration of the song's title (or a close variant). Since the song is played twice through, the title phrase is prominently stated six times, and Astaire chooses to make each repetition an intimate declaration: the dance pauses, and he sings the phrase directly to his partner. Thus, although the number is playful and takes place in a public setting, it is clearly a personal statement of the romance between Astaire and Dale, which is otherwise only sketchily suggested in this film.

The dancers enter the nightclub stage area in a confident arm-in-arm stroll, acknowledging

C 2

C 3

C 4

C 5

C 6

C 7

C 8

C 9

C 10

C 11

C 12

C 13

the applause and waving to friend Crosby in the audience (C 2). The number is set in motion as Astaire and Dale spin around each other in a sumptuous double-helix pattern (C 3), from which they emerge in close partnering. They continue to dance as Astaire begins to sing, and their movements, light and ambling at the start, gradually become fuller and travel more, subsiding only when Astaire sings the title phrase (C 4). Added are some crisp turns, a side-to-side swaying figure (C 5), and a sequence of small crossover steps. The words "I'm always right on the beat" inspire Astaire to stamp out a percussive cadenza (C 6). Then he eases up, jauntily steps around Dale, and spins her until, on his clapped command, all movement ceases momentarily while they hold an open pose facing each other (C 7).[5] But stasis is brief in this bubbling dance; as the chorus sings the next few measures, Astaire sweeps Dale in a wide circle around him (C 8), then, holding her close again (as in C 4), completes the song by singing its concluding declaration of the title phrase.

The music, played exhilaratingly by Bob Crosby's band, now returns to the beginning of the song, and the choreography develops several of the ideas already presented. Holding each other by the hand, the dancers bounce off each other accordion-style while repeating their earlier cross-stepping upstage (C 9), and then blast out a brief partnered tap cadenza in unison. A swaying pattern (C 10; compare C 5) brings them forward for another punctuating cadenza, which gives way to loving calm as Astaire again intones the title phrase to Dale.

The next sequence uses only one idea, a partnered tap turn, developed with considerable rhythmic intricacy. It begins at a brisk pace, is elaborated into a quick cadenza, slows radically in a stop-start sequence that holds back against the thrust of the music, and careens into a series of fast spins ending in a crouching pose (C 11) from which Astaire again croons the title phrase (C 12).[6]

The dance's most brilliant passage follows. The dancers separate for a series of coordinated gliding turns around the floor, come together for some partnered skittering hops (C 13), and separate again for a set of staccato turns with windmill arms (C 14), which evolve into a sequence of clipped spins on one foot punctuated by hand claps (C 15). This spin sequence is the only portion of the duet that is completely unpartnered.

Then, for Astaire's final singing of the title phrase, there is a marked change: with great deliberateness and affection, he takes Dale in his arms, presses her tightly to his body and twists gently, suggesting the deep regard that underlies this playful duet (C 16). After that the performers, side-by-side, hop out a wonderfully unexpected hitch step (C 17) and casually amble into the wings. This final promenade is identical to their entrance—except that now each has an arm around the other, and their attention is on each other, not the audience (C 18; compare C 2).

[5] The pose in C 7 occurs only once in this dance. In the romantic duet in *The Sky's the Limit* a year later, Astaire used the pose as a major motif with distinct emotional connotations (17 E 11, 15).

[6] The camera cuts to a close shot for the singing (C 12) and then cuts back to a full-figure shot—rare for Astaire, who preferred close or medium shots in a dance to be achieved not by an insert like this, but by a single cut with the camera tracking away afterward (see pp. 28–29).

D
WHITE CHRISTMAS
(2′ 35″)

Seeking a job as an entertainer, Reynolds ventures out to Holiday Inn the next day and is surprised to find that Crosby is the proprietor. After a few misunderstandings are cleared up, he shows her around his spacious, charming farmhouse, a set designed by Hans Dreier that is one of the most appealing aspects of the film. Then, as they warm themselves by the fire, Crosby sings a seasonal song he says he has just written; at the end Reynolds (her voice dubbed by Martha Mears) joins in (D 1). The scene, crowned by Berlin's simple, luminous song, has a warmth and an affecting tenderness never again captured in the film.

E
HAPPY HOLIDAY / COME TO HOLIDAY INN
(1′ 31″)

Working together, Crosby and Reynolds have the place in shape for its opening on New Year's Eve. It is packed with merrymakers from New York, whom the couple welcome with a medley of two of Berlin's less memorable songs (E 1).

F
LET'S START THE NEW YEAR RIGHT
(49″)

Another follows, sung with something less than heartfelt ardor by Crosby to Reynolds as they work in the kitchen (F 1).

C14 C15 C16 C17

C18 D1 E1 F1

G
YOU'RE EASY TO DANCE WITH
(DRUNK DANCE) (2′ 1″)

It turns out that the fickle Dale has run out on Astaire to marry a Texas millionaire. Astaire gets roaring drunk and somehow manages to wend his way to the Holiday Inn New Year's celebration to consult his old pal Crosby, "who knows about women." Astaire lurches into the inn and is soon involved in a dance with Reynolds.

This number—more a supported solo than a duet—is the first of Astaire's three drunk dances in film (the other two are in *The Sky's the Limit*—17 F—and *Blue Skies*—20 O). In most respects, this one is the most insightful of the three—perhaps because, according to Astaire, he took "two stiff hookers of bourbon before the first take and one before each succeeding take. . . . The last one [the seventh] was the best." It's a comedy dance, in part because Astaire seizes the opportunity to parody himself, allowing his characteristic coordination, his artlessly artful connections, to go amusingly awry. But it is also an amazingly apt caricature of the woozy, stumble-footed, self-pitying drunk, unable to keep mind and body synchronized.

As Astaire weaves his way around the crowded dance floor, he becomes blearily preoccupied by a dancer's wagging hand and tries to shake it (G1). That laborious task accomplished, he shuffles onward and soon bumps into the amused Reynolds. As the Bob Crosby band ironically plays a bright, swing arrangement of "You're Easy to Dance With," Astaire staggers around the dance floor with her, to the considerable delight of the other guests and to the consternation of Crosby, who senses danger in this meeting of his girl with his former partner and rival (G2).

Astaire is roused to semicoherence by his competitive instincts: seeing another man doing a vigorous, churning dance step next to him, Astaire shows he can do it, too (G3); the other dancers clear away, and soon he is partnering Reynolds with an addled smile of self-satisfaction (G4). Because things go pretty well for a while, Astaire is emboldened to lead his partner in increasingly flamboyant steps, marred only occasionally by unsteady footwork (G5).

Calamity begins, however, when he spins Reynolds away from him and then tries to wind her back into his arms—her momentum is too much for him, and he is sent staggering (G6, 7). Astaire never fully recovers his composure after this. First his feet refuse to keep up with him, and then he keeps losing track of his partner. While she frolics impishly behind him, he numbly circles the floor looking for her, his expression suggesting the morbid, sentimental self-pity of the terminal drunk (G8). Eventually he turns and, to his surprise and delight, rediscovers Reynolds. Glee is brief, however, for some missed partnering soon sends him tottering off-balance into the crowd, where an onlooker obligingly breaks his fall (G9). Then, as he continues the dance, he repeatedly looks gratefully toward the man who cushioned his fall, his body dancing onward while his mind is still several seconds behind, marveling at his rescue (G10).

Because of this preoccupation, Astaire soon finds he has his own arms, as well as Reynolds', tangled around his neck (G11). A choreographic device used by Astaire in several duets is an agile maneuver in which he insinuates himself into his partner's arms by wrapping her left arm around his neck (see p. 158); the strangling entanglement here is a deft parody of this step.

After a period of utter bewilderment, Astaire dopes out the problem and unwinds. The mental effort seems too much for him, however: dazed, his body begins to give out. Reynolds clings to him and soon finds she is his only support. He staggers, sags, and finally collapses flat on his face (G12, 13). The fall is amusing (in part because it happens so directly on the music), but it's also a little unsettling in its unvarnished realism.

H
ABRAHAM
(3′ 1″)

Upon reviving the next morning, Astaire learns what a resounding success his dance with Reynolds was. Although he only vaguely remembers her, a "hunch" tells him that she is his dream partner, and he plans to return to the inn on each holiday until he finds her again. Crosby protects his interests by trying to keep her out of sight.

The next holiday is Lincoln's Birthday, and, to disguise Reynolds from Astaire, Crosby decides they should perform in blackface. As he blackens her face in her dressing room, Crosby offhandedly proposes they get married when he has saved enough money. Though bewildered at his casualness, Reynolds accepts (H1). This scene, as well as the number that follows, are often cut when the film is shown on television,

G1 G2 G3 G4

G5 G6 G7 G8

presumably because of the offensiveness of the blackface, thereby making Crosby's romantic yearnings for Reynolds even less convincing than they are when the film is presented whole.[7]

As Astaire sorts through the audience looking for a female shape that will jog his memory, a blackfaced Crosby lethargically croons a tune that cries out for the kind of bouncy treatment it had so splendidly been given earlier, when Astaire entered the inn, by the band in the background. At the end, the blackened Reynolds, complete with fright wig, joins in (H2).

I
BE CAREFUL, IT'S MY HEART
(3′28″)

At the end of the evening, Crosby works up his courage and kisses his fiancée—on the cheek (I1). Then, since Astaire will soon be returning to the inn on Valentine's Day, Crosby seeks to consolidate his claim on Reynolds' affections by presenting her with a new romantic song as a valentine. Appropriately, the lyric uses heart imagery, but with a clumsiness startling from a songwriter as skilled as Berlin: "Be careful . . . that's not my watch you're holding, it's my heart."

At any rate, as Crosby earnestly sings such sentiments to Reynolds on Valentine's Day, his romantic plans go awry. Astaire steals into the room behind Crosby's back, instantly recognizes Reynolds as his dream partner, gathers her in his arms, and cruises around with her in a dance that is apparently to be taken at once as impromptu audition and romantic foray (I2). It's a pleasant but romantically ambiguous blend of showy wafting and fancy posturing, culminating in a bit of visual imagery as corny and misguided as anything in the lyric.

The first part of the dance is given over to a standard Astaire partnering development: he starts by partnering Reynolds gingerly from behind; then he leads her through some decorative posings, guides her in a wide circle around his body, and finally moves in on her, locking her firmly in his arms (I3–4). That point made, the dance becomes lighter, even a bit fluttery (I5), and a couple of lifts are inserted (I6). Then, in the dance's best moment, Astaire nimbly glides from one side of his partner to the other as they stroll arm in arm (I7–8).

After some lilting material, including several independent turns with windmilling arms, the dance slows and, pressing Reynolds tightly to his chest, Astaire lets his left arm drift backward, inviting her to close the pose and therefore to pull her body in toward him (I9). Although he employed this bit of sly suggestiveness in duets in other films, it was never more clear or provocative than here.[8] From there they romp to a platform behind a big paper heart, pose decoratively for an instant (I10), sweep briefly back to the dance floor, return to the platform, and then smash through the heart (I11), finishing in the middle of the floor gazing theatrically at each other (I12). Crosby's reaction suggests disappointment and alarm (I13).

J
I CAN'T TELL A LIE
(3′54″)

Delighted to discover that Reynolds is everything he had hoped for, Astaire enthusiastically

[7] On the other hand, Crosby's odd romantic reticence toward Reynolds later in the film would be a bit *more* convincing if they are not shown to be engaged. Simply snipping out this scene does not effect that improvement, however, for Reynolds later tells Astaire that she and Crosby are going to be married.

[8] Earlier: 5 E8, 10 E12, 13. Later: 18 G5, 21 B3. See also N1 and Q2 in this chapter.

G9 G10 G11 G12
G13 H1 H2 I1
I2 I3 I4 I5

proposes they start rehearsals immediately so that they can open their act at the inn on the next holiday. Crosby reluctantly goes along with the scheme.

On Washington's Birthday the film hits rock bottom. Astaire and Reynolds, bewigged and costumed like George and Martha, are shown dancing a dignified minuet during which Astaire attempts repeatedly to kiss Reynolds. But each time he gets close, Crosby instructs the orchestra to switch abruptly to noisy jazz, throwing off Astaire's timing and sending him into some incongruous, wig-flapping hot-footing. The idea, heavy and uninspired to begin with, is labored and vastly overextended in execution.[9]

For the occasion, Berlin submitted one of the worst songs in his illustrious career. I could say you're homely or stupid, the lyric muses, but this is Washington's Birthday and I can't tell a lie—one of the most clumsily backhanded compliments in the history of the love song. When Astaire sings this ditty to Reynolds, she frequently appears understandably bewildered about how to react (J 1).

Then they begin a simpering, toe-pointing duet (J 2). Watching carefully from the piano, Crosby shifts tempos whenever Astaire tries to make a pass, and each time the dancers are nonplused (J 3, 4). The joke goes on and on until the end, when, while Reynolds stands by helplessly, Astaire is launched into a desperate garble of ballet (J 5) and tap (J 6) clichés. Astaire had used a similar device in a duet with Ginger Rogers in *Follow the Fleet* (6 H); tried it again with Gene Kelly in *Ziegfeld Follies* (18 M); and developed it with the most wit in a duet in *The Belle of New York* (26 G), where abrupt shifts in orchestration are used, not shifts in tempo or musical quality. In those dances, however, the idea was applied far more sparingly and led to jokes that were integral to the choreography, not simply superimposed on it.

However, the ending of "I Can't Tell a Lie" has some merit. As Astaire spins, his wig rotates on his head so that the tail flops over his face (J 7)—an effect that would have been funnier if it had emerged directly out of the dance rather than being tacked on in a separate shot.

[9] Astaire's willingness to submit to this ordeal (called for in the script) is puzzling. In a 1922 stage show that flopped, *The Bunch and Judy,* he had done a number in similar garb with his sister and hated it.

K

EASTER PARADE

(1'45")

Romantic developments proceed by unconvincing lurches. Astaire, it happens, always falls in love with his dancing partner, so, although the minuet routine hardly gave evidence of passion, he has now predictably fallen for Reynolds. When he informs her of his feelings, she blandly explains that she is engaged to Crosby, and Astaire, crestfallen, nobly decides to bow out. But when he discovers Crosby is uncertain about his "sort of" engagement to Reynolds, Astaire reconsiders and decides to rise above nobility and "go to work."

His work commences on Easter Sunday. As Crosby and Reynolds ride back to the inn from church in a horse-drawn surrey, he serenades her with one of Berlin's golden oldies (for background on this song, see p. 277). As Crosby sings he caresses the melody but largely ignores the woman—despite the script's specific direction for him to be "exhilarated by the thought that she is his" (K 1). When the pair get back to the inn they discover Astaire there waiting for them, and, to Crosby's dismay, he moves in.

I 6 · I 7 · I 8 · I 9 · I 10 · I 11 · I 12 · I 13 · J 1 · J 2 · J 3 · J 4

L
SAY IT WITH FIRECRACKERS / SONG OF FREEDOM
(2′56″)

Skipping nimbly over Mother's Day, Father's Day, Memorial Day, and Flag Day, the film next takes up the action on the Fourth of July, a holiday right down Berlin's patriotic alley and a sensible one to emphasize in a film released in wartime.

Astaire's agent arranges for a couple of important men from Hollywood to see the show; if they like it, Astaire and Reynolds will be offered The Big Time—a movie contract. To keep Reynolds for himself, Crosby concocts a remarkably selfish scheme: he has her delayed on her way to the inn, and telephones Dale (who is back in New York after the failure of her Texas venture) to replace Reynolds in the performance.

The show begins. On a large outdoor stage, a chorus sings a song about firecrackers while distributing samples to the audience. Then Crosby appears, to do the flag waving that was all but obligatory in wartime films (L1). As he buoyantly sings about freedom, a photomontage is projected, showing military machines being manufactured and soldiers being trained. There are also heroic inset shots of General MacArthur (L2) and President Roosevelt.

M
SAY IT WITH FIRECRACKERS
(DANCE) (2′46″)

Hitchhiking to the inn, Reynolds is picked up by Dale. When Dale inadvertently reveals Crosby's scheme, Reynolds upsets it by giving her the wrong directions. With no partner, Astaire is forced to improvise a solo. He stuffs his pockets with fireworks and trots out onstage to perform a number in which he embellishes his tap sounds with explosions appropriate to the season.

Despite its plot premise, this dance is one of the least improvisatory in Astaire's career. In filming the number, Sandrich noted at the time, "Fred must have done it fifty times before music, steps, firecrackers, and smoke were perfectly coordinated." Two devices are used: torpedoes, which Astaire hurls to the floor, and small explosive charges embedded in the floor that were electrically triggered from offstage by Danny Dare playing a kind of "organ" that was constructed for the occasion. Although the explosions are real (attested to by the clearly visible smoke that rises from them), animation seems to have been used after filming to heighten the visual effect, and the explosive sounds were undoubtedly dubbed in later as well. Except for incidental effects in a couple of later numbers (22 G, 28 E), this seems to be the only time Astaire used animation in his numbers. (Actually, the animation works so well it would have been possible for Astaire to have used it alone, faking the explosions in the dance and having them drawn in later, though some of the naturalness of the rising smoke would have been lost.)

In the early 1940s, in particular, Astaire seems to have been fascinated by the sheer noisemaking capacity of tap dancing (see p. 11). In this solo he pushes the idea to its logical extreme, which he found singularly gratifying, even cathartic: "It was a great satisfaction, that dance. . . . Sometimes you want to bang your feet down so hard in a tap dance that you get shin-bucked or stone-bruised. In this one I had a completely satisfactory outlet with those dynamite noises." The effect is spectacular, and it is developed in the number with Astaire's usual highly tuned sense of theatre. But, as in some other Astaire solos, the gimmick sometimes gets in the way of the choreography, so that at times the dancing becomes filler between effects.

The number has a compelling opening. As the curtains part, Astaire skitters onstage, sportily attired, cigarette in mouth, hands in pockets, exuding heady self-confidence (M1). His light-footedness is of special benefit in this number because it contrasts so appealingly with the ground bursts, which make him seem even more buoyant than usual as he capers among the explosions and reacts to their force. The skittering becomes more complicated rhythmically, and then he unveils his gimmick: he hurls torpedoes at the floor and uses their explosions to punctuate his tap frolic (M2). It is here, in particular, that the dance sometimes degenerates into inconsequential filler, as in a repeated, but undeveloped, bit of high-stepping (M3), or in some routine tapping with pumping arms. Very fine, however, is a sequence in which several torpedos are thrown down: Astaire uses the follow-through of each throw, combined with the sound of the explosion, to propel himself into a reactive spinning jump (M4).

The dance's momentum is now arrested—rare in an Astaire number. As the band vamps expectantly, he pulls a firecracker from his pocket, lights it with his cigarette, flips it into the air, and reacts with a goofy, leg-curling jump when it explodes (M5). Then he lights a whole string of firecrackers, tosses them away, and hops around merrily, finger in ears, as explosions surround him (M6). That sets him off into some beautiful space-devouring, speed-shifting tapping while the band takes up a fragment from "Song of Freedom" (M7). Now various firecrackers embedded in the floor go off in sequence on their own, and he high-steps around reacting in counter-rhythm to the bursts.

As the band returns to the "Say It with Firecrackers" melody, Astaire romps about, the explosions punctuating his progress. Again he falls into a repeated figure—a jabbing jump to the side—that seems designed mostly to fill up time (M8; used also in 14 H9 and 20 O9).

After some more tap/explosion flurries, including one in which the bursts seem to follow him across the floor (M9), he is launched into the solo's masterful ending, which incorporates a dazzling display of speed shifts. As the explosions cease for a moment, Astaire glides through three sumptuous turns, each on a separate held note in the brilliantly supportive music (M10). Suddenly he stops, and a volley of firecrackers goes off behind him (M11), sending him bolting through one final tap burst until music and dance finish in the same instant with crisp, satisfying assertiveness, as smoke wafts through the air (M12; for a similar use of the music in dance endings, see 12 F, 12 H, 13 K, 14 F, 17 C).

N
DANCE MONTAGE
(55″)

The bedraggled Reynolds finally makes it to the inn, outraged at Crosby's bizarre, selfish trick. The visitors from Hollywood, however, are pleased with everything. They hire Astaire and her anyway, and have plans to build an entire motion picture around Crosby's Holiday Inn. Crosby reluctantly agrees to write the songs for the picture but insists on remaining at the inn to do so. Astaire and Reynolds, who is deeply hurt, take off for California. The newly launched team is shown in various multiply exposed dance fragments; in some of these Astaire repeats the held-back left-arm idea he had used in his Valentine dance (N1; compare I9).[10]

O
I'VE GOT PLENTY TO BE THANKFUL FOR
(1′10″)

Thanksgiving arrives, and a confused cartoon turkey is shown on a calendar scurrying be-

[10] The script called for a Labor Day duet to a song called "This Is a Great Country." It was to lead into an Astaire solo that would prove to the dejected Reynolds that she is not an adequate dancing partner for him.

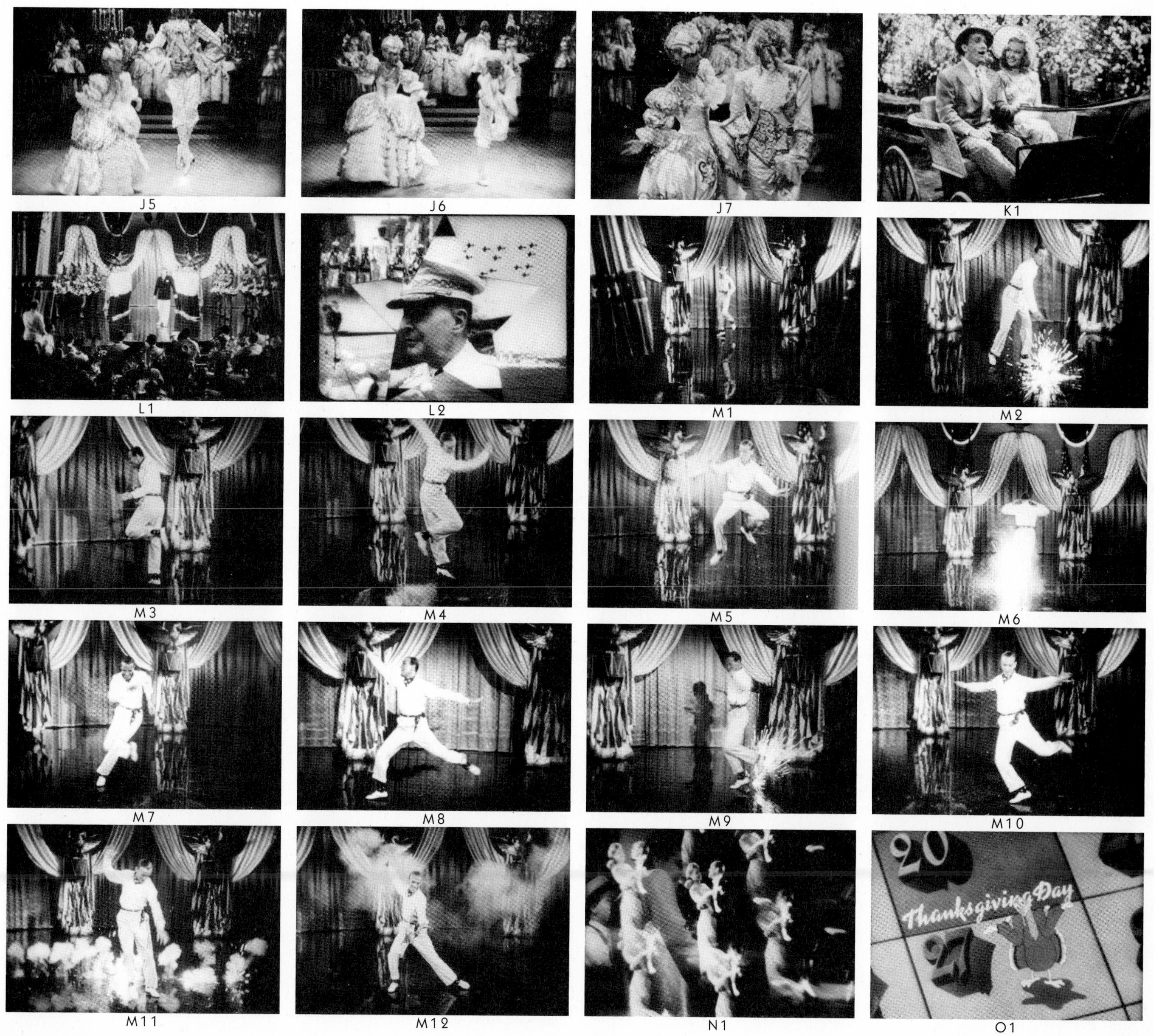

J5 J6 J7 K1

L1 L2 M1 M2

M3 M4 M5 M6

M7 M8 M9 M10

M11 M12 N1 O1

tween the third and fourth Thursdays in November—a topical joke reflecting political disagreements over the official designation of the holiday (O 1).[11]

Crosby has closed the inn and is somberly composing songs for the movie. He plays a record of a Thanksgiving song he has just written. Depressed and without appetite, he doesn't feel very thankful and mutters acidic comments as the song plays—for example, to the line "ears to hear with," he adds "or to fly with," which is amusing coming from a man who often good-naturedly joked about his protruding ears (O 2).[12]

[11] In 1939 Roosevelt sought to have the holiday celebrated on the third Thursday of the month rather than the fourth, in order to help merchants by increasing the Christmas shopping period. Many states refused to go along, and the resulting confusion was cleared up only in 1941, when Congress passed a resolution anchoring the holiday to the fourth Thursday. (The animators, incidentally, seem to have been looking at a 1941 calendar when they created this episode instead of one for 1942. All the other calendar inserts in the film are consistent with the notion that the film begins on December 24, 1940, and ends on December 31, 1942.)

[12] In Crosby's early films, his ears were pinned back with spirit gum or adhesive. Midway through the filming of *She Loves Me Not* (1934), however, he got fed up and insisted his ears be left alone. So, he says, in the first part of that film he looks "like a whippet in full flight," in the second, "like Dumbo."

P
WHITE CHRISTMAS
(REPRISE) (1' 3")

Although he knows Astaire and Reynolds are now engaged, Crosby permits himself for once to be urged into romantic assertiveness when his cook assures him that Reynolds prefers the relaxed life of the inn to the bustle of Hollywood (P 1).

Crosby journeys to Hollywood, where, on Christmas Eve, the last scene of the film is being shot. Reynolds, who is to marry Astaire the next day, portrays a woman in a somber mood; in the words of her director, "Your Hollywood success was empty, you've lost the one man you love—you know, the usual hoke." The scene is shot on the Holiday Inn set—an exact replica of the real thing, we are told. Actually, of course, it is the set that has been used throughout the film, and there is something intriguingly disorienting in the way the film calmly shatters its own artful illusion by showing its beautiful central set to be merely that—a set (P 2). Furthermore, Reynolds really *is* unhappy about Hollywood and about her marriage plans when she ventures onto the set to sing the nostalgic "White Christmas" for the camera (P 3). Then, from the shadows, Crosby joins in. Overjoyed, she rushes into his arms, ruining both the shot and Astaire's hopes (P 4).

Q
I'LL CAPTURE YOUR HEART
(REPRISE) (1'45")

But Astaire is not out in the cold for long in this happy film. A true sport, he joins Crosby and Reynolds in the reopening show at Holiday Inn on New Year's Eve. At that point, the flexible Virginia Dale—or "Miss Hit and Run," as Astaire calls her, ambles in (Q 1); she and Astaire rekindle their dancing partnership while fragments of several of the film's nonhits are spiritedly reprised (Q 2, 3).[13]

[13] This satisfying resolution is not in the script, which calls for Crosby and Reynolds to be reconciled at the inn even while Astaire is making a last, futile effort to come between them.

O 2 · P 1 · P 2 · P 3 · P 4 · Q 1 · Q 2 · Q 3

With Crosby

16.

You Were Never Lovelier

1942

Fred Astaire's first film with Rita Hayworth, *You'll Never Get Rich,* served as her introduction to stardom. By a year later, when they were paired again at Columbia, she was substantially established as glamorous star and as quintessential pinup queen. The new film, appropriately titled *You Were Never Lovelier,* is a perky comedy with memorable songs slyly built around Hayworth's peculiar screen presence: radiantly beautiful but sometimes disconcertingly cold.

Like several other Astaire films from the early 1940s, *You Were Never Lovelier* could have benefited from another dance number or two, particularly in the early part of the film, but the quality of what there is leaves little to be desired: a brash and witty solo, a couple of flavorful duets, and a sprightly duet fragment at the end. Astaire seems more comfortable than he was in the earlier film with the spectacularly glamorous Hayworth, who is here decked out in a series of clinging gowns that become increasingly luscious as the film proceeds. Most of his increased comfort, however, comes in the dialogue scenes; although his dances with her are affectionate and amiable, Astaire seems somewhat reluctant to explore in them all the romantic and erotic possibilities suggested by the script and the music.

THE SCRIPT

The film is set in Buenos Aires. To supply a Latin flavor, Xavier Cugat and his band are incorporated into the proceedings and Astaire makes some comic references to Latin steps and poses in his solo. His romantic duet with Hayworth also toys with Latin dance forms, but that probably derives from Hayworth's background as a Spanish dancer (their romantic duet in *You'll Never Get Rich* was even more Latin-oriented, and that film took place in a Stateside army camp). Beyond that, there is little effort in the film to suggest its locale. The major characters all speak plain Amurrican English, the decor is handsome but geographically unevocative, and the caprices of the plot could take place just about anywhere. The putative Argentine setting does distance the film from the contemporary reality of World War II, however, and the scriptwriters may have found that desirable.

The plot is the most ingeniously convoluted Astaire was ever involved in. It centers on a wealthy Argentine hotel owner, played with chipper gruffness by Adolphe Menjou, who is seeking to marry off his daughter, Hayworth. She is beautiful and much sought-after but has a personality "like the inside of a refrigerator." To get her into a romantic frame of mind, Menjou sends her anonymous love notes and orchids, intending to supply the young man once she has fallen for the bait. The notes are successful but, through a confusion, Hayworth comes to believe Astaire is the mysterious flower sender and falls in love with him. Since Menjou considers Astaire, a footloose and penniless professional dancer, to be a singularly undesirable match for his daughter, he spends most of the remainder of the film contriving to break up the match. There are a dazzling number of shifts and twists, all reasonably plausible, until, near the end, Menjou comes to change his mind about Astaire—only to have Hayworth change *hers* as well. Allied now with Menjou, Astaire mounts a determined final pursuit and wins.

As in much Molière, the would-be manipulator father is the central motivating force in the plot, and Menjou—who was so good at father roles that he was often, to his dismay, typecast in them—plays his part, at once foolish and crafty, with considerable depth: he is blunt, conniving, easily angered, authoritarian, yet charming and enormously likable. The scenes in which he and Astaire spar are particularly delightful. Hayworth, though far from a skilled comedienne, seems much more relaxed about the film's humor than she was in *You'll Never Get Rich.*

Although the dance numbers are all ably blended into the plot, there are none in the film's first thirty-five minutes—a considerable flaw. More important, the dances do not always do all they might to develop the plot.

THE MUSIC

Columbia Pictures boss Harry Cohn asked Jerome Kern to provide the music for the film. Kern, who always chose his projects carefully, was happy to sign on in this case, because he enjoyed writing for Astaire and because he liked the director—the easygoing William A. Seiter, who had directed Kern's (and Astaire's) *Roberta* ten years earlier.

Johnny Mercer, a friend of Astaire's, wrote the lyrics. Although Mercer was well established by this time, he was in awe of Kern. After adjusting his working methods to suit Kern's, Mercer got along exceedingly well with the older man and supplied his usual quota of witty and charming rhymes and images.

Kern was actually an unlikely choice for *You Were Never Lovelier,* since he was uncomfortable with Latin themes and rhythms—or, as he put it, "I don't write anything unless I can write it well, and I can't write Spanish songs." Instead, he poured out a succession of sumptuous ballads: "Dearly Beloved" (the film's big hit tune), "I'm Old Fashioned," "You Were Never Lovelier," and—in some respects the most arresting of all—"These Orchids," which is used mainly as background music.

Kern, also characteristically, had problems with Astaire-style rhythm numbers, but he did come up with the useful "Shorty George." He and Mercer also wrote the brilliant "On the Beam" for the film. In its shimmering, on-top-of-the-world confidence, the song is quintessential Astaire, and he made a wonderful commercial recording of it at the time; unfortunately, the song is not used in the film.[1]

Kern was at first appalled when a mere "rhumba band" was hired to play his tunes, but he was soon won over by Cugat's integrity and musicianship—so pleased, in fact, that he gave the bandleader a silver baton after the film was completed.

THE CHOREOGRAPHY

Assisting Astaire on the choreography was Val Raset, working here on his only Astaire film. Judging from his autobiography, Astaire seems to have worked out most of the duet material with Hayworth herself—much of it in a funeral parlor they used as a rehearsal studio.

[1] Mercer's lyric for the exultant release strain suggests the song's flavor: "I'm like the B-19 / Loaded with benzedrene / When I come on the scene I bust a hole in the sky. / One foot is in the groove / The other's on the move / Which only goes to prove I'm a remarkable guy."

Doing the Shorty George with Rita Hayworth

Astaire auditions for Adolphe Menjou

With Hayworth in "I'm Old Fashioned"

With Hayworth in "You Were Never Lovelier"

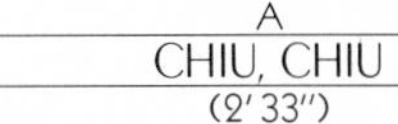

THE NUMBERS

A
CHIU, CHIU
(2′ 33″)

Having lost his last peso at the horse races, Astaire comes to Menjou's office seeking an audition for a dancing job but is unable to get past Menjou's harried, if friendly, male receptionist. As it happens, Xavier Cugat, a friend of Astaire's from New York, is in Menjou's employ and promises to try to help out.

Astaire visits Menjou's hotel nightclub, where Cugat is putting his band through a typical number. Cugat's band was at a peak in the early 1940s and featured two well-regarded soloists, Miguelito Valdes and Lena Romay, as well as a small chorus of singers imaginatively used as an instrument of the orchestra.

B
DEARLY BELOVED
(1′40″)

Cugat devises a plan. Having been hired to play at the wedding of Menjou's eldest daughter the next day, he arranges for Astaire to sing with his band, to use the event as a sort of undercover audition (B1).

The song Astaire sings is replayed often in the film as a theme for Menjou's romance-inspiring scheming. Not only was it the film's biggest hit, but it became popular as a wedding song. Though Astaire croons it affectionately, he probably would have been more comfortable if it had been taken at a somewhat brisker pace. As it is, he has trouble with some of its momentum-arresting hesitancies.[2]

C
WEDDING IN THE SPRING
(30″)

The cloaked audition has no impact on Menjou. Astaire meets Hayworth at the wedding reception and is chilled by her "refrigerated" personality (C1). Although Menjou takes an instant dislike to Astaire, he recognizes the truth in what Astaire says about his daughter's coolness toward men. To warm her up, Menjou begins sending her orchids accompanied by love notes. The notes begin "Dearly Beloved" and end "Your unknown suitor" (C2). Meanwhile, Hayworth's lovesick younger sisters, trapped by a family tradition that requires daughters to be married in order of birth, sing a brief sarcastic song about their dilemma (C3).

D
DEARLY BELOVED
(REPRISE) (1′ 32″)

Menjou's anonymous epistles eventually do the trick, and Hayworth, clutching the latest note, is shown flouncing decoratively around her bedroom (D1). Nan Wynn, a big-band vocalist of the time, sings for her on the sound track and has somewhat less trouble than Astaire with the song.

E
AUDITION DANCE
(2′ 14″)

Through a mixup, Astaire substitutes for a bellboy and delivers the next orchids and note to

[2] Observers have pointed out that the opening two and a half measures of the song's chorus are identical to a repeated motif in a portion of the love duet that concludes Act I of Puccini's *Madama Butterfly*. This was a potential problem at the time, because the opera was still in copyright. Kern expressed his philosophy about such things succinctly: "Anything that is close cannot be plagiarism. It must be coincidence. Anything that is plagiarized is whipped around so that it is not immediately noticeable."

B1  C1  C2  C3

D1  E1  E2  E3

E4  E5  E6  E7

Hayworth's house. She sees him and concludes he is the amorous letter writer.

Astaire returns to Menjou with the change from the florist and demands an audition as compensation for his errand (E1). Accompanied by members of Cugat's band, whom he has smuggled into Menjou's office, Astaire launches into the first dance of the film as the furious, sputtering Menjou looks on, a captive audience.

The dialogue suggests this slot was prepared for "On the Beam," and production records include a dance arrangement of the song. However, Astaire apparently decided to abandon that idea in favor of a dance routine on Latin themes, and so, working with Cugat's arrangers, put together a musical pastiche to accompany it, consisting of fragments of "Los Hijos de Buda" by Raphael Hernandez and Noro Morales, "Bim Bam Bum" by J. Camacho and Morales, Hungarian Rhapsody No. 2 by Franz Liszt, and "Eco" by Gilbert Valdes. The solo, at once impertinent and endearingly whimsical, carries Astaire all over the office in a frolic that cheerfully parodies everything in sight, even some of his own earlier dances. Much of the humor derives from Astaire's direct reflections of shifting nuances in the accompaniment.

The dance is in three parts. In the first, Astaire takes a gaggle of Latin dance ideas and cheerfully scrambles them with elements of his own style: exaggerations of self-consciously tempestuous Latin dancing are amusingly contrasted with his own brand of sunny understatement. At the start we find him in a Spanish mood as, one arm wrapped tightly around his own waist, he mockingly partners himself with steamy passion around the office (E2). This shifts to a brilliant blend in which a rigid, flamencolike torso rides over an Astaire specialty—a hard-driving tap pattern in which the legs wander loosely out to the side (E3) (see also 14 A1, 18 M19, 22 G15). Next some heroic, matadorlike poses are snapped out (E4) and then smilingly shrugged away (E5). A phrase that includes pelvis twitching (E6) and more foot-stomping gets the same send-up (E7). The section concludes with a spin around the floor, some exuberant breast beating that seems to owe something to the spirit of "On the Beam" (E8), and some more impudent pelvis twisting and casual shrugs.

Astaire slams his hat down on Menjou's desk and then slaps the desk several times, brightening the tempo of the music and propelling himself into the second section of the dance. Abandoning Latin themes for the moment, he snatches a cane from a convenient umbrella stand and scampers around the room with it (E9), hurdling a throw rug, and then kicking the threatening object out of the way. Now, parodying his own supposed penchant for suavely gliding over furniture, he stomps maniacally on Menjou's office couch (E10) and then jumps into an easy chair with momentum enough to send it skidding across the floor as he calmly rides along (E11). By now the music has changed, with a logic of its own, to themes from Liszt's Second Hungarian Rhapsody. Astaire advances on Menjou and slaps the desk with his cane, then crisply jumps onto the desk and taps various objects—including, finally, Menjou's skull—with the cane (E12).

To begin the last section of the dance, Astaire bounds back to the center of the floor, and the music returns to a Latin mode. After doing a brief screwball dance routine with the cane, slipping and staggering around (E13), he calmly regains stability and sails his prop across the room into the umbrella stand (E14).[3] After a reaction

[3] On this bit of business, see p. 19.

E8 E9 E10 E11
E12 E13 E14 E15
E16 E17 E18 F1

shot (unusual in an Astaire dance, but appropriate in this case) of the astonished Menjou (E 15), Astaire romps through his final burst of tricks—all filmed in a single shot. With amazing dexterity, he kicks a metal ashtray into the air, catches it, jumps on and off a low table, kicks another ashtray up, catches it, hops back onto the table, and then dashes off a Spanish fragment using the ashtrays as mock castanets (E 16). For the finish, he careens around the floor in more partnerless partnering, jumps up onto Menjou's desk (E 17), returns to the floor to bolt through several forceful spins, and then lunges at his sullen, solitary audience and demands a verdict (E 18). He doesn't get the job—the only thing in the number that defies logic.[4]

[4] Choreographer Jerome Robbins, who acknowledges Astaire as the most influential dancer in his career (see p. 3), created his first ballet, *Fancy Free,* in 1944, two years after *You Were Never Lovelier* came out. This ballet, which has become a modern classic, includes a famous solo to Latin music, originally danced by Robbins himself, that incorporates several elements from Astaire's audition dance: the impudent hip thrusts, the chest beating, the wry shrugs, the partnerless partnering, the crisp jumps from high places. In 1983 Robbins choreographed for the New York City Ballet a major work built on this film's "I'm Old Fashioned" dance as a tribute to Astaire.

F
I'M OLD FASHIONED
(4′ 37″)

Menjou angrily orders Astaire from his office. (An incidental pleasure is the wonderful little dance Astaire makes as he exits, seemingly propelled by the windy force of Menjou's shouts.) Menjou is then visited by Hayworth, who announces that she is in love with the penniless dancer and demands he be invited to visit their home (F 1). When Menjou reluctantly agrees, she dashes off excitedly ("I've only got three hours to dress!"). Astaire is bewildered by the invitation until Menjou explains the situation. The two cook up a deal: if Astaire will disillusion Hayworth on his visit (by being "your own inimitably obnoxious self"), thereby freeing her for worthier suitors, Menjou will give him a job (F 2).

So bribed, Astaire visits Menjou's home. But their plans instantly go awry when Astaire notices that Hayworth, no longer refrigerated, is dazzlingly beautiful. The two are soon out in the garden, where Astaire makes a dutiful, if halfhearted, effort to disillusion her. He explains his various faults: he is bashful, a dancer, a hopeless (and luckless) gambler, and "a plain ordinary guy from Omaha, Nebraska," an "old fashioned, everyday Middle Westerner" who is "strictly from corn." But she finds all these qualities admirable and sings warmly about their obvious compatibility—she's old-fashioned too, she sweetly observes (F 3).

This leads to a pleasant romantic duet that, like its counterpart in *You'll Never Get Rich* (14 G), seems to be placed at some distance from the plot. Although the dance is suitably affectionate, there is little effort to carry out the dramatic progression suggested by its placement in the script: it doesn't show Astaire beginning to fall in love with Hayworth, nor does it show her actively trying to break down his resistance. In fact, the choreography develops in an antiromantic direction, beginning with soft musings and then becoming showy and exhibitionistic.[5]

Kern's tender song is a marvel. Constructed sparsely in a kind of theme-and-variations form (ABA′A″), it is particularly notable for the appealing way in which the strains link up—especially

[5] Perhaps this somehow derives from the unusual setup for the number: a romantic duet that follows a love song sung by the woman. Only one other Astaire romantic duet, "Thinking of You" in *Three Little Words* (23 M), has this structure, and the dance there, too, begins intimately and becomes showy.

F 2  F 3  F 4  F 5

F 6  F 7  F 8  F 9

F 10  F 11  F 12  F 13

for the poised and dramatic transitions between the B and A′ strains and between the A′ and A″ strains. Astaire makes arresting use of this musical element in the choreography.

The singing ends, and the dance begins, with some gentle face-to-face rocking, the dancers holding hands with their arms down (F4). This soon impels them to flow around the terrace, still holding hands (F5). After some pulsating partnered turns, they separate, and a beautiful half-fall forward is used to mark the transition from the B to the A′ strain (F6, 7).

In the most ravishing passage in the dance, the dancers, now side by side, return to the rocking idea but then, as the music builds, start to turn; in the process, Hayworth coils and uncoils herself in Astaire's arms (F8, 9). On the final coiling, she sweeps around him, promenading him as she does so (F10) (on this maneuver, see p. 172n). Then, as the music subsides into the A″ strain, they glide out of the turn, dipping lightly forward and returning to their rocking (F11).

After some rapt amblings around the terrace, including a couple of partnered backbends for Hayworth which she handles reasonably well (F12), they face each other, partnering hand to hand again. Then, as the accompaniment returns to the beginning of the song, both dance and music gradually become bright and jazzy.

The jazz section includes a flurry of tap turns and miscellaneous dodgings leading to a transitional passage (from B to A′ again) as the dancers sweep around the floor (F13). All this activity comes to an abrupt halt as the A′ strain begins—the dancers, partnering close, punctuate the moment with a stamp of the foot and cease all movement as the orchestra suddenly starts playing the tune in an insistent samba rhythm (F14). Stasis is brief. Continuing to hold each other closely, the dancers softly undulate. As their movements become broader, they separate and mark the arrival of the final A″ strain with another stamp and pause. Then Astaire suddenly lights out toward Hayworth and sweeps her into his arms; together they whip off a joyous series of twirling jumps and scooting leaps—movement that scribbles over the sultry, rumbling music and pushes Hayworth to the limits of her abilities as a dancer (F15, 16).

The swirling soon simmers down for the dance's amusing but inconclusive ending: approaching an upstage doorway, they slow to a saunter, bow to each other with mock formality (F17), bump into each other trying to maneuver through the doorway, bow again, squeeze through, and swing the doors closed behind them with deft back kicks (F18).

G
REHEARSAL BITS
(15″)

A while later, Astaire is back on the terrace with Hayworth and almost kisses her (G1). Realizing he has botched his mission, he beats a hasty retreat and ruefully decides to leave Buenos Aires. But Menjou (now working on plan C) insists that Astaire stay, work in the nightclub, and never see Hayworth again. This, he reasons, will convince her that Astaire only used her to get a job, and she will shrug off her infatuation with him and be easy prey for a more suitable young man—to be supplied, of course, by Menjou.

Astaire is next seen at the club, blasting through some fragments of a dance number he is rehearsing with Cugat's band (G2).

H
THE SHORTY GEORGE
(4′10″)

Hayworth cheerily breaks in on the session and asks to see the North American number being

F14 F15 F16 F17
F18 G1 G2 H1
H2 H3 H4 H5

rehearsed. Astaire and Cugat oblige, and soon she joins Astaire in a congenial, upbeat dance that says considerably more about their mutual attraction than their earlier ballroom-style duet.

The Shorty George is a screwball jazz step of the time that calls for limp arms, bent knees, and a shuffle in place. Astaire demonstrates the step to Hayworth as he sings the song (H1), and the step reappears in the dance whenever the orchestra plays the end portion of the main strain—that is, the music under the words "named for someone about so big" or "beats his feet until his feet is beat."[6] The step is named after its probable inventor, George ("Shorty") Snowden, a champion dancer at Harlem's legendary Savoy Ballroom. Snowden stood five foot two and may have been the originator of the enormously popular Lindy (or jitterbug) dance style. His heyday lasted from the 1920s until 1938, when his doctor ordered him to stop dancing because he had beaten his feet until they were shapeless.

There is considerable dance movement under Astaire's singing. He taps and skips and once perambulates (or, as Mercer puts it, pre-ambles) around the table where Hayworth is sitting, and even goes (somewhat awkwardly) down on his knees briefly (H2). Near the end, Hayworth sings a few phrases of the song and then sashays over with chipper impudence to join Astaire in a dance to a superb arrangement of the music by big-band composer Spud Murphy. Astaire is surprised and delighted (H3).

In no time she has the Shorty George step down pat (H4), and the dancers develop the step to travel in a tight little circle. Then, still keeping arms slack and knees bent, they amble forward in a loose, shuffling tap passage (H5) that soon carries them into a low turning jump and various playful slams and wiggles (H6).

An imaginative traveling step in which the dancers move backward while thrusting forward (H7) sends them into a jaunty passage with more leg twists and twitches (H8) and some sprawling, swinging kicks (H9). They try the kicks partnered (H10), but then settle back into the Shorty George step when it is called for in the music (H11). More kicks, even broader than before (H12), and more Shorty George shuffling, sends them into a spinning lift (H13) and into sequences involving crazy-legged noodling, the latter engagingly supported by boogie-woogie piano.

Next comes the most genuinely tender moment in any of Astaire's dances with Hayworth: with clear deliberateness, but without missing a beat, he takes her lovingly in his arms and scoots around the floor with her (H14). Then, when the Shorty George music comes up, they perform the required step, still partnering. They separate again for more leg-weaving tap (H15), some snappy floor slams (H16), and an amusing, rhythmically intricate game of pat-a-cake (H17). Except that her arm work sometimes lacks clear definition, Hayworth keeps up nicely with Astaire in this difficult material.[7]

The dance is shattered by a wildly uncalled-for shot of Cugat conducting the orchestra. When the camera finally cuts back to the dancers, they are ready for the wonderful wrap-up: they gleefully hurl their arms around each other in an ingenuous hug (H18, 19), linger in that clinging pose for an instant, then begin to vibrate to the music. They separate for a final Shorty George when the appropriate phrase appears (H20), bolt into one more explosive leap

[6] Astaire had used a similar choreographic structure in "The Yam" in *Carefree* (10C).

[7] This was not accomplished without effort, however. When this dance was in rehearsal, Hayworth fell, hitting her chin on the floor, and was knocked cold.

H6 H7 H8 H9
H10 H11 H12 H13
H14 H15 H16 H17

H18 H19 H20 H21

H22 I1 I2 J1

J2 K1 K2 K3

L1 M1 M2 M3

M4 M5 M6 M7

(H21), and then, with deliberate care, resume their hug, which turns out to be terminal this time: although the music twice more announces the Shorty George call, they ignore it to remain locked in each other's embrace as they pulsate with the beat and drift out of the room (H22).

I

WEDDING IN THE SPRING

(2′ 11″)

Menjou throws a big party in order to surround Hayworth with eligible young men. He has intentionally neglected to invite Astaire, of course, and is surprised when the dancer shows up—with an invitation given him by Hayworth. Menjou quickly moves to resolve his problem by canceling Astaire's contract, thus forcing him to go back to New York. Hayworth tries to act noble and reconciled, but as Cugat's ensemble performs a rather determinedly folksy song with a tongue-in-cheek lyric for the guests (I1), Hayworth's true feelings register on her face (I2).

J

YOU WERE NEVER LOVELIER

(1′ 34″)

Eventually Astaire and Hayworth go out into the garden to say good-bye. Struck speechless by her moonlit beauty, he sings to her instead (J1). She tells him she loves him, too, and kisses him (J2).

K

THESE ORCHIDS

(41″)

Astaire is now determined to marry Hayworth, but Menjou easily convinces him that the marriage wouldn't work: Hayworth, he explains, is just in love with the mythical orchid sender, not the flesh-and-blood down-and-out dancer; if she were to discover Astaire carried the notes simply to obtain employment, she would be devastated. In fact, a plot complication soon requires Astaire to explain the whole thing to Hayworth (K1), who, on cue, becomes hurt and walks out on him. Astaire's noble confession, however, causes Menjou to think better of him—so much so that he agrees to help Astaire win his daughter (K2).

Hayworth is now besieged with orchids, including a delivery by a quartet of singing bellboys (K3). The short song they croon is a substantial mismatch: Kern's haunting melody (used as background for earlier orchid deliveries) toys arrestingly with colorful chromaticism, while Mercer's lyric is an amusing send-up of the singing telegram, incorporating even the words "quote" and "comma" into its text.

L

THESE ORCHIDS

(REPRISE) (1′ 5″)

Fortunately, Kern's melody soon receives better treatment. As part of Astaire's final scheme to win Hayworth back, Cugat's band serenades her with it from the patio (L1).

M

YOU WERE NEVER LOVELIER

(TAG) (1′ 12″)

Then, after a fanfare, Astaire enters—in armor and on a white horse, to simulate the romantic hero Lochinvar, whom he understands Hayworth idolizes (M1). When he falls from the horse, crashing ingloriously to the ground, Hayworth's heart melts and she runs out to join him.

Together they sail through a buoyant dance of celebration. It begins with a brilliant series of traveling and turning skips and hops (M2). These are then contrasted with several earthy leg jabs, which Hayworth delivers with raised shoulder in true glamour-girl fashion (M3). A spiraling double-helix spin (M4) leads to a bit of partnered swirling (M5), some partnered leaps, a pair of bows to Menjou and assorted other relatives, more swirls, an exultant promenade across the floor (M6), and a kiss at the close (M7).

A NUMBER CUT FROM THE FILM

N

YOU WERE NEVER LOVELIER

(DANCE)

According to Astaire's autobiography, he and Hayworth filmed a "romantic type of dance" to "You Were Never Lovelier," but it was cut from the film after the previews because "the studio powers . . . said it 'held up the story.' " The scene in which Astaire sings the song to Hayworth does end abruptly after their kiss (J2), and a dance certainly seems called for at that spot—although the film then would have had two romantic duets danced in the same setting. Still photographs show Astaire and Hayworth dancing in the costumes they wear for the "You Were Never Lovelier" scene (N1), though their dance poses seem mostly to quote the choreography of the "I'm Old Fashioned" duet.

N1

17.

The Sky's the Limit

1943

The Sky's the Limit is Fred Astaire's dark comedy. This remarkable film contains three excellent dances—one of them a memorable solo in which Astaire seeks to extend the tap idiom to express rage and frustration—and the film's score, created by Harold Arlen and Johnny Mercer, includes two masterful songs: the crystalline "My Shining Hour" and the somber, brooding "One for My Baby." But splendid dances and songs are hardly unusual in Astaire's films; *The Sky's the Limit* is impressive because these dances and songs are integrated into a script of considerable depth.

In several respects *The Sky's the Limit* builds on the formulas of the Astaire comedies of the 1930s. But while remaining a comedy, it reshapes these formulas into a commentary on the intensity and uncertainty of human relationships during World War II. Although almost all the action takes place within the United States, it is one of the most effective and affecting war films Hollywood ever turned out.

THE SCRIPT

The screenplay is by Frank Fenton and Lynn Root, with a number of additions and alterations by director Edward Griffith, producer David Hempstead, and Astaire.[1] Astaire plays a Flying Tiger ace, one of the legendary band of American mercenaries who fought against the Japanese in China before the United States entered the war. After Pearl Harbor, its members were inducted into the regular American forces. As the film begins, Astaire has a few days' leave in New York while awaiting reassignment, and, in order to avoid war talk, he changes to civilian clothes. Prowling the city, he soon encounters an attractive magazine photographer, played by Joan Leslie. He pursues her, but things quickly get out of hand: they fall in love and become engaged when she proposes. Knowing he will soon have to return to the war, Astaire decides, on bitter reflection, that he is unwilling to commit himself to anything permanent, and he breaks off with Leslie. However, there is a reconciliation at the end, just as he is about to fly back to the war.

Astaire plays a character that is essentially similar to the ones he had played in the 1930s: cocky, charming, highly competent. But in *The Sky's the Limit* he is "carefree" because he simply doesn't give a damn: current happenings are of no tangible or lasting consequence to him since he knows he must soon return to the war. He is effortlessly successful at everything—fighting the Japanese, playing cards, cooking breakfast, manipulating people and events, pursuing the girl. He is also widely experienced: in the past, he explains at various points in the film, he has been a professional pinball player, a journalist, a chef, a hosiery salesman, a songwriter—and also, he recalls with a wince, he has spent time on breadlines. (There is no reason why this enigmatic character couldn't also be a consummate song-and-dance man, and *The Sky's the Limit* is, in fact, the first film in which Astaire's musical ability is in no way explained.) But there are two elements he cannot control: the war and his own emotions. In an extraordinary solo near the end of the film, he becomes roaring drunk and smashes up a barroom in a rage at

[1] One additional collaborator was the Gallup Poll. When it market-tested the film's proposed title, *Look Out Below,* the survey organization included it in a list containing three other titles: two standards used in all such questions (*The Lady Takes a Chance* and *Tomorrow Never Comes*), plus one invented for this particular test, *The Sky Is the Limit.* The title invented by Gallup did far better than the one chosen by the scriptwriters, and RKO was quick to get the message.

the dilemma the war and his emotions have gotten him into.

Two other elements familiar from Astaire's 1930 musicals that are used in ingeniously altered form in *The Sky's the Limit* are Astaire's single-minded pursuit of the girl and the plot wrinkle of mistaken identity. Astaire pursues Joan Leslie as he pursued Ginger Rogers in the best-remembered films of the 1930s: he begins by annoying her but soon breaks down her resistance with a blend of casual charm and terrific dancing. But there is an important difference in this case: his intentions with Rogers were always honorable, whereas his motivations in *The Sky's the Limit,* it is made quite clear, have nothing whatever to do with marriage. And the element of mistaken identity, which created the essential plot convolutions in *The Gay Divorcee* and *Top Hat,* is intentionally introduced by Astaire in *The Sky's the Limit:* he wants Leslie to be confused about who he is.

Of Astaire's partners in the post-Rogers era, Joan Leslie is most nearly reminiscent of Rogers, particularly as an actress: attractive, intelligent, feisty, vulnerable—though not, in this role, with so highly developed a sense of humor. Borrowed from Warner Bros. for the film, Leslie had been a vaudeville performer since childhood and had made several films before *The Sky's the Limit,* appearing most notably opposite James Cagney in *Yankee Doodle Dandy* in 1942. She became identified as the quintessential homefront girl in films of the era such as *This Is the Army* and *Hollywood Canteen.* Although not a highly skilled dancer, she is generally able to keep up with Astaire in their duets.

Though she looks older in the film, Leslie was barely eighteen when it was completed. Before she reached that age, she was obligated by law to spend part of her time in the studio school, a fact Astaire apparently found disconcerting: "Gosh, the older I get, the younger they get." There is a touch of teasing fatherliness in the way Astaire relates to her in the film, to which his off-screen self-consciousness may have contributed.

The character she plays is also in the Rogers mold: an alert, desirable, self-assured career woman (Rogers was, in fact, RKO's first choice for the role). She also has a tendency, as Astaire teasingly tells her in the film, to take herself a little too seriously. Yet she seems to be less than fully serious about the war, sometimes treating it almost as a golden opportunity to advance her career as a photographer, whereas the war is just about the only thing that Astaire takes seriously—or, rather, because of the war Astaire takes nothing else seriously. At the end, seeing him return to the front, perhaps never to return, she finally seems to comprehend what the war is really about.

Astaire's rival for Leslie's affections is her magazine's publisher—ably played by Robert Benchley—a man who is cynical, unsentimental, yet lovably ineffectual. He and Astaire spar unequally throughout the film, but by the end they are friends, though neither quite realizes it or would admit it if he did. Benchley is funny in this role without being clownish or foolish.

More briefly seen are two of Astaire's Flying Tiger buddies, played by Robert Ryan and Richard Davies. Once again the characterization is apt and unorthodox—there is a strongly acidic touch to their camaraderie and to their friendship with Astaire. The men are tough, highly competitive, and capable of real cruelty to each other, but it would be difficult to imagine anyone better to have on your side when the chips are down.

In general the acting in this fluid and well-paced film is impressive: unusually natural and convincing.

One of the most remarkable aspects of the film is the way the war is handled. The war defines the mood, atmosphere, and tensions of the story, and though it is only occasionally mentioned directly, it is always there, intruding unexpectedly through a snippet of conversation, a casual reference, an overheard radio newscast, a passing, painful memory. Thus, while the romance of Astaire and Leslie is being told in light-comedy terms, the grim comedy of war is constantly lurking in the background. This is shown most clearly in Astaire's attitude toward time—of which he has very little on his brief leave—and money—of which he, as a successful Flying Tiger pilot, has a great deal. Time is precious to him, and money has no value at all; consequently, he keeps throwing money away—overpaying his landlady, buying expensive and unnecessary clothing, betting for high stakes, and calmly paying extravagantly for damages after he has smashed up a barroom.

All but obligatory in Hollywood films during World War II was a flag-waving scene in which the characters either gritted their teeth and told how they were going to grind the enemy down, or reverently praised the infinite virtues of Americanism as heavenly choirs sang. *The Sky's the Limit* has such a scene, but it is virtually thrown away—and for that reason is more affecting. Sitting at the breakfast table, Astaire offhandedly suggests to Leslie that the war is fought for the freedom to be "anything you want to be—somebody or nobody if you want to. Me—right now I want to be nobody. I guess I don't tell it very well." End of flag waving.

Moreover, the film is often astonishingly cynical about homefront patriotism—the superhawk who is 4F, the reveling dignitary who hides his champagne glass before being photographed, the self-important aircraft manufacturer who builds planes that are deathtraps for their pilots.

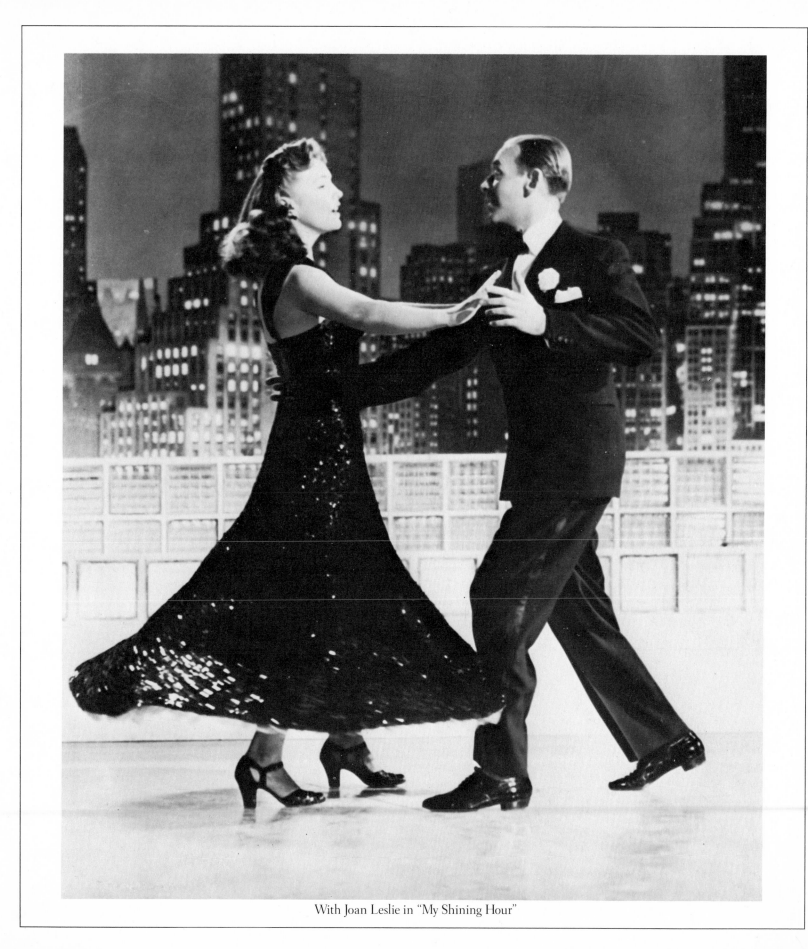

With Joan Leslie in "My Shining Hour"

What emerges, then, is a remarkably unvarnished representation of the war at home. While the characters can go for long periods without mentioning the war, it obsesses their thoughts and severely limits their options.[2]

THE MUSIC AND THE LYRICS

The Sky's the Limit is a particularly well integrated musical. Aided by Leigh Harline's excellent musical scoring, the numbers establish atmosphere, develop and consummate relationships, and clarify and amplify emotional states.

Throughout, Johnny Mercer's adept lyrics have special significance. The tender, innocent lyric for the film's signature song, "My Shining Hour," gives insight into the character Leslie plays, and later it is recalled with trenchant irony. In the "A Lot in Common with You" duet the lyric is continually changing its focus: it starts out as a bouncy love song, performed without personal relevance, but then shifts to relate directly to the singers themselves and, at one point, cleverly shifts again to make a crack about Fred Astaire and Joan Leslie as off-screen personalities. The path of Astaire's pursuit of Leslie in this number is traced through the way the lyric is handled. The dance that follows the singing of the song is essentially an affirmation and a celebration.

Finally, there is "One for My Baby," which has gone on to have a life of its own as one of the most startlingly original of popular songs. In the context of the film, however, the full significance of the song—and particularly of the lyric—can be appreciated, for the tensions and dilemmas of the story lead to, and are summed up in, this remarkable solo. Astaire rages against the insanity of his situation as the war separates him from his love and, with bitter irony, toasts them both: "Make it one for my baby, and one more for the road."

THE RECEPTION OF THE FILM

Although *The Sky's the Limit* made a respectable profit when released (see Table 1), the film caused little critical stir and soon faded into oblivion. Audiences mostly insisted on seeing the film as another frothy Astaire comedy. Comments from the preview audiences were typically of this sort: "not a war picture which is a great change"; "light, cheerful and comic"; "an entertaining war picture—I'm tired of the ones that make you cry or feel blue." Some found the film vaguely "unusual" or "different," but only a few seemed really to have appreciated what was going on: "it fairly well combines the tragedy of war with the lighter side"; "it tugged a little at the heart strings because . . . these days time is so short."

Critical reception was hardly more perceptive. In *The New York Times* Bosley Crowther dismissed the film (and the songs and dances) with a supercilious shrug. Astaire, always sensitive to negative criticism (of which he has garnered remarkably little during his long career), was especially irritated at this review, with its flip, patronizing tone and incomprehensible reference to his "quick-fitting clothes." James Agee in *The Nation* was disappointed that the film wasn't a remake along patented lines—"the first half hour has such charm and flow I half expected another *Top Hat.* I didn't get it"—while the reviewer for *Time* (possibly Agee again) bemoaned the fact that the dances are not a "pure, heart-lifting delight." Critics who liked the film thought it "gay and pleasurable" or "refreshing entertainment." Most clearly troubled by the film's tone was David Lardner in *The New Yorker.* But, rather than thinking too hard about it, he simply proclaimed that "somebody, the author or the director or the producer, presumably, was in an ugly temper during [its] creation."

The acceptance of the film as light diversion from the war, rather than a penetrating comment on the people caught up in it, was encouraged by the RKO publicity department: "Fred and Joan cat-cut all the rugs in Manhattan . . . in a hep-hot story of a Flying Tiger on leave and a fast-stepping chick in love. And they're so terrific!" This angle was ordered emphasized by studio boss Charles W. Koerner, who felt the public was tired of war pictures and wanted to get "away from any war suggestions." Astaire found the publicity campaign misguided and wrote Koerner, "Represented as such [the film] must disappoint many." The film deserves a reassessment.

THE CHOREOGRAPHY

Bernard ("Babe") Pearce, who had worked with Astaire on *Holiday Inn,* was hired as dance director for the film but was on the payroll only for three weeks, let go a few weeks before film production began. Astaire worked alone on the choreography, which was possible since there were no dancing choruses. In the titles he is given sole credit for creating and staging the dances.

[2] The film's essential seriousness about the war makes it unusual among Hollywood products of the era—particularly among homefront comedies. Even in Preston Sturges' justly praised *Hail the Conquering Hero* (1944), everyone seems to be terribly anxious to get into the fighting, treating the war as if it were a football scrimmage. The Astaire character in *The Sky's the Limit,* experienced in war, has no such illusions.

THE NUMBERS

A
MY SHINING HOUR
(SONG) (2′ 19″)

After some brief battle scenes, war hero Astaire is shown riding in triumph in a parade in San Francisco. On leave before being transferred to naval aviation, he is accompanied by a smiling unctuous southern belle who asks, "How much time you got?" He responds, with an insinuating leer, "Ten days. That time enough?" (A 1). When she takes him to her apartment, assuring him she has no roommate, it proves to be full of gabbling ladies'-club members. The disappointed Astaire is photographed by reporters as he enters the apartment. (This photograph will be used by Benchley to identify him toward the end of the film.)[3]

Later Astaire abandons a train taking him on a personal-appearance tour (A 2). In the version of the film that was first shown, he did a short dance number on the railroad trestle at this point (the number is discussed below). Tired of being hailed as a hero, he changes to civilian clothes and hitches a ride to New York with a man who, though unfit for the draft himself, has vigorous ideas about how to prosecute the war: "We gotta give 'em a taste of cold American steel."

Wandering through New York on the make, Astaire spots Leslie and follows her into what is meant to be a posh night spot, the Colonial Club (the sets in this film are definitely not a strong point). There he cheerfully horns in on her conversations with her publisher, Benchley (A 3). Benchley greets Astaire's intrusion with a combination of amusement and unperturbed irritation. Whenever Leslie attempts to photograph the celebrities at the club, Astaire playfully inserts himself in the way, arguing that he could be listed on the caption as "and friend," as in "Ginger Rogers and friend"—one of several wry outside references in the film (A 4).[4] Annoyed but also somewhat diverted by Astaire's persistence, and frustrated by the mundane nature of her photographic chores, Leslie threatens to go back to show business. To prove to Benchley she could still do so, she marches over to the club's bandleader, Freddie Slack, and requests that he accompany her as she sings "My Shining Hour" (A 5, 6).

Though the placement of this number in the script may seem contrived, the significance of the song and its setting becomes apparent later, when it is reprised. Most important, however, the song establishes the tone and point of the film: it is the perfect wartime ballad and the film's signature. When Leslie sings, the song has no specifically personal significance for her; but by the end of the film it will have become the story of her life. This is my shining hour, the singer says, now, when I'm with you; and the memory of this hour will light my nights until I'm with you again. Mercer's lyric is filled with subdued yearning and simple references: the lights of home, a watching angel. Arlen's melody is an ideal match with what Alec Wilder praises as its "spare, hymnlike translucence" and its "innocence and distilled simplicity."[5] Unfortunately, the setting for the song when it is introduced here is weak: the unassertive voice of Sally Sweetland (dubbing for Leslie) is backed by a saccharine female chorus. Slack's band then performs a chorus, which sounds fine but looks silly because the musicians have their instruments framed by tubes of fluorescent light.

B
MY SHINING HOUR
(PARODY) (49″)

Astaire continues to intrude, following Leslie from the nightclub to a lunchroom where she stops for a hamburger. Eventually he seems to be

[3] On Hollywood's stereotype about Southerners, see p. 291n. Earlier versions of the script were even more sexually explicit, both in Astaire's dialogue and in that of his two Flying Tiger buddies. Toward the end, for example, Ryan reviews the pictures of chorus girls he has been with during the leave and, "with a lecherous beam on his face," exclaims, "Oh, brother! The rest of my life is just an anticlimax." Hollywood's censorship board did running battle with the studio over such "sex suggestiveness" in this film and usually won.

[4] Another is Ryan's screen surname: Fenton, the same as one of the scriptwriters. Astaire's name in the film is "Fred." This apparently came about, not through any desire to personalize the role, but because in early versions of the script the flyer was named Phil and the publisher Fred; when Astaire agreed to do the film, the names were simply reversed. Then, when Leslie was brought in to do the role of "Jean," it was decided that if Fred was going to be Fred, Joan might as well be Joan.

[5] The song became a hit, but somewhat slowly, not reaching "Your Hit Parade" recognition until four months after the film was released (see Table 5). The key phrase, "This will be my shining hour," may have been inspired by, or a reflection of, Winston Churchill's famous wartime phrase, "This was their finest hour."

A 1 A 2 A 3 A 4
A 5 A 6 C 1 C 2

doing better with her, and as he walks her home, he happens to opine that the song she sang at the nightclub is like her—it takes itself a little too seriously. She smilingly joins him in a parody of the song in which it is suggested that the hour appears to be "shining" because the singer has had too much to drink.

C

A LOT IN COMMON WITH YOU

(3′9″)

Astaire continues his audacious and single-minded, yet curiously tender, pursuit of Leslie throughout the next day, and by evening has won her over. Not surprisingly a song and dance are what finally bring her around.

At the beginning of the day, he casually breaks into her apartment to cook breakfast for her and deliver his offhand defense of the freedom to be nobody (C1). She becomes increasingly attracted to him and fascinated by his effortless omnicompetence: Once Leslie asks Astaire, "Is there anything you haven't done?" He replies, "Couple of things. But I'll get around to them." And she responds, "Oh, you think so?" (The censors objected to the "sex suggestiveness" in the exchange when it reviewed the script, and, probably as a consequence, the lines are delivered in the film in a throwaway manner that unfortunately mitigates any unseemly implications.) Leslie is troubled, however, by the fact that he appears to have no job, and is pleased when he agrees to see Benchley the next day to seek a position on his gossip magazine, cleverly titled *Eyeful*.[6] That evening Leslie is volunteering at a local canteen, and Astaire accompanies her there, grumbling that he would much prefer being alone with her. When she is called upon to do a stage number, he amiably intrudes on her act, showing that, on top of everything else, he is very good at singing and dancing.[7] She is appropriately amazed.

Leslie skillfully handles the dramatic progression that takes place in the course of this number. Initially she fears he will ruin her number and make them both look foolish; her change in attitude occurs during the singing and is developed through intricate shifts in focus in the lyric. When they last sing, "I've got a lot in common with you," the phrase has become a direct, heartfelt declaration, and the dance that concludes the number is a celebration of this happy discovery.

When Leslie sits down on the stage steps to sing, she is joined, to her annoyance, by Astaire. Trying to ignore him, she starts singing the verse, and he startles her by chiming in on the second line (C2). Not only does he know the lyrics, but he is a fine singer (better than she is, in fact: Leslie's somewhat breathless voice is not dubbed by another singer in this number, perhaps unfortunately). Then, without waiting for her, he launches into the song's chorus, and so she finds that now *she* is joining *him* in the song. Moreover, he moves up one step as he does so, forcing her to follow him if she is to remain on the same level; this subtly sets up the idea of upstaging to be elaborated later. The lyrics of the chorus tell of a compatible pair—both are truthful and candid, both left-handed—but at one point she mutters *sotto voce,* "Get out of here, will ya?"—a suggestion he does not take.

In the final strain, Mercer's lyric modulates to refer to the singers' own personal situation in the film: looking directly at Astaire, Leslie sings, "You're woozy, you're whacked-up"; he responds, "I saw you, I cracked up"; and she replies in irritation, "You're breaking my act up." In the last phrase, they return to the love song and conclude, "I've got a lot in common with you." The difference in focus as they sing this last line is important: Leslie sings it to the audience, not to Astaire; Astaire, however, sings it directly to Leslie (C3). Later this will change.

Astaire now moves onto the stage and invites the astonished Leslie to join him, twirling his finger in the air helpfully to indicate to her the first step (C4). The lyric they sing as they amble around the stage is a commentary on the couple's current situation. "The stage was my born field, I've made it my sworn field," Astaire explains. "Get back in that corn field," Leslie advises. The next line should be "I've got a lot in common with you," but that line, which of course would not follow from the previous lines, is not sung. Instead, as the band plays the music for the line, Leslie hops in front of Astaire, trying to force

[6] Before filming began, the RKO legal office checked to make sure the title had never been used before. During production a crew member brought in a new magazine of that name that he had found in the studio barbershop, and hasty efforts were made to assure the publishers that no harm was intended.

[7] When she asks Leslie to sing, the canteen hostess innocently asks Astaire if he could "do anything" with Leslie. Astaire responds, with great enthusiasm, "*Could* I!" The censors, however, let this pass without complaint.

C3 C4 C5 C6

C7 C8 C9 C10

him off the stage (C 5). Recovering, he follows her back across the stage. She observes, "I think that we're slipping." He suggests, "You'd better start stripping," and amusedly recoils at his own audacity as she sanctimoniously declares, "My zipper ain't zipping" (C 6). (The censorship office, needless to say, at first found these lines objectionable but was argued into accepting them.) Again "I've got a lot in common with you" is not sung, and again Leslie tries to upstage Astaire.

They continue to sing of their problem: "Perhaps we'd better tell a gag" and—a pertinent comment on the era—"Perhaps we'd better wave the flag." The upstaging continues as each is determined to butt in front of the other (C 7). As they progress downstage in this staggered maneuver, the lyric invokes their recent motion-picture partners: "What's all this horseplay worth? These eggs that we lay worth?" "Where's Cagney?" "Where's Hayworth?"

The next lines are not sung. Instead, Leslie jumps in front of Astaire (stepping on his foot as she does so) and hops out a little tap dance. Astaire lifts her out of his way (C 8), but when he tries to do his own solo, he slips and staggers (presumably because of his sore foot), to her considerable delight (C 9). The mock competition is now over—he reaches for her hand (C 10) and spins her around, and with joy and affection they sing the last line of the song directly to each other as the camera cuts in for a medium shot: "I've got a lot in common with you" (C 11).

To prove it, they launch into a compatible dance, partly built on variations of an idea introduced earlier—a one-legged floor slam in which each tries to step in front of the other (C 7). After a goofy spread-legged tap shuffle as introduction (C 12), the first variation is rapped out: an outward slap of the floor with the foot (C 13). Then the dancers stop suddenly and lean off-balance into the next phrase, as Astaire wryly points out the direction with his thumb (C 14). The one-legged slam is then developed into a gleeful, noisy traveling pattern around the floor (C 15). This is followed by a quick spin in the air ending in a spread-legged pose from which the dancers waddle forward—a humorously exaggerated reprise of their first step in the dance (C 16; compare C 12). Next the one-legged slams get their most elaborate treatment: the dancers spin on one leg while wiggling the other in the air and intermittently slapping the floor with it (C 17). Some hurdling follows: she jumps over him (C 18), they do a leg-over-leg jump (C 19), and he jumps over her (C 20).[8]

The dance concludes with the brilliant big band-derived ending found in several Astaire dances of the early 1940s (see 12 F, 12 H, 13 K, 14 F, 15 M), at once unpredictable, satisfying, and seemingly inevitable. There are some beautiful skating hops to the side (C 21), a quick repeat of the spinning jump ending in a crouch (C 22), and some brilliant turns progressing downstage, which come to an abrupt halt as dance and music suddenly vanish together (C 23). As with Eleanor Powell in *Broadway Melody of 1940,* Leslie's skirt adds to the interest: when she snaps into her final pose out of the turn, it continues to make one last inertial swirl around her body in visual reverberation.

During the applause, Astaire kisses Leslie's hand in mock gallantry and she responds with a pretense of awe and modesty (C 24). "Where'd you learn to dance like that?" she mutters under her breath. "Arthur Murray," he replies.[9] At their exit, Astaire makes one last, gratuitous, leg-fluttering jump—a cabriole—while she looks back at him in breathless admiration (C 25).

D
SNAKE DANCE
(1′6″)

Astaire's triumph is interrupted, however, by the sudden arrival of his Flying Tiger buddies, Ryan and Davies, who have apparently now reached the end of their coast-to-coast personal appearance tour. Astaire seeks to keep his identity secret because he desperately wants to avoid

[8] The hurdling step seems to have been something Astaire worked out with Rita Hayworth for their "Shorty George" duet in *You Were Never Lovelier* the year before (16 H): a photograph showing them doing the step exists (see p. 212), though the step does not appear in that dance. A photograph of Astaire and Hayworth doing a leg-over-leg jump (like C 19), another step that never found its way into the Shorty George, also exists.

[9] There is irony in this remark. In 1935 the Arthur Murray dance studios had, without authorization, used a photograph of Astaire in their ads. When Astaire strenuously objected, the practice ceased. (In the late 1940s, as it happened, Astaire was to go into competition with Murray in the dancing-school business.) The RKO legal office felt it necessary to clear the other named references in the film (Hayworth, Cagney, Ginger Rogers, Margaret Bourke-White, Mischa Auer), but it apparently never cleared the use of the Arthur Murray name—possibly because it didn't know the line was going into the film (it was added on the set).

C 11 C 12 C 13 C 14

C 15 C 16 C 17 C 18

thinking about the war for as long as possible—or, as he puts it, if Leslie learns who he is, "I'll spend the rest of my leave telling her all about China." Ryan and Davies cheerfully try to make life as uncomfortable as possible for Astaire. Knowing they have him in their power, they move in on Leslie while he tries to get rid of them by suggesting, among other things, that they take a bus tour of the subway.

When Davies takes Leslie off to dance, Ryan demands that Astaire make a fool of himself by doing a snake dance on the table, to music derived from Freddie Slack's boogie tune "Cuban Sugar Mill"—a performance that is cut short by a disapproving military policeman, to Astaire's relief (D1).[10] Before Leslie returns, Astaire tries to bribe Ryan to leave, but Ryan refuses, pointing out the absurdity of the gesture and bitterly reminding Astaire of reality: "What's money? Just lettuce. We got a date in the Pacific next week and the Japs don't eat lettuce."

[10] The snake-dance routine does not appear in the script and was developed on the set by producer Hempstead, who felt the two flyers should do "something cruel" to Astaire. "I could kick him," Ryan suggested helpfully, whereupon Astaire came up with the idea of the forced snake dance—after a sturdy table was found.

E
MY SHINING HOUR
(DANCE) (2′43″)

Ryan and Davies manage to take up Astaire's entire evening, and this severely throws off his timing. Subdued, he accompanies Leslie home and they have a brief, quiet conversation on the doorstep. During it, in discussing her attitude toward her publisher, Leslie remarks that, when trying to propose to her, he always gets flustered and starts talking about the love life of a polyp—an in-joke allusion to one of Benchley's classic nonsense routines, "The Sex Life of the Polyp." When Astaire asks her what she is looking for in a man (E1), she responds with some lines from Wordsworth:

> A Creature not too bright or good
> For human nature's daily food;
> For transient sorrows, simple wiles,
> Praise, blame, love, kisses, tears, and smiles.

The description scarcely suggests the complex and troubled character Astaire plays in this film, and in sentiment it calls to mind the simple, unaffected lyric of "My Shining Hour," which is played in the background as Leslie recites the verse. Charmed, Astaire bends over to kiss her, but is stopped by a passing policeman who suggests that such activity belongs in a parlor. With this last rude disruption in his evening, Astaire takes Leslie to her door, kisses her on the cheeks (to her bewilderment), and wistfully says, "Good night, baby."

The next morning Ryan appears at Astaire's apartment with the news that their leave has been cut short—they now have to report for duty in two days. With so little time left, and realizing that he has gotten in too deep and has fallen in love with Leslie—hardly his intention—Astaire now concocts an unlikely scheme to disentangle himself and, in a sense, to provide for Leslie: he will try to marry her off to her publisher. Over a game of gin rummy, which Astaire handily wins, Benchley somewhat warily agrees to let Astaire prepare his penthouse apartment for a romantic dinner at which Benchley can propose to Leslie, with, Astaire assures him, a high probability of success.[11] But when Benchley

[11] The gin rummy business was not in the script and closely resembles one of Astaire's anecdotes about Irving Berlin: "In the middle of a game he'd sometimes ask, 'How do you like this?' And he'd test out a rhyme or sing a lyric, and I'd say 'Fine.' And then he'd throw a card down and say, 'Gin!' "

C19 C20 C21 C22
C23 C24 C25 D1
E1 E2 E3 E4

invites her to dinner, he accidentally lets slip that Astaire is in love with her—or, using the evasive language preferred by Astaire in his films, that she is the one girl Astaire can never forget.

Elated, Leslie hurries over to Benchley's apartment and, with the inadvertent complicity of Benchley's servant, Eric Blore (E 2), traps Astaire there.[12] Their roles as pursuer and pursued now reversed, she sets up a seduction routine—taking the phone off the hook, playing sweet music, showing him etchings (a word the censors suggested removing because of its "sex suggestiveness"), plying him with drinks (E 3). Amused, Astaire finally asks her to explain what this is all about; she tells him she knows how he feels about her and then informs him they are going to get married. Ensnared against his better judgment, Astaire gives in and agrees to the proposal by kissing her—after a dance.

This affecting duet of consummation is set to the music of "My Shining Hour," a pertinent choice, yet also ironic, since the lyric tells of imminent separation. The dance makes use of two opposing spatial ideas which have an emotional similarity: standing far enough apart to admire, and standing close enough to embrace.

Astaire playfully parries Leslie's marriage proposal with "How do I know my parents will give their consent?" When Leslie moves toward him in mock rage, he smiles and takes her in his arms. Then, as the "My Shining Hour" melody enters, the two spatial ideas are introduced: first the dancers separate and Astaire holds Leslie at a distance as if admiring with unspeakable delight a prize he has just won (E4); next, in contrast, he enfolds her in his arms and dances tenderly with her around the room (E 5).

Adopting the admiring pose again, Astaire gently leads Leslie by one hand out onto the main dance area (E 6) and into a flowing pattern that includes some soft kicks (E 7). He takes her in his arms again and they spin several times, easing to an exquisite halt and holding each other closely. In this pose there are some partnered back kicks for Leslie, the last of which is taken into a lift (E 8). The momentum from this sends her turning under Astaire's raised arm (E 9), but their separation is brief: she happily coils back, cradling herself in his embrace (E 10). Thus entwined, they move across the floor, then separate in the dance's signature pose of admiration, which this time closely resembles their pose at the climactic moment in the "A Lot in Common" duet (E 11; compare C 11; also used in passing in a duet in *Holiday Inn*—15 C 7). From this they plunge into each other's arms and spin rapidly upstage.

The music returns to the beginning of the song, which the orchestra plays broadly and glowingly. The choreography becomes correspondingly more showy as various overlapping and lacing figures are alternated with intricate spiraling spins (the Astaire double helix). Eventually they emerge into a pose that suggests both distance and closeness simultaneously, no matter what geometricians might say: they hold each other by the hands with stiff arms, suggesting distance, but the arms are dropped down, allowing them to bring their bodies close (E 12). In this pose, introduced but far less developed in a duet in Astaire's previous film (16 F 4), they gently rock back and forth, twice separate, turn around, return to the pose, and rock again.

Then, still holding Leslie by the hands,

[12] Blore, a familiar from the Astaire-Rogers films in the 1930s, is here making his last appearance in an Astaire film. Blore's line "If I weren't such a gentleman's gentleman, I could be such a cad's cad" is not in the script and is presumably a reference, added on the set, to *A Gentleman's Gentleman*, a film he made in 1939.

E 5 E 6 E 7 E 8
E 9 E 10 E 11 E 12
E 13 E 14 E 15 E 16

Astaire sweeps her around him (E13), and as the orchestra reaches its most dramatic rendering of the melody, the choreography becomes correspondingly extravagant, sometimes overly so, and calls for a technique and theatricality that are somewhat beyond Leslie's capabilities. Its heedless brilliance perhaps suggests the time pressures that bear on this wartime romance, when a leisurely pace was an impossible luxury. To begin, they blaze out a series of fast spins and steps while circling each other (E14). Dramatically, they suddenly emerge from their separate cadenzas and face each other for a moment in positions that are related to the earlier poses of admiration (E15; compare E4, 6, 11). There are some bold sweeps across the floor and then, during some turns, the music and the dancing finally begin to subside.

The dance concludes with an exquisite elaboration of the themes of distance and closeness. Astaire holds Leslie by one hand at a distance (E16; compare E6) and then snaps her so she winds into his arms (E17). She dreamily unwinds away from him once more and pauses, for the last time, at a distance. Finally, he pulls her toward him, turning himself around her as she spins, wrapping her in his embrace (E18), and they settle into the concluding kiss as music, dance, and scene fade out (E19).

Astaire was always reluctant to kiss in his films, considering it a Hollywood cliché and preferring to express romance by indirection and through dance. So a kiss is a special event in an Astaire number, whether it is used as a seal of acceptance on a marriage agreement (16 M7, 28 J10)—thereby becoming no more of a cliché than a handshake—or as an expression of eroticism (10 B9–11, 18 G31, 21 B6, 22 C6–7). In this dance, the kiss seems to have both connotations. Besides suggesting that Leslie's proposal (or declaration) of marriage has been accepted by Astaire, the kiss ends a scene that has a clear sexual tone: as Leslie muses earlier, "You know, this is the kind of night that doesn't belong in your life. You could just do anything and it wouldn't count."[13]

F

ONE FOR MY BABY

(4′57″)

Still trying to find Astaire a job, Leslie takes him with her the next night (his last night on leave, though she doesn't know it) to a banquet at which she has arranged for him to be interviewed by an important aircraft manufacturer (Astaire has let it slip that he knows something about airplanes). As they drive to the party, Astaire sourly switches off the war news on the radio and announces he has plans to get "slightly inebriated."[14] Leslie sternly disapproves, and Astaire, humoring her, promises to be on his best behavior.

At the banquet Benchley delivers one of his celebrated pseudo-lectures, this one a bumbling monologue (with charts) on business trends in the aircraft industry (F1). It's a form of humor that may have less lasting appeal than the dances of Astaire or the songs of Arlen and Mercer, though its zany satire remains relevant: there will doubtless always be "maximum peaks" and "probable saturation points." (When the film was released, an official at the Army Air Forces Statistical School at Harvard University requested a print of the Benchley speech to show to the student officers, explaining, "This type of entertainment would be very much appreciated by them.")

From Benchley's absurd comedy, the film jolts remarkably to the war's absurd tragedy as a war widow dedicates a new line of aircraft. A model plane glides preposterously into the scene on wires and, with tears in her eyes, she cracks a champagne bottle over its nose.

Although the rest of the people at the banquet quickly return to their revels, Astaire's mood has been soured. In his job interview, he bitterly tells the airplane manufacturer how inadequate his planes are in combat (F2). Like the other minor characters in the film, the airplane manufacturer, played by Clarence Kolb, is given some depth. Although he is pompous and huffy, the opportunity to caricature him as a buffoon is not taken. Instead he emerges as an affable businessman who happens to be incompetent: though he is being lauded as a patriot and a great contributor to the war effort at the banquet, it turns out

[13] The censors, in fact, objected to the suggestiveness of this line. The only other Astaire romantic duet that ends in a fade-out (it also ends with a kiss) occurs in the bedroom duet, "You'd Be Hard to Replace," in *The Barkleys of Broadway* (22 C). The erotic suggestiveness at the fade-out is quite clear there.

[14] In the final script, this scene in the car was preceded by a brief sequence in which Astaire talks to his landlady. She tells him that her daughter's husband is missing at sea and says how painful such things are for the wives back home. Although the scene would help to show Astaire being brought back to earth after his heady night with Leslie, it is not really necessary to explain his later actions.

E17 E18 E19 F1

F2 F3 F4 F5

the planes he is producing are so badly designed they are dangerous to fly.

Appalled at Astaire's behavior, and taking his actions to be a contemptuous dismissal of her and of all her efforts in his behalf, Leslie walks out on him (F 3).

Benchley leads Astaire to a nearby bar, where he discloses that, through gossip-column connections, he has found out who Astaire really is (F 4). Astaire urges Benchley to forget it and to keep Leslie in the dark about him, dejectedly explaining, "I'm just walking a tightrope between somewhere and somewhere else—and I've got to walk it alone, understand? So I got myself in over my head and I had to get out—that's all."

When Benchley leaves, Astaire slumps at the bar and begins to sing "One for My Baby," a song that has become a classic and, for some, an anthem. Pronounced by Astaire "one of the best pieces of material that was written especially for me," the song is highly unusual: long (58 measures), with unexpected shifts of key. Arlen himself has observed that the song is "unlike anything I'd ever done, or heard." Mercer's evocative lyric which, amazingly, was written *after* the music, is a narrative, with a beginning, a middle, and an end, and Astaire, reflecting this structure, has arranged the number so the dance occurs after he has sung the B strain of the AABA song.

The idea of breaking glass, so important to the number, is established even before it begins. (Actually, it could be argued that the idea was introduced in the previous scene, when the war widow smashes the bottle over the airplane model.) After Benchley leaves, Astaire sets his glass down on the bar. It crumbles in his hand, and he reacts with dazed bewilderment (F 5). Then he turns on the bar stool and sings to the bartender the first strain of the lyric (F 6), which concludes with a bitter salute to the two forces in Astaire's life that have brought him to his present state of despair—Leslie and the war: "Make it one for my baby, and one more for the road."

There is a dissolve to the lunchroom where he had parlayed with Leslie early in the film. He moves from the pinball machine he had operated with careless success earlier, to a small bar on the other side of the room. The music is orchestrated in an appropriately honky-tonk manner as he sends a coin spinning on the bar and sings the second A strain (F 7).

Another dissolve shows him back at the Colonial Club, where he had first met Leslie and where he heard her sing "My Shining Hour." The room is deserted now except for the bartender. Swaying, Astaire sings the B strain (F 8). But the bartender has no intention of complying with Astaire's plaintive request, "You simply gotta listen to me," or of pouring more liquor. He takes the last bottle and walks out of the room, leaving Astaire miserable and alone.

Without someone to hear, Astaire can't talk away his gloom; so he seeks to purge it with dance, a violent solo in which he expresses rage —at himself for having fallen in love with Leslie, and at the war for forcing him to leave her. Tap dancing usually has a bright, ebullient quality. In this remarkable solo Astaire instead exploits its capacity simply to generate noise. Missing are many of the qualities familiar in Astaire's work—the subtle inflections, the witty changes of tempo, the intricate playing with music and phrasing. Instead, all is given over to an unmodulated, hard-driving, ferocious effort to produce pure noise—and catharsis.[15] Throughout, Astaire stays in character: although drunk, the omnicompetent war hero remains in physical control of himself and shows he knows exactly what he is doing.

As the bartender leaves the room, Astaire sags onto a bar stool, and the orchestra begins to play the last strain of the song. When he sets his glass down on the bar, the stem breaks off (F 9), and this time he reacts violently, smashing the glass against the bar and then springing away across the room (F 10). After dancing a fragment of a tap phrase, he slams his hat furiously to the floor (F 11), where it will remain until he retrieves it at the end of the number.

Woozy, he staggers across the floor as the orchestra finishes the song. He leans against a pillar for support and finds himself gazing into the area where Leslie had sung "My Shining Hour" earlier (F 12; see A 5). As the orchestra plays a soft reprise of a portion of that ballad, Astaire blearily drifts through a partnerless duet to the remembered melody (F 13). Then he snaps out of his reverie and dashes across the room, leaping up onto the bar (F 14), where, to some blaring, agitated music, he begins his furious tap dance, slamming and sliding his way up and down the bar, heedless of danger (F 15).

Next he vaults down from the bar (F 16) and

[15] Making a lot of noise does not necessarily express despair, of course. The device is used in a very different way in a solo in *You'll Never Get Rich*, to express the giddy joy of being in love (14 F). In 15 M and 20 F Astaire also seeks to capitalize on the noisemaking capacity of tap.

F6 F7 F8 F9
F10 F11 F12 F13

continues the same savage, hard-driving tap dance across the floor (F 17). Twice he lashes out with his leg to kick glasses off a low table (F 18); then he turns, coiled and tense, caught up in his own anger, looking around for other ways to vent it (F 19). He springs back up onto the bar and continues his search, crashes and staggers his way along the bar (F 20), leaps to the back counter and kicks over three stacks of glasses (F 21), then jumps back to the floor, seizes a bar stool, and hurls it with all his might, shattering the mirror and a stack of glasses behind the bar (F 22, 23). His energy and rage spent, he sags on a stool and slumps on the bar (F 24).

When the film was in previews, RKO received a letter from a San Francisco theatre owner urging that the scene be deleted because it served "no dramatic purpose" and because such "wanton description" in wartime was "extremely distasteful if not unpatriotic." Several members of preview audiences also found the scene offensive for that reason. As it happened, real glass was used in the scene, though, as much for economy as for patriotism, RKO purchased factory rejects for the occasion. Ironically, in peacetime, breakaway glass made of sugar would have been used, but sugar was rationed in 1943. Astaire cut his shins and ankles doing the number, and the dance was dangerous in other ways as well: the bar was slippery, and the choreography called for Astaire to slide and sway his way along the edge. Two nurses stood by throughout the filming of the number, as well as Astaire's concerned wife.[16]

The bartender, dressed to go home, re-enters, jerks Astaire around by the shoulder, and demands an explanation. Astaire spills money onto the counter, inserts a tip into the bartender's pocket, and returns to the song. To make a smooth transition, he speaks the first line instead of singing, but the effect is actually a bit rough; the line "Well, that's how it goes" seems numbingly casual after the violence of the dance. As Astaire moves toward the exit, residual spurts of tap dancing ripple through his

[16] The number was shot in two and a half days, near the end of the filming schedule, after seven days of rehearsal on the set. It took half an hour for the prop men to reassemble the glasses after each take. The idea of destruction was also used by Gene Kelly in his famous "Alter Ego" dance in *Cover Girl*, released the year after *The Sky's the Limit.*

F14 F15 F16 F17

F18 F19 F20 F21

F22 F23 F24 F25

F26 F27 F28 F29

body. Then he pauses, pulls himself up, and sings the last lines of the song (F 25):

Don't let it be said
little Fred-
die can't carry his load
Make it one for my baby, and one more
for the road—
That long, long road.[17]

As he strides toward the door, he proves he is still in full control: he notices his hat on the floor, kicks it deftly into the air (F 26), snatches it in mid-flight, jams it onto his head, and exits, slamming the door behind him (F 27).

The key to the story's resolution is Benchley. He waits patiently to see if Leslie will get over her episode with Astaire, hoping to get her on the rebound. It is only after he confirms for himself that his suit is utterly hopeless that he reasons, "Well, if you won't marry me, I might as well be noble about it," his cynicism neatly puncturing one of the sappiest clichés of the Hollywood musical—the third party who becomes unaccountably noble at the end. Without explaining his motive, he gives Leslie a photographic assignment that will cause her to cross paths with Astaire in his last moments at a West Coast air base.

Leslie intercepts Astaire as he is about to climb into his bomber to fly back to the war. The moving concluding sequence reflects with almost painful realism a scene familiar to many in the film's first audiences. They sputter a few lines of awkward, disconnected dialogue and kiss; he assures her that he will return to her (F 28). (In the script he was to say "Goodbye" as he got on the plane, but this was changed on the set to "So long, baby" in echo of the lyric of his last song.) As he boards the plane, he shouts to her, almost as an afterthought, "I love you." She responds, smiling, "This is a fine time to tell me!" and then watches tearfully as the plane flies away (F 29).[18]

[17] This is usually changed to remove the name reference; a rare, possibly unique, exception is Mercer's own recording. The need for the "said"/"Fred" internal rhyme here, incidentally, may be one reason the character is called Fred in the film.

[18] Many members of the preview audience complained about the unorthodox inconclusiveness of the film's ending; some suggested a "short scene together overseas or at his destination," or having "Fred come back from his flight to Joan." Leslie seems to be muttering something in the final close-ups as she watches the plane take off. Would-be lip-readers are advised that the script calls for these final "words" to be indecipherable.

NUMBERS CUT FROM THE FILM

G
TRESTLE DANCE

Early press material for *The Sky's the Limit* announced that the film had "two solo dances for Fred himself and four new hit tunes." The missing solo occurred early in the film—on the railroad track, when Astaire is abandoning the train taking him on a personal appearance tour (A 2). The solo was cut after the film was shown to preview audiences in June 1943, but the solo apparently *was* in the print premiered in New York later. Moreover, that print (or one like it) lasted for a while: one viewer definitely recalls seeing the trestle dance when the film was shown at the Edison Theatre in New York in 1948. Here is what took place, in the words of the pressbook: "Astaire deserts the train when it stops in the mountains to let a freight pass. As the train pulls away he realizes he is free for a short time to do all the things he wants to do, and in sheer joy he starts dancing on the rails to the rhythm of the departing engine. The dance is a short one and ends when Astaire finds himself dancing out in the middle of a 100-foot trestle."

Production records suggest that the dance was thirty-two seconds long (G1). Along with the "snake dance" and "One for My Baby," this solo would have made a third dance episode in which Astaire was shown dancing on the edge of a precipice—something of a metaphor for the film's more general message, perhaps.

The press materials also cite Astaire on this solo: "After that first dance, according to Astaire, it is easier for the audience to reconcile itself to the fact that the flier can dance"—an indication that Astaire seems to have been a bit apprehensive about playing a character who has no background as a performer. The solo, of course, would not have explained *why* he could dance.

H
HARVEY, THE VICTORY GARDEN MAN

The fourth of the "new hit tunes" was sung at the banquet by Ella Mae Morse, backed by Freddie Slack's band (H1). It occurred just before Benchley's speech and related in no way to the plot.[19]

[19] Arlen and Mercer wrote one other number for the film, a jumpy love song called "Hangin' On to You": although they can ration my sugar, aluminum, silk, Grade A milk, rubber heels, I'm hangin' on to you.

G1

H1

18.

Ziegfeld Follies

1945–46

In the history of the film musical, MGM's *Ziegfeld Follies* stands as a bold experiment for its format: the film is a straightforward revue consisting of fourteen skits and musical numbers unconnected by plot or story line. Of course, the revue format was, and is, common in the theatre, and a number of Hollywood musicals in the early sound years (1929–32) followed this approach. But movie audiences, Hollywood came to believe, demanded stories in their musicals, and so legions of scriptwriters were kept busy trying to fashion plots that would link the musical numbers. By common consent it was the plots—very often contrived and mindless—that were the weakest points of most musicals, and a logical step was to try to do without them. The revue format also made a great deal of financial and logistic sense, since it was possible to incorporate into the film significant contributions from a large number of important and expensive performers without tying any of them down for the full run of the picture's production schedule.

Ziegfeld Follies is also notable for its opulence. Budgeted at an exceptionally high $3 million, the film was designed to overwhelm audiences by its sheer extravagance. In this the film sought to extend and expand upon the glamour and spectacle that were hallmarks of a certain breed of musical—particularly those from MGM—and also to carry on the tradition of the lavishly decorated revues of such Broadway impresarios as, appropriately enough, Florenz Ziegfeld.

The film was conceived by producer Arthur Freed, who, by 1944, was in a good position to lead MGM in new directions, having produced a string of successful musicals at the studio (see Table 3). His proposal for a star-studded extravaganza was especially well received by the studio brass because 1944 was MGM's twentieth year, and the film seemed an ideal way to preen in public.

Things did not work out as planned, however. When the film was shown to preview audiences near the end of the year, it was clear that its nearly three-hour length was excessive, that it contained many dead spots, and that its grand finale was a dud. Months were spent cutting, re-editing, and reshooting, and, after some experimental showings in 1945, the film emerged in final form in 1946, reduced to 110 minutes.[1] It did well at the box office, grossing better than any previous Freed film except *Meet Me in St. Louis,* but, because of its expense, was not very profitable. At any rate, Freed's idea of using the revue format was not repeated, and the film seems to mark the end of an era of opulence in Hollywood musicals.[2]

Of course, Fred Astaire, by conscious design, had largely missed this era, developing at RKO a much lighter and more intimate form of musical comedy. He had yet to meet with his first ostrich plume. Freed brought Astaire in to add luster to *Ziegfeld Follies* and signed him to a long-term contract at MGM. It was Astaire's first color film and brought him firmly back into the big-budget musical. Most of his musicals for the rest of his career were made at that studio, and most of these were produced by Freed.

Astaire appears in four of the fourteen segments—far more than any other lead performer—with mixed results. One of his numbers is something of a throwaway, a brief appearance to set the film's introductory number into motion. Another, an amusing duet-competition with Gene Kelly, is quite successful, though it does little to contribute to the film's lavish atmosphere. The other Astaire numbers, however, have the requisite opulence, with opposite results. In one of these, an Oriental dream fantasy, Astaire is submerged in phantasmagoric effects and overblown pretensions. In the other, however, his horizons seem actually to have been expanded by the film's concept and format. Liberated from any obligation to service a plot or render reality, he created a duet, "This Heart of Mine," which is extravagantly and sumptuously romantic: Effects only hinted at in earlier romantic duets are developed and expanded until they become bigger than life and shimmer with an air of splendor and genteel insolence.

[1] Among the cut material was one extended solo number for Astaire (18 O) and the finale in which he appeared more briefly (18 V). For a sidelight on Astaire's professionalism during these production agonies, see p. 17.

[2] Reviewer Bosley Crowther devoted a Sunday column to musing about the film's structure. He concluded that even though getting rid of plots was a good idea, the revue format was not satisfactory, either. His rather unhelpful suggestion: "With the great flexibility of image that the screen allows and invites, some structure entirely imaginative should be found to support variety acts."

THE PRODUCTION

Freed's idea was to formulate a film along the lines of the *Ziegfeld Follies* shows that had been a staple on Broadway from 1907 until the 1930s. Over the years, the studio had purchased the rights to hundreds of sketches, routines, and musical numbers from various stage productions, and Freed set out to blend the best of these with new material to create a varied but coherent mix. The name *Ziegfeld Follies* was purchased for $100,000 from Broadway producer Lee Shubert, who had bought all rights to the name for $27,500 when Ziegfeld died, penniless, in 1932. Dozens of people—writers, composers, directors, choreographers, designers—were called in at various times to create new sketches or to reshape existing material. Referee for the project was to be director George Sidney, but, disappointed in the results of his work, he asked to be relieved after a month of filming. He was replaced by Vincente Minnelli, who eventually directed six of the film's fourteen segments himself, including the three substantial Astaire numbers.

The film's large cast was assembled from near and far. As Minnelli reports, "Every MGM star was notified to make himself available if called." Fanny Brice, however, was the only prominent member of the cast who had actually appeared in a *Ziegfeld Follies* show.

In the spirit of a revue (as opposed to vaudeville), an effort was made to give the film unity through its overall look—clean, bright, big, colorful. The settings for many of the sequences are not supposed to be realistic; they are somewhat fanciful and often remarkably spare. The producers wanted the film to be lavish but with taste, magnificent but with fi-

With Lucille Bremer in "This Heart of Mine"

nesse. If they did not always succeed in avoiding vulgarity, they seem at least to have been aware of the problem.

Interestingly, a certain consistency of tone runs through the film, though it was apparently not consciously sought by its makers: most of the sequences have a touch of cynicism, of bitterness, of dark humor. The comedy skits find amusement in death and in watching people squirm in an almost Kafkaesque world. Of the three major dance numbers, one deals with a conniving jewel-thief and another with a doomed, pathetic dreamer, while the third is built around a song that is a sarcastic commentary on the banality of the human race. Other numbers concern themselves with the destructive power of love and with the insecurities of an adulation-craving Hollywood star. Although there are coy moments, as well as ones that are dated and/or preposterously overdecorated, this hard edge to much of the proceedings often helps to keep the film sharp and arresting.

ASTAIRE'S PARTNERS

Astaire's principal partner in the film is Lucille Bremer, a dancer who had successfully executed a modest role in *Meet Me in St. Louis* and was here being groomed by Freed for stardom. *Ziegfeld Follies* shows her to be highly accomplished at dramatic mime, and does not test her in a speaking part—the area where she was weak. She was painfully miscast in her next film, *Yolanda and the Thief* (opposite Astaire), and she largely disappeared from Hollywood after that.

Astaire also appears briefly with the twenty-one-year-old Cyd Charisse in this, her second film (and her first for MGM). She was to attain considerable success later and was to be his partner in two films in the 1950s, *The Band Wagon* and *Silk Stockings*.

Astaire's final duet in the film is with Gene Kelly, a clear Hollywood comer and, some said, the vanguard of a generation with an aesthetic and point of view that would supersede Astaire's. This was to be their only film appearance together apart from their co-hosting roles in *That's Entertainment, Part 2* in 1976. Minnelli says that he and Freed tried to team them again later, but it didn't work out.

THE MUSIC

The music, too, was gathered from various sources, old and new. Two of the songs written for the film have established themselves as standards: "This Heart of Mine," written for Astaire by Harry Warren and Arthur Freed, and "Love," written for Lena Horne by Hugh Martin and Ralph Blane, who had just completed the score for *Meet Me in St. Louis,* one of the most impressive original scores for a Hollywood musical in the 1940s or 1950s. Warren, one of the most successful, if least known, of American songwriters, was writing for Astaire for the first time. He was to provide the score for three more Astaire films at MGM: *Yolanda and the Thief, The Barkleys of Broadway,* and *The Belle of New York.*

With Gene Kelly in "The Babbitt and the Bromide"

THE CHOREOGRAPHY

The dance director for the film, Robert Alton, was an active participant in the early planning and originated the concepts for most of the dance numbers; an "idea man" of some accomplishment, he was Astaire's second-most-frequent choreographic collaborator in films, after Hermes Pan. The choreography for the Astaire-Kelly duet was created entirely by the two dancers. Important choreographic contributions to some of the non-Astaire numbers were made by two Hollywood newcomers: Eugene Loring from ballet and Charles Walters from Broadway. Both were to be important contributors—Loring as a choreographer, Walters as a director—to several later Astaire films.

THE NUMBERS

A
ZIEGFELD DAYS
(7′ 1″)

The film's opening is deadly. From heaven (where MGM has diplomatically placed him), Ziegfeld looks down and reminisces about the old days (A 1). Puppets are used to imitate Ziegfeld headliners such as the Anna Held Hour Glass Girls (A 2), who appeared in the first *Follies,* of 1907, as well as dancer Marilyn Miller, comedians Fanny Brice and Will Rogers, and singer Eddie Cantor, a Ziegfeld regular. Then Ziegfeld decides he'd like to put on one more *Follies* and calls upon Astaire to introduce it.[3]

The puppet material was created early in the production schedule, but the heavenly scene was shot nine months after the previews. The idea, apparently, was to give the film a more pertinent opening. Unfortunately, William Powell reads his lines in such a vapid, spaced-out manner that one begins to wonder what exactly is in that nectar bottle in front of him. At any rate, we never see him, or heaven, again.[4]

B
HERE'S TO THE GIRLS/ BRING ON THE WONDERFUL MEN
(8′ 18″)

Astaire appears, says some nice things about Ziegfeld and his shows, and then launches into a Roger Edens–Arthur Freed song about Ziegfeld's trademark: the girls (B 1). After flitting through a brief dance, Astaire introduces a stageful of showgirls adorned with pink ostrich feathers (twelve hundred were used in the number, according to the designer). The girls clunk hurriedly across the set and collapse into decorative poses. Now Charisse appears, in a tutu, and Astaire gallantly escorts her forward (B 2), sets her spinning into a solo dance, and then vanishes for the rest of the number.

Charisse seems a bit nervous. Her brief solo shows her to be an accomplished ballet dancer but with a tendency toward choppiness, particularly at the beginning: an inclination to slam into positions, rather than to phrase the transitions and make lyric sense of them (B 3). The choreography is fussy and cliché-ridden.

A large carousel of live horses is unveiled, and Charisse hops onto it and is rotated away. As an off-screen chorus sings a grating arrangement of the song the carousel continues to turn until, standing uncertainly (terrified, might be more accurate) on a large white horse (the Lone Ranger's Silver in private life), Lucille Ball heaves into view, desperately trying to maintain an expression of glamorous haughtiness (B 4).[5] She dismounts, takes up a whip, and puts a chorus through a slinky (if semaphoric) dance in which they pretend to be cats.

It was shortly after filming this sequence that Sidney decided he needed to be replaced as director. Although the section was kept, Freed, Minnelli, and Alton apparently decided they'd better provide an antidote and so, months later, after the previews, a new section was shot and spliced on. It shows comedienne Virginia O'Brien riding an obviously fake horse and singing a parody song, "Bring On the Wonderful Men," while trying to keep the plumes of her preposterous pink headdress out of her eyes (B 5). (The rather clever lyric for the song was by Earl Brent, O'Brien's vocal coach.)

C
A WATER BALLET
(3′ 20″)

Esther Williams, mostly underwater, is photographed through the windows of a decorated water tank (C 1).

D
NUMBER PLEASE
(7′ 51″)

Keenan Wynn has an extended encounter with the telephone bureaucracy and loses (D 1). Driven finally to insanity, he is seen chewing on the telephone at the fade-out.[6]

[3] Although Astaire never appeared in an edition of the *Ziegfeld Follies,* he was featured in a musical comedy produced by the famous showman—*Smiles,* a flop of 1930.

[4] Powell had played the title role in MGM's *The Great Ziegfeld,* a ponderous, pretentious three-hour extravaganza that won the Academy Award for best picture in 1936.

[5] Her disgusted comment on the episode: "I was tall and long legged. I couldn't sing and I couldn't dance, so MGM starred me as a costume horse . . . , cracking a whip over eight chorus-girl panthers." Also uncomfortable was Silver's trainer, who felt his charge had been sissified in the number and threatened a lawsuit.

[6] This number was shot very late, after the previews had dictated dropping several other comedy sketches. It was derived from a Fred Allen routine in a 1930 Broadway revue, *Three's a Crowd.*

A 1 A 2 B 1 B 2
B 3 B 4 B 5 C 1

E
TRAVIATA
(3′27″)

Overdecorated high culture intrudes briefly: James Melton and Marion Bell deliver Verdi's festive "Libiamo ne' lieti calici" as a chorus swirls around them in some of the film's ugliest costumes. The studio has thoughtfully supplied the performers with glasses full of a congealed substance that doesn't slosh as they waft around in Eugene Loring's choreography (E1).

F
PAY THE TWO DOLLARS
(8′3″)

This exercise in dark comedy relates the anguished demise of a man caught between the force of the law and the absurdly principled machinations of his egocentric lawyer. The lawyer insists on appealing a $2 fine for expectorating in the subway, leading the man ultimately to utter ruin (F1). This classic sketch was originally created for the Broadway revue *George White's Scandals of 1931.* Victor Moore is impressive in the central role, capturing the desperate comic pathos in the character, but never crossing the line into sentimentality.

G
THIS HEART OF MINE
(12′2″)

Subtitled "A dance story," "This Heart of Mine" is a rounded playlet involving Astaire as a gentleman jewel thief who preys on the guests at a formal ball.[7] He zeroes in on the beautiful, bejeweled Lucille Bremer and, after a voluptuous duet with her, is able to steal a kiss—and her bracelet. When they are about to part, however, she calmly removes her necklace and gives it to him. He is dumbfounded but soon deduces that she must be a bird of his particular feather. They sweep into each other's arms and are seen happily to be flocking together at the fade-out.[8]

The story, then, is one of seduction, but the would-be seducer turns out in a sense to be the seducee. The encounter is about power, and perhaps about eroticism, but not about love, and it occurs between two people who live by their wits and are wary, worldly-wise, self-reliant, and larger than life. Appropriately, their stupendous dance, captured appealingly by Minnelli's fluid camera, is extravagant and splendidly insincere. The voluptuous, full-bodied Lucille Bremer is perfectly cast in this dance—she is coolly haughty, mysterious, and desirable. As in most of his duets, Astaire exudes charm and solicitousness toward his partner, but here these qualities are, appropriately, unleavened by humor or by any question of whether he will be successful in his relentless, bee-to-honey pursuit.

Unique among Astaire's dances, this duet uses a kiss as a central element. But the kiss has a sinister implication, not a romantic one, since it is during the kiss that Astaire is able to steal Bremer's bracelet. An important theme, then, is his effort to break through her resistance in order to achieve the climactic kiss. The choreography is also notable for its extensive rotating patterns—circling, spiraling, swirling—a motif extended at times by the use of a revolving floor. In addition, imaginative use is made of strips of floor that move in opposite directions.[9] Astaire had previously used a turntable and treadmills for comic effect in a number in *A Damsel in Distress* (9 D). Here these gimmicks are used to heighten the extravagantly romantic atmosphere of the number.

Characterization, atmosphere, and circumstance are efficiently established at the beginning to music written by Roger Edens. The regal Bremer, accompanied by a duke and duchess, enters the ball, announced by a supercilious major-domo whose pronouncements are covered, and mocked, by a braying trumpet (G1).

[7] The Astaire role is based on Raffles, a dashing character developed in four popular short-story collections written around the turn of the century by Ernest Hornung (Arthur Conan Doyle's brother-in-law), and the sketch is often referred to simply as "Raffles" in the production files. The Hornung stories had been the inspiration for several films, including ones featuring John Barrymore (1917), Ronald Colman (1930), and David Niven (1940). Although Minnelli claims he wrote the story for this number, it closely follows an Alton scenario written months before Minnelli was assigned to the picture.

[8] This interpretation of the somewhat ambiguous ending is consistent with the suggestions of Douglas McVay and Stanley Green. It is not, however, particularly consistent with the one in Alton's original scenario: "Suddenly he stops, turns and looks at Lucille; sees how beautiful, how attractive and how willing she is, reaches back and takes her arm, puts on his hat and they leave the pavilion together, as she gracefully slips into a Chinchilla wrap." The number was shot in ten days for $168,023.

[9] The basic idea here was Alton's. In his scenario he excitedly suggested a "dance routine in which we use both treadmills, going in opposite directions, and the revolving surface. I can assure you that in this routine some of the most beautiful and completely original dance compositions can be executed. I will not describe this choreographically as it would be too difficult."

D1 E1 F1 G1
G2 G3 G4 G5

Lurking outside, the monocled Astaire peers in menacingly at the splendid and absurdly sophisticated gathering (G 2), then snatches an invitation from an aged, tottering guest and enters the arena. Soon Astaire is dancing with a gabby, jewel-laden countess. He catches sight of the supremely desirable Bremer (G 3).

In an instant she is in his arms—or, more accurately, he is in hers. Sending his boring countess spinning, Astaire, in one remarkably deft move, snaps up Bremer's left hand, pulls her away from her partner, and swirls her around him, wrapping himself in her arm (G 4). Then he presses her close to him, letting go with his left hand so that, to close the ballroom pose, she must pull in even closer (G5).[10] Bremer, fully up to the considerable mime requirements of this sequence, is surprised but retains her composure. She calmly begins to size him up and allows him to escort her out onto a secluded terrace for a few more waltz turns.

When she seats herself on a bench, Astaire, after glancing around to make sure they aren't being observed, leans over to kiss her (G 6), but she bolts away. Puzzled by her attitude, Astaire approaches her again (G 7) and sings to her. His heart had been doing very well until he saw her, the lyric relates, but now he finds himself singing sentimental overtures (G 8). While he sings, they plunge through a few dance fragments that are a bit too slickly showy even for this context. Approaching the end of the song, Astaire leads the still-reticent Bremer to the center of the floor. He kisses her hand and then pulls her into a sumptuous duet to Warren's lush melody. (The orchestration in this number, by Conrad Salinger, is exceptionally successful at suggesting opulence without falling, as so often happened at MGM, into pretentiousness or bathos.)

This initial duet is a showy étude on the partnered swirl. It begins as Bremer allows herself to be pulled in toward Astaire, until her body is almost enveloped in his (G 9). From that position she turns under Astaire's arm and travels around his body in a wide arc (G 10). Blended in with these figures are a series of dramatic poses, some a bit overwrought (G 11) but most of them appropriate (G 12). The duet is partnered throughout, the dancers losing touch with each other only momentarily, and is marked by Astaire's usual masterly phrasing. For instance, as the music is returning to the A strain in the middle of the ABAC song, Astaire and Bremer, tightly partnered (G 12), begin a lilting pattern across the floor that reflects the music's quality but does not always directly imitate it; then they hold back against the return of the sumptuous melody, and finally catch up with it as Bremer grandly leans backward and extends her leg outward (G 13).

The duet concludes with a variety of revolving partnered patterns (as G 14), the last of which finds the dancers clutched together describing spirals with an arm raised overhead (G 15; see also 16 M 5). At the end, Bremer falls back into a deep partnered backbend (G 16).

Encouraged, Astaire tries again to kiss her, but she abruptly turns on her heel, flashes a come-hither look (G 17), and darts away—though not too far (G 18). She pauses on a nearby platform; he catches up with her there and firmly spins her around to face him (G 19). Now come the treadmills: the platform is fitted out with a pair of them, moving in opposite directions, and these are incorporated into the next part of the dance in a remarkable variety of ways. The statu-

[10] For earlier uses by Astaire of the arm wrapping idea, see 3 E 23, 5 E 19, and 14 G 15 (parodied in 15 G 11 and, later, in 21 E 4). It seems to derive from a step devised by Vernon Castle (see 11 I 7–9). For other uses of the slyly erotic open-arm pose, see 5 E 8, 10 E 12–13, 15 I 9, and 21 B 3.

G 6 G 7 G 8 G 9
G 10 G 11 G 12 G 13
G 14 G 15 G 16 G 17

esque Bremer stands on one and glides away as Astaire darts around her in wary chase (G20). Then he joins her on the treadmills, and when they stand on opposite ones they float toward or away from each other. Soon they discover that by hopping gingerly from one treadmill to the other they can trace broad circles around each other. At the end they settle into a romantic pose as one of the treadmills pulls them along (G21), and then they jump to the other and run along it so that it speeds their progress unnaturally.

Their momentum carries them off the treadmill and back to the center of the floor, where they assume an extreme version of the crouching, enveloping pose that began their duet (G22; compare G9). Then, on a broad musical cue, Bremer explodes into a flowing lift (G23), spins under Astaire's arm (G24), and sinks suddenly to the floor while he hovers over her—posed like the figures on Keats' Grecian urn. Next the floor begins to rotate under them, bringing into view a chorus of dancers similarly posed (G25).

The dance soon resumes on this gently turning surface, with Astaire and Bremer repeating some of the revolving figures from their earlier duet (G26; compare G10) while the chorus continues to sketch out poses suggestive of flight and amorous pursuit. As the chorus moves from the revolving floor to take up positions on the treadmills, Bremer leans back in Astaire's embrace, giving herself fully to him, and together they spin exultantly around the floor, which is itself rotating (G27). It's the ultimate expression of the swirling motif.

The couple now begin their return to the ballroom, Astaire kissing her hand as she sways sensually (G28). The treadmills, which lie in their path, are cleverly built into the choreography: the dancers purposefully step on one, then the other, letting each carry them briefly to one side (G29). Back inside, Astaire spins Bremer across the floor and then moves in for the kill. With a furtive glance around, he takes Bremer's hand and approaches her to consummate the twice-delayed kiss. She starts to block his progress with her arm (G30) but, smiling, Astaire easily forces his way past this ineffectual barrier and gives her a (stage) kiss (G31) while lightly removing her bracelet with his free hand (G32).

As he is about to take his leave, however, she calls him back, strips off her necklace (G33), and coolly hands it to him (G34). He is amazed, but as it dawns on him what her true identity must be (G35), she rushes into his arms for another kiss—appropriately extravagant and now without ulterior motive (G36). Together they stroll happily off, a perfect match.

H
THE SWEEPSTAKES TICKET
(9′58″)

Re-creating her performance from the *Ziegfeld Follies of 1936*, Fanny Brice appears in the film's second classic comedy sketch. She and her husband seek to regain a winning lottery ticket he has given to the landlord. When all else fails, Brice tells the landlord the truth (H1). Startled by the news, he keels over with a heart attack; Brice snatches the ticket as he falls and, standing over the corpse, utters the punch line: "You're right, Monty. Honesty is the best policy."

I
LOVE
(4′39″)

A scene in a steamy Martinique bar begins with two women fighting over a man. When one runs desperately from the room, Lena Horne emerges to sing sultrily about the pains and pleasures of love (I1). Horne was intensely unhappy about the racially stereotyped setting for the song.

G18 G19 G20 G21
G22 G23 G24 G25
G26 G27 G28 G29

J
WHEN TELEVISION COMES (GUZZLER'S GIN)
(5′ 33″)

The comedy sketch "Guzzler's Gin" had been performed by Red Skelton for years on the radio, in theatres, and in army camps around the country. He had also used it for his successful screen test at MGM in 1940, but it had otherwise never been filmed, although he had made many films by 1944, and this seemed the ideal opportunity to record the skit for posterity. Hailed at the time as one of the film's most successful sequences, it is still considered so today. In it Skelton plays the role of a "doctor of poetry" with a sure instinct for doggerel, as well as that of an announcer who gets increasingly drunk on the sponsor's product (J 1).

K
LIMEHOUSE BLUES
(13′ 33″)

"Limehouse Blues" is billed as a "dramatic pantomime" and would have been far more successful if it had been limited to that. Unfortunately inserted into the number's drama is an elaborate "dream ballet" that is an overdecorated muddle. The number was shot in ten days for $228,226, the most expensive in the film. The music is by Edens and Salinger.

The little fable that frames this lavish spectacle is tight and affecting. Developed by Alton, Minnelli, and Max Liebman, it borders on the sentimental but is kept within bounds by the superbly controlled mime performances of its three principals: Astaire as an impoverished but proud Chinese laborer, Bremer as the haughty and desirable woman he loves (a prostitute, probably), and Robert Lewis as a sneering Chinese gentleman.

The locale, inspired by D. W. Griffith's popular 1919 film *Broken Blossoms,* is the fog-shrouded Limehouse red-light district in London, full of violence, poverty, and danger.[11] As a costermonger family (led by the animated, cigar-chomping Eugene Loring) entertains passers-by in the street (K 1), Astaire, tense and unsmiling, catches sight of Bremer (K 2). Keeping his face essentially impassive during the whole number, Astaire is nevertheless able to convey his intense longing for Bremer through the sorrowful, searching look in his eyes and the tentativeness with which he moves, following her at a respectful distance—afraid to get too close yet helplessly attracted. While he watches, she is propositioned by the businessman but rejects the offer contemptuously (K 3). Then Astaire trails Bremer as she approaches a shopwindow and gazes at a fan she covets (K 4). He enters the shop and finds the fan beyond his means. As he is leaving, gunshots ring out and hoodlums break the window and steal some of the valuables on display. During the fighting, Astaire wistfully reaches through the broken glass and picks up the fan; but a stray shot hits him and he falls.

A dissolve leads to his phantasmagoric dream-dance with Bremer (K 5–8). When he regains consciousness, he is lying on a couch in the shop, watched over by the Chinese shopkeeper and the police. Bremer and the Chinese gentleman, now a couple, stop by. Ignoring the wounded man, Bremer inquires about the fan, but then drops it in disgust when she discovers blood on it (K 9). She and the gentleman exit, laughing, as Astaire slumps back on his couch (K 10).

The Limehouse sequences were staged by Lewis, a well-known stage actor and director, with clarity and without excess. This cannot be said for the belabored dream ballet that takes up most of the number's length. In his imagination, Astaire pursues the fan as it drifts into a red-and-blue fantasy domain filled with masked creatures and assorted *chinoiserie* (K 5). Eventually he comes across Bremer, and they wander around for a while until their exotic surroundings inspire them to rip through what Minnelli calls a "precision Chinese fan dance." The duet, musically literal and rhythmically square (the usual sign Astaire had little to do with the choreography), is filled with fierce juttings and jabbings of the arms. The effect is presumably supposed to be strange and otherworldly, but it is frenetic and pretentious, and is severely weakened by the inclusion of such steps as shoulder-shrugging shimmying (K 6), Rockette-style high-kicking (K 7), and a wildly incongruous and poorly executed cartwheel for Astaire (K 8).

The dance was scored and choreographed even before the framing story was completely worked out, which may help to explain why the two bear so little relation. In the fantasy world Astaire has finally gotten his greatest wish:

[11] At the beginning and end of the number, the Philip Braham song "Limehouse Blues" (made famous on the stage in 1924 by Gertrude Lawrence) is sung in the background by Harriet Lee, a vocal coach at MGM. The original lyric's reference to "yellow chinkies" was changed for the film, to make sure there would be nothing "offensive to our allies, the Chinese," as Hollywood's censorship office put it.

G30 G31 G32 G33
G34 G35 G36 H1

Bremer; yet they show about as much desire and affection in their dance as a pair of riveting machines.[12]

L

A GREAT LADY HAS AN INTERVIEW (MADAME CREMETON)

(10′ 23″)

When Roger Edens and Kay Thompson wrote this sketch for the film, they intended it to be played by Greer Garson as self-parody. Garson, a successful stage actress, had come to Hollywood in 1939 and achieved fame in a series of Very Serious roles, in particular as the heroic title characters in *Mrs. Miniver* (for which she received an Academy Award) and *Madame Curie*.

In this sketch the Great Lady suggests, in the course of a spirited interview with the press, that perhaps she should try less dramatic roles—show a little leg, make use of her torso. When she is asked about her next role, however, she tells them that it will be along familiar lines: the story of the struggles of one "Madame Cremeton," the inventor of the safety pin—presumably a parody of the Curie story. She and the reporters then do a song-and-dance number about this improbable heroine.

When the authors previewed the sketch for Garson, however, she and (particularly) her husband were not amused. Edens then cast Judy Garland in the role instead. Although the personal point of the parody is thereby lost, Garland handles the role remakably well; it's something of a *tour de force,* in fact, and at the time was an eye-opener to the range of her talents. She slinks decoratively around the room, displaying her public psyche and pointing to her better features with her Oscar statuette (L1). In the process, especially in the early part of the number, she is able to suggest the insecurity, the desperate need for adulation and reassurance, that underlie this Great Lady's posturings.

Charles Walters, who staged the number, was crushed when Minnelli, Garland's lover at the time, was called in to do the final direction. The sketch is diverting, and Walters came up with some amusing rompings for the male chorus of reporters and photographers. But the slight theme is overcooked; eventually its point is submerged in a rather desperate, hard-sell routine accompanied by some dispiritingly raucous Edens music. The ending, however, is quite fine: Garland, surrounded by the worshipful chorus, makes grand gestures as she stands before a painting of the unaffected waif she pretends to be (L2).

M

THE BABBITT AND THE BROMIDE

(7′ 13″)

Gene Kelly came to Hollywood from Broadway in 1941 and within a year was signed by MGM to a long-term contract. By 1944 he had appeared in seven motion pictures. The last two, *Cover Girl* and *Christmas Holiday,* made on loan-out to Columbia and Universal, respectively, were highly profitable. MGM, naturally enough, now sought to cash in on this talent they owned, and from then on kept Kelly busy on the home lot, where he made his next twenty-two pictures.

Particularly after the success of *Cover Girl,* Kelly was often seen as a rival to Astaire—the new boy with an appealing screen personality and plenty of new ideas. Inevitably there were rumors of jealousy between the two, and Freed put them together in this number in part to play on the supposed rivalry; the film's revue structure facilitated such experiments. Astaire and Kelly have both repeatedly discounted any suggestion of a rivalry between them, and each has equally repeatedly expressed admiration for the work of the other, most prominently in their narrative tributes in the 1976 film *That's Entertainment.* There is no reason to doubt the genuineness of these sentiments; there was room enough for both men to be successful. When they have been asked for comparisons, Kelly and Astaire have characteristically dodged the issue by simply observing that their dancing styles are so different that any comparison is meaningless. These differences have been succinctly expressed by Minnelli: "Fred Astaire is very elegant, high up in the air and strange stops and so forth. Gene is very athletic and down-to-earth."

In their *Ziegfeld Follies* duet Astaire and Kelly chose to blend their styles rather than contrast them. Kelly has some regrets about this: "I wish we could have . . . tried to dance against each other in our own style instead of trying to amalgamate our things. Nevertheless, it was fun. . . ." Astaire, on the other hand, likes the contrasts that remain in the number: "When we were put together, the two styles *don't* go together like two chorus boys—you know, why should they? The thing is, we both were doing our thing and working together." As the two

[12] On the other hand, "Limehouse Blues" does not belong to that small collection of numbers in which Astaire's embarrassment seems palpable: 12 G, the Hoctor duet in 8 J, and the beginning portion of 26 H.

I1 J1 K1 K2

K3 K4 K5 K6

men worked out the choreography, the chief problem was not rivalry but, rather, in Freed's words, "their deference for each other. Each was willing to do whichever dance the other wanted. . . . It was a real Alphonse and Gaston routine." As Minnelli reports, "Neither wanted to be accused of foisting his quite different dancing style on the other. . . . They were both so anxious to please each other that it took a long time. We thought we'd never get it on."

The number is thus an interesting blend, in which some steps and ideas are Astaire's, others Kelly's. The overall sensibility, however, seems closer to Astaire. Kelly's choreography often takes standard steps from the tap, character, or ballet vocabulary and incorporates them wholesale into the dances. It also tends to be musically literal and to work out its dance phrases in comfortable four-square patterns. Astaire characteristically avoided these tendencies, and, with a few exceptions, so does this duet.

The idea for the number came from Freed. He had seen Fred and Adele Astaire perform the Gershwins' "The Babbitt and the Bromide" with great success onstage in *Funny Face* in the late 1920s and thought it appropriate for the Astaire-Kelly confrontation. Astaire liked the idea, but after the first rehearsal Kelly privately told Freed he would prefer to do an Indian song and dance to "Pass That Peace Pipe," a song that had been written for the film by Edens, Martin, and Blane: "a more 'up' kind of number. I guess it was purely because I wanted to do something more in my own style." Astaire deferred to Kelly's wish, but then Kelly deferred to Astaire's preference and the original idea was retained.

The George and Ira Gershwin song is rather cynical, though not aggressively so. It tells the tale of two solid citizens who meet at long intervals and find they have nothing to say to each other beyond empty clichés of greeting.[13] Costume changes reflect the advancing years, but otherwise there is no effort at characterization. Rather, Astaire and Kelly impersonate themselves, and throughout the number they engage in a friendly competition that has a nicely acid touch—at once deftly portraying and mocking the rivalry people liked to think existed in real life.

[13] Pechter has described the number as "almost a fable of the dancer's ability to transform the mundane into the lyrical . . . two men, who have nothing to say, danced by two men, who don't need to say anything." Ira Gershwin recalls that when Astaire first heard the song in 1927, he took him aside and asked, "I know what a Babbitt is, but what's a Bromide?" An hour later the show's coproducer asked Gershwin, "I know what a Bromide is—but what's a Babbitt?"

The number begins with Astaire seated on a park bench, idly tapping. He is surprised to hear himself answered in kind by the man sitting next to him (M 1). The two engage in some well-paced banter (by Alton and Irving Brecher) in which Astaire for a while pretends not to recognize the upstart Kelly. Eventually they decide to improvise a routine together—a routine like the one they've been rehearsing for two weeks, Kelly observes.

They sing the three choruses of the Gershwin song and, after each, rip through a dance duet in which they cheerfully do violence to each other.[14] Each dance is longer than the one before, and the violence becomes increasingly harsh and purposeful. The first dance episode seems a thorough amalgam of the styles of both dancers; the second seems mostly Kelly oriented; the third (and longest) seems to derive mostly from Astaire.

The violence in the first duet is rather incidental. The dancers have trouble getting coordinated—to their mutual and increasing irritation—and bump into each other a couple of times by accident. Then a step goes awry and they end up sharply kicking their feet together (M 2). They respond by staggering in pain (M 3), an idea Astaire had used before (9 C 15) and would again (in 21 A and 28 E). Then the dancers engage in two specific trademarks. First, there is some of the close sequential imitation that Kelly favored, in which one dancer hops out a step to the side and the other immediately responds in kind (M 4). (Kelly's dance with the cartoon mouse in *Anchors Aweigh* [1945], for example, uses this notion frequently, and it also appears in his dance with his alter ego in *Cover Girl*.) Second, the dancers do one of the sprawling, sliding back kicks (M 5) that are something of an Astaire signature (compare 7 D 5–6, 12 A 4, 19 F 13), though Kelly sometimes used the step as well. These two ideas are to be developed later.

Ten years pass. The Babbitt and the Bromide have grown mustaches but still wallow in the same old clichés. The dance that ensues bubbles with humorous ideas but tends to ride directly, if amiably, on the beat, in the Kelly manner. This duet begins with, and frequently reverts to, loping, casual soft-shoe, with the arms swinging freely. Kelly often lapsed into this kind of material, sometimes a bit ingratiatingly. At one point early on, there is a leg-over-leg jump (M 6), a step both dancers liked; but the fact that it is done just once, not repeated several times for effect, suggests Astaire's influence: Astaire uses the step or a variation of it in several dances (such as 7 B 27, 17 C 19, 20 O 8) but always does it just once; Kelly uses it in his mouse dance, but does it four times in a row without variation. Otherwise the dance seems to be mostly Kelly. There are several of the sequential frolicking hops to the side, one of which allows Kelly to step on Astaire's foot (M 7). He gloats as Astaire mimes agony (M 8), and then abruptly reverts to an innocent nobody-here-but-us-chickens soft-shoe as Astaire glowers at him (M 9). In retribution, Astaire deals Kelly a deft kick to the nose (M 10). There are a few more altercations and some nested vaudeville-style striding (M 11), a Kelly favorite (though Astaire used something like it before—not in a dance, but in a stage crossover to acknowledge applause, and varied with a little check step that made it more interesting [12 A 10]; another variant is found in the exit in 24 A). At the end, Kelly tips off Astaire's hat from behind, Astaire retaliates, and both glower (M 12).

[14] Astaire and Kelly sing a shortened version of the song, though all its music is used, variously arranged, in the dances.

In time both Babbitt and Bromide make it to heaven, where they are outfitted with harps and beards but retain their familiar forms of greeting. The principal device in the final dance is one Astaire had used before (and somewhat better) in a duet with Ginger Rogers in *Follow the Fleet* (6 H; see also 15 J and 26 G). The music is arranged to switch abruptly back and forth from jazzy pop to an exaggeratedly broad waltz, and the dancers follow suit.

The satiric waltz choreography looks better on the fluid Astaire than on the chunky Kelly (M 13), but both are splendid in a series of heel-clicking leaps (a Kelly trademark) made particularly memorable by the presence of the absurdly inappropriate harps (M 14). Pretending to be swept away by the gush of the music, the dancers sling their harps away and waltz together in flowery grandeur (M 15). (Embedded in this passage is a brisk pirouette, Kelly turning to the left, Astaire to the right—their preferred directions.) The image is somewhat tarnished when they bump into each other, and then it is destroyed entirely when the music changes to pop and Kelly takes the opportunity to place two kicks to the seat of Astaire's pants (M 16). Astaire soon responds in kind (three times, in fact); the idea of the return kick (M 17) may be predictable, but its timing in the music is not (unlike the hat-flipping retaliation in the previous dance, which occurred on an obvious musical cue).

Before they can come to blows, however, the

music—and therefore the dancing—returns to genteel waltzing, and then to addled jitterbug (M 18). At one point, when he and Astaire loosen hands, Kelly falls to the floor. Astaire helpfully pulls him to his feet, and the pair are launched into the finale, which seems pure Astaire. A rush of fleet-footed cavortings interspersed with precise hesitations, it incorporates some swivel-hipped tapping (M 19) of the kind Astaire also used in other dances (14 A 1, 20 O 7, 22 G 15), and develops into an explosive traveling pattern built on another Astaire signature step, the sprawling back kick used earlier (M 20; compare M 5). Kelly keeps up gamely but is pretty well outclassed in this last sequence—it may have been with this sequence in mind that Kelly once said, "I hated the third section: I thought I looked like a klotz." At the end they shake hands heartily. The harps are obligingly dropped into their arms from above (M 21), and the two performers lunge at the camera and grin (M 22). The harp-catching se-

K7 K8 K9 K10
L1 L2 M1 M2
M3 M4 M5 M6
M7 M8 M9 M10
M11 M12 M13 M14

quence is not handled with a separate shot. Rather, it is part of a twenty-six-second shot that includes all the material from the traveling back-kicks to the end of the number (M 20–22). This means that the dancers had to finish in the exactly right spot for the harp drop.[15]

N
BEAUTY
(4′56″)

Developing a suitable finale for this extravagant film proved to be a major problem. An absurdly lavish number using mountains of soap bubbles, shot in 1944 to conclude the film (see 18 V below), was badly received at the preview, and so a (comparatively) modest finale was assembled. It opens as soprano Kathryn Grayson wanders through a rocky landscape (N1) while chirping a vapid Warren-Freed tune with the airy philosophy "love is beauty." Next comes a bit of the bubbly left over from the original finale: Cyd Charisse blasting her way through a bubble mound (N2) and then wafting briefly among floating bubbles and poised showgirls (N3). At the end, a vast landscape decorated with more showgirls is shown (N4), a vision that suggests Salvador Dali much more than Florenz Ziegfeld.

[15] Production reports indicate Astaire was working with a bad leg on the second-to-last shooting day for this number; nevertheless, he insisted on working until 7:00 p.m. to finish filming one sequence, which was shot twenty-one times. The number was shot in four days for $78,726.

NUMBERS CUT FROM THE FILM

O
IF SWING GOES, I GO TOO

The most important and regrettable excision from the film was this solo routine for Astaire, in which he danced and played drums backed by a chorus of twenty-four men (O1). It was obviously a spirited number. Production notes talk of Astaire's "attack on the drums," and the routine included throwing drum sticks to the chorus and ended as "Astaire leaps onto drums." Using a set consisting of a geometric arrangement of screens, the number was shot by George Sidney early in the production schedule—the first Astaire number to be rehearsed and filmed, in fact—and then cut after the previews, apparently with Astaire's approval.[16]

Astaire himself wrote the song, and he recorded it for Decca in 1944. The music sounds slightly derivative and the lyric strains for some of its rhymes, but as a whole the song has a nice sassy bounce and infectiously high spirits.

P
THE PIED PIPER

This was a specialty number for Jimmy Durante in which he strutted along a city street singing "Start Off Each Day with a Song," interrupting himself from time to time to insert patter and jokes in characteristic manner. It was directed by Charles Walters.

[16] It took four days to shoot and cost $91,140, substantially more than "The Babbitt and the Bromide."

M15 M16 M17 M18

M19 M20 M21 M22

N1 N2 N3 N4

Q
A COWBOY'S LIFE

James Melton sang a medley of Western tunes in this number, directed by Merrill Pye. The opera singer apparently didn't fare well in this environment.

R
LIZA

Black singer Avon Long, surrounded by a female chorus, serenaded Lena Horne with this classic Gershwin song on a Southern plantation set. It was staged by Loring and directed by Minnelli (who was later to name his daughter after the song).

S
BABY SNOOKS AND THE BURGLAR

Fanny Brice was featured in a characterization she had originated on the stage in *Ziegfeld Follies of 1934* and developed as the central character in a comedy radio series between 1944 and 1951. In the sketch, Snooks drives a burglar to such distraction that he voluntarily surrenders to the police to escape the torment. It was directed by Roy Del Ruth and written by Everett and Devery Freeman.

T
DEATH AND TAXES

Durante confronted income-tax inspector Edward Arnold in a sketch written by David Freedman and directed by Minnelli.

U
WE WILL MEET AGAIN IN HONOLULU

In this elaborate number Melton sang a Nacio Herb Brown–Arthur Freed song to Esther Williams, whereupon she dived into the water for her underwater ballet. It was directed by Merrill Pye. Only the underwater routine was kept in the film, recut to fit an orchestral rendering of Warren's "This Heart of Mine" (18 C).

O1

V1

V
THERE'S BEAUTY EVERYWHERE

This is the soap-bubble finale (see 18 N). Alton's original conception was nothing if not grandiose. There would be vast heaps of soap bubbles through which the performers in the film would perambulate. Astaire and Bremer would, he visualized, dance up to the top of a bubble mountain and see "a lake of bubbles in which there are golden gondolas—one has Fanny Brice and Jimmy Durante, another Judy Garland and Mickey Rooney."

As the conception was refined in discussions with Minnelli, the golden gondolas and their hapless occupants were eliminated, but the bubble theme remained. In the version that was actually shot, James Melton sang the Warren-Freed song while Astaire, Bremer, Charisse, and the ensemble danced, or at any rate squished, around (V 1). Shaping and managing the bubbles proved to be a monumental task, and the gas used for inflating them caused some members of the cast and crew to faint. Most of the material filmed, including all of Astaire's contribution, was eventually cut. A fragment of Charisse's bubble dance was retained for the new finale (N 2, 3).

19.

Yolanda and the Thief

1945

In putting together *Yolanda and the Thief,* producer Arthur Freed made a concentrated effort to create a film that had whimsy, light fantasy, and above all charm. In the best of circumstances, these evanescent qualities are difficult to capture; under the conditions at the MGM factory, they were particularly elusive—more likely to coalesce by accident than by conscious design. What emerged was an overripe film in which humor, romance, and spontaneity have been, as if purposely, sacrificed for some ungraspable higher good. The film is a failure but, because of its high-minded and well-budgeted pretensions, an interesting one.

It bombed at the box office. This was quite an accomplishment for a film released during the movies' gold-mine years of the early 1940s, when, in director Vincente Minnelli's words, "with the industry's weekly audience of 80 million, no sensibly budgeted film . . . could fail." Nevertheless, *Yolanda and the Thief* did not even manage to recoup its production expenses—a unique event for a Freed musical of the time (see Table 3).

The film is an unlikely concoction for Fred Astaire—eggnog instead of the usual champagne. Although he does his best to enliven the proceedings, he is given remarkably little opportunity to do so in musical terms: he sings only once and has only two developed dance numbers, one of which is an overelaborate and underarticulated dream ballet. Moreover, his choreographic contribution was limited. Near the end, however, he participates for a few minutes in an agreeable festive duet that helps somewhat.

THE SCRIPT AND THE DIRECTION

The plot was derived from a magazine story by Jacques Thery and Ludwig Bemelmans and follows it quite closely. The fanciful tale concerns an American con man (Astaire) who finds himself in a fictional Eldorado-like South American country. Impressed by the wealth and naïveté of the inhabitants, he successfully swindles a trusting young heiress out of a fortune by posing as her guardian angel. In the end, however, touched by her innocence, he gives the money back—whereupon her real guardian angel manipulates events in order to allow innocent and swindler to wed happily.

The Thery-Bemelmans story is sunny and fragile and remarkably devoid of tension. The con man's dilemma is not really prepared for or developed, and the romance is precipitous and unconvincing. Besides, whereas successful fairy tales usually incorporate gnomes and witches and a little leavening cruelty, the *Yolanda* imitation is sugar, spice, and unalloyed nice.

The story's defects are, if anything, made more noticeable in the film by the opulence of the production. Many of the film's elaborate scenes, emphasizing warm yellows and reds, are beautifully atmospheric, the result of Minnelli's painterly eye. But the pace is lethargic. Then, at the last minute, Minnelli cut quite a bit of material, including several episodes involving supporting comics Frank Morgan and Mildred Natwick, as well as scenes designed to show Astaire's dawning affection for the heiress. This material had been added by scriptwriter Irving Brecher to inject some much-needed humor and romantic believability into the original story, and Minnelli's cutting was considerably damaging. Astaire himself has called the cuts "drastic" and recalls, "When I finally saw the picture, I said, 'What happened to *that*?' "

THE MUSIC

Another problem is the music. The songs are by Harry Warren, a successful Hollywood tunesmith, who had produced most of his best work in the 1930s at Warner Bros. A newcomer to MGM, he had written the sumptuous "This Heart of Mine" for Astaire in *Ziegfeld Follies* and was here producing his first complete film score for the studio. His score has a few high spots, but overall is remarkably unmemorable. Freed's lyrics are often arch, and most problematic of all are the orchestrations and musical direction by Conrad Salinger and Lennie Hayton, which rely heavily on violins and harps. The syrupy, insipid background music is constantly swarming around the characters, bathing them in a soporific haze, and the musical numbers are often similarly affected.

LUCILLE BREMER

The film was a pet project of Freed's, developed as the first starring showcase for Lucille Bremer, who had previously seen action in a secondary role in *Meet Me in St. Louis* and as Astaire's chief dancing partner in *Ziegfeld Follies*. It may well be that the failure of the film stems largely from Freed's myopic obsession with Bremer and his inability to see that she would be unable to breathe life and credibility into a difficult role. As Minnelli tersely put it, "She was a protégée of one of the studio bosses and was quite unsuitable."

On screen Bremer projected an image of statuesque desirability, a quality that had been put to good use in her duets with Astaire in *Ziegfeld Follies* and that work again in some of the dance portions of *Yolanda and the Thief*. But the role of a vulnerable young innocent seems to have been considerably beyond her limited acting abilities. She comes off stiff, bewildered, and unconvincing. Of course, the story calls for the character to fall emotionally and erotically in love with a man she believes to be an angel—a role that would challenge the most skilled actress. But it is likely that someone else might have had more success—someone like Leslie Caron, it has been suggested, or like Audrey Hepburn, or, most intriguingly, Judy Garland, who had expressed an interest in the role at the time.

With Lucille Bremer in the dream ballet

At any rate, perhaps somewhat unfairly, Bremer bore the chief blame for the film's financial failure, and it was her last major role in Hollywood. She appeared in five more motion pictures, only one of them a musical, and then, in 1948, retired from the screen.

THE SPECTER OF DE MILLE

In 1943 the choreographer Agnes de Mille had introduced into the smash Broadway musical *Oklahoma!* an elaborate "dream ballet" that is often said to be the first truly integrated dance number—one that advances the story—though, in fact, the ballet does not really change anything, but simply explicates in a fanciful manner attitudes and relationships already clearly set out in earlier dialogue.

With the sensational success of *Oklahoma!,* the dream ballet became a fixture in many Broadway and Hollywood musicals. In motion pictures it reached perhaps its most prominent development in some of the films of Gene Kelly, such as *On the Town* (1949) and *An American in Paris* (1951).

Although Astaire had actually created a dream number as early as 1938, in *Carefree* (10 B), in which the story really is advanced, he largely stayed away from the big set-piece dream ballet. The one in *Yolanda and the Thief* marks his chief participation in the field.[1]

The number, called with admirable directness "Dream Ballet," contains all the requisites—sumptuous scenic and color effects, a supporting cast of psychological types, and a studied air of otherworldly mystery. It does not, as it happens, have much to do with the plot, since it's a kind of nightmare for the character Astaire plays that he shrugs off when he wakes up, proceeding calmly to carry out his business as if nothing had happened.

It would actually have made sense if the dream ballet had occurred toward the end of the film, when it could logically be seen to summarize Astaire's dilemma at that point: his sympathy for Bremer's innocence and/or his fear about entangling, stabilizing marriage. Indeed, in his first script Brecher called for a "romantic dance" at that point, but when the idea of a dream ballet was broached, he inserted it earlier in the script. Then, later, following Astaire's suggestion that the film needed an enlivening dance routine, the proposed romantic duet became festive and lost its dramatic point.

[1] Astaire's other brushes with the genre include the "Limehouse Blues" number in *Ziegfeld Follies* (18 K), which has an elaborate fantasy-dream insert, and a ballet in *Daddy Long Legs* (28 I), in which, however, he has only a small role. He also did a couple of extended duets in dream, or dreamlike, surroundings (26 H, 28 E). See also 24 G.

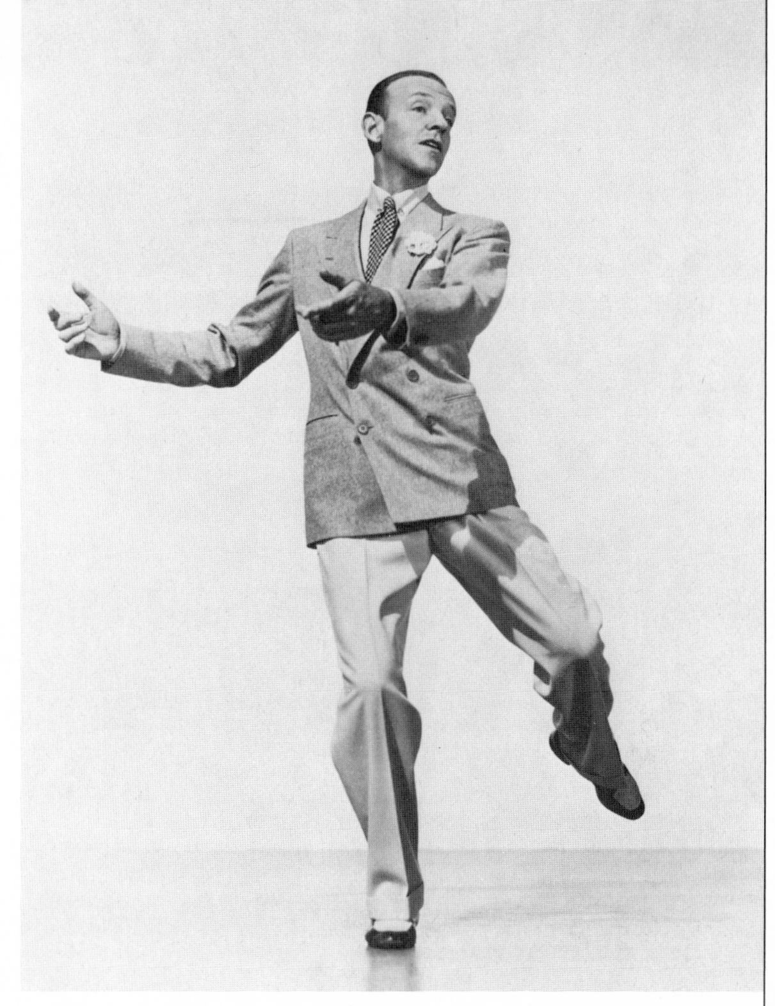

THE CHOREOGRAPHY

The choreographer assigned to the film was Eugene Loring. Like Agnes de Mille, his background was in ballet, and, also like her, his chief fame in that area had been achieved when he choreographed and danced the lead role in a highly successful cowboy ballet set to original music by Aaron Copland: Loring's was *Billy the Kid* (1938), de Mille's *Rodeo* (1942). Though Astaire made occasional contributions, the vast majority of the choreography for *Yolanda and the Thief* was apparently created by Loring. Astaire says he was in part trying to see how he liked dancing to another choreographer's designs.

Loring's first film had been *Ziegfeld Follies,* in which he had helped to stage several episodes and done a bit of character dancing in one of its Astaire numbers (18 K 1). *Yolanda and the Thief* was his first major assignment. He stayed on in Hollywood to 1960, working on at least nine more films, including two featuring Astaire, *Funny Face* and *Silk Stockings.*

THE NUMBERS

A
THIS IS A DAY FOR LOVE
(1′ 31″)

In the llama-infested hills of Patria, a kindly teacher (oddly Germanic, to which Bemelmans unavailingly objected) cheerfully instructs his second-grade pupils in the pastoral virtues of the country and leads them in their national anthem, a lilting, sugary paean to universal love (A 1). Scenes showing the happy, giggling, simple-minded citizenry follow. All sing.

B
THIS IS A DAY FOR LOVE
(REPRISE) (48″)

Yolanda is seen graduating from a convent school to take possession of the vast enterprises she has inherited. As she leaves, the mother superior gives her a lecture:[2] in pious, leaden tones, she advises Yolanda not to be concerned about her new responsibilities and assures her meaningfully that she has a guardian angel (B 1). Meanwhile, Astaire and his fellow con man, played by Frank Morgan, are entering the country to escape the American police (B 2).[3]

As Yolanda arrives at her palatial home she is accompanied by a reprise of the Patria anthem and is met by her scatterbrained aunt, played by Mildred Natwick, whose fussy ramblings supply most of the film's comedy (B 3). (In some of the original plans for the film, the aunt was to be played by Lucille Ball.)

C
ANGEL
(2′ 3″)

Learning of Yolanda's great wealth, Astaire steals out to the estate and chances to overhear her in the garden weepily praying to her guardian angel for guidance (C 1). From this he conceives a plot: he calls her on the telephone (which she answers from a wildly improbable bathtub) and identifies himself as her guardian angel (C 2–3). With monumental gullibility, she swallows the bait and agrees to come alone to his hotel to meet him.[4] As she is being dressed for the event, she sings Freed's smarmy lyric: "I've an angel . . . this angel is an angel to protect me and bring heavenly, heavenly things . . . angel divine."

D
DREAM BALLET
(15′ 42″)

Bremer rushes to the hotel, where Astaire has hastily erected a throne for himself in a corner of the lobby. He has a plan, he says, to relieve her

[2] This conversation was to have been inspired by a puppet show about guardian angels, created by the puppeteer Remo Bufano, but only the final tableau remains in the finished film.

[3] It was originally planned that Morgan's role would be played by Victor Moore, and the relationship of the two men bears some similarity to the situation in *Swing Time.* The two men, incidentally, are given middle names in the film's cast titles, although these are never mentioned in the film. The names were added at the urging of the MGM legal office in fear of nuisance lawsuits, since the "surnames are fairly common and the characters detrimental."

[4] Bremer's black-garbed duenna answers the phone and tells her it's a man. Bremer insists on talking to him and sweetly says, "There's one thing I've wanted so long (pause), to talk on the telephone"—a comedy line presumably intended to give insight into her sensual yearnings. The line is delivered so mechanically, however, that its impact is undercut. This is perhaps because Minnelli wasn't listening; he was obsessed with the framing of the shot in C2 and kept Bremer in the water for hours trying to get head, gargoyle, and telephone positioned exactly to his liking. Freed, visiting the set, exploded over the water torture his weeping protégée was undergoing. According to one account, Bremer spent twelve and a half hours in her bubble bath.

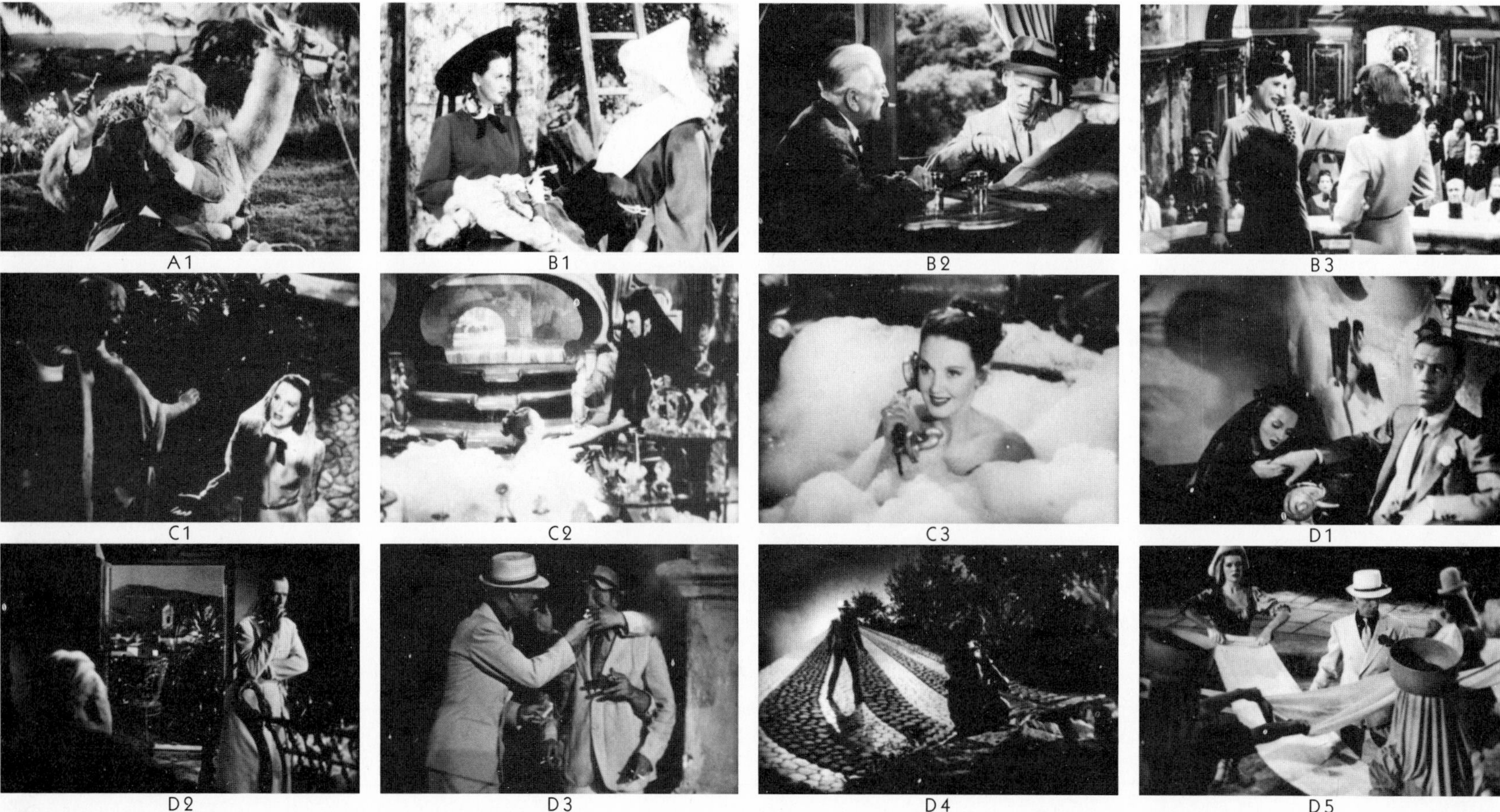

A1 B1 B2 B3

C1 C2 C3 D1

D2 D3 D4 D5

worries by taking them on himself—after she signs a simple piece of paper the next day. She is deliriously grateful and, before leaving, kisses his hand in devotion, an act he finds disconcerting (D1).

Astaire's puzzlement continues that evening. Morgan, noticing, asks whether he is getting "interested in anybody." Astaire firmly assures him there is no danger of that (D2), but when he goes to bed, he sinks into an extravagant dream in which he imagines himself dancing with, and among, various images and apparitions, including Bremer. The idea in this ballet is apparently to show him in a dilemma—his greed for her money in opposition to his dawning love for her and/or to his fear that she might entrap him in marriage. The exact impetus for this dilemma is far from clear, since there has been nothing in the script so far to suggest he has any real affection for her, and marriage hardly seems imaginable since her attitude toward him has merely been one of worshipful devotion (conceivably the dream is meant to be anticipatory).

Anyway, Art must be served and Agnes de Mille's innovations pursued, and so Astaire has this Technicolor dream. It begins with effective ambiguity. Astaire is seen to rise, restless, from bed, don a cream-colored suit, and wander through the streets, which are strangely bustling for a nighttime hour. Then he pauses to supply a cigarette and a light to an idler he had encountered earlier in the film. The man proves to have six arms and we begin to get the idea (D3).

Astaire proceeds warily, intermittently being showered by gold coins as he winds his way along a yellow stone road (D4). This leads him to a group of washerwomen who eventually entangle him in their laundry, thus setting up the entrapment theme (D5). Finally he staggers away and finds himself on a vast Daliesque landscape.[5] In the distance a billowy yellow specter emerges dry from a pool (D6), an effect accomplished by filming Bremer's double as she backed into the pool and then running the film backward; the billowing of veils was caused by an air jet strapped to her back.

Astaire follows the specter and performs spurts of dance around it as he divests it of its shrouds (D7). Underneath is Bremer, wound in an ugly spiral sash of gold coins—a get-up that cost MGM $1,500. After she and Astaire swirl around each other for a while in a pointless dance episode, she gives him some of her golden decorations. He is pleased but changes his mood when she snuggles up behind him and bursts into a saccharine song that has a surprising and brazen invitation: "Will You Marry Me?" (D8).

In the course of the song he inexplicably drops the gold he's been holding and Bremer deposits more in a chest held by three handmaidens who have conveniently materialized. The chest, according to Loring's notes, is supposed to represent her dowry. Astaire makes for the chest, but it is kept out of his reach (D9). At the end of the song Astaire slumps abruptly into a pose with crossed legs, and Bremer wraps her arms around him from behind (D10), a singularly ugly little formation, though it does perhaps suggest the theme of entrapment. Next they have a short dance, hopping and spinning around the land-

[5] *New York Times* dance critic John Martin, devoting a rare column to a Hollywood film, praised the two dance numbers and remarked that the dream ballet "has a sense of space that is altogether rare." The use of the camera's depth dimension is indeed unusual in an Astaire dance, since Astaire's approach was generally to keep the camera mobile, tightly framing the principal dancer or dancers at all times. Martin credits the innovation to choreographer Loring, though Minnelli is probably the real author of the approach and had, in fact, done similar work for Astaire earlier, in *Ziegfeld Follies* (see 18 K)—a film Martin had not yet seen, however, since it was released after *Yolanda and the Thief*.

D6 D7 D8 D9
D10 D11 D12 D13
D14 D15 D16 D17

scape, during which he manages to strip her of the remaining band of gold she wears around her waist (D11). But then he puts the gold in the chest.

Bremer disappears, and Astaire suddenly finds himself surrounded by a group of dancers who are supposed to represent his unsavory past —loose women and gamblers and jockeys and stuff. But Astaire can't join in their witless cavortings because, as he indicates by turning out his pockets, he has no money (D12).

He wanders away, perhaps in search of funds, and comes upon Bremer again, posed in the distance with one foot resting possessively on the chest (D13). Now the music turns especially soupy, and they engage in a brief duet (punctuated at one point by a reappearance of the unsavory folk who may be trying to urge Astaire on) which contains the closest thing in the number to memorable choreography. It begins with a pointed reference to her earlier gesture of kissing his hand (D14; compare D1), which he had found so disconcerting. As the duet develops, the dancers entwine their arms in various ways, neatly capturing in dance terms the theme of entrapment (D15, 16). But beyond this there is no real suggestion of either her enveloping passion for him or his concern about being caught. In fact, the dance is basically decorative, filled with fussy spins and jumps, conveying no emotional or psychological message at all, though Loring's notes say it is supposed to show that Astaire "is very much in love with Yolanda."

At the end the dancers slump to the floor (D17). The maidens and the chest reappear, and there is a wedding ceremony (D18). Bridegroom Astaire snatches up the chest and tries to run away, but becomes entangled in shrouds linked to Bremer's wedding train as she stands impassively in the background (D19). Next we see Astaire sitting bolt upright in bed (D20)—and thus ends what Minnelli has called "the first surrealistic ballet ever used in pictures."

As mentioned before, the nightmare has no perceptible effect on Astaire's attitudes or actions. After recovering, he smiles and observes twice that it was "only a dream" (a line that doesn't occur in the final script and was apparently added on the set). Then he sinks back into contented sleep, once again happily contemplating his felonious scheme.

E
YOLANDA
(2′29″)

The next day Astaire goes to Bremer's mansion to consummate the grand swindle. There is some awkward comedy when Astaire finds he must turn down offers of food and drink because Bremer has concluded that, as an angel, he doesn't eat or drink. Bremer's delivery and pacing are stilted and uncomprehending, and Astaire seems to be struggling to generate momentum. Minnelli does not appear to have been of much help.

As they wait for the servants to bring some ink so that Bremer can sign a paper for Astaire, she coyly unveils a harp to remind him "of home." Astaire strums (dubbed by jazz harpist Bobby Maxwell) and serenades her with an attractive song that rhapsodizes about the musicality of her name (E1), while Bremer struggles to look charmed (E2). Astaire shows his form by singing with a warmth and liveliness unusual in this musically listless film.

Then he brightens the tempo and raps out some amusing percussion effects by slapping the harp's sounding board, which leads to a perky little dance containing the film's most satisfying choreography. Frolicking lightly around the harp, he mixes genial tap spurts with string plucks wryly accomplished from the wrong side of the harp (E3, 4). The number ends beautifully: Astaire returns to the normal harp-playing position and, continuing to play, pivots the instrument around in a wide semicircle while Minnelli's camera follows closely, greatly adding to the effect. He comes to rest sitting beside Bremer, where he sings one final, caressing song phrase (E5). It's the only genuinely enchanting moment in a film sternly devoted to achieving charm.

F
COFFEE TIME
(5′30″)

After Astaire makes off with Bremer's power of attorney and over $1 million in bonds, he and Morgan have a brief altercation with a mysterious personage, played by Leon Ames, who had crossed their paths briefly earlier in the film (F1). (In this conversation the three men know one another's names, although the dialogue in which they were introduced was lost in the film's cutting room.) Uneasy about Ames, Astaire and Morgan try to flee the country with the money but are picked up by the police and brought back.

D18 D19 D20 E1
E2 E3 E4 E5

Now a carnival is in progress, and Astaire is treated as a national hero—Ames has let it be known that Astaire has Bremer's power of attorney and this has led to the general conclusion that Bremer and Astaire are to be married. (According to the script, Astaire is supposed to be delighted by the marriage rumor; none of that reaction survives on the film.) Bremer seems to have begun to fall in love with Astaire (the song and dance with the harp may have done the trick), but, aware that marriage with angels is unlikely, she is troubled about how to handle her dawning longing for him.

In order to get Bremer away from the mysterious, lurking Ames, Astaire pulls her through the carnival—whose bustle and turmoil are aptly captured by Minnelli's staging and camera work—to the dance floor. The dance duet that ensues might have been used to suggest, at least in passing, some of the psychological pressures the lead characters are presumably feeling—guilt, mainly: she about yearning for an angel, he about bilking a defenseless innocent. But instead we get "Coffee Time," a nicely crafted production number in which everyone seems to be having a good time; it does give the audience a respite from the labors of the plot. Bremer, too, is relieved, and she looks splendid—comfortable for once, and happy—as she joins Astaire on the dance floor.

The decor for the number is striking, especially the floor of wavy broad stripes of white and black, an inspiration of designer Irene Sharaff. Much of the dance's appeal comes from Loring's idea of setting a five-count dance phrase against a four-count musical phrase, so that, in his words, the "accents create a secondary syncopation." He was working the idea out as a duet in three different tempos—moderate, slow, and fast—when Warren came by. Intrigued, Warren observed, "You know, I have a hell of a tune for that sort of thing," and dragged out an old song he called "Java Time." Astaire, who was eager to enliven the film with a rhythm number, was delighted, as was Freed, who then provided a lyric for the tune. The rhythms and counter-rhythms, at once inevitable and unpredictable, give the dance a special buoyancy and vigor.

The number is introduced by a brief dance for a chorus deployed in formations that interweave in a manner that is imaginative and intricate but sometimes a bit cluttered visually (F2). The five-count dance phrases are clearly marked during an unaccompanied prologue, with the dancers clapping regularly on the second and fourth beats of the phrase. Then the orchestra plays the song with its four-count measures, and the rhythmic asymmetry is neatly established.

Astaire and Bremer, watching the festivities, get caught up in the compelling cadences and are urged out onto the dance floor by the others. Their opening duet, in moderate tempo, is unaccompanied except for the hand clapping, to which they contribute from time to time. The choreography is almost as hypnotically repetitive, though it builds invigoratingly from traveling kicks (F3) to partnered spins (F4), to unpartnered spin-outs, to jitterbug-derived arm loopings (F5).

The audience area darkens, the tempo slows, and the song is sung—a bit too insinuatingly—by an unseen chorus. Continuing the clapping rhythm, Astaire and Bremer, side by side, perform a lilting, rhythmically imaginative dance phrase that concludes with a wry little scooping step. This phrase is then repeated almost exactly—a fact that suggests Astaire was not the principal choreographer here. The dancers move out in the space with some partnered kicks (F6). The pleasantly casual, even dreamy, tone of the duet is shattered momentarily by a flamboyant partnered backbend during which Bremer gawkily extends a leg (F7). Soon, however, there is a more appropriate backbend (F8) and an especially ingenious development of the jitterbug arm loopings, which devolve into a pose with interlaced arms that is reminiscent of the duet in the dream ballet earlier (F9; compare D16). The slow section concludes with some repeats of earlier steps, including a final unfortunate return of the awkward backbend as the chorus dancers swarm across the floor (F10) and take over, bringing with them a brightening of the musical tempo and, for once in the film, orchestrations that are sparkling and vigorous.

Bremer and Astaire soon reappear for a final duet, this one devoted almost entirely to repeating—savoring, perhaps—the steps used earlier, though the brisk pace at which they are performed, aided by the musical setting, makes them exhilarating. There are the same kicks and hand claps (F11) and the same jitterbug partnering with the same swirling turns (F12; compare F5).[6] Toward the end there is some added mate-

[6] Also the same: after performing an eight-measure dance phrase to the first strain of the song, the dancers then repeat it almost exactly to the second strain.

F1 F2 F3 F4

F5 F6 F7 F8

rial: an Astaire-style traveling back kick (F 13; compare 7 D 5–6, 12 A 4, 18 M 5, 20), a spirited series of jumping turns, and a wonderful reverse promenade in which the woman pivots the man (F 14), an idea Astaire had used earlier (12 F 6, 16 F 10) and would again later (22 I 19, 25 C 5). At the end, the dancers thrust to the sides (F 15), exuberantly sweep past each other, and sink happily into a final pose in which they lean toward each other but do not touch (F 16).

It's still a long time—over fourteen languid minutes—to the end of the film. After the dance, Astaire, awash in smarmy background music, informs Bremer that he is going back to where he came from. She bursts into tears and tells him, "I get a feeling about you that you're not supposed to get about an angel." She kisses him impetuously and then runs off in confusion (F 17, 18).

Astaire returns to his hotel room, and *now* is when he should really have the dream he had earlier—the fanciful, disoriented juxtaposition of the money and the love-marriage themes would make some sense and sum up his dilemma. Furthermore, the entanglement motif, seen both in physical and in choreographic images in the dream ballet (D 5, 8, 9, 10, 15, 16, 19) could be taken as an ingenious distortion of some of the partnered arm work in the "Coffee Time" duet (F 9). But that's not the way MGM made the movie. Instead, we now find that Astaire has become flushed with guilt. He writes to Bremer, explaining the whole thing and returning the booty (F 19).

As it happens, Ames is Bremer's authentic guardian angel. Duly impressed by Astaire's noble act, Ames calmly performs several miracles: Astaire is interrupted as he tries to flee the country, brought back to Bremer, and married off to her. Somewhere along the line Ames apparently even causes Astaire to fall in love with her—Yolanda and her reformed thief kiss at the close to prove it (F 20). In Astaire films, miracles are not usually required to create romance, or kisses to certify it.

F9 F10 F11 F12
F13 F14 F15 F16
F17 F18 F19 F20

With Bremer in "Coffee Time"

20.

Blue Skies

1946

On the whole, *Blue Skies* is a dispirited and dispiriting film. It is based on a promising idea of Irving Berlin's: to fashion a nostalgic love story covering a thirty-year span, building the plot around a set of old and new Berlin tunes composed over the same period, with the old songs more or less arranged in chronological sequence of composition. The resulting film certainly is a cornucopia of music—over 40 percent of its length is given over to musical numbers. And although Fred Astaire's four dance episodes in the film do not maintain a consistently high level, one of them, "Puttin' On the Ritz," is a major masterpiece.

Unfortunately, music and dance are submerged in a languidly paced script centered on the romance of the somnolent Bing Crosby and the vapid Joan Caulfield. Neither performer approaches the acting task with much conviction, and it is difficult to become interested in their undermotivated passions or troubles. Even more destructively, the languor of the script is frequently reflected in Crosby's singing. He sings a deluge of songs and manages to make them all sound virtually alike, whether their intrinsic mood is somber or upbeat. With only casual musicianship, and often paying little attention to the lyric, he throws away song after song in a careless, mechanical, underarticulated manner, relying for effect on his famous deep warble.

THE SCRIPT AND THE ASTAIRE ROLE

The plot hinges on Caulfield's intolerance for what she terms Crosby's lack of "stability." He has an odd penchant for owning nightclubs: he buys them, builds them to success, and then sells them. This business behavior, which might seem shrewd to unromantic outside observers, bothers Caulfield, the scriptwriters would have us believe, because somehow it is evidence of a fundamental flaw in Crosby's character. After an on-and-off courtship they marry, have a child, argue, split up, divorce, and—following the passage of several years and without explanation—become reconciled at the end.

Astaire has a role with some potential: a perennial and increasingly pathetic also-ran. Attracted to Caulfield from the beginning, he chases her, courts her, loses her to Crosby, and tries several times—always unsuccessfully—to snap her up on the rebound. This role is unique for Astaire, in that he romances assiduously but is left in the end without a girl.[1]

The character undergoes an interesting development as the film proceeds. At first Astaire is buoyant and cocky—a carefree ladies' man who is used to getting effortlessly what he wants. Using well-tested tactics and exuding the charming lechery that was so central to his character in *The Sky's the Limit,* Astaire tries to sweep the reticent Caulfield off her feet. (When a friend calls her crazy for rejecting Astaire's offers—"I'd give my right arm for an offer like that"—Caulfield responds, "A right arm wouldn't interest him.") But Crosby, with whom Astaire enjoys an enduring and amiably acidic friendship, horns in, and she falls for him instead. As the Crosby-Caulfield romance alternately sparkles and fizzles, Astaire goes so far as to offer marriage to Caulfield (breaking his principles, he says), but she refuses, and he becomes increasingly somber and pathetic. Finally, after her divorce from Crosby, Caulfield agrees to marry Astaire—only to break off the engagement when she happens to think about her ex-husband again and to recall old longings. Astaire takes to drink and suffers an accident onstage that ends his dancing career (a plot development that is a bit un-

[1] One reason for this may be that the role was originally intended not for him but for the prominent tap dancer Paul Draper, who was dropped because he had a tendency to stutter. Joan Caulfield recalls, "We had had a week of production and scenes weren't flowing, and that is putting it mildly. Draper had a speech difficulty. So one afternoon Bing said 'I think that'll be about it.' He excused himself, went to the Front Office, and the next thing I know, Fred Astaire was going to be on the set Monday morning. And he was."

With Bing Crosby in "A Couple of Song and Dance Men"

pleasant in real-life context, since Astaire had publicly and officially announced that *Blue Skies* would be his last film). Chastened, ineffectual, and apparently crippled, Astaire is present at the end, smiling benevolently over his friends' reconciliation.

But the Astaire character's problems are not central to the plot, nor are his lively sparrings with Crosby. Instead, there are long, lethargic, melodramatic scenes between Crosby and Caulfield in which she whines about his "instability" and he croons songs and promises to do better. Astaire is off-camera for long stretches, particularly in the second half of the film, and when he reappears from time to time he seems almost to be a gratuitous, if welcome, distraction from the main event.

The film was directed by Stuart Heisler, a last-minute replacement for Mark Sandrich, who died suddenly from a heart attack at the age of forty-four just as production was beginning. Sandrich had had extensive experience with musicals—especially with Astaire musicals—and had been in charge of the previous Crosby-Astaire collaboration, *Holiday Inn,* in 1942, which has a liveliness *Blue Skies* sorely lacks. Some have suggested the film would have been much better with Sandrich at the helm, but whether he could have done much about Caulfield's insipidity, Crosby's lethargy, and the script's implausibility seems doubtful.

Although *Blue Skies* is one of Astaire's weakest and least satisfying films, the Crosby-Astaire-Berlin-Technicolor combination was highly successful at the box office, reportedly generating one of the best grosses of any Astaire film. Astaire was particularly gratified by this because of his plans to retire after the film—he wanted to go out with a hit. And the association with the famous and classy Crosby also had its special appeal and significance: "I had made my entrance with Joan Crawford and Clark Gable [in *Dancing Lady*]—now coming was the exit, with Bing Crosby." Astaire's retirement was motivated by his desire for a rest, his feeling that he was running "out of gas," and his desire to devote time to establishing a chain of dancing schools. It lasted less than two years (see p. 11).

THE CHOREOGRAPHY

Working with Astaire on the choreography was dance director Hermes Pan (on loan from Twentieth Century–Fox). Also assisting on "Puttin' On the Ritz" was Dave Robel.

With Olga San Juan in "Heat Wave"

THE NUMBERS

A
A PRETTY GIRL IS LIKE A MELODY
(3′8″)

The film covers the period from 1919 to 1946 and is presented in a series of flashbacks. Astaire relates the story to a radio audience in 1946, announcing at the beginning that the tale is "unfinished." "However," he says, "somewhere tonight there is one person who may be able to give this story its proper ending. I hope she's listening" (A1).

The first number occurs in 1919, the year the song was actually written. Astaire and Caulfield appear in an elaborate Ziegfeld-like stage show of the kind the song was written for. As usual, this Berlin classic is played in a sappy, saccharine manner by the orchestra. Astaire, however, is delightful as he frolics through a forest of preposterously overdecorated females. A spirited terrier among elephants, he mocks the women's stiffness, pretends to be smitten with their beauty, and deftly steals attention from the glamorous spectacle they are supposed to be making. He even manages to flirt with one of their number, Caulfield.

It would be difficult to imagine an aesthetic more at variance with Astaire's own than that of the big Ziegfeld (or Dillingham or Las Vegas) production numbers. These shows sought to achieve success by layering one lavish effort on another, and the "Pretty Girl" number might be taken to be Astaire's own deft send-up of such ludicrous extravaganzas.

At the beginning of this somewhat fragmented number, Astaire is scampering around and among the chorus, finding a gentle loping quality in the music that has largely been submerged in the arrangement. At one point he feigns infatuation for one of them (A2), then literally dances circles around the group (A3). After interrupting his peregrinations long enough to chat insinuatingly with the humorless and disapproving Caulfield (A4), he is off again, up some stairs. He expresses bemused admiration (and mock alarm) at one of the taller creatures he encounters (A5) and then hotfoots it down the stairs (A6), grabs Caulfield, and sweeps her off her feet in a series of rapid turns that cause her absurd costume to billow out (A7). Miraculously he is able to bring her to an abrupt and musically precise halt for a moment of calm (A8). Then he takes her flying again and ends the number by sending her swirling awkwardly into the wings.

The dance neatly establishes the cockiness and self-assurance that the Astaire character is to lose by the end of the film.

B
I'VE GOT MY CAPTAIN WORKING FOR ME NOW
(2′56″)

Astaire escorts Caulfield to the Flapjack, a club Crosby owns. After meeting the amiable singer (B1), she watches admiringly as he performs, backed up by comedian Billy De Wolfe (B2) and by some able period orchestration. Berlin wrote the song in 1919, just after World War I; it had new relevance in a film produced in 1946, a year after World War II had ended.

C
YOU'D BE SURPRISED
(1′1″)

A third Berlin tune from 1919 is sung with sassy suggestiveness by Olga San Juan (C1) at a party where the Crosby-Caulfield romance begins to heat up, to Astaire's consternation and displeasure.

D
ALL BY MYSELF
(1′27″)

Still at the party, Caulfield tells Crosby of her obsession with "stability," and Crosby croons a 1921 song to her. She harmonizes with him on the last phrases (D1).

E
SERENADE TO AN OLD-FASHIONED GIRL
(1′25″)

Later, onstage in a show, backed by a male quartet called the Guardsmen, Caulfield sings a nostalgic song Berlin wrote for the film (E1).

F
PUTTIN' ON THE RITZ
(4′34″)

Next, Astaire performs a show-stopping solo. It is set to a brilliant, breezily unsentimental Berlin song that seems so ideal for Astaire, it may come as a surprise to learn that the song was originally written for someone else: the vaudevillian Harry Richman, who used it in 1930 as the title number in the first of his two Hollywood films. Astaire heard Richman, whom he liked as a performer, sing the song in a nightclub at the time.

A1 A2 A3 A4
A5 A6 A7 A8

The song appealed to Astaire from the start, and he recorded it in 1930, complete with tap dance, for English Columbia.

Widely publicized as "Astaire's last dance," the number was shot after the rest of the film had been completed, and then only after what Astaire called "five weeks of back-breaking physical work." He wanted to retire with a dance that was a knockout, and this he accomplished. Among other things, the number uses a trick device that makes Astaire's cane seem to leap from the floor into his hand on command, and it concludes with a section applying process photography (a form of double exposure) to allow him to be backed up by a chorus of nine miniature Astaires.[2] Despite its complexities, however, the number is presented (song *and* dance) in only eight shots.

The image Astaire left with the audience in this stupendous solo was of the suave, sometimes hostile adult of the mid-1940s, not the ingratiating, likable young man of the 1930s. Indeed, his attitude toward the audience in this number is one almost of confrontation, with the chorus joining and abetting him in this at the end. Astaire's occasional smiles in the dance notwithstanding, the number is unrelievedly and cumulatively assertive, and has a rather unsettling drive. For example, throughout the dance, Astaire works with a curve-handled cane. As in other Astaire solos, the cane is used to complicate the tap rhythm; but unlike other solos, the cane in this one is soon being flung around, increasingly furiously, till it becomes almost an instrument of attack. In some respects "Puttin' On the Ritz" is similar to another famous Astaire/Berlin number, "Top Hat, White Tie and Tails" in *Top Hat* (5 D). But the occasional air of menace in "Top Hat" is undercut by the playfulness of Astaire's demeanor, a quality mostly absent in "Puttin' On the Ritz."

It is the music (even more than the lyric) that seems to have determined the look and approach of the dance. The song is in AABA form, with a verse. The central device in the A section is the use of delayed rhythmic resolution: a staggering, off-balance passage, emphasized by the unorthodox stresses in the lyric, suddenly resolves satisfyingly on a held note followed by the forceful assertion of the title phrase. The marchlike, relatively unsyncopated B section provides a literal release from these rhythmic complexities.[3] Throughout the first half of the number Astaire plays with the rhythm, usually punctuating it choreographically at the point of rhythmic resolution (the end of the held note just before the words "puttin' on the ritz"). To allow time for such articulation, he takes the music quite slowly: forty-six seconds for a chorus, as opposed to the thirty-five seconds he and Richman took in 1930. However, in the last half, the dance with the chorus, he alters his approach. The tempo is greatly speeded up—twenty-nine seconds for a chorus—changing the quality of the music considerably. Rhythmic subtleties are submerged in a voracious, hard-driving plunge to the conclusion.

For *Blue Skies* the lyric was changed. In the original version it told of the ritzy airs of Harlemites parading up and down Lenox Avenue. For the 1946 film, the strutters became well-to-do whites on Park Avenue. The patronizing, yet admiring, satire of the song is shifted, then, and mellowed in the process. The change may have had to do with changing attitudes toward race and with Hollywood's dawning wariness about offending blacks. Astaire denies this, however, suggesting instead that they were simply trying to update the song. And, indeed, the original lyric probably does apply better to the Harlem of the 1920s than to that of the mid-1940s.

The decor is a disappointment. The number opens, for no apparent reason, in a realistic set that suggests a very ordinary, book-lined office or study. The last section takes place before a drab upstage curtain.

The number begins most impressively. When the stage curtains part, Astaire is discovered poised in ascot, cutaway, striped pants, and spats, cane tucked under his left arm, holding his top hat in his hand while adjusting a cuff (F 1). He lets his cane fall, catching it behind his back with his right hand, places his hat on his head, and briefly checks out the sides of the stage in

[2] This was the last time Astaire did a solo number backed by a male chorus. In his previous attempts (5 D, 6 E, 18 O) he may have felt restrained choreographically by the abilities of the chorus dancers he had to work with. The approach here certainly avoids this problem.

[3] In his study of the American popular song, Wilder observes that the rhythmic pattern in "Puttin' On the Ritz" is "the most complex and provocative I have come upon, by any writer." George Gershwin's "Fascinating Rhythm," published five years before "Puttin' On the Ritz," is similar in musical strategy, as is Cole Porter's witty "Anything Goes," written five years after Berlin's song. Berlin's "Top Hat," written specifically for Astaire, is structured like a reverse "Puttin' On the Ritz"—the A strain is straightforward rhythmically, while the B strain has off-balance portions.

B1 B2 C1 D1
E1 F1 F2 F3

tense poses suggesting he might spring into action at the slightest provocation (F2). Relaxing slightly, but still moving as if coiled for action, he progresses toward the camera in a series of loping spins, his gaze downward (F3). Then he abruptly raises his head to look directly at the audience and, without smiling, begins to sing (F4). (This sharp shift of focus from downward to frontal will be repeated at the end of the number.) In a matter of seconds the whole tone of the number has been established—intense, controlled, with a hint of something like hostility.

Astaire delivers the lyric of the verse, underlining with gestures the words about collars, spats (F5), and "lots of dollars." Then a pickup phrase in the music propels him into motion, and he struts across the stage as he sings the first two A strains of the song's chorus (F6). To punctuate the point of rhythmic resolution in the music, he stops and jabs his cane at the floor (F7). During the singing of the marchlike release strain, the strut becomes more of a swagger, and the cane is casually slung over Astaire's shoulder. For the final A strain, he taps out an intricate counter-rhythm with his cane as he sings and struts, and punctuates the point of rhythmic resolution by tossing his cane up and forcefully snatching it out of the air (F8).

As the orchestra returns to the beginning of the song's chorus, the dance begins in mimed slow motion—taut and superbly musical. Astaire tried camera-induced slow motion twice in his career, in *Carefree* (10 B) and in *Easter Parade* (21 J)—both times, as it happens, to Berlin songs. Neither is very successful, probably because the special effect cut Astaire off from the music, which is his chief choreographic inspiration and anchor. By simply miming slow motion in "Puttin' On the Ritz" Astaire is able to relate directly to the music, gliding a long, slow choreographic line over the agitated music of the first two A strains and meeting it again at the release. To a degree, the slow-motion effect is implied in the music. In his 1930 recording of the song, Astaire essentially sings "in slow motion" at one point, rendering the A strains in a high monotone while the orchestra churns out the melody below. (Harry Richman does something similar in the 1930 film when he introduced the song.) To achieve the slow-motion effect in this dance, Astaire at first oozes his body slowly, as if pulling back against the onward thrust of the music (F9). Then, even more miraculously, he contrives to make it appear that the *cane* is dancing in slow motion, floating it from side to side and then gingerly kicking it up into his hand (F10). Toward the end of this passage he takes brief, explicit notice of what is going on in the music by tapping the top of his cane on the floor to mark the point of rhythmic resolution in the melody (F11).[4]

Astaire's return to normal speed is accomplished with a wonderful joke. He holds a brittle pose (F12) when the B strain begins, as if to resume his slow-motion dance; but then suddenly he relaxes, catching up with the music and relating directly to its rhythms. This leads to a series of tap spins.

During the final A strain Astaire returns to the strutting idea that opened the dance, but now it is embellished with additional cane taps and with a crisp jump as if in surprise (F13). To mark the point of rhythmic resolution, Astaire forcefully kicks the cane out to swing in a wide arc, and then beats out a rhythmic tattoo with it (F14; compare F11). The striking of the floor with

[4] Orchestrator Mason Van Cleave adds swirling violins for the slow-motion portion of the dance here. He repeated the idea during the camera-induced slow-motion section of Astaire's "Steppin' Out with My Baby" number in *Easter Parade* (21 J).

F4 F5 F6 F7 F8 F9 F10 F11 F12 F13 F14 F15

the cane becomes increasingly violent throughout the remainder of the solo dance.

The orchestra now repeats the song's chorus from the beginning but with a change of key. Astaire adopts an odd toed-in walk to progress upstage (F 15), spins, and sharply slaps the tip of the cane to the floor at the point of rhythmic resolution. Then he flips the cane around in his hand and, putting his full weight behind the maneuver, violently slaps the *heavy* end, the curved part, against the floor repeatedly during the course of a series of turns (F 16). The next point of rhythmic resolution is marked by a flailing, rearing lunge (F 17).

For a moment, during the release, Astaire fixes his attention on the cane—he seems almost ready to devour it (F 18)—but then a series of spins takes him upstage, and he slams the cane to the floor broadside, turns around, and forcefully back-kicks it, donkeylike, off-camera (F 19). As the A strain returns, he sidles forward, arm extended, and another cane is sharply propelled upward from the floor into his waiting hand (F 20)—an effect accomplished by a small trigger mechanism in the floor, invisible to the camera. He trots upstage with the cane and slams it broadside to the floor at the point of rhythmic resolution (F 21). Then, during an added, decorated statement of the A strain, he leaves the cane to frolic off to the side (F 22); when he returns, the dormant cane obligingly springs up into his hand—precisely at the point of rhythmic resolution (F 23).

This whole maneuver—the back kick (F 19), the retrieval (F 20), the slamming down of the cane (F 21), the frolic (F 22), and the springing up of the cane (F 23)—is shown in one shot. When Astaire frolics to the side the camera follows him, and the cane on the floor is momentarily off-camera (F 22). At that instant someone scurried onto the stage and moved the cane slightly to place it directly over the trigger mechanism in the floor, so that when Astaire returned to the cane a few seconds later, it was in firing position.

During some transitional music, Astaire trots upstage and parts the curtains to reveal a pair of mirrored doors, thus setting up the idea of dancing with images of himself. With an extravagant kick he had used earlier in the dance, he parts the doors (F 24; compare F 17) and discovers a chorus of mirror-image Astaires. For a few seconds it is not clear whether the chorus is an independent body of dancers or simply his own image multiplied by mirrors. When he leans back in amazement at the sight, they lean away in the same manner (F 25). Then he does a quick tap barrage and they mirror him precisely. Very soon the mirror illusion is broken, however. The men in the chorus do a rapid, hard-driving tap step while Astaire watches, and, with an abrupt beckoning gesture, they invite him into their midst (F 26).[5] This propels the orchestra into a greatly speeded-up repeat of the melody which emphasizes a brash, onrushing quality.

The choreography in this last section is remarkable for its clarity. The chorus is not mere decoration; it has an identity of its own and makes a definite contribution as it embellishes and punctuates the dancing of the soloist, without, however, cluttering the stage picture. Astaire joins the chorus for a unison tap phrase and then for a strut up and back on the regular rhythms of the release, during which the chorus divides into alternating figures (F 27); every other

[5] In the "Bojangles" number in *Swing Time,* where Astaire dances with three shadows of himself (7 F 7–9), he and the shadows stay synchronized for a long time so that the audience does not know whether they are his actual shadows or not (an effect that tends to distract one's attention from the choreography). In "Puttin' On the Ritz" that question is resolved immediately.

F16 F17 F18 F19

F20 F21 F22 F23

F24 F25 F26 F27

Astaire in the chorus is identical—that is, two repeated versions of Astaire-as-chorus-member were filmed and duplicated, and then these two versions were interleaved.

After some zany high-stepping stomping (F 28), a goofy shuffle with arms at the sides (F 29), and a considerable amount of violent cane thumping, all the Astaires kneel, slap the floor with their canes, and then slam them down broadside (F 30). All rise and (after a cut to a wider shot) wave their hands over the canes as if attempting to mesmerize them. Then, at the very end of the strain (not at the point of rhythmic resolution, as in the solo dance), all the canes fly up to the waiting hands (F 31).

After Astaire leads the chorus in some fast tap work featuring steps that jut out to the side, the number comes to an end: he propels himself toward the camera in a series of tapping turns while the chorus high-steps in place with their heads down (F 32), marking the soloist's progression by thrusting their arms sharply upward several times (F 33). To finish, all kneel, heads down (F 34), and on the last note, as the curtain descends swiftly, they raise their heads to face the audience (F 35), repeating the confrontational effect established at the beginning of the number.

G
I'LL SEE YOU IN C-U-B-A
(2′45″)

At his new nightclub, the Hole in the Wall, Crosby groans through a Berlin tune from 1920, and then Olga San Juan joins him, adding a snappy counterpoint (G 1). Caulfield, now in love with Crosby, proposes to him to the accompaniment of some syrupy background music. Though he is in love with her, Crosby feels he is not stable enough for her and refuses her proposal (G 2). Astaire is waiting outside and tries to catch the disappointed Caulfield on the rebound, without success (G 3).

H
A COUPLE OF SONG AND DANCE MEN
(4′55″)

A year later, Crosby happens to visit Astaire at a rehearsal. They reminisce unsentimentally and somewhat caustically about an act they used to do in the old days. On a mutual dare, they run through it once again.

This number is an obvious effort to recycle the successful "I'll Capture Your Heart" duet of *Holiday Inn,* in which Astaire and Crosby playfully, but with a lightly acid touch, mimic, mock, and one-up each other (15 A). Berlin's pleasant song, written specifically for *Blue Skies,* has its charms, and the number has a few promising moments. But it soon begins to sag and finally degenerates into a series of "impressions" whose humor is of the thigh-slapping variety.

During the singing the two performers declare and demonstrate their different talents—Crosby sings, Astaire dances (H 1). The song seems to be pitched to accommodate Crosby's baritone, but Astaire handles his low notes quite beautifully (particularly in the line that ends "a pretty girl"). In a couple of places, however, he declaims his lines rather than singing them, seeming overly eager to please.

The dance that follows is built on one joke: Crosby's ineptness as a dancer. He jumps in desperately on some of the steps at the beginning (H 2) but soon gets stuck in the wrong phrase (H 3). Later Astaire tries to help him out—for example, by turning him in a parody of a ballet promenade (H 4). Finally, Crosby essentially gives up, faking dance steps while Astaire frolics (H 5). There is nothing inherently very funny—or even interesting—in demonstrating that Fred Astaire is a better dancer than Bing Crosby. There is comedy inherent in having one dancer

F28 F29 F30 F31

F32 F33 F34 F35

G1 G2 G3 H1

calculatedly out of coordination with the other, but Crosby would have to work harder, and the dance would have to be far more intricately choreographed, for that to happen. As it is, the dance mostly seems a commentary on Crosby's famous laziness about rehearsals.

For the last half of the number, Crosby and Astaire do their "impressions," notable neither for punch nor originality. Astaire scoots across the floor as a young man out to visit his best girl (H6) and staggers as a drunk leaving a bar (H7), while Crosby does objectionable imitations of a fussy woman and a shuffling porter (H8). To conclude, the song-and-dance men demonstrate a few specialized handshakes, including that of a milkman (H9).[6]

I

YOU KEEP COMING BACK LIKE A SONG

(1′54″)

When Caulfield sees Crosby at the rehearsal, old longings are revived in both of them. Astaire proposes once again, and again she refuses. To clear the air, he takes her to Crosby's current nightclub, the Song Book, where Crosby is onstage crooning a song Berlin wrote for the film, after which Crosby and Caulfield fall wordlessly into a clinch. Astaire is left sardonically holding a useless engagement ring, and disappears for most of the remainder of the film.

[6] Crosby did a similar hand-shaking routine (including the thumb-milking bit) with Bob Hope in vaudeville in 1932, the first time the pair had worked together.

J

BLUE SKIES

(2′28″)

Berlin's 1926 ballad is warbled by Crosby to Caulfield on their honeymoon as he promises eternal steadiness and stability.

K

NIGHTCLUB MONTAGE

(1′20″)

Crosby buys and sells three nightclubs, each of which is shown while he croons a fragment of an appropriate Berlin tune off-screen: "The Little Things in Life" (1930), "Not for All the Rice in China" (1933), and "Russian Lullaby" (1927). Crosby sings all three excerpts the same way and at the same lethargic tempo, so that they are scarcely distinguishable one from another, or, for that matter, from the two preceding ballads.

L

EVERYBODY STEP

(2′50″)

Things get very slightly livelier as Crosby sings a 1921 Berlin song onstage at his latest nightclub success, the Top Hat (L1). The number includes a brief and inconsequential dance for chorus, choreographed by Hermes Pan.[7]

M

HOW DEEP IS THE OCEAN?

(1′35″)

When Crosby sells the Top Hat without consulting her, Caulfield scoops up their new baby and stomps out on him in a scene that is singularly unconvincing (M1). They are divorced.

Years later, in Crosby's new Chicago nightclub, the Cracker Barrel, Billy De Wolfe performs an excruciating six-and-a-half minute travesty monologue, "Mrs. Mergatroyd" (M2).

[7] Near the beginning of the number Crosby directs sections of the chorus in separate movement fragments. This idea is not developed here, but Pan resurrected it in the opening number of the "An Evening with Fred Astaire" television special of 1958. There Astaire teaches separate dance ideas to different sections of the chorus, and the pieces are then imaginatively developed into a full-fledged dance number.

H2 H3 H4 H5

H6 H7 H8 H9

L1 M1 M2 N1

Then Olga San Juan comes by to tell Crosby that Caulfield (and the child) are in town, and Crosby resolves to go see them. A female quartet in the club is singing Berlin's beautiful "How Deep Is the Ocean?" (1932) at a lilting tempo, and Crosby sings a musing overlay. Though brief, it's his best musical moment in the film.

N
(RUNNING AROUND IN CIRCLES) GETTING NOWHERE
(1′ 53″)

When Crosby goes to see Caulfield, he finds that she is not at home, but the maid shows him to his child, who proves to be one of those super-cute Hollywood creations guaranteed to double the size of the W. C. Fields fan club with every programmed twinkle. Charmed, Crosby sings her a new Berlin song and learns from her that Caulfield is engaged to marry Astaire (N 1).

O
HEAT WAVE
(7′ 3″)

The big production number in the film, set to a 1933 Berlin song, actually advances the plot quite directly—very unusual in a production number—but it does so in an odd and unconvincing way. Caulfield, still longing for Crosby, has broken off her engagement to Astaire and is now about to resign from the show they are in, leaving Astaire, one presumes, forever. In bitterness, he gets so drunk he cannot even walk straight (O 1). To her dismay, he staggers out onstage for the big "Heat Wave" number, which concludes with a dangerous solo for him atop a high bridge. He loses his footing, falls off the bridge, and is injured, never to dance again. Strangely, there is no effort on Astaire's part to suggest drunkenness during the number until just before his fall. Because there are no lapses or uncertainties, no tension is built about his condition. Astaire had previously done two excellent drunk dances—one about a drunk out of control in *Holiday Inn* (15 G), the other about a drunk who still retained full control in *The Sky's the Limit* (17 F). For some reason he carried over none of these remarkable insights to the "Heat Wave" number. Nor are reaction shots of Caulfield used to create tension, even though a major point is the traumatic effect of the accident on her. The only time she is clearly shown is just as he is about to fall (O 13); this seems a rare case in which Astaire's aversion to reaction shots went too far.

The dance is also odd in its inconsistent structure. The number begins, and to a degree ends, with an interesting duet of steamy, joyless desire, but patched in the middle is an incongruously bright solo for Astaire.

As the number opens, Astaire is slumped somberly in some tropical Latin marketplace (O 2). San Juan begins to sing a bowdlerized version of the "Heat Wave" song ("making her seat wave" becomes "making her feet wave"), and Astaire is wrenched from his distant thoughts by the sound of her voice. He begins to move toward her like a cat creeping up on its prey (O 3).

When her song ends, she leads him out onto the floor, and they perform a brief duet that is remarkable for its unvarnished aura of sexual desire (O 4, 5). It is an unsmiling dance of pure animal attraction, unleavened by love, tenderness, or sentiment, and is, in that respect, unique in Astaire's films. Also remarkable is the use of the music. Besides the basic melody, with its shifts and contrasts, there is a prominent, repetitive mambo drumbeat that speeds up during the duet, and this alone provides the music for most of the duet. The dancers move only on the drumbeats, but the dance is kept from becoming predictable by the ingenious parceling out of the

O 1 O 2 O 3 O 4
O 5 O 6 O 7 O 8

beat between the two soloists and the background chorus.

Suddenly Astaire spins San Juan off to the side, and the chorus surrounds him, imploring him to dance for them. He obliges with a smile: as the music becomes distinctly north-of-the-border, he dances a jazzy solo that seems completely out of keeping with the mood established in the preceding duet. This 1′ 15″ solo is shown all in one take, one of the few cases of an Astaire single-shot dance after 1941. The bouncy, boogie-like music for it was written by Astaire himself.

In its own terms, the solo is quite successful. It begins with a space-clearing jump (O 6) and is notable for its loose-legged shuffles (O 7), quick leg-over-leg vaults (O 8), and playful shifts of tempo. There is perhaps some evidence in this solo to suggest the validity of Astaire's fear at the time that his inventiveness was drying up, for the solo includes several steps lifted from dances in an earlier film, *You'll Never Get Rich*. Specifically, a space-stabbing step (O 9) had been used prominently in the "Wedding Cake Walk" (compare 14 H 9; also 15 M 8) and the loose-legged shuffles (O 7), the quick hops to the side (O 10), and the rearward tap dabs (O 11) had been used in the opening rehearsal duet with Rita Hayworth (compare 14 A 1, 3, 5). Now, it may seem absurd to suggest that some dozen or sixteen seconds of repetition—of self-plagiarism—out of the several hours of choreography Astaire had arranged by 1946 could be taken by anyone as a sign of declining power, but Astaire was supremely sensitive about the issue of repeating himself. Fortunately, he soon forgave himself and came back to create more masterpieces.

When the mood-shattering solo is over, San Juan reappears, and Astaire, no longer smiling, is enticed up some stairs to the bridge, where, suddenly overcome by dizziness, he does his final, ill-fated solo while Caulfield watches horrified from the wings (O 12–14). The show's imperturbable conductor finishes out the music despite the catastrophe on stage.

P
WARTIME MEDLEY
(1′ 35″)

After the fall, Caulfield, in despair at being the cause of Astaire's accident, vanishes for years. Astaire stops drinking, stops dancing, and takes up radio. Crosby becomes a wandering entertainer and, after World War II breaks out, serenades bond rallies and the troops with "Any Bonds Today?" (1941), "This Is the Army, Mister Jones" (1942), and, finally, "White Christmas" (1942), the sole carry-over from the previous Berlin-Crosby-Astaire collaboration, *Holiday Inn* (P 1).

Q
YOU KEEP COMING BACK LIKE A SONG / BLUE SKIES
(REPRISE) (1′ 34″)

Crosby joins Astaire on a postwar radio show, and as he warbles "You Keep Coming Back like a Song," Caulfield shows up singing "Blue Skies" (Q 1). Her sudden appearance here is cleverly planned for in the script, but in a manner so obscure as to be incomprehensible on first viewing. At the beginning of the film Astaire had mentioned that he hoped she would be listening. Miraculously, she had been. (The script calls for a shot at the beginning of the film showing Caulfield in a flower shop listening to the radio broadcast, but this was not included in the finished film.) She returns now because time has healed old wounds—or perhaps, as one critic has suggested, because Crosby is now "too old to do much of anything except stay in one place." She falls into his arms as Astaire smiles benevolently.

O 9 · O 10 · O 11 · O 12 · O 13 · O 14 · P 1 · Q 1

21.

Easter Parade

1948

As originally planned, *Easter Parade* was to be a vehicle for Gene Kelly and Judy Garland, who had been successfully teamed in two previous MGM films, most recently *The Pirate*. After the new film had started production, however, Kelly broke his ankle playing a friendly game of—depending on the source—volleyball, softball, or touch football and was unable to continue.

With Kelly's enthusiastic approval, producer Arthur Freed asked Fred Astaire if he would be interested in stepping in. Astaire had retired from the movies in 1946 but was growing restive in his self-induced leisure, during which he was busily racing horses and investing enormous amounts of money and energy in his fledgling dancing-school business. He welcomed the opportunity to get back in pictures—"for a rest." Besides, his retirement had been caused in part by his feeling that he was running out of new ideas for dances, but the creative juices had soon returned and he was beginning to feel the "urge and inspiration to go back to work." And so, after clearing things personally with Kelly, he signed to do the film.

Among the appeals of the project to Astaire was the opportunity to work with Judy Garland. Freed had been wanting to pair them at least since 1943, and *Easter Parade* proved to be a great critical and financial success—Astaire's top moneymaker at MGM, in fact (see Tables 2 and 3). None of Freed's subsequent efforts to team them again worked out, because of Garland's mental and physical illnesses, which were to end her MGM film career in 1950 and ultimately to lead to her death in 1969 at the age of forty-seven. The director originally assigned to the film was Vincente Minnelli, Garland's husband, but when her psychiatrist recommended that they not work together, Charles Walters took over, in his first major directorial assignment.

Except for a sappy plot development toward the end, when Garland petulantly and implausibly walks out (temporarily) on Astaire, *Easter Parade* retains considerable appeal. Garland and Astaire have a fine rapport as actors, and there is a relaxed, spontaneous richness to most of their scenes together—the comedy always has an edge of arresting seriousness, and the serious moments never stray too far from leavening comedy.

Though *Easter Parade* is not a cornucopia of choreographic invention, at least two of the musical numbers are outstanding: a screwball drum solo for Astaire and a clownish duet with Garland to "A Couple of Swells" that was a new departure for Astaire. There is also a sharply drawn parody of a romantic duet. Among the weaker dances are a couple of oddly inconsequential romantic duets for Astaire and Ann Miller, his other dancing partner in the film.

THE SCRIPT

Because of the unusual circumstances that brought about Astaire's participation in the film, *Easter Parade* might be considered less an Astaire film than a Gene Kelly film starring Fred Astaire: the script was completed by the time Astaire arrived on the set and the placement and basic character of the numbers had been set.

Nonetheless, the film betrays no evidence of its origins and seems ideally suited to Astaire. In particular, it handles the differences in age between Astaire and Garland (he was forty-eight when the film was shot, she twenty-five) with agility.[1] The story, set in 1911 and 1912, essentially follows the Pygmalion theme. Astaire, a successful New York dancer, has been jilted, both professionally and romantically, by his dancing partner. In a pique, he randomly plucks a young cabaret performer (Garland) out of a chorus line and vows to turn her into his costar. He is successful in this, and in the process she falls in love with him. He retains a lingering attraction to his glamorous former partner but eventually comes to realize that he is in love with his talented, if relatively plain, protégée.

The chief difference between the script on hand when

[1] The success of the pairing surprised the final scriptwriter, Sidney Sheldon, who had argued against signing Astaire on the grounds that no audience "is going to root for a young girl like Judy to wind up in bed with a guy who is a grandfather."

Judy Garland singing "It Only Happens When I Dance with You"

Astaire joined production and the final picture is that his character ended up somewhat mellowed and humanized. Originally he was brusque, even cruel, with his young protégée. Though the change was made partly in response to Astaire's suggestions, and to his screen persona, the harshness in the character had troubled Walters even before Astaire signed on, and it was in the process of being changed anyway.[2]

JUDY GARLAND

Easter Parade is one of two Astaire films in which his female partner is a singer (*Royal Wedding* is the other). Garland, of course, was also a skilled comedienne and generally could handle serious acting scenes convincingly as well. Furthermore, both in her singing and her acting, she was able to convey an innocence and a vulnerability that were ideal for her role.

As a dancer she was rather gawky and tight and would have looked foolish trying to be romantically voluptuous; in fact, Astaire exploits her limitations to produce the parodic romantic duet in the film. At the same time, Garland was an experienced and energetic show dancer with a highly sophisticated sensitivity to music. According to Astaire, she was remarkably quick to pick up the dance routines. But her greatest dance talent was in comic mime or mimicry, where, with impishly expressive face, crisply articulate gestures, and impeccable timing, she was unsurpassed—as she proves in "A Couple of Swells."

Oddly, the uncomfortable moments in *Easter Parade* come when Garland sings, not when she dances or acts. Perhaps in an effort to get away from the *Wizard of Oz* image of childlike innocence, this most naturally gifted of singers was developing a strident tone with a wide, uncertain vibrato. Fortunately, she could turn this quality off at will and did so in the first part of the film, as well as during her singing duets with Astaire, to allow their voices to blend. But by the end of the film Garland's voice has progressed from angelically pure to grating and coarse.

There is an element of autobiography in Garland's role in *Easter Parade*. However talented she was as a performer, she often felt herself to be stunted and awkward, no match for the tall, voluptuous glamour girls she was surrounded by,

[2] The original script seemed to draw elements of characterization from the successful Kelly-Garland film of 1942, *For Me and My Gal* (Kelly's first film), in which Kelly played something of a heel—a characterization that in turn partly derives from Kelly's previous portrayal on Broadway of the title character in *Pal Joey*.

and she was insecure in her relations with men.[3] Although symptoms of her illness were evident at the time the film was made—she was often late or absent from the set, and her weight and physical appearance fluctuate somewhat from scene to scene—the film was a happy experience for her, and things generally went smoothly. In particular, her working relationship with Astaire, whom she idolized, was congenial and productive.

THE MUSIC

As with *Blue Skies,* the score for *Easter Parade* was a mixture of old and new Irving Berlin songs. Berlin was paid $600,000 for the use of his name, for the title of the picture, for his services as story consultant, and for the sixteen songs (nine old, seven new). The film culminates in a performance of the title song, which had been written in 1917 under the title "Smile and Show Your Dimple" but became a hit only in 1933, when Berlin wisely and adroitly changed the lyric. As Berlin put it, "A song is like a marriage. It takes a perfect blending of the two mates, the music and the words, to make a perfect match. In the case of 'Easter Parade,' it took a divorce and a second marriage to bring out the happiest of unions."

The musical scoring was under the direction of Johnny Green and Roger Edens, who received Academy Awards for their efforts. There are some apt musical arrangements in the film—especially for "A Couple of Swells"—but there are unpleasant moments as well, particularly in the overblown "Steppin' Out with My Baby" and in some of the sentimental and mawkish background music in the last part of the film.

THE CHOREOGRAPHY

Since the numbers had all been blocked out before Astaire joined the production, he was concerned that they might not suit him. Though Kelly assured him that they could easily be changed and told him "not to worry," Astaire says that considerable revision was necessary to suit him. Kelly recalls that, though most of the ideas for the numbers were already set, Astaire superimposed his own "style" on them—by which Kelly apparently means that Astaire created the steps:

[3] As Walters, who was close to Garland for years, puts it, "You know what L. B. Mayer used to call her when she first started [at MGM]? 'My little hunchback' that's what! Imagine growing up on the back-lot in the company of Lana Turner, Elizabeth Taylor, Deanna Durbin—all of whom were getting propositioned by all and sundry. All Judy had was Mickey Rooney goosing her!"

With Ann Miller, dancing to "It Only Happens When I Dance with You"

"I think pretty much most everything was what it was but *not* the actual steps themselves. There he recharged and redid."

None of the numbers seem out of keeping with Astaire's style—from the solo that develops out of a jaunty stroll, to the solicitous romantic duets, to the lively rehearsal-audition duets, to the onstage solo that seems a pale "Puttin' On the Ritz." Only the galumphing "A Couple of Swells" duet looks at all Kelly-inspired, and this is carried out with such meticulous attention to mime and sly, throwaway humor that it seems pure Astaire at base.

Dance director for the film was Robert Alton, who had previously collaborated with Astaire on *You'll Never Get Rich* and *Ziegfeld Follies.* Alton had been working on the choreography with Gene Kelly for several weeks before Astaire joined rehearsals.

THE NUMBERS

A
HAPPY EASTER / DRUM CRAZY
(6′ 30″)

Easter Parade has the happiest possible opening. Fred Astaire is discovered jauntily strolling down a New York avenue on a sunny spring day—the perfect way to reintroduce him to the movie audience (A 1).

Walters' camera follows along congenially as Astaire sings a new, rather aggressively cheerful Berlin ditty, "Happy Easter." The song continues as he purchases a white hat and other presents for the woman in his life. Passing a toy shop, accompanied now by a retinue of present bearers, he spies a large toy rabbit in the window that catches his fancy.

Entering the shop, he is dismayed to discover that the rabbit is in the clutches of an unpleasant little boy (A 2). Undaunted, Astaire launches into a spirited routine, "Drum Crazy," in which he simultaneously sings, dances, and plays an arsenal of percussion instruments, to distract the boy long enough to snatch the rabbit away from him. One of the endearing charms of the number is the delightfully brutal way Astaire treats the child. He pilots the boy firmly around the room, mesmerizes him with a drum-tap dance, engulfs him in drums, spirits the rabbit away, and then gloats as he bolts out the door with his prize. It is a number that W. C. Fields would have found thoroughly heart-warming.[4]

The boy apparently has a limited attention span and, to keep his interest from flagging even momentarily, Astaire explodes one circus trick after another. He spiritedly sings the chorus while he raps at various drums and cymbals (A 3), and the dance begins with various tap-drum encounters, which soon lead to an unlikely sequence in which Astaire makes noise three different ways: by tapping with his feet, by bouncing drumsticks off the floor with his hand, and by banging on a bass drum with his head, all carried out, of course, with remarkable rhythmic intricacy (A 4).

[4] This is the only Astaire number that substantially uses a child. Gene Kelly, by contrast, often used children.

He then tests out a series of drums of different sizes while the boy watches intently (A 5), hangs one of them around the boy's neck, leads him in a parade out to the center of the floor (A 6), frolics around the spellbound child, firmly sits him down, goofily beats out a snappy rhythm on his own head (A 7), and then ceremoniously surrounds the boy with drums. Finally, in one continuous, amazingly efficient sequence, Astaire pays for the rabbit, takes up his hat and cane, snatches the rabbit from the boy (A 8), commits one final triumphal tap-drum barrage—adding the cane to his arsenal of implements (A 9, 10)—mockingly salutes the unfortunate child (A 11), and catapults out the door.

The number, dazzling in its inventiveness, is probably the finest of Astaire's filmed drum dances (the others: 9 J, 28 A; also 18 O). He seems to animate the entire toyshop as he makes a dance out of drawing music from snare drums, tomtoms, bells, wood blocks, toy drums, bass drums, cymbals, a xylophone, the floor, and his own head. Astonishingly, Astaire insisted on having all the drum sounds prerecorded along with the music, which meant that he had to synchronize all his slams and raps and bangs precisely with the playback.

A1 A2 A3 A4
A5 A6 A7 A8
A9 A10 A11 B1

B

IT ONLY HAPPENS WHEN I DANCE WITH YOU

(2′27″)

Astaire brings the rabbit and the other gifts to his dancing partner (Ann Miller), who promptly announces that she wants to leave the act. Unwilling to accept this, Astaire tries to seduce her with a song and a dance.

Though he insists in the song that things happen only when they dance together, the dance is apparently designed to show that those things are no longer happening, at least not to her. Astaire warms up the reluctant Miller with the song, pilots her for a few turns around the living room, and then finally takes her in his arms and kisses her. But at the end her desire to leave him has not altered.

The dramatic demands on Miller in this brief number are fairly considerable, and for the most part they defeat her. Presumably she is supposed to be torn between her remembered affection for Astaire and her new determination to leave him to pursue her own career. Some of this comes across in her pained and distant expressions, but mostly her reactions to Astaire's importunings seem self-conscious and artificial.

In the dance, Astaire repeatedly tries to break through Miller's resistance. He cuddles up to her while singing the song, but she pulls away. He closes in once more and they almost melt into a kiss (B1), but again she flees. He is able to pull her back into his arms and they do some ballroom turns with hands touching overhead (B2)—a pose that is something of a signature for their relationship and will be parodied later (see D2, E5, 6; see also 16 M5, 18 G15). There is also some of his characteristic partnering in which he holds his left arm back, tempting her to close the pose by pulling her body closer to his (B3), a slyly erotic idea most fully developed in 15 I9 and in 10 E12–13 (see also 5 E8, 18 G5). Next he urges her to join him on the outdoor terrace, where he can really show her his stuff, but she, presumably sensing what he intends, signals that it is too cold out there and draws back (B4). He returns and partners her in some quick spins across the living-room carpet and then envelops her in his arms (B5) and bends her backward into a kiss (B6), which she seems to enjoy (B7).

The significance of the kiss is ambiguous. It might be seen as a sign that Astaire has been successful in his efforts with Miller; but immediately afterward she remains determined to leave him, so his success is momentary at best. Or the kiss might be taken as an admission of failure: since the dance has not broken through Miller's reticence, Astaire reverts, in desperation, to a kiss. Thus the dance, however ingenious in concept, is puzzling and unsatisfying in execution. Cyd Charisse, who was originally intended to play Miller's part but was injured, might have been able to do more with the dance, but what it really calls for is the dance-acting savvy of the Ginger Rogers of the 1930s.[5]

C

I WANT TO GO BACK TO MICHIGAN

(2′23″)

Since Miller still insists she will leave him, Astaire turns frosty and walks out. The script written for Kelly includes a long scene at this point in which he petulantly points out that he had created her and prophesies that she'll soon return to him on her knees. When Astaire ex-

[5] Some of Miller's inflexibility in her duets with Astaire may have been due to the back problems she was having during shooting, requiring her mid-torso to be heavily taped. Some of Astaire's lack of response to Miller as a dancer may have derived from his sensitivity to her imposing size and height. (In both of their duets she wears flat slippers to avoid towering over him.)

B2 B3 B4 B5
B6 B7 C1 C2
C3 D1 D2 D3

plained that such rudeness was not in his repertory, the script was mellowed.

After a drink at the bar of a nearby club, Astaire bitterly boasts to his crony Peter Lawford and to the bartender that he can easily train any chorus girl to replace Miller (C 1). He proceeds to select one at random from the array at hand, checks her over for essential attributes (C 2), and tells her to be at rehearsal the next morning. The one he happens to pick is Judy Garland.

After she realizes who he is, Garland decides to accept the brusque and unexpected offer. First, however, she dons a milkmaid's apron and goes on stage to sing a sweet 1914 song about how she'd like to be back on the farm in Michigan (rhymes with "wish again"). Her voice here has an attractive bell-like clarity and directness (C 3).[6]

D

BEAUTIFUL FACES

(REHEARSAL) (1′ 21″)

The next day happens to be Easter Sunday. It's an unlikely time for a dance rehearsal, but that is of little concern to the preoccupied professional Astaire plays in this film. Garland arrives and proceeds to stumble through the rehearsal.

This scene is the best in the film. There is a wonderfully engaging improvisational (and perhaps autobiographical) air to it as Garland struggles awkwardly to keep up with the master —explaining with embarrassment that she has difficulty remembering which is her left foot, following his every move with a mixture of desperate concentration and intense bewilderment. (Much of the dialogue—a whole episode about a garter, for example—does not appear in the script and may have been developed on the set by the actors and director.)

At the beginning of the rehearsal she does everything wrong—twisting right when she should twist left, falling so badly out of step that she must duck to get out of Astaire's way (D 1). After a while things improve somewhat—at least it begins to look as if the two are doing the same dance. He is trying to make her over in the image of his former dancing partner, and there is a quotation of the arm-over-head partnering position used in the earlier Astaire-Miller duet (D 2; compare B 2). At the end, Astaire is for once explicit about the eroticism that permeates his romantic duets: he forcefully but tenderly bends Garland over backward (D 3), and when he abruptly breaks for lunch she lingers in the pose, dazzled and starry-eyed (D 4).

E

BEAUTIFUL FACES

(PERFORMANCE) (1′ 14″)

The little dance Astaire and Garland do as they leave the rehearsal building demonstrates their relationship with amazing precision and economy. Unthinkingly, he charges out through the door ahead of her and proceeds down the street, while she tags along timidly. Suddenly he remembers his manners and, tersely and without apology, slows to her pace and adjusts his position so that he is walking on the outside down the sidewalk. They come across Miller in the Easter parade, wearing the hat Astaire had bought for her earlier and preening for photographers (E 1). Astaire vows to Garland that a year later she will be the one attracting all the attention. Later, he wonders if she has enough appeal to catch the eye of men walking down the street; accepting the challenge, she makes grotesque faces, which do indeed cause men to turn in wonder—a funny, but also rather sad, commentary on the Garland persona (E 2).

Billed as "Juanita and Hewes," the pair perform a ballroom duet in a vaudeville show. The number is a perfect opportunity for Astaire to satirize his own romantic duets, sensually swirling the distinctly nonvoluptuous Garland around the stage. He wafts her in an extravagant spiral around him, for example (E 3), only to become strangled when she neglects to disengage her handhold on him (E 4), a neat parody of one of his own favorite partnering maneuvers (see pp. 158–59). Or a lilting side-by-side pattern goes awry when they begin to fall out of synchronization—Astaire lands as Garland takes off. Or, when he sends her fluttering across the floor, she becomes mesmerized by her own momentum and continues to twirl as he struggles to catch her on the fly.

The dance is also an opportunity for Astaire to get back at all those partners who have insisted on wearing gowns that look glamorous when immobile but prove to be choreographic nightmares when put into action. The most spectacular instance was Ginger Rogers' costume in "Cheek to Cheek" in *Top Hat* (5 E), which came apart during the dance and deco-

[6] This song is sometimes cut when the film is shown on television.

D 4 E 1 E 2 E 3

E 4 E 5 E 6 E 7

rated the air, the set, and Astaire's sweaty face with feathers. Garland's dress, which resembles the outfit Miller wore earlier in the film (see B1–7), visibly sheds throughout the dance. At one point, still having problems telling left from right, she raises the wrong arm in the romantic arm-over-head position of the earlier Astaire-Miller duet and smothers Astaire's face in feathers (E5, corrected finally in E6; compare B2 and D2).

The ending is a delicate joke: the dance concludes with what appears to be a controlled, if somewhat inelegant, partnered fall for Garland; however, at the last instant she lurches farther over onto the floor, jolting Astaire over a notch (E7).

It is conceivable (but unlikely) that there is intentional parody in the orchestration. Berlin's lovely, undeservedly obscure 1920 tune, so fresh and vibrant when played on a piano in the earlier rehearsal duet, is here given the full, blowzy MGM treatment—labored, saccharine, and pretentious.

F
A FELLA WITH AN UMBRELLA
(2′6″)

When Lawford tries to arrange a reconciliation between Astaire and Miller, Astaire is clearly willing but the haughty Miller will have none of it. (A weakness of the *Easter Parade* script is the shallowness of Miller's role. She is cast unsympathetically as a Hollywood heavy—scheming, vindictive, and self-centered—and thus does not seem a credible rival to Garland for Astaire's affections, particularly since Astaire is unable to convey the impression that she remains romantically attractive to him.) In the meantime, Lawford (to whom Miller is attracted, apparently because of his wealth) runs into Garland in a rainstorm and, sheltering her under an umbrella purchased from a passing peddler, begins to fall in love with her while enthusiastically serenading her with a relevant new Berlin song (F1).

G
REHEARSAL/PERFORMANCE/AUDITION MEDLEY
(5′36″)

Because of a chance remark of Miller's, Astaire now realizes he has made a mistake in trying to refashion Garland in the image of his former partner. When he explains this to Garland at a rehearsal at his apartment, she agrees—even going so far as to show him how silly she looks in the kind of romantic dancing shapes he has unwisely been forcing her into (G1). Astaire now seeks instead to bring out Garland's natural talents and suddenly everything clicks. In succession they rehearse (G2), perform (G3–5), and then successfully audition for Florenz Ziegfeld (G6), to a group of reliable early Berlin songs: "I Love a Piano" (1915), "Snooky Ookums" (1912), "The Ragtime Violin" (1911), and "When the Midnight Choo-Choo Leaves for Alabam' " (1913).

In "Snooky Ookums" (G4) and in parts of "Alabam'," the singers harmonize—a rarity in an Astaire film. Garland reins in her tendency toward vocal stridency, and the resulting blend is enormously appealing. Of choreographic interest is Garland's stiff-kneed rompings in the "Ragtime Violin" sequence (G5). This may be another instance of Astaire's use of a partner's peculiar characteristics: Garland frequently found the only way she could keep her legs from wobbling in stagefright was to lock her knees. The longest portion of the number is the concluding "When the Midnight Choo-Choo Leaves for Alabam'." Appropriately enough, the dance in this routine is largely a set of vaudevillian traveling-steps, most of them suggesting the churning qualities of a locomotive in motion (G6).

H
SHAKING THE BLUES AWAY
(3′19″)

Ziegfeld wants to sign the act, but Astaire turns the job down because he and Garland would have to appear in a show in which Miller is headlined. Miller, he explains to the puzzled and pleased Garland, "doesn't belong in the same show with you"—something that apparently dawned on him while they were performing their last series of routines.

Lawford arrives to take Garland to dinner, where headwaiter Jules Munshin amuses them by tossing an invisible salad (H1). Finally, in serious conversation, Lawford tells Garland he is in love with her, and she sadly tells him she is in love with Astaire (H2).

Meanwhile, Miller's Ziegfeld show is a great success, and her solo number, set to a 1927 Berlin tune, is shown—a rather overeager tap routine of the pneumatic genre (H3). From the back of the house, Astaire watches wistfully.

F1 G1 G2 G3
G4 G5 G6 H1

I
IT ONLY HAPPENS WHEN I DANCE WITH YOU
(REPRISE) (1′46″)

Astaire and Garland have landed a featured spot in a Dillingham show. In celebration, she joins him at his apartment for a romantic dinner, but when she learns he also wants to do a little rehearsing she explodes, twice calling him "nothing but a pair of dancing shoes." To prove to him that he has never taken note of her as a person, she closes her eyes and challenges him to tell her their color. He kisses her (I1) and then quietly says, "They're brown."

That improves her mood. She wanders over to the piano, on which is perched the music for Miller's song, "It Only Happens When I Dance with You." As she gently sings it to Astaire, he listens thoughtfully—mentally comparing, one presumes, Garland and Miller (I2). At the end he says, "Why didn't you tell me I was in love with you?" Hug. Fade-out (I3).[7]

J
STEPPIN' OUT WITH MY BABY
(6′1″)

After weeks of rehearsal and out-of-town tryouts, the Dillingham show opens in New York on the evening before Easter, a year after Astaire and Garland met. A solo number for Garland, "Mr. Monotony," was shot to start the show sequence but was cut from the film (see 21 P). Astaire is shown in an elaborate onstage production number in which he partners three different women, is backed by a chorus, and dances for a while in slow motion.

Although Berlin wrote the song "Steppin' Out with My Baby" for the film with Gene Kelly in mind, it seems to be developed in the spirit of "Puttin' On the Ritz" (1929), which Astaire had made his own in *Blue Skies* two years earlier.[8] Unfortunately, neither the new song nor its dance number has much of the earlier song's brassy urgency or dazzling rhythmic wit.

By far the best part of the number is Astaire's snappy little dance on a staircase as he sings the song. It is filled with darts and dashes and unexpected pauses (J1).

As he finishes the song, Astaire descends into the main stage area—which looks rather like a brothel circa 1912—and steps out with three of the resident babies in three different styles: exaggerated saunter (Patricia Jackson—J2), sultry slink (Bobbie Priest—J3), and bouncy jitterbug (Dee Turnell—J4). The second baby had made off with Astaire's cane, but now it is sailed back to him, and he snatches it out of the air and slams out a brief solo, reminiscent in parts of "Puttin' On the Ritz," featuring cane coddling, cane twirling, cane rapping, windmilling turns, and an abrupt, unkempt leap (J5), while the chorus dancers (including one "Gwyn Verdon," according to cast lists) gesticulate semaphorically in the background.

Now Astaire pauses, and the camera shifts to photograph him in slow motion while the chorus continues to mark out the song's rhythms at regular speed. Little is made of this improbable counterpoint, however. Astaire executes his twists (J6) and leaps and cane manipulations in no apparent relation to the music, while the chorus continues mindlessly to thump out repetitive patterns behind him. The return to regular speed is covered by a reaction shot—of Garland glowing proudly in the wings (J7)—a remarkably tacky device by Astaire's standards. Then, the dance's momentum having been undercut, the camera returns to a regular-speed Astaire leading the chorus in a hasty, even desperate, finish.

K
A COUPLE OF SWELLS
(4′22″)

The film's highlight, unfortunately placed almost immediately after the lengthy, hard-sell antics of the previous number, is a delicately oafish duet for Garland and Astaire. Dressed as tramps, they ingratiatingly perambulate around the stage, cheerfully explaining in song that they are on their way up the avenue to tea at the Vanderbilts' and, owing to temporary embarrass-

[7] This scene is substantially different in the script, where there is no lovemaking and Astaire brusquely tears the sheet music away when his protégée presumes to sing his former partner's song. Though he mellows somewhat in the next scene, he remains preoccupied with his former partner. Uncertainties are resolved only in the final Easter-parade scene, when he comes up to his protégée and tells her he is crazy about her—something he didn't realize until he danced once again with his former partner. The line "Why didn't you tell me I was in love with you?" was therefore added on the set; it had also been used by Gene Kelly to Garland, in a throwaway fashion, in *For Me and My Gal*.

[8] The similarity is heightened by the fact that Mason Van Cleave, who had worked with Astaire on *Blue Skies*, was brought in at Astaire's request to arrange this song. At one point, in fact (under the cane-catching section), the music seems to quote "Puttin' On the Ritz."

H2 H3 I1 I2
I3 J1 J2 J3

ment, are walking rather than taking a more elegant form of conveyance.[9] Their pretensions are rendered ludicrous by their clothes, and the choreography reflects this comic contrast as it shifts from decorative refinement to unadorned galumph. At all times, however, the couple retain a cheery dignity that is utterly captivating and, particularly in the case of Garland, endearing.

The number was inspired by the success of the "Be a Clown" duet Garland had done with Gene Kelly in *The Pirate*. Numbers like that seem to have had special appeal to her, since they liberated her from any necessity to act glamorous or even feminine, and allowed her to hide her insecurities behind a comic mask.[10] At the same time, they gave free rein to her enormous talent for mime and mimicry. In the 1950s Garland included "A Couple of Swells" near the end of her highly successful stage show; then, still in her tramp costume, she would conclude the show by sitting on the floor near the footlights to sing "Over the Rainbow." (A videotape of a 1962 television performance of the number with David Wayne suggests Garland substantially retained the film choreography for her stage act but delivered it much more broadly.)

[9] Berlin originally wrote "Let's Take an Old-Fashioned Walk" for this slot, but producer Freed turned it down. The composer calmly turned out "A Couple of Swells" in an hour and then used the other song in a 1949 stage show, *Miss Liberty*. "Let's Take an Old-Fashioned Walk" registered for nine weeks on "Your Hit Parade" while none of the songs in *Easter Parade* made it there even once.

[10] A case in point: in 1968 she was apparently so terrified of meeting one of her biographers that, after repeatedly delaying the encounter, the only way she could face him was to make herself up as a clown.

The number was important to Astaire as well. He had never before done a clown number in a film, and it seems unlikely he would have attempted it had it not been more or less forced upon him by circumstance. Following the success of "A Couple of Swells," he included clown numbers in *Let's Dance* (extreme cowboy—24 D), *Royal Wedding* (extreme Brooklyn—25 F), and *The Band Wagon* (extreme child—27 K), and was originally scheduled to do one (extreme hillbilly) with Garland in *The Barkleys of Broadway*.

Most of the movement in "A Couple of Swells" is used to underline the words of the song. Many of the jokes in this witty number arise from the precise appropriateness of the word painting and from the flair and good humor with which it is carried out. There is also a built-in extended joke about traveling: portraying a pair of eager-to-please performers in a tiny vaudeville house, Astaire and Garland suggest the idea of traveling by miming their various modes of locomotion while the backdrop rolls along behind them.

As the number begins, Astaire strolls with cheery dignity onto the stage, retreats with equal dignity to the curtain's edge, and then enters again, this time with the impishly grinning Garland in tow (K 1).[11] After adjusting their finery—including blowing dust off their sleeves—the pair, in unison and with great composure, explain who they are (K 2): a couple of sports, on their way to the Vanderbilts' for tea. They discuss and mime several methods of getting to the engagement. In medium shot they are shown making their way up the avenue, but when the camera pulls back we see that they are simply walking in place while the backdrop moves (K 3).

[11] Astaire had great difficulty with his tramp costume and kept trying new versions, showing them to Garland, and asking hesitantly, "Is this too much?" Amused, Garland finally got her own outfit worked out and then, in full clownish costume and makeup, "knocked on the door of Astaire's trailer. He opened the door and looked out in disbelief. 'Is this too much?' she asked."

The joke with the backdrop continues as they spot a buxom lady traveling on it and stalk her (K4) until she vanishes into the wings. Shrugging, they hop out a little jig and then begin the second chorus, in which they brag that they are Wall Street bankers (the backdrop has obligingly paused so that an illustrative bank is behind them) who have unfortunately lost the key to the vault (K 5), and also great ladies' men who would divulge their exploits but "can't be cads" (K 6). In further considering how to get to the Vanderbilt party, they mime such forms of locomotion as sailing while the backdrop moves in the appropriate direction (K 7). Once, when they reverse direction, however, the backdrop neglects to change with them, and, with a broad gesture they urge it into synchrony.

The song ends with great gusto (K 8) and they launch into a brief dance in which, among other things, the very refined (K 9) is embellished with some down-home knee slaps (K 10). As in most Astaire duets, the lift is saved for near the end; here it is delivered with an appropriate blend of efficient oafishness and unruffled dignity (K 11). The ending, of course, is strictly in character. As they stride toward the wings singing a parting phrase of the song, the swells discover they don't have enough space left. They solve the problem by retreating part of the way across the stage and

J4 J5 J6 J7

K1 K2 K3 K4

repeating their exit stroll (K 12). Now it dawns on Garland that in their present formation she will exit first, giving Astaire the last chance to charm the audience, just as he had had the first. (She is in front of him because of the lift, which transported her from one side of him to the other, and whose insidious character is now revealed for all to see.) The pair do an Alphonse-Gaston routine at the exit until Garland physically forces Astaire offstage (K 13) and then, head cocked appealingly, shoots the audience an eager smile as she vanishes from sight (K 14).

L

THE GIRL ON THE MAGAZINE COVER

(4′ 8″)

To celebrate their success, Astaire for some reason takes Garland to a roof-garden show in which he knows Miller is appearing. The number they witness is a preposterous spectacle based on a glamorized and labored arrangement of a once-sprightly 1915 tune. Baritone Richard Beavers intones the song as he ambles among a bevy of cover-girl-type beauties, the last two of whom are identical twins (L 1). Then Miller bursts onto the stage, accompanied by a group of top-hatted men who occasionally cluster around her reclining body in formations that might be called neo-Iwo Jima (L 2). Eventually it ends in a massed configuration (L 3).

M

IT ONLY HAPPENS WHEN I DANCE WITH YOU

(REPRISE) (1′ 14″)

Miller has learned of her former partner's new success and, for reasons no more interesting than scriptwriter-willed spite and vindictiveness, decides to seduce Astaire away from Garland and thereby break up the new act. To Garland's dismay, Miller sidles up to Astaire's table and publicly entices him to dance with her to their old melody (M 1). He reluctantly agrees and steers her through a few turns on the dance floor as Garland watches uneasily (M 2). When Astaire returns to their table he finds that she has run out on him; Miller gloats.

The plot situation, however contrived, is an interesting psychological opportunity for Astaire as choreographer: presumably it should be suggested in the dance that he is still at least somewhat attracted to Miller, and then his sudden loss of Garland at its end would cause him fully to realize whom he really loves. However, he was unable to convey much genuine attraction to Miller even in their earlier duet, when he was supposed to be madly in love with her, and makes no effort in this duet to suggest there is any lingering affection. Although he and Miller do cling together for an instant (M 3), the dance is basically a pleasantly showy and asexual exhibition piece filled with lilting turns and bright leaps (M 4), ending in a distinctly unromantic pose (M 5). (Nor are there any reprises of moments from their earlier duet, though one sequence—when Astaire sends Miller spinning and then catches up with her somewhat awkwardly at the end of the phrase—seems oddly to reflect a similar moment in the parodic "Beautiful Faces" duet with Garland.) Garland's bolt thus seems to be completely unmotivated by what she is seeing.

N

BETTER LUCK NEXT TIME

(1′ 51″)

It does, however, give her an opportunity to mope her way back to the club where she had been first discovered by Astaire. She confesses her problems to her friend the sympathetic bartender and sings a weak new Berlin song with a forced stridency and a wide, harsh vibrato (N 1).

K5 K6 K7 K8
K9 K10 K11 K12
K13 K14 L1 L2

O
EASTER PARADE
(2′ 34″)

Astaire intercepts Garland as she drags herself back to her hotel room. He tries to explain, but the scriptwriters have convinced her that he has been making a fool of her all this time, and she tells him off. Violins swarm in the background, and then, just as Garland is starting to soften, a hotel detective, convinced Astaire is disturbing her peace, sends him off in mid-explanation.

The next morning—Easter Sunday—Lawford comes to Garland's room and tells her Astaire is auditioning a new partner. (As the nice-guy-who-doesn't-get-the-girl, a rather thankless role patented by George Murphy in what seems like hundreds of motion pictures in the 1930s and 1940s, Lawford is remarkably effective: somehow he manages to maintain a certain dignity and appeal as well as a sense of humor.) Lawford's news somehow changes everything, and Garland charges over to Astaire's apartment, gives him a bunny and a snazzy new top hat, sings about it, and sweeps him off with her to stroll in the Easter parade.

The staging of the familiar song is an amusing reversal: she serenades *him* about *his* Easter bonnet. Astaire good-naturedly plays along—accepting the tribute with mock delicacy (O 1) and once pretending to sit forgetfully on her knee (O 2). Unfortunately, Garland all but murders Berlin's charming tune with her brassy delivery.

This is easy to forget, however, as the pair exuberantly circumnavigate the room (O 3) and stride out the door to join the parade, already in progress. This attractive maneuvering is the closest thing in the film to a convincing love dance. An interesting comparison can be made with Astaire's first duet with Miller, which also took place in an apartment cluttered with furniture. There the setting seemed to constrict romantic opportunities; here it seems to embellish them. It's a nice touch, possibly intended.

As they stroll along happily in the parade, Garland proffers her left hand (on her second try) and Astaire places a ring on her finger (O 4). She finds, just as he had predicted a year earlier, that she is the principal attraction for roving photographers. Ann Miller is nowhere to be seen. Then the camera cuts back, and MGM obligingly shows us what the Easter parade on Fifth Avenue must have looked like in 1912, years before Irving Berlin had immortalized it in song (O 5).[12]

A NUMBER CUT FROM THE FILM

P
MR. MONOTONY

The successful Dillingham show was originally supposed to be represented by three numbers: a 3′ 10″ singing solo for Garland, Astaire's "Steppin' Out with My Baby," and the "A Couple of Swells" duet. In sheer black tights and a short dark jacket, Garland performed "Mr. Monotony," an amusing ditty written for the film that tells the tragic saga of a monotonic slide-trombone player.

The number was recorded and shot, but the footage was cut from the film, presumably because it seemed excessive to include three samples from the show in rapid succession. Berlin successfully recycled the song in his 1949 stage show *Miss Liberty.*

[12] This film and its final image made such an impact in 1948 that the English, who have been known to take tradition seriously, were driven to create their own version of the parade in Hyde Park.

L 3 M 1 M 2 M 3
M 4 M 5 N 1 O 1
O 2 O 3 O 4 O 5

22.

THE BARKLEYS OF BROADWAY

1949

When Fred Astaire and Ginger Rogers broke up their partnership in 1939, it was not with a sense of finality. As Astaire put it, "We expected to do another picture or so when the right time came along," and in the years that followed, he says, the two often discussed the possibility of working together again. However, ten years were to elapse before the reunion took place.

After the breakup Rogers' career at first had soared. Playing in many different kinds of films—none of them a full-fledged musical—she had been so successful that by 1945 her yearly salary of $292,159 made her the highest-paid Hollywood star and, by one calculation, the eighth-highest salary-earner in the country. From that peak, however, she suffered a considerable decline. After the preview of the extremely popular *Easter Parade* of 1948, in which Astaire was teamed with Judy Garland, Rogers sent a telegram to MGM producer Arthur Freed congratulating him in glowing terms on the film—a message that presumably could also be taken as a hint of her own availability.

So confident was Freed of the success of the *Easter Parade* pairing that, even before the film was released, he was moving to create another Garland-Astaire vehicle, *The Barkleys of Broadway*. By the time the new film was in rehearsal, however, it had become painfully clear that Garland, due to physical and mental illness, would be unable to work on it—a bitter disappointment to her.

The "right time" had arrived. Rogers was called at her ranch in Oregon, and two days later she joined rehearsals. Director Charles Walters described the reunion: "I remember she came in while Fred was rehearsing. . . . Up the aisle she came and Fred stopped dead. They embraced and I wept. After all Fred and Ginger had been my dancing idols since the mid-thirties."

This last teaming of Astaire and Rogers is often compared unfavorably with their earlier efforts. It is true that their relationship in *The Barkleys of Broadway* lacks some of the buoyant spontaneity of the best moments in their films of the 1930s. On the other hand, they are here playing an older, married couple, and youthful high-jinks would be out of place. Furthermore, they play the comedy scenes in the film with the intuitive depth and responsiveness of experienced troupers—there is none of the occasional strained awkwardness that characterizes some of their earlier films.

Choreographically the film compares well with those of the 1930s: there is plenty of wit and invention. And since the film is about the married condition—about being in love rather than falling in love—Astaire is given an unusual opportunity to explore in various ways (some of them satiric) the pleasures and pains of this state of existence. However, Rogers had gained some weight in the intervening decade and had lost some of the fluidity in her upper body that is so appealing in the earlier films. Even more important, she had become less skillful at incorporating her acting ideas into her dancing. Thus, for the most part, her dancing performances do not measure up to her best efforts of the 1930s. This is seen most clearly—and regrettably—in the "They Can't Take That Away from Me" duet. Choreographically it can stand comparison with any of Astaire's greatest duets; but Rogers, a bit stiff (and unflatteringly gowned), fails to respond convincingly in it, making the duet seem less choreographically significant than it actually is.

Among the other dance highlights of *The Barkleys of Broadway* are a duet in which Astaire intricately parodies not only matrimony but also his own romantic duets ("My One and Only Highland Fling"), a pair of bright duets ("Swing Trot" and "Bouncin' the Blues"), and an ingenious solo ("Shoes with Wings On") in which Astaire handles special effects masterfully and also brings his own powers of pantomime to new heights.

THE MUSIC

In one important area, *The Barkleys of Broadway* is inferior not only to the Astaire-Rogers vehicles of the 1930s but also to virtually every other film Astaire ever made—the music—and this despite the fact that the songs were composed by one of Hollywood's most successful songwriters, Harry Warren, who had served Astaire well in earlier films.

Perhaps Warren was simply past his peak (he was to pro-

With Ginger Rogers in "My One and Only Highland Fling"

vide a set of attractive songs for one later Astaire film, *The Belle of New York,* but almost all of these had actually been written earlier, in 1945). Or perhaps he felt intimidated by the ghost and legend of George Gershwin. Warren seems to have been uncomfortable because the "famous" (his word) Ira Gershwin was selected as the lyricist for the film. Furthermore, according to Warren, Freed and Gershwin became close friends while working on the film, and "Arthur became one of the elite at the Gershwin dinner table, which usually seated the intelligentsia of the theatre crowd"—a group that apparently did not include Warren. "This was fine except that it had a little backlash for me. Freed became so much a part of the Gershwin clan that he decided he had to have a great Gershwin song in *The Barkleys.* He picked 'They Can't Take That Away from Me.' I didn't take kindly to this." (The studio's front office was also less than ecstatic about Freed's insistence on using the song: there were legal complications, and it apparently cost $10,000 to obtain the rights.)

THE SCRIPT

The dispiriting effect of Warren's uncharacteristically uninspired score is all the more regrettable because the film's screenplay, by Betty Comden and Adolph Green, is a strong one—more carefully and plausibly developed and structured, and somewhat better paced, than the typical Astaire-Rogers vehicle of the 1930s. The two central characters are especially well drawn.

Astaire and Rogers play a married couple who are a great success in Broadway musicals. Offstage, however, they are combative—particularly over Astaire's insistence that Rogers would be nothing without his directorial guidance. Encouraged by a young writer-director, Rogers walks out on Astaire and tries to do a serious play. Rehearsals are a disaster until Astaire, disguising his voice as that of the young director, telephones Rogers and gives her acting instruction. Rogers then triumphs in the play; but when she eventually discovers Astaire's ruse, she goes back to him—and to musical comedy—to spend her life simply doing "fun set to music."

It is tempting to see the script as a gloss on the real-life Astaire-Rogers relationship—particularly now, when Ginger Rogers' most frequently shown films are the light musicals she did with Astaire rather than the somewhat heavier dramas she appeared in after the pair split up. However, in the context of the 1940s this conclusion isn't justified: Rogers' career in her more serious films flourished after she separated from Astaire. Furthermore, the script of *The Barkleys of Broadway* wasn't written for Rogers but, rather, for Judy Garland, and is essentially a remake of the *Easter Parade* script with its Pygmalion theme. The chief differences are that *The Barkleys of Broadway* develops a far more believable reason for Astaire's partner to walk out on him, and at the point where, midway in the film, *Easter Parade* simply becomes sappy, *The Barkleys of Broadway* achieves a somewhat serious tone. The script written for Garland needed only minimal alteration to accommodate Rogers; the chief changes are in the numbers. A couple of Garland specialties were dropped: "Natchez on the Mississip' " (probably inspired by *Easter Parade*'s "Alabam' "), and a galumphing hillbilly routine with Astaire designed, no doubt, to cash in on the successful hobo duet "A Couple of Swells" in *Easter Parade.* "Bouncin' the Blues" was added for Rogers. An unspecified romantic duet is called for in the Garland script, but it was apparently Rogers' idea to use "They Can't Take That Away from Me" for it.

Yet in some respects the film is self-reflective, in that Rogers is so much better in the comic scenes than in the ones that try to be dramatic. The first half of the film abounds with sequences that display her considerable powers as a comedienne—as she parries with Astaire (who meets her tooth for fang), deftly undercuts her unctuous understudy, and feigns illness to cover her own thoughtlessness. In the process she creates a real human being—tough, self-centered, insecure, yet utterly appealing—and develops scenes with Astaire that are among the very best in the Astaire-Rogers series. In the last half of the film, however, when the script calls for seriousness, Rogers is sometimes out of her depth. And worst of all is a scene (written originally for Garland) in which Rogers is called upon to do "high drama" by imitating Sarah Bernhardt onstage. This is the only episode in the entire Astaire-Rogers series that is truly embarrassing.

THE TEAM

The film did well at the box office (see Table 3), and Rogers' performance was very favorably received. Critics were pleased to see the old team together again, and responses to the questionnaires distributed at the film's previews show not only that the Astaire-Rogers combination still had great drawing power, but also that Rogers significantly outscored Astaire in audience appeal: 79 percent rated Rogers' performance excellent, as against 63 percent for Astaire (top scorer, however, was Oscar Levant, at 87 percent).

Yet *The Barkleys of Broadway* was the last Astaire-Rogers pairing, and the first and last musical Rogers ever made at MGM, despite the announcement at the time that "Ginger and Fred are set to make many more dancing pictures for MGM, and both are happy about it." The reasons for this are not clear; perhaps there were practical problems of scheduling or money. According to Hermes Pan, Astaire may have considered the film "a step backwards; an effort to recapture something that had happened before." Rogers may have had similar misgivings. Moreover, according to Walters, there was no "real rapport" offscreen: "They met on the set, did their thing, and parted—no animosity, very polite . . . but you'd think they had just met." Finally, Freed was preoccupied with the idea of making another Astaire-Garland film. Garland, who was twenty-seven in 1949, seemed to be the wave of the future, while Rogers, at thirty-eight, may have been seen as a remnant of the past; and although *The Barkleys* did well financially, *Easter Parade* had done even better. The effort to team Astaire and Garland again was to take up much of Freed's time in the next three years, but in the end it was to prove futile. Meanwhile, after the boost of *The Barkleys,* Rogers' career in Hollywood continued to slide; perhaps Freed saw this as an inevitability with which he did not wish to be associated.

"Shoes with Wings On"

THE CHOREOGRAPHY

Working with Astaire on the choreography was Robert Alton, who was also in charge of shooting the dance numbers. To assist with the complicated "Shoes with Wings On" solo (which was shot first), Hermes Pan was called in.

THE NUMBERS

A
SWING TROT
(1′ 36″)

During production, Astaire kept after Warren to write a piece of music called "Swing Trot." Astaire's idea was to use the dance to promote his growing dancing-school enterprise by creating a dance craze, the secret of which could be mastered only at the Fred Astaire Dance Studios; and, after the film was released, the Swing Trot was a prominent staple in these schools. Once the number was written, choreographed, and shot, however, there seemed to be no place for it in the film. Finally someone (Ira Gershwin credits Freed) suggested running it under the opening titles. Except that the choreography is inevitably obscured, the idea was a splendid one.

The dance brilliantly reintroduced the Astaire-Rogers team to movie audiences. The first thing we see in the film are the pair's dancing feet (A 1). Then the camera pulls back to a full-figure shot and (quite unnecessarily, of course) the names of the performers appear on the screen (A 2). The dance continues as the rest of the titles are displayed and then leads directly into the opening scene of the film: musical entertainers Josh and Dinah Barkley, onstage, taking bows and making a curtain speech at what turns out to be the premiere of their successful new show.[1] A wittier and more vibrant opening for the film can scarcely be imagined.

The dance itself is essentially a set of variations on the Swing Trot step—a series of delicate, syncopated toe jabs out to the side shown in clear detail in the opening shot with the dancers side by side.[2] The step is next seen in a partnered position (A 3) and then is given a progressively more theatrical treatment. The toe jabbing becomes more exaggerated, and its direction is sometimes reversed so that one leg swings across the other (A 4). The step continues through some traveling and turning patterns, which become increasingly flamboyant. After the dancers return to the basic step, rendered broadly, they give the step its most brilliant variation by developing it into some floor-skimming leaps (A 5).

Astaire winds Rogers in and out of his arms a couple of times (A 6), and as the dance concludes he locks her close to him and gives her a quick kiss (A 7, 8). The couple's demeanor in this last sequence neatly reflects the script's characterization: Astaire controls Rogers' spins from afar, bringing her in toward him with a beckoning finger and then pushing her away to repeat the spinning maneuver, rewarding her at the end with a kiss. Rogers willingly and joyfully accepts his leadership.

[1] Two-thirds of the way through there is a dissolve covering a mismatch of shots (an absolutely unique occurrence in Astaire's filmed dances) which may have been necessary to cover reshooting occasioned by the new placement of the dance. The dissolve is not obvious: it comes when the screen is most cluttered with title material.

[2] The step has some similarities to the Piccolino step introduced in *Top Hat* (5 F). The camera work in that duet, as it happens, also begins with a medium shot of the dancers' lower bodies.

B
SABER DANCE
(2′ 34″)

In a curtain speech Astaire tells the audience that the team's success is due largely to Rogers' wonderful performances, and Rogers interrupts to insist that he is the mastermind of the act and deserves full credit. The show's composer, played by the acerbic Oscar Levant in self-impersonation, hustles the couple offstage before they can come to blows over the issue.

A 1 A 2 A 3 A 4
A 5 A 6 A 7 A 8
B 1 C 1 C 2 C 3

More disagreement occurs later, particularly at a party, when Rogers neglects Astaire to listen raptly to the flattery of an intellectual playwright-director who insists she has the makings of a "great tragic actress" and is being wasted in musical comedy. Levant is prevailed upon by the hostess (played by Billie Burke, Florenz Ziegfeld's widow) to entertain the guests with a piano performance (B1). After some noodling, he gives a spirited rendition of Aram Khachaturian's greatest hit, "Saber Dance."

C
YOU'D BE HARD TO REPLACE
(1′ 38″)

Astaire and Rogers continue their arguing at home: he is filled with petulant self-pity and she with petulant defensiveness (C1). She belts him over the head when he asserts that she couldn't cross a stage without his direction—she is Trilby to his Svengali, he says.[3] Soon, however, the argument is settled with a kiss (C2), loving reassurances, and a caressing ballad sung by Astaire (C3). In it his dependence on her is expressed with the agile indirection Ira Gershwin (and Astaire) preferred: "You'd be hard to replace." A brief swooning dance follows (C4), ending with a suggestiveness unusual in Astaire's dances: he lowers her onto a couch, she beckons him to lie down on her, and the camera fades out on a kiss (C5–7).

It's a remarkably effective scene for these two married lovers who shroud their deep mutual dependency under a cloak of stagey combativeness. And there is an improvisational feeling to the acting that gives the scene a warm believability and an engaging charm.

D
BOUNCIN' THE BLUES
(2′ 3″)

The producer of their show has hired an understudy for Rogers—a Southern woman who is pushy, unctuous, and not terribly bright.[4] Rogers meets her rival and puts her down with such deftness that the poor girl doesn't even realize what's happened (D1).

After a brief warm-up, Astaire and Rogers swing into a rehearsal of a chipper duet to be added to the show. Two-thirds of the number is side-by-side solo work, and it provides the first clear view in the film of Rogers' dancing capabilities. She looks splendid—loose and confident—and the number is the dance in the film most reminiscent of the great thirties duets. In part this is because of Rogers' costume (an attractive, loose-fitting blouse hides the tightness of her upper body, which is too evident in "Swing Trot" and especially in "You Can't Take That Away from Me") but also because her old gaiety is back, the contagious glee she projects as she joins Astaire in an exuberant dance.

As the number begins, Astaire playfully chucks Rogers under the chin—a gesture that seems in keeping with the Svengali-Trilby relationship (D2; compare C3). The opening of the dance is a cheerfully exploratory sequence to drum music—a kind of tap warm-up. There are loose shuffles that inch forward mixed with

[3] Trilby and Svengali seem to have lost some of their status as household words since 1949. The reference is to George du Maurier's 1894 novel *Trilby,* in which the title character is an artist's model who becomes a great singer under the influence of Svengali, a hypnotist. When he dies, Trilby loses her singing ability.

[4] It is curious that Hollywood, so careful not to use black people in a manner that would offend white Southern sensibilities, could get away so easily with this stereotype: if a woman is supposed to be dumb she should be given a Southern accent.

C4 C5 C6 C7
D1 D2 D3 D4
D5 D6 D7 D8

some amusingly percussive knee and pelvis jerks (D3). The sequence is all in unison except for some funny little jumps in which the dancers trade tap-question and tap-answer and then casually return to unison.

A jazz band joins the drum with a melody supplied by Warren (one of several he wrote for Astaire's approval). The dancers begin to cover more space and the dance becomes looser—more swinging—the dancers pausing from time to time to emphasize drumbeats by hammering the floor with their feet (D4). A spin and an unexpected pause in an amusing decorative pose (D5) lead to a sequence that continues the cool tap texture, embellished from time to time with some delightful cross-patterns—an awkward waddle (Rogers proves to be a terrific waddler), toed-in floor slams (D6), an explosive turning jump that ends in a rare fall to one knee (D7), and a sprawling lunge (D8).

Best of all is the ending—a series of partnered perambulations around the stage to full jazz band. Beginning with a high camera shot that is quite unusual in Astaire's work (D9), the concluding passages incorporate various bouncy variations on the strut (D10) and high-footed jog (D11), leading finally to a wonderfully witty exit in which Astaire guides Rogers toward the wings (D12) and then leans on her extended arm in mock infatuation (D13). At the last instant she yanks the curtain toward them, covering their exit like a stripper who has just dropped her last bit of drapery (D14).

Croce finds this duet "too aggressively professional," and it is true that "Bouncin' the Blues," for all its wit and high spirits, doesn't have the spontaneity of some earlier Astaire-Rogers playful duets, such as "I'll Be Hard to Handle" (4 D) and "Let Yourself Go" (6 D). Of course, some of this may be intentional, since "Bouncin' the Blues" is supposed to be a final rehearsal of a finished piece of choreography, not an exploratory improvisation. But the number's lack of spontaneity also comes from the unfortunate inclusion of a series of exclamations ("Hah!," "Yeah!") in the soundtrack. As uttered by Astaire, and presumably added after the dance was filmed, these seem forced, insincere, and calculated, partly undercutting the playfulness that had been so carefully worked into the choreography. In fact, the dance seems more spontaneous and funnier when it is viewed without the sound, a procedure that also cuts out the undistinguished music.

E
MY ONE AND ONLY HIGHLAND FLING
(5′44″)

Astaire and Rogers visit an art gallery for the unveiling of a portrait of themselves. The work proves to be a preposterous pseudo-surrealistic exercise in which he is visualized as the molding frying pan and she the molded pancake—a rather typically superficial MGM anti-intellectual swipe (E1).

After some more scenes of unfocused bickering, the couple goes onstage to do a Scottish number.

Set to the most nearly memorable original tune in the film, and the only one to achieve "Your Hit Parade" status, "My One and Only Highland Fling" is a gentle satire on marital contentment and also, in part, on Astaire's own romantic duets. Ira Gershwin's lyric, with its neat play on the word "fling," explains at length how each partner searched everywhere for the ideal mate and now enjoys utter marital bliss. In general the lyric possesses less humor, charm, and bite than one might hope for, and it becomes rather convoluted in the refrain sung by Rogers. Taking its cue from the unruffled, loping quality of the music, and also from the stereotype of

D9 D10 D11 D12 D13 D14 E1 E2 E3 E4 E5 E6

the Scotsman as inordinately reserved, the staging of the number shows what the couple's wedded state is like: contentment almost to the point of catatonia. At the same time, however, it is clear that there is a deep and genuine affection between these two comedic characters. The man may be smugly self-satisfied, but he is always clearly conscious of his wife's presence, and to make sure it is understood that his stuffy demeanor is mere pose, he gives the audience a sly wink when she is not looking.[5]

There is also choreographic self-parody in the number. Some of the most famous Astaire-Rogers duets of the 1930s developed a dramatic situation in which Astaire pursues Rogers—blocking her exit, enveloping her, enticing her to respond to his danced entreaties. "My One and Only Highland Fling" cleverly reverses the situation. Astaire is the pursued and Rogers the pursuer as she flutters around after him in worshipful, puppylike dependency. She impishly blocks his path and lingers close by, looking hopefully for some tangible sign of affection. At the end her ardent efforts are rewarded not by surrendering acquiescence, but by a condescending, if good-natured, kiss to her forehead. In some respects the number can be taken as a naïve morality fable that has relevance to the framing story of the Barkleys: their marriage will be secure and happy only when she, like the character she plays in this routine, contentedly suppresses any sense of marital rebellion.

The couple strolls onto the stage to the gentle, loping beat of the music. They halt downstage to deliver the verse; Astaire sings most of it while Rogers gazes at him adoringly (E 2). Astaire then sings the chorus, picking up its quietly insistent beat—first by swaying his body in time, and then by strolling with great decorum across the stage. Rogers tags along after him, and when he pauses briefly she scampers around to his other side so that when he continues his stroll he will have to bump into her (E 3). But without even looking at her, he simply reverses direction and, continuing to sing, leaves her behind. She resumes the chase, and when he pauses again she plants herself on one side of him or the other—confused about which way he will go next. However, now he has come to the line "In the fling I was flung with you." He sings the last word forcefully and directs it right at her—the first time he has even looked at her—a sign of attention which is so novel that it startles her (E 4). This whole sequence—the chase, the blocking of the path, the yearning gazes, the unwillingness of the pursued to return the gaze—is an astonishingly apt, if presumably unconscious, parody of the movement that occurs during the singing of "Night and Day" in *The Gay Divorcee* (3 E).

Rogers backs out of Astaire's path, and he strolls over to a tree stump and sits down. At first he neglects to leave room for her on the stump, but then graciously shifts over. From their seat the couple render a patter lyric filled with pregnant rhymes like "MacDougal" and "frugal." (Gershwin recalls he was careful to avoid "McTavish" and "lavish" since this rhyme had been prominently patented by Ogden Nash.) Regrettably, the patter lyric has to stand on its own; Warren provides almost no musical support for it.

As the second chorus begins, Astaire abruptly rises from the stump, which then tilts, toppling Rogers to the ground. Undaunted, she trots after

[5] According to Gershwin, the idea of doing a Scottish number was Arthur Freed's. He was perhaps thinking of capitalizing on—or parodying—the success of the Broadway musical *Brigadoon*, which had opened in 1947. In his autobiography Astaire calls the number a favorite, a rare commendation by him for a duet.

E7 E8 E9 E10
E11 E12 E13 F1
G1 G2 G3 G4

him, singing to her imperious Scotsman. At one point, in fact, she is able to get quite close and, to his small annoyance, she pulls his pipe from his mouth and gives him a peck on the cheek (E5). In general Rogers is a bit too cutely animated in the number, particularly when she sings her part of the song here (though she sings it well). At the same time, she fails to communicate clearly one of the jokes in the staging—the way he takes a drink of water without even considering she might like one, too.

The central joke in the brief dance that follows proceeds logically from the characterizations already established. The impassive Astaire is willing to join Rogers in a dance as long as his absurdly stuffy dignity remains intact. Accordingly, the dance consists mostly of some exceedingly stately soft-shoe steps (E6). In many of Astaire's romantic duets the choreography builds to a climax about three-quarters of the way through and then diminishes in intensity. This climactic point is usually where lifts—something Astaire never uses casually—occur. The parodic "My One and Only Highland Fling" has a comparable moment, even including a couple of lifts. Far from suggesting romance or flight, however, the lifts are terrestrial and ordinary, as if the unflappable Scot were, with minimal expenditure of energy, helping his partner over a rain puddle (E7). Then, a bit later, he joins her in some snappy highland flinging (E8), but returns, with a wink (E9), back to a calm stroll, lest he work up an unseemly sweat.

Rogers is able to detain Astaire briefly as they stroll toward the exit, and she beckons him to kiss her. After checking to see that no one is watching (E10), he gives in to passionate impulse and plants a kiss—on her forehead (E11). Dazzled (E12), Rogers lovingly takes the arm of her self-satisfied lover, and they stroll off at their usual contented pace (E13).

F
A WEEKEND IN THE COUNTRY
(2′15″)

Astaire and Rogers, with Levant in tow, accept an invitation to spend the weekend in the country and, upon arrival, spiritedly sing about country bliss while Levant sourly proclaims his preference for "the quiet of 42nd and Park" (F1). The song has a clever lyric, but the music is serviceable at best. The action is staged beautifully by Walters—the three actors sing lustily and stride toward the camera at full speed while it tracks backward.

G
SHOES WITH WINGS ON
(7′16″)

Rogers is tempted by the young director's importunings to perform in his "serious" drama. Eventually she and Astaire have a wonderfully violent argument (while posing for a cozy at-home photo session for *Look* magazine —G1) and she walks out on him to join the play in rehearsal.

Meanwhile, Astaire continues with their show, apparently replacing Rogers with her empty-headed understudy. From that show we see a solo that is one of Astaire's most elaborate trick numbers, prominently featuring intricately planned process photography which makes it appear that Astaire is doing battle with a herd of disembodied dancing shoes.[6] To achieve this effect, the set was draped in black velvet, and dancers covered entirely in black except for their brightly colored shoes were filmed dancing in it. This footage was then superimposed on the film of Astaire's dance, with animation used here and there to spruce things up. Thus no shoes were visible when Astaire was filmed, and as he performed his solo he had to position himself in such a way that the combination effect would register properly. This complicated number took two months to conceive and execute and five and a half days to shoot. It is presented in thirteen shots on the film, nine of which are used for Astaire's final solo with the multiple shoes.

As usual, the number is impressive for the ingenious way in which Astaire (assisted by Hermes Pan and MGM cinematographer Irving Ries) has taken a single idea and developed it, rather than simply layering one gimmick on top of another. And, also as usual, the most amazing parts are the ones that rely on Astaire's abilities as a dancer, not on the special effects. The number was inspired by the tale of "The Sorcerer's Apprentice," and some rehearsals were conducted to a record of the popular Paul Dukas concert piece of that name; quotations from the

[6] The "Shoes with Wings On" number may have borrowed ideas from (indeed, be a parody of) the big ballet in the popular British melodrama *The Red Shoes*. That film was not released in Britain until July 1948 (and not until October in the United States), by which time the "Shoes with Wings On" number had already been rehearsed and filmed; however, as early as March 8, 1948, *Life* had done a two-page color spread on the "Red Shoes" ballet.

G5 G6 G7 G8

G9 G10 G11 G12

Dukas score, in fact, are retained in the final music.

In his shoe-repair shop Astaire is given a pair of white dancing shoes for mending (G2).[7] After closing hours, he idly places them on the counter and is astonished to discover they can dance by themselves (G3). Understandably intrigued, he puts the shoes on, and they proceed to dance away with him. He manages brilliantly to convey the impression that the shoes are doing the dancing while his body merely follows—a demonstration of a talent for mime that Astaire had never so fully disclosed before. When his feet first begin to dance on their own he watches them in puzzlement, but soon he is leaning back, enjoying the new feeling (G4). Before long, however, the shoes are dragging him against his will out onto the floor (G5) and kicking up a little flurry on their own (G6). He tries desperately to hold his legs down with his hands, particularly when the shoes seem to be determined to go off in opposite directions (G7), but the shoes react by pushing him off the floor into the air (G8) and then into some awkward spins (G9), which trip him up and send him toppling to the floor (G10).

He is cheered, however, when he hears his own voice singing a happy song proclaiming that winged shoes have certain advantages. When they're on, the voice points out, you'll find the town full of rhythm and the world in rhyme. This seems to do the trick, for the shoes now behave, and Astaire forgets them in order to pantomime the lyric gleefully, with gestures that are precise, perfectly timed, highly original, and very funny. He shows us, for example, his guardian angel (G11) and a magician, and then tells us that the shoes (G12) with wings on (G13) can send him flying (G14).

At the end of the song, he is jubilantly frolicking around the room (G15) when two pairs of shoes hop off the shelf and onto the floor to join him. He finds this disconcerting, especially when they step on his feet (G16). Outraged, he kicks them away, but then six more pairs hop off the shelf and surround him (G17). Outnumbered, Astaire grabs a broom to swat the menace but is momentarily distracted when they are joined by a pair of pink toe shoes which parade (*sur les pointes,* of course) between his legs (G18). Eventually he abandons the ineffectual broom and retrieves a pair of pistols from behind the counter. When he shoots at the shoes they fly away.

An experience like this can reasonably be expected to drive one berserk and this, indeed, is what happens to Astaire (G19). He shoots at shoes wherever he sees them, concluding by kicking the magic shoes off his feet and shooting them as they hurtle through the air (G20). He then throws the pistols away—one of them through the shopwindow—and does a final frenzied dance that ends with dozens of shoes cascading down on him (G21).[8]

H
TCHAIKOVSKY PIANO CONCERTO NO. 1
(EXCERPTS) (6′ 31″)

The film now becomes rather earnest in tone, the bubbling comedy of the first half being partly replaced by a fair amount of soul searching that gets somewhat tiresome. The Barkleys are clearly quite a bit more interesting when they are locked in combat than when they are discovering how much they mean to each other.

Rogers is having great difficulty with her dramatic role in the play, *Young Sarah.* Astaire, after surreptitiously observing a rehearsal, telephones her and, disguising his voice to sound like that of the young director, gives her suggestions. Among other things, he explains to her that there is no important difference between musical comedy and serious drama. Bolstered by this advice, Rogers instantly improves.

Meanwhile, Levant, an unlikely matchmaker, tricks both Astaire and Rogers into agreeing to perform at a hospital benefit by telling each that the other has refused to appear. Before the benefit, however, Astaire discovers Levant's con and insists that he won't come. Yet, as Levant performs a truncated version of a Tchaikovsky piano concerto at the benefit (H1), Astaire shows up, further indicating that he regrets the separation from his wife.[9]

[7] There is an extremely rare instance of inattention to detail in this opening sequence. The customer changes from his street shoes to try a few eccentric steps with the dancing shoes. He then removes the dancing shoes, gives them to Astaire for further repair (G2), and walks out in his stocking feet, leaving his street shoes on the floor of the shop. In later shots the street shoes are no longer there.

[8] Astaire reports that the ending ideas in the number were the inspiration of an MGM prop man, Harold Turburg.

[9] The conductor is Lennie Hayton, who was musical director for this and many other MGM films. The Tchaikovsky music was prerecorded, and the performance on the film is done to the playback. Levant's backstage ritual—saying good-bye to people before performing, as if he were never going to return—was autobiographical.

G13 G14 G15 G16

G17 G18 G19 G20

I

THEY CAN'T TAKE THAT AWAY FROM ME

(4′29″)

As Astaire and Rogers wait in the wings, Levant puts them on the spot by introducing them to the audience and proclaiming they will now "brilliantly oppose each other in one of their greatest numbers." The number is set to a Gershwin classic that Astaire had introduced in *Shall We Dance* (8 I), and as he sings the song it becomes apparent that the lyric, with its nostalgic yearning for a happier romantic past, fits the Barkleys' present situation perfectly.

In the dance, Astaire tries to break through Rogers' reticence and win back her affections; it is an attempted seduction that fails. His progress is traced in the partnering patterns: in various ways he tries to entrap her in his arms, but each time she fails to respond and breaks away from him. The duet is notable also for a studied awkwardness that is built in—particularly some strange hesitant, jerky, off-center lunges that hold back against the apparent flow of the choreography and then give in at the last instant. This extraordinary idea, which gives the dance an intriguingly rough edge, seems to have been inspired by the music: portions of the song are sometimes played in a jagged, syncopated manner. For example, in the phrase "The way you wear your hat," the first five words are performed in a way that does not clearly define a beat, and this rhythmic unease is resolved only on the held note for the word "hat."

Although this duet ranks among Astaire's greatest works, the performance hardly does the choreography justice. Despite the song's importunings, they can take some things away. Rogers' stiffness and thickness, particularly in the arms and back, undercut the impact of the dance, which, with its many partnered backbends, was clearly created with the Rogers of the 1930s in mind. Her stiffness is emphasized by the unflattering gown she wears which, combined with her hairdo, gives her a heavy, matronly look. (The decor for the number—a drab upstage curtain—is also singularly unattractive.) Of course, the point of the number is that Rogers is unyielding, unwilling to give in to Astaire's ardent entreaties. But for the number to be effective, it should appear that Rogers' lack of fluidity comes from her conscious unwillingness to let go, not from her inability to do so.

In addition, much of Rogers' musical savvy is missing—the way she would react with subtle liveliness to the singing and inflect the dance with mood and poignance by acting through the dancing. In "They Can't Take That Away from Me," she adopts an appropriate expression of regret, but it often has a fixed, calculated look, stagey and unconvincing. "They Can't Take That Away from Me," then, is a rarity among Astaire works: a great dance that might well look better if it were performed by someone else.

There is quite a bit of dance movement as Astaire sings. He circumnavigates Rogers several times, lingering close (I 1) or hailing her from a distance (I 2). (The use of the camera's depth of perspective in these sequences is rather new in Astaire's work.) At one point they arrive at a beautiful pose—Astaire is drawn to her but reluctant to reach out and touch her, and she stands back from him, tense and wary (I 3).

As Astaire finishes the song, he moves determinedly toward Rogers and takes her in his arms to begin the dance. Her reluctance is palpable (I4). They separate, and the dance begins with them moving sideways side by side, haltingly, almost staggeringly. When Astaire pulls Rogers toward him, they continue the step shoulder to shoulder (I5). Then he tries to loosen her up by pulling her around by the hand so that she traces

G21 H1 I1 I2 I3 I4 I5 I6 I7 I8 I9 I10

a curved path in front of him; but she remains almost unbearably stiff and unyielding (I6).

A few more halting paces bring them shoulder to shoulder again, and as the next phrase begins in the music they hold back from it, leaning heavily to one side (I7), and then stagger in the opposite direction. After they have continued to pace side by side around the floor, Astaire snaps himself around Rogers, spinning her as he does so (I8). She lies back in his arms, and at one point he pushes her forward by the small of the back —a direct reprise of a moment in a happier dance, "You'd Be Hard to Replace" (I9; compare C4). Again Rogers seems incapable of really giving in to the movement.

The dance develops more flamboyance as the release strain is played. Taking hands, the dancers flow around the floor, and there are some rapid spins (I10) and a turning jump for Astaire (I11).

What follows, when the main strain returns, is one of those astonishing Astaire transitions—in this case from showy extravagance to quiet sensuality. During the first portion of the strain ("The way you hold your knife") Astaire spins himself around Rogers, who is herself turning, in an elaborate double-helix pattern (I12); then, on the final note (on "knife"), the flurry of activity is abruptly replaced by firm order as he grasps her tightly at the waist from behind (I13).

A stylized struggle ensues, with Rogers trying to free herself from Astaire's embrace. After repeating the same pacing hesitations as before, they stop and lean to the side (I14; compare I7). Finally Rogers spins (rather clumsily) away, and Astaire catches her by the hand (I15) and forcefully pulls her toward him until they are shoulder to shoulder once again (I16; compare I5, I7).

The dancers begin to separate (I17) and then spin around the floor, back to back, as the music of the release, played broadly and portentously, is heard again.[10] The dance, equally large-scaled, features some flowing partnered turns and another turning leap in which Rogers joins Astaire (I18; compare I11). In the midst of this activity there is a remarkable promenade: with their arms linked, Rogers circles Astaire, turning him around twice (I19) (on this maneuver, see p. 172n). This linked-arm position is an anticipation of a choreographic motif to be elaborated at the end of the dance.

Finally, as the music thunders, Astaire takes Rogers in his arms and sweeps her around in some almost violently rapid turns that travel downstage (I20). Suddenly the music subsides, and the main strain returns softly; the camera cuts in for a medium shot, and Rogers finds herself locked in the tight embrace of the yearning Astaire (I21). The dance had begun with some oddly distant shoulder-to-shoulder partnering (I5, I7) and then had progressed to a closer formation in which he clutched her firmly from behind (I13). Now, finally, he partners her from the front and holds her close. For a moment she is stunned and uncertain, but she doesn't yield. Sadly, she gently pulls away from him and releases his left hand (I22).

Astaire bends her backward and gently sways her from side to side in a final moment of tenderness (I23). After they separate, Rogers moves her arms dreamily, with raised shoulders, as they dodge lightly past each other (I24). Then they link arms as if testing their exit step (I25), and a quiet reprise of their earlier double helix (I26; compare I12) leads to one last, nostalgic partnered backbend (I27).

[10] The cut to the high camera in I17 is unusual in Astaire's duets (though common in Gene Kelly's). The idea was also used earlier in the film, in "Bouncin' the Blues" (see D9).

I11 I12 I13 I14 I15 I16 I17 I18 I19 I20 I21 I22

Again she does not respond, and again they separate. They perform some intricate, soft turns and an elaborate exploration of the linked-arm position as they prepare to exit (I 28). Then, while they settle down to stroll toward the wings arm in arm, Astaire looks at Rogers (I 29). But, refusing to meet his imploring gaze, she turns her face away—a pointed, mournful variation on the exits in their two previous duets (I 30; compare D12–14, E13, also 4 H22).

J

YOU'D BE HARD TO REPLACE

(REPRISE) (1′52″)

Backstage after the duet, Astaire asks Rogers if they can talk things over, but she insists firmly that their relationship is over. After he has sadly departed, she bursts into tears.[11] Things stay rather heavily serious for the next few minutes.

Rogers, we are given to believe, is a triumph in the role of the young Sarah Bernhardt. We see her onstage at an examination in which she wows the judges with an embarrassingly over-emotive recital of the "Marseillaise" in French (J 1).[12]

Concerned that Rogers may be falling in love with the young director, Astaire telephones her in her dressing room, again imitating the director's voice. The ruse fails when the director happens to walk into the room while she is still on the phone, and instantly—not a moment too soon—the film returns to comedy. Rogers takes great pleasure in informing the man on the phone that she loves him. Astaire is wonderful at projecting crestfallen despair at this news without engaging in pathos or self-pity (J 2).

Rogers rushes to their apartment and putters around preparing for the reunion. She puts on a recording of Astaire singing, appropriately, "You'd Be Hard to Replace."

K

MANHATTAN DOWNBEAT

(2′37″)

When Astaire arrives, she taunts him a bit and then informs him that she knows everything. Furthermore, she's made a sudden decision to give up the drama; she will happily return to musicals with him and from now on will only do "fun set to music."

They celebrate their reunion with an ineffective and insufficiently brief dance to a really terrible song, "Manhattan Downbeat." It begins in the apartment (K 1) and dissolves to finish on the musical stage (K 2), complete with moving floor panels and a chorus of high-style strutters.[13]

[11] The only other time Astaire moved Rogers to tears in their films was when, as Vernon Castle, he was killed in *The Story of Vernon and Irene Castle. The Barkleys of Broadway* is also unusual in that it calls for quite a bit of kissing (in the earlier love-spat scenes), as well as the use of a phrase never before uttered by Astaire in their films together: "I love you."

[12] When *Variety* reported that Rogers' speech was getting "loud yocks" in French Canada, MGM studio heads considered replacing it with something in English, at least for distribution in French areas. Many reviewers chortled over this scene.

[13] One version of the script called for the number to be followed by a brief curtain speech leading to another argument, at which point Levant would announce, "This is where I came in."

I23 I24 I25 I26

I27 I28 I29 I30

J1 J2 K1 K2

With Rogers in "Swing Trot"

23.

THREE LITTLE WORDS

1950

Three Little Words is especially appealing for its genial, relaxed tone, its warm good humor. The film tells a light tale, partly true, partly fanciful, of a couple of successful American songwriters, weaving into the story a splendid sampling of their best tunes. But unlike other musical biographies of its era, it effortlessly avoids pretentious melodrama and fawning hero worship. It seeks to build no legends and flatters its central subjects not by erecting monuments to them but by suggesting that they are interesting in their own right as real, flawed human beings.

The film is one of Fred Astaire's favorites—perhaps in part because he gets to play the role of a successful songwriter, an ardent fantasy in real life (see p. 21n). Cast opposite him is Red Skelton, and the pair play off each other and sing together as if they had been teamed for decades.

But the film has its infelicities as well—tacky decor (particularly for onstage numbers), and musical arrangements that often weigh down, and occasionally destroy, the very songs the film so sensibly celebrates. And choreographically the film is among Astaire's weakest. There is a brilliant solo, but it is only a fragment; beyond that, the dances are sometimes pleasantly diverting but rarely distinguished or particularly memorable.

THE SCRIPT AND THE PRODUCTION

By the late 1940s few great songs were being written for Hollywood musicals. The new songwriters didn't seem to be nearly so gifted as the crop of the 1930s, and even when songwriters of the earlier generation turned out original scores for a film, the songs were often disappointing: Harry Warren's dispiriting score for Astaire's *The Barkleys of Broadway* (1949) and Cole Porter's middle-drawer effort for the Gene Kelly–Judy Garland *The Pirate* (1948), for example.

One solution was to assemble a score of golden oldies and build a story around them, and one way to get a story was to make the film a biography of one of the songwriters. A problem was that most of those songwriters led fairly undramatic lives, at least superficially—a little struggle followed by a lot of success. This was easily solved, however: history was simply falsified. In the process there was an unfortunate tendency to become sanctimonious about the biographical subject, and the result was a series of films that are among the most dreary in the history of the Hollywood musical.

Although there had been earlier efforts (especially the successful George M. Cohan "biopic," *Yankee Doodle Dandy* of 1942), the fad really started with two Warner Bros. films in 1945 and 1946, *Rhapsody in Blue* (George Gershwin) and *Night and Day* (Cole Porter). MGM then jumped in with *Till the Clouds Roll By* (Jerome Kern) in 1947, which was a big success at the box office, and *Words and Music* (Richard Rodgers and Lorenz Hart) in 1948, which wasn't. Concluding from this that the day of the songwriter biopic was over, MGM was less than receptive to producer Jack Cummings' idea for a film biography of the songwriting team of Bert Kalmar and Harry Ruby. It was argued that Kalmar and Ruby were something other than household names, but Cummings suggested the songwriters' comparative anonymity was actually liberating. Moreover, Kalmar and Ruby were inherently amusing characters: they didn't get along all that well, neither was particularly preoccupied with the idea of writing songs, and each was obsessed with an outside hobby at which he was not so good: Kalmar wanted to be a magician, Ruby a baseball player. As Ruby tells it, "When Jack Cummings decided to make our story into a movie, he went to Louis B. Mayer and he said, 'This is gonna be a good musical, because for once we're gonna do a story about songwriters that has a *story*. . . . It's a natural—two successful songwriters. One schmuck wants to be a magician and pull rabbits out of a hat; the other one would rather play professional baseball than eat!' " Cummings' arguments stirred some interest, but it was only after he lined up two solid box-office draws, Astaire and Skelton, to play the leads that the studio bought the project.

Kalmar died in 1947—the year work on the script began—

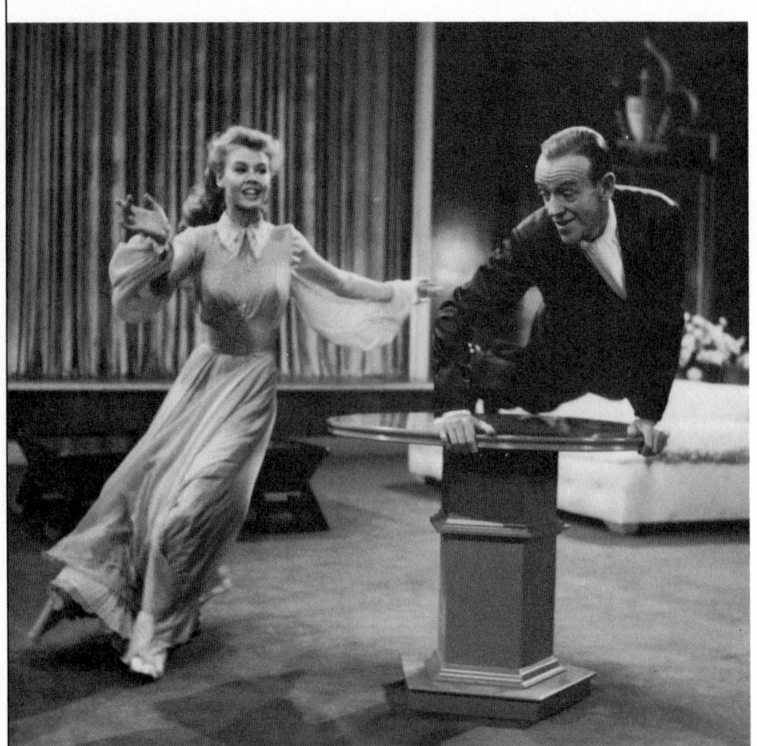
With Vera-Ellen in "Thinking of You"

but Ruby was still very much around during the filming, and, acting as a "technical adviser," he supplied a string of amusing anecdotes for scriptwriter George Wells to digest and scramble. Ruby even has a bit role in the film, as—fantasy finally fulfilled—a big-league baseball player (L 2, N1).

Although Wells and Cummings felt no compulsion to be historically accurate, *Three Little Words* is closer to a true story than the usual songwriter biopic. In particular, the film is refreshingly honest about the process of songwriting: Astaire and Skelton do not sit down and whip off a completed, fully rounded song in a few casual seconds of concentrated inspiration. Instead, they start working with a fragment of an idea and have the finished product only after a camera dissolve, which is to be taken to cover hours of agonized labor. A recurring gag in the film concerns the difficulty Kalmar had coming up with a lyric for a Ruby tune, a song that eventually became "Three Little Words." As told in the film, the magic formula finally emerged out of an argument between the songwriters, when Kalmar screamed, "I can tell you what I think of you in three little words: you're a dope!" This episode is sometimes pointed out as an instance

With Vera-Ellen in "Mr. and Mrs. Hoofer at Home"

of Hollywood's penchant for obvious contrivance and was ridiculed as such in MGM's compilation film *That's Entertainment, Part 2* of 1976. However, according to the notes Ruby gave Wells, the story is exactly true—except that Kalmar's insult was "You're a fool!"

While events are often compressed, invented, or rearranged in the film, the essential psychological relationship between the two songwriters seems to have been aptly captured—the friendly antagonism and the way the older man, Kalmar, dominated the relationship; as Ruby recalls in his notes, "Kalmar could read Ruby like a book."[1]

RED SKELTON AND VERA-ELLEN

The idea of casting Red Skelton as Harry Ruby seemed inspired to everyone except Red Skelton and Harry Ruby. Ruby, gentle and congenial, could hardly picture himself

[1] Kalmar was eleven years older than Ruby; the age difference between Astaire and Skelton is exactly the same.

Harry Ruby joins the actors—Red Skelton, Vera-Ellen, and Astaire

Astaire trying to think of words for Skelton's melody, as Vera-Ellen looks on

being portrayed by a comic noted primarily for broad humor and violent pratfalls. And Skelton was equally reluctant to take on a straight role. Cummings had to argue him into it: Skelton found the script funny, "but he didn't think it was his kind of funny. There wasn't much chance for him to do any *schtick,* like in his other pictures. 'That's exactly why you should do it,' I told him. 'If you don't do something different soon, instead of that half-crazed imitation of Bob Hope, you'll soon be washed up in the movies.' Red looked shocked that anyone would talk to him that way." With the support of the comedian's wife, Cummings finally brought Skelton around, "but it was one of the hardest sells I've ever made." Skelton does get to do a few of his characteristic comic bits in the film, but these are incidental, and his Harry Ruby is truly memorable: warm, amusing, endearingly awkward and self-conscious, and completely believable. The result pleased Ruby, too, "as long as Gable, Taylor and Cary Grant were busy in other roles," he once remarked wryly.

Also featured is the limber Vera-Ellen, the quintessential nice-girl-next-door (pretty, a little bland), who plays Astaire's vaudeville dancing partner and, eventually, wife. A skilled dance technician, she keeps up impressively with Astaire but adds little flavor of her own. Nor does she seem to have stirred his choreographic imagination in this film as she was to do in their next film together, *The Belle of New York.*

THE MUSIC

The Kalmar-Ruby songs selected for revival in the film are irresistible. Two of them, "Nevertheless" and "Thinking of You," became major hits all over again when the film (which did extremely well at the box office) was released—something that had not happened with earlier musical biopics.

The tunes used were all written between 1913 and 1931, when songs were characteristically delivered with bounce and bite; unfortunately, under the musical direction of the twenty-year-old André Previn, several of them are slowed mercilessly in the film and given pretentious thousand-violin halos in the most lugubrious MGM manner. The best musical moments come when Skelton and Astaire, supported only by piano or other light accompaniment, artlessly harmonize, delivering the songs with sincerity and warm affection.

THE CHOREOGRAPHY

Dance director for the film was Astaire's frequent choreographic sidekick Hermes Pan. The evidence in the film suggests Pan was more responsible for the choreography than usual.

Vera-Ellen in "Come On, Papa"

THE NUMBERS

A
WHERE DID YOU GET THAT GIRL?
(1′50″)

The film opens with a bright dance routine performed by Astaire and Vera-Ellen. As the dancing team of Kalmar and Brown, they are shown in action at a top vaudeville theatre in 1919.[2] The number is set to a popular song Kalmar wrote in 1912 with Harry Puck, his publishing partner and chief pre-Ruby collaborator.

The dancers are dressed alike in top hat, white tie (and socks), and tails, and the routine comes very close to being a pair of identical parallel solos rather than a true duet—a quality that may derive from its vaudevillian inspirations. The choreography rides satisfyingly, but very directly, on the music, and dance and music phrases have exactly the same length and shape—characteristic, again, of a classic vaudeville routine but quite different from Astaire's usual, more musically complex, approach to choreography. This charming little number, then, might be seen as an affectionate but slightly satiric salute to Astaire's vaudeville origins.

The dancers stride boldly onstage and belt out the song. As they sing there is a great deal of jaunty promenading (setting the basic tone of the routine), with an occasional pause for special emphasis (A 1).

To begin the dance, they skip merrily around their canes (A 2), swat the floor with the canes, frolic past each other, and toss the canes back and forth (A 3). Some of these ideas are elaborated as the dance becomes more virtuosic—an impudent little lurch is added to the high-stepping skipping, for example (A 4), and the cane taps are blended with some intricately rapid, leg-weaving taps (A 5). As the orchestration lays on the violins, the dance becomes quite explosive: an abrupt leap, a delightfully absurd step in which a leg is flung in a semicircle through the air while the cane is bounced on the floor under it (A 6), and some rapid cane twirling combined with a fluttering tap obbligato. For a finish there is some more jaunty skipping, a couple of falls to the knee (A 7), a flying leap (A 8), some broadside cane bounces (A 9), and a blistering spin that leads, right on the music, to a crisp drop to one knee (A 10).

The knee falls were new for Astaire. In all his previous films he had gone down on his knees rarely, and then rather incidentally (as in 12 A 2, 16 H 2). They were to be used in some of his later films, particularly *Let's Dance* and *Silk Stockings*—on both of which, probably not coincidentally, Hermes Pan was dance director.

B
MR. AND MRS. HOOFER AT HOME
(4′9″)

Backstage, Astaire rather off-handedly asks Vera-Ellen to marry him. Though favorably disposed, she declines for the moment, arguing that he is too busy for marriage, given all his activities—performing, songwriting, playwriting, and prestidigitating.

He is next seen at a seedy Coney Island cafe working at this last activity.[3] (When the cafe is first shown, a male quartet is onstage singing "She's Mine, All Mine!," a song written by Kalmar and Ruby in 1921.) Skelton, a pianist in the joint, is assigned to assist him in the act, and things soon go nicely awry (B 1). When Skelton timorously returns a wandering rabbit backstage, Astaire angrily throws him out of his dressing room (B 2).

Next, Astaire and Vera-Ellen are seen performing at Keith's Theatre in Washington for an audience that includes a great vaudeville fan, President Woodrow Wilson. Their act is a comedy dance skit showing the domestic intranquillity of a couple of married tap dancers. On paper the idea has potential—it might even have been used to comment ironically on the troubled romance between Astaire and Vera-Ellen. But in execution the sketch, choreographed by Hermes

[2] In real life, Astaire and his sister, Adele, had been great fans of this successful team: "We used to stand in the wings and watch Jessie and Bert with thrilled envy, wondering if we could equal their finesse and reach their headline billing."

[3] Kalmar's penchant for disappearing to do his magic is vividly recalled by Ruby: "Once we had an appointment to go to meet a producer for a big Broadway show . . . very important man, wanted us to do a whole score—a big job for us. Bert said, 'I'll be there a day later.' 'Why?' 'Harry, I gotta take care of something. . . .' He didn't show up . . . for three days! I was furious. When he finally showed up he couldn't understand why I was sore. 'Where were you?' 'Look,' he said, 'there was a big convention in Chicago, magicians came from all over the world—Australia, London. I couldn't miss it!' " Rothwell reports that Ruby has also told a remarkably similar story about himself: "Once, when he and Kalmar were called upon to finish the score for one of the Ziegfeld Follies, he couldn't be found. The New Rochelle, N.Y., Fire Department team was playing that day, with Ruby at second base."

A 1 A 2 A 3 A 4

A 5 A 6 A 7 A 8

Pan, proves to be hopelessly overdrawn and tiresomely raucous. The tacky decor doesn't help, nor does André Previn's undistinguished, movement-underlining musical score (though it does sound somewhat better if one closes one's eyes).

After a brief, fluttery solo for Vera-Ellen (B3), Astaire bounds in, and the two clutch and cling for a few seconds (B4). They soon get into a danced argument and then make up. The situation offers ample opportunity for humor; Astaire had done a wonderfully amusing tap argument before with Ginger Rogers in *Roberta* (4 D), and the danced reconciliation could have been used for artful satire of sappy romanticism. But the argument dance here consists simply of silly arm flailing and foot stamping (B5), the reconciliation of cuddles and partnered swooping (B6). That parody might be intended is conveyed more by mugging and by obvious musical effects than by the choreography.

The dancers continue their desperate effort at comedy by clanking through a mock meal (B7) and tossing around a mock baby (B8). With the battered infant nestled back in its crib (B9), they prepare to go out by swooping around the room using a hurdling lift Pan had invented for *Carefree* twelve years earlier (B10; compare 10 C14). The number ends with its best joke: missing the door by eight feet, they exit by swirling through the wall (B11).

C
MY SUNNY TENNESSEE
(51")

Coming offstage, Astaire bumps his knee and sustains an injury that puts him out of action for a considerable period of time—an event that actually happened to Kalmar. With his ambitions thus dampened, Vera-Ellen now agrees to marry him, but he backs out because he feels he can't adequately provide for her—an event that didn't. Deeply hurt, she walks out.

Astaire dejectedly seeks to pursue his songwriting career. At a music-publisher's office on Tin Pan Alley he runs into Skelton, who is working there as a song plugger. Skelton has a tune in desperate need of a good lyric, and, after working for hours, Astaire comes up with one. Like the Southern songbirds yearned for in the lyric, the two men harmonize, and Astaire's voice blends beautifully with Skelton's sweet, unaffected tenor. Accompanied only by piano, they sing with a deep appreciation of the song's bright spirit and a sure instinct for its engaging lilt (C1). This captivating song is an upbeat gloss on Stephen Foster's bleak, nostalgic "Old Folks at Home"; the first three notes of the line "All the world would not be dreary then" even go so far as to quote Foster's phrase "All de world am sad and dreary."

D
SO LONG, OO-LONG
(1' 32")

Astaire suddenly recognizes Skelton as the clumsy oaf who broke up his magic act and stomps out furiously. But "My Sunny Tennessee" becomes a big hit, and they are soon working together again. They come up with a "Japanese" song, something about a boy named Oo-long who has to leave his girl for a while, and sing it at a music store. Another delight (D1).[4]

[4] Actually, Kalmar and Ruby had known each other before the knee injury, and Ruby helped to get Kalmar a songwriting job at the music publisher's—at $60 a week (Kalmar had been getting $1,000 a week in vaudeville before the injury). Kalmar soon wrote "Oh, What a Pal Was Mary," with music by Edgar Leslie, which, according to Ruby, sold 2 million copies; Kalmar's first royalty statement on it was $90,000. The Kalmar-Ruby collaboration began at the same time. "So Long, Oo-long" came in 1920, "My Sunny Tennessee" (with some contributions by Herman Ruby) the next year.

A9 A10 B1 B2

B3 B4 B5 B6

B7 B8 B9 B10

E
WHO'S SORRY NOW?
(2′5″)

But next comes musical mayhem. Broadway headliner Mrs. Carter De Haven (impersonated in the film by her daughter, Gloria) auditions a new (1923) Kalmar-Ruby song in her dressing room (E1). Savaging the clear intent of Kalmar's brilliant lyric with its air of pointed, bittersweet accusation, she slows the song mercilessly until it becomes a dirge, to the accompaniment of MGM's regiment of swarming violins.

F
TEST SOLO
(2′1″)

Astaire, learning that Vera-Ellen is doing well in vaudeville and may take on another partner, becomes concerned and tests out his partly mended knee on a deserted stage. The exploratory dance that ensues, though brief and fragmented, is the film's choreographic highlight. The dazzle, the rhythmic intricacy, the witty surprises, the compelling authority are all there in full measure.

It opens with Astaire trying out a few steps, including one tentative knee drop (F1). Encouraged, he grinds out his cigarette and faces upstage, relaxed but poised, leaning on his cane.

Now begins a forty-two-second tap routine unsurpassed by anything in his film career. As a piano is heard in the distance playing a beguiling vamp rhythm, Astaire's attentive body begins to twist slightly, as if gradually being pulled into movement by the insistent, ghostly music. Suddenly breaking into motion, he flips his cane up, snatches it sharply out of the air (F2), raps out a brisk tap barrage, and then confidently saunters into his dance (F3). With that explosive beginning, Astaire is launched into a series of sweeping maneuvers and sumptuously gliding spins (F4, 5), punctuated by more crisp cane snatches. This is followed by tap work that is more manic: rapid tapping behind the cane (F6), a stomping promenade around it (F7), and a furious, staggering passage in which the cane is swung and kicked around so that it slaps the floor (F8). The solo routine, superbly supported by an engagingly sparse piano composition by André Previn, develops into some crazy-legged scramblings (F9) and then comes to an appropriately abrupt end with an unusual pose, as Astaire jabs the floor with his cane and kicks one leg out in front of him (F10).

His confidence in his knee restored, Astaire pauses and then throws himself into a reprise of the ending of the "Where Did You Get That Girl?" dance. He has no trouble with the rapid turns and jumps (F11, 12) but winces at the final knee drop (F13) and then collapses in pain (F14).

The ending is excruciating to watch, and the exact point of putting the audience through such agony is far from clear, since the incident has no impact on the plot. Skelton, who has been watching in the shadows, solicitously runs to Astaire's assistance and is assured that the knee has not been reinjured (F15); when next we see Astaire, he is ready to resume his dancing career.

G
COME ON, PAPA
(2′17″)

Skelton has convinced Astaire to accompany him to Buffalo, where they watch Vera-Ellen romp through a vaudeville number set to a tune Ruby wrote in 1918 with Edgar Leslie. The song, sung with insufficient sassiness by Vera-Ellen's dubber, Anita Ellis, leads to a vacuous dance routine in which the leggy, limber dancer frisks around the stage and is swung through the air by a chorus of men dressed as sailors (G1–2).

B11 C1 D1 E1
F1 F2 F3 F4
F5 F6 F7 F8

H
NEVERTHELESS
(2′17″)

Vera-Ellen is delighted to see the songwriters in the audience and invites them onstage to perform one of their songs with her. The lyric of this 1931 song is notable not only for its agile internal rhymes but also for its relevance to the Astaire–Vera-Ellen romance. Accompanied by Skelton at the piano, the couple nestle together as they sing (H1), and each assures the other that, despite misgivings, "nevertheless I'm in love with you." Each takes care to deliver the last two words of that phrase directly to the other. They are soon joined briefly by Skelton, who latches amusingly onto their nested formation for one progression across the stage (H2). The shy dignity the stocky Skelton projects as he clumps along in front of the two sleek dancers is especially endearing.

After Skelton has obligingly strolled into the wings, Astaire and Vera-Ellen sail through a dance that suggests their compatibility. The opening in particular is sweetly winning: a lilting, scooting pattern (H3) is embellished with a set of soft, intricately timed hops (H4). The rhythms in the rest of the dance, however, seem to be almost determinedly unsophisticated. For example, in the next phrase, bleeps in the music are directly echoed with little kicks (H5).

After a reaction shot of Skelton in the wings, saddened because his partner is now obviously ready to resume his dancing career, Astaire is shown planting a kiss on Vera-Ellen's cheek (H6). He partners her around the stage, sending her swirling under his upraised arm (H7), and they underline each of a series of orchestral twitches with a spinning jump (H8). Then, at the close, a running pattern onstage dissolves to a scene showing the dancers running down a train platform. The result is very cinematic, but it was extremely unusual for Astaire, who preferred clean and fully choreographed endings for his dances (H9–10).

I
ALL ALONE MONDAY
(1′42″)

Now married to Vera-Ellen, Astaire decides to abandon vaudeville for songwriting. With that problem out of the way, the script focuses on Skelton's romantic life; he is called upon to become engaged to an affected singer who is shown flouncing flirtatiously around a nightclub while irrelevantly belting out a 1926 Kalmar-Ruby ballad (I1).[5]

J
YOU SMILED AT ME
(37″)

The songwriters are soon established on Broadway and are shown auditioning singers for their 1926 hit *The Ramblers.* One of the aspirants is Arlene Dahl, who croons a portion of a *Ramblers* song that demonstrates Kalmar's virtuosic facility with internal rhyme (J1).

K
ALL ALONE MONDAY
(REPRISE) (1′19″)

Dahl doesn't get the job, however. Instead it goes, at Skelton's urging, to his fiancée, who is shown in performance singing the show's big tune (but this time doing it justice) before a stage set of monumental tastelessness (K1).

[5] During the dialogue in the nightclub after this song is sung, the club band strikes up "Who's Sorry Now?" in the background, playing it liltingly and giving evidence that someone around MGM actually did know how to do justice to this splendid song. (A portion of the song is also aptly rendered by Astaire and Skelton in 23 P.)

F9 F10 F11 F12
F13 F14 F15 G1
G2 H1 H2 H3

L
I WANNA BE LOVED BY YOU
(1′ 32″)

Astaire now discovers that Skelton's fiancée has been two-timing him. To get Skelton off the hook, Astaire and Vera-Ellen contrive to get him out of town for a while, giving the fiancée an opportunity to marry her new flame. Through the complicity of big-league baseball player Al Schacht, Skelton is shipped off to join the Washington Senators—his favorite team—in spring training, where he throws practice pitches (L1) and takes pratfalls (L3). (Catching the pitches and watching the pratfalls is the real Harry Ruby [L2].) The improbable scheme works.[6]

[6] Ruby supplied a number of anecdotes about his baseball obsession. One concerned an event in 1931 he said he "can never live down." Allowed once to play second base with the Senators in an exhibition game, he took the field as a substitute and then heard the public-address announcer tell everyone he was the composer of "Three Little Words," whereupon Al Schacht, using a baseball bat as a baton, conducted the eight thousand fans in the song. Ruby was so unnerved he forgot to cover second base in a double play. Ruby prided himself on his collection of signed photographs from famous ball players; Walter Johnson: "To Harry Ruby, who could do anything on the ball field except go to his left and right"; Joe Cronin: "To Harry Ruby, by far the best second baseman outside of baseball." He also treasured Groucho Marx's crack: "Not to listen to Ruby is a liberal education."

Then another plot-thickener is invented: Skelton concludes that a play Astaire has written will fail and, to protect him from the consequences, secretly dissuades an important backer from supporting the production, causing the play to be canceled.

Next Astaire and Skelton are seen walking down a New York sidewalk in 1928 arguing about a song, "I Wanna Be Loved by You." In sudden need of a piano, they commandeer one from some movers—an event that actually happened to them once. As they go over the song, Debbie Reynolds, in one of her earliest screen appearances, wanders into the scene and punctuates their tune by chirping "boop-boop-a-doop" (L4). The songwriters are instantly impressed and put her into their new show, *Good Boy.*

Actually, this is not quite the way in which Helen Kane became the boop-boop-a-doop girl. A well-known performer, the round-faced, pixie-voiced singer was already in the show when she was assigned the song. She disliked it and, to demonstrate her annoyance, ad-libbed the famous phrase at a performance. The song became her biggest hit, and she inserted her signature phrase into most of the songs she sang for the rest of her career, which faded out in 1930.

Twenty years later she came out of retirement to record the song for this film. Unfortunately, Kane's self-impersonation became self-parody. In her recordings from the 1920s she uses phrasing and scat interjections with wonderfully sly sexual innuendo; here she simply squeals. To make matters worse, Reynolds is given some silly and distracting stage business, clinging to and clutching at her long-suffering partner, Carleton Carpenter (L5).

M
THINKING OF YOU
(3′ 36″)

On a ship returning from London and the opening of yet another successful show, Skelton calls Astaire and Vera-Ellen into a spacious lounge where he has just finished composing a melody to a love lyric Astaire had written earlier as a surprise for Vera-Ellen. Touched by the gift, she mimes while Anita Ellis lethargically sings the 1927 song on the soundtrack (M1). Then she and Astaire dance romantically to the new melody.

Usually in Astaire's films his wedding to his woman of the hour takes place sometime after the closing credits, so he did not ordinarily have

H4 H5 H6 H7 H8 H9 H10 I1 J1 K1 L1 L2

the opportunity to perform dances of marital contentment—a condition he knew a lot about in private life. There was one such dance in *The Story of Vernon and Irene Castle* (11 L) and a fragmentary one in *The Barkleys of Broadway* (22 C), both eloquent in very different ways, and both characterized by understatement and a remarkable economy of means. This odd duet, however, is choreographically eclectic and emotionally inconclusive.[7]

It begins most promisingly, however. With the simplest maneuverings, a private, quiet mood of shared intimacy is established. The dancers hug warmly, separate by a few steps as they gaze at each other (M 2), and then, on a sigh in the music, nestle again (M 3). Equally touching are the next phrases, during which Vera-Ellen twice sweeps in a tight circle around Astaire, once with his gentle guidance (M 4), once on her own (M 5).

The choreography now becomes more showy, but the essential mood is largely preserved as Astaire leads her into an open space in the lounge where they flow through a beautiful series of soft but articulate dipping turns (M 6). Then, even better, there is a lovely sequence in which Astaire shunts his congenial partner back and forth from one side of his body to the other while they turn (M 7, 8). Some additional lilting turns follow, during which Vera-Ellen, who has been dancing a bit stiffly, loosens up.

Had the rest of the dance been as affecting and imaginative as these opening portions, the duet would have been one of Astaire's greatest. Unfortunately, the dance soon begins to fall apart. There is a mood-shattering move in which Vera-Ellen sticks one leg up into the air (just as she learned in ballet classes—M 9; see also B 4, 9), then a dopey little lift (M 10) timed to occur exactly on a coy swoop in the orchestration (which becomes increasingly oppressive as the dance progresses). In the next part of the dance they glide over the room's chunky furniture while trying to look loving (M 11), and then embark on a long series of low, effortful, leg-fluttering lifts (M 12).

The ending, however, is sweet and amusing. Coming out of the lift series, they spin gingerly back to the piano (M 13) and, as Skelton finishes playing the music, serenely subside into calm attentiveness, as if their dance duet had never taken place at all (M 14). "Nice tune, Harry," says Astaire appreciatively as the scene fades out.

N
I LOVE YOU SO MUCH
(1′ 58″)

Although the film runs another thirty-one minutes, it has no more dancing—a disproportion unique in Astaire's film career.

Skelton has another romance with an unsuitable female, and Astaire and Vera-Ellen once again cure him by sending him off to baseball practice, again with the real Harry Ruby in sardonic attendance (N 1).

Meanwhile, unsuccessful auditioner Arlene Dahl has become a big Hollywood star and, moreover, is appearing in the 1930 film version of *The Ramblers* (retitled *The Cuckoos*). The songwriters, who now move to Hollywood, see her running through a new song they wrote for the 1930 film, a song featuring one of Ruby's bounciest tunes and one of Kalmar's least inspired lyrics. Surrounded by a worshipful chorus of top-hatted men, she sashays around the set singing and fluttering a pink ostrich feather fan (N 2).[8]

O
THINKING OF YOU
(REPRISE) (1′ 36″)

At a party, Astaire learns from his drunken agent about Skelton's successful, well-meaning effort to undercut the backing for his play long ago. The songwriters argue and angrily split up.

Skelton now falls in love with the right woman—Dahl. With just symmetry, they, too, have their romance sanctioned by the film's main love song (O 1).[9]

P
AND-THEN-WE-WROTE MEDLEY / THREE LITTLE WORDS
(3′ 27″)

Much later, the songwriters' wives contrive to get the men together again by arranging a joint appearance on a radio show devoted to their music. The two men grudgingly meet to work out a routine for the show and even try to fashion a lyric for a tune Skelton wrote years before. Soon, however, they are angrily arguing over their mutually incompatible hobbies, and Astaire tells Skelton off in three little words: "You're a dope!" (P 1). Hey, that fits, observes Skelton. Astaire seems unimpressed.

At the broadcast they spiritedly reprise samples of their songs—again a musical treat (P 2)—and then Astaire springs a surprise: an old tune finally fitted out with a suitable lyric.[10] Skelton is touched (P 3), and all hatchets are happily buried (P 4).

[7] The dance may have been affected somehow by its format. Only one other Astaire romantic duet follows a love song sung by the woman—"I'm Old Fashioned" in *You Were Never Lovelier* (16 F). That duet has the same peculiar structure as "Thinking of You": it begins intimately and then becomes extroverted.

[8] One important part of the Kalmar/Ruby story largely ignored in the film was their contribution as scriptwriters to several Marx Brothers shows and films, including two of the best: *Horsefeathers* (1932) and *Duck Soup* (1933).

[9] Actually, Eileen Percy, whom Dahl impersonates, was Ruby's third wife. She had appeared in silent films in the 1920s and retired from the screen in 1927.

[10] The song was written for an Amos 'n' Andy film, *Check and Double Check*, in 1930. Among the various titles Kalmar had previously tried and rejected were "How Have You Been?," "What Do You Know?," and "Say You Are Mine."

L3 L4 L5 M1

M2 M3 M4 M5

M6 M7 M8 M9

M10 M11 M12 M13

M14 N1 N2 O1

P1 P2 P3 P4

24.

Let's Dance

1950

On paper, *Let's Dance* looks remarkably promising. The script is by Allan Scott, who had written most of the screenplays for the Astaire-Rogers films of the 1930s. The music is by Frank Loesser, an experienced Hollywood songwriter who had only recently completed the score for the Broadway hit *Where's Charley?* and was at the time working on *Guys and Dolls,* which boasts one of the finest scores in the history of the American musical theatre. The director is Norman Z. McLeod, who had to his credit several comedy classics including ones featuring the Marx Brothers, W. C. Fields, and Bob Hope. Fred Astaire's partner is the robust Betty Hutton, who, after a string of movie successes in the 1940s, had just completed *Annie Get Your Gun* at MGM, which was to become one of the highest-grossing musicals in history (see Table 3). And in there helping Astaire with the choreography was his crony and alter ego, Hermes Pan.

Somehow, just about everything went wrong. The film is lifeless, incoherent, and tediously drawn out, and the music is amazingly weak. There are a couple of high spots among the dances—a screwball solo for Astaire and a screwball duet with Hutton—but in general the level is considerably below Astaire's best.

BETTY HUTTON

It is customary, and probably fair, to place much of the blame for the film's failure on Astaire's costar. Hutton seemed able to operate on only one level—loud. She talked loud, she sang loud, she danced loud, she acted loud, and she wept loud (and repeatedly). Her style—an odd mixture of brazen hard sell and weepy sentimentality—was the opposite of Astaire's, which stressed subtlety and understatement. The idea in putting the two together was probably to see if the reaction might result in a palatable blend. The success of the Astaire partnership with Ginger Rogers, after all, is often ascribed to a complementary juxtaposition: "he gives her class, she gives him sex." In *Let's Dance,* however, there is no alchemy.

What seems to have thrown Astaire off is not Hutton's chewing-up-the-scenery approach but, rather, her inability to do anything else. In fact, he makes a considerable, and often quite successful, effort to match her style—not only in their three substantial duets but also in his solo, which is pitched almost entirely in the high-decibel range. But for contrast there was no softness, no flexibility, no real vulnerability in the Hutton persona to work with; like crystal, she had only two states of being: hard or shattered. Accordingly, when the script supplies him with an opportunity to develop a loving duet with Hutton, Astaire essentially passes it by. Like the steely Eleanor Powell, Hutton was a partner Astaire was unable to warm to romantically.

Hutton's performance style seems to have emerged at least in part from a profound insecurity about her talents. As she once told an interviewer, presumably in a lighthearted vein, "I worked out of desperation. I used to hit fast and run in hopes that people wouldn't realize that I really couldn't do anything." Hermes Pan recalls: "Poor Betty was very neurotic. . . . I said, 'Betty, hold your palms down. . . . It's better if . . . ,' and she broke down in tears and rushed off the set and said, 'Oh, you think I'm clumsy. I know you think I can't dance. . . .' I said, 'I didn't say anything.' . . . It was a very difficult period."

THE SCRIPT AND THE DIRECTION

Scott's script is filled with unlikely happenings, inconsistencies, and contrived events, and McLeod's direction is plodding. In addition, the editing is often indulgent: scenes of only incidental importance are allowed to run on far too long. These defects are not, by themselves, necessarily terminal, for they can also be found in some of Astaire's films of the 1930s—Scott's *Follow the Fleet,* for example—but in *Let's Dance* the music and the dancing do far less to enliven the proceedings.

LUCILE WATSON

One decided asset in *Let's Dance* is the performance of the seventy-year-old Lucile Watson as an authoritarian Boston dowager. The role is an ungrateful one—a stereotyped heavy who spends her time absurdly and irrationally trying to take Hutton's young son away from her until the end, when Watson becomes instantly and inexplicably mollified. Given little to work with, Watson, an experienced actress on stage and screen, is somehow able to infuse her role with such warmth, cool humor, and believability that one begins almost to root for her in her obsessive quest. At one point she has a nostalgic little dance duet with Astaire, and this is the closest the film ever gets to a convincing expression of affection.[1]

THE MUSIC

Frank Loesser had written songs for Hutton before and had turned out appropriate material that had some appeal: "Murder, He Says" in 1943 and "Papa, Don't Preach to Me" in 1947. But he seemed unable to repeat the feat in *Let's Dance*.

A highlight of the generally undistinguished score is "Oh Them Dudes," a satiric romp that forms the base for a Hutton-Astaire comedy duet and which is handled with wit and intelligence by the musical arrangers. Not so fortunate was the film's big tune, "Why Fight the Feeling," a song Astaire says he is especially fond of. The song is trashed by Hutton in the film and then overglamorized in a later dance routine for Astaire. The only time it is given its due is when it is played under the opening titles; a certain unaffected charm is evident there.

THE CHOREOGRAPHY

Hermes Pan apparently contributed considerably to the numbers, including many of the nutty ideas in Astaire's "Piano Dance" solo, such as the cascade of cats. The choreography for Astaire is unusual in that it includes several falls to the floor and drops to the knees, something that occurred only rarely in his other films—and then almost solely in numbers Pan worked on (22 G, 23 A, 23 F, 30 C, 30 H, 30 L).

[1] Watson's appeal may derive in part from her relaxed attitude toward her acting, which contrasts utterly with Hutton's congenital overanxiousness. On her retirement in 1953 Watson remarked, "I was never aura-eyed about the theatre. I think the theatre is good, hard, sordid work. It's brought me only a grim satisfaction but not any more than if I'd sewn a fine seam."

Piano Dance

THE NUMBERS

A
CAN'T STOP TALKING
(3′ 1″)

The film opens with the sound of an air-raid siren in wartime Britain blending into a prolonged note howled by the gaping Betty Hutton at a USO show (A 1)—something that might be taken as pointed commentary on her singing style. She then launches into the song, a rapid-patter ditty that seems, in her delivery at least, to be essentially tuneless. As she breathlessly relates the virtues of the man she claims to adore, she illustrates some of the words with broad gestures and sways widely from side to side (A 2).

Astaire, accompanying her at the piano, adds a bit of sung banter (A 3), and she then drags him out onto the floor for an amusing, raucous dance duet that makes use of various forms of diagonal body positions, perhaps suggested by the one she had introduced while singing the song (as in A 4, A 6; compare A 2). As a dancer, Hutton was given to slinging out gratuitous and remarkably unsensual hip swings, and she inserts several in this dance (A 5). She also performs the whole dance at the hard-sell level, while Astaire tries to vary the texture by rendering some passages with mock delicacy. As a result the performers sometimes do not seem to be doing the same dance (A 7). The number lapses into some rather conventional jitterbugging toward the end (A 8), but has a nice finish when the performers exuberantly make for the wings in a nested, staggered stride (A 9).

B
PIANO DANCE
(3′ 55″)

Astaire startles Hutton by suddenly announcing to the audience that they are going to be married. Then, in an offstage scene that ends with her weeping, she tells him that she is already married, and he walks out.

Six years later, in Boston, Hutton, now a widow with a six-year-old son, is firmly but calmly told by her husband's rich grandmother (Lucile Watson) that she is free to go back into show business as she desires, but only if the child remains in Boston to be properly cared for (B 1). Hutton weeps, then snaps up her son and, penniless, sneaks away to New York.

Which, as it happens, is where Astaire has ended up. His ambition is to be a success at high finance, but for the time being he is working as an entertainer at a Manhattan supper club. Delayed by an unsuccessful effort to close a financial deal, he cockily walks into rehearsal seven hours late. The irritated proprietor tells him to get working on a new routine. Astaire then romps through a solo that has an appropriately improvisatory feel to it. The idea is that show business is just a sideline—child's play, really—for this broadly talented man who believes his true destiny to be on Wall Street.

It begins as he ambles over to the piano, which is being played by Tommy Chambers, one of Astaire's rehearsal pianists in real life. Using the piano as a ballet barre, Astaire tosses off some exercises by way of warm-up. There is your airy arabesque (B 2), your basic plié (with attendant back pain) (B 3), your decorative rond de jambe en l'air (B 4), and your casual battement tendu (B 5).

As the music becomes bouncy, Astaire turns his attention to the piano itself and, throwing all refinement and caution aside, barrels through the most acrobatic dance of his film career. (The acrobatics were apparently at Pan's urging: "I finally convinced him he could do it.") Astaire

A 1 · A 2 · A 3 · A 4 · A 5 · A 6 · A 7 · A 8 · A 9 · B 1 · B 2 · B 3

slithers under the piano, jumps inside it while yelping gleefully (B6), hangs from it, and, after sizing it up from the floor (B7), swings himself up on top (B8) and gloats triumphantly (B9). There is a concentrated effort, largely successful, to link these raucous effects with dance material so they arise with choreographic and musical logic.

Sliding back down to the floor (B10), Astaire takes up a position at a second instrument nearby and raps out a bit of what, in *Roberta,* he had called "feelthy piano." The dance interest doesn't stop merely because Astaire is seated at a piano, of course. He remains a visual treat as he reacts happily to his own rhythms, letting the music ripple through his body, or as he cheerfully displays two fingers that are about to be put into action on the keyboard (B11). The boogie-flavored music he plays was written by Astaire himself.

Next he frolics up on top of his piano to do a tap dance there and then slaps his foot on the keys (B12). This works so well he tries it on the first piano—stroking out a piano ripple and doing a cat impersonation while the orchestra plays "Tiger Rag" (B13). When he pauses, several cats, as if called from the deep, jump from the innards of the piano and scatter (B14).

Pan recalls the origins of this gag: "It came to me that it would be very funny . . . if suddenly he'd open the piano and cats would fly out. There was a great deal of 'Oh, you can't do that,' and I said, 'Well why can't you? Just get ten cats and put them in the piano and open it and they'll scatter.' . . . There was no difficulty. . . . You can imagine the poor cats, and this noise, inside a piano—whuumpp. . . . He'd open the thing and the cats flew out. Nobody has seen one of them since."

Best of all is the ending. Astaire jumps down from the piano, retrieves his hat and coat, and sequentially hops up on three chairs, tipping each over backward (B15). The tipping is done with great control, so that the chairs topple gradually; the effect suggests that Astaire is sailing over them. He makes his way up a staircase, taking the first steps on his knees (B16), topples another chair at the top, puts on his coat, kneels before one final chair (B17), clambers up on top, tips it over, and sails out of sight—and out of the rehearsal (B18).

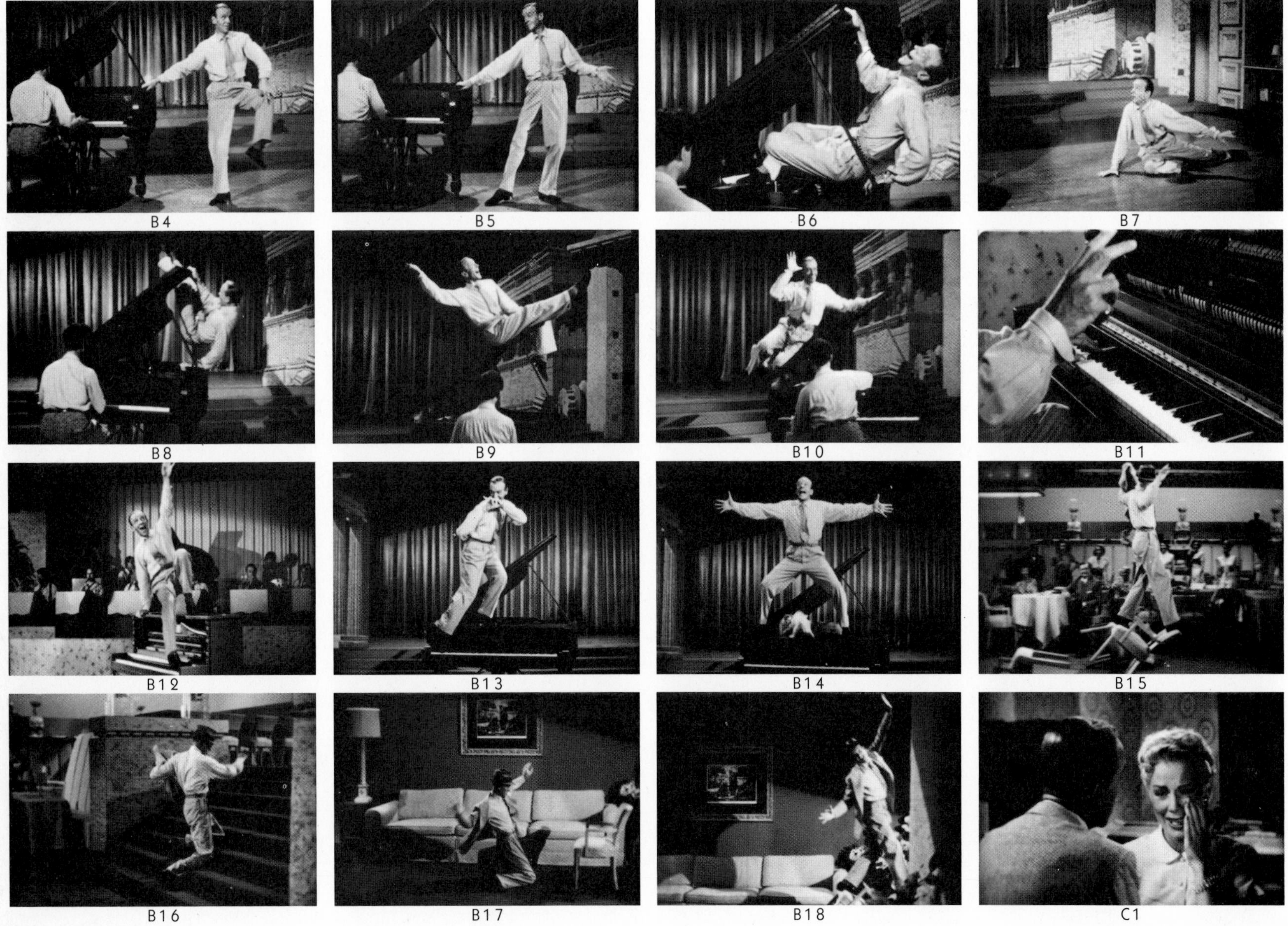
B4 B5 B6 B7
B8 B9 B10 B11
B12 B13 B14 B15
B16 B17 B18 C1

C
JACK AND THE BEANSTALK
(2′ 16″)

By chance, Astaire and Hutton run into each other, and each soon learns about the other's impecunious state. Hutton has been unable to find a job—and cries about it, of course (C1)—but Astaire promises to get her one at the club. He follows this good deed by proposing to tell her son a bedtime story.

He wins over the son by demonstrating his prowess at impersonating the alphabet—he is particularly terrific at *F* (C2) and *T* (C3). The boy asks for a story that combines *Hamlet* and "Jack and the Beanstalk," but Loesser instead has supplied a song, quite appropriate to the Astaire character, that tells the beanstalk fable from a financier's point of view: Jack's "collateral security" was "a handful of beans." (Then why, one might be set to wondering idly, wasn't the script changed to replace the *Hamlet* request with something appropriate like *Horatio Alger*?)

The lyric is rather clever, but even Astaire can't make the melody scan appealingly. In the course of the song he magically creates an illustrative beanstalk out of a rolled newspaper (C4) and concludes with a goofy little dance caper, which ends abruptly when he bumps his head on the wall (C5). He somersaults backward across the bed (C6) and comes to rest unconscious, in which condition he spends the night. His overnight stay is noted with interest by a private detective watching from the street (and so the number does, as they say, move the plot along).

D
OH THEM DUDES
(6′ 7″)

Astaire gets Hutton a job as a cigarette girl at the supper club, but Watson's lawyers find her there and seek to take custody of her son on the grounds that she doesn't make enough money to support him properly. Thinking quickly (or as quickly as the script allows), Astaire temporarily placates them by announcing that Hutton is making her debut that night as a performer in the club's show and that, if successful, she will be receiving a fine salary.

The number she and Astaire perform, which is supposed to be one of their old USO routines, is a clownish song-and-dance routine done in impersonation of a couple of swaggering cow-

C2 C3 C4 C5 C6 D1 D2 D3 D4 D5 D6 D7 D8 D9 D10 D11

boys. Astaire had done his first clown number in *Easter Parade*, with Judy Garland, and much of its humor derives from its ingenious and precisely timed contrast of the very oafish with the very refined (21 K). This duet, appropriate to Hutton's talents, eschews refinement entirely: its effects are intentionally overstated, and its humor is determinedly broad. For all that, Astaire, mustachioed and attired in grubby work clothes, still retains vestiges of his innate elegance (something he thoroughly conquered only once in his film career, in the clown duet in his next film, *Royal Wedding* [25 F]). Hutton, unhindered and unleashed, throws herself into the number with gusto and glee, punctuating every gesture with a visual exclamation point—something Astaire doesn't always find necessary.

The resulting number is actually rather delightful—charming, even—in its sheer lack of restraint, its cheerful willingness to let its hair down. And in a study of Astaire's artistry there is something almost purgative about being able to include a dance in which he mimes the scraping of horse dung off his shoe, and which concludes with a veritable fusillade of vigorous kicks to the seat of the pants. However, while the number flirts daringly with arrant vulgarity, it still maintains the careful construction and wry sensitivity that are Astaire trademarks. It's just that there is not a great deal of what might be called subtlety in its conception or execution.

The number opens with Hutton and Astaire striding menacingly into a Western saloon (D1). The customers pay no attention to the intruders, but the bartender is terrified (an odd and unnecessary inconsistency) and fearfully serves them a drink when they stomp over to the bar (D2). Their tough façade is shattered as they react to the strong liquid by wilting to the floor in agony. When they recover, their attention is caught by something in the distance, and they warily cross the room to get a closer look. It proves to be a television set showing Eastern dudes doing a Western dance. They are shocked and take the film audience into their confidence by shooting an amazed expression at it (D3) in what turns out to be one of the very few times in Astaire's film career that he looks directly at the camera. Then they turn and destroy the television set by firing a series of shots at it—no doubt an image of great appeal to the motion-picture industry, which in 1950 was facing increased competition from the new medium.

The dancers now adopt various bow-legged poses to explain in song, and at some length, their outrage at "them dudes" who are "doin' our dance" (D4). During a brief dance episode they mime your classic slip-on-horse-dung-and-sheepishly-scuff-it-off routine and then conclude the song by accompanying themselves with a series of percussive Huttonesque hip swings (D5; compare A5, H2) and by demonstrating how their dance should properly be performed—with maximum stomp, minimum gentility (D6).

They soon begin to have trouble keeping their balance and fortify themselves with another drink. This apparently does the trick, for it sends them whooping vigorously across the saloon (D7), then returning while twirling their hats on their pistols, which Astaire accomplishes by a simple side-step while Hutton adds a broad turning-in and turning-out of the legs, something she could do with remarkable speed and skill (D8).

After a raucous jumping dance over their floored hats, they try another drink, but this one causes them to collapse to the floor. There follows a belabored struggle to get up: Hutton tries hoisting Astaire by the belt (D9) and lifting him from below (D10), but both efforts ultimately fail. She then sits on him and, in the number's low spot, delivers some broad gestures as he kicks up his heels—a childish gimmick and one that is clumsily inserted into the dance without transition or choreographic motivation (D11).

Things do improve, however. The cowboys finally get to their feet and conclude the number by repeatedly kicking each other in the seat of the pants (D12, 13). What makes the sequence so endearing is the spectacularly undignified gusto with which it is carried out. The kicks are not stagey but are, rather, performed full-out, with the kickers putting all their force and weight into the effort. Moreover, the kicks escalate. The first ones are brutal enough but essentially exploratory. Then, as the orchestra picks up the rhythm and launches into a broad rendering of the main melody, the dancers punctuate the downbeats with heftier kicks—each of which is embellished when the kickees fire off their sixguns on landing. The number ends with a final stomping promenade around the saloon, which carries the cowboys out the swinging doors.

E
WHY FIGHT THE FEELING
(2′29″)

Even though Hutton's debut is a big success, Watson's lawyers have her served with a sum-

D12 D13 E1 F1

G1 G2 G3 G4

mons to appear at a judicial hearing. In the lengthy scene at the hearing, the custody of Hutton's son is discussed and Astaire's overnight stay in her apartment is explained. Astaire then announces that he will marry Hutton, thereby creating an appropriate family environment for the boy. The judge gives them sixty days to establish said appropriate environment. Since the film still has a long time to run, however, Astaire and Hutton split up after a scriptwriter-contrived fight in the marriage-license office.

Next, a rich friend of Astaire's becomes interested in Hutton. Astaire horns in on this incipient romance and they all visit the friend's lodge, where Hutton performs the film's big ballad. She sings in a languid, overemphatic manner that undercuts any appeal the song may have. As she sings, Astaire manages to give her a hot seat (E1), which ultimately sets her dress afire and sends her running into the lake for relief.

F
THE HYACINTH
(47″)

Now, for variety, a little tenderness. Astaire has impressed Watson by coming up with some financial advice that has proved successful. They get along so well that they soon find themselves briefly dancing a gentle, courtly duet to music provided by a music box (F1).

G
WHY FIGHT THE FEELING
(DANCE) (2′43″)

Meanwhile, Hutton has resolved to marry Astaire's rich friend, but at an engagement party Astaire manages to break up the alliance through a bizarre scheme: he convinces his friend that Hutton has a compulsion about tricking people into giving her their jewelry.

Astaire's decision to play this trick comes to him during a fantasy dance. After leaving the party to get some air, he wanders pensively in a nearby courtyard. As he does so, he wafts through a few unresolved partnerless dance phrases (G1). Soon Hutton materializes next to him (G2). He approaches her, then takes her in his arms and swirls her around the floor (G3, 4), but she separates from him and vanishes (G5).

The situation presents an ideal opportunity for a romantic duet, and one that has a meaningful plot point to make: during the dreamlike dance, which is set to the ballad Hutton had sung earlier, Astaire comes to realize how much he loves her. But just as obvious is Astaire's decision to pass the opportunity by. Their duet is a fragment—it runs twenty-four seconds—and makes no effort to suggest much of anything. Hutton does seem to possess enough skill and fluidity to be a suitable partner, and most of Astaire's moves are beautiful to watch, yet the number adds up to a choreographic cop-out.

At the end, Hutton's image reappears in a pool of water (G6), clutching her necklace; this gives Astaire the idea for his fraudulent scheme, we are to believe.

H
TUNNEL OF LOVE
(4′28″)

Since Hutton has not gotten married (to Astaire or anybody else) within the sixty days prescribed by the judge, Watson is able legally to take custody of the boy.[2] However, Hutton, with Astaire's complicity, abducts the boy. When Watson and the police come to the supper club in search of the child, they accost Hutton backstage; she responds by crying for the fourth time in the film (H1).

As the search for the boy continues backstage, Astaire and Hutton perform in a production number. The song is begun by Hutton in her tuneless, overstressed manner as she and Astaire emerge onstage in a tunnel-of-love gondola. The song is continued on dry land accompanied by pleasant strutting steps, some of which make use of Hutton's signature hip swings (H2; compare A5, D5). They also do a bit of camera-oriented posturing that is remarkably banal by Astaire's standards (H3).

They reboard the gondola and are cycled backstage. On the ride, Astaire tells Hutton he has given up high finance and plans to stay in show business with her. This pleases her, and when the boat stops backstage she announces (as she had twice before in the film) their plans to get married. Her son bounds into her arms, and Watson, instantly transformed, gives joyful blessing (H4).

Astaire and Hutton then ride back to the front of the stage, where they conclude the number by performing a short celebratory duet featuring some crisp leg jabs (H5). They reboard the gondola and, to suggest affection, kiss (H6).

[2] Cast-list records suggest an onstage number for Hutton, the "Ming Toy Noodle Company," may have been shot for inclusion at this point.

G5 G6 H1 H2
H3 H4 H5 H6

25.

ROYAL WEDDING

1951

In almost all Fred Astaire films the central concern is the zigzag progress of Astaire's romance with his female partner. Although the outcome is entirely predictable, much of the fun comes from watching the pair maneuver their way around (or through) various obstacles and setbacks. *Royal Wedding* is unusual in that Astaire's romance is not really central to the plot. Thus, to appreciate the film's considerable appeals takes a certain readjustment.

To be sure, the film includes the usual formula: there is a love story in which Astaire meets, falls in love with, breaks up with, and finally marries a desirable and appealing lass (Sarah Churchill). But their romance is amazingly calm and dispassionate, and Astaire never really dances with—or even sings to—the woman who attracts him. Instead the central characters are Astaire and Jane Powell, who play a successful brother-sister musical-comedy team, and the dramatic tension in the film (such as it is) derives from the circumstances that lead finally to their breakup as a performing unit: she falls in love and decides to retire from show business to marry. Though this central dilemma could have been developed with more depth and poignancy in the film, the characterizations of the brother and sister are quite rich; one believes in this attractive, talented pair from the beginning and delights in their wry banter, in which warm mutual dependency is cloaked in genial needling.

The four dance duets in the film are all onstage routines performed by Astaire and Powell, and one of them is particularly fine: a galumphing, Brooklyn-cum-zoot-suit vaudeville shtick called "How Could You Believe Me When I Said I Love You When You Know I've Been a Liar All My Life." There is also an amusing exhibition ballroom duet that takes place, in part, on a rocking ship.

But the film is best known for Astaire's two solos. In one of these he dances up the walls and across the ceiling—probably his most famous number. The other is even more remarkable and of greater choreographic interest: alone in a rehearsal room, he transforms a clothes tree into a compliant dancing partner.

DELLY, ELLIE, AND FRED

Although the film is set in 1947 at the time of the wedding of Princess Elizabeth and Prince Philip, its inspiration was the legendary adventures of Fred and Adele Astaire in the 1920s and early 1930s: enormously popular in both the United States and Great Britain, the pair finally broke up professionally when Adele decided, like the film's Ellen Bowen, to marry an English nobleman and leave show business. At about the same time Fred, like Tom Bowen, married a reserved redhead.

The film borrows other elements from history, like the dance on the rocking ship and the sister's appeal to legions of stage-door johnnies, as well as important elements of characterization. The working and personal relationship between brother and sister, in particular, seems to have been based substantially on real life: he the mastermind behind the act, always demanding endless hours of rehearsal; she the carefree butterfly, always kidding him about his devotion to work and finding it so much more interesting to have fun.

There are, of course, many differences as well. The film team has no stage mother, and Astaire's insecurity and propensity to worry (Adele liked to call him "moaning Minnie") have not really been carried over to the film character. Nor is there more than a suggestion of Adele's spirited impertinence and calculated vulgarity. But scriptwriter Alan Jay Lerner—aided by Stanley Donen, in his first assignment as solo director—has created two warmly believable and attractive characters.[1]

[1] Lerner is less than proud of his work on this, his first screenplay: "My contribution left me in such a state of cringe that I could barely straighten up." His next script was *An American in Paris* which, unlike *Royal Wedding,* is sentimental and pretentious, and which earned him an Oscar.

With Jane Powell in "Open Your Eyes"

JANE POWELL

Much of the appeal of the film can be credited to the performance of the multitalented and highly professional Jane Powell. André Previn, who worked with Powell on several films, recalls that, of "all the great artists I've worked with, in every medium, she'd come up in the top five among the professional-behaving people. . . . She was always prepared." Powell and Astaire work so well together that it is surprising to learn that she joined the film late, as a replacement for a replacement. Originally the part of Astaire's sister was to go to June Allyson, who had to bow out when she became pregnant. Judy Garland was then assigned, but when she repeatedly failed to show up for rehearsals, she was removed from the film and suspended (in quadruplicate) by MGM, never again to make a film there.

Powell seems an excellent choice as a counterfeit Adele—pretty, petite, pert, impish, full of life. Primarily known as a singer—a capable light-opera soprano in the Kathryn Grayson / Deanna Durbin mold—she is also a remarkably talented and sensitive actress, and here has a role to which she can impart some color and depth.

Moreover, Powell also proves to be a gifted dancer of considerable range. Not only can she handle the comedy and variety dance routines with flair and ease, but she also shows the requisite fluidity and sympathetic magnetism to be an excellent partner for Astaire in the film's brief ballroom number. As Astaire laconically put it, "She surprised everybody by her handling of the dances."

THE MUSIC

The film uses original songs with music by Burton Lane (whose *Finian's Rainbow* had been a smash on Broadway in 1947) and lyrics by Lerner (whose *Brigadoon* had been a smash on Broadway in 1947). Except for a couple of songs at the end, it's a fine score, tuneful and varied.

THE CHOREOGRAPHY

Dance director for the film, and Astaire's collaborator on several of his numbers, was Nick Castle, who worked on over forty films for various studios during his twenty-year career in Hollywood. *Royal Wedding* was his only Astaire assignment.

“You're All the World to Me”

THE NUMBERS

A
EV'RY NIGHT AT SEVEN
(4′ 19″)

The film opens in New York with a rather uninspired onstage duet for the central couple. Perhaps in an effort to get the film off to a royal start, Astaire plays a bored king who likes to chase the chambermaid (Powell) around the throne room. He sings her a song, and there is a brief dance (A1, 2). In general the movement under the singing is more arresting than the dance proper.

Powell is lively and appealing, responsive to Astaire's touch and to the sometimes overorchestrated rhythms of the music. But Astaire looks a bit old and tired through most of the number, as if trying to communicate two plot points: the show is in its last week, and the theatre's air conditioning has broken down. (A jarring reaction shot of the audience is inserted at one point, a clumsy device extremely rare in Astaire's musical numbers, suggesting repairs had to be made somewhere.)

B
SUNDAY JUMPS
(3′ 58″)

Soon Astaire and Powell have left New York (and Powell's collection of beaux) for London, where they will perform at the time of the royal wedding. On board ship, Powell meets a handsome English peer, Peter Lawford, and immediately forgets about a rehearsal with Astaire that was scheduled to take place in the ship's gymnasium. Abandoned, Astaire (no longer looking at all old or tired) calmly finds a willing temporary replacement: a clothes tree.[2]

Although quite a few Astaire numbers involve prop manipulation, this one is the most impressive example of Astaire's astonishing ability to animate the inanimate. Astaire also uses the opportunity to parody aspects of his own romantic duets.

The clothes tree is brought into the dance with Astaire's usual care and subtle humor. To the beat of a metronome, he tries out a few brilliant step sequences, looks at his watch, and then goes to the door to peer down the hallway to see if Powell is coming; in so doing he happens to put his hand on the clothes tree (B1), and it remains attached as he turns to go back (B2). He finds this at once surprising and interesting and gives the thing a quick audition: he sends it spinning and then stands back, observing its amblings with critical detachment (B3).

The orchestra has been playing exploratory fragments from "Sunday Jumps," as if waiting for Astaire to decide about the clothes tree's dance potential before committing itself to the song proper.[3] Many Astaire duets include a beautiful and witty transition step, the Astaire double helix: starting side by side, the dancers make independent spiraling circles around each other and wind up in a front-to-front partnering position. In this duet Astaire uses the double helix to begin the dance as he deftly spins his way

[2] The idea of using a clothes tree as a partner originated with Hermes Pan. Although he did not work on *Royal Wedding,* Pan had discussed the idea with Astaire sometime earlier. Pan receives no screen credit but is pleased, he says, that it was Astaire who used the idea, carrying it out with such taste and imagination.

[3] Lerner wrote a lyric for this bouncy Lane melody, but it is not used in the film and has never been published. It is the confession of someone who can't bear the peace and calm of Sunday and can't wait for work days to return—someone, in fact, rather like Fred Astaire, whose penchant for calling rehearsals on Sundays and holidays is legendary.

A1 A2 B1 B2
B3 B4 B5 B6
B7 B8 B9 B10

around the rotating clothes tree (B4) and tenderly takes it in his embrace (B5)—a maneuver that also serves to cue the orchestra to begin the song.

In the dazzling dance that ensues, the prop is manipulated in various ways—spun around on Astaire's hand, cradled in his arm (B6), hurdled (B7), nuzzled around his back (B8), rolled in great, loping circles around the floor (B9), carried briefly on the top of his foot, and rocked back and forth by its stand (B10). Then there is another brisk double helix (B11), a spinning partnered pattern with the performers clasping hands overhead (as it were) (B12), and a goofy, side-to-side swaying of the clothes tree that seems momentarily to mesmerize Astaire (B13). The time has now come in this duet for The Lift—something Astaire characteristically uses sparingly and carefully, usually at a point of climax near the end of a number. After dropping to one knee and pledging eternal fidelity to his partner (B14), Astaire attempts to pick it up but finds it too heavy (B15). Undaunted, he resolves to do a little body building to get himself in shape (B16).

It may be no surprise to learn (but it is worth emphasizing anyway) that this entire dance sequence—from the point where Astaire picks up his partner at the doorway (B1) to the point where he makes his decision to strengthen himself with the gym equipment (B16)—is all recorded in one continuous take: 1.4 minutes in all. At no time is editing used to create or enhance an effect.[4]

Astaire's encounter with the gym equipment, though not as exhilaratingly amusing as his dance with the clothes tree, has its screwball surprises—as when he belts the punching bag with a high kick (B17), or sends an Indian club flying with an incidental flick of his right foot during the course of a wild leap (B18).

At last he feels sufficiently strengthened to try the lift again. With mock-macho caveman virility, he ferociously grabs the clothes tree and spins with it on top of his foot (B19), developing an incidental step from earlier. Then he lifts the object to his shoulders and turns wildly (B20), presses it overhead triumphantly (B21), lowers it to the ground again, and, on the last note of the music, flips it from one side to the other so it comes to final rest in a cradled backbend (except without the bend) (B22). The dancers take a bow, and Astaire, always the gentleman, gallantly lets his partner have the preferred downstage position (B23).

[4] The medium shot in B13 is accomplished by moving the camera in and then out, not by cutting.

C
OPEN YOUR EYES
(4′ 13″)

A short while later Astaire and Powell attempt to perform a ballroom routine for the other passengers as the ship heads into heavy seas. In this sweet and amusing number, Powell shows herself to be an accomplished ballroom dancer and suggests that she could have been a compelling romantic dancing partner for Astaire had the opportunity ever arisen.

The song, a lilting waltz sung charmingly by Powell, is beautifully staged. Between phrases Astaire pilots her around the floor, so that she sings each phrase in a different locale. When she finds herself near Lawford, she warmly directs part of the phrase toward him (C1).

When she has finished singing the song, Astaire takes her in his arms for a brief exhibition duet. If her development as a dancer has suffered because she missed the rehearsal in the

B11 B12 B13 B14
B15 B16 B17 B18
B19 B20 B21 B22

gym, it is certainly not evident from this duet as she glides and spins around the floor in response to Astaire's lead (C2, 3). The duet, tender and solicitous, serves to express the couple's relationship: mutually dependent and consonant. The ending—marred somewhat by a camera that moves in too close—is quite wonderful: Powell flows voluptuously in toward Astaire (C4) and promenades him while swirling around him (C5) (on this maneuver, see p. 172n).

Now the mood changes to comedy as a storm starts to rock the ship and the dancers try to keep their aplomb as the floor tips under them. This event is based on a real-life incident: when Fred and Adele Astaire made their first voyage to London in 1923, they performed under the same circumstances, and with the same results. The scene was shot out of doors on the MGM back lot on a boat-rocking device that had previously seen service in such nonmusicals as *Captains Courageous*.

One tip sends them scooting uncontrollably until they crash into an innocent bystander, upsetting a bowl of fruit in the process (C6). The liberated fruit pursues them across the floor as the ship rocks in the opposite direction (C7). Despite the mayhem, Powell performs some remarkably fluid arm work during all this, and later, when a missed connection sends her tumbling, Astaire hauls her awkwardly to her feet from behind in a manner that shows off her pliant torso (C8). After a few more mishaps they settle into their concluding pose (C9), only to be unexpectedly swept off their feet by an ambulatory sofa (C10).

D
REHEARSAL FRAGMENTS
(1′ 30″)

In London, Astaire meets and is casually attracted to a reserved and articulate woman in the chorus of his London show. She is played by the actress Sarah Churchill, who in this, her only American film appearance, is required to do a small amount of dancing: a brief audition solo (D1) and a bit of upbeat ballroom dancing with Astaire as he asks her for a date that evening (D2). Churchill, the daughter of a famous British politician (a fact MGM was not supposed to use in its publicity for the film), had been dreaming of dancing with Astaire for seventeen years (her father's comment on this teen-age fantasy: "Humph"). On her suggestion, her role was changed from a singer to a dancer, and she reports that she found reality to be even better than the dream.[5]

E
THE HAPPIEST DAY OF MY LIFE
(2′ 22″)

Astaire learns that Churchill is engaged to a man in Chicago. A confirmed bachelor, Astaire is pleased to learn this; it means they can continue to see each other without "pressure," he opines to her confidently.[6]

Meanwhile, the Powell-Lawford romance is heating up. At the hotel, Powell rehearses one of the show's love songs under Astaire's direction and sings some of it to Lawford, who happens to be visiting (E1).

[5] Producer Arthur Freed had once thought of casting the English ballet dancer Moira Shearer (the lead in the hugely successful *The Red Shoes* of 1948), but Astaire blocked that idea: "I know she's wonderful, but what the hell would I do with her?"

[6] Her acerbic father is played by Albert Sharpe, who had created the role of Finian in *Finian's Rainbow* on Broadway in 1947. Astaire was to play that role in the regrettable film version of 1968.

B23 C1 C2 C3 C4 C5 C6 C7 C8 C9 C10 D1

F

HOW COULD YOU BELIEVE ME WHEN I SAID I LOVE YOU WHEN YOU KNOW I'VE BEEN A LIAR ALL MY LIFE

(6′8″)

Onstage at the London opening of their show, Astaire and Powell blast through a raucous vaudeville routine. The number is something of a high point for Astaire, the only time in his film career that he was able fully to repress his innate propensity to be couth. Not that he hadn't tried. As far back as *Follow the Fleet* (1936) he had been cast as a gum-chewing sailor; but he came out looking like an elegant sailor who happens to chew gum. Later he was an elegant Chinese coolie, an elegant con man, and an elegant drunk. As a tramp in a number in *Easter Parade* (21 K) and a cowboy in *Let's Dance* (24 D) he began to shrug this mantle a bit, but only here, in "How Could You Believe Me When I Said I Love You When You Know I've Been a Liar All My Life," are delicacy, refinement, wry understatement, and above all elegance finally given the wind. Of course the number is still carefully crafted, musically fastidious, intricate, and highly imaginative.

Astaire is greatly aided by his costume: a floppy zoot suit that envelops and disguises his dapper frame. Powell is sleek and appropriately vulgar in a tight-fitting skirt and sweater. Interestingly, she wears a close-cropped black wig over her blond locks, which makes her look quite a bit like Adele Astaire.[7]

The rather lengthy number is performed in a style that might be characterized as extreme Brooklyn, and the singing, as well as the movement, is intentionally broad and coarse. (Lane and Lerner, concerned that the film was becoming "so damn charming it's going to delicate itself to death," dreamed up this fine song while driving to the studio one morning.) Astaire still sounds like Astaire, but Powell's controlled soprano is considerably transformed. Astaire, playing a confirmed and unrepentant heel, takes pleasure in explaining to Powell in words unleavened by sentiment or subtlety that, contrary to any previous protestations on his part, he does not now, never has, and never will love her.

Astaire needs two full choruses of the song to explain everything. The first takes place largely on one spot on the stage. He makes his point forcefully several times (F1), and when Powell kneels to plead with him he responds by literally laughing up his sleeve (F2). The second chorus is sung amid galumphing motion: as she tags after him around the stage, accusing him of all sorts of infidelities, he suddenly turns on her with precise comic timing, stops her in her path, and gloatingly admits every indiscretion (F3). The singing ends with each trying to upstage the other (F4).

The dance that follows is an amusing set of variations on the funky slouch. There is, for example, the studied finger snap (F5), the sideways shuffle (F6), the rearing stomp (F7), the casual waddle (F8), and the splayed stride (F9). And it concludes with a traveling pattern in half-crouch with contrapuntal hand-clapping (F10). Appropriate to its style, this Astaire dance is much more directly related to the music than usual, and percussion is used, vaudeville-style, to underline comedy effects. But the dance remains delightfully surprising because the duration of a given effect is unpredictable and because there are unexpected changes in intensity in the steps. For example, the broad-gauged splayed stride (F9) explodes out of the surrounding material

[7] This apparently was a last-minute decision: MGM put out posed publicity stills from the number in which Powell does not wear the wig. Oddly, a photo of Astaire and Judy Garland in a test for the number shows Garland's dark hair covered by a *blond* wig.

D2 E1 F1 F2
F3 F4 F5 F6
F7 F8 F9 F10

and suddenly propels the dancers toward the wing, though their intended progress had seemed to be forward.

The number concludes with a broad episode that might be entitled "Left Bereft, She Wreaks Revenge." The music suddenly turns squealingly cacophonous and the dancing responds in kind (F 11), and efforts to re-establish tonal order succeed only when Astaire furiously slams his hat to the floor. Powell then vigorously stomps on the hat, breaks it over Astaire's head, thrashes him with blows that conclude with an indirect kick to the jaw (F 12), and then harangues him as he wriggles offstage (F 13). The bows are taken in character (F 14).

G
TOO LATE NOW
(3′40″)

After the show, Powell meets Lawford, and during a moonlit stroll they wistfully determine—he speaking and she in a lovely song—that they are in love and that it is too late now to think of finding anyone else (G 1). This is the third of the three ballads Powell sings in the film, and each is nicely staged to show the couple's growing attraction. The first, sung before an audience, was only incidentally directed at Lawford (C 1); the second, sung at the hotel with Astaire in attendance, was more clearly personal (E 1); and this one, in private, is a direct statement of love.

H
YOU'RE ALL THE WORLD TO ME
(4′5″)

Although we never see it happening, it turns out Astaire has fallen in love with Churchill. He doesn't sing to her about it—perhaps because she is engaged to someone else—so, back in his hotel room, he sings to her picture instead. And dances. Earlier in the script a line had been planted about how love makes you feel that you can dance all over the walls and ceiling. Astaire here proves the validity of the proposition.

He had had an idea for such a dance years before and had suggested it several times to Arthur Freed, but it never seemed to fit. Although the *Royal Wedding* script does not have a fantasy element in it, Astaire finally found a slot for his brainstorm—an idea, he says, that came to him at 4:00 a.m.

The effect was accomplished by mounting the entire room inside a cylindrical structure about twenty feet in diameter—a squirrel cage, they called it—in which the furniture and camera (and camera operator) were bolted to the floor. The whole assemblage rotated so that when Astaire was dancing on the ceiling, the room, camera, and camera operator were all upside down. There was some camera movement through the dance—from side to side, up and down, in and out—as the camera stayed tightly framed on Astaire, which meant the camera operator had to remain alert (and operating) even while hanging upside down. Astaire was asked so often about the mechanics of this number that he used to carry around a little explanatory diagram. Lighting was a tricky proposition since the room obviously needed to have a ceiling. The set was accordingly lit by the on-camera lights and by a ring of lights around the camera—all of which had to rotate with the room.

Whatever the mechanics of the number, the essential illusion is accomplished through dance, and film editing is never used to make things easier. Astaire dances two circumnavigations of the room in the number, each of which is accomplished in one or two shots. The number was rehearsed for weeks and then shot in less than a day and a half. (For a detailed breakdown of the construction and production of this number, see Table 4.)

For all its ingenuity, however, the number suffers somewhat because the choreography must be preoccupied with the effect. That is, Astaire's principal concern must be to communicate his gravity-defying illusion, to dance naturally even as his floor rotates under him. As a result, the steps themselves are less interesting than usual. The appeal of the number is further diminished by the oversweet orchestration; a perkier arrangement would have suited the dance and its mood better.

The number begins as Astaire enters his hotel room clutching a publicity photograph of Churchill. He drapes his coat, jacket, and top hat over the furniture (where they will have to be nailed down so they won't float away when the room rotates) and then slumps into an easy chair and gazes wistfully at the picture of his beloved (H 1–3). He hears his own disembodied voice singing the verse of the song and then sings the chorus himself while dancing around the room holding the picture (H 4). He places the picture on a desk and, still singing, does a terrific double helix with the desk chair, spinning it one way under his hand and circling around it in the opposite direction as it spins (H 5). He ends the song sitting on the chair (which will also have to be nailed down soon).

The dance itself begins as Astaire wafts back and forth across the room. These waftings get bolder and broader until the momentum of one carries him rather high up on one wall (H 6)—perhaps unnaturally high, but one can't be sure. From this position Astaire bounds across the floor, runs up the opposite wall, and pauses, as if experiencing an odd new sensation; soon he is prancing about on the wall (H 7).

Astaire's first circumnavigation of the room is mostly devoted to a series of happy jokes about the interesting things he can do with his new powers. For example, he finds he can jump over the chandelier (H 8) and dangle upward from a chair on the floor (H 9). When he reaches up (down) from the ceiling to grab Churchill's picture (H 10), he finds it is upside down to him and makes a deliberate show of turning it around (H 11). On reaching the other wall, he examines the picture while casually leaning at right angles to the floor (H 12).

Now he returns to what is normally considered terra firma and settles down on a chair, and there is a cut—the first since the dance began (H 13). After putting the picture down, he sets off on a second frolic around the room, which features crawling and tap dancing on the walls and ceiling (H 14–16). At the end he retrieves the picture, sinks back down on the easy chair, replaces the picture on the table, and gazes at it in exactly the same pose as at the beginning, except that now he is smiling (H 17; compare H 1). Maybe it was all a dream. (Interestingly, the number is referred to as the "dream number" in the production reports. The script calls for Astaire to fall asleep, and for his shadowy form to rise from his real form to do the dance—thus requiring that process photography be added to an already complex concept. In the finished number Astaire doesn't even bother to suggest sleep, though the idea of having his voice sing the verse off-camera does perhaps suggest fantasy.)

I
I LEFT MY HAT IN HAITI
(6′14″)

A short while later we see another number from the London show—a garish, ghastly production number on a Latin theme. Astaire spiritedly sings the song—a churning samba with a clumsy lyric (I 1). He soon finds himself in a Haiti where all the inhabitants are white and some of the women wear fedoras (I 2). There's a lot of pointless scrambling around, and Astaire does a brief, mildly interesting duet with Powell—who is *not* wearing a hat (I 3). At the end a monkey (who has the best part) jumps into Astaire's arms and gives him back his hat (I 4).

F11 F12 F13 F14

G1 H1 H2 H3

H4 H5 H6 H7

H8 H9 H10 H11

H12 H13 H14 H15

H16 H17 I1 I2

The number, presumably largely assembled by Nick Castle, is hardly worth much discussion, but a comparison with the film's opening number, "Ev'ry Night at Seven," is instructive. That number, while far from a masterpiece, at least had some point, logic, and light characterization in its chases and impish crown snatchings and concluding coronation. The "Haiti" number betrays no thought processes whatever. If Astaire is searching for the hat and the woman he left it with, why do several (but not all) of the women wear hats? And if he is going to do a duet with one of the women, why does he choose one of the hatless ones? And if he is searching for his hat, why does he do a duet anyway? Perhaps the monkey knows.

J

WHAT A LOVELY DAY FOR A WEDDING

(1' 12")

Dialogue comes as a relief. Astaire has learned that Churchill's absentee fiancé has married another woman. When he tells her, she expresses relief and pleasure, since she has fallen in love with Astaire. Although he is in love with her as well (and has, in fact, only recently done a vigorous dance to prove it), he feels he is too set in his ways to be a good husband (J1), and they part sadly and with somewhat improbable dignity.

Back at the hotel, Astaire and Powell have a discussion in which she finally decides to turn down Lawford's marriage proposal and to stay with the act (J2). Light and amusing, this well-acted and well-directed scene manages to be serious at base without slipping into pathos or weepy sentimentality.

The day of the royal wedding arrives. Keenan Wynn, who, in a double role, plays both the team's British agent and its American one, strides down the street (in his British incarnation) chiming in on a rather insipid song about the wedding (J3). Shots of the actual 1947 wedding (J4) are interspersed with shots of the two dour onlookers in the crowd (J5). The royal felicities prove contagious. In a brightly paced conclusion, Astaire and Powell simultaneously change their minds about marrying Churchill and Lawford. They decide they must get married that day. And do (J6).

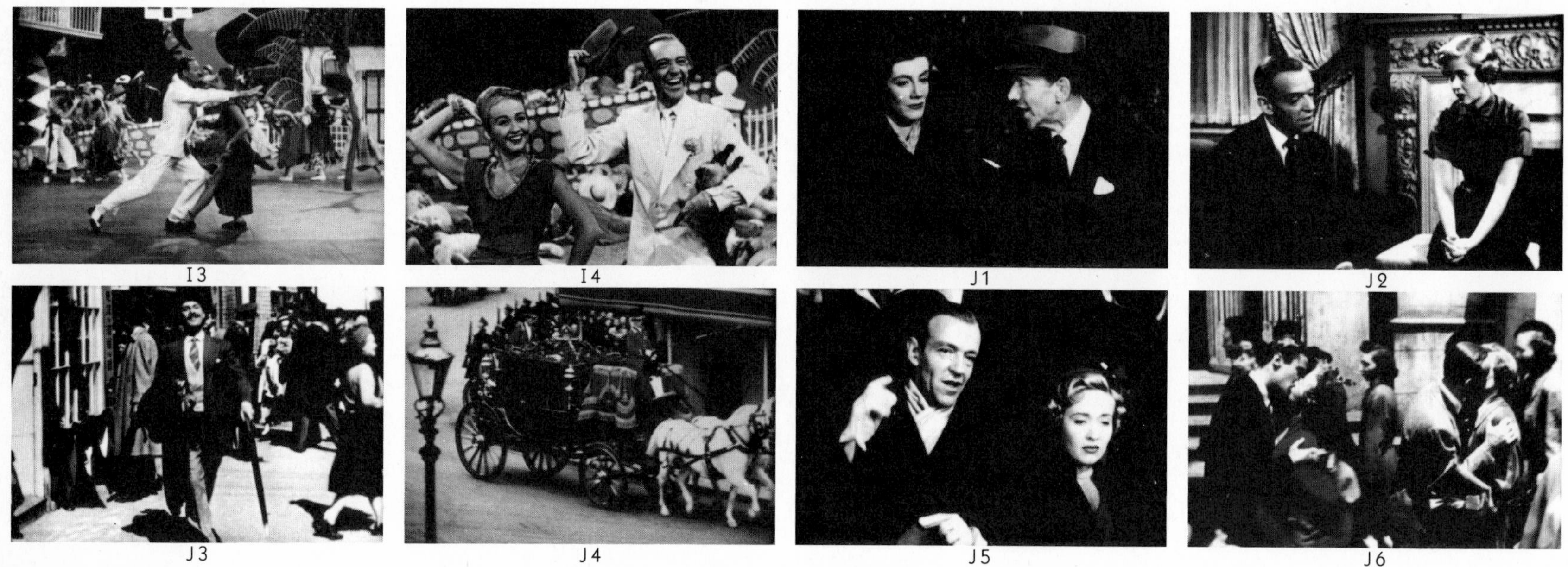

I3 I4 J1 J2

J3 J4 J5 J6

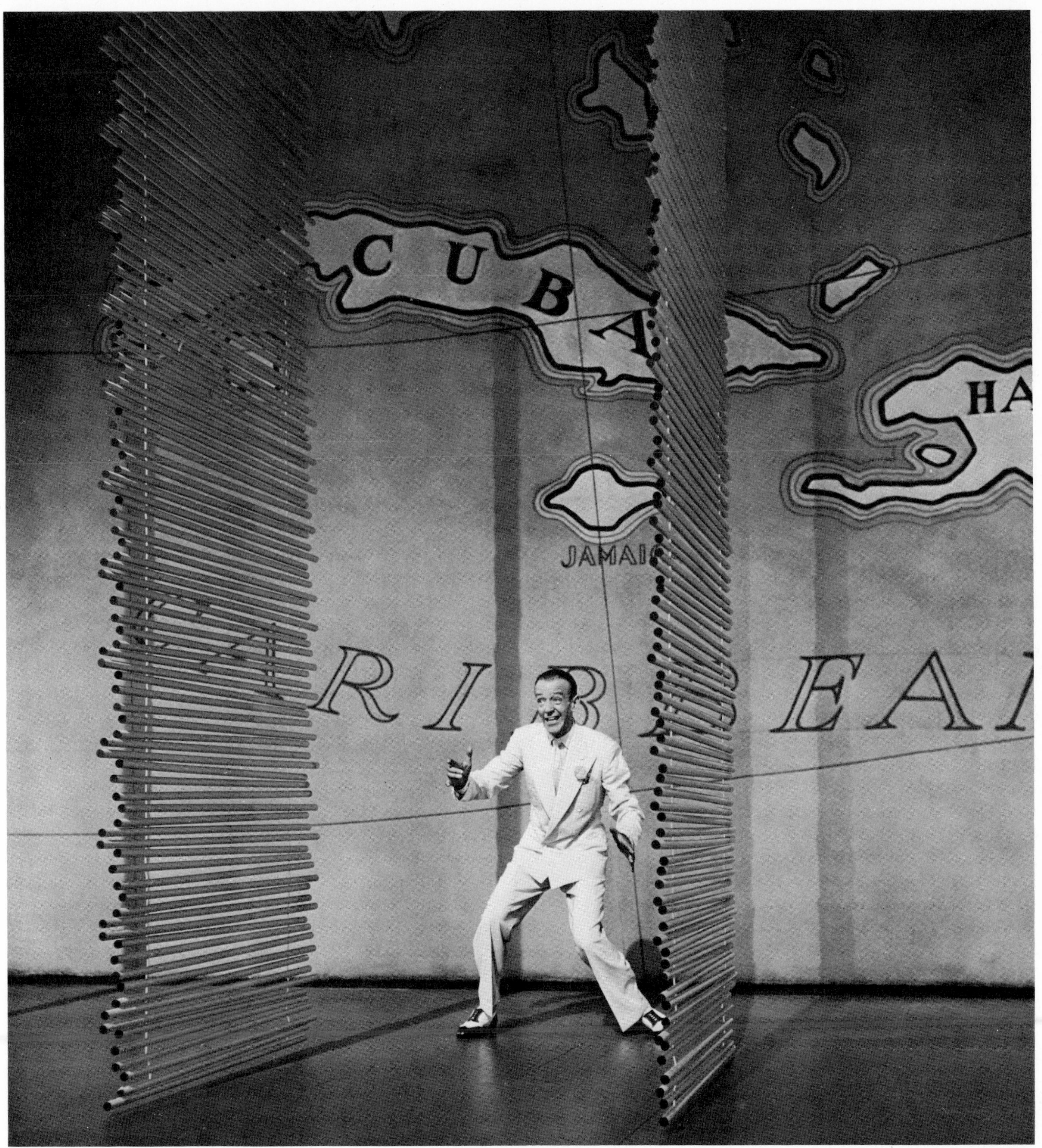

"I Left My Hat in Haiti"

26.

The Belle of New York

1952

The Belle of New York is one of the few Fred Astaire films to fail at the box office. The critics, too, rather uniformly found the film to be weak, and at least some of the participants in the film agree. The director, Charles Walters, has called it one of his least favorite of his films, and when confronted by people who like it he has suggested with amusement that they must be "sick." In his autobiography Astaire is quite harsh on the film: "The less said about it the better. . . . It bothered me to think I could try so hard with enthusiasm only to realize afterward that everything amounted to nothing." Indeed, the film's band of admirers may not number much more than three. The other two are David Shipman, who suggests it "looks suspiciously like his most enchanting work," and Douglas McVay, who has proclaimed it a "masterpiece."

A problem with the film for many seems to be the whimsicality, even the inconsequence, of the committee-created script and of the film's general tone, and it must be admitted, even by the most admiring, that the film's efforts at impish fancifulness sometimes become a bit coy. Moreover, expectations are likely to go joltingly unfulfilled: the film is populated with cartoonish, empty-headed characters who wander as best they can through various difficulties, whereas in the usual Astaire film the characters demonstrate more resourcefulness. Some also feel that Astaire was too old at that stage of his career to be effective in this sort of vehicle. In addition, the humor is somewhat elusive: much of the dialogue is very funny, but it is often understated and delivered in a throwaway manner, and the best jokes may be appreciated, if ever, only on reflection and re-viewing.

The film is unusual in its heavy reliance on dance: fully 41 percent of its eighty-two minutes is given over to dance numbers (see Table 7). Whatever his reservations about the film as a whole, Astaire recalls the dances with considerable satisfaction: "There were some awfully good dance numbers in that thing." His high evaluation seems entirely justified. Especially impressive are its three imaginative duets—bright, witty, virtuosic. The other dances include three solos and a comedy bit for Astaire, as well as a (not so splendid) solo for his partner, Vera-Ellen.

THE SCRIPT AND THE CHARACTERS

Set at the turn of the century, *The Belle of New York* is a fantasy about a New York without crime or grime, a New York of sunny, unabashed innocence. The characters who inhabit this world are in the Gilbert-and-Sullivan or Wodehouse mold: a bit childlike and not very bright. They are far more likely to solve their problems through spontaneous inspiration or luck than through craft or wile.

Fred Astaire is a naïve playboy in this film—an innocent rake. Constantly surrounded by beautiful gold diggers, he tumbles helplessly into one marriage engagement after another. His technique is sure-fire and without guile. As he puts it: "I just wait at the stage door with a bag of peanuts. Then I present them to the young lady and I say, 'Here, they're for you. I only wish they were diamonds.' The next thing I know I'm engaged."[1] He seems only dimly aware that the showgirl might be after the implied diamonds. But he never actually makes it to the wedding—something always comes up, and the brides-to-be are bought off. As he puts it in a rare moment of reflection, his problem is that he seems to "lose interest in any girl who'd marry a fellow like me"—an intricate bit of self-deprecation reminiscent of Groucho Marx's famous crack that he wouldn't want to join any club that would have him for a member.

Vera-Ellen has the opposite problem. She is, as it happens, the belle of New York—beautiful and extremely desirable—

[1] As Stanley Green observes, the writers here were making use of "a celebrated line first uttered by playwright Charles MacArthur upon meeting his future wife, Helen Hayes. Only MacArthur had wished for emeralds." Years later MacArthur parodied the line: he dumped a bag of emeralds in her lap and proclaimed, "I wish they were peanuts."

Filming "Oops" with Vera-Ellen

and men, by droves, are constantly falling in love with her. But rather than being flattered by this, she finds it irritating, since it distracts her from her work—saving souls as a member of the Salvation Army–style Daughters of Right. She is prim and cold and businesslike, and not easily impressed. Vera-Ellen's almost palpable reticence as an actress—her blandness, even—suits the role beautifully. (But it didn't suit Walters, who found her difficult to work with; she was, he says, "like a piece of moving putty.") It is inevitable, of course, that these two gently satiric characters should meet: Astaire, the hopeless romantic who is used to falling in love at a glance; Vera-Ellen, the hopeless drudge who doesn't even know what love is and seems to have very little interest in finding out.

A fantasy conceit is built into the script. Some two minutes and twenty-five seconds after first hearing her voice, Astaire informs Vera-Ellen that he is in love with her. She asserts with some impatience that this is quite unlikely, since, by his own testimony, he is merely numb and weak in the knees. When he asks her what love is in that case, she explains, as if reciting from a book she read once, that love is like billowy clouds, "and you walk on air." He ponders this revelation, and after she leaves he finds (with the aid of process photography) that he is indeed walking on air—he does a dance about it, in fact. The walking-on-air idea is then used at several points in the film as a fanciful signal of interior emotional states.

Astaire pursues his prim quarry assiduously, finding her the toughest conquest of his career—it takes him *two* dances to win her over. He is finally successful when, in the midst of the second, he makes a spontaneous gift of something much simpler than diamonds (or peanuts, for that matter): a small flower he has plucked from the grass. They celebrate their love in a fantasy production number, but then, in a fit of self-contempt, he concludes that he isn't good enough for her and breaks off their engagement. When he tries to reform himself by taking an honest job, however, she turns the tables: she pretends to be a "frivolous woman" and seeks to let him reform *her*. After some altercations, they are both walking on air.

Considering the brevity of the film and the length of the musical numbers, there is little time to develop characters other than the principal two. Nevertheless, Alice Pearce, as Vera-Ellen's plain-Jane sidekick, makes the most of her opportunities. Although she sometimes overdoes her characteristic cackling, she delivers most of her comedy lines with open-eyed innocence and apt timing (trying to cheer up Vera-Ellen as they march along in the percussion section of the band: "You know, I don't think there's anything prettier than a drum and a tambourine"). And she shows a touching vulnerability in her flustered pleasure when Astaire compliments her singing early in the film and, later, in her shy fantasizing about her own wedding during a rehearsal for Vera-Ellen's.

The monumental Marjorie Main, another highly accomplished comedienne, establishes a dominating presence as the chief of Vera-Ellen's mission, who is also Astaire's rich aunt ("Charles, you've been a problem since the day you learned how to whistle!").[2] And Keenan Wynn plays to the hilt his incidental role as Astaire's acerbic, opportunistic lawyer and friend.

VERA-ELLEN

If the quality, vivacity, and virtuosity of the three duets in this film are any indication, Vera-Ellen is the partner in the post-Rogers years who most stimulated Astaire's choreographic genius. Like most of his film partners after 1951, Vera-Ellen was an extensively trained dancer first, an actress second, and a singer not at all. Light, lithe, strong, and quick, she seems capable of doing anything Astaire chooses to dream up, and there is an unfettered quality to the choreography in the duets in this film that suggests the dancers were trying to push themselves to the limit.

Vera-Ellen's ballet background may also have suggested certain ideas that recur in several dances in the film—the frequent use of a version of the crook-legged ballet pose known as attitude being the most notable. And there are a few places in which Astaire seems to be gently parodying ballet.

THE ORIGINS OF THE FILM

Although little of it remains in the finished product, *The Belle of New York* is derived from a musical of the same name by Hugh Morton, with music by Gustave Kerker, which had first been produced on Broadway in 1897. (*Guys and Dolls*, which opened on Broadway in 1950, is partly drawn from the same source.) It was only a mild success in New York (fifty-six performances), but a great hit in London,

With director Charles Walters (left) and producer Arthur Freed

Paris, and Berlin, and it became a successful stock piece, as well as, in 1919, a silent film. The plot of the original show involves a Salvation Army lass who reforms a spendthrift playboy. The playboy's priggish father, in gratitude, wants to annul the playboy's marriage and force him to marry the Salvation Army belle. She, however, realizes the playboy is in love with his wife, not her, and alienates the father by performing a shocking French song, "At ze Naughty Folies-Bergère / My Feet Zey Fly Up in ze Air."[3]

The musical had been a favorite of MGM producer Arthur Freed since his youth, and he had long been interested in making it into a film with new songs. He wanted Fred Astaire in the role of the playboy and Judy Garland as the female lead; in the earliest script treatment of the play in Freed's files, dated October 1, 1943, the leads are named Fred and Judy.[4]

[2] According to assistant director Al Jennings, there was some tension between the two comediennes on the set: Main was afraid Pearce would steal a scene from her. Walters had originally wanted Mae West for the Main part (interesting casting against type), but West wanted too much money.

[3] The idea of the Salvation Army belle's scandalous public song was carried over in some early versions of the film's script. They called for Vera-Ellen to do a strip routine (perhaps to "Naughty but Nice") while Astaire tried to cover the number up by banging on a large drum. A song was written for the situation called "I Love to Beat the Big Bass Drum," but it was never used.

[4] At the time Freed asked Richard Rodgers and Oscar Hammerstein to do the score. Film rights to the original stage production were purchased in 1943 after a major effort to sort out who owned them. There were eleven claimants on three continents, of whom nine received payment, at a total cost to MGM of $77,000.

"Seeing's Believing"

Freed approached Astaire with the idea in the mid-1940s. Astaire was reluctant, because he would be repeating the fantasy element which had failed in *Yolanda and the Thief,* and perhaps because he had been part of a 1930 Broadway flop, *Smiles,* which had elements in common with the 1897 musical. At any rate, he escaped the Freed assignment by fleeing to Paramount for *Blue Skies* and then avoided it entirely by retiring in 1946.

When Astaire returned to movies, and to MGM, to do *Easter Parade,* Freed again approached him about the film, and they reached an agreement in the spring of 1948 to make the film with Garland—a project that never materialized because of problems with Garland's health and mental stability, problems that affected two other Astaire films, *The Barkleys of Broadway* and *Royal Wedding.* Finally, in 1951, Freed was able to bring the elements together for his dream project. Although Astaire went into it with reluctance, his attitude was in no way reflected in sagging work habits. Quite the contrary: as Walters observes, "Fred never worked so hard."

THE MUSIC

Astaire still recalls the songs with special pleasure. Most had been written in 1945, when Freed began moving toward production; "I Wanna Be a Dancin' Man" and "Naughty but Nice" were added in 1951.

Harry Warren's sweet, unaffected melodies suit the tone of the film beautifully. Johnny Mercer, among the most skillful of lyricists, shows an ability throughout the film to tailor his cleverness to fit the situation. The lyrics express sentiment in an appropriately naïve manner, and the rhymes are at once intricate and amusingly commonplace.

THE CHOREOGRAPHY

The dance director for the film, and the man in charge of shooting the numbers, was Robert Alton, Astaire's usual collaborator at MGM. This was to be his last Astaire film.

THE NUMBERS

A
WHEN I'M OUT WITH THE BELLE OF NEW YORK
(1′ 29″)

As the film opens, a chorus of men is serenading Vera-Ellen with the title song while she gazes down at them from her office window in the mission house (A1–2). Harry Warren's tune, a churning, carousellike waltz, sweetly evokes the turn-of-the-century period. (The serenader at left front is Joe Niemeyer, Astaire's longtime friend and stand-in; see p. 131n.)

B
WHO WANTS TO KISS THE BRIDEGROOM? (BACHELOR DINNER SONG)
(2′ 38″)

Under the watchful eye of the mission's chief (Marjorie Main), Vera-Ellen delivers an uplifting sermon to the men, who seem, however, to be more interested in her body than in their souls (B1). In mid-uplift there is a dissolve to another part of town, where Astaire, to be married the next morning, is presiding over a bachelor dinner at his aunt's house.

The guests at Astaire's party (the camera work is arranged so that we hear them before we see them) are all women (B2). At this, his "last soirée" before becoming a bridegroom (which Mercer rhymes with "starry-eyed groom"), Astaire salutes his "old gang" and, to an infectious Warren melody, performs a number that is an ingenious study in partnering, remarkable for the way Astaire treats each of the women individually to his courtesy and affection.

The song is sung twice. First Astaire sings it alone, and then he repeats it, alternating lines with the female chorus. As with all the numbers in *The Belle of New York,* there is a great deal of movement accompanying the singing; Astaire glides among the women and relates directly to each of them or toasts them collectively (B3).

The idea of attending to several women simultaneously is broadened into full partnering in the dance. With great élan Astaire moves from one woman to another—in the space of nineteen seconds, in fact, he manages to partner seven women in sequence (B4). But the choreography is arranged so intricately that it's as if he were dancing with only one. Moreover, no woman is summarily dumped as he moves to the next; instead, each is gently released to become part of the contributing choral frame.

Then the dance patterns change and the women come together to partner *him,* combining forces at one point to cushion his backward fall from the banquet table (B5). The dance becomes increasingly boisterous as Astaire snaps up Frenchie, a special confidante, and dances with her on top of the table while the rest of the women carouse around them. As he leans over to kiss her (B6), the revels are abruptly cut short by the entrance of the outraged Marjorie Main, Astaire's aunt.[5]

C
LET A LITTLE LOVE COME IN
(1′ 36″)

Later that evening, Vera-Ellen's crew of soul savers is shown mobilized in Washington

[5] Originally Frenchie's role (played by Lisa Ferraday) was larger, but much had been removed by the time the film emerged from the cutting room. Retained was a sequence in which the aunt hears Frenchie muttering and demands to hear "those obscene remarks she's making." Astaire replies that the remarks are not obscene, they're French. Main retorts, "French *is* obscene." When Frenchie asks what "obscene" means, Astaire says, "It means you'd better go," and she exits with "Very well then, I obscene." This exchange was considered objectionable by Hollywood's censors and the MGM legal office not on the grounds of its patent witlessness but because they felt it "unwise from the standpoint of international relations."

A1 A2 B1 B2 B3 B4 B5 B6 C1 C2 D1 D2

Square. Their anthem (contributed by Roger Edens), a gentle satire on Salvation Army themes, is sung first by Alice Pearce with bite and spirit, then by Anita Ellis (dubbing Vera-Ellen) as an unctuous ballad—an approach that vitiates the song's appeal. (Ellis had dubbed Vera-Ellen in *Three Little Words,* with generally better results.)

Now regretting his forthcoming marriage, a somber Astaire is riding by with Frenchie in an open horse-drawn carriage. Whatever the singer may be doing to Eden's song, she bewitches Astaire and, as if in a trance, he abandons the carriage (C1) to confront her (C2). (Walters' tight, fluid camera work in this scene is remarkably effective in keeping the two areas of action—the revival meeting and the carriage—separated, yet pertinently juxtaposed.)

D
SEEING'S BELIEVING
(4′42″)

Astaire, now hopelessly in love with Vera-Ellen, hears her mechanically explain to him that love is not the mere numbness he feels, but "like billowy clouds and you walk on air" (D1). Once she has left, her words reverberate in his brain, and he suddenly discovers he's able to stroll jauntily off into the night sky (D2). The magical number that ensues is one of Astaire's fine "idea" dances, less significant for the choreographed steps than for the way he toys with a gimmick, teases it around, and causes an engaging dance to emerge from the encounter.[6]

Before he's gone very far on his skyward jaunt, he comes across the top of the Washington Square arch. He regards it with some interest and then commits what may well be the first reverse jump by a character outside a cartoon—he springs from thin air onto the ledge (D3)—then gazes down in quiet wonderment. He doesn't walk on air again until almost the end of the number, instead, he flirts with the idea as he makes a dance about frolicking dangerously on a precipice. He begins to sing the song while leaning safely in toward the structure, but then ventures along the ledge, sweeping at the empty air with foot or hand, teetering gingerly on the very edge, or swinging extravagantly out over the void (D4). This last effect fits particularly well with a languorous swooping passage in the song. Mercer's lyric fits the situation in that it talks about the wonder of being in love, about feeling "miles off the ground." But it also says that the singer has been put in this state by kissing—something that hasn't yet happened to Astaire in the film.

Crooking one foot around a ladder rung, he leans backward over the edge and casually lights a cigarette as he begins the dance (D5). He darts up the ladder (D6) and, following the lilt of the music (and accompanied by fluttering white birds), he lopes over the roof of the arch—sometimes seeming to slip and lose his balance. The dance often uses the ballet pose known as attitude (D7; see also D6).

At one point he totters off the edge, but grabs a Y-shaped pipe—perhaps to prevent a fall (D8)—and then continues his roof-top romp. In one

[6] To achieve the desired effect, many of the shots in "Seeing's Believing" were made using process photography. For these shots (for example, D4) Astaire was filmed dancing in a room that was completely yellow except for the structure he was dancing upon. Then this picture was processed so the yellow portion was replaced by a filmed scene of the park as shot from above. In D11, where Astaire seems to be bounding on air, a trampoline was used and then cut out and replaced with the park scene. The camera never moves in these shots. The shots in the number (for example, D6, 7), that did *not* use process photography were filmed on a mock-up of the ledge or roof with city buildings and lights on a backdrop; in these shots the camera does move. It took four days to shoot the number.

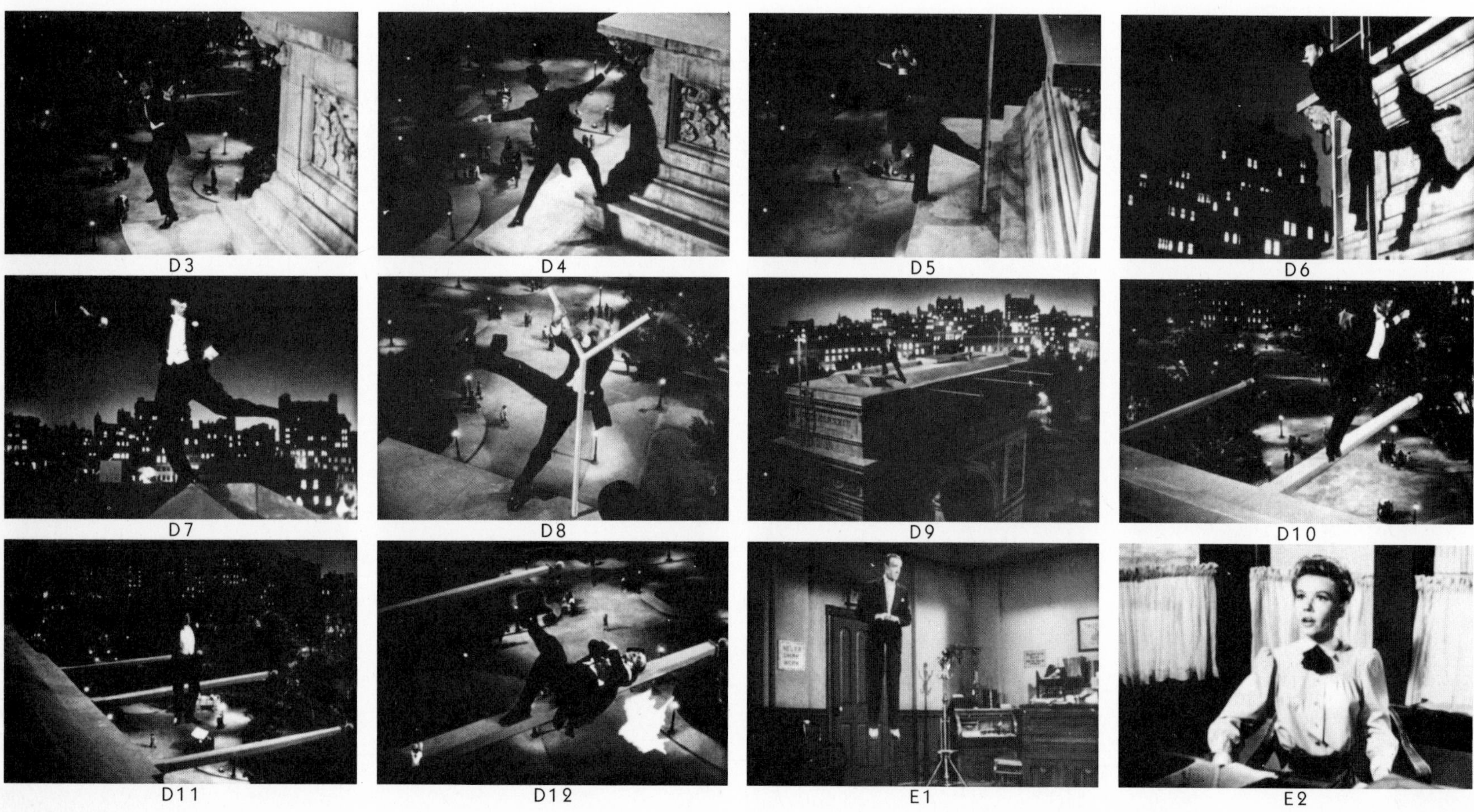

D3 D4 D5 D6
D7 D8 D9 D10
D11 D12 E1 E2

shot the camera pulls far back—extremely unusual in the middle of an Astaire dance—to give an overall view of the proceedings (D 9).

After sliding down to the edge of the roof, he ventures out onto a horizontal flagpole, where he balances dangerously. He flips his top hat through the air, spikes it with one foot, then kicks it up again, catching it on his hand.[7] Finally, he leans forward, flaps his arms, and flutters, birdlike, off the flagpole into the air (D 10). He bounces gleefully in space (D 11) and then, blissfully in love, lies down on a flagpole, flips his hat onto one foot, and dozes off as birds flutter by (D 12).

E
BABY DOLL
(3′8″)

After resting comfortably on the flagpole all night (and missing his wedding), Astaire strolls jauntily to Vera-Ellen's mission house and begins his courtship.

The next portion of the film, involving two duets and the dialogue sequences around them, is its high point and one of the most appealing extended sequences in Astaire's films. The banter is zany yet understated as the two innocents attempt to thrust and parry. And the sequence—which runs sixteen minutes—includes not only two of Astaire's most delightful duets, but also one of his most memorable bits of solo business.

In Vera-Ellen's office, plastered with signs that say "Never shirk work" and "Tell the devil where to go," Astaire seeks to prove his devotion by proudly demonstrating for her his newfound ability to walk on air (E 1). She is amazed but essentially unimpressed—you're just supposed to *feel* that way, she sputters, you're not actually supposed to *do* it (E 2). And besides, if there's anything she despises it's a show-off. Undaunted, he continues to pursue her, but on the ground.

As she bustles irritatedly off to a nearby meeting hall, he follows and engages in what might pass for reasoned argumentation. He explains that it is unfair for her to spend all her time saving the downtrodden while giving no thought to the "uptrodden" like him. She concedes that he may have something there and gives him the address of an employment agency, informing him that to be saved he must first do "an honest day's work." This comes as a jolt to Astaire, and he pauses to assess the situation carefully (E 3). Then he resolves to give in, reasoning, "Well, one day can't be so bad."

But first he sings her a song and dragoons her into a dance.[8] In the course of the number Astaire's prim, huffy quarry does loosen up, but near the end he becomes too impetuous and she draws back, shocked.

Mercer's sprightly lyric for Warren's lilting melody is suitably whimsical, and its description of the Vera-Ellen character as a "beautiful baby doll" is certainly appropriate.

A great deal of significant and intricate movement accompanies the singing. As Astaire sings the verse he tries to trap Vera-Ellen at the lectern: without actually touching her, he surrounds her with his arms (E 4). Extremely embarrassed, she nevertheless thinks quickly and ducks under his arm (E 5), then primly marches off. After stopping her progress by grabbing her wrist (E 6), Astaire begins to sing

[7] There is quite a bit of precision hat flipping in Astaire's two major solos in this film. In a dance in his next film, *The Band Wagon*, he neatly parodies the idea (27 I).

[8] The only previous Astaire film in which neither lead was given a performing background was another fantasy—*Yolanda and the Thief*.

E3 E4 E5 E6
E7 E8 E9 E10
E11 E12 E13 E14

the chorus, gently but firmly transferring her wrist from one hand to the other and moving in on her from behind. This accomplished, he lets her resume her forward progress, but now the walk has a gentle lilt to it suggested by the music and, most important, she is in his arms (E7). This smooth maneuver is impressive, even by Astaire's standards, for its agile blend of firmness and tenderness. She breaks away again, walking firmly in the opposite direction, and again he arrests her progress by grabbing her wrist. But now there are signs that he is beginning to get through to her: she pulls her hand away, but the movement is far less abrupt than before, and instead of marching out, she stops after a few steps, pausing to listen to him.

Seizing the opportunity, Astaire darts in front of her and, to the words "I'm taking you off the shelf," lifts her down onto the floor of the meeting hall (E8) (a move that is mindlessly underlined by a violin swoop in the orchestration, as is the later lift to the table [E19]). The word painting here, witty and apt, continues as he gently underscores "showing you off" and then takes her walking "holding your parasol"—an item that seems to appear magically when he mentions it in the song (E9).

As Astaire finishes the song, she suddenly runs away toward the camera. He calls out after her, singing the first words of the song ("Baby doll!"), and she stops, clearly interested (E10). As he sings "You beautiful baby doll," she allows him to move in on her (E11). Thus, by the time the singing ends and the dance begins, she has already decided to stick around for a while.

Now that she's thawed slightly, the problem is to get this living doll moving. Astaire approaches the task in a careful, experimental manner: he sets her spinning like a top, slowly at first (E12) and then faster. To stop her he twirls himself around her in a double-helix pattern and catches her on the fly just as the next phrase begins—another extraordinarily beautiful movement (E13, 14). The dancers are now in the standard partnering pose except that their extended hands are not touching. In fact, the pose is closed only incidentally in this number; not until they are near the end of the next duet do they really cling to each other. For now, they explore this open pose more thoroughly, picking up the lilt of the music (E15). A brief pause, as they admire each other at arm's length (E16), leads to a phrase that includes two gentle "off the shelf" lifts as the dance becomes increasingly jubilant, even a bit flamboyant.

As the orchestra repeats the song from the top, the dancers flow with it dodging from side to side (E17, 18). By now Vera-Ellen's hesitancy, stiffness, and tentativeness have lessened considerably, and her movements have much greater fluidity (E18; compare E15; note that both show Astaire fleetingly in the attitude pose found so often in this film). When Astaire claps his hands once, they scamper onto the platform, and he lifts her up to stand on a table (E19). On his invitation she sits down next to him on the table, and they sway cheerily with the music (E20). Keeping pace with the rocking flow of the music, they glide briefly off the table and then return to it, but only Astaire sits down. From this position he is able to partner Vera-Ellen as she playfully traces a wide circle around the table (E21). When she returns to him he slides with incredible smoothness off the table, collecting her in his arms (E22).

They spin lightly to the lectern, where they play a game by flipping down signs on the front of it—Astaire replacing signs that say "Evil has many disguises" and "Satan is at your elbow" with ones more to his liking, such as "Spread a little kindness." There is no choreographic pause for this business; rather, the sign flipping is

E15 E16 E17 E18
E19 E20 E21 E22
E23 E24 E25 E26

deftly worked into the dance as the two frolic around the lectern. Vera-Ellen joins in the game with mischievous pleasure—enjoying Astaire's discomfort when unpleasant slogans come up (E 23), accepting her fate with amusement when he triumphantly flips to "Love thy neighbor" (E 24).

He invites her back to the floor, and they jump happily off the platform, hand in hand, as the music builds. They do some confident, high-stepping cakewalking across the floor, seeming to produce with their feet the drum raps in the orchestra (E 25), and there is another pause for admiration at arm's length (E 26; compare E 16). But now Astaire gets carried away: caught up in the sheer delight of his success, he swings Vera-Ellen around himself, and himself around her, and then suddenly sweeps her into a lift, cradling her in his arms. This brings back, in an instant, her sense of propriety, and she reacts with shock (E 27). Though she tries to flee his embrace, he pulls her back to the chairs that ring the floor, and the dance ends with her curled up on the chairs, warding him off with her hand (a pose that is allowed to linger on the screen a bit too long before the fade-out) (E 28).

F
STREET-CLEANER DANCE
(1′0″)

The "Baby Doll" number is separated by only four minutes from the next duet. Part of this brief interval is given over to one of Astaire's happiest comedy dance bits.

Vera-Ellen is now clearly attracted to Astaire, and as she watches approvingly from her office window, he sets out to fulfill his promise to do his solitary day of redeeming work. He approaches the task with great good humor and thorough ineptness. His first job is as a messenger, but he crashes his bicycle when he tries to show off, by gliding in attitude, for her benefit (F 1).

Next he gets a job as a street cleaner. Although dirt hardly fits into the film's conception of what New York looked like at the turn of the century, some pieces of clean, crumpled paper have been left strategically about, and Astaire, whistling tunelessly, makes an elaborate game out of picking them up and backhanding them into his trash barrel with absurd cheerfulness and exaggerated self-importance. He does much of this with his legs comically locked together in the first position of ballet (F 2). Once more he takes the opportunity to show off for Vera-Ellen, launching into a snappy little dance with his push broom. He tries dancing while balancing the broom in his palm, totters sideways (F 3), and crashes indecorously into a nearby street vendor's wagon.

G
OOPS
(4′49″)

Astaire's third job is as the driver of a horse-drawn streetcar, a task he handles without calamity—except that he forgets to stop for passengers.

As he rides along in his empty trolley he comes across Vera-Ellen, who is out for a stroll. After a brief show of reluctance, she gives in to his entreaties to join him on the trolley. It is here that he tries his Big Line on her. As they ride long, he hands her a bag of peanuts and says, "Have some peanuts. I only wish they were diamonds" (G 1). For once the line fails resoundingly: she responds, "That's silly. You can't eat diamonds." He draws the lesson more tightly: "Diamonds can buy a lot of peanuts." As she munches, she observes with childlike logic: "I got a lot of peanuts."

E 27 · E 28 · F 1 · F 2
F 3 · G 1 · G 2 · G 3
G 4 · G 5 · G 6 · G 7

Since that didn't work, he proposes marriage in a manner that is casual and offhand even by Astaire's usual standards. His horse, he explains, is going to get married and wants to make it a double wedding. This doesn't work, either, so Astaire tries another song and dance. She joins in with much more willingness than in the "Baby Doll" number; and in the course of the dance he finally wins her.

The duet that ensues is a long one, but it never lags and it is packed with jokes and events. It plays games with the music, develops the love story with subtlety and humor, builds to an ebullient celebration, and ends with a happy surprise.

Johnny Mercer's lyric is ideally suited to the situation and characters. Sentiment is expressed plainly and directly: when I first met you, Astaire sings, my heart went oops (rhymes with "hoops," "loops," and "nincompoops"), and it's still doing that right now. Warren's melody has a goofy jocularity that complements the lyric. It is presented in the main strain as a series of fragments separated by rests, and throughout the song there is a great deal of skipping around on the scale.

As he sings to Vera-Ellen, Astaire playfully tries, as he had at the beginning of the "Baby Doll" number, to entrap her—in this case with the reins (G 2; compare E 4). She deftly maneuvers her way out of these encirclings in a way that matches his playfulness, rather than her former huffiness. When the singing ends, she darts to a seat on the other side of the trolley car, inviting him with her eyes to follow. Pausing only to stop the horse and tie up the reins (with typical attention to detail), he accepts her invitation and, to music arranged from fragments of the song, they cavort up and down the aisle. Their frolic includes some side-to-side dodging that reflects a similar idea in "Baby Doll" (G 3; compare E 17).

As the dancers hop off the trolley, the music returns to the beginning of the song. It is now played with bassoons in the lead in a manner that brings out the buffoonery of Warren's disjointed melody. The choreography matches this quality precisely: their arms pressed stiffly to their sides, Astaire and Vera-Ellen galumph through a series of jerky, mechanical turns and hops (G 4). Then the step is varied and another joke is added—a pattern featuring arm and shoulder jerks (G 5) that starts on the music, sets its own rhythm, gets out of synchronization with the music, then catches up with it.

Problems of synchronization are now elaborated as the two dancers fall out of step with each other. After various bumps and collisions they come face to face and find themselves in vertical discoordination as they perform a series of bouncy knee bends in which she is going down while he is going up (G 6).[9] Harried, Astaire grasps Vera-Ellen by the shoulders to stop her from bobbing, but as soon as he releases her she begins to hop happily. He now attempts a sterner approach: he tries to step on her foot to keep her earthbound. Unfortunately, he misses the target, and she comes down on *his* foot, to which he reacts with an expression of excruciating pain, pointing, as he does so, to where it hurts (G 7). Once again the orchestra adds to the humor—Astaire's howl of pain is suggested by squawky woodwinds.

After Astaire has laboriously extracted his trampled foot, he grabs the raised leg of his partner and cheerily circles her as she continues to hop—a parody of a ballet promenade (G 8). When he is facing front again, he flings her leg forward with a flourish of achievement. However, she continues to turn, now without his assistance, and when she completes the circle she gives him a sharp kick in the seat of the pants with her raised foot (G 9), deflating him in his moment of triumph. Then, without missing a beat, she hops forward as he glares at her (G 10). The audience can see the kick in the pants coming and, as such, it is an unusual instance of a predictable effect in Astaire's choreography. However, the kick is neatly blended into the next joke: Vera-Ellen instantly resumes her hops (in G 10), as if to say, "What kick in the pants?"

Next comes the saga of the flower, during which Vera-Ellen's heart is finally won. This episode is remarkable not only for its cartoonish zaniness but also for the intricate, if whimsical, way it is textured into the dance. Astaire is finally able to bring Vera-Ellen's seemingly interminable bouncing hops under control: he holds her firmly by the shoulders and restrains her long enough so they can return at last to synchronization. As he leads her in a march across the grass, he suddenly spots the flower

[9] Perhaps Astaire is here wryly capitalizing on one of his partner's special qualities. Walters remembers that one of the problems in dealing with Vera-Ellen as an actress was getting her to listen undistractedly to his directorial advice. In particular, he recalls, when off-camera she always seemed to be at a ballet barre doing knee bends. She would continue these bobbings as he tried to talk to her, making coherent communication rather difficult. If he asked her to stop, she would stop at the *bottom* of the knee bend.

G8 G9 G10 G11

G12 G13 G14 G15

and with great delight pounces on it (G11). As he crouches to pluck it, she trips over him with a gymnast's walkover (G12). Thus, when he turns to give her the flower she seems suddenly to have vanished (G13). She turns him around, sees the flower, takes it rapturously, and becomes his forever. Sniffing her flower, she wraps an arm around his neck and, as the camera cuts to a medium shot for emphasis, lets him hold her tight —the first time he's been able to do so in the film (G14). He holds her with his right arm while his left hangs stiffly at his side—the stiff arm being a sort of motif for this dance (see G4–6)—and the pose clarifies that it is she who is clinging.

Vera-Ellen's delight is demonstrated not only in the giddy glee with which she clings to Astaire (G15), but also in the orchestration, where the melody is rendered by squeaky violins. Then, when the orchestration abruptly changes to forceful brasses, the dance becomes exaggeratedly serious and sternly marchlike (G16). When the violins reappear, so does the clinging.[10]

After a brief Alphonse-Gaston episode over who will go first (leading to a collision reminiscent of their earlier problems), the pair reboard the trolley. Astaire rings the bell and sets the horse in motion, and their dance of celebration begins. At first the number becomes overly goofy. Astaire hops up on the back of the horse to continue the dance and Vera-Ellen, now quite willing to follow him anywhere, joins him to perform a series of leg wiggles suggesting ballet ronds de jambes (or can-can kicks) on this improbable stage (G17). The music is beautifully orchestrated for a carousel effect.

Then, after a few more ballet-derived steps, they hop off the horse and caper alongside the traveling trolley. After a brief, tender reprise of their earlier clinging dance (G18), they return to the trolley with a couple of turning strides—a move that relates splendidly to the music—and the moving trolley becomes a third member of this exuberant dance as the couple glide expansively beside it (G19) and hop on and off its running board (G20). Vera-Ellen is especially beautiful here as she flows with the dance and music. Suddenly there is a reaction shot—of the horse, who is shown looking back with what one might take to be bewilderment (G21); the insertion seems a slightly sardonic comment by Astaire on a distracting device he brought under control in his first years in Hollywood.[11]

The celebration carries the dancers through the trolley, and they briefly replay their game of dodging. Then the idea of jumping back and forth between the ground and the running board of the moving trolley is further elaborated until there is a highly significant pause in the choreography: as they ride, Astaire pulls Vera-Ellen on top of him in an intimate, lingering pose (G22), a pertinent, if subtle, contrast with the tone of the rest of the dance.

That statement made, the dancers return to the ground (in both senses) to dash to the rear of the trolley—their apparent speed increased because they are moving in the direction opposite to the trolley's progress (G23). They take up showy poses on the end of the trolley car just as it enters the car barn, and the music ends (G24). This ending is one of Astaire's most splendid. Many of his dances finish predictably by having the dancers progress out of view through a doorway or into the wings of a stage. The ending of "Oops" is an unpredictable gloss on this finish because the camera simply follows the dancers in their pose at the back of the moving trolley until suddenly all three vanish into the car barn. (As can be seen in G2, however, the audience had long ago been alerted to the fact that they were headed for the car barn by the sign on the trolley—another example of the careful attention to detail in Astaire's numbers.)

Once there, Vera-Ellen looks at Astaire with a dazed expression (G25) and underlines, by rising into the air, what the choreography has already clearly stated (G26).

H
A BRIDE'S WEDDING DAY SONG (CURRIER AND IVES)
(7′ 34″)

After a brief scene in which Astaire informs his delighted aunt of his intention to marry Vera-

[10] Astaire had previously created dances in which humor rose from the desperate efforts of the dancers to respond to shifts in the musical arrangement—shifts from bright and jazzy to broad and waltzy, for example, an idea which reached its height in "I'm Putting All My Eggs in One Basket" in *Follow the Fleet* (6 H) and its depth in "I Can't Tell a Lie" in *Holiday Inn* (15 J). The use here of shifts in orchestration is an agile development of this approach.

[11] See pp. 27–28. The reaction shot of the horse does have a practical use here: there is too much dance for the amount of trolley track on the set, and the cut to the horses is used to cover the fact that the trolley has been backed up to the beginning of the track. However, there would have been other ways to handle this—a shift of camera angle had been used earlier—so the reaction shot was a deliberate choice.

G16 G17 G18 G19

G20 G21 G22 G23

Ellen, the couple visit the Currier and Ives studio to pose for a wedding picture—and to dance again in a production number that concludes with their third remarkable duet. There are some uncomfortable moments before that duet begins, however.

Vera-Ellen selects an autumn scene for their backdrop, and as she and Astaire step in front of it, she is inspired to sing (or, more accurately, to mime as Anita Ellis sings). This soon leads to three fantasy dances that cover the remaining seasons from a Currier and Ives perspective.

The opening sequences of the number—the scene in which the song is sung, and especially the spring scene, showing the pair playing badminton—can charitably be described as catastrophic: they exude coyness, something that is usually as foreign to an Astaire number as musical insensitivity or rampant vulgarity.

The trouble begins with the music—not so much with the song itself as with the way it is performed. Actually, Harry Warren's tune has a gentle charm, and Johnny Mercer's lyric is something of a *tour de force*. Without too much condescension, the lyric reflects the musings of a young bride not usually given to deep thought: although she and her husband will age, she observes sagely, the picture they're posing for will always stay the same, showing what they looked like when they entered their comfortable, cloudless wedded state. If these naïve sentiments were handled with briskness and perhaps a wry smile, the song might come off. Instead, the tempo is lugubrious and the orchestration sappy, and the singer prettifies every note, reducing the song to sludge.

The most excruciating aspect of the first two scenes, however, is Astaire's demeanor. While Vera-Ellen manages to amble along with a certain bland conviction, Astaire shows no conviction whatever and seems, in fact, to be seething with embarrassment.

As the number begins, Astaire and Vera-Ellen take their places in front of the autumn backdrop, from where she oozes into her song while Astaire hovers near her ingratiatingly (H1). The scene then dissolves to a spring lawn setting in which Astaire and Vera-Ellen, in period sporting costume, play badminton and sway on a garden swing, each showing an absurdly fawning solicitousness toward the other (H2). These sequences are carried out with such unctuousness that they seem constantly on the verge of (intentional) parody.

Now there is a dissolve to a beautiful Currier-and-Ives winter scene showing the skating pond in Central Park. Astaire and Vera-Ellen arrive in a horse-drawn sleigh and skate a few turns around the rink. Sometimes Astaire seems to have retained a bit of his earlier embarrassed oversolicitousness (H3), but most of the skating dance has a gentle, unaffected flow. The music is played a bit more briskly, a welcome improvement, and the scene ends quite pleasantly as the pair spin on the ice, surrounded by the swirling chorus (H4).

And then all is redeemed. The scene dissolves to another animated Currier-and-Ives print, this one of the Coney Island boardwalk in summer, where the fifty-two-year-old Astaire, with his lithe, thirty-year-old partner in tow, barrels through one of the most virtuosic dances of his career. But for all its brilliance and invention, the duet is most memorable for a series of partnered backbends, sensuous and tender, that are neatly woven into its texture. The accompanying music is a reprise of "When I'm Out with the Belle of New York," done uptempo as a bright waltz but not so fast that the melody loses its satisfying lilt.

Astaire and Vera-Ellen are first seen strolling

G24 G25 G26 H1
H2 H3 H4 H5
H6 H7 H8 H9

arm in arm among the crowd (H 5). The stroll becomes slightly more flamboyant, then quite dance-like; Vera-Ellen twice spins quickly under Astaire's arm, and suddenly they are in a beguiling, partnered tap dance. Some turns in which he swoops her in circles around him (H 6; compare H 2) develop into a sequence in which Astaire repeatedly kicks his bent leg back as Vera-Ellen sweeps joyfully around him (H 7).

Emerging from this circling, the dancers, side by side, perform a rapid, cross-legged tap combination that progresses forward (H 8). Then, in contrast, they suddenly bound into a series of stamps and explosive bolts to the side (H 9) on unpredictable stresses in the music. They return to tapping, which becomes faster and more complex rhythmically. As their momentum increases, they propel themselves into a series of fast turns culminating in a quick spin in the air and a forceful landing with the arms out—a preview of the dance's concluding pose (H 10).

Astaire claps his hands, and the dancers bound jubilantly into the next phrase (H 11), which is devoted to a series of exuberant, music-propelled turns in which one foot is kicked up into attitude again (H 12). There are then some experiments with crossed-wristed arm's-length partnering, developing an idea used earlier in the film (H 13, 14; compare E 16, E 26, H 3).

The dance up to this point has been celebratory, brilliant, playful. But now, for an instant, its tone changes. The dancers spin around each other in a double-helix pattern, and Vera-Ellen falls trustingly backward across Astaire's thigh. The dancers remain momentarily oblivious of the music, which continues to bubble along. The camera cuts in closer as Astaire, with deliberate care, takes Vera-Ellen's wrists and pulls her gently out of the backbend (H 15). Then suddenly they're up there again, side by side, doing a loose tea-for-two-tippy-tap dance across the floor. The tap pattern, embellished with some snappy turns, is notable for the way it develops an intricate counter-rhythm to the music, and for the way Vera-Ellen beguilingly uses movements of her head to emphasize certain stresses in the tap phrase (H 16).

After some swirling patterns across the floor, Vera-Ellen again flings herself into a partnered backward fall (H 17). Astaire pivots her around once, and as he does so the orchestra begins a long transition back to the beginning of the song. Meanwhile, Astaire pulls Vera-Ellen to her feet, and then the backward fall, pivot, and pull-up are repeated. When she falls sharply back a third time, the pose is dramatically captured by a high camera (H 18). Then Astaire again begins to pivot her and, at the same time, she slowly rises in his arms and the backbend is gradually transmuted into a ballroom partnering pose: her left arm curves in and is placed on his right shoulder while her right arm slides down his wrist until she takes his hand (H 19, 20).[12] The impact of this exquisite maneuver and its suggestion of loving dependency is heightened by the way it is allowed to drift out of synchronization with the music. The music completes its transition back to the main melody while the dancers are still midway in their own choreographic transition. Thus, when the orchestra launches into the main melody, the dancers, unheeding and self-absorbed, drift gradually back to reality at their own pace and catch up with the music —doing a fast partnered waltz—a moment later. Like the held pose in the "Oops" duet (G 22), this is one of those eloquent moments in Astaire's playful duets that betray the seriousness at their

[12] This is all captured in one shot: the change of angle between H 18 and H 19 is accomplished by lowering the camera, not by cutting.

H10 H11 H12 H13

H14 H15 H16 H17

H18 H19 H20 H21

base. Vera-Ellen is particularly beautiful in this maneuver—confident, trusting, ecstatic.

Approaching the finish now, the dance builds up steam as the dancers explosively hit several poses in attitude (H 21). The dance has one of the most brilliantly virtuosic endings Astaire ever performed. Like Babe Ruth pointing out where he will place his next home run, the dancers anticipate their final pose (H 22; see also H 10), then retreat upstage and catapult their way back toward the camera in a blistering series of traveling spins, to conclude by launching themselves into a turn in the air (H 23), landing in the final, predicted pose exactly on the music (H 24). This image is then frozen, like a Currier and Ives print.

I
NAUGHTY BUT NICE
(5′43″)

The remainder of the film does not maintain the same level of spirited whimsy as the courtship sequence, but it comes close. With the celebration out of the way, the plot moves into the breakup phase. First there is Alice Pearce's brief but touching scene at the wedding rehearsal, when she fantasizes about her own wished-for wedded bliss (I 1). Then, through circumstances more or less beyond his control, Astaire misses his wedding and, in a moment of sour self-deprecation, concludes that he is congenitally incapable of reforming his ways and therefore not good enough for his intended bride.

There follows a beautiful scene that manages to be at once tender and absurdly funny. In full wedding regalia Vera-Ellen comes to Astaire's apartment and demands an explanation. He is touched by her beauty and overwhelmed by his own unworthiness. She still wants to marry him, but he explains that he is unreliable and selfish. "You were all those things this morning," she insists. "This is my wedding day and I want to get married." "You don't marry a fellow just because you happen to be dressed for it," he argues. To test his love for her she kisses him, but he holds on to the edge of a table behind his back and thus keeps himself from rising into the air (I 2). Shattered, she flees.

In an apparent effort to reform himself, Astaire takes a job, as a singing (and dancing) waiter at a casino. Pearce now concocts a rather improbable plan: she convinces Vera-Ellen to visit Astaire's new place of employment dressed as a vamp in order to win him back by having *him* reform *her*. When Vera-Ellen says, "How can I act like a frivolous woman?," Pearce retorts jealously, "Well, you've got every part to play it with" (I 4).[13]

As she dresses for the role in the privacy of her boudoir, Vera-Ellen performs a solo song and dance in which she shows off as many of those parts as the censors would allow. The dance, presumably choreographed by Alton, is one of those desperate attempts to be sexy, so common in Hollywood musicals of the 1950s, in which sexuality is confused with unfettered vulgarity; it consists basically of having the dancer fling her legs around (I 3). Even given the plot context, the dance seems joltingly out of character—a forgivable defect had the choreography shown some degree of wit or sophistication. Once again Anita Ellis, abetted by lethargic tempos and sappy orchestration, renders the song flaccid and cute.

Following this, Pearce does a lumpish parody

[13] Vera-Ellen's straight line, of course, should be "How can I play the part of a frivolous woman?"—a construction that adds amusing word play to the basic joke. As it happens, that is exactly the way the line is given in the script. Vera-Ellen's misreading of the line suggests that she didn't really understand the joke—and that the director and others were not being sufficiently careful about what was going on.

H22 H23 H24 I1
I2 I3 I4 J1
K1 K2 K3 K4

of the song and dance, but the comedy is heavy and badly timed (I4). Eventually Vera-Ellen joins her, and together they galumph over a bed and out the door.[14]

J
BABY DOLL
(REPRISE) (31″)

Next comes a musical highlight: the last half of the "Baby Doll" chorus, beautifully arranged for barber-shop quartet and affectionately sung by Astaire and three fellow waiters at the casino (J1). The orchestral accompaniment is subdued and supportive.

K
I WANNA BE A DANCIN' MAN
(4′5″)

Astaire is shocked to see the unlikely pair of frivolous women at the casino (K1) but is soon called away to perform onstage for the patrons. Though his number has charm and sophistication, its good humor seems a little forced, and there is noticeable strain in its effort to project casual spontaneity. Some of this may be because of the lyric: it reads as a salute to Astaire, Mercer's friend and colleague of many years, and although the tribute is carried out with grace and indirection (for example, the line "Gonna leave my footsteps in the sands of time" is undercut with an Astaire-style shrug: "At least until the tide comes in"), Astaire may have been a bit embarrassed at performing something that might be taken as directly and distinctly personal. Another possibility is that Astaire was simply tired by the time he came to film this number. By his own testimony, *The Belle of New York* was an unusually exhausting film to make, and, along with the skating sequence, this solo was filmed last.

The lyric suggests the idea of doing a sand dance (or vice versa) and the number opens with Astaire on the casino's stage spreading a hatful of sand over the floor (K2). He sings the song with humor and élan; his poses suggestive of flight before the words "free as any bird can be" are particularly amusing (K3).

The first part of the dance is an exhibition of genial sand dancing—the camera rising obligingly at one point to take in the sweeping swirls that Astaire traces in the sand (K4). At one point Astaire punctuates the loose cool of the dance with a funny, uninhibited jump (K5). At another he responds to a witty element in Warren's music: a surprising clipping of the juncture between the first statements of the A strain (the song is in AABA form). Astaire handles this with comparable wit, following the music, getting delayed, and then scampering ahead to catch up.

After sending his straw hat skimming across the floor, Astaire embarks on a vigorous solo of bandy-legged shuffles (K6) and twitchy, over-eager slams into position in direct reflection of rim shots on a drum in the orchestra (K7). At the end he sings one final line, deftly kicks his hat up to his hand (K8), and bolts into the wings (K9).

[14] The topical references in Mercer's fine lyric are apt and in period. The Bunny Hug was a racy turn-of-the-century dance that the Castles banned from their genteel dancing academy. Eva Tanguay (whose name Mercer rhymes with "gangway") was a headliner, like Sophie Tucker, during the period who was known as the "I don't care" girl.

L
WHEN I'M OUT WITH THE BELLE OF NEW YORK
(REPRISE) (33″)

Attempting to protect Vera-Ellen from the leering attentions of some male patrons, Astaire gets into a fight, the casino is broken up, and he and she somehow get into an argument over his substitution of soda water for the champagne she had ordered. But then they notice that they are forty feet in the air (L1)—still in love, you see, a condition apparently shared by no one else, because the others all remain earthbound. In a nice parallel to the opening scene, in which a mob of men had serenaded Vera-Ellen at an upstairs window, the amazed crowd gazes upward and sings the title song to the couple (L2).

Astaire and Vera-Ellen wave from on high. Magically, their clothes are changed to wedding attire, and they waltz off into the night sky as the crowd bellows the title song from below (L3).

A NUMBER CUT FROM THE FILM

M
WHEN I'M OUT WITH THE BELLE OF NEW YORK
(REPRISE)

Shortly after Alice Pearce's fantasy wedding with the policeman (I1), there was a scene in the mission house in which the men present Vera-Ellen with gifts (including some stolen silverware) and express gloom that she is getting married. To cheer themselves up they do a song-and-dance routine to the title tune, and Vera-Ellen joins in. The scene and number were filmed, but cut before release.

K5 K6 K7 K8
K9 L1 L2 L3

27.

The Band Wagon

1953

The Band Wagon is one of the most highly praised of Fred Astaire's motion pictures. Its appeals include the snappy and mildly acerbic script by Betty Comden and Adolph Green, the agile direction by Vincente Minnelli, the tasteful and imaginative sets for the numbers by Oliver Smith, and the catchy and time-tested songs by Arthur Schwartz and Howard Dietz, all colorfully packaged in the slickest MGM manner.

But there is an inconsistency of tone in this otherwise enjoyable film. In trying to satirize pretentiousness, the film sometimes becomes slightly pretentious itself; and in trying to provide a bright and sophisticated gloss on the traditional backstage musical, it sometimes ends up wallowing helplessly in that genre's hoariest clichés. True satire and lightness of touch were difficult to bring off at the MGM factory, and *The Band Wagon,* while seeking to attain the effervescent, sometimes strains for effect and becomes heavy. At times, in short, it takes itself too seriously.

The dances reflect this inconsistency of tone. When simplicity and understatement are called for, Astaire brings forth beautiful dances—the romantic "Dancing in the Dark" and the whimsical "I Guess I'll Have to Change My Plan." When elaborate effects or pointed parody is called for, he is weighed down by gimmicks or involved in incomprehensible and misguided efforts to ridicule the already ridiculous.

THE SCRIPT

A hefty percentage of the musicals produced in Hollywood in the 1930s were of the backstage variety—musicals in which putting on a show provided the major impetus for the plot. Astaire's first film, *Dancing Lady,* was one of these, but thereafter, except for *The Band Wagon,* he avoided them. Although the setting for most of his films is show business in one form or another, almost all of his films are primarily love stories—romances about two people who happen to spend a great deal of time singing and dancing, usually with each other.

It was difficult to develop fully more than one plot line in the Hollywood musicals of Astaire's era, because the films were short and so much of their time had to be given over to musical numbers. Although most backstage musicals also involve a love story, the putting-on-a-show theme tends to dominate, the love story to become incidental. This happens in *The Band Wagon,* too, though the script is perhaps slightly more successful than most in giving each plot line its due. In part this is because both revolve around the Astaire character. He plays a washed-up Hollywood hoofer who is trying to make a comeback on Broadway in a new show written for him by his friends, played by Oscar Levant and Nanette Fabray. At first the show is a disaster, run by a director (Jack Buchanan) who insists on making it "intellectual." When it fails, Buchanan willingly turns things over to Astaire, who achieves success by excising the pretentiousness and stressing that the show should be "fun set to music" —to borrow a line from an earlier Comden-Green fable, *The Barkleys of Broadway.*

The love story concerns Astaire and his ballerina partner in the show, played by Cyd Charisse. Wary of each other at the beginning, they gradually become attracted, and finally sink into a clinch at the end. In some respects it's unfortunate that the love story must be given subplot status, for the problems that beset the Astaire-Charisse romance are interesting and have considerable potential for development. The two are kept apart not by contrived plot devices like mistaken identity but for reasons that derive directly from fundamental plot premises: self-consciousness about the differences in their ages (Astaire was fifty-four in 1953, Charisse thirty) and about their different backgrounds (the high art world of ballet, the lowly world of tap). In addition, Charisse is already "taken"—she is the girlfriend of the show's choreographer, played by James Mitchell.

At first Astaire and Charisse have little interest in each other offstage and evince a considerable incompatibility during rehearsals. Eventually, however, they talk over their differences and, with tension reduced, resolve to see if they can dance together. The resulting romantic duet, "Dancing in the Dark," is the film's highlight. Not only do they discover they can dance compatibly, but, in some remarkably ingenious choreography, they begin inadvertently to fall in

Astaire watches uncertainly as James Mitchell shows him how to do a ballet lift with Cyd Charisse

love. Thereafter, however, the love story becomes incidental to the traumas of putting on the show. There are no more love dances—only brief scenes in which signs of affection between Astaire and Charisse can be glimpsed. Charisse succumbs only at the end of the film—after the show has become a success—when she makes an awkwardly affectionate, terribly serious speech to Astaire before the entire cast and then plants a kiss on him. The process by which she makes up her mind about him (and rejects Mitchell) is never clearly developed.

The point of the putting-on-a-show plot is also not entirely clear. Presumably Comden and Green were planning to parody the backstage musical, but what they ended up with is at best an affectionate tribute to that genre and at worst an unrepentant rehash of the same old clichés. In his autobiography Astaire argues that "our intention was more or less to rib the theatrical side of this story mercilessly in the playing," but the ribbing simply doesn't come off. What does get ridiculed is intellectual pretentiousness. Buchanan is supposed to be a theatrical whiz kid who sets out to convert the innocent script Levant and Fabray have written into a modern-day version of *Faust*. We never really see much of this improbable artistic miscegenation but are given to understand that it is hopelessly dreary and dull. The message seems to be that art and entertainment don't go together, or, more pointedly, that art can't be entertaining.[1]

THE ASTAIRE CHARACTER

Most of the main characters in *The Band Wagon* are based on real people. The writers, played by Fabray and Levant, are based on Comden and Green themselves—though parallels with Garson Kanin and Ruth Gordon and with Oscar and June Levant have also been suggested. The flamboyant actor-director-impresario played by Buchanan[2] was, accord-

[1] The scriptwriters' attitude on this issue is suggested by a behind-the-scenes event. At one point in the original script, Astaire was supposed to say, "I am not Nijinsky, I am not Marlon Brando—I'm just Mrs. Hunter's little boy, Tony—an entertainer." The implication, obviously, is that Brando (and Nijinsky) do heavy art and can't, therefore, be entertaining. (When Brando was asked his permission to use his name—a standard studio practice—he refused until the word "entertainer" was changed to "song and dance man.")

[2] Buchanan, a well-established British song-and-dance man, was billed as a costar in England, as a featured player elsewhere. Astaire had seen Buchanan perform on stage in the 1920s and was "tremendously impressed." When the film was previewed in March 1953 the predominantly young audience was also impressed by Buchanan, now sixty-two years old: 78 percent rated his performance excellent, as compared to 74 percent to Charisse, 71 percent to Fabray, 66 percent to Astaire, and 46 percent to Levant. (Audiences were apparently souring on the acerbic Levant: compare the data on p. 289.)

"Triplets"—Astaire, Nanette Fabray, and Jack Buchanan

ing to Vincente Minnelli, "a cross between Orson Welles, stage designer Norman Bel Geddes and Jose Ferrer, who had at that time done similar pretentious productions." Minnelli has also seen parallels with George S. Kaufman, while others have suggested Noel Coward, Laurence Olivier, and, in some respects, Minnelli himself.

There is no ambiguity about the inspiration for the Astaire character—it was Astaire himself. According to Minnelli, Astaire's probable appearance in the film "sparked an idea" when the script was being planned. "Why not base his part on the Astaire of a few years back, who'd been in voluntary retirement? Why not develop the situation further by suggesting that fame had passed him by?" Comden and Green built on this idea, and there are many references in the character to Astaire's own personality and professional approach: his sensitivity about the height of his partner, his wariness about lifts, his sometimes petulant self-consciousness about his age, his willingness to work long and hard in rehearsal, his problems in trying to match his style to that of ballet-trained partners. In case anyone misses these references, his hat and cane are referred to as "perhaps the most famous top hat and stick of our generation," and he is remembered as the star of the film *Swinging Down to Panama*.

A major difference between Astaire and the character he plays in the film, of course, is that Astaire never was down and out. But fear of failure and of becoming a has-been always bothered him inordinately: "I have a horror of not delivering." Given his sensitivity on the issue (heightened, perhaps, by the box-office failure of his last picture, *The Belle of New York*), it's impressive that he was so willing to take on the *Band Wagon* script. Comden reports that she and Green were "very nervous" about the character when first presenting it to Astaire, but he took to it immediately and worked extensively with them in story conferences. What he saw, presumably, was a role with some depth and potential, and that took precedence over any problems of ego. Moreover, he nowhere allows his off-screen personality to infect the characterization. As Stephen Harvey notes: "Playing a soured version of himself . . . Astaire makes Tony Hunter so compelling by refusing to color his performance with pathos or self-pity."

THE MUSIC

In 1951 and 1952 Arthur Freed had produced five musicals at MGM. The most successful of these were fashioned around established music rather than original scores: a remake of *Show Boat* as well as *An American in Paris,* which was built around Gershwin music, and *Singin' in the Rain,* which used

With Charisse in the "Girl Hunt" ballet

With Buchanan in "I Guess I'll Have to Change My Plan"

A publicity pose with Charisse

a collection of classic songs that had been written by Nacio Herb Brown and Freed thirty years earlier.

The formula was continued with *The Band Wagon,* again with success. The score, selected by associate producer Roger Edens, draws on songs written by Arthur Schwartz and Howard Dietz for Broadway shows produced between 1923 and 1937. Several of the songs came from *The Band Wagon* of 1931, a revue featuring Fred and Adele Astaire in their last stage appearance together before her retirement from show business. In addition, the songwriters supplied a new song for the film, "That's Entertainment," and the music for the "Girl Hunt Ballet."

THE CHOREOGRAPHY

The dance director was Michael Kidd, contributing here to his second film after some ten years of experience in ballet and on Broadway. A choreographer with a predilection for acrobatics and sight gags, Kidd had a sensibility that was quite different from Astaire's, though the two apparently got along well on the set. Of Astaire's numbers, Kidd seems to be largely responsible for "Girl Hunt Ballet," most of "Triplets" and "That's Entertainment," parts of "A Shine on Your Shoes," and perhaps portions of "Dancing in the Dark."

The rehearsal with Charisse goes awry in "You and the Night and the Music"

THE NUMBERS

A
BY MYSELF
(1′22″)

The film begins with some heavily satiric references to Astaire. The familiar top hat and cane shown behind the titles (A1) are the property of the washed-up musical film star Tony Hunter (Astaire) and are about to be auctioned off. (This opening seems a direct, if obscure, reference to *Top Hat,* which also displayed the titles over a top hat; see 5 A2.) They garner no takers, even though the asking price is only 50 cents. Then a conversation on the train that is taking Astaire to New York confirms his has-been status, and he is further humiliated when reporters at Grand Central Station abruptly desert him to interview and photograph the passenger they had come to meet—film star Ava Gardner, playing herself.[3]

Astaire reacts with a bemused shrug. Strolling jauntily down the train platform, he sings to himself a chorus of the wistful "By Myself" (A2), thus clearly establishing the strength and self-confidence of the character.

B
A SHINE ON YOUR SHOES
(4′16″)

Astaire is met by his friends Levant and Fabray, who carry signs proclaiming themselves the Tony Hunter Fan Club (B1). They enthusiastically tell of a show they have written with him in mind. He is interested but wary—particularly when he learns the show will be produced and directed by a "genius" who has never done a musical before. Appalled at how Forty-second Street has deteriorated in the years he's been in Hollywood, Astaire sends his friends off and sets about exploring the neighborhood.[4] He ventures into a tacky penny arcade and is soon involved in a musical number that lifts his spirits.

"A Shine on Your Shoes" is one of Astaire's task-oriented solos—a dance in which he seeks, Keaton-like, to make machines and objects do his bidding. In this case he conquers an entire amusement arcade. As he cheerily wanders into the area, most things go wrong—he is given a hot dog he doesn't want; a vibrating machine sends him flying; a "fun" machine refuses to function (B2); and a distorting mirror seems to belie the message he has just received from the "love appeal" machine, which has proclaimed him "gorgeous." A shoeshine quickly corrects all problems, however. When he returns to play among the machines at the end of the number (pausing proudly to photograph his shine in the photo booth), they all cooperate. Even the fun machine (which cost MGM $8,000) functions under Astaire's forceful entreaties, and Astaire is congratulated by the crowd for his achievement.

Dance is submerged by task in this number, but there are some beautiful moments during the singing of the song. After singing the verse to the bootblack while standing beside the shoeshine stand, Astaire uses a full eight measures of the song's chorus to mount the stand and sit in the chair (B3). The little dance he makes out of this simple maneuver is a masterpiece of controlled flow and musical sensitivity. Also remarkable is the control with which Astaire delivers a series of sharp kicks while holding himself in the air propped on the arms of the chair (B4). The final dance around the penny arcade, accompanied by the blaring jazz arrangement of Skip Martin and partly abetted by the bootblack, is broad and obvious by Astaire's usual standards. In particular there is quite a bit of slamming into position, often underlined by percussive effects in the orchestra (B5). This raucous quality infected several Astaire solos during the 1950s, such as 29 G, 30 L, and, to a degree, 26 K.[5]

[3] The script was originally even rougher. It included a brief scene in which a motion-picture exhibitor is quoted as calling Tony Hunter "box-office poison." In the 1930s an exhibitor had carelessly and inaccurately characterized Astaire with those words—an incident he recalls with some pain in his autobiography.

[4] This scene is loaded with personal references. Green, returning once to New York in a state of dejection, had been met at Grand Central by Comden carrying a placard saying "Adolph Green Fan Club." Astaire looks for the New Amsterdam Theatre, where, he says, he had last appeared. The New Amsterdam was the theatre in which the original 1931 *Band Wagon* had played. (It was here, Green recalls fondly, that he first saw Astaire in action.) There are also references to Levant's hypochondria, leading to a quintessential Levant line, "I can stand anything but pain." The ever-cautious MGM front office, incidentally, was uneasy about a scene in which Forty-second Street was deprecated; there are important exhibitors there, it observed anxiously.

[5] MGM's method for casting the bootblack was to find a bootblack who could dance, rather than a dancer who could be trained to shine shoes. The choice was LeRoy Daniels from downtown Los Angeles. According to a studio blurb, Daniels' "antics with his bebop rags and boogie woogie brushes keep his customers entertained while they get a shine. He also inspired the [1950] tune made popular by Bing Crosby, 'Chattanooga Shoe Shine Boy.' "

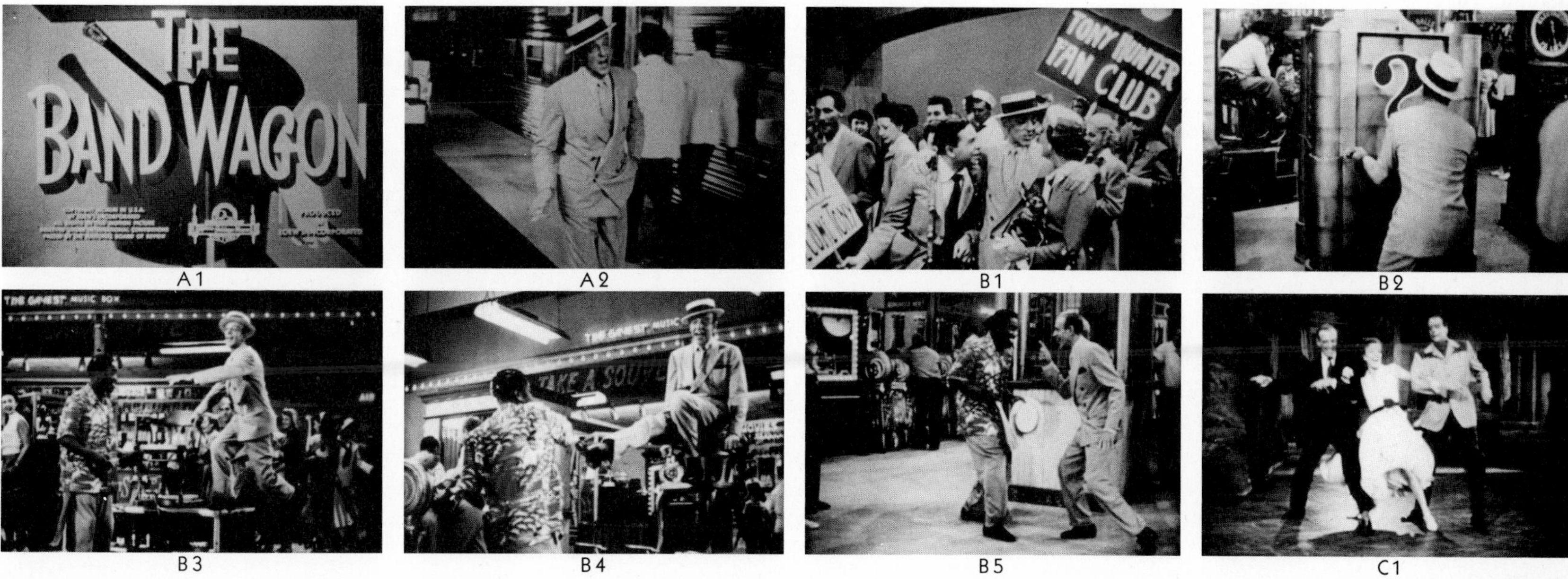

A1 A2 B1 B2

B3 B4 B5 C1

C
THAT'S ENTERTAINMENT
(3′24″)

Astaire soon meets Buchanan, the manic actor-director-impresario who, on hearing Levant and Fabray describe their show, agrees to produce the show and even to appear in it himself. (Levant's giddy enthusiasm as he jumps around declaring "I'm so glad!" when Buchanan says he likes the script seems a bit out of keeping with the character who is otherwise usually given to Levantesque sourness. According to Minnelli, Levant's behavior here is a direct emulation of the excitable Adolph Green.) The Buchanan character is a surprisingly sympathetic one. His faults seem to derive from an unrealistic flamboyance of vision, rather than, as one might expect, from an excess of ego. Thus Comden and Green have chosen to bypass some obvious comic possibilities in order to create a character of believable human dimensions. Because of this, Buchanan's thoughtful and self-effacing conversion to Astaire's notion of what a musical should be later in the film does not come as a jolt.

When Buchanan enthusiastically proclaims his plan to "angle" the Levant-Fabray book so that it will become a modern-day version of *Faust* (thus attaining "meaning" and "stature"), Astaire is skeptical. But the others manage to convince him (temporarily) that all art, from highest Shakespeare to lowest musical comedy, is just entertainment, and therefore that Buchanan's proposed mix is possible.

Their views are expressed in a number set to a new Schwartz-Dietz song, "That's Entertainment," and staged with affectionate hoke—and little else.[6] For example, Astaire, Fabray, and Buchanan perform some close-order tap and show-biz clichés, including a one-upping crossover step (C1), an idea that is merely delivered without development (and had been far more imaginatively used by Astaire in 17 C). After some other vaudevillian shticks, the number ends with the quartet of singers parading around ingratiatingly, seeking to put over its little aesthetic philosophy by sheer force of declaration (C2).

D
BEGGAR'S WALTZ
(2′19″)

Astaire's proposed partner in the new show is a well-established ballet dancer, played by Cyd Charisse. He goes to see her perform onstage.

Her brief dance, consisting of a set of classroom steps embellished with a few tricky lifts, is set to ballet music written for the original *Band Wagon* revue of 1931 (D1). Charisse proves to be a rather formidable ballet performer with good balances and beautiful legs and feet. Her rather steely, brittle technique gives the impression of considerable strength—which, according to choreographer Eugene Loring, who worked with her on several films, is an illusion (see p. 398n). In this exhibition she tends—particularly in the arms and upper body—to jolt rather abruptly from one position to the next, without phrasing the transition and without really projecting a position satisfyingly when she does hit it. This regrettable quality is absent in most of her duets with Astaire, where her dancing is much softer.

E
DANCING IN THE DARK
(2′46″)

Charisse and Astaire finally meet at a party for the show's backers and he tries, without her noticing, to make sure she is not too tall for him—another biographical reference (E1).[7] Although they soon find themselves arguing over his age and her artistic pretensions, Buchanan is able to dragoon them into the show.

Things do not go well at rehearsals.[8] Astaire feels out of place and has difficulty managing the lifts and other feats urged on him by the show's high-pressure, patronizing choreographer, James Mitchell (E2). Frustrated and furious, Astaire finally throws a tantrum and walks out (E3). At the instigation of the choreographer (who is also her boyfriend), Charisse visits

[6] The lyric is quite clever—as in the reference to a Shakespearean play "Where a ghost and a prince meet / And everyone ends in mincemeat." According to Schwartz, he and Dietz got the idea for the song as Astaire and the others were reading through this scene. The songwriters wrote it in another room in forty-five minutes and brought it in before the actors had finished their reading.

[7] The height testing in the film reflects real life. Before Charisse was selected for *The Band Wagon,* Astaire came by when she was rehearsing for another film with Hermes Pan: "He came in, nonchalantly, pretending he was just visiting his old friend. . . . I could see that he was there to size me up—for size. . . . Even though we had danced in the same number together . . . when we did *Ziegfeld Follies* [see 18 B2] he wanted to make sure, I guess, that I hadn't grown any. . . . He did it very subtly, very tactfully. Then he just smiled and strolled out."

[8] Two Astaire musical numbers were originally part of these rehearsal sequences; see 27 O and 27 P.

C2 D1 E1 E2

E3 E4 E5 E6

Astaire in his room at the Plaza Hotel and awkwardly tries to calm him down.

In a scene that strains Charisse's acting ability to the limit, the two dancers finally talk things out and are able to smooth over many of their differences, most of which have been caused, they discover, by their defensiveness toward each other.[9] Charisse asks, "Can you and I really dance together?" (E4). To find out, they take a horse-drawn cab to Central Park (E5), where they seek out a place to dance.

Eventually they come across a secluded open-air dance floor. The music of the most famous Schwartz-Dietz song of all, "Dancing in the Dark," wafts through the trees, and to its accompaniment they do discover, to no one's great surprise, that they can indeed dance together, and quite well.

This dance is often seen as a crucial metaphor for the central problem in the putting-on-a-show plot: the successful blending of the high art of the ballerina with the low art of the hoofer and ballroom dancer. This notion should not be pushed too far, however, since, after all, the show is *not* a success when Buchanan attempts to blend high art with popular art, but only when Astaire takes over and throws out all the high-art pretensions. Besides, the ballroom/ballet blend characterizes all of Astaire's romantic duets with ballet-trained partners: Vera-Ellen, Leslie Caron, the Charisse of *Silk Stockings,* even Audrey Hepburn. The duet is remarkable not so much for its ingenious blending of art forms as for the way it develops a subtle emotional transformation. Astaire and Charisse, now wary friends, set out with a task before them that seems straightforward: to discover if they can dance together even though they come from different worlds and different generations. In the course of the dance, however, something unexpected happens: quite contrary to their wills and intentions, they begin to fall in love. Two choreographic devices are used to trace this: an elaborate game of touching and partnering, and the use of stunned hesitations.

The progress of the romance in the dance is most clearly charted in the way the dancers touch each other. At first they are distant and reluctant to touch. However, as the dance, and the romance, build, the partnering gradually becomes closer and progressively more confident and joyous, and lifts and elaborate partnered spins are worked into the texture. Finally, the climax of the dance is reached during an elaborate progression across the floor in which Charisse makes a great, deliberate show of wrapping her arms around Astaire's neck rapturously (E28). Touching, in fact, is used neatly to mark out the emotional change in the scenes that frame the dance: as they ride to the park in the horse-drawn cab, Astaire and Charisse are steadfastly *not* touching—to emphasize this, Astaire has his arms folded across his chest (E5); in the ride *from* the park, by contrast, they are holding hands (E33).

At the same time, the second choreographic device is being developed. One of the most remarkable aspects of Astaire's dancing and choreography is his ability to alter and shade the tempo within a single phrase. In "Dancing in the Dark" these modulations of tempo are used to dramatic purpose: several times the dancers sink to the floor and hesitate in apparent surprise and wonder at what is happening to them; then they are impelled back into the dance (E14, 17, 20). Later, when romantic inhibitions have been overcome, the idea is reprised, altered now to suit the dancers' new relationship: the sinking and rising are done in cooperation—as if the pair are mocking their earlier uncertainty and hesitancy (E23–25, 31).

The arrangement and orchestration of the music, by Conrad Salinger, is quite beautiful: sensual and dramatic, avoiding the tendency toward sappiness or lugubriousness that so often prevailed in MGM musicals. Another special appeal of the number is its attractive, understated decor, which contrasts markedly with the gaudy excess of the Broadway show Buchanan is trying to put on. Especially impressive is the simple, becoming costume Charisse wears, a copy of a $25 dress that had been purchased from an Arizona supplier by costume designer Mary Ann Nyberg. It cost the MGM wardrobe department $1,000 to make copies of the dress for the dance number.

At the beginning of the number, Astaire and Charisse leave the cab to wander silently through Central Park in search of a place to dance. They cross a crowded ballroom floor (where a band is playing the contemplative "High and Low" from 1930) and eventually come upon a secluded

[9] Many people in the preview audience, particularly women, said they disliked this scene—especially the way Charisse cries in it. Charisse could probably have benefited from better directorial advice: under the guidance of a more communicative director, Rouben Mamoulian, Charisse did better with a far more difficult acting role in her next Astaire film, *Silk Stockings.*

E7 E8 E9 E10

E11 E12 E13 E14

dance area (E 6). Their walk is somber, reflective; they are obviously ill at ease with each other. They do not touch; Astaire, in fact, mostly keeps his hands in his pockets.

Entering the dance area, Charisse, without looking at Astaire, inserts a brief, swooning dance phrase into the stroll, by way of invitation. Astaire answers with a danced turn that causes him to pull his hands from his pockets. But then he realizes that he doesn't know what to do with his hands; he reaches out, splays his fingers, and uncertainly pulls his hands back toward his body (E 7). Rather than touch her, he deliberately clasps his hands behind his back (E 8). In this tense and strangely restrained pose, the "Dancing in the Dark" melody enters, and the dance begins.

In the first phrases the dancers flow sometimes with the melody (richly rendered by cellos), sometimes with the countermelody. Astaire's hands are finally freed in a turn, and he reaches out to touch Charisse—from a distance—and sends her into some quick spins. This leads to turns that begin with the dancers close (E 9) but soon develop into a remote embrace (E 10). Separating, they glide back to the edge of the dance floor.

The music now returns to the opening phrase, and the dancers repeat their reflective, musically intricate dance-walk, but with an important difference—Astaire is now loosely partnering Charisse, hand to hand (E 11). She turns in his arms, and they resume the walk in a tighter pose, with him partnering her from behind (E 12). Out of this emerges a partnered pirouette (the first of several in the dance), which Charisse ends by sinking to the ground (E 13, 14). The dancers hesitate in this pose, in apparent bewilderment, and then return to the dance.

They sweep liltingly side by side around the floor (E 15), and then once again Charisse spins into a fall. This time the fall emerges not from a partnered pirouette but from a lift (E 16), and this leads to the second bewildered hesitation (E 17).

They are again pulled back into the dance by the music and are soon moving across the floor, Astaire firmly partnering Charisse from behind (E 18). The themes of touching and of hesitancy are intricately linked here as Charisse's right hand slowly moves upward—as if it were being impelled, reluctantly, by an outside force—to take Astaire's hand (E 19).

Another partnered pirouette leads to the third of the fall-hesitations (E 20), and then, all hesitation gone, the dancers flow across the floor, their progress punctuated by a pair of exultant lifts (E 21). At the far end of the floor (after the first of the two camera cuts in the dance), there are more partnered pirouettes, now elaborated with shifts of direction and extensions of arm and leg (E 22). After the dancers separate briefly, Charisse sinks down on a bench, her back to Astaire. Unlike her previous falls, this one does not suggest bewilderment or uncertainty. She simply waits, proffering her hand with full confidence that Astaire will come around behind her, take it, and pull her back into the dance (E 23). This he does, exactly as the orchestra returns full-throatedly to the main theme. He pulls her upward (E 24) and then off the bench and into his arms (E 25).

After more partnered pirouettes comes the emotional climax, in a final progression across the floor that displays to advantage Charisse's remarkable arms. (It is of interest that, where other choreographers were understandably mesmerized by Charisse's long, shapely legs, Astaire saw the choreographic possibilities in her long, shapely arms.) Charisse turns in Astaire's arms and then locks her left arm around his neck. In that position she performs two voluptuous back-

E15 E16 E17 E18
E19 E20 E21 E22
E23 E24 E25 E26

bends (E 26). Then she pauses, leaning against him (E 27), and finally, with great deliberateness, wraps her other arm around his neck in an embrace that is at once dramatic and intimate as he presses her tightly to his body (E 28).

With that, the dance and the dancers have made their statement, and all that remains is to blend the dance back into the story. After a camera cut, Astaire and Charisse dart toward some stairs that lead up from the dance floor and spin their way up them—one of those difficult steps that look so easy in Astaire's work (E 29). At the top they form dramatic poses with diagonal arms, first in opposition, then together (E 30). Charisse sinks to the floor for a final mocking reprise of her earlier falls; where those were uncertain and bewildered, this one is confident and trusting (E 31). Astaire pulls her to her feet again, and they climb back into the cab—Astaire pausing to dance his re-entry (E 32; compare B 3). As the music fades, they settle back into the seat of the cab, contentedly holding hands (E 33).[10]

In the hotel-room scene that precedes the "Dancing in the Dark" duet, the scriptwriters had Astaire call "human speech" the "greatest means of communication." Astaire delivers the line dutifully—and then calmly proceeds in this duet to show how much more richly dance can communicate.

F
YOU AND THE NIGHT AND THE MUSIC
(REHEARSAL SEQUENCES)

Unfortunately, after "Dancing in the Dark" the Charisse-Astaire love story largely vanishes from the film. Charisse, as we are well aware, is now strongly attracted to Astaire, but she has not broken off her relationship with the show's choreographer. Astaire is uncertain how he stands with Charisse, and she is apparently uncertain about that as well.

However, while the dimensions of this love conflict are not really developed in the film, it is clear that Astaire and Charisse enjoy being together very much, and the film does include one brief sequence that, with nice indirection, shows the warmth of their relationship. They are sitting side by side during a pause in rehearsals, and Astaire absently offers Charisse a cigarette. When he had done that earlier she had refused with a disdainful "Dancers shouldn't smoke," which had angered him. Now, after hesitating, she takes the cigarette and puffs on it amateurishly (F 1). When Astaire suddenly realizes what has happened he laughs, takes the cigarette away from her, and apologizes gently.

Meanwhile, Buchanan's preposterously overdecorated *Faust* musical is now in its final rehearsals. Astaire and Charisse are seen working on part of a dance to "You and the Night and the Music" (1934), first in a rehearsal area, then onstage, where explosive effects go awry all around them (F 2). The choreography in these rehearsal fragments is appropriately parodic: much of the time the dancing naïvely underlines the music—one move for each beat—and the dancers jolt from one position to the next.

[10] The idea of returning to the cab was apparently something that was dreamed up on the set, since it is not mentioned in the final shooting script. The thing that Astaire, not notably a sentimental person, remembered most about the duet twenty-seven years later was the trouble he had "getting back into that damned cab." Salinger's musical arrangement at the end of the number is very fine: the "dancing in the dark" melody for violins, and a bold, dramatic counter-melody for brasses blend effortlessly into some jaunty, quietly contented phrases for strings as the dancers reboard the cab and sit back.

E27 E28 E29 E30
E31 E32 E33 F1
F2 G1 G2 H1

G
I LOVE LOUISA
(2′31″)

Buchanan's show finally opens in New Haven and proceeds to lay an egg. We never actually see the show, but, to the accompaniment of some wonderful Greco-Broadway dirge music by Salinger, Minnelli takes care to show us the egg (G1).

After the show Astaire comes across an impromptu party, or wake, being held in a hotel room by the members of the cast ("the kids"). He is warmly welcomed, as, later, are Charisse, Fabray, and Levant. Soon Levant cajoles Astaire into leading the group in a spirited rendition of "I Love Louisa." Fabray joins in and impishly impersonates the title character (G2; compare 1 F15). (The script had originally called for Astaire and Charisse to do a "cut-up dance" to "Never Marry a Dancer" [from a 1934 show] at this point.)

H
NEW SUN IN THE SKY
(1′1″)

There is a feeling of letdown after the exuberance of "I Love Louisa," and in this pause Levant, more in sadness than irony, suggests that we "kids" find a barn someplace and put on a show. Astaire leaps at the suggestion and decides to sell his $60,000 worth of paintings and produce the show himself—but with all the artistic pretentiousness thrown out. It will now have, he points out, "laughs and entertainment." Buchanan sees the error of his ways and agrees to work under Astaire's direction. This, of course, is a classic scene of the traditional backstage musical, but here it is handled quite seriously, even realistically, and without parody.

Charisse's choreographer-beau, Mitchell, declares he will leave the show since it is no longer going to try to be artistic. Charisse decides to stay with Astaire and "the kids," though this apparently does not mean she is breaking off her romance with Mitchell.

The restructured show is soon taken on the road. Astaire says he is going to follow the original Levant-Fabray script, but the final result is apparently a revue, not a book show, very much in the tradition of the Hollywood backstage musical. In Philadelphia we see Charisse dancing and singing (dubbed by India Adams) a chorus of "New Sun in the Sky."[11] As in her ballet number, Charisse's movements tend to be punchy and frequently lack subtlety of phrasing (H1).

[11] This had been an Astaire solo in the original *Band Wagon*. He made a dance out of getting dressed to go out, an idea he recycled (to different music) in *The Gay Divorcee* (3 C).

I
I GUESS I'LL HAVE TO CHANGE MY PLAN
(1′47″)

Then, from a stage in Boston, Astaire and Buchanan, in top hat and tails, perform a jaunty soft-shoe. The tune certainly calls for jauntiness, but the lyric, which tells of a shattered love affair, doesn't match it very well. In large measure this is because the original lyric was changed for the film. Originally it told of a man who is about to have an affair—he's bought blue pajamas for the occasion, in fact—only to discover the woman is married. By the end, however, he observes that "forbidden fruit I've heard is better to taste" and jauntily resolves to toss any scruples to the wind. This was too much for Hollywood, where it was usually forbidden even to mention pajamas (no matter what their color), much less love affairs with married women. Accordingly, the lyric was mellowed and the mismatch of melody and lyric created.

At any rate, the performers essentially ignore the import of the lyric (rare in an Astaire number) as they perambulate around the imaginative, colorful Oliver Smith set. Like the music, the number is a masterpiece of droll understatement and stands in vivid contrast to the frantic hard-sell antics of the other numbers in this last part of the film.

The music is an ABACA form, and the B and C sections contain a bit of dramatic tension that is absent from the A sections, which project a relaxed cool. The choreography plays with this contrast, both during the singing of the song and in the dance proper: things seem to build up, but then, before they can lead to anything too energetic, they are amusingly brought back under control. For example, during the dance portion of the number, the buildup in the B section leads to a series of quick crossover steps (I1) and then to some bold turns, which continue into the A section only to subside into a calm stroll a measure or two later (I2), catching up belatedly with the music (the orchestration contributes to the joke by following the choreography, not the sense of the melody).

At the end, the two soft-shoe veterans coolly topple their hats from their heads. Their intention is to catch the tumbling hats with their feet —but they miss (I3). (There had been quite a bit of precision hat tossing and catching in Astaire's solos in his previous film, *The Belle of New York*, and the gesture here seems a bit of casual self-parody.) Unruffled and amused, Astaire and Buchanan toss their canes after the lost hats and stroll off arm in arm (I4).[12]

The number is really more a simultaneous pair of identical solos than a true duet—the only Astaire dance of which that is true (though 23 A comes close). Buchanan, perhaps because of his billing as "the British Fred Astaire," was terrified of doing the number, and it certainly would have been easy for Astaire to show him up. (Moreover, Buchanan frequently was in great physical pain during the shooting of the film because of dental surgery he was undergoing at the time.) But the steps in this number are comfortably within his range, and the two hoofers look as if they've been performing together for years.

[12] The ending joke emerged during rehearsals. The tricks with hat and cane frequently went awry, and so, according to Astaire, they decided to end the number that way. The sequence was shot five times; the dancers apparently had difficulty getting the missed catch exactly right.

I1

I2

I3

I4

J
LOUISIANA HAYRIDE
(2′2″)

Next, in Washington, D.C., Nanette Fabray leads the ensemble through a song from 1932 (J 1). Although the song, the musical arrangement, and the staging of the number are not particularly impressive, Fabray is a delight to watch. She phrases beautifully, with wit and a keen musical sense, and seems to be a natural mover. Toward the end of the number, for example, she struts twice across the stage, backed up by a group of male dancers; she makes a fluid and quite sexy little dance out of this simple sequence, whereas the men merely slam unthinkingly into position.

K
TRIPLETS
(2′25″)

On the train between road engagements, Astaire admits to Levant (and to himself) that he is in love with Charisse. But she seems still to be involved with Mitchell.

In Baltimore, Astaire, Buchanan, and Fabray perform "Triplets," a novelty number devised by Kidd in which the performers are dressed as babies and, for part of the time, frolic on their knees. Neither Astaire nor Buchanan looks as if he is having much fun, but the reliable Fabray throws herself into it wholeheartedly (K 1).

L
GIRL HUNT BALLET
(11′56″)

Finally the show opens in New York. Charisse and Astaire run into each other at the stage entrance and converse briefly and awkwardly. He is still uncertain how he stands with her, and she isn't giving him any clues; she has yet, it appears, to make up her mind.

Onstage, they perform in a big production number that attempts to parody the enormously popular tough-guy detective novels of Mickey Spillane. The number, set to music composed by Edens using themes supplied by Schwartz, was devised and written by Minnelli, who, in his autobiography, points out a major problem with the effort: "Applying the term satire to a ballet based on this school of fiction was actually a bit redundant, for in practically every page the writing contained the seeds of its own parody." The script, which is read in a voice-over by Astaire, is, as Minnelli suggests, "disjointed" and makes "little sense" while incorporating "all the Spillane clichés." Actually, there is a certain strained logic to it, but, oddly, the way Minnelli has filmed it makes the story unnecessarily confused, even incomprehensible.

At the beginning Astaire, alone on a city street, hears a trumpet player practicing. A distraught blonde (Charisse) enters and throws herself at him (L 1). Then a man in an overcoat enters and picks up a bottle with liquid in it. On a high note from the trumpet, the bottle explodes—a connection that is not made clear. As the blonde runs off, Astaire discovers that all that's left of the man is "a rag and a bone and a hank of hair." Audiences were presumably supposed to recognize this as a line from an 1897 poem by Rudyard Kipling, "The Vampire"—a line that is used there to characterize the female title character. (The MGM legal office took the trouble to clear the quotation with the Kipling estate.) From this one might deduce that the blonde is not so innocent as she seems.

Astaire concludes that the dead man has been "trying to tell me something." Then he picks up an emerald ring the blonde had left behind and is immediately knocked unconscious by some thugs. The thugs steal the ring—another action that is not at all clear. When he regains consciousness, Astaire resolves to follow his hunches about the three "clues" to find the man's killer.

He is led to a couturier's shop because the rag matches some fabric in the window. The emerald ring is on display in the shop. A brunette (also played by Charisse) leads him to the stockroom (L 2), where he defends himself against the ambush of three men, then pursues a fourth ("Mister Big," he concludes) through the streets of Manhattan. He pauses, exhausted, in a subway station. Now the mysterious blonde reappears, and she and Astaire engage in a slinky adagio while gangsters tumble around and shoot one another in the background (L 3). One shot is aimed at Astaire but hits someone else. The blonde again runs off.

The hank of hair leads him to a beauty shop where he is again knocked unconscious. Upon reviving, he is led by the bone clue to the Dem Bones Cafe. He enters, amusingly trying to disguise himself as one of the habitués (L 4), and soon finds himself doing a jazzy adagio with the leggy brunette. This duet is notable for its strained efforts at hard sell, its ersatz sexiness, and its lack of musical wit and sophistication—qualities that strongly suggest Astaire had little to do with the choreography (L 5, 6).

Suddenly Astaire somehow figures everything out. When the trumpet player in the cafe's band plays a high note, a glass of nitroglycerine on the bar will explode (recall scene I). But after a fight Astaire tosses the glass away; it explodes harmlessly and he emerges unscathed. He then shoots the trumpet player ("Mister Big"), who, dying in his arms, proves to be the blonde, still wearing the emerald ring (L 7). At the fade-out, Astaire strolls off with the brunette—his kind of woman, he tells us.

"Girl Hunt Ballet" has often been highly praised—by Astaire, among others. It is dazzlingly colorful in design, but it seems misguided in conception and confused in execution. Kidd's choreography becomes really imaginative only in some of the tumbling effects for the gangsters, and these are just brief shards of movement with little cumulative impact. Stephen Harvey has suggested interestingly that the number is "really a sly pastiche of those achingly serious Gene Kelly ballets which some esthetes felt had exalted the musical into the realm of Art." But there seems to be no evidence that such a parody was intended, and even if it had been, the point could have been made with less silliness and more, well, art.

J 1

K 1

L 1

L 2

M
THAT'S ENTERTAINMENT
(REPRISE) (1′6″)

The show is, needless to say, a tremendous success. Nevertheless, Astaire finds himself apparently abandoned backstage in his dressing room.[13] He bolsters himself against this disappointment by singing a fragment of "By Myself." When he emerges from his dressing room, however, he discovers the entire cast assembled there to give him a surprise tribute, which is spoken by Charisse, who concludes: "As far as I'm concerned, [the show] is going to run forever" (M1). To clarify any ambiguity in her phraseology, she kisses him (M2).[14]

It's a heavy, stilted moment, and in an effort to lighten things for the ending, Buchanan, Fabray, and Levant eagerly join Astaire and Charisse for a bouncy concluding reprise of "That's Entertainment," with lyrics that seem to make the film's position quite plain: "A show that is really a show sends you out with a kind of glow. . . . No death like you get in *Macbeth,* no ordeal like the end of *Camille,* this goodbye brings a tear to the eye. . . . *That's* entertainment" (M3).

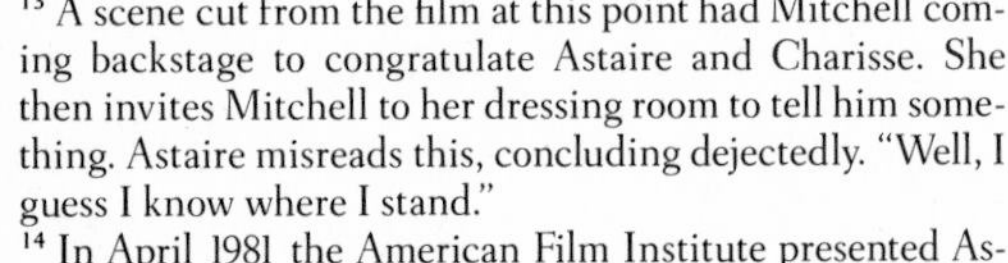

[13] A scene cut from the film at this point had Mitchell coming backstage to congratulate Astaire and Charisse. She then invites Mitchell to her dressing room to tell him something. Astaire misreads this, concluding dejectedly. "Well, I guess I know where I stand."

[14] In April 1981 the American Film Institute presented Astaire with its lifetime-achievement award. For her contribution to the award ceremony, Charisse recited her *Band Wagon* speech (but without the kiss) as a tribute to Astaire.

NUMBERS CUT FROM THE FILM

When editing on *The Band Wagon* was completed in January 1953, the film was two hours and twenty-nine minutes long. By the following summer it had been cut to a final length of one hour, fifty-two minutes. Four musical numbers and part of a fifth were among the excised footage.

N
SWEET MUSIC

This number took place at the end of the backers' meeting at Buchanan's apartment. After Astaire and Charisse are reluctantly introduced as the stars of Buchanan's new show, Levant seats himself at the piano and he and Fabray do a 4′45″ rendition of "Sweet Music," a song Fred and Adele Astaire had performed in the original *Band Wagon* revue. As part of the routine Levant plays fragments of various well-known piano compositions (N1, 2).

O
YOU HAVE EVERYTHING

Shortly after this, Astaire and Charisse go separately to the "Rollo Rehearsal Hall" to practice. Although they are unaware of it, they happen to occupy adjacent rehearsal studios, each equipped with a portable record player. The camera observes them simultaneously with their shared wall in the center of the screen (O1). In the dance, to a 1937 tune, Astaire performs in his style, Charisse in hers. The music reflects this, abruptly alternating a jazz arrangement with a sweet, violin-dominated arrangement. At one point Astaire's record gets stuck. The number ran three minutes and obviously was a splendid opportunity to contrast the two performers and to emphasize the differences in the worlds and eras they are supposed to represent in the film.

P
GOT A BRAN' NEW SUIT

This solo for Astaire was included in the rehearsal montage sequence as the cast seeks to put together Buchanan's *Faust* show. It occurred before Astaire gets fed up and walks out—indeed, the number is one of the reasons he throws his tantrum.

Designed to show the development of a musical number, it was in five sections, perhaps separated by other bits of rehearsal business as part of the broader rehearsal montage. (1) In the orchestra pit Fabray auditions the 1935 song for Astaire, spiritedly singing a chorus of it to piano accompaniment. (2) Astaire likes the song and begins to work with it in the theatre lobby, trying to come up with some ideas for a dance routine. (3) Working in the theatre lounge, Astaire discovers an idea with his cane that he finds satisfactory. (4) In a hallway backstage, he continues to work to improve the cane idea accompanied by drum. (5) Finally, the number perfected, Astaire performs it at a rehearsal onstage—he sings one full

L3

L4

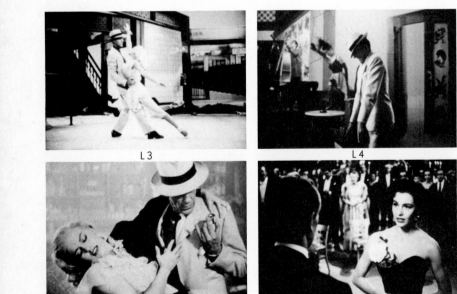

L5

L6

L7

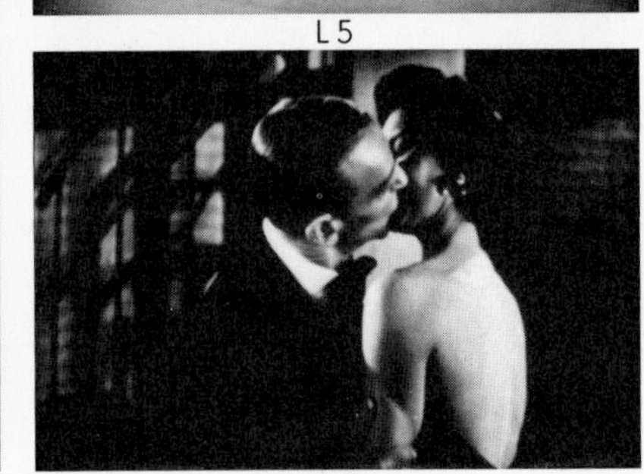

M1

M2

M3

chorus and then dances a chorus (P1). The final song-and-dance sequence ran a minute and a half. Fabray and Levant, apologizing for not mentioning it earlier, arrive to inform him that the song has been cut from the show. Astaire, panting, is disgusted and deflated (P2).

Q
TWO-FACED WOMAN

Later, at a dress rehearsal for the *Faust* show (after the "Dancing in the Dark" number), Charisse performs a number choreographed by Kidd to this 1932 song, backed by a female chorus—half of them dressed in white to represent the woman's good side, the other half in red to represent her bad side.

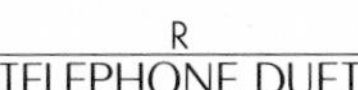

R
TELEPHONE DUET

In her autobiography Charisse mentions a duet with Astaire that was cut. It involved a telephone: "He was at a desk in his office, I was in my apartment. And we had a conversation about making a date, using dance as our means of communicating. No words were spoken, only the way we danced conveyed our meanings. I think that was chopped because it was improperly shot." The duet appears to have been not a separate number but part of "Girl Hunt Ballet" (R1).

N1

N2

O1

P1

P2

R1

28.

Daddy Long Legs

1955

Largely, it seems, on the strength of its script, Fred Astaire ranks *Daddy Long Legs* as a personal favorite among his films. The screenplay, crafted by Phoebe and Henry Ephron from a popular and affecting 1912 novel, traces with wit and charm the reluctant romance of an engagingly eccentric middle-aged millionaire and a spirited orphan whom he puts through college. Particularly remarkable is the way the script builds its plot complications out of the June-September aspect of the romance rather than simply ignoring it, thus allowing Astaire comfortably to play his age—something that undoubtedly appealed to him enormously.

Contributing greatly to the success of the film are the vivid and appealing performances by Leslie Caron as the object of Astaire's philanthropy (and, eventually, desire) and by the supporting cast, led by Fred Clark and Thelma Ritter as involved members of Astaire's staff. The direction, sympathetic and amiable, is by Jean Negulesco and the score is by Astaire's old crony Johnny Mercer, who came up with "Something's Gotta Give," by far the most successful song written for Astaire in the 1950s. The film is also handsomely designed.

The dances are something of a problem. Although Astaire's numbers are not among his very finest, most of them are solidly constructed and show in considerable measure the wit, inventiveness, and musicality that are trademarks of his choreography. However, his partner, the ballet-trained Caron, proves to be an uncongenial foil. She is remarkably chunky for a dancer, and she often dances uncomprehendingly. Worse, the producers disfigure the film with a ponderous and pretentious dream ballet created by the then fashionable French choreographer Roland Petit.

SHAPING THE SCREENPLAY

The film takes its story from *Daddy-Long-Legs,* a novel by Jean Webster. Webster fashioned her novel into a play, which became a hit on Broadway and was performed throughout the country between 1914 and 1919. The novel and play provided the basis for a silent film treatment in 1919 with Mary Pickford and Mahlon Hamilton, and for two sound films: one in 1931 with Janet Gaynor and Warner Baxter, and, less directly, one in 1935 called *Curly Top,* in which Shirley Temple played cupid to Rochelle Hudson and John Boles.

Twentieth Century–Fox owned the film rights, and in 1951 the company's resident tycoon, Darryl F. Zanuck, began to look into the possibility of using it again, essentially as a remake of the 1931 film. The thinking was that the central role could be played by a singer-dancer like Mitzi Gaynor, while possibilities considered for the male lead included Gregory Peck, David Niven, Cary Grant, John Lund, and Ray Milland—all of whom were in their thirties or forties.

Nothing came of these casting ideas, but the notion of fashioning the story as a musical was established. Then, in late 1953, Zanuck saw Astaire, whose contract at MGM had now run its course, dining at a nightclub, and things quickly fell into place. With Astaire signed, and then Caron, Zanuck turned the project over to the Ephrons, who were jubilant at the opportunity: "Knowing it was Astaire and Caron," Henry Ephron later wrote, "we would have made the supreme sacrifice if they had asked us—taking a cut in salary. Maybe."

Mostly rejecting previous scripts and treatments, the Ephrons went back to the original Webster novel for inspiration. The novel is written as a collection of letters from the foundling to her anonymous benefactor, whom she impishly calls "Daddy-Long-Legs" because her only glimpse of him was as an elongated shadow at the orphanage. The letters range over the four years of the girl's college career and richly portray her character: perceptive, talented, bubbling with humor, and voraciously curious about everything.[1] There are moments of disappointment, and petulance, too, as she grows older and wiser. With skillful lightness Webster blends into the girl's commentary some elements of reform protest—about the dreary state of orphanages and about

[1] These were also apparently qualities Webster had in abundant measure. The character reflects the author in other ways as well. Although no orphan, Webster had attended a Northeastern women's college (Vassar), and had begun to write stories while there, achieving her first book-length publication shortly after graduation. Also like her character, she decided to change her first name while in college. Webster died in childbirth in 1916 at the age of forty.

Leslie Caron in the nightmare ballet

women's rights—as well as occasional devastating characterizations of others, such as: "She never lets ideas interrupt the easy flow of her conversation." (The orphanage reform ideas were put forward far more directly in the play version—a flowery, melodramatic tearjerker that hardly seems to have been written by the same hand—and survives in the earlier films as well, quite heavily in the 1919 Pickford film.)

Understandably charmed and intrigued by the letters, the rich man visits the girl, but without revealing his identity as her benefactor, and eventually proposes marriage. Overwhelmed by their class differences, she refuses, and then, miserable and desperate, she resolves to go to her mysterious benefactor for advice. The meeting, of course, resolves everything.

Some adjustments in the original story were made for the film. Since Caron is French, it was arranged that Astaire would discover her while he was on a diplomatic mission to France. And, following earlier film treatments, the story was reset in the present day—a change Astaire would doubtless have insisted upon anyway, since he had an aversion to period dramas following the failure of *The Belle of New York* two years earlier. Removed from the story was the issue of orphanage reform—hardly a peak issue in 1955.

Partly following the 1931 film version, the dilemma of the romance revolves directly around the differences in age and financial status of the two central characters, not their class differences as such. And it is the millionaire who grows uncertain, not the girl. Caron falls rather readily in love with Astaire; in fact, she is quite forward about encouraging his advances. But he, self-conscious about the age gap and concerned that the young woman may have been only temporarily dazzled by his wealth and maturity, breaks off the romance in guilt and chagrin.

In the novel the age difference is not nearly so severe—a significant, but not terribly monumental, fourteen years. But when the film was made Astaire was fifty-five, and Caron, who was twenty-four, is convincingly cast as a college student. The Ephrons wisely allowed this age issue to stand at the heart of their story rather than seeking to minimize it.

The characters they developed are rich and captivating. Astaire is free-spirited and unconventional, the black sheep of his priggish family and the despair of his orderly staff. Caron is girlishly appealing and touchingly vulnerable, yet self-confident and often assertive. She tends to be a bit more weepy than Webster's character and is less of a reflective intellectual—she dreams where the original toys at philosophy

"History of the Beat"

—but she has the same giddy delight in life and much the same inner seriousness.

Ephron's happiest creations, however, are among the supporting characters, particularly Astaire's dyspeptic chief of staff (Fred Clark), always trying to bring order to his employer's chaotic and capricious life style, and Astaire's sentimental secretary (Thelma Ritter), quick to take up Caron's cause. (Ritter, who seems effortlessly to dominate every scene she is in, has, according to one compilation, the distinction of being the performer most often nominated for an Academy Award without winning.) Also noteworthy are Astaire's friend (Larry Keating), a diplomat who finally gets Astaire to see himself as others see him, and Astaire's sister-in-law (Kathryn Givney), acerbic and officious.

There seems to have been a concentrated effort by all concerned with making the film to keep it from lapsing into sentimentality. As in Webster's novel, this is accomplished by keeping the touch light. The dialogue between Astaire and Caron, in particular, appealingly cloaks serious matters in the amusingly indirect banter that Astaire always favored. The musical numbers have been smoothly blended into the script and arise naturally out of the action.

The Ephrons worked quickly on the script over the summer of 1954. Henry Ephron reports that Astaire came by each Friday to read over what they had written. He was delighted and had only one suggestion: he didn't like the way one love scene ended in a kiss. "That love scene," he told the writers, "Cary Grant can play it. I can't. I don't make love by kissing; I make love by dancing."

The script was completed by early August and sent off for approval to Zanuck, who pronounced it "sensational" and furnished a battery of thoughtful and perceptive suggestions for improvement. (Zanuck's remarkable talent as an editor of scripts was something that impressed even those who disliked him personally.) The final script was ready by the end of September. There are only minor differences between this document and the finished film—an occurrence that may well be unique in Astaire's career in musicals.

THE MUSIC

Astaire had long admired "Dream," a Johnny Mercer song hit of 1945, and suggested it be incorporated throughout the film—an idea that may have inspired the Ephrons to make their heroine a congenital daydreamer. At Astaire's urging, Mercer was then signed to provide all the songs for the film —something of a gamble, since he had never before produced both lyrics and music for an entire film.

Besides "Something's Gotta Give," with its rhythmically intriguing melody and its brilliantly appropriate lyric, Mercer came up with several pleasant, lightweight tunes. Oddly, most of the songs in the film are sung by choruses (usually off-screen), which means that most of the lyrics provided by this master lyricist are difficult to understand on the soundtrack.

The music for the big Petit ballet was composed by Alex North, a specialist in background music for dramatic films.

LESLIE CARON

As an actress, Caron is beautifully cast in *Daddy Long Legs.* She is wide-eyed yet poised and resourceful—qualities that suit the role (or one interpretation of it) perfectly. Caron had been discovered in Paris by Gene Kelly, who brought her to Hollywood to appear opposite him in his highly successful 1951 film *An American in Paris.* She had had extensive ballet training at the Paris Conservatory and had been a member of the Ballets des Champs-Elysées. Her dancing in *Daddy Long Legs,* however, is singularly undistinguished, lacking in flow and motivation, and her movements often seem bewildered and perfunctory. Some of this may have been caused by the intimidating presence of Astaire; Henry Ephron reports that Caron was "shy and frightened she would never measure up to Fred." But she doesn't look much better in her solo material, even though it was created for her by a Parisian colleague, Petit.

Caron seems to be rather unmusical (she herself has commented on the musical deficiencies of her French training), which would pose major difficulties for her in Astaire's choreography. In his autobiography Astaire even goes so far as to imply criticism of her in this regard: "One day at rehearsals I asked her to listen extra carefully to the music, so as to keep in time. Her reply, 'Oh, I know, I know—I am so slow at learning. My mother used to send me to see all of your pictures to learn how to keep in time with the music.'" She also seems to have been rather inflexible. The story is told of a step Astaire wanted her to do in which she was required to toe in with one foot. She had enormous difficulty with the step and eventually got up the courage to say, "Oh, a dancer cannot point her toe in"—an observation that must have seemed nearly incomprehensible to a man who had spent his life cheerfully shattering such mindless rules. "She can if she wants to," Astaire replied. Caron agreed to work on it.

Daddy Long Legs was Caron's last dance musical. Relying thereafter solely on her considerable acting abilities, she appeared in one more musical (the danceless *Gigi* of 1958) and then only in nonmusicals.

THE WIDE SCREEN

As Astaire put it at the time, *Daddy Long Legs* "is my first go at CinemaScope, or is it the other way around?" Although he reports that Negulesco kept telling him, "You gotta keep those sides filled," the dances in *Daddy Long Legs* are generally kept as much center-screen as ever. The chief exception to this is the romantic duet "Something's Gotta Give," in which he and Caron try to make choreographic use of the larger space they could comfortably put between them.

ASTAIRE AND THE PRODUCTION OF THE FILM

Daddy Long Legs was produced at a time of personal tragedy for Astaire. In the spring of 1954 his beloved wife, Phyllis, underwent major surgery for lung cancer. For a while the surgery seemed to have been successful, but in August she suffered a setback and soon after lapsed into a coma from which she never recovered. She died, at the age of forty-six, on September 13, a few days before shooting was to begin.

Despondent, Astaire at first tried to get out of the film—at one point he even offered to pay for the production expenses thus far incurred. Zanuck and Samuel Engel, the film's producer, urged him to continue, as did many of his friends. (Meanwhile, however, Zanuck quietly lined up the sixty-six-year-old Maurice Chevalier as a possible replacement.) Realizing that work would probably be the best therapy, and remembering that his wife had wanted him to make the film, Astaire appeared in Engel's office two days after the funeral and told him, "I don't know if I can make it, Sam, but I'll try. I'm reporting for work."

The production schedule was arranged to make it as easy as possible for Astaire—the Petit ballet, in which he appears only intermittently, was produced first—and gradually he worked his way back. But as Engel recalls, "It was a frightful ordeal for the poor man. He'd be dancing as if nothing had happened, and then he'd come over in a corner and talk to me. He'd say, 'I don't know if Old Dad can make it,' and tears would come to his eyes. I'd say, 'It's O.K. It's all right to cry.' He'd say, 'It's rough Sam, real rough. Especially going home and she's not there.' "

Although there may be evidence of strain on Astaire's face during his brief appearances in the Petit ballet (15,6), there is no other suggestion in the film of the personal tragedy he was undergoing at the time. As Engel observes, "When *Daddy Long Legs* was finally released, Fred was so good in it that I'm sure the audience never guessed his heart was breaking. His class emerged when he wrote me a letter saying, 'Thanks for standing by Old Dad.' It should have been the other way around."

THE CHOREOGRAPHY

Astaire's choreographic assistant on the film was David Robel, who had previously worked on *Blue Skies* and later assisted on two of Astaire's television specials.

The film's ballet choreographer, Roland Petit, had established his stage reputation over the course of the previous decade with a series of steamy and highly theatrical ballets on such eternal themes as sex and death, which reportedly shocked some sensibilities when they were premiered. He had done the choreography for two Hollywood films before he came to *Daddy Long Legs,* including Caron's most recent previous effort, *The Glass Slipper.* Petit's predilection in his ballets is for naked passion, flashy effects, and violent overstatement, all delivered with remarkable musical insensitivity. It would be difficult to find a choreographer whose instincts were more at variance with Astaire's, and yet the two did manage to collaborate productively on the film's daydream number. The big ballet near the end of the film is the product of Petit's imagination alone.

THE NUMBERS

A
HISTORY OF THE BEAT
(1′ 30″)

The film deftly establishes Astaire's condition of casual extravagance at the opening. As a gaggle of timorous art devotees is led around the first floor of his palatial New York house (A 1) (on the walls are originals, not prints, according to a Fox press release), Astaire holds forth in an office upstairs, simultaneously banging on a set of drums and making firm financial decisions (A 2).

This leads to a short solo routine performed for the uncomfortable amusement of his harried and long-suffering aide, Clark. It's one of the oddest solos in Astaire's career—half formed and half baked. It begins with him singing a song fragment at the drum set while holding brushes. The fragment is clearly the prologue to a longer song, but the rest is never sung and was apparently cut (see 28 K). After a reaction shot of Clark (there are three of them in this brief number), Astaire is suddenly seen to be holding drumsticks, which he proceeds to flip around. Next he darts out into the center of the room and frolics while bouncing the sticks off the floor (A 3), the furniture, and the walls. The number ends as he repeatedly bashes a pair of cymbals with one stick (A 4), bursts back into the center of the room, spins quickly, and gestures toward the unimpressed Clark for approval.

Astaire owned an elaborate drum set himself and liked to spend hours slamming away at the traps to the accompaniment of jazz records. It was relaxation, or release, for him, and the idea of building this into a musical number was perhaps natural. But he apparently never fully developed the idea and, uncharacteristically, was willing to have the routine represented in the film as a collection of fragments demonstrating tricks he could perform with his drumsticks. This was probably the first substantial Astaire number to be filmed, and it may have been particularly affected by his grief.

B
C-A-T SPELLS CAT
(59″)

Astaire is next seen on a tour in France with a State Department group. When his car runs into a ditch, he goes to a nearby orphanage for help and discovers Caron cheerfully caring for a group of younger children. She gives them a musical spelling lesson in English, and he is charmed (B 1).

C
DADDY LONG LEGS
(1′ 30″)

From the motherly proprietress of the orphanage, Astaire learns that Caron's likely destiny in life is to marry a most unsuitable local farmer. When he reaches Paris, Astaire arranges with the American ambassador to send Caron to a women's college in the United States. To avoid any doubts about his motives, Astaire agrees that his financial sponsorship will remain anonymous, and Caron's only requirement will be to send a letter every month to a post-office box telling him of her progress.[2]

Caron receives the news with dreamy delight. Taking her image of him from the long-legged shadow he cast as he left the orphanage after delivering the news to the proprietress, Caron childishly draws a caricature of her "Papa Faucheux" on a blackboard while an off-screen female chorus distantly sings the title song (C 1). The song is quite a charmer, and it is regrettable it is given very little prominence in the film. The melody is wonderfully gentle and wistful, and the naïve lyric (only partly decipherable on the soundtrack) aptly suggests Caron's girlish state of mind.

D
WELCOME EGGHEAD
(40″)

At college Caron is welcomed with a brief hazing song, but she is soon acclimated and quickly picks up the slang ("Hi!" and "Wow!"), which at first bewildered her. Following a well-worn Hollywood tradition, the film shows college life as a thing of proms and romances, a place where books are sometimes carried, but never read.

E
DAYDREAM SEQUENCE
(7′ 36″)

For two years Caron regularly sends her anonymous benefactor letters. These are read only by

[2] In all earlier versions of the story, the orphan is a feisty rebel in a cruel and largely uncaring institution (in the 1919 Pickford film she is punished by having her hand forced onto a hot stove); her benefactor (a trustee of the orphanage) is charmed by her indomitable high spirits.

A 1 A 2 A 3 A 4

B 1 C 1 E 1 E 2

Clark and the weepily sympathetic secretary, Thelma Ritter. Touched by the letters, Clark and Ritter finally demand that Astaire read them. Astaire somewhat reluctantly obliges (E 1).

The letters describe Caron's images of her mysterious Daddy Long Legs. She sees him variously as a Texas millionaire, as an international playboy, and as her guardian angel, and the film obligingly allows Astaire to materialize in each of these imagined states.

As the Texan he clomps about grandly in cowboy boots, shedding coins whenever he raises his ten-gallon hat (E 2). Included in the routine is a brief song in which he bawls that down in Texas they're always asking him, "Daddy, Daddy, why's your legs so long?" His voice is (obviously) dubbed—by basso profundo Thurl Ravenscroft—apparently the only time Astaire was dubbed in his career. Mercer's lusty melody for this song is highly derivative: it is a close relative of Richard Rodgers' "Bloody Mary" from *South Pacific*.

Astaire's amusing caper as the Texan, based on a square dance figure, is, appropriately enough, not only long-legged but bow-legged, a cheerfully galumphing routine in which he flails his legs in little curlicues and stomps around on the outside of his feet (E 3). Toward the end he has an altercation with an invisible obstruction on the floor. In an effort to stamp it out (E 4) he stubs his foot, hops and staggers around in pain for a while (E 5), but recovers in time to end the routine with a zany series of springs into the air (E 6).

As an international playboy he is shown imperiously making his way, to a tango, through legions of fawning females (one of whom—in a blond wig—is Barrie Chase, who was to be Astaire's partner in his television specials between 1958 and 1968) (E 7; see also 30 A 3). Eventually one woman rejects him, an event he finds as fascinating as it is unexpected. As he makes a play for her (E 8), Caron quickly decides to change her dream.

The final portion of the number is a lovely duet in which Astaire solicitously hovers over Caron as her ever-attentive guardian angel. The dance can be seen essentially as a balletic solo for Caron around which Astaire lovingly invents intricate and amusing embellishments. And, it seems, that's exactly the way it was choreographed. As Petit recalls, "The first rehearsal was just a catastrophe. So I said, 'You should let me go, because I can do nothing. You don't need me.' So he said, 'Yes, yes, I need you because I like you and I feel comfortable with you. You do Leslie's dance and everything, and I will try to manage by myself and I will ask someone who worked with me before. . . . I will manage.'"

The dream-Astaire comes upon the dream-Caron in a pastel alley of shops where he calmly sets about granting her every wish and protecting her from every mishap: he buys her an ice-cream cone and prevents loose scaffolding from falling on her. When Caron is impressed by a ballerina doll in a shopwindow, he obligingly transforms her into a toe dancer (E 9)—an act that causes some problems because (influenced, perhaps, by *The Red Shoes*) she delightedly finds her slippers running away with her, and he has some trouble keeping up.

Eventually they settle down in an open space and, to a beguilingly lush melody, dance a sweet, harmonious duet in which they scarcely touch. In it Astaire glides around Caron, framing her balletic moves and poses in figures of his own (E 10, 12), or mesmerizing her from a distance with his incredibly articulate hands (E 11). A sequence involving leaps to the side leads to a circling of the floor in a beautiful series of sidelong, space-devouring strides—probably the step, mentioned earlier, with which Caron had trouble because it required her to turn in with the left foot (E 13). (In two or three places in this duet the dancers come to the end of a dance phrase and hold a pose, waiting for the next phrase of the music to begin; the pauses are brief, indeed scarcely noticeable, but they are extremely unusual in an Astaire dance.)

After various grand traveling patterns, some of which repeat the mesmerizing idea on a broader scale (E 14, 15), Astaire sends Caron spinning into a series of traveling turns on toe and strolls along after her approvingly (E 16). Then he dramatically darts around her, draws her in toward him (E 17), plucks a star from the sky (E 18), and presents it to her. Delighted, she wanders away, as he gazes after her protectively (E 19).[3]

F
DREAM

Enchanted by the letters, Astaire, a man of action (and caprice), immediately arranges to go to Caron's college on the pretext of seeing his niece, who is her roommate. Clark is appalled, and Astaire's sister-in-law is bewildered; but the visit is arranged and takes place at the time of a spring dance, presided over by the Ray Anthony Orchestra.

Astaire meets his niece (whom he hasn't seen since she was a baby) and soon finds himself conversing with Caron in a garden. He finds her remarkably grown up and flirtatious—something the childlike daydream ballet certainly didn't prepare him for (F 1). (It is also likely to come as something of a jolt to the viewer, or to the reader of the Webster novel; but, then, she *is* French, after all.) In the background a vocal group, accompanied by the Anthony Orchestra, croons "Dream." This is the song's first use in the film, and it is here directly associated with the Astaire-Caron romance, for the couple dance to it briefly while continuing their banter. Caron draws Astaire a rather unflattering picture of what she imagines her elderly guardian to be like and then startles Astaire by asserting that she plans to live with her benefactor after she graduates.

G
THE SLUEFOOT
(4′ 38″)

To Astaire's irritation, Caron's rather pushy boyfriend comes to collect her for the next dance, the improbably entitled "Sluefoot." As demonstrated by the college-student dancers, the Sluefoot seems to be built mostly out of a step combination that includes leg jutting and arm jabbing, and finishes with a hand clap and a scooping thrust forward. The general demeanor is loose—the "lackadaisiest," suggests Mercer (rhymes with "craziest").

Astaire, watching from the sidelines, gets jostled by the crowd into the middle of the dance floor—alongside Caron, he is pleased to discover. He quickly picks up the spirit of the dance, even yelling out "Sluefoot!" at one point, then shrinking in amused embarrassment when he realizes that no one else has joined him.

After a bit of arm flailing and some spirited careening, he and Caron perform a variant of some of the Sluefoot steps: there are the leg juttings fore and aft (G 1), the leg thrusts to the side (G 2), the arm jabs (G 3), and the scooping thrust forward in conclusión (G 4). Having established his credentials, Astaire snaps Caron up and, holding her around the waist with one arm while the other hangs limp at his side (a typical part-

[3] The star effect is, of course, achieved through animation, a technique rarely used (and then only incidentally) by Astaire in his films: 15 M, 22 G.

nering configuration in this film), circles the floor with her. This idea is blended in with various elaborations of the Sluefoot steps—some of them carried out during partnering—and with a slinging lift (G5, 6).

After a sequence in which Caron and Astaire playfully spin and dodge past each other several times, there is a cut to a medium shot, and as the camera pulls back, the two dancers blast their way into a brilliant (if temporary) finish that is the dance's highlight. The step combination is rhythmically complex and involves some blistering quick turns, a crossover behind-the-back tap (G7), and a sudden plunge to the knee (G8).

Astaire and Caron are now joined by the rest of the dancers for more boisterous Sluefooting, which eventually develops into a wonderful screwball cadenza for Astaire. As the others watch, he scampers and shuffles and flaps and twitches comically to raucous drum accompaniment (G9). The cadenza is a great success with everyone except Astaire's embarrassed sister-in-law (G10), and all join in again as the dance comes to an arm-flailing finish. At the end,

E3 E4 E5 E6
E7 E8 E9 E10
E11 E12 E13 E14
E15 E16 E17 E18
E19 F1 G1 G2

Astaire and Caron are exultantly carried around the floor by the other dancers.

Although the number is performed as an exhibition of sorts, it establishes an important plot point: Astaire is shown to be able to compete effortlessly for Caron on her own ground. It also brings out a particularly appealing aspect of the Astaire character: his utter lack of interest in putting up a stuffy front. He is quite willing to risk making a fool of himself, and there is something especially gratifying in the way he triumphs over the generational challenge with such cheery composure.

Rather oddly, however, the dance does very little to develop the Astaire-Caron romance. They seem to be having fun together, but the focus is really on Astaire—it's almost the only duet he ever created in which he inserts a solo segment for himself. Caron seems simply to be along for the ride, and for the most part the dance would be equally successful had her role been danced by one of the other college women at the dance.

H

SOMETHING'S GOTTA GIVE

(6′20″)

Whatever the romantic impact of the Sluefoot dance, the evening as a whole has clearly had a romanticizing effect on Astaire. When next seen, he is back in his New York mansion sitting behind his drum set, feelingly—and beautifully—singing a fragment of "Dream" (H1).

Eagerly he reads Caron's next letter to her Daddy Long Legs. Soon afterward, he finds it convenient to arrange for Caron's boyfriend to be sent to work as an engineer in Bolivia. He next invites Caron and his niece to come to New York for a weekend and is only temporarily disconcerted when Caron arrives at the airport alone: his niece, it happens, is ill.

Caron is set up in a luxurious hotel suite, and Astaire joins her there for dinner. The conversation lightly turns to talk of Astaire's peripatetic and thus far inconclusive love life, and he is soon musing in song over the obvious attraction he and Caron feel for each other (H2). Mercer's lyrics are singularly appropriate:

> When an irresistible force such as you
> Meets an old immovable object like me,

G3 G4 G5 G6 G7 G8 G9 G10 H1 H2 H3 H4 H5 H6 H7 H8

You can bet as sure as you live,
Something's gotta give.

Even the diction—with polysyllabic adjectives like "implacable"—perfectly suits the experienced and mature character Astaire plays. (By contrast, the lyric in Caron's "Daddy Long Legs" song contains only one word that has more than two syllables, and that is "Cinderella's.")

As with many songs composed for Astaire, the melodic line is built around a figure involving some rather intricate syncopation. In the first lines, for example, the first seven syllables are sung with an off-the-beat rhythmic complexity that resolves only at the end of the line (on "*force* such as you" and "*ob*ject like me"). Throughout his dance duet with Caron, Astaire makes use of this engaging rhythmic device, reflecting it in various walking, darting, and hopping figures.

A drama is played out in the dance: overcoming her initial hesitations, Caron gradually becomes warmer and more intimate with Astaire. During this process the dancers several times separate widely and seem to be groping for each other in a dreamlike haze—an idea that may have been inspired by the fact that the film was shot in CinemaScope, giving the dancers much more lateral space to fill.[4] But these promising choreographic ingredients are not fully or convincingly developed, and much of their effect is undercut by Caron's performance: she is stiff, unyielding, uncomprehending. The elements for a great romantic duet are there, but they never fuse satisfyingly.

The dance begins as Astaire tenderly leads Caron by the hand out onto the floor (H3). The impulse of the music's syncopation is reflected in the unevenness of their walk and then later in some dodging sidelong hesitations as they face each other. A soft spin (articulated by Astaire, merely delivered by Caron) leads to a passage in which Caron wafts from side to side under Astaire's direction (H4) and then is neatly spun into a linked-arm stroll (H5).

Again the syncopation of the melody is visualized: first in a lush partnered figure—sometimes with the outside arm hanging limp at the side

[4] The only other Astaire duet in which the dancers spend so much time separated is "Stereophonic Sound" in *Silk Stockings* (30 C), which parodies the wide screen.

H9 H10 H11 H12
H13 H14 H15 H16
H17 H18 H19 H20
H21 I1 I2 I3

(H6; compare G5)—and then in a side-by-side dodging pattern, in which Caron's bewilderment at the choreography seems palpable (H7).

Next comes the dance's most remarkable moment: Astaire spins Caron and then deftly moves in on her so that when she stops turning she finds herself locked in his embrace (H8–10). Apparently disconcerted by this, she pushes herself away from him in some confusion, but soon they are together again for some lovely partnered hops on the syncopated figure in the music (H11). Once more they separate (H12)—Caron's upper-body stiffness is particularly evident here—and then are drawn together for some hand-to-hand swirling that begins with an especially unattractive partnered pose in which Caron thrusts out one leg horizontally (H13).

There are more partnered hops and a figure in which the dancers seem to be groping for each other in a fog (H14). Soon they link up again and Caron does some fleeting, uncommunicative thrusts around Astaire's body (H15). Together they swirl toward the doorway, pause nestled together for an instant (H16), and then jubilantly scamper out the door for a night on the town (H17).

The number continues in double exposure as the dancers are seen to frolic over images suggesting various nightclubs. As locales vary so does the musical arrangement, going into a Latin phase, for example, and then into American jazz. The choreography reflects these changes somewhat, and near the end there is even a reprise of some of the Sluefoot steps.

Back in the hotel corridor after having danced the night away, Astaire and Caron playfully blend a convenient tea cart into their dance (H18) and then finally cool down enough to sing a last phrase of the song. The number ends quite beautifully: the dancers swirl in each other's arms to the door of Caron's room and then separate and settle into reflective calm, gazing at each other as the music subsides (H19).

The Ephrons supply them with musing dialogue in which they gingerly imply their regard for each other. After Caron eventually goes into her suite, Astaire has a final gesture that tells more about his feelings than any words. After slyly checking to make sure no one is looking, he hops on the tea cart and glides down the hallway with childlike glee (H20). Suddenly the elevator doors open and a stuffy couple, startled at Astaire's undignified behavior, get out. With characteristic composure, he calmly dismounts and lets them pass (H21). (This wonderful episode with the tea cart was apparently dreamed up on the set or when the number was choreographed. It is not mentioned in the script, though otherwise the setting of the number and the dialogue surrounding it are there virtually intact.)

I
NIGHTMARE BALLET
(12′ 7″)

Astaire apparently gets little sleep, for he is next seen buying a large (but simple) engagement ring (under the blissfully encouraging gaze of Ritter and the disapproving scowl of Clark) and then meets Caron at her hotel suite for breakfast (I1).

Meanwhile, however, it happens that his friend the ambassador has moved into the suite next door. After overhearing the loving conversation between Astaire and Caron as they clink orange-juice glasses on the terrace, he calls Astaire to his room and demands to know what is going on (I2). In a well-paced and well-developed scene, he forcefully argues that Astaire has taken advantage of his wealth and position to sweep the orphan girl off her feet (while sweeping her boyfriend off to Bolivia). Astaire finally and reluctantly sees the reasonableness of all this. He telephones Caron and tells her that he has been abruptly called abroad—and vanishes from her life.[5]

Time passes, and Caron's only association with Astaire is through the newspaper clippings she collects telling of his world travels. While her phonograph plays "Dream," she writes to her Daddy Long Legs, telling him that she desperately needs to see him for advice. As she writes, she drifts off into a disturbed sleep in which she imagines herself following Astaire to some of the locales he has visited, only to have him reject her each time.

It's a fairly viable idea for a phantasmagoric dream ballet, and it might have served poignantly to underline Caron's state of mind. Unfortunately, the ballet, choreographed by Petit and set to Alex North's raucous and undistinguished musical noodlings, just lies there, twelve minutes of pretentious nonsense, a deadening interlude that television stations—with impeccable, if uncharacteristic, taste—often omit when they show the film.

In her dreams Caron visits a pastel-colored

[5] As he leaves the ambassador's room, Astaire remarks acidly on the coincidence that, of all the hotel suites in New York, the ambassador was placed in the one next to Caron—a sly device the Ephrons used to take the edge off an obvious plot contrivance.

I4 I5 I6 I7

I8 J1 J2 J3

version of the hotel corridor she and Astaire had once frolicked through (I 3). In quest of Astaire, she opens three different doors. The first takes her backstage at the Paris Opéra, and soon she is onstage, where, in a tutu, she clunks with some desperation through a vapid ballet routine (I 4). The sole member of the audience is the unsmiling Astaire (I 5), who mysteriously vanishes when she goes to the box where he is sitting. The second adventure occurs in a steamy Hong Kong den where Caron, wildly out of character, tries to do a slinky, seductive adagio for Astaire's delectation (I 6, 7). He is unmoved and again vanishes. Finally, she finds herself dressed in a Pierrette costume in the midst of a carnival in Rio de Janeiro, where acrobats and other revelers block her path to Astaire, who wanders mysteriously in the distance (I 8).[6]

J

DREAM

(1′ 8″)

Coming to the film's rescue after this choreographic catastrophe are Thelma Ritter and Fred Clark. Caron's last letter to Daddy Long Legs mobilizes Ritter into action. She arranges with Clark to send a fraudulent telegram that will bring Astaire home immediately, goes to the college to collect Caron on her graduation day, and brings her to Astaire's mansion. In the meantime Astaire has discovered that Caron's boyfriend is going to marry his niece, and, with that hurdle tidily out of the way, things are lined up for the film's splendid final scene.

It takes place in the first-floor art gallery of the mansion—the same locale that opened the film. As Caron enters, an art tour is again under way, and the guide repeats his patter, complete with the same small, self-conscious jokes. Astaire joins Caron there and she is, of course, delighted to see him after all this time, though a little wary. She finally realizes Astaire's identity—not from anything he tells her, but from his resemblance to the portraits of her benefactor's ancestors that hang on the wall (J 1).[7]

The concluding dialogue, carried out over an appropriate reprise of "Dream," is masterful in its indirectness, playful but tender. Continuing the game, Astaire tells Caron he has been to see the owner of the mansion, and she asks what they discussed. "Since he's your guardian," Astaire explains, "I felt I should ask his permission before asking you to marry me." "What did he say?" "He said I'd have to wait my turn, that he wants to ask you himself first." "Why don't you?" (J 2).

What follows is one of the most touching gestures of love in Astaire's film career. He jubilantly pulls Caron toward him (J 3), but then pauses (J 4) and, with great seriousness—made all the more intense by the contrasting lightness of the preceding dialogue—gently and deliberately enfolds her (J 5) so that her arm and head are nestling softly on his shoulder, cradling his young bride-to-be in his embrace (J 6).

The film concludes with a brief dance of celebration—a double dance, really, for as Astaire and Caron glide around the floor, utterly engrossed in each other, Clark and Ritter enter the room and watch over the proceedings benevolently. Pleased with the outcome, they engage in an exquisitely paced mime dialogue—he asks her to dance (J 7), she suggests they have a drink instead, and they exit arm in arm.

Meanwhile, Astaire and Caron continue their dance, which, highly unusual for Astaire, incorporates a kiss. It is intricately choreographed: beginning at arms' length (J 8), the dancers pull in toward each other, and then Caron spins dreamily (J 9), gliding yieldingly into Astaire's welcoming embrace (J 10). Continuing to cling after the kiss, they revolve happily as the film fades out (J 11).

A NUMBER PARTIALLY CUT FROM THE FILM

K

HISTORY OF THE BEAT

The conductor's score for the film suggests the opening Astaire solo originally included the singing of a lengthy Mercer song that bouncily details the progress of "the beat" from ragtime through jitterbug and swing to bop and "cool," wherein "the beat is broken but unbowed" (clever man, that Mercer). The verse of the song is included in the film, but not its sixty- or seventy-measure chorus. The dance that followed the singing of the song is, however, shown complete.

[6] On the issue of the fashionable "dream ballet," see p. 255.

[7] This device is a considerable improvement on all previous versions of the story, where the orphan simply goes to visit her benefactor in his office and is greeted with "Couldn't you guess that I was Daddy Long Legs?"

J 4 J 5 J 6 J 7

J 8 J 9 J 10 J 11

29.

Funny Face

1957

During the course of his career, Fred Astaire made quite a few motion pictures in which the dance numbers carry the show: the dances are so fine that one is quite willing to ignore weakness in the material surrounding them. In *Funny Face* the opposite comes close to being true, and that makes it remarkable among Astaire's films.

Its strong points are Stanley Donen's agile direction, Leonard Gershe's amiable script, the timeless George and Ira Gershwin songs, the quality of the acting by the leads, and, especially, the ingenious and imaginative photographic effects inspired by the film's "special visual consultant," fashion photographer Richard Avedon. These all add up to a film that is, to use that most overworked of film-review adjectives, stylish. In contrast, the dance numbers are disappointing by Astaire's standards. The dances do show taste, wit, originality, and craftsmanship: no number is a thorough dud. But none ranks among Astaire's truly important numbers.

THE PRODUCTION AND THE MUSIC

Gershe had originally intended his script, entitled *Wedding Day,* to be the book for a stage musical. The script interested Roger Edens, Arthur Freed's associate producer at MGM, who decided to try to make a film of it. His ideal cast was Fred Astaire and Audrey Hepburn, and he discovered that both were very interested in doing the picture and in working together. Both had commitments at Paramount, however, and it eventually proved easier to move major elements of MGM's "Freed unit" to Paramount than to move the two stars to MGM. So in many respects *Funny Face* is an MGM musical made on a foreign lot.

At first Edens wanted to have new music composed for the film. But one day when he, Donen, and Gershe were reading over the script, the line "I think my face is perfectly funny" sent them running to the score of *Funny Face,* the Gershwin stage musical of 1927 (which had featured Fred and Adele Astaire). They found several eminently appropriate songs from that show (and one, "Clap Yo' Hands," from the Gershwins' *Oh, Kay!* of 1926) and were delighted to discover that, in Edens' words, "the music itself was as fresh in its melody and as modern in its structure as if it had just been written."

One of the splendid features of the film is the skill with which these thirty-year-old songs are blended into the script. They suit the situations so well that the lyrics seem a natural extension of the dialogue. However, it is unfortunate, after Edens' inspired discovery, that he didn't trust Gershwin more. As performed in the film, the songs for the most part lack the briskness and sharpness the composer strongly preferred.[1] Furthermore, two of the dances inspired by Gershwin songs are actually set to newly composed music that has dated, whereas the Gershwin songs themselves still retain the freshness Edens found so impressive in 1956. It is particularly unfortunate that both of these songs—"Clap Yo' Hands" and "Let's Kiss and Make Up"—have exactly the kind of rhythmic spikiness ideal for Astaire.

The score also includes three new songs written for the film by Edens, with lyrics by Gershe. In general, the quality of the new songs gives further evidence of Edens' wisdom in relying principally on Gershwin.

THE SCRIPT

As in *Easter Parade,* Astaire is here cast in a Pygmalion role: he plays an established fashion photographer (modeled on Richard Avedon) who discovers a petulant young Greenwich Village intellectual (Hepburn) and converts her into a successful fashion model. They fall in love (she first).[2] But she idolizes a charismatic Left Bank Parisian philosopher (fashioned not too vaguely after Jean-Paul Sartre), which leads to a breakup with Astaire, who insists the philosopher is interested in her body, not her mind. She soon discovers that Astaire is right and comes back to him.

[1] In the introduction to his *Song-book* of 1932, George Gershwin gives his "chief hint" about performing his music: "The rhythms of American popular music are more or less brittle; they should be made to snap, and at times to crackle. The more sharply the music is played, the more effective it sounds."

[2] Avedon had trained and then married a fashion model, and Gershe, a friend of Avedon's, built from this premise. Gershe didn't even bother to disguise the origins of his inspiration much: the name of the character Astaire plays in the film is Dick Avery.

The script has ample opportunity to satirize both the extroverted pretentiousness of the fashion world and the in-group pretentiousness of Parisian intellectual society—the best satire might have been to show how similar the two worlds are at the core. But, mostly, the film passes the opportunity by. Though there are a few mild verbal swipes at the world of high fashion, the film ends up further glamorizing it. And the cafe intellectuals are simply dismissed as a group of phonies, lechers, free-loaders, and hypocrites, giving the film a somewhat sour, anti-intellectual tone (an element also present, though to a lesser degree, in *The Barkleys of Broadway* and *The Band Wagon,* as well as in quite a few non-Astaire musicals of the period). Looking back, Donen says the charge of anti-intellectualism is "probably true . . . although it certainly wasn't intentional on my part."

Instead of satire, the script's first order of business is the Astaire-Hepburn romance—in fact, except for an over-adrenalized fashion editor, convincingly played by Kay Thompson and apparently modeled on Diana Vreeland, there are no other roles of any substance in the film. Much of the charm of this remarkably intimate film arises from the interest and appeal these two experienced and warmly compatible actors are able to bring to their parts—Astaire's fashion photographer is assured, mature, composed, gentle, and professionally preoccupied; Hepburn's Greenwich Village intellectual is desirable, insecure, occasionally feisty, and touchingly vulnerable.[3]

AUDREY HEPBURN

Like *A Damsel in Distress* (with Joan Fontaine) and *Second Chorus* (with Paulette Goddard), this is a film in which Astaire is paired with a woman who was primarily a straight actress rather than a musical-comedy performer. There is a benefit—the love scenes have a natural richness and a believability not matched in Astaire's films with dancers like Cyd Charisse and Vera-Ellen. But there is a cost, too. Unlike Fontaine and Goddard, who had virtually no background in dance, Audrey Hepburn had undergone a little dance training—she studied ballet as a child and did some dancing early in her professional career—and that may be worse than none at all. In her major duet with Astaire, "He Loves and She Loves," Hepburn keeps trying to project as a lyric dancer, and the results are awkward and sometimes embarrassing.

[3] Donen later found its dependence on the leads to be a fault in the film: "It is such a creaky, old, sick script, and to have made a picture out of that! . . . No situations, nothing, nothing, nothing, just going on air. That picture really travels on the charm of those two people. . . . What's missing is the whole spine of the picture."

Audrey Hepburn in "Basal Metabolism"

Some of the problem may arise from Hepburn's position in the film. She was riding high at the time, and to a considerable extent this was *her* film, *her* musical debut. Her name preceded Astaire's in the credits (the only other female partners for whom that was the case were Judy Garland and Betty Hutton), and he was there to present her. She was able to insist that her singing voice not be dubbed—which is fortunate—but it may also be that she was overconfident of her dancing ability and allowed herself (and was allowed by Astaire) to get out of her depth.

RICHARD AVEDON

The most memorable feature of *Funny Face* is its visual style, and much of that was the work of Avedon, who worked closely with Donen on the film.[4] The photography is extraordinarily imaginative—as in the darkroom scene, lit entirely in red, and the scene at the churchyard, with its soft, gauzy, romantic haze. And best of all is a beautiful sequence in the center of the film in which Hepburn poses for a series of fashion photographs at various locales around Paris. The montage is the most arresting photographic sequence in any of Astaire's films.[5]

THE CHOREOGRAPHY

The film is the first of Astaire's to use the word "choreography" in the titles. Sharing billing with, and ahead of, Astaire is Eugene Loring, a ballet choreographer who had previously worked with Astaire on the unsuccessful fantasy film *Yolanda and the Thief.* Besides collaborating on Astaire's numbers, Loring created the dance numbers for Hepburn and Thompson. Loring calls working with Hepburn "the happiest . . . experience I had . . . with any star. . . . She would try anything. . . . It was just divine working with her."

[4] The working situation was complicated by Hollywood's rigid caste system. Any of Avedon's instructions to the crew had to be communicated through the director. Avedon and Donen, who became close friends as a result of the collaboration, would often work out their ideas in the evenings, and then Donen, alone, would convey their conclusions to the technicians the next day. They also invented signals such as coughs, hair smoothings, and tie straightenings to communicate on the set.

[5] The innovativeness of the photography is suggested in co-choreographer Eugene Loring's recollection: "We wanted [one] number . . . smoky and for the spotlight to hit the lens of the camera—directly into it. When they brought the prints back, the dailies, Paramount had leveled it off in the development of the film. Instead of being dark and smoky . . . they had it all lit up."

With Kay Thompson in "Clap Yo' Hands"

THE NUMBERS

A
OVERTURE (FUNNY FACE / 'S WONDERFUL)
(1' 33")

Heard under the titles is almost the only Gershwin music in the film performed in a manner that would have pleased the composer: a chorus of "Funny Face" beautifully sung by Astaire at an appropriately brisk tempo in the clipped, snappy style Gershwin advised.[6] The music then goes over to a lugubrious rendering of part of "'S Wonderful," sung by a chorus.

B
THINK PINK
(2' 21")

Wasting no time, the film starts off with a splashy visual treat—if not a musical or a choreographic one. Kay Thompson, as the high-strung editor of the fashion magazine *Quality,* has decided that women henceforth shall be clothed in pink (though she wouldn't be caught dead in it herself). She issues her decree in a number set to an Edens-Gershe song that includes some witty and impudent Avedon-inspired posings in pink by fashion models Suzy Parker and Sunny Harnett (B1, 2). The number concludes with a brief chorus routine that includes a high-kicking lunge (B3), a step that recurs later in the film several times.

C
HOW LONG HAS THIS BEEN GOING ON?
(4' 13")

Thompson, Astaire, and crew invade a Greenwich Village bookstore, Embryo Concepts, in order to do some fashion photography (Thompson is now on an "intellectual" kick). The waif in charge is Hepburn, and she watches helplessly as the invaders rearrange the books for visual effect.

Astaire stays behind to help her clean up the mess, and at one point he gives her a matter-of-fact kiss as a demonstration of the philosophy of empathy, which they have been discussing—"I put myself in your place and I felt that you wanted to be kissed" (C1).

After he leaves, she muses in song over the romantic longings this brief kiss has inspired in her. She sings the remarkably appropriate Gershwin song quite well, though the extremely slow tempo, while emphasizing a suitable dreamy quality, threatens at times to cause the song to fall apart. The song is beautifully staged by Donen. The fashion people have left behind a wide-brimmed sun hat, and in the course of the song Hepburn absently picks it up. Its glowing pastels clashing with the drab atmosphere of the bookstore (C2), she swirls it around during a short dance, then with it on looks at herself in the mirror with yearning dismay. As the number ends, she pensively puts the hat down and wanders away.

D
FUNNY FACE
(3' 23")

Upon studying his photographs from the bookstore session, Astaire realizes that Hepburn could make an ideal fashion model—one with "character, spirit, and intelligence." This unusual idea intrigues Thompson, and she orders some books to be delivered to her office by Hepburn in order to size her up. Appalled at the prospect, Hepburn slips from Thompson's clutches and, in full flight, finds refuge in Astaire's darkroom, which is bathed in red light.

Astaire gently explains their plans for her—plans that include a trip to Paris, where she could see her philosopher idol. The trip interests her, but she says she could never be a model because her face is "funny." Astaire's response is typical of the amused, slightly patronizing banter he uses with her in the first half of the film—an experienced adult dealing with a talented but naïve child. Remembering that she had earlier berated him for spending his time photographing "silly women" rather than something beautiful like a tree, he tells her: "When I get through with you you'll look like—what do you call beautiful?—a tree—you'll look like a tree."

He sings the Gershwins' "Funny Face" to her—another song that proves remarkably appropriate. The dance that emerges from it is only a fragment, but it is the best in the film. Astaire continues to busy himself with his darkroom work as he sings, and she watches, pleased and fascinated. The whole number is carried out as if it were simply incidental to his work. By the end of the number, Astaire has come up with the

[6] In recordings of the song made in the late 1920s, Fred and Adele Astaire took about forty-three seconds to sing the chorus, and a piano recording by Gershwin was even faster: thirty-seven seconds. In the film, Astaire sings the song here at the bright tempo of the Gershwin piano rendering; then, later in the film, he sings it slower—about forty-eight seconds for the chorus.

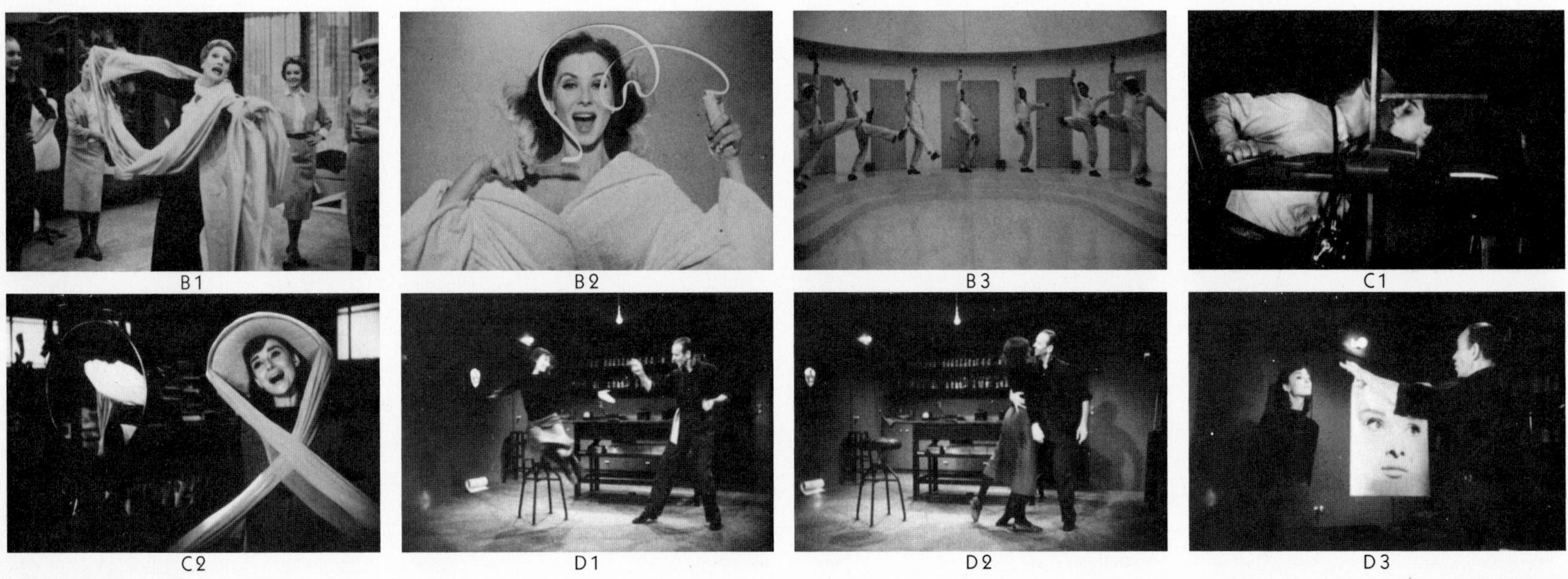

B1 B2 B3 C1

C2 D1 D2 D3

striking Avedon photograph (shown in D3) of Hepburn's wide-eyed, disembodied face that was used as the central publicity image for the film.

During the singing of the song, Astaire sets up the masked projection of her face on a vertical enlarging surface at the left. The setup is completed when he finishes singing, and he has some time on his hands as he waits for the enlargement to expose. He bumps into her in the semidarkness and, with nothing else to do for a while, proceeds to dance with her.

They come forward in the room, Astaire making sure she crouches down so as not to interrupt the cross-room projection. A casual little dance ensues in which a stool becomes a third party. As she sits on it, he grandly promenades her and then makes a game of spinning her on it rapidly (D1). The tone is one of innocent play in which he is the player and she the playee (and loving it). There is a sense of shared improvisation as they discover the stool and explore ways to build it into their dance. Finally, after some open-armed partnered rocking steps (D2) and a few quick spins around the floor, he swings her up, depositing her on the stool again as he returns to his work.

He sings the song through once more as he develops the enlargement. He shows it to her—but only after teasingly holding the wrong side toward her (D3). Suddenly he turns on the enlarger light, framing her (real) face in it. The abrupt change from red light to full color is stunning. (The idea of filming the darkroom scene in red light was Donen's; Avedon suggested adding the contrasting white light of the enlarger.) As the number ends, Astaire crosses the room to examine her face more closely (D4). Not too much depth, perhaps, but certainly not funny. And quite as beautiful as a tree.

E
BONJOUR, PARIS!
(4′51″)

Having arrived in Paris to promote their new fashions and to unveil Hepburn as a model, Thompson, Astaire, and Hepburn take time out to explore the city. To another Edens-Gershe tune they develop an ebullient travelogue number that tries to do for Paris what "New York, New York" did for that city in Donen's *On the Town* (E1).

F
BASAL METABOLISM
(3′30″)

Hepburn's next stop is a murky Parisian cafe, in eager quest of the intellectual life. She has never troubled to learn French, which would seem likely to slow her down a bit, but she proceeds undaunted; besides, in this place at least, communication seems to be primarily nonverbal.

Astaire seeks her out at the cafe (F1).[7] He is impressed neither by the surroundings nor by the twitchy, eccentric dance she does with two male patrons to demonstrate to him what a free spirit she has become (F2). The episodic dance, set mostly to jazzed-up arrangements of "How Long Has This Been Going On?" and "Funny Face," generally misfires as parody: in this film even studied freakiness comes out looking innocent and glamorous. However, Loring is quite successful at making use of Hepburn's abilities, and he avoids pushing her too far. And there is a nice finish: Hepburn collapses across the laps of two cafe patrons, who go on talking unconcernedly.

G
LET'S KISS AND MAKE UP
(4′17″)

Leaving the cafe, Astaire and Hepburn argue over her philosophic quest. Hurt, she returns to her apartment, and Astaire decides to cheer her up with a warm and amusing song and dance. He throws a stone against her second-story window, and when she comes out on her balcony, he clambers up and serenades her with a thirty-year-old Gershwin song that suits the situation perfectly, "Let's Kiss and Make Up."

The solo—apparently one of Astaire's personal favorites—has elements of great appeal: Astaire's gracious singing, the craftsmanship and ingenuity of the prop manipulation in his dance with the umbrella and raincoat, and the wit and integrity of the concluding mock bullfight. Moreover, the number serves the plot purpose well: Astaire is able to mollify Hepburn, and by indirection to apologize for his harsh words earlier.

The number's weaknesses seem to stem largely from the music. The Gershwin song—chosen mainly for its appropriate lyric—is fairly unimpressive. Furthermore, because the song was considered temperamentally ill-suited to the

[7] The two people having the lovers' quarrel at the sidewalk table as he enters are Roger Edens and Hepburn's mother (F1).

D4 E1 F1 F2
G1 G2 G3 G4

mock-Spanish capers of the dance solo, some new, singularly unappealing music was written for most of the dance by house arranger Alexander Courage. Broadly obvious and pointlessly raucous, it is also often unnecessarily imitative of the dance. Astaire had apparently worked out the dance to different Spanish-style music, and then Courage came in to write new music to fit the movements; the resultant score often simply underlines dance steps or provides vague atmospheric background.[8]

The number begins most engagingly. When Hepburn steps out on her balcony, Astaire surprises her by launching into the verse, without spoken prologue. Moving closer when he begins to sing the chorus, he picks a flower and hands it to her as a peace offering. But she is still a bit miffed and reluctant to take the gift, so Astaire urges her on by giving emphasis to the words "come on" in the lyric. The tactic works: she smiles and takes the flower (G1).

When he finishes the song, Astaire jumps from the balcony to the courtyard below. To the Gershwin song, which is played through once more, he does a brief dance, using his furled umbrella as a prop—flipping it from hand to hand (G2), swinging it around, tossing it into the air, and catching it behind his back. He had done a similar solo with an umbrella (also to Gershwin) in *A Damsel in Distress* (9 A) twenty years earlier, which, for sheer dazzle and witty surprise, is quite a bit better. This one starts out splendidly but mellows toward the end, and the final toss and catch are uncharacteristically predictable. Again, some of this may derive from the way the music is handled. As Alec Wilder notes, the Gershwin song has an interesting rhythmic jaggedness to it, and when it is performed straight at the beginning of the dance, Astaire plays arrestingly with its crisp rhythms. But in the last part the rhythms of the song are flattened in Courage's arrangement, and the choreography seems to flatten as well.

A placid cow is pulled through the courtyard in a cart (G3), and this odd event turns Astaire's thoughts, by amusing if unlikely association, to the bullfight arena. In preparation for a contest, he deftly tosses his umbrella into a distant trash can (G4). (On this bit of business, see p. 19.) Then he grandly salutes his special señorita in the stands (G5) and launches into a wry send-up of the macho, show-off antics of Spanish heroics.

As the music gives out with assorted Spanishisms, Astaire uses his red-lined raincoat, inside out, to suggest the toreador's cape (G6) and then frolics around the courtyard with it. As usual, he shows a remarkable ability to make the object come to life in his hands. However, the shapeless raincoat, even with weights sewn in to make it more manipulable, proves to be somewhat recalcitrant, and the solo, though ingenious, lacks the magician's flair of Astaire's best solos with props. In particular, an episode in which he runs around the courtyard dragging the coat along the ground behind him comes off as choreographic filler.

Things quickly improve, however. Flinging the coat to the ground, he decides that it now represents the exhausted but still dangerous bull. To music that attempts (unsuccessfully) to be comically grandiose, Astaire makes a great, funny show of extracting his umbrella from its receptacle (G7) and prancing toward the downed raincoat to render it lifeless with one well-placed jab. He caps this grand deed with an unkempt jump of triumph (or surprise) (G8).

The solo continues with another brief umbrella dance in which the prop variously becomes a baseball bat and a golf club—perhaps his success as a bullfighter has led him to try his hand at other simulated sports. Then he slams the umbrella around, kicks it into the air with his knee, and uses it to scoop up his hat and coat from the ground. Saluting his enraptured audience of one, he swaggers from the arena with his coat draped dramatically around his shoulders like a cape (G9). This last section of the dance is accompanied by some of the most witlessly overblown music Astaire was ever associated with. Hepburn's reaction at the end is not shown. In fact, the only shot of her during the entire dance is the one much earlier, just before Astaire becomes a bullfighter (G5). Given that Astaire's dance is supposed to be for her benefit, his stricture against reaction shots may have been taken a bit too far in this case.

H
HE LOVES AND SHE LOVES
(4′44″)

The big romantic duet of the film takes place on the misty grounds of a French chapel and is a

[8] Astaire says he was improvising before a mirror in a raincoat "and noticed that the coat moved rather well." His rehearsal pianist Walter Ruick ad-libbed some Spanish music, which gave him the idea of using the coat as a bullfighter's cape. Assisting on the solo was Dave Robel.

G5 G6 G7 G8

G9 H1 H2 H3

celebration of the love between Hepburn and Astaire. The process by which they fall in love, however, is shown not in a dance number but, rather, in a beautiful montage sequence that precedes the duet—a sequence that has the feel, if not the standard properties, of a fine musical number.

The five-minute montage shows Astaire coaching and photographing Hepburn as she models Hubert de Givenchy fashions in various Parisian locales: before the Arc de Triomphe, at a train station, in a flower shop, at the Opéra, while fishing on the Seine, near a fountain, and on the staircase of the Louvre in front of the *Winged Victory* statue. In each case the finished photograph captures her in mid-flight (Avedon's approach to fashion photography) and is held in freeze frame on the screen. Sometimes a picture is shown in the various color separations used to prepare the photograph for publication.

The sequence is remarkable not only for its visual beauty and chic but also for the way it is developed to show Hepburn's growth as a fashion model. At the beginning she has to be told everything—what her mood is supposed to be, which direction to move (H1). Soon she is confidently mocking Astaire's instructions to her (he observes with wry pleasure, "You've outgrown me"), and in the last sequence she calls her own shots as she glides down the stairs in a glamorized commentary on the sculpture behind her (H2).

Throughout, Astaire treats her with the preoccupied solicitude of a skilled craftsman. He fails even to grasp the significance of the tears in her eyes, the result of a businesslike kiss he has given her in one scene in an effort to get her into the proper mood. (His response: "Good. Now wet your lips.")

This leads to a scene near an idyllic chapel in the forest of Chantilly, a nineteenth century hunting-lodge chapel made to look more church-like by being given different windows and door. Hepburn is wearing a bridal gown but can't get into the requisite happy mood. Astaire moves close to her to explain the situation: "This is your wedding day. . . . You're going to marry the man you love . . . the man who loves you. . . . He's the only . . . and you're . . ." The background music swells, and they impetuously melt into a kiss (H3). It's a classic Hollywood situation and exactly the kind of love scene Astaire had been telling scriptwriters for twenty-five years he couldn't perform convincingly. Here he proves how right he was—although his embarrassed awkwardness does have a certain charm.

Exhilarated, Hepburn blurts out that she loves him. At once puzzled and pleased by this startling pronouncement, Astaire responds by singing a convenient old Gershwin song, "He Loves and She Loves." The song emerges from the dialogue with gratifying naturalness—enhanced, perhaps, by the device of having Astaire begin it facing away from the camera—and the lyric, which has an appropriate musing quality (if they love, why can't we?), places the singer's declaration of love at the end.

Then they dance. After the visual splendor and wispy humor of the photography sequence, and after the gentle charm of the dialogue-and-song scene, everything is set for a great romantic duet. Unfortunately, the dance is a letdown.

Like several other Astaire duets, the dance emerges from a quiet, introspective stroll. Arm in arm, the dancers perambulate around the lawn, engrossed in their newly declared love (H4). The stroll is embellished with some musically subtle hesitations and a fleeting partnered backbend, which Hepburn handles fairly well (H5).

The texture gradually becomes more flamboyant. Flowing across a little bridge over a stream, they spin in a double-helix pattern into a partnered arabesque (H6). Then the idea of strolling is greatly broadened: beginning with a lunging kick (H7; compare B3, K6), Astaire and Hepburn lope side by side around the grass. Another kick leads to some swirling partnered turns for Hepburn and then to a pair of leaning lifts (H8, 9). This lift sequence is quite possibly the ugliest moment in Astaire's entire dance career. The dancers simply clunk into position, and Hepburn seems gangling and all feet, an effect emphasized by the awkward little flutter kick she inserts in the second lift. Furthermore, the choreography between the lifts—a labored turn—is astonishingly uninspired by Astaire's standards.

Next they glide over to a waiting raft, which obligingly floats them across another stream. They stand on their raft swaying and clinging as birds fly by (H10).

Having landed on the far shore, they dash around the area in a repetitive sequence that is an unconvincing and stagey approximation of rapture (H11). Hepburn finally sinks uncertainly to the ground and is raised by Astaire into a turning backbend (H12). They softly link arms again and stroll lovingly into the distance as the

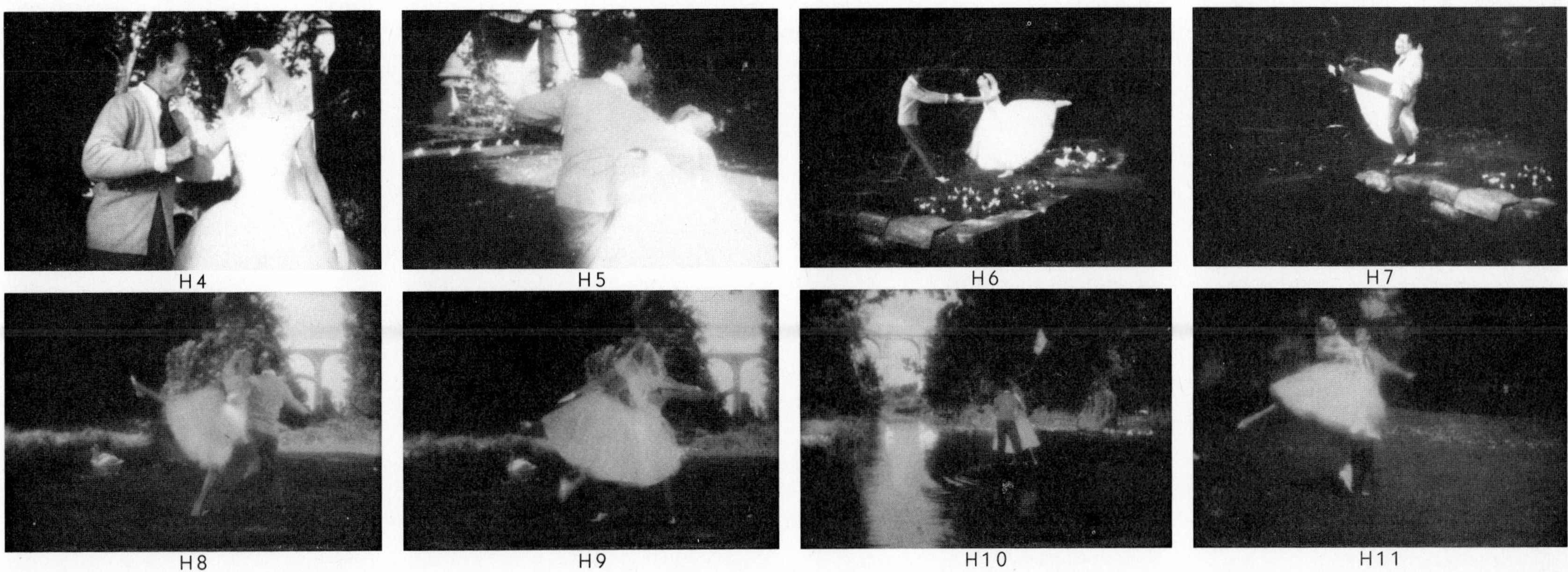

H4 H5 H6 H7

H8 H9 H10 H11

camera cuts back and the music wafts to its conclusion (H13). This sort of quiet ending, with a distant, receding camera, had been used several times by Gene Kelly in his films, but never before—or since—by Astaire.

The choreography for the duet shows admirable restraint and economy as it develops its statement out of the dancers' tender, contemplative stroll. However, as a whole it lacks Astaire's usual ease and flow, and its efforts at a climax in the last section (H11–12) fall back on effects that simply repeat rather than cumulate. In general, choreographic invention takes second place to romantic photographic atmosphere in this number. The gauzy focus is no problem, but such effects as the slow raft ride across the stream (H10), however appealing they may be as photography, tend to break the dance into segments and to dampen its momentum. Throughout, there seems to be a somewhat self-conscious striving to be memorable, and the associated decision to take the Gershwin song at a droopy pace doesn't help, either.[9] The idea of performing the dance in the out-of-doors rather than in the studio created special problems for the choreography, of course. As Astaire put it after the film was completed, "There's nothing worse than dancing up and down hill." To complicate matters further, it kept raining, and the ground was so soft that they had to spread sand on it and then cover it with sod. Hepburn's comment: "Here I have been waiting for 17 years to dance with Fred Astaire, and what do I get? Mud!"[10]

Another major problem in the dance is that Hepburn simply can't make it work: she is often stiff, held back, gawky, and angular, and shows little conception of flow or line—as, for example, in her self-conscious efforts at lyricism (H8, 9, 12). Perhaps her limited training intimidated her, making her aware there was some ideal shape she should be forming without giving her the skill to attain it. Moreover, the costume designer and the director were not kind to her. The bouffant skirt of her wedding dress makes the rest of her slim body appear almost skeletal, and the white gloves seem pawlike at the end of her slender arms. The camera is often placed unusually low (see H11), which tends to make her look like a voluminous skirt with feet attached, and medium shots of her partnered backbends (H12) emphasize her uncertain arm work and exaggerate the incongruity of the mitts she is wearing.[11]

Astaire tries to help her along—he stays close, partnering all the way through—and the dance has none of the side-by-side parallel solo work found in almost all of his other duets. But the combined obstacles of this dance defeat even him in the end.

[9] Each chorus of the song takes about eighty-two seconds in the film. By contrast, it takes less than sixty seconds for Adele Astaire and Bernard Clifton (of the original *Funny Face* cast) to sing a chorus on their recording from the 1920s.

[10] Astaire's other out-of-studio duet, in *A Damsel in Distress* (9 E), was also problematic. In that case, however, he largely triumphed over the obstacles. As in "He Loves and She Loves," the duet is built out of a stroll and Astaire has a partner who is primarily an actress. But the earlier duet has an ease and lilt that are lacking in "He Loves and She Loves" and is far less preoccupied with trying to make an effect.

[11] There is one very odd directorial boner. The photography makes heavy use of the wide-angle lens, which exaggerates distances, giving a feeling of spaciousness. However, it can also produce distortions of objects close to the lens (in a portrait it can make a nose seem longer, for example). In H12 Hepburn is close to the camera and there is an ugly moment as her arm swings by the lens—the arm appears to get longer and then shorter again.

I

ON HOW TO BE LOVELY

(2′37″)

Preparing for their big fashion show, Kay Thompson and Hepburn perform some brightly satiric Loring choreography to an appealing Edens-Gershe song. Pretty ballet poses are often used to underline the word "lovely" (I1). (This number is sometimes cut when the film is shown on television.)

J

MARCHE FUNÈBRE

(1′6″)

Astaire and Hepburn get into another argument over her French philosopher-guru (who turns out to be young and attractive). Astaire's objections appear to be partly paternal—he distrusts the man's intentions toward Hepburn—and partly jealous. Their increasingly noisy argument continues backstage at the fashion-show premiere, and a fountain is knocked over, spraying the audience in the film's one bid for thigh-slapping laughs.

Hepburn runs out. Astaire and Thompson, disguised, infiltrate the philosopher's salon in an effort to recapture her. At the salon a singer moans, in French, an Edens effort called "Marche Funèbre," a feebly satiric, Edith Piaf-like song about love and death.

H12 H13 I1 K1

K2 K3 K4 K5

K
CLAP YO' HANDS
(4′0″)

Astaire and Thompson discover that the philosopher has Hepburn in an upstairs room. They romp through a song and dance that is supposed somehow to show their compatibility with the others in the salon while allowing them to maneuver their way up the stairs.

The duet, set to an old Gershwin tune, is one of Astaire's rare efforts at sustained broad comedy. Astaire's dance humor, in general, is dry and understated, and it tends to emerge naturally from the choreographic texture. In "Clap Yo' Hands," however, just about all the jokes are on the surface. And like the "Ritz Roll and Rock" number in his next film, *Silk Stockings* (30 L), the number seems at times an almost desperate effort to parody those popular music trends and fads of the 1950s from which Astaire felt himself to be distant.

Things are made worse by the musical arrangement. There is plenty of potential for floor-stomping comedy in Gershwin's music, with its ample rhythmic wit and complexity.[12] But the song is submerged in some new material—"knocked-out jazz," Edens calls it—composed for the film by Skip Martin. It seems significant that the best moments in the number come during the Gershwin material and the worst during the Martin material.

Thompson and Astaire begin the number by spiritedly harmonizing on an introduction (by Edens and Gershe) in which the lyric mentions their need to get up the stairs (K 1). The verse of the Gershwin song is next, and the performers reconvene in the center of the smoke-filled salon to deliver it. As Thompson sings the lyric, Astaire frolics around her in a slouching, zoot-suity shuffle (K 2).

The best part of the number is the transition from verse to chorus of the Gershwin song. Astaire has a cadenza in which he keeps rotating, emerging to face front just in time for the chorus. Then, as Thompson sings the chorus, she and Astaire march forward and back, or from side to side, Astaire punctuating the song with brisk hand claps and broadly exaggerated squawks of mock alarm (K 3). Although hand clapping never really gets used much in the number (despite the song's title and message), Thompson supplies a substitute by slapping Astaire's guitar, and Astaire embellishes this idea by back-kicking the guitar (K 4).

There is a quick, raucous runaround to some equally raucous Martin music in which Astaire repeats his squawking routine from a prone position (K 5). Then the performers lunge into the center of the floor (K 6) and go right into a funny little soft-shoe to the Gershwin music (K 7). The unexpected shift from the absurdly rambunctious to the absurdly exquisite is amusing, but the humor ends there: Astaire and Thompson exchange a few Mr. Interlocutor-type lines while continuing their incongruous soft shoe, but the lines lack humorous punch and fall flat.

Things pretty much disintegrate in the ending, which is pure Martin and hard-sell comedy. Astaire pretends to slap his guitar so hard he hurts his hand, shuffles funkily around (K 8), thrashes about on the floor (K 9), and clumps up the stairs on his knees (K 10).

L
'S WONDERFUL
(2′14″)

Hepburn refuses to be rescued from her philosopher, and Astaire, in a rage, makes plans to go back to New York immediately. But Hepburn soon discovers that the philosopher really is a mere lecher, as Astaire had insisted. Escaping his clutches, she goes back to the fashion show, humbled (L 1). Then, thinking Astaire has abandoned her, she sadly returns, still in her fashion-show wedding dress, to the chapel yard. Astaire learns she has rejected the philosopher and, through empathy, dopes out where she must be.

There is no dialogue in the final scene—apt Gershwin lyrics make it unnecessary. Coming up behind her, Astaire assures her that, still, "I love your funny face." They kiss—for the fourth time in the film, a record for Astaire (L 2)—and then sing a chorus of "'S Wonderful" to each other. Hepburn alone sings the astonishingly appropriate words of the release strain: "You've made my life so glamorous, you can't blame me for feeling amorous."[13] They glide briefly around the lawn, board their raft, and float atmospherically away as the film ends (L 3).

[12] The song struck that note when it was first performed on Broadway. According to Ira Gershwin, it was "exclaimed and stomped by Harlan Dixon and Ensemble in a Long Island drawing room"—a situation not unlike that of the film.

[13] It need hardly be added that the song is taken at an extremely slow pace: sixty-three seconds for the chorus. By contrast, the singers on the original-cast *Funny Face* recording sing it in forty-four seconds, whereas Gershwin's recorded piano solo takes about thirty-eight seconds.

K 6 K 7 K 8 K 9

K 10 L 1 L 2 L 3

30.

Silk Stockings

1957

Silk Stockings is more brilliant than buoyant. The script is joke-filled, fairly hard-sell, and briskly paced, and contains brassy satire both of Soviet dreariness and of Hollywood superficiality. The Cole Porter songs are snappy and attractive, and the central love story for Fred Astaire and Cyd Charisse is convincing, if not always compelling or affecting.

Astaire's dances in the film vary considerably in quality. The most satisfying are two duets: "Fated to Be Mated," a jubilant and relaxed dance of celebration for Astaire and Charisse, and "All of You," a duet of urgent seduction that is amusing and ingenious. There are also a couple of numbers of broad satire: one salvo is aimed at Hollywood and hits dead-on; the other, aimed at rock and roll, misses entirely.

THE *NINOTCHKA* ORIGINAL

This film is the first of Astaire's to be substantially derived from a Broadway musical since *Roberta* in 1935. The stage show *Silk Stockings,* a hit of the 1955 season, was itself derived from a story by Hungarian playwright Melchior Lengyel and from a classic 1939 MGM motion picture based on this story: *Ninotchka,* directed by Ernst Lubitsch, with Greta Garbo and Melvyn Douglas in the leading roles. Lengyel's story was fabricated to suit a proposed advertising slogan. MGM had had great success in 1930 by billing Garbo's first talkie as "Garbo talks!" and it now wanted a film that could be trumpeted with the slogan "Garbo laughs!" Lengyel came up with a three-sentence idea, which he then read to Garbo at her poolside. "I like it. I will do it," she said, and then dived back into the pool. As Lengyel recalled later, the three sentences from which he then developed his story were: "Russian girl saturated with Bolshevist ideals goes to fearful, capitalistic, monopolistic Paris. She meets romance and has an uproarious good time. Capitalism not so bad, after all."

The story he wrote from these sentences was very substantially altered by the *Ninotchka* scriptwriters. It concerns Ninotchka, a stiff, inhibited female functionary from the Soviet Union, who is sent to Paris to check up on a trio of endearingly bumbling Soviet agents who have become seduced by Western luxury. In the process she meets and soon falls in love with a mature man-about-town who determinedly breaks down her monumental resistance with a combination of playful humor and agile charm. Eventually she breaks off the romance and returns to Moscow, but by the end she and her suitor have become reconciled, and she agrees to marry him and to live in the West.

Although the story derives much of its momentum and humor from the contrasts of radically different political life styles, its treatment of the two cultures is naïve, even trivializing. The Soviet system is satirized for its rigidity, capriciousness, and drabness, but its brutality is laughed off with bone-chilling cracks: in the 1939 film the purges are referred to as producing "fewer but better Russians," whereas *Silk Stockings* contains jokes like "Tchaikovsky and Borodin have what is in Russia today a great advantage: they are dead."[1] The West is depicted as a place of irresponsible luxury, and freedom is casually and repeatedly equated with arrant frivolity.

But incisive political commentary is hardly the point of the story in any of its incarnations. As Leland Pogue observes, Lubitsch was concerned in his film about "the happiness rightly due to lovers . . . who love fully and unselfishly; and he leaves the world and its political madness to take care of itself." Or, as Cole Porter succinctly puts it in one of the *Silk Stockings* songs, "love is ev'rything."

SILK STOCKINGS ON THE STAGE

It is tempting for film reviewers to compare the *Silk Stockings* film with *Ninotchka* and to lament the loss of the "Lu-

[1] The *Ninotchka* film makes a modest effort to be evenhanded in this, including a few lines in which the czarist regime is characterized as brutal and uncaring; none of this found its way into either version of *Silk Stockings.* Because of its unflattering portrayal of the Soviet system, *Ninotchka* was subject to censorship efforts in various countries for years. On the other hand, MGM rereleased the film in 1947, as part of Hollywood's efforts to show that the industry was not overrun with subversives. *Ninotchka* opened in the fall of 1939, shortly after the joint German-Soviet invasion of Poland (though the filming was completed before that event). *Silk Stockings* opened on Broadway in 1955 during relative Cold War calm. The film version was released in the summer of 1957, at a time of comparative crisis.

bitsch touch." But by the time the story reached Broadway, lightness had already been sacrificed in a calculated effort to achieve a comedy tone of clipped brashness and loud, if essentially innocent, mockery. The result was jokier than the original, but without its high style and airy insouciance.

The original stage script, written by George S. Kaufman and his wife, Leueen MacGrath, apparently made an effort to capture the flavor of the *Ninotchka* film, but in extensive out-of-town tryouts, the producers, Cy Feuer and Ernest Martin, became convinced the show needed more bounce and push to succeed on Broadway. Kaufman, who had been directing, was replaced in that job by Feuer himself; Abe Burrows was brought in to rewrite the book; and Cole Porter was kept in his hotel room turning out new tunes to fit new scenes. Before the New York opening, several scenes from the original script were reinserted, and the resulting mix was apparently about half Burrows and half Kaufman-MacGrath.

In the refashioning of the original story as a musical, the leading male character was given a real occupation: he is a theatrical agent in the *Silk Stockings* play and a film producer in the film version. He has engaged a Soviet composer for a project, and the female Soviet agent comes to Paris to bring the composer back home. When the agent/producer seeks to seduce her from her mission, then, he is acting not only to serve his romantic desires (as in the *Ninotchka* film), but also to service his business interests. And Ninotchka's abrupt decision to return to Moscow may be slightly more believable in *Silk Stockings:* she becomes outraged at the way the Russian composer's music is vulgarized by the filmmakers; in *Ninotchka* she is essentially bribed to leave by a jealous woman.

The authors of the Broadway musical also added another object for satire: the monumental superficiality of Hollywood. It's an easy target, perhaps, but one the authors knew well; and in this case the parody occasionally verges on the trenchant. To this end an important new character was fashioned: a dumb vulgar Hollywood sex queen.

SILK STOCKINGS ON THE SCREEN

The principal task facing the producers of the *Silk Stockings* film was not how to remake the old *Ninotchka* film but, rather, how to transfer the successful Broadway musical to the screen. And a central problem was to refashion the leading roles, created for a pair of singing actors (Hildegarde Neff and Don Ameche), to fit a pair of acting dancers.

The *Silk Stockings* film is actually far closer to *Ninotchka* than was the *Silk Stockings* stage musical. The authors of the stage version used almost none of the dialogue from the classic *Ninotchka* screenplay, whereas the screenwriters went back to the original film and devised a screenplay that is an ingenious blend of the two sources, including dialogue sequences and substantial episodes taken directly from the 1939 film that do not appear in the stage musical.

To oversee this blending, producer Arthur Freed chose Rouben Mamoulian as the film's director. There was a great deal of resistance to this selection among the studio brass, since Mamoulian's last picture, a 1948 MGM musical, *Summer Holiday,* had failed miserably at the box office. But Freed insisted, possibly because he felt Mamoulian's directorial style was close to that of Lubitsch. Both had turned out seminal light comedies in the 1930s, and, like Lubitsch, Mamoulian had once directed Garbo in a classic—*Queen Christina* in 1933.

Mamoulian's chief initial task was to convince Astaire to take the leading role—Astaire had previously turned it down because he felt himself to be too old for the part. Over lunch, Mamoulian brought the dancer around, stressing the importance of dance in his conception of the film and assuring Astaire of his continued attractiveness on the screen. Judging from the film, Mamoulian's assurances were fully justified: the character Astaire plays is engaging—suave, mature, confident, generous, and likable. The script may have particularly appealed to Astaire because it concerns the romance of two self-reliant grownups, getting him away from the May-September aspects of his previous few films.

Although the *Silk Stockings* film retains much of the brashness of the Broadway musical, Mamoulian and the scriptwriters mellowed it somewhat. Perhaps with the image of Astaire before them, they made the central male character less cynical; while still an operator, he is more amiable and charming, less like a used-car salesman.[2] Moreover, the love story is made more important, and is more tender and jocular, less combative, than it was on the stage. These changes, which edged the new film closer to the tone of the *Ninotchka* film, seemed especially necessary to Mamoulian. As he put it in an early memo to the scriptwriters, "The love story . . . is the main theme of our picture. If we fail with it, all the shooting is for nothing. This is, now, the weakest

[2] Leonard Gershe, one of the scriptwriters, was uncomfortable with the change, feeling that the conniving film producer needed more "commonness," a quality he thought Astaire was not very good at projecting. Astaire, on the other hand, was pleased with the role: "Me? I play Gene Kelly. . . . It's a guy who produces, directs, acts, sings, dances. . . . Who could it be but Kelly?"

Cyd Charisse, Astaire, Joseph Buloff, Jules Munshin, and Peter Lorre

point in the script. It is abrupt, unprepared for and unbelievable. It also greatly lacks charm."

In reshaping the stage musical for film, Mamoulian strove to make the dance element pre-eminent: "I had two of the best dancers in the world, and what interested me was to give greater importance to the dancing than to the action proper. . . . The psychological and dramatic development existed only in the dances." This approach was hardly new in an Astaire film. Still, dance is used effectively and consequentially at several points: to trace Charisse's surrender to Astaire's charms and to Western luxury, and to celebrate their love.

Mamoulian was remarkably successful in casting the secondary roles. Janis Paige, as the dumb movie star, gives a fine performance—manic, noisy, and utterly endearing. Equally endearing are the three frazzled commissars, one of them played by Peter Lorre in a brilliant bit of casting against type. A superb actor, Lorre was best known in sinister roles, but here the glint in his eye becomes a twinkle, and he emerges triumphant as the world's least likely, and most cherubic, song-and-dance man.[3]

CYD CHARISSE

Silk Stockings gave Charisse the most challenging acting role of her career and she does quite well. She tends to be somewhat stiff and self-conscious, but these qualities are not inappropriate to the character she portrays. Unlike Garbo, she is unable convincingly to leaven her apparatchik persona with flashes of insecurity and vulnerability, and so her succumbing to Western temptation is more surprising. On the other hand, under Mamoulian's direction she is touching in her scenes of giddy, champagne-laced lovemaking with Astaire.

[3] Lorre's success is all the more impressive because of his physical problems at the time—he was ill and alarmingly dependent on drugs.

MGM apparently lacked the courage to flatten her makeup in the opening scenes, and so, much more than Garbo, Charisse gives the impression of a glamorous Hollywood star stuffed incongruously into a stiff uniform. However, once Charisse changes to civilian clothes, the designers, headed by Helen Rose, have been ingenious in fashioning garb for her that suggests severity but looks attractive, while allowing her the freedom to dance.

THE FILMING OF THE DANCES

Like *Daddy Long Legs, Silk Stockings* was filmed in super-wide-screen CinemaScope (which Mamoulian has called "the worst shape ever invented by the distorted initiative of man"). Astaire makes no effort in his love duets to explore the space at the edges of the screen, but amusing use of the wide screen is made in the satiric "Stereophonic Sound" number (see C13).

There is an unusual amount of cutting in the Astaire dances in the film. Moreover, most of it involves changing from a full-figure shot to a medium shot of the upper body (with the camera tracking away afterward) rather than the more typical cuts between different full-figure shots. Astaire had used the full-to-medium cut before, but usually only when there was some special value in getting in closer to the dancers at that point. In *Silk Stockings* the full-to-medium cut is the standard, not the exception. Nonetheless, the dances are still filmed with Astaire's usual sensitivity; the cuts are informative and never jarring.

THE MUSIC

Porter wrote twenty-seven songs for the stage show, of which thirteen were used. Attesting to the considerable success of the score, all but two of these thirteen were incorporated into the film—a remarkably high percentage for the time. Porter wrote two more songs expressly for the film: the bouncy "Fated to Be Mated," and, at Astaire's suggestion, "The Ritz Roll and Rock," a rhythm song that attempts to parody a musical development of the era. According to Astaire, the composer had little interest in the film version of his two-year-old stage show and never appeared on the set; he was far more interested in the new songs he was writing at the time for an original MGM musical, *Les Girls,* starring Gene Kelly.

THE END

Silk Stockings is the last of Astaire's classic Hollywood musicals. He was to appear in many films after *Silk Stockings* as an actor, and he made one other musical eleven years later—but of a very different kind. In addition, he turned his attention to television, where he took on a number of acting roles and produced and starred in four extremely successful musical specials during the next decade. But the Hollywood musical as Astaire had known it—indeed, defined it—was in its last glow in 1957. The genre was losing its popularity and being squeezed out by economics as the studio system crumbled, competition from television became severe, and popular music moved into the era of rock and roll.

The film itself contains amusing commentary on these developments (at one point Astaire, playing the role of a movie producer, says he is reluctant to make a film into a musical because "it's too expensive"), and, indeed, the film's celebration of luxury and decadence may have a certain self-reflective irony. There are also musical numbers that satirize rock and roll, hard-sell choreography, and Hollywood's desperate efforts to remain afloat by grasping at such highly touted technological straws as wide screens and stereophonic sound.

Silk Stockings is a twilight film in many ways. Although it was brought in neatly under budget and turned a tidy profit, it was the last dance musical Arthur Freed ever produced and the last film Rouben Mamoulian ever directed. It was also the last musical Cyd Charisse made in Hollywood. Perhaps twilight came with the property: the Broadway version of *Silk Stockings* turned out to be Cole Porter's last stage musical and George S. Kaufman's last produced play.

THE CHOREOGRAPHY

Eugene Loring had been the choreographer for the stage version of *Silk Stockings,* and he was asked to choreograph the film as well. Loring had worked with Astaire on *Funny Face* the year before and on *Yolanda and the Thief* in 1945, and he preferred "not to choreograph for Astaire again. He's very difficult to work with. By that I mean it's hard to create for him and get something new and fresh that also pleases him. He's very set in his ways." Accordingly, Astaire's frequent collaborator Hermes Pan was brought in to work with Astaire, while Loring took charge of all the non-Astaire numbers.

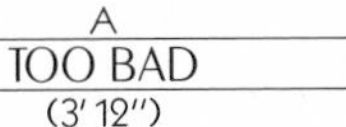

THE NUMBERS

A
TOO BAD
(3′12″)

The film opens with a nice Mamoulian touch: Fred Astaire's feet are seen briskly hurrying across Paris past strewn newspapers whose headlines identify him as a film producer who has signed a Russian composer to do movie music for him. The camera follows the feet into a theatre, where the entire body meets the composer backstage. Between bows, the composer frantically complains that Moscow has sent three commissars to take him back home.

Astaire intercepts the commissars in an ensuing scene and invents a tale: the composer's father is a French citizen, and therefore the son can be taken out of the country only with the permission of the French courts—which will take time. Furthermore, he argues, there may be great propaganda advantage in having a Soviet musical score in an American film. He sweetens the trio up with food, drink, and feminine companionship in a luxury hotel in a scene derived from the *Ninotchka* original (A1, 2). The commissars quickly agree to stay on in this "decadent town" to oversee the venture and jubilantly sing about this prospect.[4]

The song leads to a dance of celebration set to a nicely incongruous cha-cha-cha arrangement of the music. Throughout, Astaire eggs on the commissars in his calculated campaign to seduce them with the pleasures of Paris. After romping briefly with two of the pleasures and then deftly pairing them off with a couple of commissars, he takes on the third—Barrie Chase, who was to become his partner in his highly successful television specials between 1958 and 1968 (A3; see also 28 E7). He finds he can't pair her off, however, because the remaining commissar, Lorre, has devised a solo routine for himself: propped between table and chair, a knife clenched in his teeth, he determinedly raps out a Russian folk step (A4). As the others finish their frolic by toppling onto a sofa, Astaire leaves the room, satisfied, while Lorre desperately continues his dance routine, apparently unable to get out of it.

B
PARIS LOVES LOVERS
(3′43″)

Meanwhile, back in Moscow, in a scene taken directly from the Broadway show, the Commissar of Art, whose office is in a ballet studio, is arrested and carried off while the dancers calmly go on with their class. The new Commissar of Art (B1) is ordered to send an envoy to Paris to check on the earlier delegation. Selected for the task is Ninotchka, a humorless, hard-bitten female apparatchik, played by Cyd Charisse.[5]

Meeting the anxious trio in Paris, she scornfully lets her views of capitalistic society be known. Eying some lingerie in a display case, she reacts as Garbo did to a frivolous hat in the 1939 film: "How can such a civilization survive where women are permitted to wear things like these?" (B2, 3).[6]

As she grills the commissars in their hotel room, Astaire enters with a forged affidavit asserting that the composer is half French. He is fascinated by this creature and tries to charm her as "one oppressor to the other." When they are alone he sings to her of the appeals of the city, but she is unmoved, responding to his paean of praise with a derisive countermelody: "capitalistic, imperialistic, militaristic." Following the script of the stage show, the song is neatly blended with dialogue: talk separates verse from chorus and the first chorus from the second. This was a fairly common procedure on Broadway but an unusual one in Hollywood, and all but unknown in Astaire films.

The song boasts a beautiful verse and a chorus

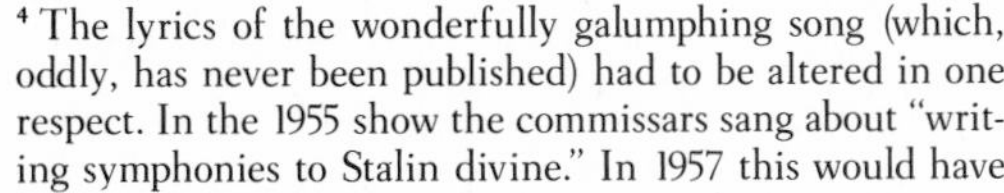

[4] The lyrics of the wonderfully galumphing song (which, oddly, has never been published) had to be altered in one respect. In the 1955 show the commissars sang about "writing symphonies to Stalin divine." In 1957 this would have been anachronistic because of Nikita Khrushchev's campaign to discredit the dead dictator, which had begun in 1956. Accordingly, the reference was changed to "Russia divine," and the joke lost much of its punch.

[5] George Tobias, who plays the new Commissar of Art, had the same role on Broadway, the only member of that cast to appear in the film. As it happens, he also appeared in one scene in *Ninotchka*—as a Soviet diplomatic clerk who refuses Melvyn Douglas a visa to visit Russia (see L2).

[6] When a porter offers to carry her bags, she refuses because "that's social injustice." In 1939, however, the porter had responded, "That depends on the tip," an exchange that wittily encapsulates the central contrast between immobilizing socialist principle and practical capitalist expediency. The porter's rejoinder was included in early versions of the *Silk Stockings* screenplay, but dropped (perhaps accidentally) in the first of Gershe's re-writes.

A1

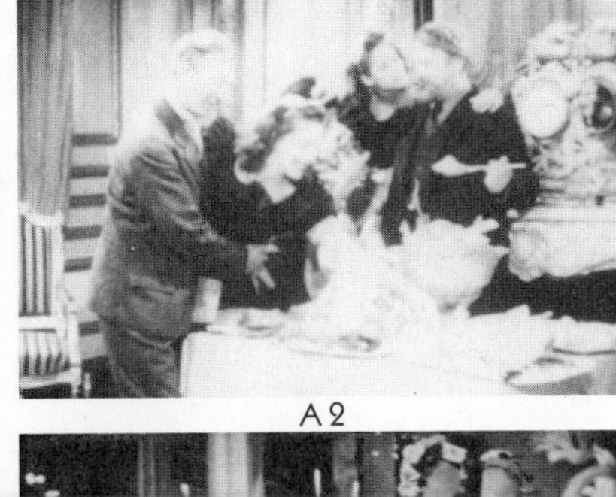
A2

A3

A4

B1

B2

B3

C1

melody of grace and remarkable economy. But the lyric of the chorus alternately wallows in hopeless cliché ("love" is actually rhymed with "heaven above") or leaden cleverness ("the urge to merge with the splurge of the spring"). This scene shows the film's blending of sources. The opening, where Charisse grills the commissars while typing a report, comes from *Ninotchka,* while the rest of the scene, from the point where Astaire enters until the end, comes from the stage show.

C
STEREOPHONIC SOUND
(3′52″)

Enter Janis Paige as the Hollywood star. She has come to Paris to work on a film for Astaire—a "boiled-down" version of *War and Peace.* It will be her first nonswimming picture, she eagerly observes at a press conference, pausing a moment to knock water from her ear (C1).[7]

Soon she and Astaire are launched into a robust number that pointedly satirizes Hollywood's efforts in the 1950s to maintain its audience through such frantically promoted technological gimmicks as wide screens, glaring color, and stereophonic sound. The performers vigorously scamper around the room and mime as they sing three choruses of the song. Paige is particularly wonderful while, among many other things, mocking a famous Betty Grable pinup pose (C2) and giving her impression of Lassie (C3). To simulate stereo, she and Astaire bellow into the innards of a piano (C4).[8]

A new chorus, written especially for the film, has wry pertinence to Astaire's situation in the 1950's, and is mimed with precision and wit:

> There was a time when dancing was so
> intimate and sleek
> A fella hugged his partner as they
> cuddled cheek to cheek [C5]
> Now he doesn't even know if she's around
> Because they're in glorious Technicolor,
> Breathtaking CinemaScope and
> Stereophonic sound.
> It's not enough today to see a dancer at
> his ease
> He's got to throw his back out and come
> sliding on his knees,
> He's got to have glorious Russian ballet
> [C6—folkish]
> Or modern ballet [C7—angular]
> Or English ballet [C8—stiff and proper]
> Or Chinese ballet [C9]
> Or Hindu ballet [C10]
> Or Bali ballet [C11]
> Or any ballet and
> Stereophonic sound,
> And stereophonic sound.

Unfortunately, the brief dance that follows is not nearly so imaginative. It is set rather directly on the music and its comedy becomes unduly effortful and silly, as the dancers flutter, collide, clutch (C12), and gesticulate. One effect, however, is quite fine: they squirm toward each other from opposite ends of a long table, filling the film's elongated CinemaScope screen (not

[7] In Kaufman's stage script the character had been a dancer. It was rewrite man Burrows who converted her to a swimmer and who invented the zany water-in-the-ear business. Paige's stock response, "There's absolutely no truth to the rumors, we're just good friends," was an inspiration of the screenwriters.

[8] There is some bowdlerization for the film: in the line "Unless her lips are scarlet and her bosom's five feet wide," "bosom's" is replaced by "mouth is." MGM also saw to it that references to rival Darryl Zanuck were removed and that Metrocolor got listed in the song's catalogue of Hollywood's color processes.

C2 C3 C4 C5
C6 C7 C8 C9
C10 C11 C12 C13

fully represented in the frame enlargement) with their prone bodies (C 13). The dance ends with further scrambles around the table and an improbable joyride from table to floor on the chandelier (C 14). (To manage this ride with smoothness—and to minimize the danger of injury to the two performers—the chandelier is lowered as they swing forward, gliding them downward.)

D
IT'S A CHEMICAL REACTION, THAT'S ALL/ALL OF YOU
(6′ 16″)

The next day Astaire takes Charisse on a tour of Paris; he tries to show her the glamour spots, but she prefers the factories.

Later, back at his hotel room, he confesses he finds her "absurd and irresistible" and, when prodded, she allows that "the arrangement of your features is not entirely repulsive to me." This leads to a discussion of romance. In Russia, Charisse observes, someone who wants someone, simply says, "You! Come here!" And then, in song, she matter-of-factly explains that love is merely a chemical reaction (D 1).

Astaire responds with a song of his own, which rejects chemistry in favor of geography. In a lyric that is unusually suggestive by Hollywood standards, he expresses a consuming interest in making a tour of her, exploring, in order, her east, west, north, and south. Although Hollywood's censorship office specifically demanded the song be sung in "a non-suggestive manner," Astaire makes no effort to undercut the words' impact in his delivery; on the contrary, he sings the song with a dramatically appropriate air of seething desire (D 2).

As in "Paris Loves Lovers," the singing is expertly blended with dialogue, but now the musical number is expanded into a dance scene. Of the various treatments showing Ninotchka's transformation from repressed ideologue to sentient woman, this seems the most thoroughly convincing. In the 1939 film, her rigidity was finally shattered when Douglas got her to laugh by taking a pratfall. In the 1955 stage musical, Ameche brought her around by serenading her with Porter's fine song in a booming baritone. Here Astaire lets dance do the work. In point and general outline the dance resembles Astaire's famous first romantic duet, in *The Gay Divorcee*, which was set to another apt Porter song, "Night and Day" (3 E). Though both are dances of determined pursuit, "All of You" is more concerned with manipulative seduction than with stylized lovemaking. In "Night and Day" Astaire is ardent and imploring; here he is more distanced—almost scientific—as he experiments with various devices to animate his stiff and uncooperative prey, and stands back from time to time, calmly assessing his progress.

He begins by trying a brief, enticing solo scamper across the room; she remains unmoved. Amused at his own frustration, he snatches up a nearby chair and does an ironic little dance, cleverly making the chair serve as his pliant partner (D 3).

Turning serious now, he thrusts the chair aside, moves determinedly toward Charisse, and, as the music voices the "All of You" melody, firmly pulls her out onto the floor with him. As he does so he observes with wry delight that her leg floats outward into an involuntary, if modest, arabesque, as if the dancer in her were struggling timidly to come to the surface (D 4). To get her to move, though, he has to pilot her firmly around the floor by grasping her by the upper arms, even as she continues to fold them protectively in front of her as if to push him away. When he releases her momentarily, she begins

C14 D1 D2 D3
D4 D5 D6 D7
D8 D9 D10 D11

to wander off, and he has to arrest her progress by grabbing her wrist. Again he tries to get her moving—at first by example and then, when that fails, by direct physical manipulation. He sends her spinning and is pleased to see her come to rest in ballet's fifth position (D5). She sheepishly tries to shrug the incident off, but he presses the point home by wagging his finger at her.

Now, a bit overconfident perhaps, Astaire seats himself on a chair and gestures for her to dance. At first she coolly declines and begins to walk away, but then she pauses and waits, letting him catch up with her. However, when he does a mocking little frolic around her stationary body, she again starts to leave. Once more Astaire grabs her by the wrist, pulls her close, and locks her in his arms as she protects herself with her arms (D6).

They move gingerly in this position to music that ruminates expectantly, but when the orchestra begins to play a romantic, full-bodied rendition of the song, the lush melody sends the dancers gliding across the floor. For the first time Charisse yields to Astaire's touch: her body loses its stiffness, and she moves with empathic fluidity (D7). The change in her demeanor is probably a bit abrupt choreographically, but it is given firm support by the shifting mood of the musical arrangement.

The new mood continues as Astaire swirls Charisse in wide, gliding arcs around his body (D8) until she wraps herself voluptuously around his waist (D9). Then, as he sends her wafting along on her own, he stands back to survey his handiwork with satisfaction and a certain humor (D10). The dance becomes suitably flamboyant, with broad kicks (D11) and a ballet-style partnered pirouette (unusual for Astaire) that is spun off with clipped precision. Now Charisse gives herself over entirely to Astaire's lead, falling into his arms (D12) and leaning luxuriously backward into his body (D13). The dancers do a couple of cantilevered hip lifts (D14), which will be elaborated (and parodied) in their later duet. Then, as the music slows, there is a beautiful partnered fall for Charisse: as Astaire holds her by the hands, she sweeps past him, slides to the floor (D15), twists her body around, and is pulled back to her feet (D16)—all in a single, sumptuous phrase.

The ending is almost too understated. The dancers stroll quietly over to a rug in front of the fireplace (D17) and sink to the floor—Astaire's pose is ardent and importuning; Charisse's is contented and dreamy (D18).

E
SATIN AND SILK
(2′ 35″)

Charisse is mellowed enough to admit that there are pleasures in music and dancing, but she feels guilty: "Pleasure itself is an indulgence; only by denying selfish interests can one properly serve the state." Astaire decides to try the Russian approach—"You! Come here!" he demands—and then kisses her. To his surprise and delight, she asks for another, and then responds in kind (E1). This scene is derived from a typical amalgam of sources: the sequence of kisses and her line "That was restful" are from the *Ninotchka* film (E2), the line about using silk for parachutes is from the stage version of *Silk Stockings,* and the "You! Come here!" line is invented for the screenplay.

The demands of this scene help *Silk Stockings* to set a record: it is the film in which Astaire most often kisses his partner. There are six kisses in all, shattering the achievement of *Funny Face,* which chalked up four. (Astaire's previous average, of course, was close to zero.)

D12 D13 D14 D15
D16 D17 D18 E1
E2 E3 E4 E5

The scene's potential alarmed the censors, who demanded that the kissing not be open-mouthed and that the protagonists "not be in a prone position."

Next, pushy Janis Paige bursts into the room. She complains that she has heard the music of the Russian composer that Astaire wants to use in their planned motion picture and finds it "lousy." Enraged by this insult to Russian culture, Charisse leaves the room in a huff. But Astaire soon convinces Paige of the value of the Russian's music. In fact, they decide to make the film into a musical, and Paige agrees to try to convince the highbrow composer to let his music be used for this purpose.

Back in her hotel room, Charisse is seen to be transformed—idly tapping the typewriter to the remembered rhythms of "All of You." In a scene derived from the *Ninotchka* film, she muses dreamily on the beauties and joys of Paris in the spring, observing in an odd comparison, "We have the high ideals but they have the climate" (E 3, 4).

Next, at a lavish fashion salon, Paige warms up the Russian composer by animatedly and insinuatingly singing a paean to the transforming effects of fancy underwear on "a gal's morale" (E 5). Paige's comic timing is excellent—for example, in the darting inflection of her eyes and in the slight pause she puts before the last word in the line "and her g-string is made of rope."[9]

F
SILK STOCKINGS
(4′25″)

Charisse has also, it happens, succumbed to the attraction of decadent Western attire. In the privacy of her hotel room she carefully turns a picture of Lenin face down on a table, locks the door, and stealthily extracts articles of alluring feminine clothing from various hiding places around the room, starting with a pair of silk stockings (F 1).

In the comparable scene in *Ninotchka,* Garbo had pulled a frivolous hat from hiding (F 2). The screenwriters have here imaginatively expanded the idea to provide an opportunity for a solo dance for Charisse in which her utter surrender to Western pleasures, and to love, can be expressed in choreographic terms.[10] She slinks around the room, gradually clothing herself in her decadent garments. (At one point she ducks behind a lace curtain to change underwear; although she wore a flesh-colored body suit for this sequence, the censors ruled that she must at no time be shown full-figure in the body suit.) At the beginning she sometimes shows signs of uncertainty (F 3), but she is soon swooping about (F 4) and preening (F 5). Loring's dance is concerned with advancing an idea rather than developing steps, but it serves its plot purpose well, and its ulterior motive—to give the audience an extended look at Charisse's terrific legs—even better.

G
WITHOUT LOVE
(2′28″)

Decked out in her new finery, Charisse meets Astaire for a date. She is uneasy, concerned she

[9] This entire scene is taken directly from the stage musical; however, Paige's addressing the composer as "Mr. Boroff, baby" is new. The song had at least one more chorus on-stage, but the provocative lyric is otherwise only minimally altered for the film: the word "hell" is excised and "she can flatten Lord Mountbatten" becomes "she can flatten any Latin."

[10] There was no comparable scene in the *Silk Stockings* stage show. Porter's beautiful song is sung by Ameche later in the story, after Ninotchka has returned to Russia, as he muses softly over their (temporarily) shattered romance.

F 1 F 2 F 3 F 4

F 5 G 1 G 2 G 3

G 4 G 5 G 6 G 7

might look foolish, but Astaire is as startled and pleased by the transformation as Douglas was in 1939 (G1, 2).

After a night on the town they return to her hotel room glowing with champagne. Giddily in love, Charisse serenades Astaire about her feelings (G3). Porter's lyric is offensive and, more to the dramatic point, too extreme for the character: "A woman to a man is just a woman, but a man to a woman is her life."[11]

Next there is the famous execution sequence from the 1939 film. Tipsily, she expresses guilt at being so happy and says she should be punished. Obligingly, she is placed against the wall, blindfolded, and given a last kiss (G4, 5). At the pop of a champagne bottle she slumps to the floor announcing, "I have been punished" (G6, 7). Charisse then topples over, adding, "I feel better," and Astaire helps her to a sofa and leaves quietly.

Charisse handles the considerable demands of this scene remarkably well, especially considering the inevitable comparison with the luminous Garbo performance that must have haunted her. Swept away by wine and romance, she is charming, affecting, and convincing.

H
FATED TO BE MATED
(3'45")

The next day Astaire and Charisse meet at a studio to watch a rehearsal for the motion picture he is producing. But first Astaire brings her to a vacant sound stage for some serious business: he tells her that his story about the Russian composer's having a French father was fraudulent. When she observes that she then no longer has any reason to stay in Paris, he proposes marriage as the soundest reason he can imagine and caps the proposal by singing a song newly written for the film by Porter.[12]

When he finishes singing, he takes her in his arms and moves lightly across the floor with her and into a jubilant love dance that travels through various stage sets and is set to reprises of two of their love songs: "Paris Loves Lovers" and "All of You." The splendid dance, choreographed mostly by Hermes Pan, is spirited and buoyant, and more acrobatic than usual for Astaire, featuring the knee work and hefty lifts that he characteristically avoided. It is also somewhat more musically literal than usual.[13]

It begins with a loving hug (H1) and a romp around some poles (H2)—ideas that recur at the end of the dance, neatly framing it. The dance's single most felicitous image is a cantilevered hip lift.[14] The idea had been presented in the "All of You" duet (see D14), but here it is developed so

[11] Far better is Garbo's beautiful fragmented speech: "Comrades! People of the world! The revolution is on the march. . . . I know . . . wars will wash over us . . . bombs will fall . . . all civilization will crumble . . . but not yet, please . . . wait, wait . . . what's the hurry? Let us be happy . . . give us our moment. . . ."

[12] Except for this new song (replacing "As On through the Seasons We Sail") the scenes at the movie lot follow the stage script quite closely; there is nothing from *Ninotchka* in them.

[13] As a joke, Pan and the dancers created a dance to this song which was certainly bizarre by Hollywood standards: it took place entirely on the floor. Explaining they had "a different idea," they brought Mamoulian in and performed it for him with straight faces. He was very amused: "In a way I wish I had photographed that; it was an extraordinary achievement."

[14] The idea has antecedents in *Carefree* (see 10 E10) and in *Three Little Words* (23 M12)—films Pan worked on. It can also be found in some of Astaire's television duets in the 1950s, on which Pan also worked.

H1 H2 H3 H4
H5 H6 H7 H8
H9 H10 H11 H12

that it can be used to travel: Charisse exultantly swings her legs out into space and plants her feet at a distance, pulling Astaire around after her (H 3). Charisse is particularly beautiful in this, animating the move by swinging—propelling—her weight in a wide, spacious arc around Astaire, who supports her. She moves with unaffected joy in what is probably her finest single dance moment in the two films she made with Astaire.

Once the traveling lift has carried the dancers onto a stage set that suggests a Latin locale, the orchestra launches into an arrangement in which the melody of "Paris Loves Lovers" is played over an assertive Latin-style counter-rhythm. Pan had the idea to set the dance entirely to the accompaniment: while the melody soars, the dancers move only in direct reflection of the percussive undercurrent, bolting about in space-devouring, floor-slamming lunges (H 6) embellished by an occasional quick spin on the knee (H 4) or a crisp jump (H 5). The sequence is marred by some momentum-arresting business involving the seating of Charisse on a pillar (H 7), but things quickly improve: side by side, the dancers lope around the floor in a figure that gradually evolves back into the traveling hip lift—a superb transition (H 8, 9).

The lift carries them into a waterfront set, where they slow to a cool saunter as the music shifts to an upbeat, jazzy arrangement of "All of You" (H 10). In the dance that follows, the sauntering alternates with various lifts during which Charisse kicks her legs around somewhat overemphatically, and at times even vulgarly (H 11, 12).

There follows a passage that is particularly gratifying in its relation to the music: a hand-in-hand traveling pattern that starts from the saunter and then sweeps exhilaratingly across the floor (H 13). It brings the dancers to a corner where some crates are stacked; they scamper over the obstacle, repeating some of their percussive limb thrusts and kicking lifts (H 14). Another broad lunge takes them back to the main floor, where they perform a parody of their hip lift: Astaire, holding Charisse up, looks the other way and grimaces as she kicks out in reflection of percussive blasts in the orchestra (H 15).

The ending of the dance number is an exuberant rapid-fire reprise of several dance ideas developed earlier. The dancers swoop back and forth under a pair of horizontal bars (H 16), as they had maneuvered through vertical ones earlier (H 2). After a repeat of one of their space-devouring lunges (H 17; compare H 6), they do another spin on one knee (H 18; as in H 4), and another plunge-and-catch (H 19; see H 14).[15] At the end they throw themselves into an exultant hug (H 20), as at the beginning (H 1).

I
JOSEPHINE
(1′ 25″)

Charisse and Astaire join the others on another sound stage, where Paige is going through a full-dress rehearsal of one of the musical numbers from the motion picture Astaire is producing (I 1). In the stage version this was a broad production number built around a parody of a striptease. Loring prepared both a short and a long version for the film; what survives is a shortened version of the short version.

[15] Astaire had to be persuaded to try the plunge-and-catch routine—he was afraid he would drop Charisse, who weighed in at 112 pounds. Because this last sequence involves a knee spin, Charisse wears a divided skirt for the shot (particularly obvious in H 17), as she had for the shot that included the other knee spin (H 4).

H13 H14 H15 H16
H17 H18 H19 H20
I1 J1 J2 K1

J

SIBERIA

(2′9″)

Paige's song in praise of "undulating hips" and "lubricating lips" is interrupted by the Russian composer, who flies into a rage at this travesty of his music. Charisse takes his side, and soon she and Astaire are arguing over what she sees as a severe insult to Russian culture (J1). Angrily Astaire accuses her of reverting to her previous condition as a "carefully trained robot." Guilty at having betrayed her way of life for "an emotional attachment," Charisse orders the composer and the three commissars to head back to Moscow with her.

The commissars, struck glum by this devastating turn of events, muse in song and dance over the prospect of ending up in "cheery Siberia." The routine, which apparently follows the stage version closely (a number modeled on the show-stopping "Brush Up Your Shakespeare" from Porter's *Kiss Me Kate*), is less funny than it should be. To be sure, the central joke fully registers: three stocky men of wildly dissimilar sizes, dressed in floppy, ill-fitting business suits, are shown attempting a delicate, high-strutting routine while singing bouncily of the misery that awaits them—a cornucopia of improbable juxtapositions. But the joke would be most effective if their movements were precisely articulated and rendered in Rockette-like synchronization. The performers seem capable of such an effort, but are instead allowed to inflect the movements variously, and frequently they fall out of exact coordination (J2). As a result they often look clumsy and underrehearsed, conforming to expectations rather than offering humorous contrast with them.[16]

K

THE RED BLUES

(4′39″)

Back in Moscow, Charisse invites the three commissars and the composer to her crowded apartment for a reunion dinner, where they reminisce warmly about Paris. A letter arrives from Astaire, but it has been completely blacked out by the censors—an event that dampens their merrymaking, as it had in *Ninotchka* (K1, 2). To brighten things, the composer brings in a group of musicians and, announcing that he has now become fascinated by Western popular music, plays his "latest and most decadent composition."

Revelers emerge from the woodwork, and Charisse is soon leading a group of male dancers in a vigorous romp around the room. This dance is an eclectic gaggle of Russian folk steps, ballet pyrotechnics, jitterbugging, tap fragments, and Broadway dance clichés. There is even, for some reason, a kind of reprise of the cantilevered hip lift (K3).[17] At the scene's fade-out, the dancers collapse, happy and exhausted; their exhaustion is understandable, but their happiness hardly fits the melancholy of the scene.

L

THE RITZ ROLL AND ROCK

(3′29″)

Onstage, *Silk Stockings* ended with the scene in Ninotchka's Moscow apartment. Ameche has obtained a visa and enters at the end of the "Red Blues" number, embraces Ninotchka, and then fast-talks everyone into defecting to the West on a large airplane provided by the Commissar of Art, who plans to make big money in the United States by confessing as an ex-Communist and publishing his memoirs. There is a slight air of improbability about the scene (as Ameche puts it at one point in the script, "This is silly. They wouldn't even do this on television") and the romance gets lost in the talky shuffle. The *Silk Stockings* film abandons the stage show's ending for one much closer to the *Ninotchka* original.

Astaire, like Douglas, tries to get a visa but is refused by a suspicious Soviet bureaucrat (L1, 2).[18] Eventually, the three commissars are sent to Paris, where they again succumb to capitalist temptation. Although she is reluctant to go, Ninotchka is once more sent on a mission to bring them back. When Charisse arrives, the three commissars eagerly escort her to a nightclub where Astaire is performing as part of the opening-night program.

The number is thus rather clumsily shoe-

[16] As an elaborate joke on Mamoulian, the cast prerecorded a satire on this song ("When you work for sweet Mamoulian, it's like working for Na-pooleon") which was played back as the director began to shoot the number.

[17] Charisse blasts through this number with considerable gusto, an effect apparently possible only on film. According to Loring, "She has bursts of energy, not for long, and then she gives up. I had planned the shooting so that the tough stuff came in the morning when she was energetic and I'd do the easy scenes in the afternoon." The musical arrangement of the song is overblown; its arrangement on the stage-cast recording is far superior—lighter and bouncier.

[18] Douglas ends the scene with the visa official by knocking him down in frustration. There is no such altercation in Astaire's scene.

K2 K3 L1 L2

L3 L4 L5 L6

horned into the script as a means of granting Astaire's request to do "a sock solo" in the film. He proposed a number that would be a "twist on the rock-and-roll craze," an idea Porter at first greeted with bewilderment, arguing that he didn't know how to write a rock-and-roll song. After some study of this genre, however, he came up with a useful and suitably sassy ditty. The very idea of Fred Astaire doing a rock-and-roll number is inherently funny, and Porter's lyric takes off from this improbable miscegenation of styles: rock and roll is dead and gone, it (hopefully) trumpets, now that the ritzy set has taken it over. Porter's concept led to the obvious conclusion that Astaire should do the number in top hat and tails—something he initially resisted because he felt the garb to be passé (he had managed to avoid it in his two previous films).

The number is one of Astaire's rare attempts at obvious satire and, like the others—the ribbing of ballet in *Shall We Dance,* of gutsy detective fiction in *The Band Wagon* (27 L), and of intellectual phoniness in *Funny Face* (29 K)—it tries too hard and accomplishes too little. The humor is forced, even a bit desperate, and as satire the number is simply uncomprehending. Besides, as Astaire once wryly observed, it "didn't do any good."[19] In retrospect, Astaire regrets the way he sang the song: "It wasn't a great song to begin with, but it didn't have to be *that* bad. . . . I overdid, overplayed it." He doesn't seem all that pleased by the dance, either: it "was all right because there were a lot of other people involved in it"—faint praise, indeed.

The number begins promisingly enough. Astaire is first seen in unmistakable silhouette: in top hat and tails, leaning jauntily on his cane (L 3). The music is swarmy mock Tchaikovsky, but as the lights come up it suddenly shifts to rock and roll, and this launches Astaire into a goofy little danced prologue during which he slams brusquely to one knee (L 4), saunters with an affectation of coolness, his shoulders raised up almost to his ears (L 5), and startles onlookers by suddenly springing wildly at them like a Halloween spook (L 6).

As he begins to sing, the men of the chorus drop to the floor behind him, and when he resumes his slouchy cool-cat saunter-parody, they roll over behind him (L 7). Astaire slumps to the floor himself toward the end of the song and then is lifted to his feet by two of the men for the dance, which involves a lot of screaming and flailing and scrabbling on the floor (L 8), all laid on the music with a complete lack of rhythmic sophistication, presumably as a conscious send-up of the elementary rhythmic patterns of rock and roll. Someone apparently thought it would be funny to see Astaire biting his cane and shinnying up the edge of a mirror, so some of that is thrown in (L 9, 10).[20] After some hat juggling by Astaire, and some careening by the chorus, the dance ends with everybody sprawled on the floor. As Astaire falls, his hat topples from his head (Mamoulian reports that the toppling hat was not intended—it was a "lucky accident" that, after some consideration, was kept). Astaire takes careful aim (L 11) and then, with savage glee, terminates his last dance in his last major musical by smashing his top hat flat (L 12).

[19] In an interview at the time, Astaire voiced his opinion without reservation: "What's happened to music, anyway? The songs you hear pouring out of radios and jukeboxes sound sick, sick, SICK! What's happened? Is there some kind of contest to see who can write the ugliest songs? There's just a terrible sameness to this junk on the air."

[20] The mirror routine seems misjudged, even on its own terms. The joke (one presumes) is to give the illusion that Astaire is rising magically into the air, in which case the camera should have been placed so that only his leg is duplicated in the mirror, not his head as well.

M
TOO BAD
(REPRISE) (16")

Well, back to the plot. In an anteroom at the nightclub the three commissars cheerfully inform Charisse that they own the place: they have become rotten capitalists, Lorre giddily observes, and have hopes of becoming much more rotten. They now represent, they say, the Russia of good will and hospitality.

Astaire enters, and, as in *Ninotchka,* confusions are soon cleared up (M 1). The last moment, however, is original to the *Silk Stockings* film. Charisse crisply ends all uncertainty with her Soviet-style command: "You! Come here!"[21] Astaire happily complies, but, amusingly, the terminal clinch is never shown. Instead, Mamoulian's camera turns to show the three commissars in a final frolic of jubilation, and the film's concluding image is of ex-Commissar Lorre, wedged again between table and chair, gleefully stomping out his most famous dance step (M 2).

[21] This is apparently an idea that emerged on the set; it is a major improvement over the screenplay, which called for *Astaire* to deliver this line.

L7 L8 L9 L10

L11 L12 M1 M2

31.

FINIAN'S RAINBOW

1968

The blame for *Finian's Rainbow* seems to rest primarily with its twenty-nine-year-old auteur, director Francis Ford Coppola, a man who had never before had anything to do with musicals. The film, a screen adaptation of a twenty-one-year-old Broadway musical hit, attempts, like the original, to blend whimsy with social commentary about racial brotherhood. Both whimsy and racial brotherhood were rather unfashionable in the politically tumultuous year of 1968, when the film came out, and to handle them in that atmosphere one would need wit, lightness of touch, detachment, and warmth without sentimentality. What Coppola came up with was a film in which the attempted whimsy becomes leaden and the social commentary becomes trivial and self-conscious.

Above all, just about everything in the film is ill-paced. Virtually all the dialogue scenes (as well as most of the jokes) are belabored. The musical numbers are also tedious. Although he was working with some of the most attractive songs imaginable, Coppola obviously viewed them with impatience, distrust, and incomprehension. Instead of letting the songs speak for themselves, he chose to festoon the numbers with distractingly manic camera work—a desperate effort to enliven that has the result of undercutting the effect of the numbers by making them all look and sound alike.

Embedded in all this is Fred Astaire playing the central role of Finian, an aged yet remarkably agile repository of Irish blarney. Astaire was quite willing to shed his usual dapper demeanor for the grizzled look appropriate to the role—a transformation some critics found disconcerting. In fact, he gives one of the liveliest and most endearing performances of his career.

With a great dancer, however aged, heading his cast, one might expect Coppola to allow his star an occasional extended opportunity to dance. But the director was well aware that the era of the dance musical had passed in Hollywood—*Silk Stockings,* Astaire's last previous musical, eleven years earlier, had been one of the last specimens. So all Astaire is given is a brief romp here and a fragmentary jig there. And even this material is dismembered by Coppola's frenetic camera work, which even includes inset shots of Astaire's dancing feet, the first in thirty-five years.

Beyond this, most of what passes for dance in *Finian's Rainbow* involves what Stephen Harvey has aptly described as "hordes of black and white extras streaming through meadows in a desperate facsimile of spontaneous energy." Here and there, however, a few bits and pieces emerge that are worthy of attention, and there is one fleeting moment of great beauty—the ending of the "Look to the Rainbow" dance number (31 E).

COPPOLA'S DISASTER

Astaire, rarely critical of others in public, has called *Finian's Rainbow* his "biggest disappointment." Coppola has been even less generous about the film, terming it "a disaster." He has sometimes been (understandably) defensive about the film in interviews, observing that he was "brought in to direct a project that had already been cast and structured." However, he admits that "I had my way, within the limitations of time and money. I was very responsible." The problem, in part, was that he was in well over his head: "I was . . . working in a big studio, in a methodology I didn't understand very well. . . ."

Actually, some of the best things about the film had already been decided before Coppola signed on as director. For example, there was the casting of Astaire as Finian and of pop singer Petula Clark as his daughter. Clark sings with an engaging individuality, but, unlike many vocalists, she never achieves distinctiveness by distorting the intent of the song. She is, in addition, a skilled actress, having begun acting in British films in 1944, at the age of twelve. *Finian's Rainbow* was her twenty-third film. Nor is Coppola responsible for the film's other great virtue, the luminous Burton Lane–E. Y. Harburg songs, which had been written for the Broadway stage version when Coppola was eight years old.

The book, by Harburg and Fred Saidy, clearly bewildered Coppola: he found it "terrible," "sort of ridiculous," and saw no way to handle its odd mixture of caprice and social satire. Yet he felt there was "something warm" about the old show: "I fought very hard not to change it, which was probably a mistake. I had the idea that if you do *Finian's Rainbow,* you shouldn't rewrite it or update it. I guess I was wrong." Instead, he says, he merely tried to "zip it up."

There are two linked plot lines in the show. One concerns a mercurial Irishman who comes with his daughter to Rainbow Valley, near Fort Knox, to plant a crock of gold he has

Francis Ford Coppola directs Astaire

"borrowed" from a leprechaun so that it might grow.[1] The other concerns the valley's happily integrated group of sharecroppers, or cooperative farmers, who are being dispossessed by a bigoted Southern senator. Eventually the Irishman's daughter falls in love with the sharecroppers' leader, the magic of the gold is used to turn the senator black temporarily (so he can see what it's like), and a leprechaun in pursuit of his stolen gold decides to become mortal and to marry a valley girl.[2]

The screenplay was written by the authors of the stage play, with substantial contributions by Coppola. As Coppola suggests, the film follows the stage script closely. The dialogue is tightened somewhat and a number of Harburg's more pointedly political barbs are removed, as are a few bawdy cracks. Also excised are references to such things as poll taxes and Jim Crow laws, which, fortunately, had begun to be dated in 1968. However, the film then *adds* a subplot, about a black botanist in the valley who is working to create a breed of tobacco blended with mint to achieve a naturally mentholated cigarette. This subplot, unrelated to any of the musical numbers, simply clutters and lengthens the film.

In confronting the musical, Coppola says he did not want to "get fancy" but, rather, sought to achieve "a lot of warmth and affection." A commendable goal, unquestionably, but his failure in this area is truly monumental: the film is almost completely devoid of either quality. One story element with potential for "warmth and affection" is the relationship between Finian and his devoted but feisty daughter. In the film's opening scenes Astaire and Clark are allowed a few touching moments in which one can catch glimpses of their love for each other, but thereafter their relationship is largely ignored. A similar opportunity existed in the love story between Clark and the sharecropper leader, played by a hairy-chested Canadian baritone, Don Francks, who proves to be a capable actor. But the romance is handled perfunctorily—the lovers meet, kiss, sing, argue a little, and get swept along by events.

Intruding on all this is the energetic Tommy Steele as the world's most overbearing leprechaun. He plays everything at a manic high pitch, an effect that quickly becomes enervating. To his credit, Coppola was aware of the problem, but he proved incapable of handling it: "I felt the leprechaun should be more shy and timid and bewildered. . . . And at my insistence Tommy started to do just that in rehearsal, and he was really good at it. . . . Somehow during the actual shooting, little by little, he slipped back into his familiar character. . . . He eluded me." The suffering viewer can sympathize with Coppola's problem, but the suspicion remains that a stronger director could have kept the actor under control —perhaps by taking him off carbonated beverages or something. Failing that, it was certainly possible to reduce his damaging impact in the film—in the scriptwriting stage, in the shooting phase, or, ultimately, in the cutting room. Coppola seems to have passed these opportunities by.

THE CREATION OF THE MUSICAL NUMBERS

Though the dialogue scenes are ill-paced, shallow, and humorless, it is in the musical numbers that true mayhem is committed. For it is here that some of the finest songs of the modern musical theatre are systematically dismembered and trivialized.

Appropriately enough, Coppola had an idea for each of the

[1] In the stage original, Finian was not required to do more than a few scraps of singing and dancing, so the role had to be modified to suit Astaire's talents in those areas. The original Finian was the Irish actor Albert Sharpe, who played the role of Sarah Churchill's pub-tending father in *Royal Wedding*.

[2] It is sometimes asserted that the reason it took twenty-one years to bring this popular show to the screen was that Hollywood found its racial and political commentary too hot to handle during the cautious days of the McCarthy era. However, various efforts to produce the show as a film (even, once, as a cartoon) were made during the 1950s. An important stumbling block was Harburg's very capitalistic demand of $1 million for rights to the property.

numbers: "I said, 'Grandish.' I'll shoot it on a hill and have Petula Clark hanging white bed sheets. And 'If This Isn't Love' will be done with children's games." However, these "ideas" emerge in the film purely as frantic bits of visual business that have little to do with the point of the songs, and invariably distract from the music and the lyric without adding much of anything of their own. For example, in "Something Sort of Grandish" leprechaun Steele is supposed to be telling Clark of his highly human infatuation for her, but the two spend the number desperately running up and down a hill swirling bed sheets and getting entangled in them while their disembodied voices dutifully render the song on the soundtrack.

Some of Coppola's problems with the musical numbers can be attributed to his insensitivity to choreography. Few of his concepts leave much room for dance steps. Hermes Pan was signed, "at Fred Astaire's insistence," to provide this material, but Coppola, although proclaiming "I know nothing about dancing," found Pan's work "abysmal . . . we fired the choreographer halfway through the picture." As a result, Coppola says, "I improvised all the dancing." (Astaire says he made some suggestions to Coppola but these were ignored.) Moreover, and rather incredibly, the shooting went faster than Coppola expected and he soon used up the material he had prepared. By the second week of filming he was "faking it," and the film, he concludes dismally, "was basically a cheat." For his part, Pan calls Coppola "a real pain. . . . He knew very little about dancing and musicals. He would interfere with my work and even with Fred's. . . . These schoolboys who studied at UCLA think they're geniuses, but there is a lot they don't understand."

Even allowing for these circumstances, however, the staging and filming of the musical numbers are still amazingly incompetent. Even the most naïve improviser knows enough to vary the pace and to develop more than one kind of movement material. But almost everything in Coppola's film is taken at a pell-mell pace, and almost all the numbers involve the same idea: performers romping through field and stream, down road and railroad track, across bridge and hillock.

Then Coppola employs another technique that further eviscerates the songs: the purposeful mismatching of shots during musical numbers. A performer will be shown falling down at the end of one shot, for example, and then suddenly sloshing through a stream at the beginning of the next. The approach does sometimes have the effect of giving energy to a sequence, but it also invariably distracts, and the cuts seem to be arranged arbitrarily or mechanically, without any musical point or effect in mind.

With Petula Clark

THE MUSIC

Despite the visual mayhem, the songs generally receive affectionate and sensitive musical performances in the film. It is here, however, that Coppola applies his most ingeniously diabolical stroke. Closing one's eyes is no escape: in the many sequences where the chorus is shown romping about, Coppola has mixed into the track the sounds of people giggling and gurgling, thus adding aural clutter to visual clutter (though these extraneous sounds are fortunately not included in the fine "soundtrack" recording from the film). Spontaneity, lightness, humor, warmth, joy, charm, and life are systematically sacrificed in a wildly misguided effort to be cinematic.

THE CHOREOGRAPHY

Presumably, the bulk of what passes for choreography in this film must be credited to Coppola. Astaire undoubtedly remained in basic control of his brief solo material, and some scraps of crowd movement may owe something to Pan.

THE NUMBERS

A
LOOK TO THE RAINBOW
(4′8″)

Actually, for all the tedium to follow, the first twenty minutes of the film do contain a few appealing moments. Quite promising, for example, is the opening: under the titles Clark and Astaire (or sometimes their doubles) are seen to be wandering across spectacular American landscapes while Clark is heard luminously singing the film's central song (A1). There is a wonderful improbability to this sequence—to cover all the territory shown, the wanderers would have to trek thousands of miles. The juxtaposition of these scenes with the fanciful Lane-Harburg ballad sets exactly the right wistful tone.

B
THIS TIME OF THE YEAR
(2′13″)

Fancy is quickly fractured, however. The film's opening dramatic scene is staged with unnecessary meanness and ill-humor. A rednecked Southern sheriff is shown trying to run the simple, happy sharecroppers off their land. As they wait for their leader, Francks, to arrive to pay off their back taxes, the sharecroppers terrorize the sheriff by romping all over his dusty Cadillac while an off-camera chorus, their words muffled by crowd noises, sing the song.

C
ASTAIRE'S JIG
(23″)

Upon nearing his goal, the sharecroppers' valley near Fort Knox, Astaire bursts into a happy little dance of celebration (C1–2). His frolic is one of the film's rare—and characteristically fleeting—delights. Its impact is severely undercut, however, by the incompetent way in which the voices of Astaire and Clark—obviously recorded separately from the action—have been added to the soundtrack.[3]

D
HOW ARE THINGS IN GLOCCA MORRA?
(2′9″)

Clark and Astaire briefly reminisce about Ireland, and she is led to sing sweetly the show's most popular song. This is the only musical number filmed with restraint—for the most part, Coppola is content simply to let the audience watch this beautiful woman sing this beautiful song—and a bit of warmth is even allowed to show between Astaire and Clark (D1). The scene ends on a tartly antisentimental note: Clark's song moves Astaire to tears (D2), which he then defensively shrugs off by calling it "cheap Irish music."

E
LOOK TO THE RAINBOW
(5′27″)

In a scene too long by half, Astaire helps Francks pay off the back taxes and obtains for his investment an acre of land close to Fort Knox. In the process Francks discovers Clark and becomes very interested in her. Now there is a reprise of "Look to the Rainbow," which evolves into the film's most extensive dance number. The number, disjointed and underdeveloped choreographically, is further dismembered by directorial whim; but it contains glimmers of wit, and its ending is masterful.

Astaire begins by singing to a group of children. Clark, who has been sitting by Francks, sings a phrase and strolls over to join Astaire. When she comes to the words "my own true love's eyes," she steals a shy glance at Francks. Then, embarrassed at her own feelings and forwardness, she looks away—a brilliantly understated bit of acting. Equally touching is the next sequence, in which Astaire and Clark harmonize briefly, once again giving the audience a glimpse of the tenderness of their relationship (E1).[4]

Astaire now leaps up onto a platform built around a tree and begins a gentle little dance. Soon he collects Clark, and she joins him in some wryly dignified neobaroquery filled with courtly bows and genuflections. Their dance takes them around the tree, and when they complete their circling the music shifts to a bit of Irish jiggery sending them into some appropriate limp-armed hopping and stamping (E2), embellished with an amusing rearing lunge (E3). This

[3] Incredibly, the film garnered an Academy Award nomination for the sound.

[4] At first Astaire and Clark were uncomfortable working with each other: she was petrified at the thought of having to dance with him, and he was worried about having to sing with her. She discovered his concern during the playback of their recording session, when he jumped up and shouted, "I sang with her! I sang with her!"

A1 C1 C2 D1

D2 E1 E2 E3

is followed by another partnered circling of the tree and some leg-shifting jumps in place.

This brief duet has charm and humor and presents ample material from which to develop a complete dance number. But Coppola's idea of choreography is to have hordes of people romping mindlessly through fields, and that's what we get instead. Astaire abandons his lovely partner to Francks and then, with sprightly pied-piper-like enthusiasm, leads the chorus in their frolic. As usual, the noise of a laughing crowd is clumsily mixed into the soundtrack, adding a forced note to the gaiety.

At one point the field is given over to the dancing chorus performing hillbilly stomps, and then Astaire reappears, shown in several disconnected episodes. In one he tries to retrieve his satchel, which is playfully kept from him by several dancers; in others he is shown dancing down a stream (people are always sloshing through streams in this film), engaging in a bit of business with his bag that is incomprehensible because the camera is too close, or leading the group in a fragmented but appealing romp that lopes and spins through the fields.

The music gradually evolves into a wonderful sequence in which a churning idea is alternated with a held note. The number, and the music, begin to fade away as Astaire and Clark leave to journey down the road,[5] presumably to inspect the property Astaire has just purchased (E4). As they do so, Astaire capers along during the churning episodes in the music and freezes on the held notes, alternating bubbling activity with moments of stasis, while Clark ambles along agreeably behind him (E5). Then, on his final episodic caper, Astaire takes Clark in his arms and spins along with her until together they hit a final pose, and the scene fades out. The moment is magical.

[5] Coppola's distrust of dance reaches its highest point in this otherwise excellent episode. In the held pose of E4, it is clear the performers are bidding good-bye to each other. Apparently afraid this obvious gesture of farewell wouldn't communicate, he mixed in a coarse and redundant "Bye!" on the soundtrack.

F
ASTAIRE'S ROMP, WITH TREE, THROUGH WOODS
(1′ 10″)

The bag Astaire is so protective of contains gold "borrowed" from a leprechaun. Astaire plans to bury it here, near Fort Knox, so that it will grow. On a moonlit night he ventures out with bag, shovel, and jug of whiskey—and finds himself pursued by a mobile tree. Astaire and his unlikely pursuer make an amusing little dance out of this bit of business.

G
OLD DEVIL MOON
(3′46″)

The film now begins its terminal slide into coyness and tedium as the leprechaun, in the person of the hyperkinetic Tommy Steele, emerges from the pursuing tree. He and Astaire have an unrelievedly agitated dialogue scene that keeps straining for humor.

Looking for Astaire in the woods, Clark bumps into Francks. After a dialogue scene that even Clark is unable to keep well paced, they kiss and sing a haunting love song as Coppola distracts the viewer with gyrating, shallow-focus cameras and pointlessly mismatched cuts (G1).

H
SOMETHING SORT OF GRANDISH
(2′56″)

Eventually, Astaire buries his gold in secret. Then, after an excursion into the gratuitous mentholated-tobacco sub-subplot, the valley's resident black botanist gets a job as shuffling butler to the film's black-hearted bigoted Southern senator, played by Keenan Wynn. In a routine brought over from the stage show, the botanist does a vengeful slow-motion shuffle while serving a bromo to the anxious senator—a heavy, noisy joke that is allowed to linger on the screen for a full forty-nine seconds (H1).

Leprechaun Steele now meets Clark and, we are to believe, falls in love with her. Though they sing about love, the song is staged as a playful, overactive romp through the laundry that is occasionally visually arresting but never emotionally relevant (H2).

I
IF THIS ISN'T LOVE
(3′38″)

Now Clark breaks up with Francks, apparently because he is impractical. But they somehow get together again during the course of the next number, a desperate frenzy of field romping (Clark even gets to chase a pig while ostensibly singing) superimposed over an exuberant, scale-

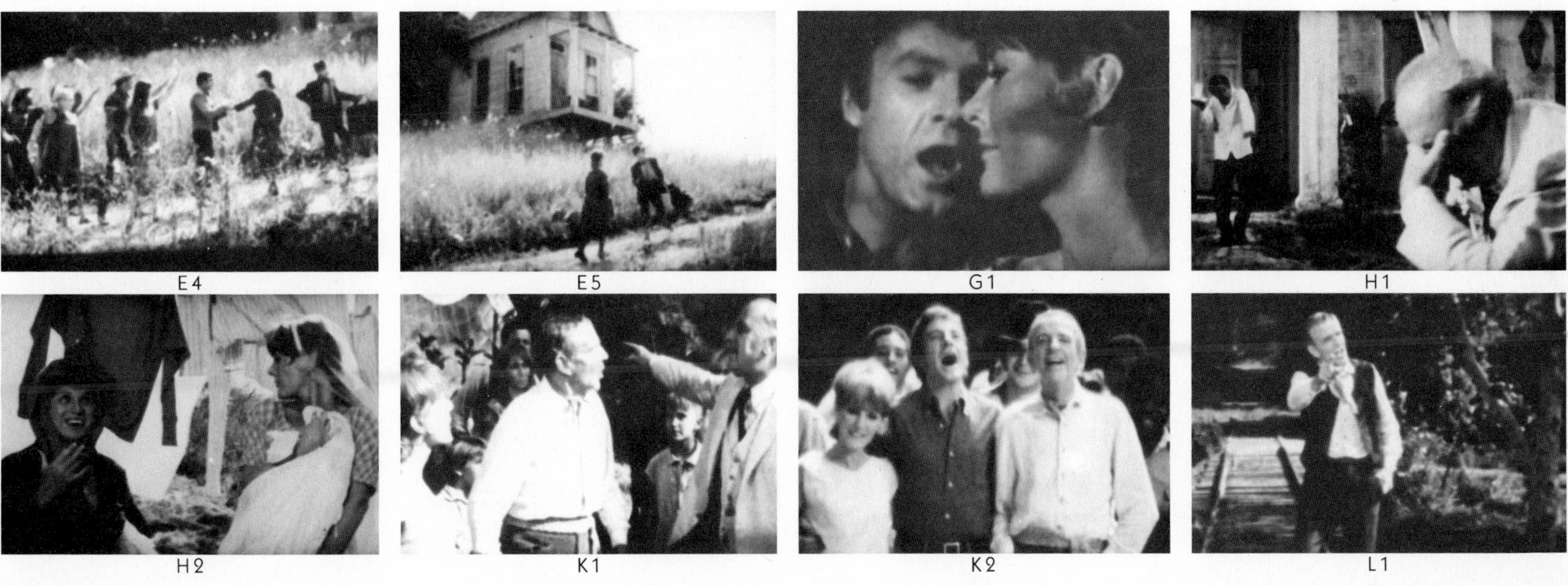

E4 E5 G1 H1

H2 K1 K2 L1

ascending song quite capable of standing on its own.[6]

J

SOMETHING SORT OF GRANDISH

(REPRISE) (58")

Using quotes from the lyric of "Night and Day," Steele animatedly informs Astaire of his love for Clark. (The quotations from the famous Cole Porter song were actually in the original play, but Astaire's presence here gives them a peculiar resonance.) Steele says this is a sign of incipient mortality, which he can reverse only if he gets back his crock of gold. Astaire refuses, and Steele, in an eminently cuttable scene, tries to enlist the aid of some children to look for the buried treasure. As they run around looking, he sings and does funny things like taking a shower fully clothed and falling out of a tree.

K

THAT GREAT COME-AND-GET-IT DAY

(3'50")

Wynn comes to the valley seeking the gold he has heard is in the ground. He orders the people out because they are violating a law he has just enacted forbidding the mixing of races (K 1). Astonishingly, Wynn is able to handle his acting chores in this scene with a certain disarming humor and lightness: there is an engaging dignity—even charm—in the vicious bigot he plays. In a fury, Clark wishes that Wynn would become black. Because she is standing near the crock of gold, he does, and runs off terrified into the woods, chased by his own dogs.

Francks then returns from somewhere and sings about a charge account the valley has been given on the strength of rumors that there is gold in the ground (K 2). Everyone romps happily through the fields, well trodden by now.

L

WHEN THE IDLE POOR BECOME THE IDLE RICH

(4'43")

Next Astaire sings a song that has one of Harburg's most pointedly satiric lyrics (L 1).[7] Meanwhile, the mob, gurgling noisily as usual, is shown celebrating the bounty brought by the charge account. The lyric is either mindlessly undercut with irrelevant business or simple-mindedly underlined with broadly illustrative, and often distractingly busy, matter: when Astaire sings about a poor man's rejection, Hermes Pan (in one of his rare film appearances) throws a towel at him (L 2); and when the lyric mentions horses, real ones are shown nearly trampling the singer. Coppola refrains from showing people romping through fields in this number; instead they are shown romping along a railroad track (L 3).

The number concludes with a dance solo for Astaire. It runs less than two minutes, but it still takes Coppola thirteen shots to record it, including an inset shot of Astaire's flickering feet (L 4). However, the dance is weak, so Coppola's damaging direction has little artistic effect. The routine most resembles the misfired satire of Astaire's last solo in films, "The Ritz Roll and Rock" in *Silk Stockings* (30 L). Almost all the movement involves percussive twitches and jolts set mechanically one to the beat—an effect emphasized by the drummer's monotonously regular rim shots. According to earlier dialogue, Finian is supposed to be arthritic. It is conceivable, though far from obvious, that Astaire's dance evolved from that premise.

Astaire begins the dance with a series of quirky knee thrusts (L 5) and soon is bolting his way over some packing boxes, clambering up a ladder, and clinging to a pole (L 6). He returns to earth to sing a final fragment of the song and to perform some additional kinetic sputters and an-

[6] Coppola says of this number: "After the song . . . we were supposed to go into a big production number. Well, it was so awful that I got little Barbara Hancock (Silent Susan, in the film) and we went back and I shot her with a 500-mm lens going in and out of the trees. She was just faking it. And that's the way the numbers were done." The romp through the trees, however, represents less than half a minute of the number's length. Hancock was a twenty-one-year-old ballet dancer from Georgia with a fair amount of musical-comedy experience onstage; she reportedly got the part after winning an audition with 250 other ballet dancers.

[7] In the stage show, "That Great Come-and-Get-It-Day" ended Act 1 and "When the Idle Poor Become the Idle Rich" opened Act 2 (led by Finian's daughter), the charged articles having arrived during the intermission. (The second song is given more point by having the sharecroppers parade around in improbably fancy duds, a device abandoned by Coppola for some reason.) In its initial showings, the film, too, was designed to have an intermission at that point.

L 2 L 3 L 4 L 5

L 6 L 7 M 1 M 2

atomical pixilations. The number has an imaginative conclusion: the music under the last phrase loops repeatedly, so the precise ending of the dance is not predictable and it comes as an amusing surprise when Astaire abruptly drops to the floor (L7).

M

OLD DEVIL MOON / RAIN DANCE

(4′ 3″)

Francks and Clark decide to get married, and they are so happy that they reprise their love song while sloshing through a stream (M1). Francks' mute sister sees them, is infected by the romantic mood, and flounces around balletically as it begins to rain. She gets very wet. Then the soggy ground opens and she discovers the buried crock of gold, which she carries off (M2).

N

THE BEGAT

(3′8″)

In the woods the newly blackened Wynn meets leprechaun Steele, who uses magic to transform him into a nice person. The converted Wynn then joins up with a trio of black singers, and they happily harmonize while racing their jalopy around the countryside (N1). Perhaps the witty song is destroyed this way so that Coppola could apply some of the car-chase formulas he once learned at the knee of drive-in exploitationist Roger Corman. There can be no conceivable musical reason.

O

LOOK TO THE RAINBOW

(REPRISE) (1′ 14″)

The marriage of Francks and Clark, for which "Look to the Rainbow" serves as an attractive wedding march, is broken up by the law. Clark is accused of being a witch for turning Wynn black. There is a nice 1960s touch as she furiously thrashes at the threatening rifles of her accusers with her wedding bouquet (O1).

P

WHEN I'M NOT NEAR THE GIRL I LOVE

(4′ 9″)

Astaire obtains a temporary delay: his daughter will not be burned as a witch if Wynn is turned white by dawn (although Wynn now seems to have no objection to remaining black). Meanwhile, Steele comes across Francks' sister and promptly falls in love with her. He sings about that, and they celebrate by dancing through the woods. Their dance does contain one sweet idea: a rocking phrase in the music is visualized in some scampers over a pair of hillocks (P1).

Q

LOOK TO THE RAINBOW

(REPRISE) (45″)

Eventually the crock is recovered, and the remaining two wishes are used to cure Francks' sister's muteness and to whiten Wynn. The latter event somehow disposes of the charge of witchcraft against Clark, and everyone is happy except that a barn burns down (an event added for the film, presumably to give Coppola a chance to do his barn-burning routine) and Astaire's gold, its wishes spent, is now worthless. The charred survivors celebrate the delayed wedding (Q1).

R

HOW ARE THINGS IN GLOCCA MORRA?

(REPRISE) (1′ 57″)

With his daughter married off and his gold vanished, Astaire concludes, in a quintessential Harburg sentiment, that "things are hopeless, but they're not serious" (R1). He cheerfully bids her and the others good-bye and goes off in quest of another rainbow. The final images in Astaire's last film musical show him frolicking down the road, and far away (R2–4).

A NUMBER CUT FROM THE FILM

S

NECESSITY

The only song written for the Broadway show that is not used in the film version is the philosophically satiric "Necessity." The number was shot (it fell between J and K) and is included on the "soundtrack" recording from the film (sung by Brenda Arnau and chorus), but it was cut when the film was finally released. Perhaps it was felt that the film was too long.

N1 O1 P1 Q1

R1 R2 R3 R4

Tables

Casts and Credits

Notes

References

Index

TABLES

TABLE 1
ASTAIRE AND ROGERS AT RKO

			PRODUCTION COST	GROSS FILM INCOME DOMESTIC	FOREIGN	TOTAL	PROFIT (LOSS)
1931	The Tip-Off	R	159	204	42	246	(15)
	Suicide Fleet	R	373	376	106	482	(75)
1932	Carnival Boat	R	217	224	58	282	(35)
1933	Professional Sweetheart	R	122	225	49	274	50
	Flying Down to Rio	A R	462	923	622	1545	480
	Chance at Heaven	R	150	193	50	243	2
1934	Rafter Romance	R	130	174	63	237	21
	Finishing School	R	156	219	61	280	17
	The Gay Divorcee	A R	520	1077	697	1774	584
1935	Romance in Manhattan	R	289	357	143	500	26
	Roberta	A R	610	1467	868	2335	770
	Star of Midnight	R	280	575	256	831	265
	Top Hat	A R	609	1782	1420	3202	1325
	In Person	R	493	495	219	715	147
1936	Follow the Fleet	A R	747	1532	1175	2707	945
	Swing Time	A R	886	1624	994	2618	830
1937	Shall We Dance	A R	991	1275	893	2168	413
	Stage Door	R	952	1250	512	1762	81
	A Damsel in Distress	A	1035	1010	455	1465	(65)
1938	Vivacious Lady	R	703	830	376	1206	75
	Having Wonderful Time	R	966	771	237	1008	(267)
	Carefree	A R	1253	1113	618	1731	(68)
1939	Star of Midnight (reissue)	R	—	80	—	80	57
	The Story of Vernon and Irene Castle	A R	1196	1120	705	1825	(50)
	Bachelor Mother	R	509	1170	805	1975	827
	Fifth Avenue Girl	R	607	950	420	1370	314
1940	Primrose Path	R	702	898	302	1200	110
	Lucky Partners	R	733	880	510	1390	200
1941	Kitty Foyle	R	738	1710	675	2385	869
	Vivacious Lady (reissue)	R	—	212	60	272	155
	Tom, Dick and Harry	R	806	1223	405	1628	234
1942	Once Upon a Honeymoon	R	1441	1805	720	2525	282
1943	The Sky's the Limit	A	871	1410	775	2185	625
1944	Tender Comrade	R	789	1927	725	2652	843
1946	Heartbeat	R	1560	1650	685	2335	126

Figures represent thousands of dollars
Source: Bender.

TABLE 2
RANK ACHIEVED BY EACH ASTAIRE FILM IN ITS YEAR OF RELEASE, BASED ON GROSS RECEIPTS

RELEASE YEAR	WORLD WIDE	US AND CANADA	
1933	10	11–15	Dancing Lady
1933	15	16–20	Flying Down to Rio
1934	3–5	3–5	The Gay Divorcee
1935	6	6	Roberta
1935	2	2–5	Top Hat
1936	5–8	6–9	Follow the Fleet
1936	6–9	5–8	Swing Time
1937	15	16–20	Shall We Dance
1937	28–30	38–40	A Damsel in Distress
1938	23–25	28–30	Carefree
1939	14–15	17–20	The Story of Vernon and Irene Castle
1940	?	c. 31–40	Broadway Melody of 1940
1941	?	?	Second Chorus
1941	30–34	31–35	You'll Never Get Rich
1942	5	6	Holiday Inn
1942	46–49	48–52	You Were Never Lovelier
1943	c. 48–50	c. 65	The Sky's the Limit
1946	c. 12	16–19	Ziegfeld Follies
1945	c. 50–80	c. 50–80	Yolanda and the Thief
1946	3	3	Blue Skies
1948	1–2	1–2	Easter Parade
1949	10	15	The Barkleys of Broadway
1950	c. 12	12	Three Little Words
1950	c. 17	19–21	Let's Dance
1951	c. 18	18–20	Royal Wedding
1952	c. 84	84–86	The Belle of New York
1953	c. 13	28–29	The Band Wagon
1955	c. 32	40–44	Daddy Long Legs
1957	c. 23–25	33–36	Funny Face
1957	c. 26–30	38–43	Silk Stockings
1959	13–15	15	On the Beach
1961	c. 25	24	The Pleasure of His Company
1962	c. 28–35	31	The Notorious Landlady
1968	?	25–27 or 37	Finian's Rainbow
1969	?	100+	Midas Run
1974	15	15	That's Entertainment
1974	1	1	The Towering Inferno
1976	?	74	That's Entertainment Part 2
1976	?	100+	The Amazing Dobermans
1977	?	100+	The Purple Taxi
1981	?	31–32	Ghost Story

Note: Rankings preceded by "c." (for "circa") are educated guesses; those without that designation are reasonably firm. A question mark denotes an area of complete murkiness. In general, grosses followed a pyramidal structure; that is, a gross ranked 30th is far closer to one ranked 50th than it is to one ranked 10th. Statistics compiled from *Variety* and other sources by James Mark Purcell.

TABLE 3
THE FREED MUSICALS AT MGM

		COST	GROSS
1939	The Wizard of Oz	2,777,000	3,017,000[1]
1939	Babes in Arms	748,000	3,335,000
1940	Strike Up the Band	838,661	3,494,000
1940	Little Nellie Kelly	665,300	2,046,000
1941	Lady Be Good	863,461	1,692,000
1942	Babes on Broadway	940,069	3,859,000
1942	Panama Hattie	1,097,908	4,326,000
1942	†For Me and My Gal	802,981	4,371,000
1943	Cabin in the Sky	662,141	?
1943	†DuBarry Was a Lady	1,239,223	3,496,000
1943	Best Foot Forward	1,125,502	2,704,000
1943	Girl Crazy	1,410,851	3,771,000
1944	Meet Me in St. Louis	1,707,561	7,566,000
1946	*†Ziegfeld Follies	3,240,817	5,344,000+
1946	The Harvey Girls	2,524,315	5,175,000
1945	*Yolanda and the Thief	2,443,322	1,791,000+[2]
1947	Till the Clouds Roll By	2,841,608	6,724,000+
1948	Summer Holiday	2,258,235	1,609,000+[3]
1948	†The Pirate	3,768,496	2,956,000[4]
1947	Good News	1,662,718	2,956,000+
1948	*Easter Parade	2,503,654	6,803,000+
1948	Words and Music	2,799,970	4,552,000+
1949	†Take Me Out to the Ball Game	1,725,971	4,344,000+
1949	*The Barkleys of Broadway	2,325,420	5,421,000+
1949	Any Number Can Play	1,465,641	3,205,000+
1949	†On the Town	2,111,250	4,440,000+
1950	Annie Get Your Gun	3,768,785	8,010,000+[5]
1950	Pagan Love Song	1,906,265	3,205,000+
1951	*Royal Wedding	1,590,920	3,925,000
1951	†An American in Paris	2,723,903	8,005,000+
1951	Show Boat	2,295,429	8,650,000
1952	†Singin' in the Rain	2,540,800	7,665,000
1952	*The Belle of New York	2,606,644	1,993,000
1957	†Invitation to the Dance	1,419,105	615,000
1953	*The Band Wagon	2,169,120	5,655,505+
1954	†Brigadoon	2,352,625	3,385,000
1955	†It's Always Fair Weather	2,062,256	2,485,000
1955	Kismet	2,692,960	2,920,000
1957	*Silk Stockings	1,853,463	4,417,753
1958	Gigi	3,319,335	13,208,725[6]
1960	Bells Are Ringing	2,203,123	3,985,950
1961	Light in the Piazza	553,281	2,345,000

* Astaire film
† Kelly film

[1] Additional grosses: re-release 1948–49 $1,564,000; re-release 1954–55 $465,000
[2] Net loss $1,644,000
[3] Loss $1,460,000
[4] Net loss $2,290,000
[5] Includes 1956–57 re-release
[6] Includes 1966 re-release

Source: Fordin.

TABLE 4
THE CREATION OF THE CEILING DANCE IN ROYAL WEDDING, 1950

(Pre-production rehearsal period: May 1–July 5)
Rehearsal: August 15, 16, 17, 18, 19
Silent photo tests: August 21
Rehearsal: August 25, 28, 29, 31, September 1
Pre-record music and singing: September 5 (morning)
Rehearsal: September 5 (afternoon), 6

Shooting log: September 7

8:00–9:20 Line and light dolly shot: bringing Tom into bedroom—London hotel suite—Stage 26—Rig for light change
SHOT 2 9:20–9:30 Rehearse, check setup
9:30–9:45 Shoot 6 takes (print takes 5 & 6), take 1 good—hold takes 2-3-4: unfinished, light change bad
9:45–9:55 Rehearse director riding boom—set marks for next setup—add more track
9:55–11:20 Line and light dolly & pan for 1st shot of number: lyrics & start into dance
11:20–11:35 Rehearse, check setup
SHOT 3 11:35–11:45 Shoot 5 takes—all unfinished for dance action
11:45–11:53 Reload camera
11:53–12:00 Shoot 3 takes—takes 6 & 7 no good for camera: boom movement bad—take 8 good, hold—Mr. Astaire not too happy
12:00–12:10 Sound reloading
12:10–12:15 Shoot 2 takes—print takes 9 & 10
SHOT 7 12:15–12:20 Rehearse, check setup & marks to shoot tag section of number
12:20–12:25 Shoot 5 takes—print takes 4 & 5—takes 1-2-3 unfinished, dance action
12:25–1:25 LUNCH 1 hr—1/2 hr crew
1:25–2:30 Line & Lite 1st cut of dance routine—meantime strap camera operator into harness
SHOT 4 2:30–2:50 Rehearse, check set & setup—check dance routine
2:50–2:52 Shoot 1 take
2:52–3:28 Unharness camera operator—re-rig harness
3:28–3:30 Shoot 1 take—print takes 1 & 2
3:30–3:40 Changing lens—relines and relight for next cut
3:40–3:50 Check setup—reharness camera operator
SHOT 5 3:50–4:15 Shoot 5 takes—takes 1-2-4-5 all unfinished dance routine, take 3 good—Mr. Astaire wanted another
4:15–4:25 Reload camera
4:25–4:26 Shoot 1 take—print takes 3 & 6
4:26–4:45 Decided not to make final cut in revolving set—but to shoot interior hallway—hotel corridor—instead—Leaving one shot to do in revolving set tomorrow morning—select setup after cleaning out corridor set—NOTE: This decision made due to Mr. Astaire being very tired
SHOT 1 4:45–5:10 Line and light medium full shot: Tom crossing to his room
5:10–5:19 Rehearse, check setup
5:19–5:20 Shoot 1 take (1)
COMPANY DISMISSED 5:20 PM

Shooting log: September 8

8:00–8:30 Line and light last cut of Dream number: interior Tom's bedroom London hotel suite—Revolving set—Stage #26
8:30–9:00 Waiting for Mr. Astaire—due at 9 am
SHOT 6 9:00–9:20 Rehearse & check setup
9:20–9:30 Shoot 2 takes
9:30–9:50 Resting Mr. Astaire & camera operator—reloading camera meantime—also fixing arc which had stopped rotating
9:50–9:52 Shoot 1 take (print takes 1 & 3)—take 2 unfinished dance routine
9:52–10:45 Making stills
10:45 COMPANY DISMISSED

The complete scene and number consists of seven shots (see 25 H and the frame enlargements on p. 329):
1. Astaire crosses the hotel corridor (10″–H 1)
2. he enters the room, turns on the light, and sits in a chair (38″–H 2)
3. he sings the song and begins the dance (1′4″—H 3–5)
4. he dances once around the room and sits down again (1′41″—H 6–12)
5. he rises and begins to scramble around the room a second time until he is lying down on the right wall kicking his feet in the air (28″—H 13–15)
6. he gets up, travels back around the room, and resumes his seat (51″—H 16)
7. he is shown gazing fondly at the picture (5″—H 17)

TABLE 5
HIT SONGS FROM THE ASTAIRE FILMS

SCORE/HIGHEST RANK	
	Dancing Lady (November 30, 1933) Burton Lane–Harold Adamson
70/3	"Everything I Have Is Yours" (January 6, 1934)
	Flying Down to Rio (December 21, 1933) Vincent Youmans–Gus Kahn/Edward Eliscu
42/5	"Flying Down to Rio" (January 20, 1934)
77/3	"Carioca" (January 27, 1934)*
27/5	"Orchids in the Moonlight" (March 3, 1934)
	The Gay Divorcee (November 15, 1934) Con Conrad–Herb Magidson
47/1	"The Continental" (October 13, 1934)*
	Roberta (March 7, 1935) Jerome Kern–Dorothy Fields
74/1	"Lovely to Look At" (February 23, 1935)*
79/1	"I Won't Dance" (March 2, 1935)
	Top Hat (August 29, 1935) Irving Berlin
88/1	"Cheek to Cheek" (September 7, 1935)*
4/7	"No Strings" (September 21, 1935)
1/10	"The Piccolino" (September 21, 1935)
22/2	"Top Hat, White Tie and Tails" (October 5, 1935)
39/4	"Isn't This a Lovely Day" (September 28, 1935)
	Follow the Fleet (February 20, 1936) Irving Berlin
56/2	"I'm Putting All My Eggs in One Basket" (March 14, 1936)
44/3	"Let Yourself Go" (March 14, 1936)
27/3	"Let's Face the Music and Dance" (March 14, 1936)
	Swing Time (August 27, 1936) Jerome Kern–Dorothy Fields
98/1	"The Way You Look Tonight" (October 3, 1936)*
39/3	"A Fine Romance" (October 3, 1936)
	Shall We Dance (May 13, 1937) George and Ira Gershwin
20/6	"They Can't Take That Away From Me" (June 5, 1937)*
4/7	"Let's Call the Whole Thing Off" (June 5, 1937)
	A Damsel in Distress (November 24, 1937) George and Ira Gershwin
47/3	"Nice Work If You Can Get It" (November 27, 1937)

Derived from Brooks, who lists the top ten hit songs for each week. To calculate a hit's score, each 10 ranking is given 1 point, each 9 ranking 2, and so forth. (This is a severe test of a hit; a song could do very well and be considered a hit without ever entering the top ten.) The song's highest ranking and the date it first entered the charts are also indicated, as is the date of the New York premiere for each film.

SCORE/HIGHEST RANK	
	Carefree (September 22, 1938) Irving Berlin
69/1	"Change Partners" (October 1, 1938)*
	Broadway Melody of 1940 (March 28, 1940) Cole Porter
12/6	"I've Got My Eyes on You" (March 2, 1940)
	Holiday Inn (August 4, 1942) Irving Berlin
83/2	"Be Careful, It's My Heart" (July 25, 1942)
129/1	"White Christmas" (October 17, 1942)*
	You Were Never Lovelier (December 4, 1942) Jerome Kern–Johnny Mercer
64/3	"Dearly Beloved" (October 24, 1942)*
	The Sky's the Limit (September 2, 1943) Harold Arlen–Johnny Mercer
4/8	"My Shining Hour" (January 22, 1944)*
	Blue Skies (October 16, 1946) Irving Berlin
60/3	"You Keep Coming Back Like a Song" (October 12, 1946)*
	Easter Parade (June 30, 1948) Irving Berlin
13/6	"It Only Happens When I Dance with You" (September 4, 1948)
	The Barkleys of Broadway (May 4, 1949) Harry Warren–Ira Gershwin
2/9	"My One and Only Highland Fling" (July 9, 1949)
	Three Little Words (August 9, 1950) Harry Ruby–Bert Kalmar
98/1	"Nevertheless" (October 7, 1950)
66/2	"Thinking of You" (October 14, 1950)
	Daddy Long Legs (May 5, 1955) Johnny Mercer
70/1	"Something's Gotta Give" (June 18, 1955)*
	SPECIAL MENTION
	Fred Astaire–Johnny Mercer
15/4	"I'm Building Up to an Awful Let-Down" (February 15, 1936)

* Nominated for Academy Award for best song. Also nominated: "Love of My Life" *(Second Chorus)*, "Since I Kissed My Baby Goodbye" *(You'll Never Get Rich)*, "Too Late Now" *(Royal Wedding)*. The winners: "The Continental," "The Way You Look Tonight," and "White Christmas."

TABLE 6
SHOTS IN THE ASTAIRE-ROGERS "CARIOCA" DUET (2 C)

(Duration of dance: 90 seconds)

Shot

1. Medium shot: Astaire asks Rogers to dance (C 2)
2. Full-figure shot: Astaire and Rogers enter dance floor

The dance

3. Full-figure shot of the two dancing—dance begins (C 3–4)
4. Long shot of entire floor, shot framed by members of audience (C 5–6)
5. Same as 3 (full-figure shot) (C 7)
6. Reaction shot of members of audience (C 8)
7. Same as 4 (long shot, framed) (C 9)
8. Same as 3 (full-figure shot) (C10)
9. Medium shot of dancers—top two-thirds of body (C 11)
10. Same as 3 (full-figure shot) (C 12)
11. Reaction shot of members of audience (C 13)
12. Same as 3 (full-figure shot)—dancers bump heads (C 14)
13. Same as 4 (long shot, framed)—audience is seen to laugh (C 15)
14. Same as 3 (full-figure shot)—dance ends (C 16)
15. Immediate cut to applauding audience (C 17)

TABLE 7
MUSICAL PROPORTIONS IN THE ASTAIRE FILMS

PERCENTAGE OF THE FILM GIVEN OVER TO:			
MUSICAL NUMBERS	NUMBERS THAT INCLUDE DANCE	NUMBERS THAT INCLUDE ASTAIRE	
20	17	7	Dancing Lady 94 min.
32	28	28	Flying Down to Rio 89 min.
31	30	25	The Gay Divorcee 107 min.
37	26	28	Roberta 105 min.
26	26	26	Top Hat 99 min.
30	22	24	Follow the Fleet 110 min.
25	20	25	Swing Time 105 min.
29	26	28	Shall We Dance 116 min.
30	20	27	A Damsel in Distress 98 min.
19	17	19	Carefree 80 min.
24	20	22	The Story of Vernon and Irene Castle 93 min.
38	36	27	Broadway Melody of 1940 102 min.
27	10	21	Second Chorus 83 min.
24	22	24	You'll Never Get Rich 88 min.
37	21	21	Holiday Inn 101 min.

PERCENTAGE OF THE FILM GIVEN OVER TO:			
MUSICAL NUMBERS	NUMBERS THAT INCLUDE DANCE	NUMBERS THAT INCLUDE ASTAIRE	
25	14	18	You Were Never Lovelier 97 min.
17	13	14	The Sky's the Limit 89 min.
62	54	37	Ziegfeld Follies 110 min.
26	22	22	Yolanda and the Thief 108 min.
43	22	19	Blue Skies 104 min.
46	38	30	Easter Parade 103 min.
35	25	27	The Barkleys of Broadway 109 min.
32	18	19	Three Little Words 102 min.
23	21	21	Let's Dance 112 min.
41	33	33	Royal Wedding 93 min.
46	41	35	The Belle of New York 82 min.
33	31	28	The Band Wagon 112 min.
29	26	26	Daddy Long Legs 126 min.
38	26	24	Funny Face 103 min.
36	30	21	Silk Stockings 117 min.
35	22	9	Finian's Rainbow 145 min.

CASTS AND CREDITS

The information given here includes some people who were uncredited in the actual film titles. The credits have often been reworded for consistency, so people who performed the same function in different films are presented in the same way; however, the main choreographic credit is given exactly as it appears in the film titles. In the cast lists, all speaking parts—and a few notable nonspeaking parts—are listed, arranged in order of appearance; "n.k." (for "not known") indicates a player who could not be identified.

1. DANCING LADY

Metro-Goldwyn-Mayer, 94 minutes; New York premiere November 30, 1933, Capitol Theatre and Loew's Metropolitan (Copyright November 27, 1933)

Producer David O. Selznick *Associate producer* John W. Considine, Jr. *Director* Robert Z. Leonard "Musical Ensembles Directed by Sammy Lee and Eddie Prinz" *Songs* music by Burton Lane, lyrics by Harold Adamson ("That's the Rhythm of the Day": music by Richard Rodgers, lyric by Lorenz Hart; "My Dancing Lady": music by Jimmy McHugh, lyric by Dorothy Fields; "Hold Your Man": music by Nacio Herb Brown, lyric by Arthur Freed) *Musical director and conductor* Louis Silvers *Arrangements* Maurice de Packh, Wayne Allen *Additional arrangements* Jack Virgil, Charles Maxwell, Paul Marquardt *Screenplay* Allen Rivkin and P. J. Wolfson (from the novel by James Warner Bellah) *Director of photography* Oliver T. Marsh *Special effects* Slavko Vorkapich *Recording* Douglas Shearer *Art director* Merrill Pye *Set decoration* Edwin B. Willis *Gowns* Adrian *Editor* Margaret Booth

Barker at burlesque house Jack Baxley *Blonde with Tone* n.k. *Tod Newton* Franchot Tone *Man with Tone* Pat Somerset *Mr. Farnsworth* n.k. *Woman with Tone* n.k. *Man in audience* Charles Williams *Rosette La Rue* Winnie Lightner *Janie Barlow* Joan Crawford *Policeman* Frank Hagney *Court orderly* n.k. *Judge* Ferdinand Gottschalk *Policeman at court* n.k. *Woman jail attendant* n.k. *Man at slot machine* n.k. *Actress with Southern accent* Eve Arden (Eunice Quedens) *Her agent* Matt McHugh *Steve (Gable's assistant)* Ted Healy *Patch Gallegher* Clark Gable *The Three Stooges* Moe Howard, Jerry Howard, Larry Fine *Vivian Warner* Gloria Foy *Jasper Bradley, Sr.* Grant Mitchell *Miss Allen (Bradley's secretary)* Cecil Cunningham *Junior Bradley* Maynard Holmes *Stagehand* n.k. *Ward King* Robert Benchley *Singer at party* Art Jarrett *Grandma* May Robson *Grace Newton* Florine McKinney *Chorus girls* Shirley Aranson, Bonita Barker, Katherine Barnes, Dalie Dean, Marion Weldon *Show authors* Harry C. Bradley, John Sheehan *Pinky (another author)* Sterling Holloway *Babe (blond chorus girl)* Lynn Bari(?) *Fred Astaire* Fred Astaire *Rehearsal coach* n.k. *Man at club* n.k. *Proprietor of club* Charles C. Wilson *Singer in "That's the Rhythm of the Day"* Nelson Eddy

2. FLYING DOWN TO RIO

RKO Radio Pictures, 89 minutes; New York premiere December 21, 1933, Radio City Music Hall (Copyright December 29, 1933)

Associate producer Lou Brock *Executive producer* Merian C. Cooper *Director* Thornton Freeland "Dance director Dave Gould" *Assistant dance director* Hermes Pan *Songs* music by Vincent Youmans, lyrics by Edward Eliscu and Gus Kahn *Musical director and conductor* Max Steiner *Arrangements* Eddie Sharpe, Bernhard Kaun, R. H. Bassett, and others *Screenplay* Cyril Hume, H. W. Hanemann, Erwin Gelsey (from the play by Anne Caldwell, based upon an original story by Lou Brock) *Director of photography* J. Roy Hunt *Special effects* Vernon Walker *Art directors* Van Nest Polglase, Carroll Clark *Costumes* Walter Plunkett *Editor* Jack Kitchin *Recording* P. J. Faulkner, Jr. *Sound editor* George Marsh *Associate director* George Nicholls, Jr.

Hotel manager (Mr. Hammerstein) Franklin Pangborn *Assistant hotel manager (Mr. Butterbass)* Eric Blore *Honey Hale* Ginger Rogers *Fred Ayres* Fred Astaire *Roger Bond* Gene Raymond *Plane mechanic* Harry Bowen *Del Rio's aunt (Titia)* Blanche Frederici *Belinha de Rezende* Dolores Del Rio *Women at table* Betty Furness, Lucile Browne, Mary Kornman *Waiter* Francisco Maran *Bus boy* n.k. *Maid* Alice Ardell *Orchid seller* n.k. *Members of Yankee Clippers band* Eddie Borden, Jack Rice, Ray Cooke, Howard Wilson, Eddie Tamblyn, Jack Good *Airplane mechanic* Eddie Boland *Rodriguez (Del Rio's aunt's chauffeur)* Sidney Bracy *Haitian golfer* Clarence Muse *Julio Rubeiro* Raul Roulien *Carioca Casino manager* Luis Alberni *The Turunas (Carioca Casino orchestra)* The Brazilian Turunas *Leader of the Turunas* n.k. *Carioca Casino patrons* n.k. *First Carioca singer* Alice Gentle(?) *Second Carioca singer* Movita Castaneda *Third Carioca singer* Etta Moten *Black dancing couple in "The Carioca"* n.k. *Billboard workers* Julian Rivero, Pedro Regas *Banker in Rio (Alfredo Vianna)* Reginald Barlow *The Greeks* Roy D'Arcy, Maurice Black, Armand Kaliz *Del Rio's father* Walter Walker *Brazilian policemen* n.k. *Police official (Toranta)* n.k. *Chorus girls* n.k. *Messenger* Gino Corrado *Hotel Atlantico manager* Adrian Rosley *Bellhop* n.k. *Pilot-messenger* n.k. *Mayor of Rio* Paul Porcasi *Pilot of airliner* Wallace MacDonald

3. THE GAY DIVORCEE

RKO Radio Pictures, 107 minutes; New York premiere November 15, 1934, Radio City Music Hall (Copyright October 11, 1934)

Producer Pandro S. Berman *Director* Mark Sandrich "Dance Ensembles Staged by Dave Gould" *Assistant Dance Director* Hermes Pan *Songs* "Night and Day": music and lyrics by Cole Porter; "The Continental" and "A Needle in a Haystack": music by Con Conrad, lyric by Herb Magidson; "Don't Let It Bother You" and "Let's K-nock K-neez": music by Harry Revel, lyrics by Mack Gordon *Musical director and conductor* Max Steiner *Orchestrations* Clifford Vaughan, Maurice de Packh, Bernhard Kaun, Howard Jackson, Eddie Sharpe, Gene Rose *Screenplay* George Marion, Jr., Dorothy Yost, Edward Kaufman (from the stage musical *Gay Divorce*, book by Dwight Taylor, musical adaptation by Kenneth Webb and Samuel Hoffenstein) *Director of photography* David Abel *Special effects* Vernon Walker *Assistant director* Argyle Nelson *Production associate* Zion Myers *Art directors* Van Nest Polglase, Carroll Clark *Costumes* Walter Plunkett *Sound recording* Hugh McDowell, Jr. *Music recording* Murray Spivak, P. J. Faulkner, Jr. *Finger doll chorus dance* Frank Warde *Editor* William Hamilton *Sound editor* George Marsh

Singer in "Don't Let It Bother You" n.k. *Egbert Fitzgerald* Edward Everett Horton *Guy Holden* Fred Astaire *French waiters* George Davis, Alphonse Martell *Proprietor of French nightclub* Paul Porcasi *Messenger at docks* Little Charlie Hall *Customs official* Cyril Thornton *Chief customs inspector* E. E. Clive *Hortense Ditherwell* Alice Brady *Custom official* n.k. *Mimi Glossop* Ginger Rogers *Porter* n.k. *Delivery boy at London hotel* n.k. *Astaire's valet* Charles Coleman *English car driver* n.k. *Horton's secretary* n.k. *Singer in "Let's K-nock K-neez"* Betty Grable *Waiter at seaside hotel* Eric Blore *Rodolfo Tonetti (co-respondent)* Erik Rhodes *Woman at hotel* n.k. *Singer in "The Continental"* Lillian Miles *Cyril Glossop (Rogers' husband)* William Austin

4. ROBERTA

RKO Radio Pictures, 105 minutes; New York premiere March 7, 1935, Radio City Music Hall (Copyright February 26, 1935)

Producer Pandro S. Berman *Director* William A. Seiter "Dances Arranged by Fred Astaire" "Assistant Dance Director Hermes Pan" *Songs* music by Jerome Kern; "Let's Begin": lyric by Otto Harbach, revised by Dorothy Fields; "I'll Be Hard to Handle": lyric by Bernard Dougal, rewritten by Dorothy Fields; "Yesterdays" and "Smoke Gets In Your Eyes": lyrics by Otto Harbach; "I Won't Dance": lyric by Dorothy Fields, after the original by Oscar Hammerstein II; "Lovely to Look At": lyric by Dorothy Fields *Additional music* "Indiana" by James F. Hanley and Ballard MacDonald *Musical director and conductor* Max Steiner *Orchestrations* Gene Rose, Wayne Allen, and others *Screenplay* Jane Murfin, Sam Mintz, Allan Scott (from the stage play, book by Otto Harbach, based upon the novel *Gowns by Roberta* by Alice Duer Miller) *Additional dialogue* Glenn Tryon *Director of photography* Edward Cronjager *Art director* Van Nest Polglase *Associate art director* Carroll Clark *Set decoration* Thomas K. Little *Gowns* Bernard Newman *Editor* William Hamilton *Sound recording* John Tribby *Music recording* P. J. Faulkner, Jr. *Sound editor* George Marsh *Production associate* Zion Myers

Candy (trick-voice comedian) Johnny (Candy) Candido *Voyda (proprietor of Cafe Russe)* Luis Alberni *Ship's officer* William B. Davidson *Huck Haines* Fred Astaire *John Kent* Randolph Scott *Other Wabash Indianians* Hal Borne, William Carey, Phil Cuthbert, Delmon Davis, Ivan Dow, William Dunn, Howard Lally, Muzzy Marcellino, Paul McLarind, Charles Sharpe, Gene Sheldon *Ladislaw (doorman)* Victor Varconi *Stephanie* Irene Dunne *Aunt Minnie (Roberta)* Helen Westley *Lord Henry Delves* Ferdinand Munier *Lizzie Gatz/Countess Scharwenka* Ginger Rogers *Maid at Roberta's* Bodil Rosing *Waiter at Cafe Russe* Michael Visaroff *French teacher* Adrian Rosley *Mrs. Teale* Mary Forbes *Sophie Teale* Claire Dodd *Dressmaker (female)* n.k. *Yvonne* n.k. *Leonne (model)* Jane Hamilton *Albert (chief dressmaker)* Torben Meyer *Newspaper reporter* Grace Hayle *Anna (saleslady at Roberta's)* n.k. *Bartender at Cafe Russe* n.k. *Cossacks in Cafe Russe* Mike Tellegen, Sam Savitsky *Mannequins* Lucille Ball, Virginia Carroll, Diane Cook, Lorraine DeSart, Betty Dumbries, Maxine Jennings, Lorna Low, Margaret McChrystal, Wanda Perry, Virginia Reid (Lynne Carver), Donna Roberts, Kay Sutton

5. TOP HAT

RKO Radio Pictures, 99 minutes; New York premiere August 29, 1935, Radio City Music Hall (Copyright August 29, 1935)

Producer Pandro S. Berman *Director* Mark Sandrich "Ensembles staged by Hermes Pan" *Songs* Music and lyrics by Irving Berlin *Musical director and conductor* Max Steiner *Orchestrations and arrangements* Edward Powell, Maurice de Packh, Gene Rose, Eddie Sharpe, Arthur Knowlton *Screenplay* Dwight Taylor, Allan Scott (based upon an original story by Dwight Taylor) *Director of photography* David Abel *Special effects* Vernon Walker *Art director* Van Nest Polglase *Associate art director* Carroll Clark *Set decoration* Thomas Little *Gowns* Bernard Newman *Editor* William Hamilton *Sound recording* Hugh McDowell *Music recording* P. J. Faulkner, Jr. *Sound editor* George Marsh

Thackeray Club waiter Tom Ricketts *Jerry Travers* Fred Astaire *Horace Hardwick* Edward Everett Horton *Thackeray Club desk clerk* n.k. *Bates (Horton's valet)* Eric Blore *Dale Tremont* Ginger Rogers *London hotel manager* Edgar Norton *Flower shop salesman* Leonard Mudie *Flower shop assistant* Lucille Ball *London hotel desk clerk* Robert Adair *Alberto Beddini* Erik Rhodes *Telegram delivery boy* n.k. *London hotel doorman* n.k. *London hotel maid* n.k. *Astaire's valet (George)* n.k. *Callboy at London theatre* Peter Hobbes *Madge Hardwick* Helen Broderick *Waiter at Lido* n.k. *Venice hotel manager* Gino Corrado *Waiter with steak* Frank Mills *Venice hotel maid* n.k. *Waiter at festival* Tom Costello(?) *Venetian fisherman* Genaro Spagnoli

6. FOLLOW THE FLEET

RKO Radio Pictures, 110 minutes; New York premiere February 20, 1936, Radio City Music Hall (Copyright February 20, 1936)

Producer Pandro S. Berman *Director* Mark Sandrich "Ensembles Staged by Hermes Pan" *Songs* music and lyrics by Irving Berlin *Musical director and conductor* Max Steiner *Additional music* "Let's Face the Music and Dance": adapted by Max Steiner, orchestrated by Maurice de Packh *Arrangements* Gene Rose *Additional arrangements* Maurice de Packh, Clarence Wheeler, Walter Scharf, Roy Webb *Screenplay* Dwight Taylor, Allan Scott (based upon the play *Shore Leave* by Hubert Osborne) *Director of photography* David Abel *Special effects* Vernon Walker *Art director* Van Nest Polglase *Associate art director* Carroll Clark *Set decoration* Hugh McDowell, Jr. *Gowns* Bernard Newman *Editor* Henry M. Berman *Music recording* P. J. Faulkner, Jr. *Sound editor* George Marsh *Technical adviser* Commander Harvey S. Haislip, U.S.N., Retired

Bake Baker Fred Astaire *Bilge Smith* Randolph Scott *Sailor* n.k. *Sailor* Frank Jenks *Dopey Williams* Ray Mayer *Ship announcer* n.k. *Coxswain* Bud Geary *Ticket seller at ballroom* Constance Bergen *Connie Martin* Harriet Hilliard *Ticket taker at ballroom* n.k. *Other sailors* Tony Martin, Edward Burns, Frank Mills, Frank Sully, Billy Dooley, Eddie Tamblyn *Waiter at ballroom* James Pierce *Sherry Martin* Ginger Rogers *Kitty Collins* Lucille Ball *Singing trio in "Let Yourself Go"* Joy Hodges, Betty Grable, Jeanne Gray *Waitress at ballroom* Jane Hamilton *Ballroom emcee* n.k. *Chief competitors in dance contest* Dorothy Fleisman, Bob Cromer *Proprietor of ballroom (Mr. Weber)* Herbert Rawlinson *Iris Manning* Astrid Allwyn *Policeman* Thomas Brower *Ship deck officers* n.k. *Astaire's partner in dancing lesson* Frank Moran *Marines on ship* n.k. *Captain Hickey* Harry Beresford *Captain Jones* Frederick Blanchard *English woman* Doris Lloyd *English officer* Huntley Gordon *Ensign Gilbert* William Smith *Telephone girl in Nolan's office* Kay Sutton *Jim Nolan* Russell Hicks *Office boy* Allen Wood *Hicks' assistant (Sullivan)* Brooks Benedict *Man at party* n.k. *Naval officer (Lt. Williams)* Addison (Jack) Randall *Butler at party* Eric Wilton *Marine* Max Wagner *Executive officer* Commander Harvey S. Haislip(?) *Deck officer* George Lollier *Quartermaster* George Magrill *Women at gambling table in "Let's Face the Music and Dance" number* Jane Hamilton, Lucille Ball, Maxine Jennings, Lita Chevret

7. SWING TIME

RKO Radio Pictures, 105 minutes; New York premiere August 27, 1936, Radio City Music Hall (Copyright September 27, 1936)

Producer Pandro S. Berman *Director* George Stevens "Dance director: Hermes Pan" *Songs* music by Jerome Kern, lyrics by Dorothy Fields *Additional music* Robert Russell Bennett, Hal Borne *Musical director and conductor* Nathaniel Shilkret *Orchestrations* Robert Russell Bennett *Screenplay* Howard Lindsay and Allan Scott (from the story "Portrait of John Garnett" by Erwin Gelsey) *Additional scriptwriting* Dorothy Yost *Director of photography* David Abel *Special effects* Vernon Walker *Art director* Van Nest Polglase *Associate art director* Carroll Clark *Silver Sandal set and "Bojangles" costumes* John Harkrider *Set decoration* Darrell Silvera *Gowns* Bernard Newman *Editor* Henry Berman *Recording* Hugh McDowell, Jr. *Sound editor* George Marsh *Assistant directors* Argyle Nelson, Syd Fogel

Dr. Edward Cardetti ("Pop") Victor Moore *Stagehand* Harry Bowen *John Garnett ("Lucky")* Fred Astaire *Red* Frank Jenks *Other dancers in Astaire's show* Bill Brand, Frank Edmunds, Jack Good, Donald Kerr, Ted O'Shea *Margaret Watson (Astaire's fiancée)* Betty Furness *Judge Watson (Furness' father)* Landers Stevens *Stagehand* Harry Bernard *Man at wedding* Jack Rice *Minister* Howard Hickman *Tailor (Schmidt)* Abe Reynolds *Maid at Furness house* Fern Emmett *Train conductor* n.k. *Railroad ticket seller* Frank Hammond *Man in N.Y. street* Tom Curran(?) *Penny Carrol* Ginger Rogers *Policeman on N.Y. street* Edgar Dearing *Mr. Gordon (proprietor of dance academy)* Eric Blore *Mabel Anderson (Rogers' friend)* Helen Broderick *Cab driver* Little Charles Hall *Hotel desk clerk* Ralph Byrd *Eric Facannistrom (drunk)* Gerald Hamer *Ricardo Romero* Georges Metaxa *Announcer at Silver Sandal* Joey Ray *Al Simpson (owner of Silver Sandal)* Pierre Watkin *Dice Raymond* John Harrington *Roulette dealer (Tony)* Jean Perry *Raymond's boys* Olin Francis *(Muggsy)*, Frank Mills *(croupier)*, Bob O'Conor *Porter in Furness' room* n.k. *Metaxa's valet* Floyd Shackleford *Minister at Rogers' wedding* Ferdinand Munier

8. SHALL WE DANCE

RKO Radio Pictures, 116 minutes; New York premiere May 13, 1937, Radio City Music Hall (Copyright May 7, 1937)

Producer Pandro S. Berman *Director* Mark Sandrich "Ballet staged by Hermes Pan and Harry Losee" *Songs* music by George Gershwin, lyrics by Ira Gershwin *Additional music* George Gershwin *Musical director and conductor* Nathaniel Shilkret *Arrangements and orchestrations* Nathaniel Shilkret *Additional arrangements* Robert Russell Bennett *Screenplay* Allan Scott, Ernest Pagano (based upon a story by Lee Loeb and Harold Buchman, adapted by P. J. Wolfson) *Director of photography* David Abel *Special effects* Vernon Walker *Art director* Van Nest Polglase *Associate art director* Carroll Clark *Set decoration* Darrell Silvera *Ginger Rogers' gowns* Irene *Editor* William Hamilton *Recording* Hugh McDowell, Jr.

Jeffrey Baird Edward Everett Horton *Delivery boy* n.k. *Doorman* n.k. *Ballet masters* Marek Windheim, Rolfe Sedan *Peter P. Peters (Petrov)* Fred Astaire *Linda Keene* Ginger Rogers *Rogers' rhumba partner* Pete Theodore *Rogers' show manager* n.k. *Rogers' maid (Tai)* Emma Young *Arthur Miller (Rogers' manager)* Jerome Cowan *Denise (Lady Tarrington)* Ketti Gallian *Ship announcer* n.k. *Newspaper photographers* n.k. *English steward* Douglas Gordon *Singer in "Slap That Bass"* Dudley Dickerson *Ship's waiter* Leonard Mudie *Radio officer* Henry Mowbray *Purser* n.k. *Bar stewards* n.k. *Mrs. Fitzgerald* Ann Shoemaker *Other passenger* Helena Grant *Dispatcher* Sam Hayes *Ship steward* George Magrill *Cecil Flintridge* Eric Blore *Jim Montgomery (Rogers' fiancé)* William Brisbane *Rooftop headwaiter* n.k. *Rooftop band leader* Ben Alexander *Charlie* Sam Wren *Newsboy* Sherwood Bailey *Policeman in Central Park* Charles Coleman *Justice of the Peace* William Burress *Hotel desk clerk* Jack Rice *Hotel carpenter* Harry Bowen *Flower seller on ferry* Tiny (Elizabeth) Jones *Bellhop* n.k. *Process server* Frank Moran *Police officer in jail* n.k. *Ballet soloist in "Shall We Dance"* Harriet Hoctor *Rogers' attorney* Richard Tucker

9. A DAMSEL IN DISTRESS

RKO Radio Pictures, 98 minutes; New York premiere November 24, 1937, Rivoli Theatre (Copyright November 19, 1937)

Producer Pandro S. Berman *Director* George Stevens "Dance Director Hermes Pan" *Songs* music by George Gershwin, lyrics by Ira Gershwin *Additional music* aria by Friedrich von Flotow *Musical director and conductor* Victor Baravalle *Arrangements and orchestrations* Robert Russell Bennett *Additional arrangements* Ray Noble, George Bassman *Screenplay* P. G. Wodehouse, Ernest Pagano, S. K. Lauren (from the novel by P. G. Wodehouse and the play by P. G. Wodehouse and Ian Hay) *Director of photography* Joseph H. August *Special effects* Vernon Walker *Art director* Van Nest Polglase *Associate art director* Carroll Clark *Set decoration* Darrell Silvera *Editor* Henry Berman *Recording* Earl A. Wolcott *Assistant director* Argyle Nelson

Butler (Keggs) Reginald Gardiner (singing dubbed by Mario Berini) *Page (Albert)* Harry Watson *Footman (Thomas)* John Blood(?) *Cook* Mary Gordon *Maid* Violet Seton(?) *George Burns* George Burns *Gracie Allen* Gracie Allen *Jerry Halliday* Fred Astaire *Lady Alyce Marshmorton* Joan Fontaine *Woman in street* n.k. *English bobby* Frank Moran *Cockney street dancer* Joe Niemeyer *Man in street* n.k. *Lord John Marshmorton* Montagu Love *Reggie* Ray Noble *Lady Caroline Marshmorton* Constance Collier *Footman (Henry)* Clive Moran(?) *Madrigal singers* Pearl Amatore, Betty Rone, Jac George, and others *Barker at carnival* Charles Bennett *Drunks in fun house* Jack Walklin, James Clemens, Kenneth Terrell, James Fawcett *Female singing trio in "Nice Work If You Can Get It"* Betty Rone, Jan Duggan, Mary Dean

10. CAREFREE

RKO Radio Pictures, 80 minutes; New York premiere September 22, 1938, Radio City Music Hall (Copyright September 2, 1938)

Producer Pandro S. Berman *Director* Mark Sandrich "Ensembles staged by Hermes Pan" *Songs* music and lyrics by Irving Berlin *Musical director* Victor Baravalle *Arrangements* Robert Russell Bennett, Conrad Salinger, Gene Rose *Orchestrations* Robert Russell Bennett, Leonid

Raab, Conrad Salinger, Max Reese *Screenplay* Allan Scott, Ernest Pagano (story and adaptation by Dudley Nichols and Hagar Wilde, based upon an original idea by Marian Ainslee and Guy Endore) *Director of photography* Robert de Grasse *Special effects* Vernon Walker *Art director* Van Nest Polglase *Associate art director* Carroll Clark *Set decoration* Darrell Silvera *Ginger Rogers' gowns* Howard Greer *Wardrobe* Edward Stevenson *Editor* William Hamilton *Recording* Hugh McDowell, Jr. *Assistant director* Argyle Nelson

Stephen Arden Ralph Bellamy *Doorman* Charles Coleman *Elevator operator* Jack Arnold (Vinton Haworth) *Connors* Jack Carson *Tony Flagg* Fred Astaire *Dr. Powers* Walter Kingsford *Amanda Cooper* Ginger Rogers *Skeet judge (Roland Hunter)* Franklin Pangborn *Judge Travers* Clarence Kolb *Aunt Cora* Luella Gear *Golf pro (MacPherson)* James Finlayson *Headwaiter at club* Richard Lane *Waiter* Ray Hendricks *Rogers' maid* Hattie McDaniel *Astaire's secretary (Miss Adams)* Kay Sutton *Elevator starter* Paul Guilfoyle *Truck driver* James Burtis *Policeman* Edward Gargan *Radio announcer (Harrison)* Harold Minjur *Sponsor* Harry Bailey *Band leader* n.k. *Cab driver* Frank Moran

11. THE STORY OF VERNON AND IRENE CASTLE

RKO Radio Pictures, 93 minutes; New York premiere March 30, 1939, Radio City Music Hall (Copyright March 30, 1939)

Producer George C. Haight *Executive producer* Pandro S. Berman *Director* H. C. Potter "Dance Director Hermes Pan" *Songs* "Only When You're in My Arms": music by Con Conrad, lyric by Bert Kalmar and Herman Ruby; other songs from various composers and lyricists (see text) *Musical director* Victor Baravalle *Arrangements* Robert Russell Bennett *Additional arrangements* Edward Powell, Hugo Friedhofer, Roy Webb, David Raksin, Leonid Raab *Screenplay* Richard Sherman (based upon the book *My Husband* and the magazine series "My Memories of Vernon Castle" by Irene Castle, adaptation by Oscar Hammerstein II and Dorothy Yost) *Director of photography* Robert de Grasse *Special effects* Vernon Walker *Art director* Van Nest Polglase *Associate art director* Perry Ferguson *Set decoration* Darrell Silvera *Ginger Rogers' costumes* Irene Castle *Wardrobe and ensembles* Walter Plunkett *Editor* William Hamilton *Montage sequence* Douglas Travers *Recording* Richard Van Hessen *Assistant director* Argyle Nelson *Technical adviser* Irene Castle

Streetcar conductor Fred Sweeney *Vernon Castle* Fred Astaire *Flower delivery boy* James Adamson(?) *Lew Fields* Lew Fields *Claire Ford* Frances Mercer *Stagehand* n.k. *Singing quartet at beach* n.k. *Messenger at beach* Allen Wood *Irene Foote Castle* Ginger Rogers *Walter Ash* Walter Brennan *Mrs. Annie Foote* Janet Beecher *Dr. Hubert Foote* Robert Strange *Plump tap dancer* Sonny Lamont *Train conductor* Dick Elliott *Rogers' girlfriends* Marjorie Bell (Marge Champion), Eleanor Hansen, Ethyl Haworth, Mary Brodel *Man in "Hen Pecks" skit* n.k. *Man in audience* Hal K. Dawson *Emile Aubel* Rolfe Sedan *Papa Aubel* Etienne Girardot *French cab driver* Jacques Lory *French landlady* Adrienne d'Ambricourt *Maggie Sutton* Edna May Oliver *Lady Bolton* Elspeth Dudgeon(?) *French painter* Leonid Kinskey *French singer* Louis Mercier (singing dubbed by Jean Sablon) *Louis Barraya (cafe owner)* Clarence Derwent *Russian nobleman* Victor Varconi *Lady in revolving door* Tiny (Elizabeth) Jones *Elderly man in montage* Jack Richardson(?) *Elderly woman in montage* n.k. *Newsboys at train* Wesley Giraud, Joe Polosci *Stage managers at benefit* Don Brodie, Frank Mills *Dresser at benefit* Armand Cortez(?) *Drag dancer in "Who's Your Lady Friend?"* Emmett O'Brien *Frank* n.k. *Announcer* Tom Chatterton *Soldiers* n.k. *Recruiting officer* Milton Owen *Airman assistant* n.k. *Commanding officer* n.k. *French man in hotel* Max Luckey *Officer in hotel* n.k. *French woman in hotel* n.k. *Movie director* Bruce Mitchell *Actor* Roy D'Arcy *Fort Worth hotel manager* Donald MacBride *Military messenger* n.k. *Student pilot* Douglas Walton *Mechanic* Lynton Brent *Colonel* Russell Hicks *Colonel's aide* George Irving

12. BROADWAY MELODY OF 1940

Metro-Goldwyn-Mayer, 102 minutes; New York premiere March 28, 1940, Capitol Theatre (Copyright February 9, 1940)

Producer Jack Cummings *Director* Norman Taurog "Dances Bobby Connolly" *Additional choreography* Albertina Rasch *Songs* music and lyrics by Cole Porter *Additional music* Walter Ruick, Roger Edens *Musical direction* Alfred Newman *Arrangements* Roger Edens *Vocal arrangements and orchestrations* Edward Powell, Leo Arnaud, Charles Henderson *Additional arrangements* George Bassman, Murray Cutter, Wally Heglin *Screenplay* Leon Gordon and George Oppenheimer (based upon an original story by Jack McGowan and Dore Schary) *Additional scriptwriting* Preston Sturges, Albert Mannheimer, Walter DeLeon, Eddie Moran, Thomas Phipps, Vincent Lawrence, Sid Silvers *Directors of photography* Oliver T. Marsh, Joseph Ruttenberg *Art director* Cedric Gibbons *Associate art director* John S. Detlie *Art director for musical numbers* Merrill Pye *Set decoration* Edwin B. Willis *Gowns* Adrian *Men's costumes* Valles *Editor* Blanche Sewell *Recording* Douglas Shearer

Man selling bus-tour tickets n.k. *Johnny Brett* Fred Astaire *Dawnland barker* n.k. *Bride (Miss Martin)* Gladys Blake *Groom (Mr. Jones)* George Chandler *Dawnland manager* Joseph Crehan *King Shaw* George Murphy *Bob Casey* Frank Morgan *Pearl de Longe (Morgan's girlfriend)* Ann Morriss *Dawnland worker* James Flavin *Sailor at Dawnland* Chic Collins *Theatre ticket-taker (George)* Jack Mulhall *Clare Bennett* Eleanor Powell *Man with hat in theatre audience* n.k. *Bert Matthews (Morgan's partner)* Ian Hunter *Morgan's chauffeur* Hal LeSeuer *Morgan's secretary (Amy Blake)* Florence Rice *Casey and Matthews receptionist* Barbara Jo Allen (Vera Vague) *Juggler* Trixie Firschke *Unemployed actor (Dan)* Joe Yule *Press agent (O'Grady)* Hal K. Dawson *Soda jerk* Irving Bacon *Powell's maid (Angel)* Libby Taylor *Emmy Lou Lee (Morgan's Southern girlfriend)* Lynne Carver *Emmy Lou's old friends* William Tannen, Alphonse Martell(?) *Audition singer* Charlotte Arren *Her accompanist* Johnny Broderick *Silhouette artist in cafe* Herman Bing *Waiter* Paul Burns or Jean Del Val *Unicyclist (The Great Capolio)* Blair Woolstencroft *Theatre usher* n.k. *Baritone in "I Concentrate on You"* Douglas McPhail *Pop (stage-door man)* E. Alyn Warren *Astaire's Dawnland bride* Mary Field *Soprano in "Begin the Beguine"* Carmen D'Antonio (singing dubbed by Lois Hodnett) *Singing quartet in "Begin the Beguine"* The Music Maids

13. SECOND CHORUS

Paramount, 83 minutes; New York premiere January 15, 1941, Paramount Theatre (Copyright January 3, 1941)

Producer Boris Morros *Director* H. C. Potter "Dance director Hermes Pan" *Songs* lyrics by Johnny Mercer; "Would You Like to Be the Love of My Life": music by Artie Shaw; "Poor Mr. Chisholm": music by Bernard Hanighen; "Dig It": music by Hal Borne *Additional music* Artie Shaw; also Maceo Pinkard, Victor Young, Johnny Green *Associate musical director* Eddie Paul *Arrangements* Gregory Stone, Johnny Guarnieri, Artie Shaw, Eddie Paul *Screenplay* Elaine Ryan and Ian McLellan Hunter (based upon an original story by Frank Cavett) *Additional scriptwriting* Johnny Mercer *Director of photography* Theodor Sparkuhl *Art director* Boris Leven *Set decoration* Howard Bristol *Wardrobe* Helen Taylor *Editor* Jack Dennis *Assistant editor* Fred Feitshans *Recording* William Wilmarth *Associate producer* Robert Stillman *Associate director* Frank Cavett *Assistant director* Edward Montagne *Production manager* Joe Nadel

Danny O'Neil Fred Astaire (trumpet playing dubbed by Bobby Hackett) *Stu (Goddard's date)* Frank Melton *Ellen Miller* Paulette Goddard *Hank Taylor* Burgess Meredith (trumpet playing dubbed by Billy Butterfield) *Mr. Dunn (collection agent)* Jimmy Conlin *Elderly lady* n.k. *Man at bar* n.k. *College man in sunglasses* n.k. *Artie Shaw* Artie Shaw *The Artie Shaw Band* Billy Butterfield, Jack Cathcart (trumpet), Vernon Brown (trombone), Les Robinson (alto sax), Bus Bassey, Jerry Jerome (tenor sax), Johnny Guarnieri (piano), Nick Fatool (drums), and strings; also probably George Wendt (trumpet), Jack Jenney (trombone), Neely Plumb (alto sax), Al Hendrickson (guitar), Jud de Naut (bass) *Shaw's managers* n.k. *The Perennials* Hermes Pan and others *Messenger telling of Shaw's arrival* n.k. *Blond college boy* Billy Benedict *Telegram delivery man* Ben Hall *Elevator operator* n.k. *Elevator starter* n.k. *Cleaning woman* n.k. *Shaw's receptionist* n.k. *Stage-door man* n.k. *Lester Chisholm* Charles Butterworth *Whiteman's secretary* n.k. *Dorsey's secretary* n.k. *Desk clerk* Don Brodie *Waiter* n.k. *Disappointed man at stage door* n.k.

14. YOU'LL NEVER GET RICH

Columbia Pictures, 88 minutes; New York premiere October 23, 1941, Radio City Music Hall (Copyright September 25, 1941)

Producer Samuel Bischoff *Director* Sidney Lanfield "Dances staged by Robert Alton" *Songs* music and lyrics by Cole Porter *Additional music* Charles Bradshaw, Nico Grigor *Musical director* Morris W. Stoloff *Assistant musical director* Paul Mertz *Arrangements* Carmen Dragon, Leo Arnaud, Paul Mertz *Orchestrations* Leo Shuken *Screenplay* Michael Fessier, Ernest Pagano *Director of photography* Philip Tannura *Art director* Lionel Banks *Costumes* Irene Sharaff *Editor* Otto Meyer *Music recording* P. J. Faulkner *Assistant director* Gene Anderson *Technical adviser* Jack Voglin

Martin Cortland Robert Benchley *Jenkins (his chauffeur)* Emmett Vogan *Jewelry salesman* Jack Rice *Robert Curtis* Fred Astaire *Joe (at rehearsal)* Robert Homans *Sheila Winthrop* Rita Hayworth *Marge (chorus girl)* Sunnie O'Dea *Cummings (Benchley's secretary)* n.k. *Julia Cortland* Frieda Inescort *Headwaiter* n.k. *Newspaper photographer* Lester Dorr *Aunt Louise* Marjorie Gateson *Tom Barton* John Hubbard *Policeman* Tim Ryan *Army doctor* Edward McWade *Corporal* n.k. *Foreigner at Grand Central Station* Harry Burns *Information clerk* Hal K. Dawson *Swivel Tongue* Cliff Nazarro *Conductor* n.k. *Kewpie Blain* Guinn ("Big Boy") Williams *His mother* Dorothy Vernon *Top sergeant* Donald MacBride *Soldier-messenger* n.k. *Guard* n.k. *Would-be sleeper in barracks* Monty Collins *Sentry at camp entrance* Jack O'Malley *Mrs. Barton* Ann Shoemaker *Singers in guardhouse* The Four Tones (Rudolph Hunter, John Porter, Lucius Brooks, Leon Buck) *Musicians in guardhouse* Chico Hamilton (drums), A. Grant (guitar), Joe Comfort (jug), Red Mack (trumpet), Buddy Colette (clarinet) *Captain Williams* Harold Goodwin *Captain Nolan* Paul Phillips *Army chauffeur* Eddie Coke *Guard at guardhouse door* n.k. *Prisoners* Frank Wayne, Tony Hughes *Astaire's guards* Frank Sully, Garry Owen *Colonel Shiller* Boyd Davis *Shiller's orderly* Harry Strang *Sonya* Osa Massen *Singer in "Wedding Cake Walk"* Martha Tilton *Solo dancer in*

"Wedding Cake Walk" Forrest Prince *Justice of the Peace* Frank Ferguson *Soldiers* Larry Williams, James Millican

15. HOLIDAY INN

Paramount Pictures, 101 minutes; New York premiere August 4, 1942, Paramount Theatre (Copyright June 12, 1942)

Producer and director Mark Sandrich "Dance Ensembles staged by Danny Dare" *Assistant dance director* Babe Pearce *Songs* music and lyrics by Irving Berlin *Musical director* Robert Emmett Dolan *Assistant musical director* Arthur Franklin *Vocal arrangements* Joseph J. Lilley *Additional arrangements* Paul Wetstein, Gilbert Grau, Herbert Spencer, Walter Scharf *Specialty accompaniments* Bob Crosby's Band *Screenplay* Claude Binyon (based upon an idea by Irving Berlin, adaptation by Elmer Rice) *Director of photography* David Abel *Art director* Hans Dreier, Roland Anderson *Gowns* Edith Head *Makeup* Wally Westmore *Editor* Ellsworth Hoagland *Recording* Earl Hayman, John Cope *Assistant director* Charles C. Coleman, Jr.

Ted Hanover Fred Astaire *Cab driver* n.k. *Three dancing boys* n.k. *Santa Claus* Bud Jamison *Jim Hardy* Bing Crosby *Lila Dixon* Virginia Dale *Callboy* n.k. *Danny Reed (agent)* Walter Abel *Linda Mason* Marjorie Reynolds (singing dubbed by Martha Mears) *Proprietor of flower shop* Leon Belasco *Man at nightclub table* Harry Barris *Waiter at nightclub* Jacques Vanaire *Gus (cab and sleigh driver)* Irving Bacon *Mamie* Louise Beavers *Daphne* Joan Arnold *Vanderbilt* Shelby Bacon *François* Marek Windheim *Hat-check girl* Katharine (Karin) Booth *Drunken woman* Kitty Kelly *Man applauding* Edward Emerson(?) *Irritated man on dance floor* n.k. *Parker (Hollywood man)* John Gallaudet *Dunbar (Hollywood director)* James Bell *Assistant director* Keith Richards or Reed Porter *Pop* Bob Homans

16. YOU WERE NEVER LOVELIER

Columbia Pictures, 97 minutes; New York premiere December 4, 1942, Radio City Music Hall (Copyright October 19, 1942)

Producer Louis F. Edelman *Director* William A. Seiter "Dance Director Val Raset" *Songs* music by Jerome Kern, lyrics by Johnny Mercer ("Chiu Chiu": music and lyric by Nicanor Molinare) *Additional music* Raphael Hernandez, Noro Morales, J. Camacho, Gilbert Valdes, Franz Liszt *Musical director* Leigh Harline *Assistant musical director* Paul Mertz *Arrangements* Conrad Salinger (arrangement of "The Shorty George" by Lyle [Spud] Murphy) *Screenplay* Michael Fessier, Ernest Pagano, Elmer Davis (based upon a story by Carlos Olivari and Sixto Pondal Rios) *Director of photography* Ted Tetzlaff *Art Director* Lionel Banks *Associate art director* Rudolph Sternad *Set decoration* Frank Tuttle *Gowns* Irene Sharaff *Editor* William Lyon *Music recording* P. J. Faulkner *Assistant director* Norman Deming

Robert Davis Fred Astaire *Bellhop* n.k. *Fernando (Menjou's secretary)* Gus Schilling *Eduardo Acuna* Adolphe Menjou *Clothes designer* n.k. *Juan Castro* Douglass Leavitt *Mrs. Maria Castro* Isobel Elsom *Xavier Cugat* Xavier Cugat *Singers with Cugat's band* Lina Romay, Miguelito Valdes *Cecy Acuna (Hayworth's sister)* Leslie Brooks *Lita Acuna (Hayworth's sister)* Adele Mara *Julia Acuna (Hayworth's married sister)* Catherine Craig *Maria Acuna* Rita Hayworth (singing dubbed by Nan Wynn) *Mrs. Delfina Acuna* Barbara Brown *Tony (Cecy's fiancé)* Larry Parks *Roddy (Lita's fiancé)* Stanley Brown (Brad Taylor) *Volunteer bridegrooms* Kirk Alyn and others *Hayworth's maid (Louise)* Mary Field *Grandmother Acuna* Kathleen Howard *Bellboy quartet* n.k.

17. THE SKY'S THE LIMIT

RKO Radio Pictures, 89 minutes; New York premiere September 2, 1943, Palace Theatre (Copyright August 21, 1943)

Producer David Hempstead *Director* Edward H. Griffith "Dances created and staged by Fred Astaire" *Songs* music by Harold Arlen, lyrics by Johnny Mercer *Additional music* Freddie Slack *Musical director* Leigh Harline *Arrangements and orchestrations* Leigh Harline, Roy Webb, Phil Green, Phil Moore, Sid Cutner, Maurice de Packh, Jack Virgil, Gilbert Grau *Screenplay* Frank Fenton, Lynn Root (based upon their story "A Handful of Heaven," derived from the story "On Special Service" by William T. Ryder) *Additional scriptwriting* S. K. Lauren *Director of photography* Russell Metty *Special effects* Vernon Walker *Associate producer* Sherman Todd *Art directors* Albert S. D'Agostino, Carroll Clark *Set decoration* Darrell Silvera, Claude Carpenter *Gowns* Renie *Recording* Richard Van Hessen *Prerecording* James G. Stewart *Editor* Roland Gross *Assistant director* Ruby Rosenberg *Technical adviser* Robert T. Smith

Fred Atwell Fred Astaire *Chinese official* Joseph Kim *Reginald Fenton* Robert Ryan *Richard Merlin* Richard Davies *Southern girl in motorcade* Amelita Ward *Navy officer on train* Neil Hamilton *Second navy officer* Frank Melton *USAF Commander* Peter Lawford *4F man driving car* Olin Howlin (Howland) *Doorman at Colonial Club* Clarence Muse *Joan Manion* Joan Leslie (singing of "My Shining Hour" dubbed by Sally Sweetland) *Bartender at Colonial Club (Mac)* Ed McNamara *Phil Harriman ("Eyeful" publisher)* Robert Benchley *Freddie Slack (bandleader)* Freddie Slack *Pamela (at Colonial Club)* n.k. *Mr. Reed (at Colonial Club)* n.k. *Sir Charles* n.k. *Short-order cook (Mr. Kiefer)* Ferris Taylor *Mrs. Fisher (landlady)* Elizabeth Patterson *Police officer at docks* n.k. *Dock foreman* Paul Hurst *Benchley's secretary* Dorothy Kelly *Workers in "Eyeful" office hall* n.k. *Sergeant at canteen door* Al Hill *Canteen hostess* Marjorie Gateson *Dancing soldier at canteen* Larry Rio *Police officer on street* n.k. *Jackson* Eric Blore *Radio announcer* n.k. *Harvey J. Sloan* Clarence Kolb *Mrs. Leo Roskowski* Norma Drury *First bartender* Vic Potel *Second bartender* Joe Bernard *Third bartender* Al Murphy *Lieutenant at air base* n.k.

18. ZIEGFELD FOLLIES

Metro-Goldwyn-Mayer, 110 minutes, Technicolor; roadshow premiere (Boston) August 20, 1945; New York premiere March 22, 1946, Capitol Theatre (Copyright January 15, 1946)

Producer Arthur Freed *Director* Vincente Minnelli (E, G, K, L, M, N) *Additional direction* Norman Taurog (A, B), George Sidney (B, F, J), Merrill Pye (C), Robert Lewis (D), Roy Del Ruth (H), Lemuel Ayers (I) "Dance Direction Robert Alton" *Additional dance direction* Eugene Loring, Charles Walters, Roy Del Ruth *Songs* music by Harry Warren, Roger Edens, Hugh Martin; lyrics by Arthur Freed, Earl Brent, Ralph Blane, Kay Thompson, Roger Edens *Additional music* Roger Edens, Conrad Salinger, Giuseppe Verdi, Charles Ingle, George and Ira Gershwin, Philip Braham *Conductor* Lennie Hayton *Arrangements* Roger Edens, Lennie Hayton, Conrad Salinger *Additional arrangements* Ted Duncan, Calvin Jackson, Paul Marquardt *Orchestrations* Wally Heglin, Conrad Salinger *Scriptwriting* Peter Barr (D), David Freedman (H), Harry Tugend (J), Kay Thompson (L), Roger Edens (L), and others *Directors of photography* George Folsey, Charles Rosher, Ray June *Photography of puppet sequence* William Ferrari *Color consultant* Natalie Kalmus *Associate color consultant* Henri Jaffa *Settings* Merrill Pye, Jack Martin Smith, Harry McAfee, Edward Carfagno, Lemuel Ayers, Irene Sharaff *Statuary* Tony Duquette *Costumes* Helen Rose, Irene Sharaff *Makeup* Jack Dawn *Hair* Sydney Guilaroff *Editor* Albert Akst *Recording* Douglas Shearer

(A) *Florenz Ziegfeld* William Powell *Ziegfeld stars* Bunin's Puppets (B) *Fred Astaire* Fred Astaire *Ballet dancer* Cyd Charisse *Woman with whip* Lucille Ball *Singer* Virginia O'Brien (C) *Swimmer* Esther Williams (D) *Caller* Keenan Wynn *Voices on telephone* Robert Lewis, Peter Lawford, and others *Voice of telephone operator* Audrey Totter *Texan* Grady Sutton *Woman* Kay Williams (E) *Tenor* James Melton *Soprano* Marion Bell (F) *Victor Moore* Victor Moore *His lawyer* Edward Arnold *Woman on subway* n.k. *Judge* Joseph Crehan *High-court judge* William B. Davidson *Warden* Harry Hayden *Police officers* Ray Teal, Eddie Dunn, Garry Owen (G) *The Flunky* Sam Flint *Major-domo* Charles Coleman *The lieutenant* Feodor Chaliapin *The princess* Lucille Bremer *The duke* Count Stefanelli *The duchess* Naomi Childers *Man waltzing Bremer* n.k. *The countess* Helen Boice *Her companion* n.k. *The imposter* Fred Astaire *Retired dyspeptic* Robert Wayne (H) *Norma* Fanny Brice *Telegraph boy* Arthur Walsh *Monty* Hume Cronyn *Mr. Martin (landlord)* William Frawley (I) *Singer* Lena Horne (J) *Announcer* Red Skelton *J. Newton Numbskull* Red Skelton (K) *Singer* Harriet Lee *Tai Long* Fred Astaire *Man with cane* n.k. *Head of costermonger family* Eugene Loring *Moy Ling* Lucille Bremer *Chinese gentleman* Robert Lewis *Proprietor of shop* n.k. *Hoodlums* n.k. *Police officers* George Hill, Jack Deery(?) (L) *Butler* Rex Evans *Great lady* Judy Garland (M) *Fred Astaire* Fred Astaire *Gene Kelly* Gene Kelly (N) *Singer* Kathryn Grayson *Ballet soloist* Cyd Charisse

19. YOLANDA AND THE THIEF

Metro-Goldwyn-Mayer, 108 minutes, Technicolor; New York premiere November 22, 1945, Capitol Theatre (Copyright November 15, 1945)

Producer Arthur Freed *Director* Vincente Minnelli "Dances Staged by Eugene Loring" *Songs* music by Harry Warren, lyrics by Arthur Freed *Additional Music* "Dream Ballet": Lennie Hayton *Musical director* Lennie Hayton *Orchestrations* Conrad Salinger, Wally Heglin, Lennie Hayton *Additional orchestrations* Robert Franklyn, Ted Duncan *Screenplay* Irving Brecher (based upon a story by Jacques Thery and Ludwig Bemelmans) *Additional scriptwriting* George Wells, Robert Nathan, Joseph Schrank *Director of photography* Charles Rosher *Color consultant* Natalie Kalmus *Associate color consultant* Henri Jaffa *Special effects* A. Arnold Gillespie, Warren Newcombe *Art directors* Cedric Gibbons, Jack Martin Smith *Set decoration* Edwin B. Willis *Associate set decorator* Richard Pefferle *Costumes* Irene Sharaff *Makeup* Jack Dawn *Editor* George White *Recording* Douglas Shearer

Schoolteacher Ludwig Stossel *Patria boys* n.k. *Mother Superior* Jane Green *Yolanda* Lucille Bremer (singing dubbed by Trudy Erwin) *Gigi (child at breakfast table)* Ghislaine (Gigi) Perreau *Puppeteer* Remo Bufano *Johnny Parkson Riggs* Fred Astaire *Victor ("Junior") Budlow Trout* Frank Morgan *Waiter on train* Marek Windheim *Child at door* n.k. *Aunt Amarilla* Mildred Natwick *Emilio (servant)* n.k. *Plumber* n.k. *Gaston (cook)* Chef Milani *Servant* n.k. *Marcel (major-domo)* Michael Visaroff *Ludwig (child)* n.k. *Ludwig's father* George Humbert *Conchita* Danna McGraw *Fruit vendor* n.k. *Man bumming cigarette* n.k. *Cab driver* Leon Belasco *Mr. Candle* Leon Ames *Duenna* Mary Nash *Dancers in "Dream Ballet"* n.k. *Mr. Banillo* Oscar Lorraine *Butler (Otto)* n.k.

Waiter at hotel n.k. *Police officer* Charles La Torre *Festival official* n.k. *Officer on train* n.k. *Waiter on train* n.k. *Padre* Francis Pierlot

20. BLUE SKIES

Paramount Pictures, 104 minutes, Technicolor; New York premiere October 16, 1946, Paramount Theatre (Copyright December 27, 1946)

Producer Sol C. Siegel *Director* Stuart Heisler "Dances staged by Hermes Pan" *Dance assistant* Dave Robel *Songs* music and lyrics by Irving Berlin *Additional music* solo dance in "Heat Wave": Fred Astaire *Musical director* Robert Emmett Dolan *Associate musical director* Troy Sanders *Arrangements* Mason Van Cleave, Hugo Frey, Charles Bradshaw, Ralph Hallenbeck, Matty Matlock, Sidney Fine *Vocal arrangements* Joseph J. Lilley *Screenplay* Arthur Sheekman (based upon an original idea by Irving Berlin, adaptation by Allan Scott) *Directors of photography* Charles Lang, Jr., William Snyder *Color consultant* Natalie Kalmus *Associate color consultant* Robert Brower *Special effects* Gordon Jennings, Paul K. Lerpae *Process photography* Farciot Edouart *Art directors* Hans Dreier, Hal Pereira *Set decoration* Sam Comer, Maurice Goodman *Gowns* Edith Head *Costumes* Waldo Angelo *Costume execution* Karinska *Makeup* Wally Westmore *Editor* LeRoy Stone *Recording* Hugo Grenzbach, John Cope

Radio announcer n.k. *Jed Potter* Fred Astaire *Mack (stage manager)* Frank Faylen *Mary O'Hara* Joan Caulfield (singing dubbed by Betty Russell) *Bubbles (Caulfield's friend)* n.k. *Junior (Bubbles' sugar daddy)* John M. Sullivan *Jeffrey (Astaire's valet)* Jimmy Conlin *Jim (door opener at nightclub)* n.k. *Johnny Adams* Bing Crosby *Drunk in nightclub* Jack Norton *Tony* Billy De Wolfe *Nita Nova* Olga San Juan *Charles Dillingham* Roy Gordon *Singers in "Serenade to an Old-Fashioned Girl"* The Guardsmen *Stage manager in Dillingham show* n.k. *Stagehand with flowers* n.k. *Mom (Caulfield's maid in dressing room)* n.k. *Mr. Rakopolis (buyer of Hole in the Wall)* Charles La Torre *Tough guy in Hole in the Wall* John Kelly *Angie (chorus girl)* n.k. *Cliff (pianist)* Cliff Nazarro *Nurse in hospital* Frances Morris *Doctor* n.k. *Woman patron at Top Hat* n.k. *Female quartet at Top Hat* Vicki Jasmund, Norma Crieger, Joanne Lybrook, Louise Saraydar *Martha (Caulfield's maid)* Victoria Horne *Mary Elizabeth Adams (child)* Karolyn Grimes *Dan (Detroit stage manager)* Will Wright *Callboy* n.k.

21. EASTER PARADE

Metro-Goldwyn-Mayer, 103 minutes, Technicolor; New York premiere June 30, 1948, Loew's State Theatre (Copyright May 26, 1948)

Producer Arthur Freed *Director* Charles Walters "Musical numbers staged and directed by Robert Alton" *Songs* music and lyrics by Irving Berlin *Musical director* Johnny Green *Associate musical director* Roger Edens *Orchestrations* Conrad Salinger, Mason Van Cleave, Robert Franklyn, Paul Marquardt, Sidney Cutner, Leo Shuken *Vocal arrangements* Robert Tucker *Screenplay* Sidney Sheldon, Frances Goodrich, Albert Hackett (based upon an original story by Frances Goodrich and Albert Hackett) *Additional scriptwriting* Guy Bolton *Associate producer* Roger Edens *Director of photography* Harry Stradling *Color consultant* Natalie Kalmus *Associate color consultant* Henri Jaffa *Special effects* Warren Newcombe *Art directors* Cedric Gibbons, Jack Martin Smith *Set decoration* Edwin B. Willis *Associate set decorator* Arthur Krams *Women's costumes* Irene Sharaff *Men's costumes* Valles *Hair* Sydney Guilaroff *Makeup* Jack Dawn *Editor* Albert Akst *Recording* Douglas Shearer

Don Hewes Fred Astaire *Models* n.k. *Proprietress of shop* Helene Heigh *Bearers* n.k. *Florist* Margaret Bert *Boy in drum number* Jimmy Bates *Salesgirl in drum number* Fern Eggen *Essie* Jeni Le Gon *Nadine Gale* Ann Miller *Johnny Harrow III* Peter Lawford *Mike (bartender)* Clinton Sundberg *Waiter* Albert Pollet *Hannah Brown* Judy Garland *Rehearsal pianist (Marty)* Wilson Wood *Sam (Astaire's valet)* Peter Chong *Dog act* Hector and His Pals (Carmi Tryon) *François (headwaiter)* Jules Munshin *Waiter at drug counter* Nolan Leary *Drugstore customers* Howard Mitchell, Bob Jellison *Peddler with umbrella* Angie Poulis *Ziegfeld aide* Dick Simmons *Cab driver* Jimmy Dodd *Policeman* Robert Emmet O'Connor *Stage manager at Dillingham show* n.k. *Anna (Garland's maid backstage)* Doris Kemper(?) *Astaire's partners in "Steppin' Out with My Baby"* Patricia Jackson, Bobbie Priest, Dee Turnell *People backstage* n.k. *Callboy at roof garden* Sig Frohlich *Singer in "Magazine Cover" number* Richard Beavers *Showgirls* Joi Lansing, Elaine Sterling, Patricia Vaniver, Shirley Ballard, Ruth Hall, Gail Langford, Lola Albright, Patricia Walker, Marjorie Jackson *Twin showgirls* Lynn and Jean Romer *Front-desk clerk at hotel* Harry Fox *Hotel detective* Ralph Sanford *Delivery man* n.k.

22. THE BARKLEYS OF BROADWAY

Metro-Goldwyn-Mayer, 109 minutes, Technicolor; New York premiere May 4, 1949, Loew's State Theatre (Copyright March 15, 1949)

Producer Arthur Freed *Director* Charles Walters "Musical numbers staged and directed by Robert Alton; Dance number 'Shoes with Wings On' Directed by Hermes Pan; Dancing shoes effects Irving G. Ries" *Songs* music by Harry Warren, lyrics by Ira Gershwin ("They Can't Take That Away from Me" by George and Ira Gershwin) *Additional music* Aram Khachaturian, P. I. Tchaikovsky *Musical director and conductor* Lennie Hayton *Additional conducting* Adolph Deutsch *Arrangements* Conrad Salinger, Leo Arnaud, Paul Marquardt, Wally Heglin, Robert Franklyn *Vocal arrangements* Robert Tucker *Orchestrations* Conrad Salinger, Wally Heglin, Robert Franklyn *Screenplay* Betty Comden, Adolph Green *Additional scriptwriting* Sidney Sheldon *Director of photography* Harry Stradling *Color consultant* Natalie Kalmus *Associate color consultant* Henri Jaffa *Special effects* Warren Newcombe *Art directors* Cedric Gibbons, Edward Carfagno *Set decoration* Edwin B. Willis *Associate set decorator* Arthur Krams *Ginger Rogers' costumes* Irene Sharaff *Men's costumes* Valles *Hair* Sydney Guilaroff *Makeup* Jack Dawn *Editor* Albert Akst *Recording* Douglas Shearer *Associate producer* Roger Edens *Assistant director* Wallace Morsley

Josh Barkley Fred Astaire *Dinah Barkley* Ginger Rogers *Ezra Millar* Oscar Levant *Doorman* Mahlon Hamilton *Millie Belney* Billie Burke *Blonde at cast party* Dee Turnell *Husband at cast party* Reginald Simpson *Cleo Fernby (Levant's friend)* Lorraine Crawford *Jacques Pierre Barredout* Jacques François *Bert Felsher (show producer)* Clinton Sundberg *Shirlene May (Rogers' understudy)* Gale Robbins *Ladislaus Ladi (surrealist artist)* Hans Conried *Larry (Barkleys' press agent)* Wilson Wood *Cab driver* Allen Wood *Gloria Amboy (Levant's friend in the country)* Carol Brewster *Pamela Driscoll (Rogers' "Sarah" rival)* Inez Cooper *Mr. Perkins of "Look"* Frank Ferguson *"Look" photographers* George Boyce, John Albright, Butch Terrell *Dancer in "Shoes with Wings On"* Les Clark *Stage-door man* Nolan Leary *Genevieve (Levant's friend)* Joyce Mathews *Waitress (Helen)* n.k. *Players in "Young Sarah" rehearsal* Joe Granby *(Duke de Morny)*, Esther Somers *(mother)*, Helen Eby-Rock *(aunt)* *Announcer at benefit* Bob Purcell *Orchestra conductor* Lennie Hayton *Henrietta (Levant's friend)* Roberta Johnson *Director of ceremonies at "Young Sarah" performance* n.k. *Judge* George Zucco *Clementine Villard* Mary Jo Ellis *Joe (in box office)* Jack Rice *Reader of "Macbeth" speech* Mimi Doyle *Marie (Levant's friend)* Claire Carleton *Man in dressing room* n.k. *Mary (Rogers' maid)* Margaret Bert

23. THREE LITTLE WORDS

Metro-Goldwyn-Mayer, 102 minutes, Technicolor; New York premiere August 9, 1950, Loew's State Theatre (Copyright July 6, 1950)

Producer Jack Cummings *Director* Richard Thorpe "Dances Created and Staged by Hermes Pan" *Songs* music by Harry Ruby, lyrics by Bert Kalmar ("Where Did You Get That Girl?": music by Harry Puck; "Come on, Papa": lyric by Edgar Leslie; "My Sunny Tennessee" also by Herman Ruby; "Who's Sorry Now" also by Ted Snyder; "I Wanna Be Loved by You" also by Herbert Stothart) *Additional music* André Previn *Musical director and conductor* André Previn *Orchestrations and arrangements* Leo Arnaud, Wally Heglin, Robert Franklyn *Additional arrangements* Conrad Salinger *Screenplay* George Wells (based upon the lives and songs of Bert Kalmar and Harry Ruby) *Director of photography* Harry Jackson *Color consultants* Henri Jaffa, James Gooch *Special effects* Warren Newcombe *Montage sequence* Peter Ballbusch *Art directors* Cedric Gibbons, Urie McCleary *Set decoration* Edwin B. Willis *Associate set decorator* Arthur Krams *Costumes* Helen Rose *Hair* Jack Dawn *Editor* Ben Lewis *Recording* Douglas Shearer *Technical adviser* Harry Ruby

Bert Kalmar Fred Astaire *Jessie Brown Kalmar* Vera-Ellen (singing dubbed by Anita Ellis) *Charlie Kope (agent)* Keenan Wynn *Mendoza the Great* Harry Mendoza *Callboy* Mickey Martin *Barker* Syd Saylor *Singing quartet* n.k. *Boy with ball score* Elzie Emanuel *Harry Ruby* Red Skelton *Pianist* Sherry Hall *Clanahan* Harry Shannon *Assistant in magic act* Pat Williams *Stagehand with fire extinguisher* Douglas Carter *Prop man* Harry Cody *Messenger with flowers* Sig Froelich *Al Masters (music publisher)* Paul Harvey *Johnny (waiter)* Charles Wagenheim *Mrs. Carter De Haven* Gloria De Haven *Man in wings* n.k. *Waiter on train* John B. Williams *Terry Lordel* Gale Robbins *Eileen Percy* Arlene Dahl *Philip Goodman (producer)* Pierre Watkin *Al Schacht* George Metkovich *Baseball coach* Pat Flaherty *Ball player* Harry Ruby *Other ball players* Frank Kelleher, George Woods, Jerry Priddy, John McKee, Jack Paepke, Edward F. Nulty, Lou Stringer, Fred Millican *Grape juice vendor* Fred Santley *Piano movers* Dwight Martin, George Magrill *Helen Kane* Debbie Reynolds (singing dubbed by Helen Kane) *Dan Healy* Carleton Carpenter *Skelton's shipboard girlfriend* Beverly Michaels *Photographers* William Tannen, Bert Davidson *Hollywood director* George Sherwood *Maid (Lily)* n.k. *Piano player at party* Harry Barris *Newspaper man (Marty)* Alex Gerry *Phil Regan* Phil Regan

24. LET'S DANCE

Paramount Pictures, 112 minutes, Technicolor; New York premiere November 29, 1950, Paramount Theatre (Copyright November 23, 1950)

Producer Robert Fellows *Director* Norman Z. McLeod "Dances staged by Hermes Pan" *Songs* music and lyrics by Frank Loesser *Additional music* "Piano Dance": Tommy Chambers, Mason Van Cleave, Fred Astaire *Musical director* Robert Emmett Dolan *Associate musical director* Troy Sanders *Vocal arrangements* Joseph J. Lilley *Dance music arrangements* Robert Van Eps *Additional orchestrations and arrangements* Van Cleave *Screenplay* Allan Scott (suggested by a story by Maurice Zolotow) *Additional dialogue* Dane Lussier *Director of photography* George Barnes *Color consultant* Monroe W. Burbank *Special effects* Farciot Edouart *Art directors* Hans Dreier, Roland Anderson *Set decoration* Sam Comer, Ross Dowd *Gowns* Edith Head *Makeup* Wally Westmore *Editor* Ellsworth Hoagland *Recording* Hugo Grenzbach, John Cope *Assistant director* Edward Salven

Kitty McNeil Everett Betty Hutton *Don Elwood* Fred Astaire *Milton DeLugg (accordionist)* Milton DeLugg *Soldier to pick up bags* Paul Lees(?) *Edmund Pohlwhistle* Roland Young *Serena Everett* Lucile Watson *Charles Wagstaffe* Melville Cooper *Nurse Gorman* Esther Somers *Richie* Gregory Moffett *Carola Everett* Ruth Warrick *Butler in Boston* Jack Trent *Watchman (Tom)* Chester Conklin *J. P. Pierce (Wall Street broker)* Charles Evans *Pierce's secretary* n.k. *Trumpet player* Eddie Johnson *Bubbles Malone* Peggy Badey *Larry Channock (proprietor of supper club)* Barton MacLane *Tommy (pianist)* Tommy Chambers *Waiter at chili parlor* Herbert Vigran *George (customer at chili parlor)* n.k. *Jewelry salesman* Rolfe Sedan *Astaire's cab driver* Ralph Peters(?) *Dugan (detective)* Oliver Blake (Prickett) *Customer at club* Harry V. Cheshire(?) *Herman (waiter at club)* Syd Saylor *George (club bartender)* James Burke *Marcel (cook in club)* Harold Huber *Henri* n.k. *Timothy Bryant* Shepperd Strudwick *Process server* Sayre Dearing *Waiter* Duke York(?) *Elsie* Virginia Toland *Mary* Charmienne Harker *Bartender in "Dudes" number* Bobby Barber *Square-dance caller* Paul A. Pierce *Judge* George Zucco *Court reporter* Charles Dayton *Clerk at marriage license office* Dick Keene *Mrs. Thorpe* n.k. *Mr. Thorpe* n.k. *Mrs. Bryant* Nana Bryant *Nurse* Mary Field *Hutton's cab driver* n.k. *Police lieutenant* Harry Woods *Stagehand* n.k.

25. ROYAL WEDDING
("WEDDING BELLS" IN UNITED KINGDOM)

Metro-Goldwyn-Mayer, 93 minutes, Technicolor; New York premiere March 8, 1951, Radio City Music Hall (Copyright February 5, 1951)

Producer Arthur Freed *Director* Stanley Donen "Dances by Nick Castle" *Dance assistants* Marilyn Christine, Dave Robel *Songs* music by Burton Lane, lyrics by Alan Jay Lerner *Musical director* Johnny Green *Orchestrations* Conrad Salinger, Skip Martin, Robert Franklyn *Additional orchestrations* Albert Sendrey *Screenplay* Alan Jay Lerner *Director of photography* Robert Planck *Color consultants* Henri Jaffa, James Gooch *Special effects* Warren Newcombe *Art directors* Cedric Gibbons, Jack Martin Smith *Set decoration* Edwin B. Willis *Associate set decorator* Alfred E. Spencer *Makeup* William J. Tuttle *Hair* Sydney Guilaroff *Editor* Albert Akst *Recording* Douglas Shearer *Assistant director* Arvid Griffen

Tom Bowen Fred Astaire *Ellen Bowen* Jane Powell *Pete Cumberly (Powell's admirer)* Jack Reilly *Chester (Astaire's valet)* Alex Frazer *Eddie (stage-door man)* Wilson Benge *Irving Klinger* Keenan Wynn *Dick (Powell's admirer)* William Cabanne *Billy (Powell's admirer)* John Hedloe *Lord John Brindale* Peter Lawford *Linda (Lawford's girlfriend)* Kerry O'Day *Stewards* Andre Charisse, Albert Pollet *Barbara (Lawford's girlfriend)* Pat Williams *Purser* Henri Letondal *Edgar Klinger* Keenan Wynn *Anne Ashmond* Sarah Churchill *Charles Gordon (London stage manager)* Francis Bethancourt *London cab driver* James Finlayson *James Ashmond* Albert Sharpe *Drinker in Sharpe's pub* Wilson Wood *Telephone operators* Mae Clarke, Helen Winston *Chorus girl at rehearsal* Wendy Howard(?) *Sarah Ashmond* Viola Roache *Cab driver* Stanley Mann *Man backstage* n.k. *Singers in "What a Lovely Day for a Wedding"* Phyllis Morris *(woman)*, Tommy Hughes *(man)*, Leonard Mudie *(doorman)*, Richard Lupino *(elevator operator)*, David Thursby *(London bobby)*

26. THE BELLE OF NEW YORK

Metro-Goldwyn-Mayer, 82 minutes, Technicolor; New York premiere March 5, 1952, Loew's State Theatre (Copyright February 12, 1952)

Producer Arthur Freed *Director* Charles Walters "Musical numbers staged and directed by Robert Alton" *Assistant dance directors* Alex Romero, Marilyn Christine *Songs* music by Harry Warren, lyrics by Johnny Mercer ("Let a Little Love Come In": music and lyric by Roger Edens) *Musical director* Adolph Deutsch *Vocal arrangements* Robert Tucker *Orchestrations* Conrad Salinger, Maurice de Packh, Robert Franklyn, Alexander Courage *Screenplay* Robert O'Brien, Irving Elison (from the musical play by Hugh Morton, adaptation by Chester Erskine) *Additional scriptwriting* Irving Brecher, Fred Finklehoffe, Sally Benson, Jerry Davis, Joseph Fields *Director of photography* Robert Planck *Color consultants* Henri Jaffa, James Gooch *Special effects* Warren Newcombe, Irving G. Ries *Art directors* Cedric Gibbons, Jack Martin Smith *Set decoration* Edwin B. Willis, Richard Pefferle *Women's costumes* Helen Rose *Men's costumes* Gile Steele *Makeup* William Tuttle *Hair* Sydney Guilaroff *Editor* Albert Akst *Recording* Douglas Shearer *Associate producer* Roger Edens *Assistant director* Al Jennings

Angela Bonfils Vera-Ellen (singing dubbed by Anita Ellis) *Officer Clancy* Henry Slate *Mrs. Phineas Hill* Marjorie Main *Elsie Wilkins* Alice Pearce *Gilford Spivak* Clinton Sundberg *Derelict* Benny Rubin(?) *Charles Hill* Fred Astaire *Frenchie* Lisa Ferraday *Frenchie's girls* Lyn Wilde, Dorinda Clifton, Carol Brewster, Meredith Leeds, Pamela Drake, Mary Jane French, Helen Kimbell, Jean Corbett, Betty Jean Onge, Beverly Thomas, Lola Kendrick, Jetsy Parker *Max Ferris* Keenan Wynn *Chauffeur* Buddy Roosevelt *Dixie "Deadshot" McCoy* Gale Robbins *Judkins (butler)* Roger Davis *Mr. Currier* Oliver Blake *Mr. Ives* Billy Griffith *Men in mission house* Tom Dugan, Percy Helton, Dick Wessel *Other Bowery bums* Joe Niemeyer, Walter Ridge, Donald Kerr, Sandee Marriott, Joe Evans, George Boyce, Bud Penny, Al Gallagher, Charles Cross *Headwaiter in casino* Reginald Simpson *Bartender in casino* n.k. *Customers in casino* n.k. *Policeman* n.k.

27. THE BAND WAGON

Metro-Goldwyn-Mayer, 112 minutes, Technicolor; New York premiere July 9, 1953, Radio City Music Hall (Copyright July 3, 1953)

Producer Arthur Freed *Director* Vincente Minnelli "Dances and Musical Numbers Staged by Michael Kidd" *Dance assistants* Alex Romero, Pat Denise *Songs* music by Arthur Schwartz, lyrics by Howard Dietz *Additional music* Roger Edens *Musical director* Adolph Deutsch *Orchestrations* Conrad Salinger, Skip Martin, Alexander Courage, Roger Edens, Robert Franklyn *Screenplay* Betty Comden, Adolph Green *Directors of photography* Harry Jackson, George Folsey *Color consultants* Henri Jaffa, Robert Brower *Special effects* Warren Newcombe *Art directors* Cedric Gibbons, Preston Ames *Art director for musical numbers* Oliver Smith *Set decoration* Edwin B. Willis, Keogh Gleason *Costumes* Mary Ann Nyberg *Makeup* William Tuttle *Hair* Sydney Guilaroff *Editor* Albert Akst *Recording* Douglas Shearer *Associate producer* Roger Edens *Assistant director* Jerry Thorpe

Auctioneer Douglas Fowley *First rider on train* Emory Parnell *Second rider on train* Herb Vigran *Tony Hunter* Fred Astaire *Porter* Ernest Anderson *Woman getting off train* Barbara Ruick *Man getting off train* Steve Forrest *Photographer* Donald Kerr *Reporters* Frank Scannell, Stu Wilson, Roy Engel *Ava Gardner* Ava Gardner *Lester Marton* Oscar Levant *Lily Marton* Nanette Fabray *Man on 42nd Street* Steve Forrest(?) *Kid at penny arcade* Curtis Jackson *Tall woman at penny arcade* Sue Casey(?) *Knock-the-cans concessionaire* Wilson Wood *Shooting-gallery operator* Al Hill *Bootblack* LeRoy Daniels *Jeffrey Cordova* Jack Buchanan *Hal Benton (Buchanan's manager)* Robert Gist *Paul Byrd* James Mitchell *Gabrielle Gerard* Cyd Charisse (singing dubbed by India Adams) *Men in Charisse ballet* Bert May, Matt Maddox, William Lundy *Colonel Tide (backer)* Thurston Hall *Woman at backers' meeting* Madge Blake(?) *Other backers* George Sherwood, Stuart Holmes, Harry Stanton, Marion Gray, Bess Flowers, Estelle Eterre, Lillian Culver *Plaza doorman* Jack Gargan *Driver of horse-drawn cab* Joe A. Brockman *Set designer in "Faust" show* Betty Farrington *Conductor in "Faust" show* Henry Corden *Stagehands* Dick Alexander, Al Ferguson, Charles Regan, Jack Stoney *Col. Tide's chauffeur* Smoki Whitfield *Caterer at cast party* Manuel Paris *Cast members at party* Dee Turnell, Jimmie Thompson, Bert May, Elynne Ray, Judy Landon, Ann McCrea, Robert R. Stebbins, Ted Jordan, Lyle Clark, Peggy Murray *Bartender at cast party* n.k. *Buchanan's chambermaid* Lotte Stein *Women in "New Sun" number* n.k. *Women in "Girl Hunt" ballet* Dee and Eden Hartford, Julie Newmeyer (Newmar) *Other dancers* Bill Foster, Shirley Lopez, Lysa Baugher *Bobby (Astaire's valet)* Bobby Watson

28. DADDY LONG LEGS

Twentieth Century–Fox, 126 minutes, CinemaScope, Color by DeLuxe; New York premiere May 5, 1955, Roxy Theatre (Copyright May 5, 1955)

Producer Samuel G. Engel *Director* Jean Negulesco "Ballets by Roland Petit" "Dances staged by Fred Astaire and Dave Robel" *Songs* music and lyrics by Johnny Mercer *Additional music* Ray Anthony, George Williams; Nightmare ballet: Alex North *Music director and conductor* Alfred Newman *Arrangements and orchestrations* Edward B. Powell, Skip Martin, Earle Hagen, Bernard Mayers, Billy May for the Ray Anthony Orchestra, Nelson Riddle, Walter Ruick, Cyril J. Mockridge *Vocal-music director and vocal arrangements* Ken Darby *Screenplay* Phoebe and Henry Ephron (from the novel and play by Jean Webster) *Director of photography* Leon Shamroy *Color consultant* Leonard Doss *Special effects* Ray Kellogg *Art directors* Lyle Wheeler, John De Cuir *Set decoration* Walter M. Scott, Paul S. Fox *Wardrobe* Charles Le Maire *Modern wardrobe* Kay Nelson *Ballet costumes* Tom Keogh *Makeup* Ben Nye *Hair* Helen Turpin *Editor* William Reynolds *Recording* Alfred Bruzlin, Harry M. Leonard *Assistant director* Eli Dunn

Guide at Pendleton House Joseph Kearns *Woman on tour* Lillian Culver *Griggs* Fred Clark *Jervis Pendleton* Fred Astaire (singing in Texas number dubbed by Thurl Ravenscroft) *Mr. Bronson* Ralph Dumke *Mrs. Carrington* Kathryn Card *Commission members* Carleton Young, Paul Power *Boy at orphanage gate* n.k. *Julie André* Leslie Caron *Marie* n.k. *Paul* n.k. *Codene* n.k. *Mme. Sevanne* Ann Codee *French farmer* Frank Krieg *Alexander Williamson (ambassador)* Larry Keating *Cab driver* Harry Seymour *College girls* n.k. *Pat Withers* Sara Shane *Sally McBride* Charlotte Austin *Linda Pendleton (Astaire's niece)* Terry Moore *Trunk delivery men* J. Anthony Hughes, Bob Adler *Miss Pritchard* Thelma Ritter *Caller in daydream number* n.k. *Dancers in daydream number* Barrie Chase and others *Gertrude Pendleton (Astaire's sister-in-law)* Kathryn Givney *Band at spring dance* Ray Anthony and Orchestra *Jimmie McBride* Kelly Brown *Girl athlete at dance* Janice Carroll *Older woman at dance* Gertrude Astor(?) *Butler at Pendleton House* n.k. *Vocal group* members of Six Hits and a Miss *Larry Hamilton* Damian O'Flynn *First hotel manager* Charles Anthony Hughes *People on elevator* n.k. *Second hotel manager* Olan Soule *Jewelers* David Hoffman, Paul Bradley *College girl* n.k. *Dancers in nightmare ballet* n.k. *College dean at graduation* Helen Van Tuyl *Butler* Larry Kent

29. FUNNY FACE

Paramount Pictures, 103 minutes, VistaVision, Technicolor; New York premiere March 28, 1957, Radio City Music Hall (Copyright March 28, 1957)

Producer Roger Edens *Director* Stanley Donen "Choreography by Eugene Loring and Fred Astaire" "Songs staged by Stanley Donen" *Dance assistants* Dave Robel, Pat Denise *Songs* music by George Gershwin, lyrics by Ira Gershwin ("Think Pink," "Bonjour Paris!," "On How to Be Lovely," bridge for "Clap Yo' Hands": music by Roger Edens, lyrics by Leonard Gershe; "Marche Funèbre": music by Roger Edens, lyric by Lela Simone) *Additional music* Bullfight dance: Alexander Courage; dance music for "Clap Yo' Hands": Skip Martin; "Basal Metabolism": Alexander Courage *Musical director and conductor* Adolph Deutsch *Arrangements and orchestrations* Conrad Salinger, Mason Van Cleave, Alexander Courage, Skip Martin *Screenplay* Leonard Gershe (from his unproduced stage play *Wedding Day*) *Director of photography* Ray June *Color consultant* Richard Mueller *Special visual consultant and main title backgrounds* Richard Avedon *Special effects* John P. Fulton *Process photography* Farciot Edouart *Art directors* Hal Pereira, George W. Davis *Set decoration* Sam Comer, Ray Moyer *Costumes* Edith Head *Audrey Hepburn's Paris wardrobe* Hubert de Givenchy *Makeup* Wally Westmore *Hair* Nellie Manley *Editor* Frank Bracht *Recording* George and Winston Leverett *Assistant director* William McGarry

Receptionists Marilyn White, Dorothy Colbert *Lettie (Thompson's secretary)* Ruta Lee *Maggie Prescott* Kay Thompson *Babs* Virginia Gibson *Laura* Sue England *Junior editors* Louise Glenn, Heather Hopper, Cecile Rogers *Models in "Think Pink" number* Suzy Parker, Sunny Harnett *Dovitch* Alex Gerry *Dick Avery* Fred Astaire *Steve (Astaire's assistant)* Paul Smith *Marion (model)* Dovima *Jo Stockton* Audrey Hepburn *French tour man* n.k. *Male dancers in "Bonjour, Paris!" number* n.k. *Paul Duval* Robert Flemyng *Sidewalk cafe patrons* Baroness Ella van Heemstra, Roger Edens *Gigi* Karen Scott *Man in cafe* n.k. *Man standing on head* Jerry Chiat *Man nearby* Gabriel Curtiz *Drinking companions* George Dee, Marcel de La Brosse, Albert Godderis *Mimi* Diane du Bois *Dancers in "Basal Metabolism"* n.k. *Marcel (Astaire's assistant)* n.k. *Priest* n.k. *French woman* n.k. *Professor Emile Flostre* Michel Auclair *Woman at door at Flostre's* n.k. *Bouncer* Jerry Lucas *Singer at Flostre's* Elizabeth Slifer(?) *Woman crying at Flostre's* Jan Bradley *Mr. Barker* Nesdon Booth *Mrs. Barker* Fern Barry *Announcer at fashion show* n.k. *Clerk at hotel* n.k. *Telephone operator at hotel* n.k. *TWA clerk* Donald Lawton *Airport announcer* n.k. *Man buyer* Peter Camlin *Woman buyer* Elsa Petersen

30. SILK STOCKINGS

Metro-Goldwyn-Mayer, 117 minutes, CinemaScope, Metrocolor; New York premiere July 18, 1957, Radio City Music Hall (Copyright May 13, 1957)

Producer Arthur Freed *Director* Rouben Mamoulian "All dances in which Fred Astaire appears choreographed by Hermes Pan; All other dances choreographed by Eugene Loring" *Dance assistants* Dave Robel, Pat Denise, Angela Blue *Songs* music and lyrics by Cole Porter *Musical director and conductor* André Previn *Arrangements and orchestrations* Conrad Salinger *Additional orchestrations* Skip Martin, Al Woodbury, Robert Franklyn *Music coordinator* Lela Simon *Screenplay* Leonard Gershe, Leonard Spiegelgass (based upon the original musical play by George S. Kaufman, Leueen McGrath, and Abe Burrows; also based upon the screenplay *Ninotchka* by Charles Brackett, Billy Wilder, Walter Reisch, and Ernst Lubitsch [earlier version by S. N. Behrman]; all versions derived from "Ninotchka," an original story by Melchior Lengyel) *Additional scriptwriting* Harry Kurnitz *Director of photography* Robert Bronner *Color consultant* Charles K. Hagedon *Art directors* William A. Horning, Randall Duell *Set decoration* Edwin B. Willis, Hugh Hunt *Costumes* Helen Rose *Makeup* William Tuttle *Hair* Sydney Guilaroff *Editor* Harold F. Kress *Recording* Robert Tucker *Assistant director* Al Jennings

Steve Canfield Fred Astaire *Peter Ilyitch Boroff (composer)* Wim Sonneveld *Stage manager* Rolfe Sedan *Bibinski* Jules Munshin *Brankov* Peter Lorre (singing dubbed by Ernest Newton) *Ivanov* Joseph Buloff (singing dubbed by William B. Lee) *Fifi* Tybee Afra *Suzette* Betty Uitti *Gabrielle* Barrie Chase *Arresting officer* Frank Arnold *Arrested Commissar of Art* Leonid Snegoff *Vassili Markovitch (Commissar of Art)* George Tobias *Russian ballet master* Michel Panaieff *Vera (ballet dancer)* Belita *Voice of receptionist (male)* n.k. *Ninotchka (Nina Yoshenko)* Cyd Charisse (singing dubbed by Carol Richards) *Messenger* n.k. *Porter* Peter Camlin *Peggy Dayton* Janis Paige *Reporters* Paul Bryar, Stephen Ellis, Eugene Borden, Roger Etienne, Jean Heremans, Francis Ravel, Albert Carrier, George Sorel, Marcel de la Brosse, Olga Borget, Geneviève Pasques *Pierre* n.k. *Proprietor of fashion salon* Florence Wyatt *Fashion models* June McCall, Virginia Bates, Susan Avery, Arlene Karr, June Kirby *Gate attendant at film studio* n.k. *Man entering film studio* n.k. *Al* n.k. *Film director* Jan Arvan *Stagehands* n.k. *Postwoman* Kaaren Verne *Musicians* n.k. *Visa official* Ivan Triesault *Doorman at nightclub* Manuel Paris

31. FINIAN'S RAINBOW

Warner Brothers–Seven Arts, 145 minutes, PanaVision, Technicolor; New York premiere October 9, 1968, Penthouse Theater (Copyright October 1, 1968)

Producer Joseph Landon *Associate producer* Joel Freeman *Director* Francis Ford Coppola "Choreography by Hermes Pan" *Songs* music by Burton Lane, lyrics by E. Y. Harburg *Musical director and conductor* Ray Heindorf *Associate musical director* Ken Darby *Screenplay* E. Y. Harburg, Fred Saidy (from the Broadway play by E. Y. Harburg and Fred Saidy) *Additional scriptwriting* Francis Ford Coppola, Joseph Landon *Director of photography* Philip Lathrop *Art director* Hilyard M. Brown *Set decoration* William L. Kuehl, Phillip Abramson *Costumes* Dorothy Jeakins *Makeup* Gordon Bau *Hair* Jean Burt Reilly *Editor* Melvin Shapiro *Assistant editor* Fred Talmage *Recording* M. A. Merrick, Dan Wallin *Music recording* Richard C. Harris *Dialogue supervisor* Ronald Colby *Continuity* Betty Levin *Assistant directors* Fred Gammon, Howard Kazanjian

Finian McLonergan Fred Astaire *Sharon McLonergan* Petula Clark *Sheriff* Dolph Sweet *Buzz Collins* Ronald Colby *Howard* Al Freeman, Jr. *Henry* Louis Silas *Susan the Silent* Barbara Hancock *Sharecroppers* Brenda Arnau and others *Woody Mahoney* Don Francks *Elderly black man* n.k. *Og the leprechaun* Tommy Steele *Senator Billboard Rawkins* Keenan Wynn *Geologists* Robert Cleaves, Vince Howard *Postman* n.k. *District Attorney* Wright King *His assistant (Rogers)* n.k. *Passion Pilgrim Gospeleers* Avon Long, Roy Glenn, Jester Hairston *Minister* n.k. *Deputies* Peter Virgo, Martin Eric

NOTES

(Asterisked notes are to material in footnotes.)

INTRODUCTION

"inventing 'up' to the arty . . . just happens": Astaire 1959, pp. 6–7.

On dancers' opinions: Balanchine: Nabokov and Carmichael, p. 48; Cunningham: Cunningham; Nureyev and Robbins: Heeley; Fonteyn: Fonteyn, pp. 3, 4, 37; Baryshnikov: Baryshnikov. For similar comments, see also Harris 1973, 1981; Siegel 1980; Vaughan 1956, p. 91; Park, p. 29.

THE YEARS BEFORE HOLLYWOOD

This discussion of Astaire's early career is based principally on his autobiography (1959) and also on Barnett, Davidson, and other sources as indicated. All quotations from Adele Astaire are from her 1936 article.

Wayburn's script: a copy survives in the University of Southern California Library, as does a later, considerably shortened version that Wayburn may have tried to recycle with other child performers.

"Adele had the faculty . . . ": Wodehouse and Bolton, p. 198. They go on: "Fred struggled on without her for a while, but finally threw in his hand and disappeared. There is a rumor that he turned up in Hollywood. It was the best he could hope for after losing his brilliant sister." In 1933 Wodehouse published *Heavy Weather,* a novel with a central character who seems to have been inspired by Adele Astaire.

"I don't think . . . ": Benchley.

Serge Diaghilev: Haskell, p. 200; Dolin.

Fellow vaudevillian: Niemeyer, p. 24.

Particularly influential: Astaire 1959, pp. 18, 238–39; Conrad, p. 11.

John Bubbles: Astaire 1980b; Pan, 1980; Crosby 1953, p. 332; Levant 1941, p. 179; B. Thomas 1984, p. 27. See also Murphy 1970, p. 49; Dietz 1974, p. 12. Bubbles claims that Astaire once took an hour-long lesson from him on the stage of the Ziegfeld Theatre and paid four hundred dollars for it (J. Goldberg 1978).

"learn how to twiddle . . . ": Dolin.

". . . well known as real brother and sister": Astaire 1959, p. 151.

"Come on, Fred . . . ": Luce.
"Saying 'I love you'. . . ": J. Lewis; or: "we thought [the love story] would come out in the dancing" (Astaire 1980a). Appalled at the sexual explicitness of R-rated movies in the 1980s, Astaire observed, "Why do they have to be so *obvious?*" (1980b).

THE HOLLYWOOD MUSICALS

"I am tremendously . . . " and "I am a little uncertain . . . ": Behlmer, pp. 50–51.
"a helluva dancer . . . ": Haver, p. 76.
"You can get dancers . . . ": quoted by composer Burton Lane in B. Green 1979, p. 54, and reaffirmed in Lane 1983.
On Broadway stars' failure in Hollywood, see especially Mordden, pp. 50–66.
By RKO's standards: For complete statistics and for an excellent discussion of RKO's corporate history, see Jewell; also useful is Jewell and Harbin.
* "Fred Astaire steals picture . . . ": Jewell, p. 207.
* Goldwyn petitioned: RKO files; Mosley, pp. 159–60.
". . . be-glamoured and be-pixied": Agate, pp. 223–26.
Berman journey: Berman.
Astaire letters: February 9, February 12, 1934. Berman telegram: February 26, 1934. "I'm a bit . . . ": letter of April 4, 1934. See also Jewell, pp. 219–20.
In his autobiography: Astaire 1959, p. 184.
"Your work . . . ": Britton. See also B. Thomas 1984, pp. 37–38.
"cannot be overemphasized": Jewell, p. 258.
* "The girls always think . . . ": Lawrenson, p. 108.
"We *never* fought": Astaire 1980a; Rogers on Heeley; Reagan 1984, p. 158. Hermes Pan, their colleague, strongly agrees: Pan 1980.
"There is no setup . . . ": Jablonski and Stewart, p. 250.
Comparative statistics on top ten money earners: Purcell.
* Film version of *Lady Be Good!*: Skolsky 1935.
* "I thought . . . ": Marshall, pp. 82–83. See also A. Astaire 1935.
Astaire's new contract: For a discussion of his displeasure with the financially insecure studio, see Jewell, pp. 270–71, 318–21.
"I don't want . . . ": Sullivan.
Studio's hottest property: See also Table 1. In a lengthy magazine article about Rogers in 1943, S. J. Woolf discussed her life and career without ever mentioning the films she had done with Astaire.
On the Astaire-Rogers breakup at RKO, see also Jewell, pp. 546–47, and D. Churchill.
* "The infectious . . . ": Milton.
* Increase in metal-tap business: *Literary Digest* 1936, p. 21.
* "he carefully removed . . . ": Davidson, p. 182.
* "his style no longer . . . ": S. Harvey 1975, p. 108; see also Hirschhorn 1974, p. 139.
On the dancing school trauma, see Astaire 1959, pp. 284, 289–90.

THE YEARS AFTER THE HOLLYWOOD MUSICALS

"A four wood . . . ": J. Lewis.
"I didn't realize . . . ": Astaire 1981.

THE AUTHORSHIP OF THE CHOREOGRAPHY

"You know . . . nobody could ever . . . ": Saltus, p. 12.
Pan as behind-the-scenes figure: See, for example, de Mille, pp. 89–90.
"Fred Astaire creates . . . ": Pierre, p. 11.
Astaire's dominance in the choreographic process: "Fred invented everything he ever did" (Adele Astaire in Heeley); "[Astaire] is his own choreographer . . . [he] works out his own steps and those of his partner" (Eustis, pp. 103, 110); "He creates every step, every intricate routine himself" (Hall); "Fred always had the final word" (Pan 1980); "[Astaire] is his own dance originator" (Barnett, p. 19); "All of his steps are of his creation" (Baskette, p. 96); "[Astaire] always arranges his own routines" (Creelman); "He figured out all his own routines" (H. Warren, p. 304). Astaire: "I create all of my own routines" (Crowther 1937); "I do all my own choreography" (Conrad, p. 13; Astaire 1980b); "I have had to do most of my choreography. I would say most of it, with help from various choreographers that I've worked with" (Astaire 1978; see also B. Thomas 1984, p. 98). Astaire apparently contributed a smaller portion of the choreographic material on his television shows—about 40 or 50 percent, estimates Pan (1983, 1980; see also Knight 1960). On Astaire's creative process, see also Davidson, p. 190; Croce 1972, pp. 89–96; Winge; *Literary Digest* 1936, p. 20; Burnet; Richards, p. 162.
* Soloists fashioned their own material: See Guest.
* Frederick Ashton: Vaughan 1977, pp. xvii–xix.
Astaire on Gershwin and the prop man: Astaire 1959, pp. 134–35, 295.
"Barrie would contribute . . . ": Saltus, p. 14.
* "You would be surprised . . . ": Newnham.
* "We all pitched in": J. Goldberg 1976.

ASTAIRE'S WORKING METHODS

* Never did much exercising: Creelman; Moss.
"You go to a rehearsal . . . ": Astaire 1979a.
* "I used to do it . . . ": Saltus, p. 14.
Recording the numbers live, post-recording in the 1930s: Astaire 1959, p. 200; Borne, pp. 53–55; Pan 1980.
"How do you think . . . ": Evans.
* "Astaire has found out . . . ": Winge.
"I have a horror . . . ", "I always need . . . ", etc.: Astaire 1959, pp. 244, 186, 203, 198.
"He lacks confidence . . . ": Schickel, p. 260; also Walters.
"I remember . . . ": Lerner, p. 89.
"not a ham": Walters.
"too lightfooted . . . ", "I am really bad-tempered . . . ": Astaire 1959, p. 7.
"stupid, small-minded . . . ": Jampel; see also Reagan, p. 156.
"He gets very annoyed . . . ": BBC, p. 30.
Never "100% right . . . ": Zeitlin.
"We worked hard . . . ": Pan 1980.
* Running gag about drink of water: Davidson, p. 89.
* "keeping the laughs going . . . ": Astaire 1959, p. 254.
"first concern was the film . . . ": Fontaine, p. 143.
"Of all the actors . . . ": Mamoulian.

ASTAIRE'S CHOREOGRAPHY: STYLE AND CONSTRAINTS

"I think it's probably . . . ": Astaire 1979a.
"Working out the steps . . . ": Eustis, p. 110.
"Get it as perfect . . . ": Astaire 1979b.
"Astaire's dancing . . . ": Anderson.
"Just try and keep up . . . ": Evans.
"outlaw style": Astaire 1959, p. 325. On the issue of style, see also Parrish.
On running his previous films, see Davidson, p. 190; Fordin, p. 167.
* "oompah trot" or "runaround": Astaire 1959, pp. 82–83.
For Astaire on choruses, see Eustis, p. 107.
* Richard Rodgers on the two-minute plot: Delamater 1978, pp. 613–14.
"little tonal contrast" etc.: Hamm, pp. 361–78.
Astaire on making money: See Saltus, p. 10.

ASTAIRE'S CHOREOGRAPHY: SOURCES OF THE MOVEMENT VOCABULARY

* "Gestures . . . family relation . . . ": Balanchine, p. 255.
"I find that . . . ": Eustis, p. 109.
* Steps and music adopted: Astaire 1979a; Baskette, p. 96; Winge.
"Every song . . . ": Wilder, p. 109.
"the world's greatest . . . ": Lane 1981.
"He knew . . . ": S. Green 1973, p. 1; Berlin prefers Astaire: O'Hara, p. 77.
Jerome Kern: Bordman 1980, p. 142.
"Fred Astaire is the best singer . . . ": Levant 1965, p. 204.
"He has a remarkable ear . . . ": Crosby 1975.
"He makes every song . . . ": Balliett; see also Harris 1973.
* George Gershwin on Astaire's singing: Jablonski and Stewart, p. 281; but see also Croce 1972, p. 118.
* Does not like his own singing voice: Wixen, p. 11; Kreuger.
* "serious hobby of mine": Astaire 1959, p. 46.
Astaire's influence on song composition: on the general subject of the collaborative process between music director and choreographer, see the interesting discussion by MGM's John Green in Delamater 1978, pp. 617–21.
"Astaire *can't* . . . ": BBC, p. 29.
"You give Astaire . . . ": Wilson.
"made listeners think . . . ": Wilder, pp. 155–56, 110.
Four in the morning: Astaire 1959, pp. 210, 229, 234.
"Except for the times . . . ": Davidson, p. 186.
"If I may say it . . . ": Modell. See also Vecchi.
"To catch the public . . . ": Fleming.
"It is extremely important . . . ": Eustis, p. 111.
For an extended discussion of Astaire's contribution to the integrated musical, see Mueller 1984.
Dance films with plots: see Croce 1965, p. 26; Croce 1972, p. 7; Kisselgoff 1980; see also Vaughan 1966.
"merely adornments": Hirschhorn 1974, p. 140; "like cherries . . . ": Taylor and Jackson, p. 20; "unity of expression" etc.: Kobal 1971, p. 218. Similar assertions: Fordin and Chase; Sonnenshein, pp. 500–1; Taylor and Jackson, p. 81; Kobal 1977, p. 147; Delamater 1974, p. 130; Delamater 1981, pp. 132, 163–65, 286–87; Sennett, p. 237; Solomon, pp. 73–74; Honeycutt; Schatz, pp. 207–20; Basinger, p. 139. On this issue, see also M. Wood, pp. 152–53; Mueller 1984; J. Feuer 1983, p. 73.
* "this may seem . . . ": Hillier, p. 27.

ASTAIRE'S USE OF THE CAMERA

For additional discussion of some of these issues, see Mueller 1981.
"Either the camera will dance . . . ": Winge.
"The history of dance . . . ": Heeley.
Approach forged by indirection: Astaire 1980b. Pan recalls: Pan 1980. Rogers recalls: Evans, p. 11.
"In the old days . . . ": Eustis, p. 106.
On three-camera dance filming, see Eustis, pp. 108–9; Croce 1972, pp. 126–27.
Knew how the dance would look: Pan 1980.
"a terrifying, tiresome thing . . . ": Saltus, pp. 12, 14. See also Pan's comments in BBC, p. 16; and in Georgakas.
* " 'Top Hat' . . . ": Saltus, p. 14.
"In every kind of dancing": Eustis, p. 107.
On spatial phenomena of choreographing for the camera, see Mueller 1978.
* Astaire preferred CinemaScope: Fordin, p. 444.
* "an abomination": Delamater 1981, p. 218.
* On Minnelli's use of the camera in dance, see Genne.
* No important difference: Astaire 1980b.
* Walters observes: Walters.
Ross' *The Turning Point:* A startling revelation is Ross' assertion that he prepared for the production, in part, by screening Astaire films (*New York Times,* June 15, 1978).

ASTAIRE'S CONTRIBUTION

"I don't think about what I do . . . ": Astaire 1980b.

1. DANCING LADY

On Astaire's attitude toward the film, see Astaire 1959, pp. 183–84.
On the preview audience, see Haver, p. 148. This work also includes an excellent, lavishly illustrated discussion of the production of the film (pp. 134–48).

THE SCRIPT AND THE PRODUCTION

* Crawford and Gable: B. Thomas 1978, pp. 81, 88, 94.
* Crawford and Tone: Haver, p. 145.

THE MUSIC

For Richard Rodgers on the film, see Rodgers, pp. 163–64.

THE CHOREOGRAPHY

"required a lot . . . ": Astaire 1959, p. 184.

C. EVERYTHING I HAVE IS YOURS

On the discovery and use of the song, see Haver, p. 145.

E. HEIGH-HO (REHEARSAL)

"Gosh . . . ": Astaire, 1959, p. 183.
* Gable was ill: Haver, p. 146.
* Crawford dancing with broken ankle: Crawford, p. 97.

F. HEIGH-HO / LET'S GO BAVARIAN

* Written by Lane and Adamson: Lane 1983. For an illustrated discussion of the process used to achieve the photographic effect in this sequence, see Haver, p. 145.

2. FLYING DOWN TO RIO

On Astaire's surprise at his success, see Astaire 1959, pp. 189, 196.

ASTAIRE AND ROGERS

"only in the sense . . . ": Croce 1972, p. 24.

THE MUSIC

For an overview of Youmans' career, see Wilk, pp. 33–39. For an assessment of his music, see Wilder, pp. 292–312.

THE CHOREOGRAPHY

On Pan, see Pan 1980; BBC, p. 21; B. Green 1979, p. 60; Pierre, p. 11; *Literary Digest* 1936. On Borne, see Borne, pp. 50–53.

A. MUSIC MAKES ME

* "Sweet Music": See also Dietz 1974, p. 12.
"one of the greatest . . . ": Park, p. 21.

B. ORCHIDS IN THE MOONLIGHT

* "lifted bodily . . . ": *Vanity Fair,* February 1934. For sober analysis of the "equator" line, including the colorful suggestion that it "eroticizes the globe," see Henderson.

C. THE CARIOCA

"I thought Ginger and I . . . ": Astaire 1959, p. 196.
Dance gimmick an inspiration of Hermes Pan: Croce 1972, p. 26.

3. THE GAY DIVORCEE

* Using Luce in the film: Berman.
For an excellent discussion of the production of *The Gay Divorcee* and of the personalities behind it, see Croce 1972, pp. 37–41.
"I was amazed . . . ": Astaire 1959, p. 196.

THE FILM AND THE CENSORS

On the 1934 changes in the production code, see McClure, p. 147.

C. A NEEDLE IN A HAYSTACK

* Astaire liking for "After You, Who?": BBC, p. 24.
* he will tie . . . ": Barnett, p. 29; also Skolsky 1934. On Astaire's clothes-consciousness, see also A. Astaire 1936, Gallico.

D. LET'S K-NOCK K-NEEZ

On the number's contribution to Betty Grable's career, see D. Warren, pp. 26–27.
* Routine choreographed by Pan: Croce 1972, p. 33.

E. NIGHT AND DAY

* "made things as easy as possible . . . ": C. Schwartz 1977, p. 120.
Producer suggested song be dropped: Eells 1967, p. 99. On the song, see also Wilder, pp. 230–32.
* 'I think that will work": Eells 1967, p. 99.
* ". . . Mohammedan call to worship . . . ": Kimball 1971, p. 110.
* More mundane stories: C. Schwartz 1977, p. 142.
"Claire was a beautiful dancer . . . ": Astaire 1959, p. 176.
"Ginger was a Charleston dancer . . . ": BBC, p. 23.

F. THE CONTINENTAL

* Porter wrote an amusing song: See Kimball 1983, p. 110.
* "worked out the steps . . . ": BBC, p. 23.
"hardly compare with . . . Berkeley . . . ": Croce 1972, p. 36.
"in many languages": Borne, p. 52.

G. TABLE DANCE

"a spectacular thing . . . ": Astaire 1959, pp. 176, 193.
Luce's recollection: Luce.

4. ROBERTA

THE SCRIPT

For discussions of the stage show, see Bordman 1980, pp. 335–43; S. Green 1971, pp. 91–93; Gottfried, pp. 172–73; Freedland 1978, pp. 116–18.
On the importance of *Roberta* to Bob Hope's career, see Hope, pp. 106–13; Morella, Epstein, and Clark, pp. 12–15, 61–64, 204; Faith, pp. 87–94, 124–25, 322–23. For Murphy's recollections, see Murphy, pp. 150–57.
* ". . . mistakes you make": Jewell, p. 270.
* Astaire had seen show: Lederer, p. 58.

THE MUSIC

Astaire's suggestion on "I Won't Dance": Bordman 1980, p. 248.

THE FILMING OF THE DANCES

* Seiter assigned: Croce 1972, p. 51.

A. ORGAN NUMBER

Vaudevillian gag: Hope, p. 107.

B. LET'S BEGIN

For an extended appreciation of the song, see Wilder, pp. 66–67. Wilder especially likes the way the opening phrase of the verse is used again as a tag at the end of the chorus. However, neither verse nor tag is used in the film; nor, apparently, were they sung in the stage show. This wonderful song played a much bigger part in the stage version—it opened the show (sung by a male quartet) and was reprised at least four times, with appropriate alterations in the lyric to suit the changed situations. The lyric, which speaks of the dilemma of choosing between "love or gin, wife or sin," was considerably bowdlerized for the film.

D. I'LL BE HARD TO HANDLE

"three minutes": Croce 1972, p. 47.
* Floor of hard maple: See Baskette, p. 96.
* "by tapping out . . . ": ibid.

E. YESTERDAYS

* "Sweet and Hot" reference: S. Green 1973, p. 92.
* Fay Templeton: A reigning Broadway beauty at the turn of the century, Templeton weighed two hundred and fifty pounds in 1933 and had such severe arthritis that she was unable to stand for any length of time. Accordingly, the role was arranged so that she played most of it sitting or lying on a couch—an element partly carried over to the film staging (see Freedland 1978, pp. 116–17).
Death scene: In the stage version, the music used in the death scene was an operatic duet, "The Touch of Your Hand," sung without plot relevance by the Dunne character and the doorman; the film's use of "Yesterdays" is obviously a considerable improvement. (In the novel, the death of the aunt is handled quite perfunctorily.) Some of the long shots at the end of the scene showing Dunne singing (such as E1) are out of synchronization with her voice on the soundtrack. The original idea, apparently, was to have her conclude the song and then exit with the others. This was changed so that she exits while still singing and then concludes the song in the anteroom as the aunt slumps in death.

F. I WON'T DANCE

Borne's second piano: Borne, p. 55.
* "chicken stew . . . ": Baskette, p. 96.

H. LOVELY TO LOOK AT

* Fields, Kern, and the lyric: Wilk, p. 43.
* "It's a very good song . . . ": BBC, p. 26.
* "keep the melody . . . ": Wilder, p. 72.
* Kern's ambivalence about "Smoke Gets In Your Eyes": See Wilder, pp. 71–72; Bordman 1980, pp. 341–42.

5. TOP HAT

For some retrospective appreciations of the film, see Crowther 1978, pp. 31–35; Grieves.

THE SCRIPT

"There's a lot . . . ": Croce 1972, p. 68. For a tabular presentation of many of the points of plot similarity between *Top Hat* and *The Gay Divorcee,* see S. Green 1973, p. 98.
For an excellent extended consideration of the writing, and rewriting, of the *Top Hat* script, see Croce 1972, pp. 67–78.
* "In the first place . . . ": See also Jewell, p. 299.

THE MUSIC AND THE ASTAIRE-BERLIN FRIENDSHIP

* "Your Hit Parade" ranking: Williams, pp. 70–71.
On Berlin's pride over the *Top Hat* songs, see J. Wilson; Freedland 1974, pp. 125–26; S. Green 1981, p. 285.
For Astaire on Berlin, see Lederer; Astaire 1959, p. 55.
"closest and best friend": J. Wilson.
"He's a real . . . ": J. Wilson. When Berlin took up painting in the 1970s, he often sent samples to Astaire. One of these, a small picture of a bird wearing a top hat, came with a note: "I started to paint a bird, and I was thinking of you. So I stuck a top hat on his head" (Lederer, p. 57). Berlin also supplied at least two songs not used in the film, both written in 1934: "Get Thee Behind Me, Satan" and "Wild About You"; the first was eventually used in *Follow the Fleet,* the second in Berlin's 1940 Broadway show *Louisiana Purchase* (Jay, p. 77).

C. ISN'T THIS A LOVELY DAY

* "quite earnestly bawdy": Greene, pp. 30–32.
* Occur at a zoo: Croce 1972, pp. 67–68.
* "they made it rain . . . ": J. Wilson.
Dance similar to minuet: See minuet description by Wynne, p. 44.

D. TOP HAT, WHITE TIE AND TAILS

* Only idea that survives in film: Croce 1972, p. 70.
For photographs from the *Funny Face* stage solo (which, like "Top Hat," seems to have used a chorus-craning idea), see S. Green 1973, p. 26; B. Green 1979, pp. 34–35.
The "Young Man of Manhattan" idea came to Astaire at 4:00 a.m. Inspired, he jumped out of bed and pranced around with an umbrella as a prop, inadvertently waking his sister in the next room. "Hey," she called out, "what the hell are you doing?" "I just got an idea for the 'Manhattan' number." "Well, hang on to it, baby—you're going to need it in this turkey" (Astaire 1959, p. 164).
On the genesis of the film number, see also Lederer, p. 56; B. Green 1979, pp. 41–42; Bordman 1978, p. 456; S. Green 1981, p. 285.
On Berlin's song, see Wilder, p. 110.
For another discussion of this number, see Mast, pp. 21–24.
* Placement of the number in the original script: Croce 1972, p. 68.
Astaire could not "routine": Astaire 1959, p. 210.

E. CHEEK TO CHEEK

On the decor, see Croce 1972, pp. 75–76.
* Melody "based on" Chopin: Jay, p. 77.
* "The melody line . . . ": J. Wilson.
For firsthand accounts of the feather-shedding event, see Astaire 1959, pp. 207–10; Niven, p. 250; Eells 1976, pp. 41–42; BBC, pp. 30–31; Davidson, p. 187. According to Rogers (1984), the dress was ice-blue in color.
* Joke track: Pan 1980.

F. THE PICCOLINO

"I love it . . . ": J. Wilson.

6. FOLLOW THE FLEET

THE SCRIPT

* Rogers helpful to Hilliard: Nelson, pp. 107–9.
* Lela Rogers as Ball's coach: Morella and Epstein, pp. 26–29.
* Ball purchased studio: Jewell, pp. 286–87.

THE MUSIC

Berlin wrote two songs for the film that were not used: "Moonlight Maneuvers" and "There's a Smile on My Face." They were published independently in 1935 (Croce 1972, p. 96).

THE CHOREOGRAPHY

Pan choreographed Rogers' solo: Pan 1980.

C. GET THEE BEHIND ME, SATAN

* "supplied the best joke . . . ": Greene, pp. 68–69.

D. LET YOURSELF GO (DANCE)

* Footage inserted in Astaire-Rogers dance: Croce 1972, p. 85.
* Final contestants: *New York Evening Journal,* December 9, 1935.

H. I'M PUTTING ALL MY EGGS IN ONE BASKET

* "an old burlesque gag": Croce 1972, p. 88.

J. LET'S FACE THE MUSIC AND DANCE

On the limp-kneed pose, see J. Harvey, which also contains another analysis of this number.
* Song written with Astaire in mind: J. Wilson.
* Song was freed up: Croce 1972, p. 96.
* Martin's great disappointment: Martin and Charisse, p. 57.
* Posed stills with grins: See, for example, Freedland 1976, pp. 68–69; Springer, p. 86; Kobal 1971, p. 145; Sennett, p. 97.

In two parts: The final script calls for two separate dances in this number. The first begins "with a frenzy because both expect to die at the end of it" and concludes as "their dance infects them," turning frenzy to "a kind of exaltation." Then Astaire throws his gun and a letter of hers overboard, and a cutaway shot is inserted to show these objects splashing into the water. Finally, there is a second dance, which is supposed to be "triumphant."
* Fortunate "accident": Pan 1983.
* "I kept on dancing . . . ": Astaire 1959, pp. 214–15.

K. WE SAW THE SEA (TAG)

Concluding scenes: The ending was developed on the set. The final script mostly reworks *Roberta:* after "Let's Face the Music and Dance," it calls for Scott and Hilliard to become quickly reconciled, and Astaire and Rogers to return to the stage to encore their last number, "only this time there is gay rhythmic movement." However, unlike *Roberta,* the script did not include an Astaire-Rogers proposal scene.

7. SWING TIME

The greatest Astaire-Rogers film: Croce 1965, pp. 25, 32. For discussions of the remarkable Art Deco sets, see Croce 1972, pp. 112–113, and Spiegel.

THE MUSIC

Bennett brought by Kern: Bennett's arrival at RKO caused some strain with the studio's resident music director, Max Steiner (Bordman 1980, p. 354).
* ". . . shadow boxed . . . ": Nugent.
* "Although I don't think . . . ": Kimball and Simon, p. 203.

THE SCRIPT

"stupid": Saltus, p. 16. Reviewing the film in 1936, Wilford Beaton voiced sentiments with which Astaire would probably agree: "Pan Berman no doubt would get in bad with the other fellows who produce musicals if he supplied one of his with a coherent story having some appeal to an intelligent audience, but I think he should have a go at it. The innovation might provoke the box-office into hearty response." On script development, see Croce 1972, pp. 108–9; Croce 1965, pp. 33–35; Richie, p. 38.
"Two more . . . ": Milton.

GINGER ROGERS

"He gave us . . . ": Rogers; see also Richie, p. 39. For a less generous assessment of Stevens' abilities by another actress, see Fontaine, pp. 90, 115–16.
* Rogers having affair with Stevens: Eells 1976, pp. 46–48. On Stevens' attraction to his leading ladies, see Fontaine, p. 90.

A. IT'S NOT IN THE CARDS

Not very good: Pan 1980.

C. THE WAY YOU LOOK TONIGHT

"The producers lacked . . . ": Croce 1972, p. 105. Fields recalls that when Kern first played the song for her, she started to cry: "The release absolutely killed me. I couldn't stop, it was so beautiful" (Wilk, p. 44).

D. WALTZ IN SWING TIME

* "They can't wait . . . ": Croce 1972, p. 102.
* "put them together . . . ": Bordman 1980, p. 358. "composing": Bennett. Borne insists: Borne, p. 57. The music as originally published reads "Music by Jerome Kern" and, in smaller letters, "Constructed and Arranged by R. Russell Bennett"; in a later edition there were some fairly minor changes, and Bennett's name was dropped from the credits (Wilder, p. 75). Fields wrote some lyrics for part of the composition, and these are sung by a chorus under the opening titles, but the words are incomprehensible.

The piece is unified: "Waltz in Swing Time" can be broken down into eight sections: 1. introduction; 2. fanfare melody (sixteen measures); 3. waltz passage that rises chromatically (sixteen measures); 4. waltz with syncopation (two against three) (thirty-two measures); 5. fanfare (sixteen measures); 6. soft waltz derived from C section of "Never Gonna Dance" (forty measures); 7. fanfare (sixteen measures); 8. coda, beginning with a broad waltz (eight measures), which then alternates with repeats of the syncopated waltz, fading away finally with a soft repeat of the fanfare idea.
Astaire suggests pit band: Croce 1972, p. 112.

F. BOJANGLES OF HARLEM

For a discussion of Robinson and Bubbles, see Stearns, pp. 180–88, 212–19. On the music, see also Bordman 1980, pp. 357–60; Croce 1972, p. 112; Croce 1965, p. 34; Freedland 1978, p. 129.
* "Fred took me aside . . . ": Wilk, p. 44.
* "Jig Piano Dance": Bordman 1980, pp. 358–60.
* "got paid . . . ": Borne, p. 57.
* ". . . blank white screen . . . ": Walker.

"I just pointed . . . ": Pan 1980.
Ending: The shadow dance was incorporated in the "Hot Fields" scenario, except that there the shadows were to do three different routines, and when the Bojangles dancer tries to match all three, he loses his balance and falls down a flight of stairs. The scenario included the sighting of Astaire's fiancée in the number itself, shortly before the end. The Bojangles dancer is dangling by his fingertips from the edge of a stage dance floor suspended high in the air over a city. He is startled to see his fiancée and then, "with a wry smile," he "waves a hail and farewell to her, and drops off into space."

G. NEVER GONNA DANCE

* Songs also relate in lyric: Solomon, p. 62.

Side-by-side walk reflects earlier dance: Croce 1972, p. 108.
* On shooting the dance: B. Green 1979, p. 82; BBC, p. 39; RKO files; Croce 1972, p. 113.

8. SHALL WE DANCE

"afraid his public . . . ": Rodgers, p. 171.
For an account of Balanchine's traumatic two and a half years at the Metropolitan Opera, see Taper, pp. 177–90.
Less convincing film: Astaire has characterized the film as "one of the weaker sisters" (1978). Leo Braudy argues that the point of the film is to contrast "the emotionally detached and formal patterns of high art with the involved and spontaneous forms of popular art" and to suggest that "tap dancing is superior to ballet as movies are superior to drama, not merely because they are more popular, but because they contain more life and possibility" (pp. 143–44). While that seems a fair, if somewhat generous, estimate of the film's intent, the film's contrived and distinctly unspontaneous texture undercuts the impact of its message.

THE GERSHWINS, ART, AND THE TRIP WEST

For discussions of the Gershwins' dealings, see Jablonski and Stewart, pp. 247–50; Schwartz 1973, p. 274. On Kern's, see Bordman 1980, p. 357.
". . . out to write hits": Gershwin's concern about writing hits in Hollywood explains Alec Wilder's admiring observation that despite Gershwin's work on "more ambitious compositions," his "last songs became *less* rather than more complex" (p. 122).

B. RHUMBA SEQUENCE

* The song "Hi-Ho!": The lyric and Ira Gershwin's recollections of the matter are in Kimball and Simon, p. 203. See also Ewen 1970a, pp. 269–70; Borne, p. 124.

Choreographed by Pan: Pan 1980.
The rhumba: Gershwin's accompanying music to this number, called "Ginger Rhumba" in the film production records, bears some resemblance to portions of "Just Another Rhumba," a song the Gershwins wrote for the 1938 film *The Goldwyn Follies.* Not used in that film, the song was first published in 1959.

D. SLAP THAT BASS

The song: Alec Wilder's comment is apt: "By 1937 it's simply too late for that kind of don't-worry-about-me-I-know-all-about-jazz kind of writing. It comes off as what a friend calls 'ole folks makin' rhythm' " (p. 156). Embedded in the song is a coy and heavy-handed reference to "I Got Rhythm."
* "Fred began to dance . . . ": Georgakas, p. 28; BBC, p. 41.

E. WALKING THE DOG

Gershwin's comment: Levant 1941, p. 208; I. Goldberg, p. 343.

G. THEY ALL LAUGHED

Lyric's origin: I. Gershwin, p. 258.

I. THEY CAN'T TAKE THAT AWAY FROM ME

* Gershwin unhappy: Jablonski and Stewart, p. 281.

J. SHALL WE DANCE

* "Naturally I prefer . . . ": Cullum, p. 41. On Hoctor's career, see also Hering; Cocuzza.

The Ginger dancers: The music when they enter is "Wake Up Brother and Dance," a song the Gershwins wrote for the film that was otherwise unused. The song, fitted out with a new lyric and considerably altered in character, resurfaced in the 1964 Billy Wilder film *Kiss Me, Stupid* as "Sophia" (C. Schwartz 1973, p. 349).
The title song: This song was designed to help plug the film and was written last, after the film's title had finally been decided upon, on a suggestion of Vincente Minnelli's (Jablonski and Stewart, pp. 266–67; Minnelli, p. 95). It bears some resemblance, not too surprisingly, to the song it replaced, "Wake Up Brother and Dance." For a view of this number as "an implicit attack against the [Busby] Berkeley emphasis on anonymous spectacle," see L. Braudy, pp. 143–47.

9. A DAMSEL IN DISTRESS

* *Damsel* set Fontaine's career back: B. Green 1979, p. 88.
* Casting Ruby Keeler: Astaire 1959, p. 228. Casting Lombard: RKO archives. Jessie Matthews unavailable: S. Green 1973, p. 165; S. Harvey 1975, p. 73.

"sort of a right-legged dancer . . . ": Burns 1980, p. 150.

THE FILM AND GEORGE GERSHWIN

* "used his considerable influence . . . ": Wodehouse 1982, p. 5.
* "a sort of musical comedy . . . ": B. Green 1981, p. 126.

Wodehouse has suggested: Wodehouse 1982, p. 5.

"He complained . . . ": Schwartz 1973, pp. 191–92. See also Kimball and Simon, pp. 200, 216; Ewen 1970, p. 142.

Wodehouse meets Gershwin: See Wodehouse and Bolton, pp. 81–86.

THE MUSIC

"so deceptively authentic . . . ": Levant 1941, pp. 207–8.

"other singers than Fred and Ginger . . . ": Jablonski and Stewart, p. 281.

Baravalle brought in on Astaire's urging: RKO archives.

On Borne's contribution, see Borne, p. 60.

THE SCRIPT

"going to make . . . ": Wodehouse 1953, pp. 97–100. The book had been made into a silent film in 1920 by Pathé and had been a success on the stage in London in 1928 using a script written by Ian Hay and Wodehouse that is much closer to the novel than is the screenplay.

"Friends have often . . . ": Wodehouse 1982, pp. 5–6.

* "Contrary to opinion . . . ": Burns 1955, p. 106.

A. I CAN'T BE BOTHERED NOW

* Niemeyer became stand-in: Niemeyer.

B. THE JOLLY TAR AND THE MILKMAID

* The song: Its lyric can be found in I. Gershwin, pp. 196–97.

C. PUT ME TO THE TEST

* Idea brought in by Burns: Astaire 1959, p. 228. Burns' accounts: Burns 1955, pp. 192–93; 1980, pp. 50–51.
* Lyric used in *Cover Girl:* See I. Gershwin, pp. 90–92. This source also reprints the lyric.
* "great Irish dancer": Burns 1955, p. 193.

Robinson's exit step: an observation by tap expert Jane Goldberg.

D. STIFF UPPER LIP

Local fair: The scene may not be entirely authentic. One British critic has pointed out sternly that it is "a little hard to stomach" the idea of "a Coney Island-type fairground right in the heart of the English countryside" (Conrad, p. 13).

Stylistic tribute: See B. Green 1981, p. 122.

* Lyricist looked up: I. Gershwin, pp. 156–58; this source also reprints the complete lyric, including a second chorus.
* Pan's idea: Pan 1983; see also Georgakas, p. 28.

E. THINGS ARE LOOKING UP

Underappreciated ballads: For other exclamations about the high quality of this song, see Wilder, pp. 159–60; I. Gershwin, p. 345. The number was shot at the RKO ranch in Malibu, California (as was the "Foggy Day" number).

* Fontaine's tap lessons: Fontaine, p. 88.
* "terrified": Pan 1983.

"Isn't she AWFUL?!": Fontaine, p. 89.

F. SING OF SPRING

The song: Played as sweet background music several times during the film, it can be heard most clearly in Fontaine's first scene with her father in his garden. The melody of this unpublished song seems intended to be taken seriously, though the lyric is a parody, filled with such nonsense patter as "tally-tally-til-lo" and "jug-a, jug-a jug." It was first performed in its entirety in 1969 (C. Schwartz 1973, p. 279) and was first recorded in 1976. According to Ira Gershwin, the song was originally written as a "contrapuntal exercise" called "Back to Bach" (p. 198).

H. NICE WORK IF YOU CAN GET IT

* Lyric inspired by English cartoon: I. Gershwin, p. 97.

J. NICE WORK IF YOU CAN GET IT (DANCE)

Zoom lens: *New York Times,* August 29, 1937, sec. 10, p. 3.

* ". . . if you got off . . . ": Astaire 1959, p. 227.

10. CAREFREE

On the film's "feel," see also Mordden, p. 140.

THE SCRIPT

Rogers' penchant for mischief: Her abilities in this area had been used earlier, in the mishap-prone "I'm Putting All My Eggs in One Basket" dance in *Follow the Fleet* (6 H). They were fully exploited (perhaps overexploited) in a 1952 film, *Monkey Business,* in which she and Cary Grant, under the influence of a drug, spend most of the film running amok. (For an appreciation, see McGilligan, pp. 127–28.)

On Rogers and RKO, see Jewell, pp. 425–27.

A. GOLF SOLO

* Borne's piano: Borne, p. 54.

"fooling around," rehearsal data: Astaire 1959, pp. 234–35. For a somewhat fanciful recollection of the filming of the golf solo, see Bellamy, p. 157.

B. I USED TO BE COLOR BLIND

* Intended use of "The Night Is Filled With Music": Croce 1972, p. 150.

On black and white: Berman, Freedland 1976, p. 79.

Astaire's wife and the rumors: Astaire 1959, pp. 233–34.

C. THE YAM

* The Black Bottom's most provocative form: Sims.

Lift a creation of Hermes Pan: Croce 1972, p. 147.

D. CHANGE PARTNERS (SONG)

* Written years earlier: S. Green 1973, p. 180.

E. CHANGE PARTNERS (DANCE)

Lively waltz tempo: The music used for this portion of the dance is the release (B) strain of the AABA song. On the waltz implications of Berlin's song, see Wilder, p. 113. In triple meter, the release resembles the opening phrase of an earlier Berlin song, "Oh, How I Hate to Get Up in the Morning."

11. THE STORY OF VERNON AND IRENE CASTLE

THE SCRIPT

"We were young . . . ": Castle 1919, p. 41.

"of common sense . . . ": Croce 1972, p. 155.

"In *The Castles* . . . ": Ager.

RKO AND MRS. CASTLE

"technical adviser": *Time* magazine, in an article on the film, characterized this term as "Hollywood lingo for a big name hired mainly for publicity purposes" (1939, p. 51). For Irene Castle's dawning suspicions about the accuracy of this characterization, see I. Castle 1958, pp. 245–46.

Payment of $5,000: She also received a $15,000 salary as technical adviser, bringing her total payment for the film to $40,000. Representing her in these negotiations was George Enzinger, a Chicago advertising executive who was her lover at the time and later her fourth (and final) husband. For her recollections of the settlement, see I. Castle 1958, p. 247. See also Jewell, pp. 515–20.

"Irene Castle had her thousands . . . ": *Time* 1939, p. 49.

* "When I was . . . ": Saltus, p. 10.

For photographic comparisons of the Castle and Rogers costumes, see Ager; *Life* 1939. See also Croce 1972, pp. 152–53; S. Green 1973, pp. 186–99.

* She wanted one sequence . . . ": Croce 1972, p. 165; see also BBC, p. 47.

For Mrs. Castle on the nationwide search, see I. Castle 1959, pp. 244–45.

Her suspicion was correct: Berman. Mrs. Castle's contract with RKO committed her to approve Ginger Rogers if "we are unable to agree upon another actress," an ingenious way of saying Mrs. Castle had the right to veto whoever RKO proposed for the role except Ginger Rogers. It may be that her secret desire was to play the role herself. She was a well-preserved forty-four in 1937, and although the film character is supposed to be around twenty, Rogers herself was in her late twenties at the time (though skilled at playing teen-age roles). Irene Castle had had considerable experience as a film actress in silent movies (see Stainton, Fanger). (If the idea was ever seriously considered at RKO, Astaire may have rejected it, as he felt Irene Castle was too old and too tall for him —Saltus, p. 10; BBC, p. 46.) When the film came out, Hedda Hopper remarked in her April 4 column: "The greatest mistake was not letting Irene play herself." RKO offered Mrs. Castle the part of her own mother, but she declined (D. Churchill). She had been interested in a Hollywood comeback as early as 1934, when she made a screen test for Warner Bros. In a letter to RKO, Mrs. Castle says she was hoping the *Castles* film would help her "to get located in Hollywood."

The Castles and the Astaires; Astaire was embarrassed: *Stage.*

"a tremendous influence . . . ": Astaire 1959, pp. 238–39.

"He was always . . . ": I. Castle 1919, p. 65.

* "happy-go-lucky": I. Castle 1958, p. 149.
* "argued over money . . . ": ibid., p. 138.
* Both Castles profligate: Marbury, p. 247.

"Vernon was a delight . . . ": Hayes and Doty, pp. 55–56.

On Vernon Castle's proportions and effeminacy, see I. Castle 1958, pp. 34, 150.

DANCE AND SENSUALITY

On the Castle approach to dance, see Castle 1958, pp. 86–87; Seldes, p. 239; Allen, p. 15; especially Erenberg.

In their dance manual: Castle and Castle, pp. 32–33.

"humor that permeated . . . ": I. Castle 1958, p. 87.

THE MUSIC

Songs not modernized: See also D. Churchill.

On the cost of music rights: *Variety,* April 12, 1939.

CHOREOGRAPHY

Pan's research: Pan 1980.

Mrs. Castle had forgotten steps: I. Castle 1958, p. 188.

"I had frequently . . . ": Crowther 1939.

A. THE YAMA YAMA MAN

Fondness for animals: Vernon Castle once got out of a car on a country drive to help a turtle cross, and his letters to his wife from the war zone urgently and repeatedly inquire after the health and happiness of their numerous pets (I. Castle 1919). Irene Castle felt the same way and expressed the hope in her autobiography that she would be remembered for her animal shelter work, not "as a dancer or style leader" (1958, p. 225).

* Cheek spot on opposite side: Allen, p. 12; Langford, p. 115.

"She swings on her heel . . . ": Brinkley. See also Langford, p. 263; Farnsworth, p. 61; *Life* 1939, p. 28; Ager, p. 23. McCoy's dance was staged by Gus Sohlke.

* Racial transformation: I. Castle 1958, p. 247. Berman finds: Berman.

C. THE HEN PECKS

Historically accurate: Mrs. Castle has reprinted her husband's notes for the sketch (1958, p. 48). The woman behind Rogers and to her right in C 2 is Marjorie Bell, later to become Marge Champion.

D. REHEARSAL SEQUENCE

Zowie: The original dog is pictured in I. Castle 1919, p. 28. He was named after the comic character Vernon Castle played in "The Hen Pecks."

F. WAITING FOR THE ROBERT E. LEE

* Irene Castle alone auditioned for Fields: I. Castle 1958, pp. 35–39.
* Duet audition: Hayes and Dody, pp. 58–59.

Derives from cakewalk and polka: Sims 1983.
"a kick and a hop . . . ": Stearns and Stearns, p. 323.
On the yo-yo step and the Texas Tommy in general, see Caffin and Caffin, pp. 270–71.

G. CASTLE WALK REHEARSAL

* Mrs. Castle given bonnet by friend: I. Castle 1958, p. 115.

I. TOO MUCH MUSTARD

Though unprepared: Although called upon to dance before they were fully ready, the Castles had actually rehearsed once with the band leader (I. Castle 1919, p. 39).
The Castles' acrobatic duet: In early writings Irene Castle says they developed their acrobatic dance from memories of Blossom Seeley's solo performances in the United States (1919, pp. 21, 36). In her later autobiography she asserts, remarkably, that they concocted it from press clippings (1958, p. 54). For a different version of these events, see Marbury, p. 248.
Dance historically advanced: This dance event is also shown in the Castles' semi-autobiographical film *The Whirl of Life*, and there, too, the dance is built out of later steps—a blend of Castle Walk and maxixe steps—performed in a more historically accurate small, narrow corridor between tables.
"more as rest . . . ": I. Castle 1919, p. 54.
"raise yourself up . . . ": Castle and Castle, p. 47. See also I. Castle 1958, p. 79.
The Wind Up: Castle and Castle, pp. 61–65.

J. MEDLEY MONTAGE

* Mrs. Castle's regret: Crowther 1939.
* "If Vernon had ever . . . ": I. Castle 1958, p. 87.

"It was Jim Europe . . . ": Margolis.

* Hairpin story: D. Churchill; Duncan 1956. Hospital story: Treman; Castle 1958, p. 116, also p. 27.

"mashish": Castle and Castle, p. 107.

* "All too fast . . . ": Marin 1939. Sims agrees: Sims. Castles stress: Castle and Castle, pp. 161–62.

Forty-foot tower: Croce 1972, p. 162.

K. HELLO! HELLO! WHO'S YOUR LADY FRIEND?

On "eccentric dancing," see Stearns and Stearns, pp. 231–38.

* Cagney role first offered to Astaire: Cagney, p. 104.

L. THE LAST WALTZ

"Sometimes, in the midst . . . ": *Literary Digest* 1918; see also I. Castle 1919, p. 52; 1958, pp. 130–31, 137.
Castle did fly: The mission was repeated not because the first photographs had been hit by a bullet (as in the film) but because Castle, wary of enemy fire, had failed to get close enough. Dressed down by his commanding officer for his lack of courage, Castle went back and, heedless of danger, accomplished the mission, winning the officer's approval and friendship (I. Castle 1918, pp. 85–88; 1959, p. 151).
"By counting . . . ": Castle and Castle, p. 72.

M. ONLY WHEN YOU'RE IN MY ARMS (REPRISE)

"We did have . . . ": I. Castle 1919, p. 113.

12. BROADWAY MELODY OF 1940

Technicolor plans: Astaire 1959, p. 241.
"a big Metro mess . . . ": Lederer, p. 57.

* MGM assured Astaire about Murphy: Murphy 1940, p. 22.

THE SCRIPT

The series: This was the last in the *Broadway Melody* series. At one point MGM planned to do a 1943 version, teaming Powell with Gene Kelly, but that never materialized (S. Green 1981, p. 40).
The doormat role: On Murphy's distaste for this, see Murphy 1970, pp. 203, 229–30, 241.

THE CHOREOGRAPHY

"Fred dances . . . ": Powell 1939a.
"hoping I'd shrink . . . ": Powell 1974, p. 30.
Powell recalls: ibid., pp. 30–31. Also on the choreographic chores: Duncan 1961; Astaire 1959, p. 241; Delamater 1981, p. 286; Powell 1939b, 1981.
On Rasch's credit: Powell 1981; Duncan 1961, p. 43. On Rasch's work, see Ries.

A. PLEASE DON'T MONKEY WITH BROADWAY

"a classic . . . ": Murphy 1970, p. 210.
"Fred instantly brightened . . . ": Murphy 1940, p. 86.

C. BETWEEN YOU AND ME

* Doc Shurr: Murphy 1970, p. 159.

E. I'VE GOT MY EYES ON YOU

"Astaire's most convincing . . . ": S. Harvey 1975, p. 85.

G. I CONCENTRATE ON YOU

* Powell took only ten tap lessons: Duncan 1961, p. 43; Powell 1974, pp. 25–26.

H. BEGIN THE BEGUINE

On the origins of the song, see C. Schwartz 1977, pp. 142–43. In *Jubilee* the song was sung by June Knight and danced by her and Charles Walters, with choreography by Albertina Rasch; for photographs, see Kimball 1971, pp. 136–37; Hamm, p. 353; Gottfried, pp. 208–9. See also Bordman 1978, pp. 495–96. On the Shaw recording, see Wilder, p. 240; C. Schwartz 1977, pp. 146–47; Simon, pp. 415–16; Eells 1967, p. 129. The recording was made almost by accident: everyone assumed it would be the other side—a boisterous version of Friml's "Indian Love Call"—that would sell the record. "Begin the Beguine" brought Shaw and his band almost instant fame and fortune, a transformation Shaw recalls with amazement, and uneasiness, in his autobiography (pp. 333–44).

* Longest popular song: Wilder, p. 240. For the complete lyric, see Kimball 1971, p. 134 or Kimball 1983, p. 133.

The glass floor: Powell 1981.
Chorus work: The chorus' bend-back-and-thrust-forward maneuvers in the opening portion of the number reflect chorus passages in the "Dancing in the Dark" number Rasch choreographed for the *Band Wagon* revue on Broadway in 1931, a number that also took place on a mirrored stage (for a photograph of the chorus in action, see Gottfried, p. 63). However, Powell says the chorus material in "Begin the Beguine" was entirely the work of Connolly (1981).
Powell's pride in the arm work: Powell 1981.

* "We did that thing . . . ": Powell 1974, p. 31. There is a Colombian folk dance, the Bambuco, that may have inspired some of the choreography at the end of the Spanish duet. In it the man and woman dance separately, alternately whirling and facing each other.

13. SECOND CHORUS

"the worst film . . . ": Graham.

* "smaller budget": Astaire 1959, p. 242; "a quicky": Graham.
* RKO statistics: Jewell, pp. 760–61.

THE SCRIPT AND THE PRODUCTION

Artie Shaw saga: Simon, pp. 415–21; Korall; Frank, pp. 140–49; Blandford, pp. 31–33; Shaw, pp. 335–60. For Turner's account of their brief, tumultuous marriage, see Turner, pp. 48–66. Shaw says he was attracted to Hollywood because producer Boris Morros proposed to have him work on a film version of *Porgy and Bess* directed by Rouben Mamoulian. The project never materialized.
On the genesis of the film, see S. Green 1973, pp. 214–15; Astaire 1959, p. 242; Freedland 1976, p. 89.

B. EVERYTHING'S JUMPING

* "ultra-suave and urbane . . . ": Simon, p. 504.

C. I AIN'T HEP TO THAT STEP BUT I'LL DIG IT

New step: For one set of instructions on the Dig It, see *Look*.
"just once . . . ": Parish, p. 381.

E. LOVE OF MY LIFE

* "If you bring a song . . . ": Korall.

J. CONCERTO FOR CLARINET

"People make . . . ": Korall. At the end of 1940, Shaw put together an expanded (9′18″) version of the piece, which was issued on two sides of a 78-rpm record. Brian Rust calls it "rather an exhibitionist piece, concluding with the soloist reaching ever higher into the tonal stratosphere until the sound ceased to be acceptable as normal music and became merely a demonstration of Shaw's undoubted and never-questioned technique" (pp. 130–32).

M. ME AND THE GHOST UPSTAIRS

Description of dance: Pan 1980. The music track for the number is in Miles Kreuger's Institute of the American Musical.

14. YOU'LL NEVER GET RICH

RITA HAYWORTH

Life: 1941.
"It was news . . . ": *Time* 1941, p. 90.
On Hayworth's rise, see Kobal 1977; B. Thomas 1967.
"saintly quality": Kobal 1977, p. 135.
A quick study: *Time* 1941, p. 95; Kobal 1977, p. 134.
Unbending aspect: In his biography of the actress, John Kobal observes that her screen persona "contained the ingredients of all that wartime taste dictated: she was desirable, yet could be a sex symbol for servicemen without offending the women back home" (p. 130). It may be that women felt unthreatened by Hayworth because they sensed the inaccessibility of the image she projected.
"I guess the only jewels in my life . . . ": Hallowell.

THE MUSIC

For Porter on the songs and their use, see Eells 1967, p. 203.

THE CHOREOGRAPHY

"I insisted . . . ": Othman.

D. SHOOTING THE WORKS FOR UNCLE SAM

* "you fellows . . . ": Information from Joseph and from *Brooklyn Daily Eagle*. Voglin also let the sentry who stops Hayworth's car in one scene be at shoulder arms rather than the required port arms because it would have taken him too long to show the man how to do it right. Hayworth had the sniffles the night the scene was shot, and Voglin reports he was afraid the delay might cause her to catch a bad cold.

E. SINCE I KISSED MY BABY GOODBYE

Cole Porter tune: Although Astaire doesn't sing the song in the film, he did make a record of it, backed by another black singing group, the Delta Rhythm Boys. That rendition is much more upbeat and less dreamy than the one in the film. The song's lyric (complete with verse, which is sung on neither film nor record) is given in Kimball 1971, p. 178, and 1983, pp. 209–10.

* "only in the movies . . . ": S. Green 1973, p. 228.

F. MARCH MILASTAIRE

Guardhouse drummer: According to Stanley Green (1973, p. 225), the drummer is Chico Hamilton, aged twenty. Hamilton was to develop into a top jazz musician—particularly in avant-garde jazz—in the 1950s.

G. SO NEAR AND YET SO FAR

Serviceable song: Porter wrote a verse for this song, but it is not sung in the film, perhaps because it is rather suggestive—there are urgings about "going native." Astaire's recording of the song includes the verse and treats the music in a livelier manner than in the film. The complete lyric can be found in Kimball 1971, p. 178 and 1983, p. 210.

15. HOLIDAY INN

THE SCRIPT AND THE PRODUCTION

On the development of the film, see "Tap Dance"; Cameron; S. Green 1973, p. 232.

The Crosby character: At this point in his career, Crosby was in a good position to dictate how his character would be handled. As Sandrich observed at the time, "Crosby always plays himself, and that is his strength. When he undertakes a part it's a sort of metabolization. . . . Before rehearsals end, the character and the dialogue have been chewed up and thoroughly digested into Bing's own personality" ("Tap Dance"). On Crosby's antipathy to love scenes, both on and off screen, see Shepherd and Slazer, p. 286.

* Dare remembered Reynolds: Cameron.

THE SAGA OF "WHITE CHRISTMAS"

"White Christmas": Record sale figures are from Schneider; "Your Hit Parade" statistics are from Williams; see also Table 5. Sheet-music sales at the end of 1982 were 5,772,271 in the United States and Canada, making it close to the top seller of all time in that form as well. *The Guinness Book of World Records* says that the top-selling copyrighted songs in sheet music are "Let Me Call You Sweetheart" (1910) and "Till We Meet Again" (1918), each with sales of over six million by 1967. However, "White Christmas" has continued to sell and probably has surpassed the competition. Crosby's first recording of the song (for Decca) was made on May 29, 1942, and released on July 30, a few days before the film's premiere. It was included in an album of six 78-rpm records of songs from the film and was not issued as a single until 1946 (Levine).

Crosby reluctant to sing it: C. Thompson, p. 94; Carpozi, on the other hand, characterizes this story as "gibberish" (p. 59).

"We thought . . . ": Freedland 1974, p. 146.

Berlin expected modest success: Yoder. Reporter Sidney Skolsky, after visiting the set in 1941, wrote about the film's music at length and mentioned "White Christmas" only in passing. On the other hand, the leader of the vocal group that accompanies Crosby on his recording of the song has a different recollection: "Ken Darby remembers that 'when we first recorded "White Christmas" all who participated recognized a potential smash hit of endless duration'" (Zwisohn, p. 47). Though Berlin may have had modest expectations for the song, he told one reporter during filming that he considered it the best thing he had done since "Easter Parade" (Chapman).

"a meaning . . . ": C. Thompson, p. 95.

* Song written in the mid-1930s, copyrighted in 1940: Schneider. Its first public performance was apparently on Christmas day 1941, when Crosby sang it on the radio on the "Kraft Music Hall" (Levine). It includes a rarely heard verse in which the singer complains of the warm weather in Beverly Hills and yearns for a snowy Christmas back east. The verse is included in the Joan Morris/William Bolcom recording issued in 1979; this may well be the first time the verse was recorded. See also Wilk, pp. 276–77.

"I sang it": C. Thompson, p. 95; see also Ewen 1950, pp. 136–37; Yoder; Lingeman, p. 214.

A. I'LL CAPTURE YOUR HEART

* "Having heard . . . ": Astaire 1959, p. 249; see also C. Thompson, p. 93.

* ". . . tap dancer like Fred Astaire": Ulanov, pp. 182–83.

G. YOU'RE EASY TO DANCE WITH (DRUNK DANCE)

"two stiff . . . ": Astaire 1959, p. 250.

J. I CAN'T TELL A LIE

* 1922 stage show: For a photograph, see S. Green 1973, p. 24. See also Astaire 1959, pp. 93–99; Bordman 1980, pp. 225–30.

L. SAY IT WITH FIRECRACKERS/SONG OF FREEDOM

Selfish scheme: For the suggestion that such self-interested cruelty was an aspect of Crosby's off-screen personality, see Shepherd and Slatzer; Crosby and Firestone.

M. SAY IT WITH FIRECRACKERS (DANCE)

"Fred must have . . . ": "Tap Dance." Crosby recalls, "Fred Astaire danced himself so thin that I could almost spit through him. . . . He started the picture weighing one hundred forty pounds. When he finished it he weighed one hundred twenty-six" (1953, p. 173).

The "organ": "Tap Dance."

"It was a great . . . ": Astaire 1959, p. 249.

O. I'VE GOT PLENTY TO BE THANKFUL FOR

* "like a whippet . . . ": The problem is discussed in Crosby 1953, pp. 121–23.

16. YOU WERE NEVER LOVELIER

THE SCRIPT

Menjou's dismay: Menjou, pp. 217, 335.

THE MUSIC

On signing Kern, see Wilk, p. 141; Freedland 1978, pp. 157–59.

On Mercer, see Burrows, p. 259.

"I don't write . . . ": BBC, p. 50.

Kern and Cugat: Cugat, pp. 141–42.

THE CHOREOGRAPHY

On working out duets with Hayworth, etc., see Astaire 1959, pp. 252–54.

A. CHIU, CHIU

On the Cugat band, see Simon, pp. 140–41.

B. DEARLY BELOVED

* "Anything that is close . . . ": Freedland 1978, p. 159. See also Wilder, p. 83; Bordman 1980, pp. 393–94.

F. I'M OLD FASHIONED

For appreciations of the song, see Bordman 1980, pp. 393–94; Wilder, pp. 82–83.

H. THE SHORTY GEORGE

On George Snowden's career, and for a photograph of the man in action, see Stearns and Stearns, pp. 315–27, 334.

* Hayworth fell: Kobal 1977, p. 151.

N. YOU WERE NEVER LOVELIER (DANCE)

"the studio powers . . . ": Astaire 1959, pp. 253–54.

For additional relevant photographs, see S. Green 1973, pp. 252–53.

17. THE SKY'S THE LIMIT

World War II: Despite its effectiveness, this film often goes unmentioned in studies of the films of World War II. See, for example, Lingeman; Jacobs; Morella, Epstein, and Griggs; Kagan; Manvell; Suid.

THE SCRIPT

"Gosh . . . ": Astaire 1959, p. 256.

On the flag-waving issue, see Lingeman, pp. 197–210.

THE RECEPTION OF THE FILM

"quick-fitting clothes": Crowther 1943. On Astaire's reaction, see Astaire 1959, pp. 256–57.

"the first half hour . . . ": Agee, p. 51.

"pure, heart-lifting delight": *Time* 1943.

"somebody . . . ": Lardner.

THE CHOREOGRAPHY

Astaire sole choreographer: Leslie.

A. MY SHINING HOUR (SONG)

Freddie Slack: For a brief profile of this popular boogie-woogie specialist of the time, see Simon, p. 483.

"spare, hymnlike translucence . . . ": Wilder, p. 275.

C. A LOT IN COMMON WITH YOU

* Photograph of leg-over-leg jump: S. Green 1973, p. 250.

* Astaire photograph in Arthur Murray ads: A sample can be found in *The New Yorker,* April 13, 1935, p. 69.

D. SNAKE DANCE

* "something cruel": see Todd.

E. MY SHINING HOUR (DANCE)

"A Creature . . . ": From a Wordsworth poem beginning, "She was a phantom of delight."

* "In the middle . . . ": Lederer, p. 56.

F. ONE FOR MY BABY

"one of the best . . . ": Jablonski, p. 144.

"unlike anything . . . ": Wilk, p. 160. Arlen has often expressed amazement at how brilliantly Mercer fitted the lyric to his brooding and unorthodox melody: "I wrote it as if it were natural to me to write that kind of song, but then I started thinking, 'Jesus, how could a lyric writer dig *this,* or even understand it?' . . . And yet John put on that line the best torch-song lyric of our time." Mercer himself casually ascribes his success to "luck" (Jablonski, p. 144; Wilk, p. 139).

On the song, see also Wilder, pp. 277–78; Ewen 1970b, p. 255. For accounts of the shooting of this number, see Mainwaring; Niemeyer. See also Astaire 1959, p. 257. The song was a late bloomer. Although popular, it rose to its classic status only years later, through countless renditions by such singers as Tony Bennett and Frank Sinatra. Astaire recorded the song in 1945 for Decca (backed by a rendition of one of his own songs, "Oh, My Achin' Back"), but the record was not released. A copy that survives in Miles Kreuger's Institute of the American Musical shows why: although he sings the song beautifully in the film, it is very badly performed on the record—hurried, unmodulated, undermotivated, the lyric partly muddled. In 1959 Astaire finally recorded the song to his satisfaction, and it was released as part of "Now," a long-playing record issued by Kapp.

G. TRESTLE DANCE

Solo in New York print: Kate Cameron in her *New York Daily News* review of the film refers to both "his solo dances."

One viewer: Miles Kreuger.

H. HARVEY, THE VICTORY GARDEN MAN

* "Hangin' On to You": The sprightly lyric is published in Jablonski, p. 145.

18. ZIEGFELD FOLLIES

On the origins of the film, see Fordin, pp. 121–46; this source also contains a wealth of other production material. All financial and shooting-day statistics are from Fordin.

Sheer extravagance: When production began, studio executives let it be known that the film had a "ceilingless" budget and that its costs could easily mount to four or five million dollars, making it "the most expensive musical of all time," outstripping Paramount's *Lady in the Dark* (which had starred Ginger Rogers) by a million dollars (*New York Times,* May 7, 1944, sec. 2, p. 3).

On the era of opulence, see MGM art director Jack Martin Smith's comments in Delamater 1981, pp. 254–55.

* "With the great flexibility . . . ": Crowther 1946.

THE PRODUCTION

On buying the title, see Carter, p. 158.

On Sidney's replacement, see Fordin, pp. 121, 128. Minnelli was later to direct two other Astaire films, the unsuccessful *Yolanda and the Thief* (1945) and the highly successful *The Band Wagon* (1953). Before coming to Hollywood in 1940, Minnelli had worked as designer on *Ziegfeld Follies of 1936* (a show produced by the Shuberts four years after Ziegfeld's death).

"Every MGM star . . . ": Minnelli, p. 141.

ASTAIRE'S PARTNERS

On subsequent efforts to pair Astaire and Kelly, see Minnelli, p. 144.

B. HERE'S TO THE GIRLS

* "I was tall . . . ": Morella and Epstein, p. 58.
* Silver's trainer: Fordin, p. 127n.

D. NUMBER PLEASE

* Other sketches dropped: Fordin, pp. 144–46.
* Derived from Allen routine: S. Green 1973, p. 269.

G. THIS HEART OF MINE

* Minnelli claims: Minnelli, p. 142.
* Suggestion of McVay: McVay 1967, p. 54. Suggestion of S. Green: S. Green 1973, p. 274.

I. LOVE

Horne was unhappy: Fordin, p. 134. The white establishment in Knoxville, Tennessee, was also unhappy, though not for the same reasons. The number was cut from prints shown there, and Horne's name was blacked out on all advertising posters, because, as one theatre manager put it, the scene "might prove objectionable to some people in Knoxville" (*New York Times*, July 24, 1946, p. 30). That was not an uncommon thing to happen to numbers featuring blacks at the time (see Horne and Schickel, p. 109).

J. WHEN TELEVISION COMES (GUZZLER'S GIN)

Successful sequence: The scene was rehearsed and shot in one day. The sketch had originally been written for the Fred Allen radio show in the 1930s, and Skelton had latched on to it and made it his own—without bothering to pay or credit the author, Harry Tugend. Skelton's business manager (and ex-wife) was paid $5,000 by MGM for the rights to the script. As it happened, Tugend was working on the lot at the time and got wind of what was going on. If she got $5,000 for not writing the sketch, Tugend demanded, he deserved $6,000 for writing it. He was successful. Later Tugend cheerfully acknowledged that Skelton "may have stolen 'Guzzler's,' but he does it a hell of a lot better than we did it on the Fred Allen show" (A. Marx, pp. 109–13).

K. LIMEHOUSE BLUES

* Sung by Harriet Lee: Fordin, p. 136.

Costermonger scene: The song is "Wot Cher!" by Charles Ingle. The street setting had previously been used in MGM's *The Picture of Dorian Gray* (1945).

The scenario for this number bears some similarity to that of "The Beggar's Waltz," which Astaire performed on Broadway in *The Band Wagon* in 1933.

For a list of participating dancers, see Fordin, p. 554.

"precision Chinese fan dance": Minnelli, p. 142.

L. A GREAT LADY HAS AN INTERVIEW (MADAME CREMETON)

On the origins of the number, see Fordin, p. 140; Cutts, p. 14. Charles Walters' reaction: Cutts, p. 14. Actually, Minnelli says, he and Garland had broken up temporarily at the time this sketch was shot; later, in 1945, they were married (pp. 142–45).

M. THE BABBITT AND THE BROMIDE

"Fred Astaire is very elegant . . . , " "Neither wanted . . . ": Lehman, et al., p. 66.

For Kelly's comments on the number, see Hirschhorn 1974, pp. 138–39; Delamater 1981, p. 226. For Astaire's, see Saltus, p. 10. "their deference . . . ": T. Thomas 1974, p. 69. According to Minnelli, "Gene Kelly, in retrospect, feels that since [this] . . . was the only time he and Fred Astaire worked together, it shouldn't have been so light and unchallenging. I disagree. This was a revue, they should have been kidding their rightly exalted stations. . . . When I told Fred what Gene thought about the number, he cracked back, 'What does Gene mean by unchallenging? Didn't we beat hell out of the floor together? We were supposed to be a popular team. We weren't trying, after all, to do *L'Après-Midi d'un Faune*'" (p. 144).

On the choreographic process in this number, see T. Thomas 1974, p. 69; Minnelli, p. 144; Delamater 1981, p. 266; B. Green 1979, pp. 94–95. See also Hirschhorn 1974, p. 137.

"a more 'up' . . . ": T. Thomas 1974, p. 69. See also Fordin, pp. 129–30; Delamater 1981, p. 226. An early idea submitted by Alton for "Pass that Peace Pipe" had Astaire, Kelly, and Mickey Rooney dressed as Indian braves doing a routine in which they passed a peace pipe back and forth. The song was eventually used in MGM's *Good News* (1947).

* "almost a fable . . . ": Pechter, pp. 79–80.
* Ira Gershwin recalls: I. Gershwin, p. 25.
* Shortened version of song: The complete lyric is given in I. Gershwin, pp. 23–24.

"I hated . . . ": Fordin, p. 130.

O. IF SWING GOES, I GO TOO

* For additional photographs from this dance, see Fordin, p. 124; *Consumer Guide*, pp. 82–83.

V. THERE'S BEAUTY EVERYWHERE

On the bubbles, and for another photograph, see Fordin, pp. 140–43; Astaire, p. 266. For Charisse's agonized recollections of what it was like to dance on pointe among the shoe-shrinking bubbles, see Martin and Charisse, p. 118.

19. YOLANDA AND THE THIEF

"with the industry's . . . ": Minnelli, p. 169.

THE SCRIPT AND THE DIRECTION

"When I finally . . . ": Astaire 1978, p. 35.

THE MUSIC

For Warren's comments on the film, see T. Thomas 1975, p. 236.

LUCILLE BREMER

"She was a protegee . . . ": S. Green 1973, p. 285.

On Garland's interest in the role, see Fordin, p. 155.

THE SPECTER OF DE MILLE

On the *Oklahoma!* "dream ballet," see also Mueller 1984.

THE CHOREOGRAPHY

Dancing to another's designs: Astaire 1978, p. 36.

A. THIS IS A DAY FOR LOVE

Bemelmans' objection: Fordin, pp. 170–71.

C. ANGEL

* Freed exploded: Fordin, p. 167.
* Twelve and a half hours: *Life* 1945a.

D. DREAM BALLET

* "has a sense of space . . . ": Martin 1945.

Bremer's double: Fordin, p. 170; Minnelli, p. 157.

"the first surrealistic ballet . . . ": Minnelli, p. 156.

E. YOLANDA

Dubbed harpist: H. Warren.

F. COFFEE TIME

Floor decor by Sharaff: Fordin, pp. 166–67.

Origins of the dance: Delamater 1981, pp. 232–33; Fordin, p. 166.

"Dream Ballet" in proper sequence: It is possible for the intrepid film programmer to insert the "Dream Ballet" at its more logical place. One skips past the first hotel bedroom scene and its dream (D 2–20) and then shows it immediately after the kiss-and-run scene (F 17–18). When Astaire sits bolt upright in bed after the dream (D 20), cut back to the letter-writing scene (F 19) and finish off the film without further improvement.

20. BLUE SKIES

Cornucopia of music: In addition to the songs given major treatment in the film, several other Berlin tunes are used as background. In order, they are "Tell Me Little Gypsy" (1920), "Nobody Knows" (1919), "Mandy" (1918), "I Wonder" (1919), "Some Sunny Day" (1922), "When You Walked Out Someone Else Walked In" (1923), "Because I Love You" (1926), "Homesick" (1922), "How Many Times" (1926), "The Song is Ended" (1927), "Lazy" (1924), "Always" (1925), "I Can't Remember" (1933). None of the songs Berlin wrote for Astaire in the 1930s is included; Crosby prerecorded a medley that included "Cheek to Cheek" and "I'm Putting All My Eggs in One Basket," but it was not used.

Crosby's famous deep warble: By contrast with this film, Crosby stressed his upper range in his early days as a singer and often sang with urgency and a keen sense of rhythm. On the change, see Giddins, pp. 14–21.

THE SCRIPT AND THE ASTAIRE ROLE

* "We had had a week . . . ": B. Green 1979, p. 96. For a somewhat different story, see B. Thomas 1984, p. 191.

On the film's cost and receipts: *Time* 1946; S. Green 1973, p. 301; S. Harvey, p. 106; Hirschhorn 1981, p. 277.

"I had made . . . ": Astaire 1959, p. 282.

THE CHOREOGRAPHY

Robel's help: Astaire, p. 283.

F. PUTTIN' ON THE RITZ

Astaire heard Richman: Saltus, p. 12.

"five weeks . . . ": *Time* 1946.

* "the most complex . . . ": Wilder, p. 104.

Astaire on the lyric change: Saltus, p. 12. There may have been an additional reason for changing the lyric. In its original form the lyric might suggest that the number be done in blackface, something Astaire seems to have had little interest in. Furthermore, in the only blackface number he ever did, "Bojangles" in *Swing Time* (7 F), he danced with shadows of himself; since he intended to dance with images of himself in "Puttin' On the Ritz," that parallel would be close and might violate his almost obsessive rule about not repeating himself. Between the films *Puttin' On the Ritz* and *Blue Skies*, the song, with the original lyric, had been used in another film, *Idiot's Delight* of 1939, where it is spiritedly sung and danced by Clark Gable. This improbable sequence is included in the 1974 film *That's Entertainment*.

Trigger mechanism: Pan 1980.

H. A COUPLE OF SONG AND DANCE MEN

* Crosby and Bob Hope in vaudeville: Hope, pp. 103–4.

Q. YOU KEEP COMING BACK LIKE A SONG / BLUE SKIES (REPRISE)

"too old . . . ": S. Green, 1973, p. 292.

21. EASTER PARADE

Volleyball: Hirschhorn 1974, p. 156; Freedland 1976, p. 112; Hirschhorn 1981, p. 295. Softball: Frank, p. 235. Touch football: Fordin, p. 226; Cutts, p. 15; Finch, p. 159; B. Thomas 1984, p. 203.

"for a rest . . . , " "urge and inspiration . . . ": Astaire 1959, pp. 290–91. See also Smith; Hirschhorn 1974, p. 157; Minnelli, p. 195; B. Green 1979, p. 101.

On the psychiatrist's ruling out Minnelli as director, see Minnelli, pp. 194–95.

THE SCRIPT

* ". . . a grandfather": Frank, p. 235.

On changing the Astaire character, see Kobal 1971, pp. 239–40; Frank, p. 234; Fordin, p. 225; Freedland 1976, pp. 117, 120.

JUDY GARLAND

Quick to pick up dance routines: Minnelli, p. 196; Frank, p. 236; Finch, p. 159.

On the change in Garland's voice, see Pleasants, pp. 279–90; Pechter, p. 80. Pleasants argues that Garland was able to temper this stridency during the years after her break with MGM (1951–61) but then declined again in the late 1960s. He quotes a cruel description by Oscar Levant of Garland as she developed in her last years: "a vibrato in search of a voice."

On Garland's self-image, see Edwards, pp. 54–55; Finch, p. 81; Frank, pp. 81–82.

* "You know . . . ": Cutts, p. 16.

On Garland's experience working on the film, see Frank, pp. 236–37; Minnelli, p. 196; Miller, pp. 149–50.

THE MUSIC

$600,000: *New York Times,* November 5, 1947.

"A song is like . . . ": Fordin, p. 225.

THE CHOREOGRAPHY

"not to worry": Hirschhorn 1974, p. 157. For Astaire on revisions, see Astaire 1959, p. 292. For Kelly on revisions, see Delamater 1981, pp. 226–27. Jack Martin Smith, one of the film's art directors, says, "Choreography passed over from Gene Kelly to Fred Astaire would be non-existent" (Delamater 1981, p. 253).

A. HAPPY EASTER / DRUM CRAZY

Drum sounds prerecorded: Winge.

B. IT ONLY HAPPENS WHEN I DANCE WITH YOU

Cyd Charisse's injury: Miller, p. 147.

* Miller's back problems: Miller, p. 149.

C. I WANT TO GO BACK TO MICHIGAN

Script mellowed: Freedland 1976, pp. 117, 120.

G. REHEARSAL-PERFORMANCE-AUDITION MEDLEY

Garland's locked knees: Frank, pp. 109–10.

J. STEPPIN' OUT WITH MY BABY

The song: The release (the B section of the AABA song) was lifted by Berlin from his 1942 song "The President's Birthday Ball" (Jay, p. 115).

* Astaire requests Van Cleave: Fordin, p. 228.

K. A COUPLE OF SWELLS

* Berlin originally wrote: Fordin, p. 225.

Inspired by "Be a Clown": Minnelli, p. 194. A year later, a similar duet—a hillbilly routine called "Heavenly Music," again with Kelly—was scheduled for Garland's next (and last) film at MGM, *Summer Stock* (Hirschhorn, p. 192).

* Garland terrified: Frank, p. xv.

On Garland's stage show, see Cutts, p. 15; Frank, pp. 331, 414, 441, 446; Edwards, p. 157; Finch, p. 182.

* ". . . Is this too much?": Finch, p. 159.

O. EASTER PARADE

* English version of parade: Conrad, p. 28.

For a discussion of the technical procedures used in creating the final shot, see Fordin, pp. 231–33.

P. MR. MONOTONY

For a photograph of Garland in costume, see Fordin, p. 233.

22. THE BARKLEYS OF BROADWAY

"We expected . . . ": Astaire 1959, pp. 238, 294. After *The Story of Vernon and Irene Castle* was filmed in 1939, a *Time* cover story on Rogers reported, "Astaire and Rogers both announced their desire to continue working together. They may do so after her next [two] pictures" (p. 52). See also Shipp, p. 15.

On Rogers' career, see McGilligan; Eells 1976; Scott.

Rogers' telegram is reprinted in Fordin, p. 234; see also Eells 1976, pp. 60–61.

On Garland and *The Barkleys,* see Minnelli, pp. 197–99; Fordin, p. 246; Frank, pp. 237–42; Edwards, pp. 119–20; Finch, p. 160.

"I remember . . . ": Cutts, p. 15; see also BBC, p. 53.

Rogers' pay was $12,500 per week, whereas Garland's had been $5,769 per week. There was an awkward moment during rehearsals when Garland appeared on the set, parading around importantly and holding up production. Rogers became upset and went to her dressing room. Finally Walters took Garland by the arm and "led her out as she hurled imprecations about Ginger" (Levant 1965, pp. 195–96).

THE MUSIC

"Arthur became . . . ": Thomas 1975, p. 250; on Warren, see also Fordin, p. 247.

THE SCRIPT

On the off-screen parallels, see Croce 1972, p. 178; B. Green 1979, p. 106; J. Feuer 1977; J. Feuer 1982, pp. 99–102.

Rogers' idea to use "They Can't . . . ": McGilligan, p. 121; Eells 1976, p. 61.

THE TEAM

"Ginger and Fred are set . . . ": Shipp, p. 71.

"a step backwards . . . ": BBC, p. 52.

"They met on the set . . . ": BBC, p. 53.

THE CHOREOGRAPHY

Alton shot the numbers: Walters.

A. SWING TROT

On the origins of the dance, see Fordin, p. 245. "Swing Trot" in the Astaire schools: Dzhermolinska.

Gershwin credits Freed: S. Green 1973, p. 325.

D. BOUNCIN' THE BLUES

Warren wrote several versions: Warren 1972.

"too aggressively professional": Croce 1972, p. 176.

E. MY ONE AND ONLY HIGHLAND FLING

The lyric: reprinted in I. Gershwin, pp. 59–61.

* According to Gershwin: I. Gershwin, p. 61.

* Astaire calls number a favorite: Astaire 1959, p. 294.

"McTavish" and "lavish": I. Gershwin, pp. 61–62.

F. A WEEKEND IN THE COUNTRY

The clever lyric: Originally it had Levant yearning to be frolicking at a bar drinking "rye that's alcoholic." The MGM head office, however, pointed out that the new Republic of India had banned all scenes showing drinking and, with distribution in that country in mind, suggested dropping the line. It is not used in the final picture. A version of the lyric, shorter and somewhat different from that used in the film, is reprinted in I. Gershwin (pp. 125–26). Walters staged another striding number in his 1953 film *Dangerous When Wet* (see Casper, p. 169).

G. SHOES WITH WINGS ON

On the photographic process, see *American Cinematographer;* BBC, p. 52.

On the connection with "The Sorcerer's Apprentice," see BBC, p. 52.

Toe-shoe sequence: This was shot separately and then superimposed. The rest of the dancer, Dee Turnell, can be seen earlier—she is the Russian ballet dancer in the number's opening sequence. She also plays the blonde whom Levant mistakes for his friend Cleo at Billie Burke's party early in the film.

* Ideas of Harold Turburg: Astaire 1959, p. 295.

H. TCHAIKOVSKY PIANO CONCERTO NO. 1

* Music prerecorded: Fordin, p. 247.

* Levant's backstage ritual autobiographical: Levant 1965, p. 263.

J. YOU'D BE HARD TO REPLACE (REPRISE)

"Marseillaise": Actually, Bernhardt had refused to perform a Molière scene at the examination because she would have had to do it with a boy she didn't know; instead, she decided to recite La Fontaine's gentle fable "Les Deux Pigeons" and, after two false starts, performed so well that she was admitted to the Conservatoire before she had finished the recitation (Baring, pp. 13–14).

23. THREE LITTLE WORDS

THE SCRIPT AND THE PRODUCTION

Dreary films: Astaire himself may have contributed somewhat to the overserious approach to musical biography: In *The Story of Vernon and Irene Castle* he had played the lively, fun-loving Vernon Castle with undue sobriety.

"bio-pics": Other early biographical films of composers include *Swanee River* (1940), which tackled Stephen Foster, and *Alexander's Ragtime Band* (1938), which some consider a sort of spiritual biography of Irving Berlin. Berlin, however, had always steadfastly opposed being the subject of a film biography and was confirmed in that judgment when the crop of biopics came out in the late 1940s: "There's only been one biographical movie of a songwriter that hasn't made me too embarrassed to sit and watch it, and that was . . . *Yankee Doodle Dandy.* I couldn't take the risk of one about me turning out to be a syrupy tribute." (On this issue, see Freedland 1974, pp. 100, 196–97, 205–6.) Astaire has also firmly resisted any plan to become the subject of a film biography.

Cummings and MGM: A. Marx, pp. 144–46.

"When Jack Cummings decided . . . ": Wilk, p. 31.

RED SKELTON AND VERA-ELLEN

"but he didn't think . . . ": A. Marx, p. 146.

"as long as Gable . . . ": Rothwell.

A. WHERE DID YOU GET THAT GIRL?

* "We used to stand . . . ": Conrad, p. 11.

B. MR. AND MRS. HOOFER AT HOME

* "Once we had an appointment . . . ": Wilk, p. 31.

* ". . . with Ruby at second base": Rothwell; see also Adamson, p. 71.

Choreographed by Hermes Pan: Pan 1983.

C. MY SUNNY TENNESSEE

An event that actually happened: As Ruby once recalled, "Bert and his wife got together a big new act. He spent almost $11,000 on scenery and costumes; it was a beautiful act. They opened in Washington. President Wilson was there—he loved vaudeville, you know. Coming offstage—this scene is in the picture—Bert hit something backstage and hurt his leg. He couldn't go on, and they had to cancel the act. He couldn't dance. He came back to New York and he was broke" (Wilk, p. 30). (ASCAP biographical material, however, places the mishap in Boston.) On Wilson's fondness for vaudeville (he particularly liked Primrose, a minstrel dancer, and often said he wished they could exchange jobs), see E. Wilson, pp. 145, 325–26. The Keith's Theatre circuit later became the K in RKO.

Song plugger: Working in this capacity, Ruby once played tunes for the young vaudeville team of Fred and Adele Astaire (Rothwell).

D. SO LONG, OO-LONG

* Sales of "Oh, What a Pal Was Mary": Wilk, p. 30.

L. I WANNA BE LOVED BY YOU

* On Ruby at the Senator's exhibition game, see Ruby 1967.
* Signed photographs: Ruby 1959.

On Kane's career, see Bedoian. The Kane style was used for the voice of Betty Boop in a famous cartoon series of the 1930s, but Kane herself did not do the voice for the character.

N. I LOVE YOU SO MUCH

* On the Kalmar/Ruby contribution to Marx Brothers material, see Adamson.

24. LET'S DANCE

BETTY HUTTON

"I worked . . . ": *Theatre Arts,* p. 15.

"Poor Betty . . . ": Pan 1983; see also Davidson, p. 186.

LUCILE WATSON

* "I was never aura-eyed . . . ": *Theatre Arts,* p. 16.

THE MUSIC

Astaire fond of song: Astaire 1959, p. 297.

B. PIANO DANCE

"I finally convinced him . . . ": BBC, p. 17.

"It came to me . . . ": BBC, p. 17.

25. ROYAL WEDDING

DELLY, ELLIE, AND FRED

* "My contribution . . . ": Lerner, p. 140.

JANE POWELL

"all the great artists . . . ": Bookspan and Yockey, p. 44.

For the studio point of view on the Garland firing, see Fordin, pp. 299–301; Schary, pp. 215–16. For the Garland point of view, see Frank, pp. 274–82; Edwards, pp. 129–33; and especially Finch, pp. 171–74; all of these also discuss Garland's attempted suicide in response to the MGM action. See also Allyson, pp. 134–36. Charles Walters had originally been scheduled to direct *Royal Wedding,* but he withdrew when Garland was assigned to the film. He had directed her in *Summer Stock* the year before and did not feel up to the emotional demands of doing another Garland picture (Frank, pp. 274–76).

"she surprised everybody . . . ": Astaire 1959, p. 298.

THE CHOREOGRAPHY

For Castle's comments on working with Astaire, see Stearns and Stearns, pp. 226, 228.

B. SUNDAY JUMPS

* Clothes tree idea was Pan's: Astaire 1980b.
* Pan is pleased: Pan 1980.
* Astaire's Sunday rehearsals: Borne, p. 52.

C. OPEN YOUR EYES

On the 1923 incident, see Astaire 1959, pp. 103–4.

Boat-rocking device: Fordin, p. 302; Delamater 1981, p. 261.

D. REHEARSAL FRAGMENTS

On Sarah Churchill, see S. Churchill, pp. 194–204.

* "I know she's . . . ": Fordin, p. 298.

F. HOW COULD YOU BELIEVE ME . . .

* Publicity stills without wig: See, for example, Freedland 1976, p. 129.
* Photo of Garland in blond wig: Fordin, p. 299.

"so damn charming . . . ": S. Green 1973, p. 360.

H. YOU'RE ALL THE WORLD TO ME

The idea: Astaire 1959, p. 299; Fordin, p. 301. In an interview in the November 1945 issue of *Lion's Roar,* an MGM publicity publication, Astaire mentions the idea and says he hopes "some screenplay writer finds a reason for it." Lerner apparently has convinced himself that the idea was his: "One night I dreamed that Fred was dancing up the wall, all across the ceiling and down the other wall. I mentioned it to Arthur at lunch the following day and lo, in the film Fred danced up one wall, across the ceiling and down the other wall" (p. 140).

Squirrel cage: For comments by its inventor, art director Jack Martin Smith, see Delamater 1981, pp. 260–61; see also Fordin, p. 303.

Explanatory diagram: Astaire 1978.

The music and orchestration: As Kreuger has observed, the Lane music can be heard in another (brighter) rendition in the 1934 Eddie Cantor film *Kid Millions,* where it is spiritedly sung by the ten-year-old Harold Nicholas and a chorus of Goldwyn Girls as part of a production number. The song on that occasion (with a lyric by Harold Adamson) was called "My Minstrel Man."

26. THE BELLE OF NEW YORK

"sick": Walters; see also Cutts, p. 16; B. Green 1979, p. 107.

"The less said . . . ": Astaire 1959, p. 299. Astaire's disappointment in the film may have been magnified by the fact that it came out just after Gene Kelly's triumphantly successful, Oscar-winning *An American in Paris,* and at the same time as Kelly's almost equally successful *Singin' in the Rain* (see Table 3). For later, more favorable evaluations of the film by Astaire, see Saltus, p. 12; Fordin, p. 366; Chase.

"looks suspiciously like . . . ": Shipman, p. 28. "masterpiece": McVay 1975, p. 30. Other possible members of the small band of admirers are John Cutts (p. 16) and Michael Freedland (1976, pp. 132–33); see also Sutton.

"there were some . . . ": Saltus, p. 12.

THE SCRIPT AND THE CHARACTERS

* "a celebrated line . . . ": S. Green 1973, p. 374. For the actress' spirited account, see Hayes and Dody, pp. 142–43.

"like a piece of moving putty": Cutts, p. 16.

* Tension between Main and Pearce: Fordin, p. 364.
* Mae West: Cutts, p. 16; Fordin, p. 364.

THE ORIGINS OF THE FILM

Plot of the original show: See Bordman 1978, p. 154.

* Rodgers and Hammerstein asked to do score: Fordin, p. 152.

On Astaire's reactions to the project, see Astaire 1959, pp. 161–63, 281–82, 299.

"Fred never . . . ": Cutts, p. 16.

THE MUSIC

Astaire still recalls: Astaire 1980b.

THE CHOREOGRAPHY

Alton in charge of shooting the numbers: Walters.

E. BABY DOLL

The lyric: One slight lapse, perhaps, occurs in the verse where Astaire suggests he is worried about uttering a platitude or striking an attitude (rhymes with "gratitude")—concerns that may be a bit too intellectual for the character he plays in this film. They seem more suitable for his character in *Daddy Long Legs* (lyrics again by Mercer), who is given to ruminating in song about immovable objects and irresistible forces.

She reacts with shock: The "Baby Doll" duet is quite similar in form to the pas de deux in August Bournonville's 1851 ballet *Kermesse in Bruges,* in the course of which a shy, reticent, proper young woman is gradually attracted to her attentive and eager partner. Her coldness breaks down and she is soon happily kicking up her heels. But toward the end he becomes overconfident and impetuously grabs her by the hand. Startled, she draws away from him a bit, and they finish the dance with a series of side-by-side pirouettes and a chaste pose—friends, but not improperly so. In fact, the entire film has an element of charm and innocence characteristic of Bournonville.

G. OOPS

* Walters' problems with Vera-Ellen: Walters.

H. A BRIDE'S WEDDING DAY SONG

Winter scene: This backdrop and the equally beautiful summer scene are derived from the Currier and Ives prints shown to the couple in the studio: "Central Park—Winter: The Skating Pond" and "Coney Island Boardwalk." According to one of the art directors for the film, Jack Martin Smith, the prints were "very hard to reproduce in cube form, because of the perspective. . . . We used a dry brush effect on the set pieces and the backdrop, to make it look like a lithograph" (Fordin, pp. 365–66).

K. I WANNA BE A DANCIN' MAN

This mellow song is sometimes erroneously credited to Burton Lane and Alan Lerner (see Burton, p. 273; Taylor and Jackson, p. 105; McVay 1975, p. 33; Woll, p. 90). Astaire also filmed the number in mustache and waiter's garb, but this was rejected in favor of the more formal costume (Haley).

27. THE BAND WAGON

Most highly praised: As Arlene Croce observes, "Movie critics pressed for their favorite musical will generally name one of [Gene] Kelly's or, if it's an Astaire film, *The Band Wagon*" (1977, p. 437). When the film came out, Bosley Crowther of the *New York Times,* not trusting his first impression, went to see it again, and then, reinforced, proclaimed it "one of the best musicals ever made" (Fordin, p. 419). Archer Winsten in the *New York Post* called it "the best musical of the month, the year, the decade, or, for all I know, of all time" (Fordin, p. 397). See also Pechter. For a less ecstatic reception, see Knight 1953a, 1953b.

Colorfully packaged: For a discussion of the imaginative use of color in this film, see Hogue.

THE SCRIPT

"our intention . . . ": Astaire 1959, p. 302.

Art can't be entertaining: As Jane Feuer suggests, in films like *The Band Wagon* MGM seems to be responding to "charges of infantilism from the citadels of high art" (1977, p. 325; see also Feuer 1982; M. Wood). On the other hand, Pechter argues that "what is mocked is not . . . high culture, but the pretension of theatre people who don't know the limits of their capabilities" (p. 79).

THE ASTAIRE CHARACTER

"a cross between . . . ": S. Green 1973, p. 385; other Fabray, Levant, and Buchanan parallels: Fordin, p. 401; S. Green 1973, p. 385; Minnelli, p. 261; S. Harvey 1975, p. 129; Marshall, p. 210.

* "tremendously impressed": Astaire 1959, p. 105.

"sparked an idea . . . ": Minnelli, p. 261.

"I have a horror . . . ": Astaire 1959, p. 244.

"very nervous": Fordin, pp. 400–1.

"playing a soured version . . . ": S. Harvey 1975, p. 130.

THE MUSIC

For a thoughtful discussion of Schwartz's songs, see Wilder, pp. 313–30. For discussions of Astaire and the original *Band Wagon,* see Dietz 1953; Astaire 1959, pp. 166–70.

THE CHOREOGRAPHY

On Kidd and Astaire, see Minnelli, p. 272; Fordin, pp. 409, 416.

A. BY MYSELF

* Recalls with some pain: Astaire 1959, pp. 235–36.

Strength and self-confidence: For an interesting discussion of the "aloneness" of the Astaire character in this film, see Corliss, pp. 200–2. See also Hogue; Telotte. The obscure Schwartz-Dietz song "By Myself" had first been sung, interestingly enough, by Jack Buchanan in the 1937 Broadway show *Between the Devil,* which ran for only ninety-three performances. The complete lyric is given in Dietz 1974, pp. 229–30. See also A. Green, p. 38.

B. A SHINE ON YOUR SHOES

* "Adolph Green Fan Club"; first saw Astaire: A. Green, p. 38.

The song: This comes from a 1932 revue, *Flying Colors*. The lyric for the verse was rewritten for the film; the original is given in Dietz 1974, pp. 169–70.

For the cost of the fun machine and details of its design, see Fordin, pp. 404–5. For Minnelli's comments on this number, see Delamater 1981, p. 269.

C. THAT'S ENTERTAINMENT

Levant emulates Green: Minnelli, p. 262.

* The lyric: Reprinted in Dietz 1974, pp. 296–98.

* Idea for song: A. Schwartz.

D. BEGGAR'S WALTZ

Original revue: The original "Beggar's Waltz" was essentially a duet for Astaire and ballet dancer Tilly Losch, choreographed by Albertina Rasch, and dealt with a beggar's dream-fantasy about dancing with a star ballerina (Astaire 1959, p. 169). It is somewhat similar in outline to Astaire's "Limehouse Blues" number in *Ziegfeld Follies* (18 K). For photographs, see Freedland 1976, p. 35; S. Harvey 1975, p. 34; B. Green 1979, p. 40; Ries, p. 112.

E. DANCING IN THE DARK

* "He came in . . . ": Martin and Charisse, p. 203.

* On Charisse and the director, see Martin and Charisse, p. 203.

For commentary on the duet, see Solomon, p. 100; Casper 1977, p. 153; J. Feuer 1977, p. 319; J. Feuer 1982, p. 18; Delamater 1981, pp. 102, 110; Schatz, p. 214; S. Green 1973, p. 390; Scheuer, pp. 314–15; Kobal 1971, p. 231; Sennett, p. 247; Kuyper.

On the $1,000 dress, see Fordin, p. 407.

"Dancing in the Dark" melody: The song's lyric, which is suggestive of a deep romance, is inappropriate for the Astaire-Charisse situation at this point in the story and is not sung. Of course, since the point of the number is to see if the performers can dance together, not sing together, singing might be doubly inappropriate. In one version of the script it was suggested, rather remarkably, that the melody from "I Guess I'll Have to Change My Plan" be used here instead. In the original 1931 *Band Wagon* revue, "Dancing in the Dark" was sung by John Barker while ballerina Tilly Losch, backed by a female chorus, danced on a mirrored floor. (For photographs, see Dietz 1974, pp. 201–3; Gottfried, p. 63; Ries, p. 115.) The lyricist says he first thought the song dull, but "time and applause have taken the dullness out of it." Schwartz recalls that he composed the music in the dark in one minute, "as if I'd known it all of my life"; he then turned on the light to write it down (A. Schwartz; also B. Green 1979, pp. 45–46). The form of the music is AA'BAA'. The B section is often omitted when the song is performed, and that convention is followed in the dance arrangement here.

* ". . . that damned cab": Astaire 1980b.

F. YOU AND THE NIGHT AND THE MUSIC—REHEARSAL SEQUENCES

The love conflict: For the intricate, if somewhat cheerless, argument that Charisse plays a "phallic mother" to Astaire in this film, and that in order for "the stage to be set for love" she must (metaphorically) "castrate herself" even while Astaire (equally metaphorically) castrates and/or kills Buchanan and Mitchell, see Giles.

"dancers shouldn't smoke": For biographical aspects, see Martin and Charisse, p. 202.

G. I LOVE LOUISA

After the show: The beautiful song in the background in the postshow sequences is "Something to Remember You By" from *Three's a Crowd* of 1930.

Impersonates the title character: Astaire had performed this song, together with Adele Astaire, Tilly Losch, Helen Broderick, and Frank Morgan, as part of a Bavarian merry-go-round number in the original *Band Wagon*. (For photographs, see S. Green 1973, p. 28; B. Green 1979, p. 43; Dietz 1974, p. 197.) The song, Dietz says, was written for a chambermaid who loved the team's music but never got around to cleaning their suit (1974, p. 143). The lyric contains the line "I love a great big boo-som," which was sanitized in Hollywood to "I never want to lose 'em."

H. NEW SUN IN THE SKY

Revue tradition in backstage musicals: see Mordden, p. 83n.

I. I GUESS I'LL HAVE TO CHANGE MY PLAN

The tune, the lyric: The song had first been performed by Clifton Webb, in top hat and tails, in a 1929 revue, *The Little Show*, and it went on to become Schwartz's first big hit. Interestingly, Webb was Freed's first choice for the role Buchanan plays in the film, but Webb thought it too small a part and suggested Buchanan. Vincent Price and Edward G. Robinson were also considered for the role (Fordin, pp. 401–2; Minnelli, p. 262; Marshall, p. 210).

The mismatch was created: Actually, things are more complicated than that. The music was first written by Schwartz to a lyric by Lorenz Hart when both were counselors at a boys' camp in the Adirondacks. The song, performed in the camp show, was "I Love to Lie Awake in Bed," and the lyric is filled with ingenious internal and multisyllabic rhymes. Schwartz pulled the song out of his trunk when he was working on *The Little Show* in 1929 with Dietz, who then fashioned the new lyric. The story and both sets of "original" lyrics are given in Dietz 1974, pp. 124–26.

* Ending joke: Marshall, p. vii.

Buchanan in pain: Marshall, pp. 215–16; Fordin, pp. 407–11.

K. TRIPLETS

For a discussion, with pictures, of the apparatus and rehearsal procedures used in this number, see Fordin, pp. 410–13. The considerable agonies of putting on the number are discussed at some length by Fabray in Marshall, p. 214. See also B. Thomas 1984, pp. 224–26. The lyric, as used in *Beat the Devil* of 1937, is given in Dietz 1974, pp. 229–31. Dietz also furnishes a picture (p. 311) from a later stage performance of the song by an improbable cast: Danny Kaye, Vivien Leigh, and Laurence Olivier.

L. GIRL HUNT BALLET

Music by Edens, etc.: Fordin, p. 416.

"applying the term . . . ," "disjointed," etc.: Minnelli, p. 270. Minnelli's script is reprinted in Minnelli, pp. 270–72.

Praised by Astaire: Astaire 1959, p. 301.

"really a sly pastiche . . . ": S. Harvey 1975, p. 131.

NUMBERS CUT FROM THE FILM

Excised footage: The music track for the "You Have Everything" and "Got a Bran' New Suit" numbers is available on Out Take Records. The music track for the "Sweet Music" number is on file at Miles Kreuger's Institute of the American Musical. The music track for "Two-Faced Woman" (sung by India Adams) was recycled and used as a number for Joan Crawford in MGM's *Torch Song* of 1953.

P. GOT A BRAN' NEW SUIT

For another still from this number, see Fordin, p. 409.

Q. TWO-FACED WOMAN

For a still from this number, see Fordin, p. 412.

R. TELEPHONE DUET

"He was at a desk . . . ": Martin and Charisse, p. 204.

28. DADDY LONG LEGS

Personal favorite: Astaire 1959, pp. 311–12.

SHAPING THE SCREENPLAY

Two sound films: For completeness of the record, *Vadertje Langbeen* should be mentioned. It was a 1938 Dutch film that apparently was never shown outside Holland because the producers had not acquired the film rights to the story. Fox's successful effort to block this film is discussed, and the film is very favorably reviewed, in *Variety*, October 26, 1938.

Fashioning the story as a musical: In 1952 the Webster story had been made into a stage musical in London, titled *Love from Judy*, with songs by Hugh Martin and Timothy Gray. At one point Zanuck considered having the songs for the film written by Alec Wilder, who was seen as a "new talent" at the time.

At a nightclub: Astaire 1959, pp. 305–6.

"Knowing it was . . . ": Ephron, p. 131.

Ritter's distinction: Wallechinsky et al., p. 201.

"That love scene . . . ": Ephron, p. 133.

On Zanuck as a script editor, see Gussow, pp. 140–64.

THE MUSIC

Astaire's urging: BBC, p. 29.

LESLIE CARON

"shy and frightened . . . ": Ephron, p. 137. The crew found her defenses charming: "Every day, when she came on the set, she would gravely say 'Good morning,' and shake hands with everyone from Negulesco to the electricians. . . . The stagehands nicknamed her 'The French Corporal.' " Soon she became "the most loved person on the set." Frank Sinatra took a fancy to her, and "[every morning] there was a bouquet of roses left on her doorstep and . . . every morning, when Caron came out, she read the card, picked up the roses, and dropped them into the garbage pail. When the story hit the set, the stagehands changed her name to 'Stonewall Caron' " (Ephron, pp. 137–39).

She herself has commented: Heeley.

"One day at rehearsals . . . ": Astaire 1959, p. 311.

THE WIDE SCREEN

". . . my first go . . . ": H. Thompson.

ASTAIRE AND THE PRODUCTION OF THE FILM

"I don't know . . . ," "It was a frightful . . . ," "When *Daddy Long Legs* . . . ": Davidson, pp. 199–201; see also Astaire 1959, pp. 306–11; Ephron, pp. 136–37; Niven, pp. 255–56; Reagan, p. 158. A year later, in an interview held in New York to publicize the film, Astaire's loss was still very evident: "It's not the same anymore, without her. . . . When I wake up the way I did at three this morning, I say to myself, 'What's the use?' I always needed her judgment too. I especially wanted her opinion of this new picture" (H. Thompson).

A. HISTORY OF THE BEAT

On Astaire's drumming hobby, see Ephron, p. 136; Davidson, pp. 185–86. Astaire had previously performed splendid, fully developed drum solos in *A Damsel in Distress* (9 J) and *Easter Parade* (21 A); perhaps he had simply run out of ideas.

E. DAYDREAM SEQUENCE

"The first rehearsal . . . ": Heeley.

29. FUNNY FACE

THE PRODUCTION AND THE MUSIC

For details on the move to Paramount, see Astaire 1959, pp. 313–15; Fordin, pp. 442–43; S. Green 1973, pp. 408–9.

"the music itself . . . ": Edens, p. 18.

Lack briskness: The slowing down of popular music in the 1940s and 1950s is well illustrated by Doris Day's performance of "Love Me or Leave Me" in the 1955 film of that name. Portraying Ruth Etting, she takes nearly two minutes to sing a chorus of the song; Etting, in her recording from the 1920s, does it in one minute, eighteen seconds.

THE SCRIPT

On Gershe and Avedon, see Knight 1957, p. 19.

"probably true . . . ": S. Harvey 1973, p. 7; on anti-intellectualism, see also J. Feuer 1977.

* ". . . creaky . . . script . . . ": S. Harvey 1973, p. 7.

RICHARD AVEDON

* Avedon and Donen's working methods: see Knight 1957, p. 19; S. Harvey 1973, p. 7.

* "We wanted . . . ": Delamater 1981, p. 232.

THE CHOREOGRAPHY

"the happiest . . . ": Delamater 1981, p. 231.

C. HOW LONG HAS THIS BEEN GOING ON?

The extremely slow tempo: Hepburn is not unusual in taking this song at a very slow tempo; see Wilder, p. 141. Written for the original *Funny Face* in 1927, it was dropped when the show was still on the road and replaced by "He Loves and She Loves." The song was recycled with success in a Ziegfeld show, *Rosalie*, in 1928. For the film the lyric of the verse has been entirely rewritten. The original lyric is given in I. Gershwin, pp. 277–79.

D. FUNNY FACE

On Donen's idea and Avedon's idea, see Knight 1957, p. 22.

F. BASAL METABOLISM

* Sidewalk lovers: S. Green 1973, p. 407.

G. LET'S KISS AND MAKE UP

Music by Courage: Edens.

* "and noticed . . . ": Astaire 1959, p. 315; also Astaire 1971b.

Song's rhythmic jaggedness: Wilder, pp. 139–40.

Weights in raincoat: Astaire 1971b.

H. HE LOVES AND SHE LOVES

On the photographic process in the montage sequence, see Knight 1957. The process is illustrated in *Life*, April 15, 1957, pp. 88–91.

On the chapel alterations, see Blair.

"There's nothing . . . ," "Here I have . . . ": Beaufort; see also Blair; Astaire 1959, p. 316. A February freeze had killed the grass, and so some fast-growing seed was brought in from California. When the rain turned that into a quagmire, sod was imported.

K. CLAP YO' HANDS

* "exclaimed and stomped . . . ": I. Gershwin, p. 213.

"knocked-out jazz": Edens, p. 19.

30. SILK STOCKINGS

THE *NINOTCHKA* ORIGINAL

On the Lengyel and Garbo incident, see Stanley.

The story Lengyel wrote from his three sentences: In this Ninotchka falls in love with the man in Paris, but she becomes convinced he is not serious and returns to Moscow. When he comes to Moscow to conduct some negotiations, her superiors order her to win him over. Not willing to be his lover, she marries him (later she can divorce him "by postcard" under the Soviet system). She vengefully refuses to consummate the marriage, they argue, and he storms back to Paris. Reconciliation is achieved in later negotiations in Paris.

* On politics and *Ninotchka*, see Carringer and Sabath, pp. 144–45.

"the happiness . . . ": Pogue, p. 119.

SILK STOCKINGS ON THE STAGE

For the most extensive account of the tumultuous, agonizing, and often hilarious backstage drama, see the leading lady's remarkable autobiography (published under her real name), Knef, pp. 280–347. Other accounts are in Eells 1967, pp. 288–94; Teichmann, pp. 234–35, 308–9; Meredith, pp. 615–17; Schwartz 1977, pp. 252–55; Goldstein, pp. 442–45; Burrows, pp. 268–75. Tensions were increased by a series of mishaps: one of the leads became pregnant and had to be replaced, and leading lady Hildegarde Neff came down with the measles ("With measles you have to stay in the dark, don't you?" "We can turn the spots on the audience, we'd probably get a prize for being avant-garde.") Kaufman stopped talking to Feuer and Martin (whom he referred to as "Mr. Hyde and Mr. Hyde"), and Porter privately resolved never to work with them again. In a pique, Kaufman, MacGrath, and Porter refused to attend the Broadway premiere. At one point Neff asked to be released from her contract, because "Ninotchka has nothing more to do with the part I signed for"; her request was refused.

SILK STOCKINGS ON THE SCREEN

Authors of the stage version: C. Feuer. Lengyel had also made his story into a three-act play in the late 1940s, and it received a few stagings in Europe (including Paris) in the early 1950s. The play is arranged to take place on a single set, a suite in a luxurious hotel in Paris. About the only things from this source that survive in the film are the names given to the three commissars, the line about using silk for parachutes rather than neckties, and the references to the electromagnetic theories of the fictitious Soviet sexologist Kamachev. This play is much more preachily anti-Soviet than any other version of the story.

Sequences and episodes from 1939 film: Attesting to its remarkable appeal and resilience, the *Ninotchka* screenplay has been published four times: in Wald and Macauley; in Brackett, Wilder, and Reisch; in Anobile; and (somewhat abbreviated) in Weinberg.

Resistance to Mamoulian: Fordin, p. 443.

Mamoulian convinces Astaire: Mamoulian; BBC, p. 59.

* More "commonness": BBC, p. 59.

* "Me? . . . ": Smith.

"The love story . . . ": Fordin, p. 445. On Lubitsch's equally careful overseeing of the scriptwriting process, see Weinberg, pp. 276–77.

"I had two . . . ": Milne, p. 149.

* On Lorre and drugs, see Martin and Charisse, p. 212.

THE FILMING OF THE DANCES

"the worst shape . . . ": Mamoulian.

THE MUSIC

Porter's lack of interest: Lederer, pp. 57–58; Fordin, p. 444.

THE CHOREOGRAPHY

Choreographer: The first choice for the Broadway show was Michael Kidd, who had choreographed Porter's previous musical, *Can-Can*. To Porter's disappointment, Kidd refused the assignment, "because he felt relations between the two atomic powers were too strained to stand kidding" (Eells 1967, p. 291).

"not to choreograph for Astaire . . . ": Delamater 1981, p. 229.

B. PARIS LOVES LOVERS

Charisse grills the commissars: In the comparable scene in *Ninotchka*, Garbo asks Commissar Buljanoff if he spells his name with one or two *f's*. Here Charisse asks Commissar Bibinski if he spells his name with two or three *b's*. Score one for *Silk Stockings*.

C. STEREOPHONIC SOUND

* Converted her to a swimmer: Eells 1967, p. 293.

A robust number: Onstage this number had been a solo for Gretchen Wyler. The song was not published until 1958, after it had been given added exposure on the screen.

On the saga of the Grable photograph, see D. Warren, pp. 77–80.

Chandelier ride: Pan 1980.

D. IT'S A CHEMICAL REACTION, THAT'S ALL/ALL OF YOU

Merely a chemical reaction: In "It's a Chemical Reaction" Porter has ably fashioned a song from a suggestion in one of Garbo's lines in the 1939 film ("Love is a romantic designation for a most ordinary biological, or shall we say chemical, process"), as well as from some dialogue in the Lengyel play discussed in a note above. Only the first half of the song is sung by Charisse.

F. SILK STOCKINGS

On this scene in general, see R. Wood; Milne, p. 151.

The censors: Fordin, p. 448.

G. WITHOUT LOVE

Execution sequence: The stage version also included this sequence (one of the few places it directly followed the 1939 film) and then ended the scene (and the first of its two acts) with an added soliloquy for Neff as she tosses in her sleep. In it she tries to defend her happiness against imagined prosecutors.

H. FATED TO BE MATED

Choreographed mostly by Hermes Pan: Pan (1983) says Astaire performed the dance as he set it, with "one or two changes." Also Pan 1980.

* "In a way . . . ": Mamoulian.

* Astaire had to be persuaded: Pan 1980; BBC, p. 57.

* 112 pounds: Martin and Charisse, p. 201.

I. JOSEPHINE

On Loring's versions, see Fordin, pp. 450–51. Onstage the number was led by the imposing, 156-pound Gretchen Wyler, who had signed on to understudy the understudy for the role. Through various mishaps to the others, she got her big chance and, in classic fiction come true, stopped the show and became an overnight sensation (Eells 1967, pp. 292–94). The show's leading lady characterizes her as "a plump blond with a voice like a fanfare" (Knef, p. 313).

J. SIBERIA

* Joke on Mamoulian: Mamoulian; Fordin, pp. 449–50. The joke routine, which had to be cleared with studio heads because of its expense (several thousand dollars), was actually filmed; the director retains the film as a memento.

K. THE RED BLUES

* "She has bursts . . . ": Fordin, p. 448; see also Delamater 1981, p. 231.

Melancholy of the scene: For different perspectives on the point of this number, see Milne, p. 152; R. Wood, p. 152.

L. THE RITZ ROLL AND ROCK

"sock solo": Astaire 1959, p. 319; also on the evolution of this number, see Eells 1967, p. 303; Freedland 1976, p. 147; Lederer, p. 57.

"didn't do . . . ": Astaire 1971a.

* "What's happened . . . ": Smith.

"It wasn't . . . ," "was all right . . . ": Lederer, p. 57.

"lucky accident": Mamoulian.

31. FINIAN'S RAINBOW

"hordes of black and white . . . ": S. Harvey 1975, p. 143.

COPPOLA'S DISASTER

"biggest disappointment": Harmetz; see also Lederer, p. 59.

"a disaster": Farber, p. 220.

"brought in . . . ": Murray, p. 65.

"I had my way . . . ": Gelmis, p. 186.

". . . working in a big studio . . . ": Murray, p. 65.

"terrible": Garber, p. 220.

"sort of ridiculous . . . ," "something warm": Gelmis, p. 183.

"I fought very hard . . . ": Farber, p. 220.

"zip it up": Gelmis, p. 183. For additional information, see Johnson, pp. 61–69. The stage script has been published twice: Harburg and Saidy; Saidy and Harburg.

* Bringing the show to the screen: Druxman, pp. 121–23; P. Scheuer; Gelmis, p. 183.

"get fancy," ". . . warmth and affection," "I felt the leprechaun . . . ": Gelmis, pp. 183–85.

THE CREATION OF THE MUSICAL NUMBERS

"I said, 'Grandish' . . . ": Gelmis, p. 184.

"at Fred Astaire's insistence": Gelmis, p. 184.

"I know nothing . . . ": Farber, p. 220.
". . . fired the choreographer . . . ": Gelmis, p. 184.
"I improvised . . . ": Farber, p. 220; see also S. Braudy, p. 70.
Astaire's suggestions: Maltin, p. 5.
"faking it": Gelmis, p. 184.
"basically a cheat": S. Braudy, p. 70.
"a real pain . . . ": Georgakas, p. 27.
Purposeful mismatching of shots: Coppola discusses his filming approach with apparent pride of discovery in Gelmis, p. 185. See also Johnson, p. 68. But such cutting had been used before in Hollywood musicals, of course, most notably by Stanley Donen in the "New York, New York" number in *On the Town* in 1949 and the "Bonjour, Paris!" number in *Funny Face* in 1957 (29 E). But the technique there has some point as an exuberant travelogue, and it is used in only one number in each film, not in all of them. Even earlier the approach was masterfully used in the "Isn't It Romantic" number in Rouben Mamoulian's *Love Me Tonight* of 1932. Richard Lester had employed the Coppola approach with far more success (the cuts are often informative and/or funny) in *A Funny Thing Happened on the Way to the Forum* (1966).

D. HOW ARE THINGS IN GLOCCA MORRA?

Most popular song: For Harburg's warm reminiscences about the evolution of the lyric for this evocative song, see Wilk, p. 228.

E. LOOK TO THE RAINBOW

* "I sang with her! . . . ": Freedland 1976, p. 166.

I. IF THIS ISN'T LOVE

* "After the song . . . ": Gelmis, p. 184. On Hancock, see Roman, p. 95.

REFERENCES

The interviews, letters, and published materials indicated below are specifically cited in the notes. In addition, this study has made extensive use of unpublished documentary sources which, to reduce clutter, are not usually referenced —though the source is generally obvious in context. Chief among these have been the Arthur Freed and Roger Edens Collections at the University of Southern California Library, and the RKO Collection. These are rich mines of production records, business and legal files, contracts, cast lists, letters, publicity and music materials, and day-by-day production schedules; especially helpful were the chronological arrays of scripts and treatments for each film, some of them annotated by participants, which give evidence about the progress of developing the finished product.

Additional material of this sort (particularly script, cast, and music information) was found in Miles Kreuger's Institute of the American Musical, the Library of the American Academy of Motion Picture Arts and Sciences, the Astaire Scrapbooks in the Boston University Library, and the Theatre, Dance, and Music Collections of the Library of the Performing Arts of the New York Public Library, Lincoln Center.

Adamson, Joe. *Groucho, Harpo, Chico, and Sometimes Zeppo.* New York: Simon and Schuster, 1973.

Agate, James. *First Nights.* London: Nicholson and Watson, 1934.

Agee, James. *Agee on Film.* New York: McDowell, Obolensky, 1958.

Ager, Cecelia. "Castles in Hollywood." *Stage,* February 1939, pp. 20–23.

Allen, Frederick Lewis. "When America Learned to Dance." *Scribner's Magazine,* September 1937, pp. 11–17, 92.

Allyson, June (with Frances Spatz Leighton). *June Allyson.* New York: Putnam, 1982.

Altman, Rick, ed. *Genre: The Musical.* London: Routledge and Kegan Paul, 1981.

American Cinematographer. "The Dancing Shoes." September 1949, pp. 318–19, 335–36.

Anderson, Jack. "Robbins Thinks Big About Dances." *New York Times,* May 29, 1983, sec. 2, p. 1.

Anobile, Richard J., ed. *Ernst Lubitsch's Ninotchka.* New York: Darien House, 1975.

Astaire, Adele. "I'm Getting What I Want Out of Life." *Hearst's International—Cosmopolitan,* November 1935, pp. 59, 162–63.

———. "He Worries, Poor Boy." *Variety,* March 18, 1936, p. 3.

Astaire, Fred. *Steps in Time.* New York: Harper and Bros., 1959. (Reprinted by Da Capo Press, 1981.)

———. Interview with Hugh Fordin, Beverly Hills, October 12, 1971a. Tape recording, Special Collections, University of Southern California Library.

———. Interview on "Dick Cavett Show," ABC Television, October 13, 1971b.

———. "Reminiscences of Fred Astaire," interview with Ronald L. Davis, Beverly Hills, July 31, 1978, SMU Oral History Project on the Performing Arts.

———. Interview with Margot Fonteyn for "The Magic of Dance," BBC Television, 1979a.

———. Interview with Johnny Carson, "The Tonight Show," NBC Television, December 21, 1979b.

———. Interview with Barbara Walters, "20/20," ABC Television, March 6, 1980a.

———. Interviews with John Mueller, August 7 (telephone) and 12 (Beverly Hills), 1980b.

———. Speech on "The American Film Institute Salutes Fred Astaire," CBS Television, April 18, 1981.

Balanchine, George. "The Dance Element in Stravinsky's Music." *Dance Index* 6, 10–12 (1947): 250–57. (Reprinted in *Ballet Review,* Summer 1982.)

Balliett, Whitney, "Jazz: A Nice Place to Be." *The New Yorker,* January 1, 1979, pp. 56–57.

Baring, Maurice. *Sarah Bernhardt.* London: Peter Davies, 1933.

Barnett, Lincoln. *Writing on Life: Sixteen Close-Ups.* New York: William Sloan, 1951. (Chapter 2, on Fred Astaire, originally published in 1941; chapter 3, on Adele Astaire, in 1945.)

Baryshnikov, Mikhail. Interview with Mike Wallace, "60 Minutes," CBS Television, February 18, 1979.

Basinger, Jeanine. *Gene Kelly.* New York: Pyramid, 1976.

Baskette, Kirtley. "My Companion Said: 'I'd Just Love to Dance with Fred Astaire!' " *Photoplay,* April 1935, pp. 30–31, 96.

BBC. *The Fred Astaire Story.* London: BBC, 1975.

Beaton, Wilford. "Swing Time." *The Hollywood Spectator,* August 29, 1936. (Reprinted in *American Film Criticism,* ed. Stanley Kauffmann [New York: Liveright, 1972].)

Beaufort, John. "Fred Astaire Recalls 'Funny Face' Dance." *Christian Science Monitor,* March 23, 1957.

Bedoian, Jim. Liner notes for "Helen Kane: The boop-boop-a-doop girl," Take Two Records TT210, 1981.

Behlmer, Rudy, ed. *Memo from David O. Selznick.* New York: Viking, 1972.

Bellamy, Ralph. *When the Smoke Hits the Fan.* Garden City, N.Y.: Doubleday, 1979.

Benchley, Robert. "Hail to the King!" *The New Yorker,* November 29, 1930, pp. 33–36.

Bender, R. D. "Statistics of Feature Releases." RKO Radio Pictures, June 1952.

Bennett, Robert Russell. Letter to John Mueller, March 20, 1981.

Berman, Pandro S. Interview with John Mueller, Beverly Hills, August 20, 1982.

Blair, W. Granger. "On the Seine in the Rain with 'Funny Face.' " *New York Times,* July 15, 1956.

Blandford, Edmund C. *Artie Shaw: The Man and His Music.* Hastings, Sussex, England: Blandford, 1974.

Bookspan, Martin, and Yockey, Ross. *André Previn.* Garden City, N.Y.: Doubleday, 1981.

Bordman, Gerald. *American Musical Theatre: A Chronicle.* New York: Oxford University Press, 1978.

———. *Jerome Kern: His Life and Music.* New York: Oxford University Press, 1980.

Borne, Hal (interviewed by Arlene Croce). "Music for Astaire & Rogers: A Conversation with Hal Borne." *Ballet Review* 4, 3 (1972): 50–60.

Brackett, Charles; Wilder, Billy; and Reisch, Walter. *Ninotchka.* New York: Viking, 1972.

Braudy, Leo. *The World in a Frame: What We See in Films.* Garden City, N.Y.: Doubleday, 1976.

Braudy, Susan. "Francis Ford Coppola: A Profile." *Atlantic,* August 1976, pp. 66–73.

Brinkley, Nell. "That 'Yama Girl' Is Wonderful." *New York Evening Standard,* July 6, 1908, p. 12.

Britton, Jimmy. "Stage and Hall: Mr. Fred Astaire's Return to Birmingham—His Opinion on Stage and Screen." *Birmingham* [England] *Mail,* October 26, 1933.

Brooklyn Daily Eagle. "18-Acre Camp Erected For Draft Film Musical." October 26, 1941.

Brooks, Elston. *I've Heard Those Songs Before.* New York: Morrow Quill, 1981.

Burnet, Dana. "Watching His Step: A Portrait of Fred Astaire." *Pictorial Review,* January 1936, pp. 10–11, 40, 42.

Burns, George (with Cynthia Hobart Lindsay). *I Love Her, That's Why!* New York: Simon and Schuster, 1955.

Burns, George. *The Third Time Around.* New York: Putnam, 1980.

Burrows, Abe. *Honest Abe: Is There Really No Business Like Show Business?* Boston: Little, Brown, 1980.

Burton, Jack. *The Blue Book of Hollywood Musicals: Songs from the Sound Tracks and the Stars Who Sang Them Since the Birth of the Talkies a Quarter-Century Ago.* Watkins Glen, N.Y.: Century House, 1953.

Caesar, Irving. Interviewed on "All You Need Is Love," BBC Television, 1980.

Caffin, Caroline and Charles H. *Dancing and Dances of Today.* New York: Dodd, Mead, 1912. (Reprinted by Da Capo Press, 1978.)

Cagney, James. *Cagney by Cagney.* Garden City, N.Y.: Doubleday, 1976.

Cameron, Kate. " 'Holiday Inn' Premiere for Navy." *New York Sunday News,* August 2, 1942.

———. "The Sky's the Limit." *New York Daily News,* September 3, 1943.

Carpozi, George, Jr. *The Fabulous Life of Bing Crosby.* New York: Manor, 1977.

Carringer, Robert, and Sabath, Barry. *Ernst Lubitsch: A Guide to References and Resources.* Boston: G. K. Hall, 1978.

Carter, Randolph. *The World of Flo Ziegfeld.* New York: Praeger, 1974.

Casper, Joseph Andrew. *Vincente Minnelli and the Film Musical.* New York: Barnes and Co., 1977.

Castle, Mr. and Mrs. Vernon. *Modern Dancing.* New York: Harper and Brothers, 1914. (Reprinted by Da Capo Press, 1980.)

Castle, Irene. "My Memories of Vernon Castle." Serialized in *Everybody's Magazine,* November 1918–March 1919.

———. *My Husband.* New York: Scribner's, 1919. (Reprinted by Da Capo Press, 1979.)

———. *Castles in the Air.* New York: Doubleday, 1958. (Reprinted by Da Capo Press, 1980.)

Chapman, John. "The Happiest Man on Broadway." *Saturday Evening Post,* January 9, 1943, pp. 15, 81–82.

Chase, Robin. Liner notes for "The Belle of New York," DRG Records D5-15004, 1978.

Churchill, Douglas W. "Building Castles in Hollywood." *New York Times,* February 22, 1939.

Churchill, Sarah. *Keep On Dancing.* New York: Coward, McCann and Geoghegan, 1981.

Cocuzza, Gininne. "An American Premiere Danseuse." *Dance Scope* 14, no. 3 (1980): 36–51.

Conrad, Derek. "Two Feet in the Air." *Films and Filming,* December 1959, pp. 11–13, 28, 35.

Consumer Guide, Editors of. *The Best, Worst & Most Unusual: Hollywood Musicals.* New York: Beckman House, 1983.

Corliss, Richard. *Talking Pictures: Screenwriters in the American Cinema 1927–1973.* Woodstock, N.Y.: Overlook, 1974.

Crawford, Joan (with Jane Kesner Ardmore). *A Portrait of Joan.* Garden City, N.Y.: Doubleday, 1962.

Creelman, Eileen. "Fred Astaire Talks of Dancing and Movies and His Latest Comedy, 'Second Chorus.' " *New York Sun,* January 15, 1941.

Croce, Arlene. "Notes on la Belle, la Perfectly Swell, Romance." *Ballet Review* 1, no. 1 (1965): 23–35.

———. *The Fred Astaire & Ginger Rogers Book.* New York: Outerbridge and Lazard, 1972.

———. *Afterimages.* New York: Knopf, 1977.

Crosby, Bing. *Call Me Lucky.* New York: Simon and Schuster, 1953.

———. Liner notes for "Attitude Dancing," United Artists Records UAS 29888, 1975.

Crosby, Gary, and Firestone, Ross. *Going My Own Way.* Garden City, N.Y.: Doubleday, 1983.

Crowther, Bosley. "Up the Astaire-Way to Success." *New York Times,* November 28, 1937, sec. 11, p. 5.

———. "Castles in Pictures." *New York Times,* April 2, 1939, sec. 10, p. 5.

———. "The Sky's the Limit." *New York Times,* September 3, 1943.

———. "The Revue and the Screen." *New York Times,* March 31, 1946, sec. 2, p. 1.

———. *Reruns: Fifty Memorable Films.* New York: Putnam, 1978.

Cugat, Xavier. *Rumba Is My Life.* New York: Didier, 1948.

Cullum, Winifred. "Hoctor Dances with Astaire." *The American Dancer,* May 1937, pp. 14–15, 41.

Cunningham, Merce. Conversation with John Mueller, Washington, D.C., 1973.

Cutts, John. "On the Bright Side: An Interview with Charles Walters." *Films and Filming.* August 1970, pp. 12–18.

Davidson, Bill. *The Real and the Unreal.* New York: Harper and Bros., 1961.

Delamater, Jerome. "The Musical," in *American Film Genres: Approaches to a Critical Theory of Popular Film,* ed. Stuart M. Kaminsky. Dayton, Ohio: Pflaum, 1974, pp. 120–140.

———. "A Critical and Historical Analysis of Dance as a Code of the Hollywood Musical." Ph.D. dissertation, Northwestern University, 1978.

———. *Dance in the Hollywood Musical.* Ann Arbor, Mich.: UMI Research Press, 1981.

De Mille, Agnes. *America Dances.* New York: Macmillan, 1980.

Dietz, Howard. "The Musical Band Wagon Keeps On Rollin' Along." *Look,* August 11, 1953, pp. 92–95.

———. *Dancing in the Dark.* New York: Quadrangle, 1974.

Dolin, Anton. Letter to John Mueller, February 9, 1983.

Dorris, George, and Croce, Arlene. "An Interview with Gordon Boelzner." *Ballet Review* 3, no. 4 (1970): 51–62.

Druxman, Michael B. *The Musical: From Broadway to Hollywood.* New York: Barnes and Co., 1980.

Duncan, Donald. "Irene Castle in 1956." *Dance Magazine,* October 1956, pp. 87–89.

———. " 'The Dance with the Noise.' " *Dance Magazine,* August 1961, pp. 42–44. (On Eleanor Powell.)

Dzhermolinska, Helen. "Swingtime on Park Avenue." *Dance Magazine,* April 1947, pp. 24–26, 34.

Edens, Roger. "Labor Pains." *Film and TV Music,* Spring 1957, pp. 18–20.

Edwards, Anne. *Judy Garland: A Biography.* New York: Simon and Schuster, 1974.

Eells, George. *The Life That Late He Led.* New York: Putnam, 1967.

———. *Ginger, Loretta and Irene Who?* New York: Putnam, 1976.

Ephron, Henry. *We Thought We Could Do Anything: The Life of Screenwriters Phoebe and Henry Ephron.* New York: Norton, 1977.

Erenberg, Lewis A. "Everybody's Doin' It: The Pre-World War I Dance Craze, The Castles, and the Modern American Girl." *Feminist Studies,* Fall 1975, pp. 155–70.

Eustis, Morton. *Players at Work: Acting According to the Actors.* New York: Theatre Arts, 1937. (Includes "Fred Astaire: The Actor-Dancer Attacks His Part," originally published in *Theatre Arts Monthly,* May 1937, pp. 371–86.)

Evans, Harry. "Ginger, Leila, and Fred." *Family Circle,* May 8, 1936, pp. 10–12, 22.

Ewen, David. *The Story of Irving Berlin.* New York: Holt, 1950.

———. *George Gershwin: His Journey to Greatness.* Englewood Cliffs, N.J.: Prentice-Hall, 1970a.

———. *Great Men of Popular Song.* Englewood Cliffs, N.J.: Prentice-Hall, 1970b.

Faith, William Robert. *Bob Hope: A Life in Comedy.* New York: Putnam, 1982.

Fanger, Iris. "Irene Castle." In *Notable American Women: The Modern Period,* ed. Barbara Sicherman and Carol Hurd Green. Cambridge, Mass.: Harvard University Press, 1980, pp. 142–43.

Farber, Stephen. "Coppola and the Godfather." *Sight and Sound,* Autumn 1972, pp. 217–23.

Farnsworth, Marjorie. *The Ziegfeld Follies.* New York: Putnam, 1956.

Ferguson, Otis. "Words and Music." In *American Film Criticism,* ed. Stanley Kauffmann. New York: Liveright, 1972.

Feuer, Cy. Letter to John Mueller, November 22, 1982.

Feuer, Jane. "The Self-Reflective Musical and the Myth of Entertainment." *Quarterly Review of Film Studies,* August 1977, pp. 313–26.

———. *The Hollywood Musical.* Bloomington: Indiana University Press, 1982.

———. "College Course Film: The Hollywood Musical." *Journal of the University Film and Video Association,* Fall 1983, pp. 70–78.

Finch, Christopher. *Rainbow: The Stormy Life of Judy Garland.* New York: Grosset and Dunlap, 1975.

Fisher, John. *Call Them Irreplaceable.* New York: Stein and Day, 1976.

Fleming, Warner. "What Puts Fred Astaire Over?" *Shadowplay Magazine* (Chicago), February 1935, pp. 30, 61–63.

Fontaine, Joan. *No Bed of Roses.* New York: Morrow, 1978.

Fonteyn, Margot. *The Magic of Dance.* New York: Knopf, 1979.

Fordin, Hugh. *The World of Entertainment: Hollywood's Greatest Musicals.* Garden City, N.Y.: Doubleday, 1975.

Fordin, Hugh, and Chase, Robin. "Hollywood Puts on Its Dancing Shoes Again." *New York Times,* June 25, 1978, sec. 2, p. 8.

Frank, Gerold. *Judy.* New York: Harper and Row, 1975.

Freedland, Michael. *Irving Berlin.* New York: Stein and Day, 1974.

———. *Fred Astaire: An Illustrated Biography.* New York: Grosset and Dunlap, 1976.

———. *Jerome Kern.* London: Robson Books, 1978.

Gallico, A. T. "Costumes by Fred Astaire." *New York News,* January 29, 1933.

Gelmis, Joseph. *The Film Director as Superstar.* Garden City, N.Y.: Doubleday, 1970.

Genné, Beth Eliot. "The Film Musicals of Vincente Minnelli and the Team of Gene Kelly and Stanley Donen: 1944–1958." Ph.D. dissertation, University of Michigan, 1984.

Georgakas, Dan. "The Man Behind Fred and Ginger." *Cineaste* 12, no. 4 (1983): 26–29.

Gershwin, George. *George Gershwin's Song-book.* New York: Simon and Schuster, 1932.

Gershwin, Ira. *Lyrics on Several Occasions.* New York: Knopf, 1959.

Giddins, Gary. *Riding on a Blue Note.* New York: Oxford University Press, 1981.

Giles, Dennis. "Show-Making." *Movie,* Spring 1977, pp. 14–25.

Goldberg, Isaac. *George Gershwin: A Study in American Music.* New York: Ungar, 1958.

Goldberg, Jane. "Taps for Ginger Rogers." *Village Voice,* March 15, 1976, p. 129.

———. "John Bubbles: A Hoofer's Homage." *Village Voice,* December 4, 1978, p. 112.

Goldstein, Malcolm, *George S. Kaufman: His Life, His Theater.* New York: Oxford University Press, 1979.

Gottfried, Martin. *Broadway Musicals.* New York: Abrams, 1979.

Graham, Sheila. "Fred Astaire: Still Dancing Man." *Newark Evening News,* September 22, 1968.

Green, Adolph, "The Magic of Fred Astaire." *American Film,* April 1981, pp. 36–37.

Green, Benny. *Fred Astaire.* London: Hamlyn, 1979.

———. *P. G. Wodehouse: A Literary Biography.* London: Pavilion, 1981.

Green, Stanley. *Ring Bells! Sing Songs! Broadway Musicals of the 1930s.* New Rochelle, N.Y.: Arlington House, 1971.

——— (with Burt Goldblatt). *Starring Fred Astaire.* New York: Dodd, Mead, 1973.

———. *Encyclopedia of the Musical Film.* New York: Oxford University Press, 1981.

Greene, Graham. *The Pleasure-Dome: Collected Film Criticism 1935–40.* London: Secker and Warburg, 1972.

Grieves, Jefferson. "Top Hat." *Films and Filming,* October 1962, pp. 45–48.

Guest, Ivor. *The Romantic Ballet in Paris.* London: Pitman, 1966.

Gussow, Mel. *Don't Say Yes Until I Finish Talking: A Biography of Darryl F. Zanuck.* Garden City, N.Y.: Doubleday, 1971.

Haley, Jack, Jr. Telephone conversation with John Mueller, January 9, 1984.

Hall, Leonard. "That Cute Astaire." *Delineator,* December 1935, pp. 68–69.

Hallowell, John. "Rita Hayworth: Don't Put the Blame on Me, Boys." *New York Times,* October 25, 1970, sec. 2, pp. 15, 38.

Hamm, Charles. *Yesterdays: Popular Song in America.* New York: Norton, 1979.

Harburg, E. Y., and Saidy, Fred. *Finian's Rainbow: A Musical Satire.* New York: Random House, 1947.

Harmetz, Aljean. "Astaire, Nearing 80, Is Still a Very Private Person." *New York Times,* May 8, 1979.

Harris, Dale. "Fred Astaire: Singer." *New York Times,* April 29, 1973.

———. " 'I Just Dance.' " *Ballet News,* August 1981, pp. 22–27.

Harvey, Jim. "Fred and Ginger." *Dance Life,* Winter 1977, pp. 1–17.

Harvey, Stephen. "Stanley Donen Interviewed." *Film Comment,* July–August 1973, pp. 4–9.

———. *Fred Astaire.* New York: Pyramid, 1975.

Haskell, Arnold. *Balletomania Then and Now.* New York: Knopf, 1977.

Haver, Ronald. *David O. Selznick's Hollywood.* New York: Knopf, 1980.

Hayes, Helen, and Dody, Sanford. *On Reflection: An Autobiography.* New York: M. Evans and Co., 1968.

Heeley, David, producer and director. "Fred Astaire: Puttin' on His Top Hat" and "Fred Astaire: Change Partners and Dance" (two television programs written by John L. Miller), PBS, March 1980.

Henderson, Brian. "A Musical Comedy and Empire." *Film Quarterly,* Winter 1981–82, pp. 2–16.

Hering, Doris. "Don't Forget the Backbend, Harriet!" *Dance Magazine,* December 1965, pp. 112–17.

Hillier, Jim. "Interview with Stanley Donen." *Movie,* Spring 1977, pp. 26–35.

Hirschhorn, Clive. *Gene Kelly: A Biography.* Chicago: Regnery, 1974.

———. *The Hollywood Musical.* New York: Crown, 1981.

Hogue, Peter. "The Band Wagon." *Velvet Light Trap: Review of Cinema,* Winter 1974, pp. 33–34.

Honeycutt, Kirk. "Gene Kelly: Dancing on Film and Strolling Down Memory Lane." *New York Times,* June 1, 1980, sec. D, pp. 1, 15.

Hope, Bob (as told to Pete Martin). *Have Tux, Will Travel.* New York: Simon and Schuster, 1954.

Horne, Lena, and Schickel, Richard. *Lena.* New York: Signet, 1965.

Jablonski, Edward. *Harold Arlen: Happy with the Blues.* Garden City, N.Y.: Doubleday, 1961.

Jablonski, Edward, and Stewart, Lawrence D. *The Gershwin Years.* Garden City, N.Y.: Doubleday, 1973.

Jacobs, Lewis. "World War II and the American Film." In *The Movies: An American Idiom,* ed. Arthur F. McClure. Rutherford, N.J.: Fairleigh Dickinson University Press, 1971, pp. 153–77.

Jampel, David M. "Astaire in Japan Muses on Show Biz." *Variety,* August 21, 1957, pp. 2, 54.

Jay, Dave. *The Irving Berlin Songography 1907–1966.* New Rochelle, N.Y.: Arlington House, 1969.

Jewell, Richard. "A History of RKO Radio Pictures, Incorporated." Ph.D. dissertation, University of Southern California, 1978.

Jewell, Rick, and Harbin, Vernon. *The RKO Story.* New York: Crown, 1982.

Johnson, Robert K. *Francis Ford Coppola.* Boston: Twayne, 1977.

Joseph, Robert. "This Army Moves on Its Paycheck." *New York Herald Tribune,* October 12, 1941.

Kael, Pauline. *Reeling.* Boston: Little, Brown, 1976.

Kagan, Norman. *The War Film.* New York: Pyramid, 1974.

Kerr, Walter. *The Silent Clowns.* New York: Knopf, 1975.

Kimball, Robert, ed. *Cole.* New York: Holt, Rinehart and Winston, 1971.

———. *The Complete Lyrics of Cole Porter.* New York: Knopf, 1983.

Kimball, Robert, and Simon, Alfred. *The Gershwins.* New York: Atheneum, 1973.

Kinkle, Roger D. *The Complete Encyclopedia of Popular Music and Jazz 1900–1950.* New Rochelle, N.Y.: Arlington House, 1974.

Kisselgoff, Anna. "Film Unit Pays Tribute to the Artistry of Astaire." *New York Times,* May 2, 1973.

———. "The Old Movie Musicals." *New York Times,* March 2, 1980.

Knef, Hildegarde. *The Gift Horse: Report on a Life.* New York: McGraw-Hill, 1971.

Knight, Arthur. "Hommage à Fred Astaire." *Saturday Review,* July 25, 1953a, p. 28.

———. "*The Band Wagon:* MGM's Gift Horse." *Dance Magazine,* September 1953b, pp. 68–69.

———. "Choreography for Camera: Fashion and Dance Meet with Delight in 'Funny Face.' " *Dance Magazine,* May 1957, pp. 16–22.

———. "Hermes Pan: Who Is He?" *Dance Magazine,* January 1960, pp. 40–43.

Kobal, John. *Gotta Sing, Gotta Dance.* London and New York: Hamlyn, 1971.

———. *Rita Hayworth: The Time, the Place and the Woman.* New York: Norton, 1977.

Korall, Burt. Liner notes for "1940–1941: Shaw Returns with a Fine Band," RCA Records AXM2-5572, 1980.

Kreuger, Miles. Conversations and correspondence with John Mueller, 1980–84.

Kuyper, Erik de. "Step by Step: Reflexions on the 'Dancing in the Dark' Sequence from Vincente Minnelli's *The Band Wagon.*" *Wide Angle* 5, no. 3 (1983): 44–49.

Lane, Burton. Appearance on "The Song Writers: Burton Lane," CBS Cable, 1981.

———. Letter to John Mueller, March 3, 1983.

Langford, Gerald. *The Richard Harding Davis Years.* New York: Holt, Rinehart and Winston, 1961.

Lardner, David. "Jaundiced Eye." *The New Yorker,* September 4, 1943, p. 58.

Lawrenson, Helen. "It's Better to Remember Fred." *Esquire,* August 1976, pp. 92–96, 106, 109–10.

Lederer, Joseph. "Fred Astaire Remembers . . . Gershwin, Porter, Berlin, Kern, and Youmans." *After Dark,* October 1973, pp. 55–59.

Lehman, Peter; Campbell, Marilyn; and Munro, Grant. " 'Two Weeks in Another Town': An Interview with Vincente Minnelli." *Wide Angle* 3, no. 1 (1979): 64–71.

Lerner, Alan Jay. *On the Street Where I Live.* New York: Norton, 1978.

Leslie, Joan. Conversation with John Mueller, Vagabond Theatre, Los Angeles, August 28, 1984.

Levant, Oscar. *A Smattering of Ignorance.* New York: Doubleday, Doran, 1941.

———. *The Memoirs of an Amnesiac.* New York: Putnam, 1965.

Levine, Howard. Conversations with John Mueller, January-February, 1983.

Lewis, Draper, writer. "Fred Astaire Salutes the Fox Musicals" (produced by Alan P. Sloan, directed by Marc Breaux), ABC Television, 1974.

Lewis, Jerry D. "Interview: Fred Astaire." *Glendale Federal Magazine,* Summer 1982, pp. 8–10.

Life. "The Movie of the Week: Astaire and Rogers Revive *The Castles.*" March 27, 1939, pp. 27–30.

———. "Rita Hayworth Rises from Bit Parts into a Triple-Threat Song & Dance Star." August 11, 1941, pp. 12, 33.

———. "Bubble Bath: Seventeen Experts Assist Actress as She Spends 12½ Hours in Tub." March 12, 1945a, pp. 55–57.

———. "Astaire's Last Dance." December 31, 1945b, pp. 54–56.

Lingeman, Richard R. *Don't You Know There's a War On? The American War Front, 1941–1945.* New York: Putnam, 1970.

Literary Digest. "Vernon Castle, Redeemed from Frivolity by War." March 2, 1918, pp. 66, 68.

———. "Dancing with Astaire and Rogers." December 12, 1936, pp. 20–21.

Look. "The Dig It." November 5, 1940.

Luce, Claire. Telephone interview with John Mueller, June 7, 1981.

Mainwaring, Dan. "Astaire Dance on Bar So Risky Two Nurses Wait During Film." *New York Herald-Tribune,* May 2, 1943.

Maltin, Leonard. "Astaire." *Film Fan Monthly,* May 1973, pp. 3–6.

Mamoulian, Rouben. Lecture and discussion at University of Southern California, December 7, 1975. Tape recording, Special Collections, University of Southern California Library.

Manvell, Roger. *Films and the Second World War.* New York: Delta, 1974.

Marbury, Elizabeth. *My Crystal Ball.* New York: Boni and Liveright, 1923.

Margolis, Max. "Swing Music and Popular Dance." *Dance Herald,* February 1938, pp. 1, 7.

Marshall, Michael. *Top Hat & Tails: The Story of Jack Buchanan.* London: Elm Tree Books, 1978.

Martin, John. "The Dance: Castle Style." *New York Times,* April 16, 1939, sec. 10, p. 6.

———. "Fred Astaire: A Distinguished Art in an Unpretentious Medium." *New York Times,* November 2, 1941, sec. 2, p. 9.

———. "The Dance: Astaire et al." *New York Times,* December 16, 1945, sec. 2, p. 2.

Martin, Tony, and Charisse, Cyd (as told to Dick Kleiner). *The Two of Us.* New York: Mason/Charter, 1976.

Marx, Arthur. *Red Skelton: An Unauthorized Biography.* New York: Dutton, 1979.

Marx, Samuel. *Mayer and Thalberg.* New York: Random House, 1975.

Mast, Gerald. *Howard Hawks, Storyteller.* New York: Oxford University Press, 1982.

McCarthy, Albert. *Big Band Jazz.* New York: Putnam, 1974.

McClure, Arthur F. "Censor the Movies! Early Attempts to Regulate the Content of Motion Pictures in America, 1907–1936." In *The Movies: An American Idiom,* ed. Arthur F. McClure. Rutherford, N.J.: Fairleigh Dickinson University Press, 1971, pp. 117–52.

McGilligan, Patrick. *Ginger Rogers.* New York: Pyramid, 1975.

McVay, Douglas. *The Musical Film.* London: Zwemmer, 1967.

———. "The Belle of New York." *Velvet Light Trap: Review of Cinema,* Winter 1975, pp. 30–33.

Menjou, Adolphe, and Musselman, M. M. *It Took Nine Tailors.* New York: McGraw, 1948.

Meredith, Scott. *George S. Kaufman and His Friends.* Garden City, N.Y.: Doubleday, 1974.

Miller, Ann (with Norma Lee Browning). *Miller's High Life.* Garden City, N.Y.: Doubleday, 1972.

Milne, Tom. *Rouben Mamoulian.* Bloomington: Indiana University Press, 1969.

Milton, Paul R. "S-O-S Fred Astaire." *Dance,* December 1936, pp. 12, 28.

Minnelli, Vincente (with Hector Arce). *I Remember It Well.* Garden City, N.Y.: Doubleday, 1974.

Modell, Samuel S. "In the Dance World: Fred Astaire Airs His Views." (Unidentified New York newspaper, February [?] 1933, in Astaire scrapbooks in Boston University Library.)

Mordden, Ethan. *The Hollywood Musical.* New York: St. Martin's, 1981.

Morella, Joe, and Epstein, Edward Z. *Lucy: The Bittersweet Life of Lucille Ball.* Secaucus, N.J.: Lyle Stuart, 1973.

Morella, Joe; Epstein, Edward Z.; and Clark, Eleanor. *The Amazing Careers of Bob Hope: From Gags to Riches.* New Rochelle, N.Y.: Arlington House, 1973.

Morella, Joe; Epstein, Edward Z.; and Griggs, John. *The Films of World War II.* Secaucus, N.J.: Citadel. 1973.

Morning Post (London). "At the Palace: Gaiety and Charm." November 3, 1933.

Morros, Boris (as told to Charles Samuels). *My Ten Years as a Counterspy.* New York: Viking, 1959.

Mosley, Leonard. *Zanuck: The Rise and Fall of Hollywood's Last Tycoon.* Boston: Little, Brown, 1984.

Moss, Morton. "Fred Astaire Doesn't Dwell in the Past." *Los Angeles Herald-Examiner,* November 25, 1977.

Mueller, John. "Films: Choreographing for Camera." *Dance Magazine,* April 1978, pp. 109–12.

———. "Fred Astaire's 'Dancing in the Dark.' " *Dance Magazine,* May 1979, p. 163.

———. "The Filmed Dances of Fred Astaire." *Quarterly Review of Film Studies,* Spring 1981, pp. 135–54.

———. "Fred Astaire and the Integrated Musical." *Cinema Journal,* Fall 1984, pp. 28–40.

Murphy, George (as told to Jerry Asher). "My Friend Fred!" *Photoplay,* March 1940, pp. 22, 86.

Murphy, George (with Victor Lasky). *"Say . . . Didn't You Used to Be George Murphy?"* New York: Bartholomew House, 1970.

Murray, William, "Playboy Interview: Francis Ford Coppola." *Playboy,* July 1975, pp. 53–68, 184–85.

Nabokov, Ivan, and Carmichael, Elizabeth. "Balanchine: An Interview." *Horizon,* January 1961, pp. 44–56.

Nelson, Ozzie. *Ozzie.* Englewood Cliffs, N.J.: Prentice-Hall, 1973.

Newnham, John K. "Dance Film Notes." *Dancing Times,* July 1937, p. 459.

Niemeyer, Joe. "Take It from His Stand-in!" *Silver Screen,* July 1948, pp. 24–25, 60–62.

Niven, David. *Bring on the Empty Horses.* New York: Putnam, 1975.

Nugent, Frank S. "Swing Time." *New York Times,* August 28, 1936.

O'Hara, John. "There's No One Quite Like Astaire." *Show,* October 1962, pp. 76–77, 138–39.

Othman, Frederick C. "Movie Dancers' Sitdown Wins Raise." *New York World Telegram,* May 12, 1941.

Pan, Hermes. Interview with John Mueller, Beverly Hills, December 26, 1980.

———. Interview with Ronald L. Davis, Beverly Hills, January 12, 1983, SMU Oral History Project on the Performing Arts.

Parish, James Robert. *The Paramount Pretties.* New Rochelle, N.Y.: Arlington House, 1972.

Park, William. "To Fred and Ginger with Love." *Sarah Lawrence Journal,* Spring 1970, pp. 21–29.

Parrish, Linda. "Fred Astaire: A Study in Style." Master's thesis, University of California, Los Angeles, 1975.

Pechter, William S. "Movie Musicals." *Commentary,* May 1972, pp. 77–81.

Pierre, Dorathi Bock. "Dancing to Fame." *American Dancer,* September 1936, pp. 10–11. (On Hermes Pan.)

Pleasants, Henry. *The Great American Popular Singers.* New York: Simon and Schuster, 1974.

Pogue, Leland A. *The Cinema of Ernst Lubitsch: The Hollywood Films.* London: Yoseloff; New York: A. S. Barnes, 1978.

Powell, Eleanor. "Letter to the Troupers." *Dance Magazine,* July 1939a, p. 19.

———. "Hollywood Jottings." *Dance Magazine,* December 1939b, p. 18.

———. "Eleanor Powell Talking to John Kobal: I Would Rather Dance Than Eat!" *Focus on Film,* Autumn 1974, pp. 22–31.

———. "Eleanor Powell Talking to John Kobal: Work and Play in Hollywood." *Focus on Film,* Spring 1975, pp. 33–42.

———. Letter to John Mueller, November 9, 1981.

Purcell, James Mark. Correspondence and conversations with John Mueller, 1983.

Reagan, Ron. "Performers of the Century: Fred Astaire." *Ladies' Home Journal,* January 1984, pp. 105, 156–58.

Richards, Dick. *Ginger: Salute to a Star.* Brighton, England: Clifton Books, 1969.

Richie, Donald. *George Stevens: An American Romantic.* New York: Museum of Modern Art, 1970.

Ries, Frank. "Albertina Rasch: The Broadway Career." *Dance Chronicle* 6, no. 2 (1983): 95–137.

Rodgers, Richard. *Musical Stages: An Autobiography.* New York: Random House, 1975.

Rogers, Ginger. Interview on "Today," NBC Television, June 18, 1984.

Roman, Robert C. "Finian's Rainbow." *Dance Magazine,* March 1969, pp. 94–95.

Rothwell, John. "Another Hollywood Tin Pan Alley Saga." *New York Times,* April 9, 1950, sec. 10, p. 4.

Ruby, Harry. "A Face That Launched a Thousand Quips (Or Why Was I Born?)." *Variety,* January 7, 1959.

———. "Why I'm Sorry I Wrote 'Three Little Words.' " *Dramatists Guild Quarterly,* Spring 1967, p. 15.

Rust, Brian. *The Dance Bands.* New Rochelle, N.Y.: Arlington House, 1972.

Saidy, Fred, and Harburg, E. Y. "Finian's Rainbow." *Theatre Arts,* January 1949, pp. 55–76.

Saltus, Carol. "The Modest Mr. Astaire Talks with Carol Saltus." *Inter/View,* June 1973, pp. 9–16.

Schary, Dore. *Heyday: An Autobiography.* Boston: Little, Brown, 1979.

Schatz, Thomas. *Hollywood Genres.* Philadelphia: Temple University Press, 1981.

Scheuer, Philip K. "The Gold at 'Rainbow' End." *Los Angeles Times,* October 15, 1967.

Scheurer, Timothy E. "The Aesthetics of Form and Convention in the Movie Musical." *Journal of Popular Film,* Fall 1974, pp. 306–24.

Schickel, Richard. *The Men Who Made the Movies.* New York: Atheneum, 1975.

Schneider, Hilda (secretary to Irving Berlin). Telephone conversation with John Mueller, March 4, 1983; letter to John Mueller, July 21, 1983.

Schwartz, Arthur. Interview on WYLF, Rochester, N.Y., September 5, 1983.

Schwartz, Charles. *Gershwin: His Life and Music.* Indianapolis: Bobbs-Merrill, 1973.

———. *Cole Porter: A Biography.* New York: Dial, 1977.

Scott, Allan. "Ginger Rogers: Up from the Chorus." In *Close-Ups,* ed. Danny Perry. New York: Workman, 1978, pp. 66–69.

Seldes, Gilbert. *The Seven Lively Arts.* New York: Barnes and Co., 1957.

Sennett, Ted. *Hollywood Musicals.* New York: Abrams, 1981.

Shaw, Artie. *The Trouble with Cinderella (an Outline of Identity).* New York: Farrar, Straus and Young, 1952.

Shepherd, David, and Slatzer, Robert F. *Bing Crosby: The Hollow Man.* New York: St. Martin's, 1981.

Shipman, David. *The Great Movie Stars: The Golden Years.* New York: Crown, 1970.

Shipp, Cameron. "How to Dance like Four Antelopes." *Colliers,* January 8, 1949, pp. 15, 70–77.

Siegel, Marcia B. *The Shapes of Change.* Boston: Houghton Mifflin, 1979.

———. "Mediadance." *Soho News,* February 6, 1980, p. 54.

Simon, George T. *The Big Bands.* New York: Macmillan, 1967.

Sims, Ed. Interviews with John Mueller, New York City, August 3, 1982, November 4, 1983.

Skolsky, Sidney. "Tintypes." *New York News,* November 20, 1934.

———. "Film Flam." *Chicago Tribune,* February 13, 1935.

———. "Watching Them Make Pictures." *Hollywood Citizen-News,* November 21, 1941.

Smith, Cecil. "Astaire Prefers 'Good Old Days' of the Present." *Los Angeles Times,* July 14, 1957, sec. 5, p. 3.

Solomon, Stanley S. *Beyond Formula: American Film Genres.* New York: Harcourt Brace Jovanovich, 1976.

Sonnenshein, Richard. "Dance: Its Past and Its Promise on Film." *Journal of Popular Culture,* Winter 1978, pp. 500–6.

Spiegel, Ellen. "Fred and Ginger Meet Van Nest Polglase." *Velvet Light Trap: Review of Cinema,* Fall 1973, pp. 17–22.

Springer, John. *All Talking! All Singing! All Dancing!* New York: Citadel, 1966.

Stage. "Names In Lights—Fred Astaire." April 1, 1939.

Stainton, Walter H. "Irene Castle Was One of the First International Celebrities to Take the Movies Seriously." *Films in Review,* June-July 1962, pp. 347–55.

Stanley, Fred. "How Garbo Laughed: Writer of 'Ninotchka' Tells of His Feat." *New York Times,* January 4, 1948, sec. 2, p. 4.

Stearns, Marshall and Jean. *Jazz Dance.* New York: Macmillan, 1968.

Stern, Lee Edward. *The Movie Musical.* New York: Pyramid, 1974.

Suid, Lawrence H. *Guts and Glory: Great American War Movies.* New York: Addison-Wesley, 1978.

Sullivan, Ed. "Looking at Hollywood." *Chicago Tribune,* December [day unknown], 1938, p. 29.

Sutton, Martin. "The Belle of New York." *Movie,* Spring 1977, pp. 54–55.

"Tap Dance to Firecracker Beat Tests the Skill of Even Astaire." (Unidentified New York newspaper, July or early August 1942, in Astaire clipping file, Theatre Collection, New York Public Library.)

Taper, Bernard. *Balanchine.* New York: Macmillan, 1974.

Taylor, John Russell, and Jackson, Arthur. *The Hollywood Musical.* New York: McGraw-Hill, 1971.

Teichman, Howard. *George S. Kaufman: An Intimate Portrait.* New York: Atheneum, 1972.

Telotte, J. P. "Dancing the Depression: Narrative Strategy in the Astaire-Rogers Films." *Journal of Popular Film and Television,* Fall 1980, pp. 15–24.

Theatre Arts. "Offstage." December 1953, pp. 14–16.

Thery, Jacques, and Bemelmans, Ludwig. "Yolanda and the Thief." *Town & Country,* July 1943, pp. 58–62, 78, 81–83.

Thomas, Bob. *King Cohn.* New York: Putnam, 1967.

———. *Joan Crawford: A Biography.* New York: Simon and Schuster, 1978.

———. *Astaire: The Man, The Dancer.* New York: St. Martin's, 1984.

Thomas, Tony. *The Films of Gene Kelly: Song and Dance Man.* Secaucus, N.J.: Citadel, 1974.

———. *Harry Warren and the Hollywood Musical.* Secaucus, N.J.: Citadel, 1975.

Thompson, Charles. *Bing.* New York: McKay, 1975.

Thompson, Howard. " 'Daddy Long Legs' Sits One Out to Reflect." *New York Times,* May 15, 1955.

Time. "Dancing Girl." April 10, 1939, pp. 49–52. (Cover story on Ginger Rogers.)

———. "California Carmen." November 10, 1941, pp. 90–95. (Cover story on Rita Hayworth.)

———. "The Sky's the Limit." September 20, 1943, p. 96.

———. "The New Pictures: 'Blue Skies.' " October 14, 1946, p. 103.

Todd, John. "Fred Astaire Does Film Snake Dance." International News Service, February 27, 1943.

Topper, Suzanne. *Astaire and Rogers.* New York: Leisure Books, 1976.

Treman, Irene Castle. "I Bobbed My Hair and Then—" *Ladies' Home Journal,* October 1921, p. 124.

Turner, Lana. *Lana.* New York: Dutton, 1982.

Ulanov, Barry. *The Incredible Crosby.* New York: Whittlesey House, 1948.

Variety. "Flying Down to Rio." December 26, 1933.

Vaughan, David. "After the Ball." *Sight and Sound,* Summer 1956, pp. 89–91, 111.

———. "Grace and Spirit: Notes on Recent Dance Films." *Ballet Review* 1, no. 3 (1966): 13–20.

———. *Frederick Ashton and His Ballets.* New York: Knopf, 1977.

———. "TV." *Ballet News,* June 1980, p. 41.

Vecchi, Nina. "His Feet Are Not Eloquent by Accident." *Brooklyn Eagle,* [June 11?], 1933. (Clipping in Astaire scrapbooks in Boston University Library.)

Wald, Jerry, and Macauley, Richard, eds. *Best Pictures 1939–1940.* New York: Dodd, Mead, 1940.

Walker, Vernon L. "Rhythmic Optical Effects for Musical Pictures." *American Cinematographer,* December 1936, pp. 504, 514.

Wallechinsky, David, Wallace, Irving, and Wallace, Amy, *The Book of Lists.* New York: Morrow, 1977.

Walters, Charles. Interview with John Mueller, Malibu, Calif., August 19, 1980.

Warren, Doug. *Betty Grable: The Reluctant Movie Queen.* New York: St. Martin's, 1981.

Warren, Harry. Interviews with Irene Kahn Atkins, August 12–November 29, 1972, American Film Institute / Louis B. Mayer Foundation Oral History.

Weinberg, Herman J. *The Lubitsch Touch: A Critical Study.* New York: Dutton, 1971.

Wilder, Alec. *American Popular Song: The Great Innovators 1900–1950.* New York: Oxford University Press, 1972.

Wilk, Max. *They're Playing Our Song.* New York: Atheneum, 1973.

Williams, John R. "This Was 'Your Hit Parade.' " *Rockland [Maine] Courier-Gazette,* 1973.

Wilson, Edith Bolling. *My Memoir.* Indianapolis: Bobbs-Merrill, 1939.

Wilson, John S. "Irving Berlin Tips Top Hat to Fred Astaire." *New York Times,* November 19, 1976, sec. C, p. 1.

Winge, John. "How Astaire Works." *Film and Theatre Today,* January 1950, pp. 7–9.

Wixen, Joan. "The Real Fred Astaire." *Modern Maturity,* April-May 1975, pp. 9–11.

Wodehouse, P. G. *A Damsel in Distress.* London: Herbert Jenkins, 1919.

———. *Performing Flea: A Self-Portrait in Letters.* London: Herbert Jenkins, 1953.

———. *A Damsel in Distress.* London: Hutchinson, 1982.

Wodehouse, P. G., and Bolton, Guy. *Bring on the Girls! The Improbable Story of Our Life in Musical Comedy, with Pictures to Prove It.* New York: Simon and Schuster, 1953.

Woll, Allen L. *Songs from Hollywood Musical Comedies, 1927 to the Present: A Dictionary.* New York and London: Garland, 1976.

Wood, Michael. *America at the Movies.* New York: Basic Books, 1975.

Wood, Robin. "Art and Ideology: Notes on *Silk Stockings.*" *Film Comment,* May-June 1975, pp. 28–31.

———. "Never, Never Change, Always Gonna Dance." *Film Comment,* September-October 1979, pp. 28–31.

Woolf, S. J. "Highest Paid Movie Actress." *New York Times Magazine,* December 5, 1943, pp. 18, 45.

Wynne, Shirley. "Research for the Film." In *Baroque Dance 1675–1725.* Los Angeles: UCLA Dance Department, 1977.

Yoder, Robert M. "Sure Sign That Christmas Is Coming." *Saturday Evening Post,* November 17, 1951.

Yorkin, Bud. "Fred Astaire: A Touch of Class." In *Close-Ups,* ed. Danny Perry. New York: Workman, 1978, pp. 70–71.

Zeitlin, David. "Old Dog's New Tricks at 66." *Life,* October 29, 1965, pp. 87, 91–92, 96–97.

Zwisohn, Laurence J. *Bing Crosby: A Lifetime of Music.* Los Angeles: Palm Tree Library, 1978.

INDEX

A key to locating the musical numbers appears at the end of this index.

THE MUSICAL NUMBERS

A NOTE ON THE TYPE

The text of this book was set in a digitized version of Fairfield, a type face designed by the distinguished American artist and engraver Rudolph Ruzicka (1883–1978). Fairfield displays the sober and sane qualities of a master craftsman whose talent has long been dedicated to clarity.

Rudolph Ruzicka was born in Bohemia and came to America in 1894. He designed and illustrated many books and was the creator of a considerable list of individual prints in a variety of techniques.

Composed by New England Typographic Service, Inc., Bloomfield, Connecticut. Printed and bound by Kingsport Press, Inc., Kingsport, Tennessee. Designed by Iris Weinstein.